THE
CHICANO
HERITAGE

OUR CATHOLIC HERITAGE IN TEXAS
1519-1936

THE MISSION ERA:

THE END OF
THE SPANISH REGIME

1780-1810

CARLOS E. CASTAÑEDA

VOLUME V

ARNO PRESS

A New York Times Company

New York — 1976

Editorial Supervision: LESLIE PARR

———◆———

Reprint Edition 1976 by Arno Press Inc.

Reprinted from a copy in the State
  Historical Society of Wisconsin Library

THE CHICANO HERITAGE
ISBN for complete set: 0-405-09480-9
See last pages of this volume for titles.

Manufactured in the United States of America

———◆———

Library of Congress Cataloging in Publication Data

Knights of Columbus. Texas State Council. Historical
    Commission.
    Our Catholic heritage in Texas, 1519-1936.

    (The Chicano heritage)
    Prepared under the auspices of the Knights of Columbus
of Texas.
    Reprint of the ed. published by Von-Boeckmann-Jones
Co., Austin, Tex.
    Includes bibliographies.
    CONTENTS: v. 1. The mission era: the finding of
Texas, 1519-1693.--v. 2. The mission era: the winning
of Texas, 1693-1731.--v. 3. The mission era: the
missions at work, 1731-1761. [etc.]

    1. Spanish missions of Texas. 2. Catholic Church--
Missions. 3. Missions--Texas. 4. Catholic Church in
Texas. 5. Texas--History--To 1846. I. Castañeda,
Carlos Eduardo, 1896-1958. II. Title. III. Series.
F389.K62 1976   976.4   76-1471
ISBN 0-405-09488-4

OUR CATHOLIC HERITAGE IN TEXAS

IN SEVEN VOLUMES

1519-1936

PREPARED UNDER THE AUSPICES OF
THE KNIGHTS OF COLUMBUS OF TEXAS

JAMES P. GIBBONS, C. S. C., *Chairman*
TEXAS KNIGHTS OF COLUMBUS HISTORICAL COMMISSION
St. Edward's University
Austin

REV. PAUL J. FOIK, C.S.C., Ph.D., DECEASED EDITOR OF *OUR CATHOLIC HERITAGE IN TEXAS*

OUR CATHOLIC HERITAGE IN TEXAS

1519-1936

PREPARED UNDER THE AUSPICES OF
THE KNIGHTS OF COLUMBUS OF TEXAS
JAMES P. GIBBONS, C. S. C., *Editor*

THE MISSION ERA:

THE END OF
THE SPANISH REGIME

1780-1810

by

CARLOS E. CASTAÑEDA, Ph. D., LL. D., K. H. S.

VOLUME V

Austin, Texas
VON BOECKMANN-JONES COMPANY, PUBLISHERS
1942

TEXAS KNIGHTS OF COLUMBUS HISTORICAL COMMISSION

Honorary Chairman of the Commission

THE MOST REV. ARCHBISHOP ROBERT E. LUCEY, D. D., LL. D.

Executive Committee

THE REV. JAMES P. GIBBONS, C. S. C., A. B., Chairman
THE RIGHT REV. MONSIGNOR JOSEPH G. O'DONOHOE, LL. D., Secretary
THE MOST REV. BISHOP M. S. GARRIGA, D. D., LL. D.
THE RIGHT REV. MONSIGNOR PETER GUILDAY, PH. D., LL. D.
HON. JOSEPH I. DRISCOLL, LL. D., K. S. G., Past State Deputy
HON. GUS STRAUSS, State Deputy.

Diocesan Historians

REV. ALOIS J. MORKOVSKY, Archdiocese of San Antonio
RIGHT REV. MONSIGNOR JOHN S. MURPHY, LL. D., Diocese of Galveston
RIGHT REV. MONSIGNOR JOSEPH G. O'DONOHOE, LL. D., Diocese of Dallas
REV. DANIEL A. LANING, Captain, U. S. Army, Diocese of Corpus Christi
REV. ARNOLD A. BOEDING, Lieutenant, U. S. Army, Diocese of Amarillo
REV. DAVID J. KIRGAN, Diocese of El Paso

Historiographer

CARLOS E. CASTAÑEDA, PH. D., LL. D., K. H. S.

PREFACE

A series of untoward circumstances delayed the completion of the present volume. The untimely death of the editor, the Rev. Dr. Paul J. Foik, C.S.C., after a prolonged illness from which he had begun to recover, was a stunning blow to his many friends, and constituted an irreparable loss to the author. His kindly and intelligent criticism, his gentle guidance, and his contagious enthusiasm for a work into which he had placed his whole heart and soul have been sorely missed in the continuation of this volume, half finished at the time of his lamented death. The author wishes to pay the highest tribute to the memory of his friend and fellow-worker, Father Foik, for the invaluable assistance in the production of the first four volumes of *Our Catholic Heritage in Texas,* the pride and constant goal of all his endeavors during the last fifteen years of his life.

The present volume continues the complete narrative of the history of Texas. The panorama of the closing years of the Eighteenth Century, full of momentous events in the history of the world, as well as in that of Texas, is unfolded largely from the sources gathered for the purpose by the Texas Knights of Columbus Historical Commission. The cession of Louisiana to Spain in 1763 brought about a complete reorganization of the northern frontier of New Spain and converted Texas into an interior province. This change affected the work of the missionaries and resulted in the ultimate abandonment of the mission as a frontier institution. In the present volume, the full story of the secularization of the missions, which marks the official end of the mission era, is told for the first time.

But the missionary zeal was not spent. In spite of the new policy to abandon the mission as an agency for the control of the Indians in Texas, the enthusiastic Father Silva succeeded in founding a new mission Nuestra Señora del Refugio, the last bloom of missionary endeavor on the northern frontier of New Spain. The details of its establishment and its development are presented in connection with the last efforts at missionary control, upon which discredit was brought by the fantastic plans of the illiterate Brother Alberola, an incident of the greatest significance heretofore unknown by historians.

The need for the effective defence of Texas made it imperative to establish connections between the outlying provinces of northern New Spain Here we see the details of the steps taken to blast trails between Texas and New Mexico, which eventually were to lead enterprising American pioneers to the gates of Santa Fe. The retrocession of Louisiana to France and the purchase of this vast province by the United States had a profound effect on Texas. The filibustering activities of Nolan and his successors, the ambitious aims of Burr's conspiracy, the unscrupulous character of Wilkinson, American commander on the Louisiana frontier at the time, and the disturbing spirit of the western frontiersmen as reflected in the public press, all contributed to arouse Spanish officials to make frantic efforts to safeguard Texas. The reaction of these events and circumstances are given in detail for the first time in the present volume and here are to be found the origins of foreign colonization in Texas, which are traceable to 1803.

The spread of the ideas of the French Revolution and the direct intervention of Napoleon in Spain had its repercussion in Texas. The effect of this blow to Spanish authority in the peninsula and of the appearance of French agents in Texas, is, likewise, traced in detail and fitted into the general narrative to place in proper perspective the events that followed. Throughout the volume the aim has been to present the complete picture of the social, economic, and political conditions that underlie the main events that mark the end of the period of the Spanish régime by portraying realistically the personal considerations and human emotions that often determine the course of history.

The author wishes to acknowledge his indebtedness to the Knights of Columbus, under whose auspices this work has been carried out; to Rev. Dr. Paul J. Foik, C.S.C., of St. Edward's University, for his unwavering enthusiasm and wise counsel to the very last day of his life; to Rev. James P. Gibbons, C.S.C., likewise of St. Edward's University, who succeeded the deceased chairman in his duties as editor, for a critical revision of the manuscript of the present volume; to Dr. Charles W. Hackett, Dr. Eugene C. Barker, Miss Winnie Allen, and E. W. Winkler, all of the University of Texas, for useful suggestions, friendly advice, and continued coöperation in checking materials and sources; to the Manuscript Division of the Library of Congress for the courtesies extended to him while consulting source materials; and to Elisa, his wife, for uncomplaining endurance in checking details.

C. E. CASTAÑEDA,
University of Texas

CONTENTS

ILLUSTRATIONS AND MAPS

THE END OF THE SPANISH REGIME

CHAPTER I

REORGANIZATION AND NEW POLICIES, 1770-1800

Contrary to the statement made by a pioneer historian of the state that "There is little to be recorded of Texas during the last two decades of the century,"[1] these years are replete with significant details of new policies and developments essential to the understanding of subsequent events. The immediate effect of the cession of Louisiana to Spain was the abandonment of the frontier establishments in East Texas and the reorganization of the line of presidios from California to the Gulf of Mexico. This, however, was followed by a series of changes in the traditional Indian policy along the entire frontier, dictated by the increasing danger of aggression on the part of the English colonies and by the realization that the northern tribes which crowded upon the outposts of Spain's dominions in North America could no longer be controlled by the time-honored institution of the mission. The ascension of Charles III to the throne inaugurated a period of political reorganization both at home and abroad, that was to result in fundamental changes in the administrative machinery of the northern provinces of New Spain. These changes were to have a profound effect on distant Texas. Closely related to the administrative reforms was the revision of the missionary system and the policies of the government pertaining to the conversion and civilization of the natives. This resulted in the secularization of the old missions of San Antonio and La Bahía. The innovations of the energetic Charles III were to affect profoundly the social and economic life of Texas.

Indian policy. The abandonment of East Texas made more urgent than ever the control of the northern tribes, the traditional enemies of Spain and the loyal friends of France in America. The adoption of Rubí's recommendation to wage a war of extermination against the faithless Lipan-Apaches required the coöperation of their northern rivals. This meant a complete reversal of the Indian policy pursued during the greater part of the century. An equally important consideration, and one that did not escape the minds of frontier officials, was the danger lurking in the development of bonds of interest and friendship

---

[1]Bancroft, H. H., *North Mexican States and Texas*, I, 634.

between these Indians and the aggressive English pioneers. Powerful and warlike, the northern nations could not be brought under subjection by the Spanish mission. Prolonged contact with Europeans had acquainted them with the use of firearms, and the growing intensity of national rivalry had taught the Indians the value of their material assistance. A sharp break in the policy, long pursued with success by the French, would result in the total loss of their friendship.

When O'Reilly took possession of Louisiana in 1769, he realized all these facts and wisely chose one of the most remarkable men on the French frontier to win the support of the northern tribes. Athanase de Mézières, son-in-law of the redoubtable St. Denis, brother-in-law of the Duke of Orleans, an experienced and tried officer, was appointed lieutenant-governor of the Natchitoches district, with jurisdiction over the Red River Valley. This area included a large portion of eastern and northern Texas and most of Arkansas and Oklahoma.[2] The instructions given him reveal the general policy to be adopted in dealing with these Indians. Licensed traders were to be appointed for the friendly tribes. Hostile nations, however, were to be deprived of the advantages of trade, whether conducted by the Spaniards or the French. Traffic in stolen horses and Indian captives was to be discouraged and rigorously suppressed. The center of this reprehensible exchange had long been the villages of the Taovayas on Red River. Here the Comanches, when at peace, obtained firearms, munitions, and agricultural products for their stolen horses and Indians taken in raids made upon Spanish outposts. Spanish captives, while not so numerous as Apaches, were not infrequent, but these were generally taken to San Antonio for ransom.[3]

The work of De Mézières. De Mézières proved himself eminently successful in his first expedition. He visited some of the tribes in the upper Red River, appointed traders for the friendly Yatasi and Cadodacho, conferred medals on Chiefs Tinhioüen and Cocay, expelled all unlicensed traders and white vagabonds, and held a council at San Luis, a Cadodacho village near present Texarkana. The chiefs of the Taovayas, Tawakonis, Yscanis, and Kichais attended the council and promised to

---

[2]Bolton, H. E., *Athanase de Mézières*, I, 1-48. The introduction to the letters, diaries, and reports of this outstanding figure constitute the best biographical sketch and appraisal of his work. A brief summary of his various visits to the northern tribes in Texas is found in Morfi, J. A., *History of Texas*, Part 2, Chapter X, translated by Carlos E. Castañeda.

[3]Bolton, *op. cit.*, I, 47-48; 88-92; 127-193.

visit San Antonio to cement a lasting peace. The visits to the Indians of the north by Pablo le Blanc and Father Fray Pedro Ramírez in 1771 followed, but the Comanches and Tonkawas still distrusted the Spaniards.[4]

Rumors of English traders, the desire to learn more about the country recently visited, and the actual strength of the northern tribes prompted De Mézières to undertake a new expedition in 1772. Setting out from Natchitoches in March, accompanied by a few soldiers and some interpreters, he went west to the Trinity, where he visited the villages of Kichais, Yscanis, and Tawakonis near the site of Palestine. He then continued in the same direction to the Brazos and visited two Tawakoni pueblos located near Waco. Going up the Brazos for about two hundred miles he arrived at the village of the Wichitas. Here he sent word to the Taovayas on Red River, and, accompanied by seventy Indians, returned south to San Antonio. In eighty-eight days he had traversed over a thousand miles of country seldom if ever frequented by white men; he had learned much about the northern Indians, and had won their good will.[5]

During this expedition he found that the Taovayas were carrying on an extensive and lucrative trade with the English who furnished them with goods in exchange for stolen Spanish horses. This he attempted to stop. He also learned that the northern tribes, who had recently made peace with the Spaniards, were being hard-pressed by the Osages. He suggested that they move southward to be under the protection of a Spanish presidio. The Indians expressed their willingness to do it after the fall harvest. On his return he, therefore, proposed to Governor Ripperdá the establishment of a presidio in the country of the Cadodachos. Although the governor enthusiastically endorsed the plan, Spanish officials were dubious of its practicability, and wary of the expense involved. The plan, consequently, was abandoned. At the same time De Mézières and Ripperdá proposed a joint campaign with the new allies against the Apaches, as previously suggested by Rubí. But nothing came of this. On his return to Natchitoches, De Mézières spent several days among the Bidais and in the villages of the Hasinais, in order to disrupt a dangerous friendship that was beginning to form between these Indians and the Apaches.

Temporary failure of De Mézières' plans. In spite of the zealous efforts of De Mézières and the determined support of Governor Rip-

---

[4]Bolton, H. E., *Texas in the Middle Eighteenth Century*, 121-122.
[5]Bolton, *De Mézières*, I, 95-99; 283-351.

perdá, many of the advantages secured by the work of these two men in gaining control of the northern tribes were lost through the personal rivalries of other officials. Particularly was this true in regard to the opposition offered by Hugo Oconor. From the first he and his friends suspected the natives, De Mézières, and Ripperdá. They emphasized the bad faith of the Indians, exaggerated the extent to which French traders were profiting individually through these illicit relations, and accused Ripperdá of partiality towards the French and participation in illegal profits. Viceroy Bucareli y Ursua was won over to the Oconor faction and ended by not only prohibiting all trade with Louisiana, but also by eventually removing Ripperdá from office. Although he was notified as early as November 15, 1776, of his transfer to Comoyagua, Honduras, the peculiar circumstances prevailing during this time in Texas kept him from departing until 1778.[6]

Croix's plans for the extermination of the Apaches. Early in 1776 a new administrative unit was created with the appointment of Teodoro de Croix, generally known as Caballero de Croix, as commandant general of the Interior Provinces, who chose Chihuahua as his capital. The new commander set out shortly thereafter to inspect the frontier, accompanied by Fray Juan Agustín Morfi, who was to write a history of Texas after his return.[7] The first task of the new commander was to devise a plan to check permanently, if possible, the Indian hostilities that in recent years had devastated the frontier settlements of Texas, Coahuila, New Mexico, and Chihuahua, and to chastise in particular the Apaches, the worst offenders. The Caballero de Croix counted heavily in his plan on the coöperation of the brilliant young governor and soldier of Louisiana, Bernardo de Gálvez. It was his intention to unite the nations of the north, who, aided by three hundred *Chausseurs* from Louisiana under the command of Gálvez, were to fall simultaneously upon the eastern Apaches while Croix attacked them from the south and west with the entire available forces of the Interior Provinces.

Pursuant to his plan, he held a council of war at Monclova in December, 1777, in which he presented for discussion sixteen questions

---

[6]*Ibid.*, I, 107-108; II, 13-81; Viceroy Bucareli to Arriaga, April 26, 1776. *A. G. I., Audiencia de Guadalajara,* 103-5-21 (Dunn Transcripts, 1776).

[7]Morfi wrote the well-known but unpublished *Memorias* and a history of Texas based on these notes, the existence of which was doubted until it was discovered and translated by the writer and published by the Quivira Society as Volume VI of its *Publications.* See Castañeda, *Morfi's History of Texas,* Part I, 27-36.

"regarding the Apache on the one hand and the nations of the north on the other hand, their divisions, habitat, fighting strength, and depredations; the possibility of making an offensive alliance with the Apaches against the other group, or *vice versa.*" The council approved Croix's plan for uniting with the northern Indians against the Apaches and recommended that the details of the proposed campaign be worked out by a council to be held in San Antonio.[8]

Junta held in San Antonio, January 5, 1778. The meeting was presided over by the Caballero de Croix. Governor Ripperdá, Captains Rafael Martínez Pacheco, Luis Cazorla, and Domingo Díaz, and the adjutant-inspector and secretary of the commandancy-general, Antonio Bonilla, fully discussed the recommendations of the previous *Junta* held in Monclova. They agreed that the peace sworn to by the Apaches had been repeatedly and flagrantly violated; that the enmity of the northern nations was provoked by the friendship of the Spaniards for the Apaches; and that the only remedy for the evils afflicting the Interior Provinces was a war of extermination against the perfidious nation. To that end the plan proposed by Croix was adopted and the council unanimously recommended that De Mézières, who was now in Louisiana, be transferred to Texas and commissioned to explain the details of the plan to the northern tribes.[9]

De Mézières lost no time in answering the summons. By February 20 he was in San Antonio, where he outlined the essential features of the plan regarding the coöperation of the northern allies. He proposed that one thousand Indians be assembled in the villages of the Taovayas. These he would lead personally to the Colorado, where they were to join three hundred Spanish troops. Their forces having been split into two sections, they were to march west to the Pecos and northern Coahuila, and drive the Apaches before them toward the advancing troops of the Interior Provinces under the command of the Caballero de Croix. Mindful of the ill-treatment accorded to captives, he proposed that all Indians taken prisoner should be bought by the missionaries at a prearranged price to swell the thinning ranks of the neophytes.[10]

---

[8]Bolton, *De Mézières*, I, 110-112; II, 147-170. The text of the questions and the deliberations of the *Junta* held in Monclova on December 9-11, 1777, are found in *A. G. M., Provincias Internas*, Vol. 64, pp. 58-71.

[9]Junta de Guerra, *A. G. M., Provincias Internas*, Vol. 64, pp. 71-78.

[10]Bolton, *op. cit.*, II, 172-186.

New expeditions of De Mézières and his untimely death. The plan
outlined by De Mézières had to be submitted to the various Spanish
officials before it was put into execution. Unwilling to remain idle in
San Antonio, he now revisited the northern tribes. In March, 1778, he
set out from San Antonio with a small escort and went first to the
new settlement of Bucareli on the Trinity. He proceeded to the pueblos
and *rancherías* of the Kichais, the Tonkawas, and the Tawakonis on the
Brazos. Following the Cross Timbers, he went on to the villages of the
Taovayas on the Red River. While among the Taovayas, he sent a stern
message to the Comanches who had been lukewarm in their attitude
towards the proposed alliance with the Spaniards. He learned to his
amazement that since his last visit several English traders had penetrated this area and successfully disposed of their wares. To prevent
such incursions in the future and to strengthen the influence of .Spain
over these Indians, he dispatched an urgent appeal to Croix for the
establishment of a Spanish settlement among the Taovayas. But this,
like many other proposals, was disregarded. Shortly afterwards he left
the site of what is now known as Old Spanish Fort and went to Natchitoches, taking with him the two cannons abandoned by Parrilla in his
hasty retreat almost twenty years before. These he left at Bucareli.[11]

In the meantime Croix had returned to Chihuahua. The plan drawn
up by De Mézières was carefully considered in several councils and
approved in principle, but it was concluded that its execution required
more troops than were available. While the matter was being decided
by the viceroy, De Mézières was formally transferred to Texas, and his
permanent residence was established in San Antonio. The purpose was
to have him continue his work out of San Antonio among the nations
of the north, particularly the Comanches who had not been won over
completely. The change seems to indicate that the authorities in New
Spain had eventually adopted the recommendations of Ripperdá in this
regard and decided to transfer the control of the northern tribes from
Natchitoches to San Antonio. But fate decreed otherwise. In May, 1779,
De Mézières set out from Natchitoches for Texas. Instead of going
directly to San Antonio, he decided to call upon the new allies in an
effort to win the friendship of other tribes and strengthen the good
will of those who were now at peace. When he reached the Atoyaque
River, he suffered a severe fall from his horse which stumbled and threw
him on his head. He went back to Natchitoches, or rather was carried

---

[11]*Ibid.*, I, 113-116.

back on an improvised stretcher. Here he remained until early in August when he again undertook the journey, going first to the Nabedache. From these he continued to the villages of the Kichais and the Tawakonis, proceeding to San Antonio by way of the San Xavier (San Gabriel) River. Shortly after his arrival in San Antonio, he learned that his faithful and loyal services had been rewarded by his appointment as governor. But he never fully recovered from the severe fall near the Atoyaque. Before taking office, he died on November 2, 1779.[12]

Events moved rapidly during these years. Simultaneously with the untimely death of De Mézières, Spain had joined France as an ally of the rebellious English colonies in their war for independence; Governor Gálvez had become indispensable in Louisiana; the troops needed for the proposed campaign against the Apaches could not now be spared. Temporarily the doomed Apaches were once more saved from annihilation.

Fighting the Apaches. Spanish officials in Coahuila and Texas, however, did not abandon the new policy. They soon became convinced that the Mescaleros of New Mexico, the Lipans of Texas, and the Apaches proper were all blood kin and inseparable allies. It was now decided to arouse rivalry and enmity among them in a desperate effort to pit one against the other. Spanish agents in Coahuila were partially successful in attaining their object. In 1780 the Apaches and the Mescaleros attacked the Lipans in Coahuila. The latter were forced to move into the area between present Laredo, San Antonio, and Goliad. With their range of activity reduced, they renewed (under the guise of friendship) their thieving and raiding expeditions on the settlements in Texas, particularly along the Río Grande, with greater audacity than ever.[13]

The Mescaleros and Apaches, who continued their depredations in Coahuila, Nuevo Santander, and Nueva Vizcaya (Chihuahua), soon made peace with the Lipans of Texas with whom they were reconciled by the end of 1781. Needing arms and ammunition, they decided to obtain them from the Tonkawas who at this time lived between the Brazos and the Colorado. The latter secured their arms and ammunition from French traders who frequented their lands. The emissaries of the Mescalero-Apache-Lipan group found a ready welcome by the chief of

---

[12]*Ibid.,* I, 116-122; II, 239-288.

[13]Domingo Cabello to Viceroy Matías de Gálvez, September 30, 1784. *A. G. I., Provincias Internas,* Vol. 64, pp. 132-134. This excellent report on Indian relations from 1680 to 1784 deserves to be published in full. It consists of sixty pages.

the Tonkawas, called El Mocho (The Mutilated), because he had lost an ear in battle. His real name was Toquet. This Indian was really not a Tonkawa but an Apache, who had been captured while very young and who had risen to the position of the great chief of the Tonkawas through his personal prowess and ability. In vain did Governor Cabello attempt to dissuade him from becoming an ally of the Apaches. Neither gifts nor threats moved him. The governor repeatedly invited him to come to San Antonio, but fearful of treachery, he as steadfastly refused. In January, 1783, while visiting La Bahía with a group of Apache friends, he became involved in an argument and was killed. His death, which Cabello claimed was not entirely accidental, temporarily checked hostilities.

Governor Juan de Ugalde, of Coahuila, had personally taken the field against the Apaches in 1781 and 1782, and he had succeeded in inflicting a series of defeats upon them in northwestern Coahuila and the lower Pecos. These victories brought him considerable renown, but did not put an end to the depredations. An idea of the extent of their marauding activities may be gathered from the fact that in June, 1784, alone, the Apaches killed forty-six persons and took six hundred horses and mules.[14]

Plan conceived by Governor Cabello. Viceregal officials were really puzzled by the unsolved problem of the continued hostilities of the *Apachería* in the Interior Provinces. Viceroy Gálvez even contemplated the negotiation of peace with the Lipans of Texas and the Mescaleros of Coahuila in the hope of obtaining a temporary respite. To this proposal Governor Cabello emphatically replied in the negative. To make peace with the Lipans would be tantamount to opening the door wide to the Apaches and their kinsmen, the Mescaleros, who, feigning friendship, would penetrate the provinces of Coahuila, Nuevo Santander, Nuevo León, and Nueva Vizcaya, commit their accustomed depredations with impunity, and discover the poor state of the frontier defences. Such a peace would soon reduce the prosperous establishments of the Interior Provinces to the miserable condition of those of Coahuila and Texas. On the contrary, Cabello argued, the war against the Apaches and their blood allies should be intensified and no quarter given until "only the memory of their existence in this province remains."

In order to carry out this purpose, a number of troops was essential, adequate to prevent these Indians from penetrating from Coahuila and

---

[14]*Ibid.*, pp. 135-140.

Texas into Nuevo León and Nuevo Santander. To safeguard Nuevo León, soldiers from the Presidio of Coahuila (Monclova) should patrol regularly the country from that post to Laredo. Similarly a group of soldiers from Monterrey should make inspections at regular intervals as far as Pesquería. These patrols would soon drive the raiding bands of Apaches east of the Río Grande. The Indians would then naturally come to prey upon the settlements of Laredo, Dolores, San Ambrosio, San Ignacio, Revilla, Camargo, and Reynosa, as well as upon the ranches in their vicinity. In all these establishments there were numerous ranches on either side of the Río Grande with an abundance of stock and cattle.

To protect the lower Río Grande settlements and their ranches, Governor Cabello suggested the establishment of a competent detachment of troops at Camargo. But more important still was the reënforcement of Laredo, located east of the river and constituting the natural defence for the rich ranches of Dolores and San Ignacio. With an adequate garrison at this point and sufficient troops in the neighboring presidios and outposts of Coahuila and Texas, the settlements in the two provinces would have ample protection; and the Apaches, unable to continue their habitual thievery, would be starved into submission.

The larger garrison at Laredo could then send out at regular intervals a detachment to reconnoiter the country in the direction of La Bahía. This detachment would meet another at the half-way point in the vicinity of the mouth of the Nueces where Corpus Christi stands today. If the troops at La Bahía were increased, the commander at this point could also send a similar detachment to meet one from San Antonio at Rancho de San Bartolo, located about midway. The Presidio de Béjar would also send another patrol in the direction of San Juan Bautista to meet the one from that place at Palo Alto, located about the same distance from the two. By this means the country between these three strategic points would be regularly patrolled and the Apaches kept constantly at bay.

He further proposed the patrol of the country along the east bank of the Río Grande by detachments from San Juan Bautista and Laredo. He was fully aware of the large number of additional troops needed for this elaborate plan. But, in his opinion, the benefits accruing to the two provinces and their wretched settlers from the effective protection afforded them against the Indians would in a short time more than offset the initial expense.[15]

The military resources of Texas. The actual number of men in the two remaining presidios after the reorganization of the northern frontier in accord with the new regulations of 1772 was one hundred seventy-six soldiers, nine officers, and two chaplains. This gave the Presidio of Béjar and the Presidio of La Bahía eighty-eight men each, not including the officers. But not all this force could be used to fight the Lipans and Apaches because some had to do guard duty, while others had to look after the horses, provide escorts, and carry the mail. These indispensable duties left only sixteen men available in San Antonio for campaigns against the Indians and thirty-three in La Bahía.

It was preposterous to rely on any effective aid from the friendly Indians of the north in the war against the Apaches and the Comanches. Indian allies were more of a liability than an asset. They had to be humored constantly, supplied with horses, arms, ammunition, and provisions; and they could never be relied upon on account of their lack of discipline, their fickle nature, and their irresponsible character.

Governor Cabello called attention to the fact that the Gileños, while belonging to the same family as the Lipans, Mescaleros, and Apaches, and while having the same habits and customs, lived far to the west along the Gila River from which they derived their name. They, therefore, constituted no danger to the Interior Provinces of Nuevo León, Nuevo Santander, and Texas.

"If His Majesty," declared the governor, "cannot afford at this time the expense necessary for the war [against the Apaches], the time will soon come when his dominions in this region will be totally lost and his vassals will find themselves obliged to abandon their homes and property and move to places where, in spite of poverty and misery, they may find protection for their lives and those of their wives and children." The commandancy-general, with its limited resources, could neither afford any effective aid nor remedy the sad situation of the Interior Provinces.[16]

Danger from the United States. A French Indian agent, Juan Gasiot, with remarkable foresight, called the attention of the new commandant general, Felipe Neve, in 1783 to the grave danger which

---

[15]Governor Cabello to Viceroy Gálvez, September 30, 1784. *A. G. M., Provincias Internas*, Vol. 64, pp. 142-149.

[16]*Ibid.*, pp. 150-157.

the attainment of independence by the English colonies presented to the interests of Spain. "It is necessary to keep in mind that a new independent power exists now on this continent," he declared. "It has been founded by an active, industrious, and aggressive people, who, free from the war sustained for many years against their mother country, from which they have at last succeeded in obtaining independence, are already considering the means that will cause it to be respected in the future. These men, freed from the hardships of war that have engaged them so long, will turn their industrious genius to agriculture, the arts, and commerce. Their development," he said, "will constantly menace the dominion of Spain in America and it would be an unpardonable error not to take all necessary steps to check their territorial advance by strengthening the outposts of Spain, particularly in Texas Coahuila, and New Mexico.

"If we fail to do so, your lordship will see that the citizens of the United States of America, led by the advantages for trade offered by the uncontrolled Indians in the territories lying between their [western] frontiers and our provinces of New Mexico and Texas, will make frequent incursions and establish trade relations with the natives, who will thus become attached to them. They will next establish forts among them and will continue to advance until they reach the limits of our possessions where they will have to be checked. By this time, they will have become formidable by their new acquisitions and the winning of numerous allies."

To forestall this impending danger Spain had to take immediate steps to win the support of the Indians in the intervening area and enrich her resources with the resultant trade. There was gold in the country of the Taovayas, the Comanches, and the lands beyond, and all the natives had valuable pelts and furs. While peace reigned, this was the time to prepare for the future struggle.

Significant, indeed, is the profound observation of Gasiot concerning the fundamental power inherent in a free people. "The character of their republican government," he said, "has great influence over the individual. The voice of public interest binds them and moves them as one, and in this union of action their strength is found. Such a people may be exposed to suffer more internal disturbances than any other, but they are likewise capable of undertaking and accomplishing greater things than any other. A Senate, that is ready to meet at any time, that is always ready to deliberate upon anything that may benefit the states, and that has the necessary means at its command for the accomplishment of the purposes desired must keep the people of a monarchical government always on the alert, with the spring of its resources far removed and the need of waiting for decisions and resources that must come from [the seat of power] more than two thousand leagues away."

The governor of Texas, he pointed out, could not possibly maintain friendly relations and, from this distant residence in San Antonio, attend to the exigencies of trade with the Taovayas, Wichitas, Tawakonis, Iscanis, and Quitseys. These Indians were well-disposed towards the Spaniards at this time. Advantage of their receptive mood should be taken. Their request that a fort be established in their midst should be granted immediately. Such an act would give great power to the Spaniards in holding the area indicated. It would serve as a trade center and a rallying point for allies in the event of hostilities.

The country occupied by the nations enumerated offered easy access to the provinces of Louisiana, New Mexico, and Texas. With the proper commander in a post established among them, foreigners could be effectively kept out of the three provinces. Kind and fair treatment of the warlike nations would win their friendship, and the establishment of trade would develop ties of interest that would strengthen their attachment. Gasiot further pointed out that through these Indians the Comanches also could be brought under the influence of Spain.

The plan suggested by Nicolás Lamathe to accomplish this was impracticable. Special commissioners to deal with the various Indian nations gave rise to conflicting policies. Too many administering officials resulted in inconsistencies. Gasiot advocated the appointment of one agent or governor of Indian affairs to handle all the northern nations. One Indian agent could and should be placed under the immediate direction of the governor of Texas, the nearest important official. He could easily go to San Antonio once or twice a year for instructions and to secure the presents to be distributed among the new allies.

He concluded by stressing the importance of establishing trade relations with Louisiana through La Bahía and by way of the mouth of the Trinity River. Such trade would bring the settlers of the two provinces closer together, increase their prosperity, build ties of union, and make effective their mutual coöperation in resisting the advance or penetration of the English.[17]

---

[17]Juan Gasiot to Felipe Neve, October 9, 1783. *San Francisco El Grande Archives,* XXXIII, pp. 151-162.

Indian policy of Viceroy Gálvez.   In 1785, Bernardo Gálvez, count of the same name, who had distinguished himself by his services in Louisiana during the struggle of the English colonies for independence, was appointed viceroy of Mexico. His experience and intimate acquaintance with Indian affairs had prepared him in a large measure for his new task. It was natural that he should turn his attention to the most pressing problem, that of the northern frontier. On August 26, 1786, he prepared a long set of instructions for Jacobo Ugarte y Loyola, the new commandant general of the Interior Provinces, designed to guide him and all the frontier commanders in their relations with the Indians in their respective provinces. The influence of Rubí, Croix, Ripperdá, and Cabello, as well as that of Lamathe and Gasiot, is evident in the general instructions.

He emphatically stated that the Apaches were the worst enemies of the Interior Provinces. "They are the cause of their desolation," he declared, "the enemies most to be feared because of their treachery, their warlike customs, their habit of stealing for a livelihood, and their knowledge of our strength." While their actual number has been greatly exaggerated, nevertheless, their rapidity of movement and constant roaming made them a formidable enemy.

In view of these facts, the first concern of commanders should be to protect all exposed frontiers and wage an incessant campaign against bands marauding in the vicinity of their respective posts. This would prevent attack. Frequent raids at unexpected times should be made upon their temporary camps. Experience had shown the futility of large scale operations or formal campaigns against them. Such enterprises had proved costly and worthless on account of the inability to maneuver with the necessary dispatch and secrecy.

In fighting Indians on the frontier it was necessary to adopt their own strategy. The chief element was surprise. Success depended on it. Quick and telling blows alone would eventually either exterminate or bring to subjection these nomadic tribes. The ideal number for such campaigns was from one hundred fifty to two hundred soldiers, well mounted and armed, and unimpeded by trains of supplies or bulky baggage. Frontier troops, furthermore, should be commanded by officers who were experienced in Indian warfare, regardless of their age or rank.

Troops in frontier presidios should always be ready to pursue raiding Indians. The report of marauders should be followed up by tracking them down immediately. Time was the most important element. The

Indians had the advantage over the Spaniards in that they knew the country better, were generally less impeded in their movements, and better mounted. Immediate pursuit, consequently, was essential to success. The most effective method of destroying the largest number of Indians possible was to follow them to their *rancherías,* feign a retreat, and thereby draw them into an ambush. The viceroy urged frankness and honesty in reporting all Indian engagements, and condemned the practice of those officers, who continually exaggerated the strength of the enemy in order to exalt their own prowess. Such reports were responsible for numerous misrepresentations.

In the relentless war against the Apaches, the settlers had a moral obligation to aid the troops whenever necessary. The government would supply them with arms and munitions. If settlers proved indifferent, the governors of the various provinces not only could, but also would be obliged to conscript them.

The war against the Apaches was to be persistently and vigorously prosecuted, but after the Indians had been vanquished and had sued for peace, a treaty was to be granted and its stipulations enforced. Reasonable and even generous terms, it was hoped, would make the peace permanent. Treachery, however, should be punished with harshness in order to compel obedience to authority.[18] In time the Indians would develop respect for the Spaniards.

Recommendations concerning El Paso and New Mexico. Presidio del Paso del Norte was strategically located to prosecute the war against the Apaches. The viceroy instructed the new commandant general of the Interior Provinces to make a special study of the condition, the state of the defences, and the needs of the post. If more arms and ammunition were required by the settlers to defend themselves and coöperate with the garrison, these would be supplied. Because of its location as a half-way station between Chihuahua and the Province of New Mexico, and the habit of the various Apache tribes of visiting this post, this presidio was in position to learn much about the plans of the Indians, influence them for peace, and keep open the line of communication between Nueva Vizcaya and New Mexico.

With regard to New Mexico, the settlements and presidios in that province were too distant from El Paso to expect any material aid from

---

[18]Bernardo Gálvez to Jacobo Ugarte, August 26, 1786. *Nacogdoches Archives,* VI, pp. 222-241.

its garrison. They would have to depend on the support of the settlers for defence. For the same reason, help from Sonora or Nueva Vizcaya was an even more remote possibility. The Indian policy in New Mexico was to have as its cardinal point the maintenance of peace and the cultivation of the friendship of the Yutes to use them in opposing the Comanches on the northern and eastern frontier. It was equally important to stir up still more the enmity between the Navajos and Gila-Apaches, in order to set one against the other so as to secure their ultimate destruction or subjection. At Taos the Jicarilla-Apaches and the Comanches were both to be courted and their friendship and confidence won through kind treatment, judicious distribution of gifts, and the establishment of trade.[19]

Recommendations concerning Nuevo León and Nuevo Santander. For military purposes the provinces of Texas, Coahuila, Nuevo León, and Nuevo Santander were placed under the immediate command of Colonel Juan de Ugalde, who had previously served as governor of Coahuila and had successfully campaigned against the Apaches in this region. Ugalde, being subordinate to the commandant general only in a general way, was given authority over the available troops in the four provinces and full discretion to conduct the war against the Indians.

The viceroy pointed out that in these four provinces the chief enemies were the Mescalero-Apaches. Their kinsmen, the Lipans, maintained a nominal peace in Texas and Coahuila, as also did the Comanches further to the north. But all Indians, including the various tribes generally designated as nations of the north, were to be distrusted. All officers, however, should scrupulously observe the terms of peace negotiated by Governor Domingo Cabello and other agents, giving no justification for the renewal of open hostilities with any Indians now at peace. But every unprovoked violation or infraction of these terms by the natives was to be severely punished. Caution was to be exercised in ascertaining the perpetrators of outrages, because it was well known that the Lipans in particular took great pains to blame either the Mescaleros or the northern tribes.

While firmly enforcing the terms of peace, they were to court the friendship of all these tribes and to build bonds of interest by developing active trade with them. At the same time the traditional rivalry between the Apaches and the northern Indians was to be tactfully kept alive

---

[19]*Ibid.*, pp. 220-222.

and fostered in order to remove all possibility of the two great factions uniting against the Spaniards.

Commanders and officials in the four provinces were to exercise great secrecy in the execution of their plans, and place no confidence in the friendly nations. The Indians, in visiting the Spanish outposts and settlements, observed everything that was going on and revealed the plans to the enemy, even joining them in many instances. All troop movements were watched closely by the perfidious Lipans. From San Juan Bautista to Espíritu Santo there were more than one hundred leagues of unprotected country. In this area and along the Río Grande to Reynosa there were many ranches and small settlements exposed to the treachery of friendly Indians and the fury of the open foe. From San Juan Bautista (near Eagle Pass) to La Junta (present Presidio) the country was equally unprotected. These facts should cause settlers and officers in Nuevo León and Nuevo Santander to redouble their vigilance and keep themselves ready at all times to repel attack or avoid surprise.[20]

Colonel Ugalde lost little time in putting into effect the instructions of the viceroy. His vigorous pursuit of the Mescaleros and Lipan-Apaches met with success both in Coahuila and Texas and abated to a large extent the impudent raids and depredations of these Indians who suffered severe losses. In his campaigns he was effectively aided by the new governor of Texas, Rafael Martínez Pacheco, former captain of the ill-fated Presidio de San Agustín near the mouth of the Trinity.

San Antonio helps defeat the Apaches. In 1789, Colonel Ugalde made an expedition from Monclova to the site of the former Presidio of San Sabá (Menard), pursuing the Mescalero and Lipan-Apaches. The Villa de San Fernando and Presidio de Béjar were suddenly stirred into action the night of December 21 by the arrival of Lieutenant Casimiro Valdez, an Indian scout named Joaquín Gutiérrez, and Chief Sofías of the Comanches, who, accompanied by a small escort of soldiers, brought an urgent message from Colonel Ugalde. These men had set out from the old and abandoned Presidio of San Sabá on the 19th. They brought a request for eighty-five men and two thousand cartridges. These soldiers, or as many as could be mustered, were to set out within forty-eight hours in order to join at San Sabá the force of Colonel Ugalde and two hundred Comanche allies with their eight chiefs to deal a

---

[20]*Ibid.*, pp. 222-230.

ATTEMPTED ASSASSINATION OF GOVERNOR RAFAEL MARTÍNEZ PACHECO

decisive blow to a large party of Lipans and Mescaleros. The messengers related how a few days before, Colonel Ugalde had encountered the enemy on the Pedernales, where after a brief skirmish, they had fled, leaving one warrior and one squaw dead and abandoning two little girls who had been captured.

Spontaneous and instant was the response to the appeal for aid. Soldiers and settlers wanted to go immediately. For two days the blacksmith shops blazed, shoeing horses and forging swords, mending stirrups and casting lead bullets. On December 24 all the preparations were completed and fifty-two volunteers, all that could be armed, started for San Sabá with eleven soldiers, Lieutenant Valdez, and his companions to join Colonel Ugalde. Martínez Pacheco later informed the viceroy in his report that many more wished to go but had been prevented by lack of arms and ammunition. They took the two thousand cartridges, some supplies, a bolt of white domestic for arm bands for the Indian allies, and a large flag bearing the royal arms of the king and an inscription: "Given by Ugalde to the chief of the Comanches, Soquiné."[21]

Battle of Soledad Creek. Reënforced by eleven soldiers and the fifty-two volunteers from San Antonio, Ugalde marched to Soledad Creek where the Lipans and Mescaleros had pitched camp on a large *ranchería*. Besides the troops from Coahuila, he had a large number of Comanches, Tawakonis, Taovayas, and Wichitas who had joined the Spaniards. On January 9, 1790, Ugalde surprised the enemy, who offered stout resistance for several hours, but finding themselves completely surrounded and outnumbered, made a brave dash and succeeded in breaking through the line of the Indian allies. More than two score were killed and a large number of women and children were captured, as well as a large herd of horses and mules. The Indian allies were favorably impressed by the determined and vigorous charge of the Spaniards under the leadership of Ugalde.[22]

The campaign had originally been directed against the Mescaleros of Coahuila. But shortly afterwards, these were joined by the Lipans who flocked to their ranks in the hope of loot. One of the parties left the vicinity of San Antonio where they had been visiting, under the guise of friendship, to ascertain the amount of help that might be given

---

[21]Diary of events by Rafael Martínez Pacheco, December 3-29, 1789. *Nacogdoches Archives,* VI, pp. 113-119.

[22]Rafael Martínez Pacheco to the Viceroy, March 1, 1790. *Nacogdoches Archives,* VI, pp. 132-139.

Ugalde. On August 25, a Lipan chief and a group of warriors had taken friendly leave of Martínez Pacheco. That night they stopped at the ranch of Curbelo, eight leagues west of San Antonio. The old settler, a member of one of the oldest families of the Villa de San Fernando, received them as friends. Early the next morning he was informed that his guests had departed during the night and taken with them a herd of horses. Curbelo, still unaware of their treacherous intent, mounted his best horse and set out, unarmed and unescorted, to overtake them to ask them to return the horses. When he came up to the ungrateful visitors and remonstrated with the chief, he was attacked from the rear, killed, and scalped.

This was not the only act of barbarous treachery committed by the Apaches on their way to join the Mescaleros in the vicinity of San Sabá. A day or two later they arrived at Los Almagres where a group of civilians from San Antonio had gone to try to work the mines in that area. Unaware of the hostile character of their visitors, who they thought were still at peace, they welcomed them into their camp. That night the miners, five in number, were killed in their sleep and their stock was stolen.[23]

Indian complications in San Antonio. The policy of keeping peace with all Indians tried the skill of Spanish officials. Martínez Pacheco had a difficult situation on his hands when on December 5, 1789, a group of three Lipans arrived, supposedly on a friendly mission. The next day Chief Juan of the Bidais, accompanied by eighteen warriors, twenty-seven squaws, and nine boys were welcomed. That same day an Orcoquisac chief, seven warriors, five women, and three boys also came on a peace mission. These last two groups were enemies of the Lipans. On December 9, a party of eleven Tawakonis arrived with their chief to inquire when the war against the Apaches was going to begin. They expressed their readiness to join the Spaniards. Martínez Pacheco entertained them with similar graciousness and distributed presents to all of them, but his actions were unconvincing. It is to be kept in mind that at this very time Colonel Ugalde was on his way to San Sabá in pursuit of the Mescaleros.

---

[23]Rafael Martínez Pacheco to Viceroy Revillagigedo, March 1, 1790. *Nacogdoches Archives*, VI, pp. 123-131. A group of Lipans who visited San Antonio on December 5, when asked about the incident, said it was the Mescaleros who committed the outrage. They declared that the Lipans had gone to the Pedernales to hunt, but were on the way back to the Medina River. Diary of Rafael Martínez Pacheco, December 3-31, 1789. *Nacogdoches Archives*, VI, pp. 113-119.

The Lipans left on December 10, to join their friends, no doubt, and report what they had seen. The northern Indians remained in San Antonio until the 17th, when the Bidais and Orcoquisacs returned to their country and the Tawakonis set out to join Ugalde.

Martínez Pacheco escapes assassination. The Lipans seem to have reported the duplicity of the governor. This prompted them to take revenge. On December 29, early in the morning, six Lipan warriors entered the residence of the governor unannounced and walked stealthily into his bedroom. Martínez Pacheco realized their sinister intent, and smiling faintly as he raised himself in his bed, welcomed them, explaining he was sick with fever. He reached for some tobacco on a nearby table and offered it to his visitors. Slowly he began to dress without revealing his feelings, inquiring what he could do for them. The Indians eyed him in sullen silence. The governor suggested they have some roast meat and motioned them to the kitchen. The Indians followed him, observing his every move. He told the cook to roast some meat and casually signalled a soldier in the patio to call the guard and send twelve men through the rear. The Indians now became suspicious and started to move toward the patio. The governor tried to reassure them, telling them the meat was almost ready and urged them to stay. At that instant the soldiers appeared in the doorway, covering them with their guns.

The governor ordered the men to tie up the astonished Indians, who, realizing they had been trapped, drew the knives hidden under their clothes and made a desperate effort to cut their way out of the room. Chief Santa Rosa, the leader, grabbed Martínez Pacheco as the soldiers came in to disarm the Indians. A rough and tumble fight followed, in which the chief of Valero Mission wrestled with Santa Rosa and rescued the governor. Martínez Pacheco finally succeeded in unsheathing his sword and transfixing the Lipan chief. The thrust inflicted a skin wound on the Valero chief as it went through the Lipan. In a few minutes four others were dead. The sixth was overpowered, taken out into the patio and killed. After the scuffle "The room was smeared with blood— the floors, the walls, the chairs, and the table," said the governor. One soldier was seriously wounded.

In his report Martínez Pacheco assured the viceroy that the Indians had come to kill him and to spy upon the movements of the Spaniards. Fortunately not one escaped to carry information to the enemy, and contributed in part to the surprise at La Soledad.[24]

---

[24]Diary of Events of Martínez Pacheco. *Nacogdoches Archives*, VI, pp. 113-119.

Friendship with northern tribes. Martínez Pacheco was able to report in the spring of 1790 that steady progress had been made in consolidating peace with the Indians of the north. When he first took over the government of the Province of Texas on December 5, 1786, the Taovayas had been alienated by the killing of two members of their tribe in San Antonio. The rumor reached him that two hundred warriors were coming to avenge the death of their companions. On January 29, 1787, a group of seventeen Taovaya spies were reported in the vicinity. That night one entered San Antonio but was captured and held prisoner. A few days later fourteen others were trapped. These were not punished or maltreated, but the circumstances of the death of their two companions were explained to them, presents were distributed, and four of the prisoners released to take a message of friendship to their chief and an invitation to come for the hostages. The policy of moderation produced the desired results. The chief came, the prisoners were all released, and a lasting peace negotiated.

The Comanches had been won over similarly. Spanish soldiers had rescued a three-month-old Comanche baby from the Lipans. The infant and its mother were to be eaten at a festival. The governor had kept the child, who was now almost two years old, and had sent the mother back to her people.

The coast Indians were also at peace. Many of the former neophytes of Mission Rosario had returned, and recently forty-three children had been baptized. On February 15, 1790, a delegation of Karankawas, Copanos, and Cujanes visited San Antonio, where they feasted and were given presents. They had come to request Fray José Mariano Reyes, who was on the point of leaving Texas, to stay to found a mission for them. The good friar was persuaded to remain and await authorization for the founding of the contemplated mission. In the meantime, the governor had sent seven soldiers to help rebuild Rosario Mission which had been almost abandoned.[25]

Progress in Indian relations. Contrary to general belief, the new policy instituted by Viceroy Gálvez proved successful to a considerable extent in curbing the widespread depredations of the Apaches and in winning the friendship of the northern tribes. The immediate effect was to cause many of these Indians to sue for peace and to agree to dwell

---

[25]Martínez Pacheco to Viceroy Revillagigedo, March 1, 1790. *Nacogdoches Archives*, VI, pp. 123-131. See Chapter VI.

in the vicinity of presidios or Spanish settlements and to seek, in general, protection under the supervision of Spanish officials.

We find Viceroy Revillagigedo, therefore, issuing in 1791 a new set of instructions concerning relations with the Indians of the Interior Provinces which reveals the progress made. Officers were told to welcome peace proposals, but to explain clearly the terms under which peace was to be granted. The Spaniards were now in position to dictate terms and to demand and enforce their observance. In the first place any tribe or nation desiring peace had to give up its nomadic life and settle within four leagues of a presidio. If they agreed to this essential condition, they would be allowed rations for a reasonable period of time in order to enable them to establish themselves on the new site and make arrangements for the raising of crops. Furthermore, the Spaniards would protect them thereafter against all their enemies as long as they continued to live peaceably. Again, they were to be given to understand that the Spaniards expected them to take part in all campaigns against enemies, whether they be former friends or kinsmen. Lastly, and most significantly, the Indians who made peace and agreed to the terms outlined, were admonished that in the future they might not, without permission from the commander of the nearest presidio, leave or absent themselves from the *rancherías* where they were established.

The details of this provision were explicit and clear, tending to supervise in a general way the movements of the friendly Indians to prevent treachery. Warriors and young men of the tribes might leave the new *rancherías* and take their own horses to go hunting, but each had to have a passport or identification card to show to any Spanish officer to prove his peaceful character. To insure his return and good behavior while away, the women and children had to remain in the *rancherías* as hostages. The same condition was to be observed respecting visits to friends and relatives who had not made peace or settled near presidios.

The officials carefully informed those agreeing to the new terms the amount of rations to be allowed to enable them to establish their *rancherías* near a presidio. Each married Apache was to receive two pecks of corn or wheat, four packages of cigarettes, a *piloncillo* (loaf of brown sugar), a handful of salt, and one thirty-second part of a beef each week until the first crop was harvested. Chiefs and important members of the tribe were to be allowed an extra loaf of brown sugar, two extra packages of cigarettes, and occasional gifts of clothes for themselves and their families. Those, who after making peace distinguished themselves in campaigns against other Indians, were to be encouraged in their zeal by the distribution of special gifts and extra allowances comparable to those received by chiefs.

In the new *rancherías* established by the former nomadic Apaches, practical independence was to be allowed the Indians in the administration of their affairs and the chiefs were to be permitted to administer justice in the less important cases. The chief was to be shown special consideration. In the event that there were more than one chief in the same *ranchería,* the most capable and loyal to Spanish interests was to be singled out, given a baton, and appointed Indian governor. The advantages of keeping the peace were to be emphasized to the chiefs and all the Indians. No insults were to be tolerated from them. They should be made to respect the Spaniards. Petty thefts were to be severely punished to discourage repetition and prevent graver abuses. Friendly Indians, who absented themselves without permission, or ran away to join the enemy, were to be severely punished, if they were caught or returned.

It is of interest to note that the linguistic handicap was fully realized. In his instructions the viceroy urged frontier officers to learn the language of the natives in order to dispense with interpreters. He recommended that the children of the soldiers be allowed to play with the little Indian boys. This was the easiest and best way of learning their language and of winning their confidence.

Indians taken in battle were not to be released to their people either for ransom or in an exchange of prisoners, nor as a gesture of good will. Such captives were to be turned over to the missions or sent to the interior where they could be Christianized and made useful members of society. No Apache chief was to be granted permission, except with the consent of the commandant general, to visit Chihuahua to negotiate peace. From those who were at peace, the frontier commanders were to obtain all information possible concerning the life and habits of the hostile nations, the location of their principal *rancherías,* and their favorite haunts and meeting places. Whenever hostile Indians were known to have congregated in the vicinity of an outpost within twenty to forty leagues, they were to be attacked instead of being permitted to begin hostilities.

Such Indians as made peace and came to live near the presidios were to be treated kindly as long as they observed the terms of the treaty negotiated. Women and children should be given employment in the tasks that they were able to perform, but the warriors, who were not in the habit of working, were to be allowed to do only what they wanted. Fair wages should be paid to all those employed, but if no monetary recompense was made, the workers in the field were to receive all the fruits of their labor.[26]

Let it not be supposed that the Indian menace had completely disappeared. Governor Manuel Muñoz, writing to the commandant general in 1793, reported marauding bands of Lipans under Chiefs Jacinto and Mariano still active in the vicinity of La Bahía. Chiefs Canoso (Grayhair), Chiquito (Shorty), and Moreno (Darky) had a disagreement with the herders of San José and were threatening to abandon their *rancherías* near San Antonio, while a band of Tonkawas had recently stolen ten head of cattle from the mission. Governor Muñoz deplored the facility with which hostile Indians kept themselves informed of the movements and plans of Spanish troops and broadly hinted that unscrupulous citizens of San Antonio were largely to blame.

Commandant General Pedro Nava still complained of the tendency of frontier commanders to report incidents in vague and general terms, exaggerating facts to enhance their own merits, and omitting pertinent and essential details that might serve to shape a more effective policy. In respect to the citizens who persisted in carrying on trade and in maintaining relations with hostile Indians, Nava grew impatient and emphatically instructed officials on frontier outposts to exercise the greatest severity in repressing so injurious and disloyal a practice.[27]

Economic reform.   The series of administrative and economic reforms in Spain and in the colonies that marked the ascension of Charles III were directed primarily to the correction of abuses in the government of the vast colonial empire and to the increase of the royal revenue. In the earnest desire to attain the latter purpose, careful stock was taken of the economic resources of the Spanish dominions in order to adopt measures that should bring to the royal coffers the latent wealth of America.

In Coahuila and Texas there were no mines to speak of, agriculture yielded meager returns without irrigation, the population was not sufficiently dense to produce the natural revenue that results from the

---

[26]*Nacogdoches Archives,* Vol. 6, pp. 157-176.

[27]Governor Manuel Muñoz to Pedro Nava, May 20, 1793; Pedro Nava to Governor Muñoz, June 20, 1793. *Saltillo Archives,* Vol 5, pp. 217-220; 221-223.

exchange of commodities and the fruits of personal industry. The only
source of wealth worthy of consideration was the cattle industry. In
Texas this had been fostered and successfully developed by the missions, where the Indians, under the wise direction of the missionaries,
had multiplied their slender resources into many large herds of horses,
mules, asses, and cattle. Rubí, and later Croix, had noted the countless
herds that roamed the plains and filled the rich river valleys. Branded
and unbranded, the majority of these belonged to the missions scattered
throughout Texas from Los Adaes to Laredo and from San Antonio
to the establishments in the lower Río Grande. The extent of the branded
herds has been pointed out in the previous volume. The ones at La Bahía
alone, when branded and counted in 1778, numbered over fifteen thousand
head.[28]

Herein, then, is to be found the reason for the increasingly bitter
attacks on the mission system in Texas and the growing impatience of
officials with a state of affairs which kept out of the reach of the royal
treasury the only possible source of revenue. Texas had been a constant
drain upon the crown from the time of its first occupation. Not a cent
of revenue had ever reached the coffers of His Majesty from this remote
province. What mattered, thought Croix, whether the natives were
Christianized and civilized with the proceeds of this wealth created at
such sacrifices, if the king did not receive a share?

The idea grew and became a conviction firmly fixed in the mind of
officials that the missions had served their purpose and reached adult-
hood. The surplus wealth created under the protection of the crown
should now revert to the king. The conclusion was logical, but it ignored
a number of fundamental factors that were to result not merely in the
suppression of the mission system but in the economic ruin of the weak
and insecure civil settlements of the province and in the arrest of its
future development until the appearance of the Anglo-American colonists.
The civil settlements and the presidios themselves had been maintained
and aided constantly by the reserve food supply accumulated by the
missions. The affluence that excited the envy of the settlers and the
cupidity of the crown officials had made possible the attraction of new
converts and the appeasement of many Indian tribes. A modification
or reorganization of their economic resources was needed to meet the

---

[28]Fray José Francisco López, Razón e Ynforme que el Padre Presidente de las
Missiones de la Provincia de Texas, ó Nuevas Filipinas, remite . . . *University of
Texas Archives.*

changing conditions inevitably brought about by the progress made, but the measures adopted for the purpose were too drastic.

Missionaries take the lead.   No one realized the need of a change in the temporal administration of the missions more than the missionaries themselves. For many years the *Padres* had felt that the administration of temporal property was foreign to their sacred calling. But they also perceived the irrefutable fact that the Indians gathered in the missions were really only children, unaccustomed to and incapable of managing their own affairs. They, just as the royal officials, fully realized that the mission was a center for both the Christianization and the civilization of the natives. In the accomplishment of the second purpose, the Indians had to be instructed patiently in gainful occupations and taught habits of self-restraint, of sustained effort, and of industry in order that they might fit themselves to take their places as useful citizens in a civilized community. It was for this reason that the missionaries had become the administrators of the communal property of the neophytes as well as their guardians and preceptors.

The *Discretorio* (Senior Council) of the College of Nuestra Señora de Guadalupe of Zacatecas, which, since the withdrawal of the missionaries of Querétaro, had taken over the administration of the missions in Texas, addressed a petition to the new commandant general, Caballero de Croix, on January 13, 1780. They earnestly entreated him to relieve the missionaries in Texas of the grave responsibility of the temporal administration of the missions, a task alien to their ministry. While this had been a duty necessary in the early years, it was now felt that a continuation of the practice only served as a constant source of disagreement with royal officials. Many who looked with envy upon the material success of the missions accused the missionaries unjustly of private interest in defending the neophytes from exploitation and despoliation.

It should, however, be kept in mind, they pointed out, that the neophytes were constantly being replaced in these missions by new arrivals and that, even among those who had been in residence for relatively long periods of time, individually there were few who could be entrusted with the administration of their share of the mission property. The Indians, they declared, were by nature and experience simple, not understanding the wiles of civilization. They had no conception of material values. For example, they would gladly exchange a copper kettle, an ax, a hoe, or even a *metate* (grindstone) for a piece of brown sugar or for two or three ounces of powder. A horse, a cow, or any other possession would be traded for a pint of liquor. The Spaniards knew this and were anxious to take advantage of them.

Contrary to the general belief, the mission communal property, if divided among the neophytes, was insufficient to furnish each one the means of an independent livelihood. They depended chiefly on the crops raised from year to year, and these were the result of the sympathetic but firm supervision of the missionaries.

Nevertheless, the *Discretorio* concluded that the best thing to do would be to distribute equitably all common property among the neophytes, giving each his share of the stores in the mission farms, and dividing among them the cattle, the farm implements, and all other belongings. The missionaries would keep only the churches, the priest's quarters, and the things necessary to continue their spiritual ministration. The royal salary, if continued, would suffice to meet their needs. They would expect nothing from the neophytes. They would require only a boy to run errands for them and a young Indian girl to grind their corn and make *tortillas* (corn cakes) for them. The signers of the petition were the elders of the college, Fathers Joaquín María Manzano, Anastasio de Jesús Romero, José Patricio García de Jesús, Ignacio María José Lanunza, and Ignacio Benigno del Río.[29]

Royal order for new regulations for administration of missions. In June of the same year (1780) the king issued an order instructing the viceroy to formulate new regulations for the administration of the missions. He was to request the oldest and most experienced missionaries, as well as the civil officials, who were qualified by experience to speak authoritatively, to make suggestions for the improvement of mission administration. These proposals were to be analyzed and incorporated in the new regulations which were to be submitted to the bishops of Guadalajara and Durango for their final revision and approval. Such regulations as were thus drawn up could be put into operation by the viceroy, subject to final confirmation by the Council of the Indies.

When the royal order was transmitted to the commandant general of the Interior Provinces, the Caballero de Croix, he referred the matter to Galindo Navarro, his assessor. By this time the petition of the *Discretorio* had been received. Galindo replied that in the adoption of new regulations, the most important point was the administration of the

---

[29]Petition of the *Discretorio* of the College of Guadalupe to Caballero de Croix, January 13, 1780. *Saltillo Archives*, Vol. 5, pp. 2-4.

temporal property of the missions. The matter was of such vital interest to the future welfare of the provinces that a hasty decision should be avoided at all costs. He advised, therefore, that the request of the College of Zacatecas, namely, that missionaries in Texas be relieved of the temporal administration of the missions, be not granted until other opinions concerning the subject were secured, and the whole question of a general policy concerning mission temporalities was fully discussed.[30]

Question of ownership of unbranded cattle and stock. Upon his return to Chihuahua, the Caballero de Croix issued an order in which he declared that all unbranded cattle and other stock found on the king's domain (*mesta*) and generally designated as *mesteño,* were the king's property. Citizens and private individuals could round up such cattle and stock to brand them upon paying a fee of fifty cents per head. Croix had just made an inspection of the frontier in company with Father Fray Juan Agustín Morfi, and the numberless herds that roamed the plains were still fresh in his mind. The order was intended to prevent the natives from using this reserve food supply exclusively, to encourage the settlers to make use of the wild cattle and horses, and to increase thereby the revenues of the crown. The fee of fifty cents a head seemed reasonable, but it proved excessive for the destitute Spanish pioneers of Texas to whom money was almost unknown, and who depended on barter for all their needs.[31]

The decisions of the commandant general, however, ignored the fact that a large number of the unbranded cattle and horses roaming the plains were not wild, but belonged to the various missions and to the ranches of the more industrious settlers, particularly those in the vicinity of San Antonio. The hostility of the Indians in the years immediately preceding the order of Croix and the lack of protection had kept many of the citizens and the neophytes of the missions from the annual round-ups during which the new cattle and horses were generally branded.

Payment of tithes on wild cattle and stock. As long as the majority of the wild stock had belonged to the missions, the newly erected bishopric of Nuevo León had made no claims to tithes. But after the publication of the new order by Croix, Bishop Rafael José Verger, of Nuevo León,

---

[30]Royal *Cédula* of June 14, 1780; Galindo Navarro to Croix, July 20, 1781. *Saltillo Archives,* Vol. 5, pp. 5-6.

[31]Fray José Francisco López, *Razón e Ynforme . . .,* p. 14. *University of Texas Archives.*

Nuevo Santander, and Texas, instructed Juan Barrera in San Antonio to take steps to collect the proper tithes from the citizens of the Villa de San Fernando. Barrera appeared before the Reverend Pedro Fuentes, curate and ecclesiastical judge of San Fernando, to request the payment of tithes for the years 1780-1783 on all wild cattle and stock caught and branded. He argued in the name of the bishop that whenever a private individual rounded up cattle and stock for the purpose of branding them, whether these be from his private ranch or from the public domain, he was duty bound to pay tithes to the church. Thus the wild cattle and stock declared to be the property of the crown were subject to payment of tithes. The bishop went further and claimed that tithes were likewise payable on the fees collected by royal officials for granting permission to hunt, catch, and brand wild cattle.[32]

The curate, Father Fuentes, granted the request and ordered that a copy of the bishop's proclamation be sent to Governor Cabello for him to take notice of the section which pertained to the tithes due on fees collected for the right to catch wild cattle and horses.[33] The governor was somewhat taken aback by the unexpected request. He politely acknowledged receipt of the summons, ordered that a copy be filed, but withheld fulfillment of the request for payment until he could consult on the matter with the commandant general. This he did on May 20, 1784.[34]

Protests and efforts to establish legal claim to unbranded cattle and stock. The order of Croix, which had not as yet received royal sanction, was vigorously contested by private individuals and missionaries alike, and frantic efforts were made to round up and brand as many of the wild cattle and horses as possible before a royal decree concerning the matter was issued. In the meantime during the years between 1780 and 1787 many abuses were committed. Soldiers and unscrupulous individuals wantonly slaughtered large numbers of wild cattle for their hides or for a piece of fresh meat; others drove large herds to the neighboring provinces where they sold them at ridiculously low prices; and the Indians,

---

[32]Proclamation of Bishop Rafael José Verger, April 19, 1784. *Saltillo Archives*, Vol. 5, pp. 7-11.

[33]Pedro Fuentes to Domingo Cabello, May 13, 1784. *Saltillo Archives*, Vol. 5, pp. 11-18.

[34]Decreto del Gobernador Cabello, May 18, 1784; Domingo Cabello to Croix, May 20, 1784. *Saltillo Archives*, Vol. 5, pp. 18-21.

enemy and friend alike, were allowed to prey upon the wild herds to their hearts' delight.[35]

For their own protection, the ranch owners of San Antonio and La Bahía and the missionaries entered into a mutual agreement to round up their respective cattle and horses whether branded or unbranded. Simón de Arocha and Juan José Flores represented the eighteen or twenty ranchers and Father Fray Luis Mariano de Cárdenas represented the interests of the missions of San Antonio and La Bahía. The agreement declared that for fourteen years no real round-up had been held because of the hostility of the Indians and the inadequate protection afforded by the garrison. The neophytes of Mission Espíritu Santo were to round up all cattle and stock from the point where Arroyo Alonso entered Cleto Creek to the headwaters of the said creek, hence north to Mina de Manar, hence east to Arroyo Rosario, hence to Nogales Creek, hence to the mouth of Tulillo Creek, and hence to the Guadalupe. The missions of San Antonio and the citizens of Villa de San Fernando were to round up the cattle and stock found between the limits of the Villa and Presidio and the Guadalupe River.[36]

Having reached an agreement, they now appealed to the governor *ad interim,* Rafael Martínez Pacheco, to secure permission from Commandant General Jacobo Ugarte y Loyola, to round up their cattle in the specified area, mainly in the country south and west of the Guadalupe and to brand them, pending the final decision of the king as to the payment of a head tax. The order of Croix of 1780 had been seriously questioned and uniformly protested and the matter had been submitted to the king for final confirmation.

Martínez Pacheco was sympathetic with the outraged cattle raisers and the missionaries. He pleaded earnestly in their behalf and sent to the commandant general a complete list of all the owners of cattle ranches in the vicinity of San Antonio. He pointed out that they should be allowed an opportunity to brand their rightfully owned cattle before the new regulations were put in force, because Indian hostilities for the last few years had prevented them from holding their annual round-ups. Furthermore, these people had endured untold hardships because of severe droughts and unusually cold winters, particularly in 1786 when there

---

[35]Fray José Francisco López, *Razón e Ynforme* . . ., pp. 15-17. *University of Texas Archives.*

[36]Acuerdo entre los vecinos y misioneros, May 21, 1787. *Nacogdoches Archives,* Vol. VI, pp. 87-99.

was much snow and ice, and because they had to abandon their ranches frequently for lack of adequate protection. These facts accounted for the large number of unbranded cattle and stock, many of which rightfully belonged to the ranchers and missions. If they were permitted to round up the cattle and stock found south and west of the Guadalupe River as proposed, the petitioners were willing to forego all claims to the not inconsiderable herds that strayed beyond this river. The commandant general made no reply to the request of Martínez Pacheco.[37]

Late in November, Ugarte y Loyola sent the governor a copy of the royal decree of September 21, 1787, concerning the ownership of unbranded cattle in Texas. According to the terms, Governor Martínez Pacheco was instructed to declare formally that all unbranded cattle and stock found on the king's domain were the property of the crown. Citizens and missionaries were to be allowed a period of grace, four months from the time of publication of the decree, in which to claim and brand all such cattle and stock as they could round up. After the expiration of the grace period they were to advance no further claims on any unbranded stock.[38]

Martínez Pacheco hastened to remonstrate that the citizens of the Villa de San Fernando and the missions of San Antonio and La Bahía had solicited the recognition of their right to the unbranded cattle and stock found within the respective jurisdictions of their ranches and in the country to the east as far as the Guadalupe River, to the west as far as the Medina, and to the north as far as the hills. In lieu of this right, they were willing to forego their claims to any and all cattle and stock that had strayed or might in the future stray beyond these limits. The governor made bold to suspend the operation of the decree, pending the disposition of the request of the citizens and missionaries. He urged in his pleadings in their behalf that the four-month period allowed was too short. Lastly, he declared that serious difficulties would arise from the need of guarding and protecting the royal herds. There would be a continual temptation to hunt and brand wild cattle without paying the royal fee required.[39]

---

[37]Rafael Martínez Pacheco to Jacobo Ugarte y Loyola, October 14, 1787. *Saltillo Archives*, Vol. V, pp. 36-48.

[38]*Cédula* of September 21, 1787. Summarized in letter of Ugarte y Loyola to Martínez Pacheco, December 1, 1787. *Saltillo Archives*, Vol. 5, pp. 43-46.

[39]Martínez Pacheco to Jacobo Ugarte y Loyola, December 1, 1787. *Saltillo Archives*, Vol. 5, pp. 43-48.

Some idea of the number of cattle that were caught and branded as a result of the new policy, first instituted by Croix and finally confirmed by royal decree, may be gathered from the official reports on the revenues collected at fifty cents per head. The money thus collected was kept in San Antonio in a special chest under three locks, in keeping with an old Spanish custom. Governor Martínez Pacheco had the key to one, Juan José de los Santos, *alcalde,* had the key to the other, and Juan Arocha, *alcalde,* had the key to the third. In order to deposit or take out any of the funds from the chest, all three officials had to be present, each to open his respective lock.

Up to January 1, 1787, a total of eight thousand eight hundred five *pesos* had been collected. This indicated that over seventeen thousand head of unbranded or wild cattle had been caught and killed or shipped out of the province. It is further to be kept in mind that the hunters of wild cattle were not particular about reporting accurately the number caught or killed because the more accurate the report was, the greater the amount that would be due the royal treasury. An idea of the distribution of the cattle at this time may be obtained from the annual reports made. For example, in 1786, there were two hundred twenty-eight head paid for at La Bahía, seven hundred twenty at Nacogdoches, and one thousand two at San Antonio, according to reports made by Governor Pacheco, Captain Luis Cazorla, and Antonio Gil Ibarbo in January, 1787. The number that the friendly and hostile Indians killed or drove away is not known.

But the wild cattle had not by any means been exhausted in spite of the ruthless destruction. On March 16, 1788, Martínez Pacheco reported that as the result of special round-ups executed by the ranchers and the missions to take advantage of the four months' period of grace granted by the royal decree of September 21, 1787, as many as six thousand two hundred thirty-one head of cattle and one hundred eighty-three horses were caught in the country west of the Guadalupe alone, and one thousand four hundred eighteen head in the former pastures of Mission Espíritu Santo. The governor explained that the San Antonio missions were unable to participate in these round-ups because of their lack of neophytes and tame horses.[40]

Thus in two round-ups in the winter and spring of 1787-1788, without participation by the San Antonio missions, more than seventy-five

---

[40]Reports on Mesteños, 1786-1788. *Saltillo Archives,* Vol. V, pp. 49-53; 56-62.

hundred head of wild cattle were herded, and from 1780 to 1788, according to official records, over twenty-four thousand were caught, killed, or driven to market in the adjoining provinces. The injudicious waste of this valuable asset was the forerunner of the economic ruin of the missions and the Spanish civil settlements of Texas.

Population statistics, 1783-1794. Census reports giving remarkable details not generally suspected, appear to have been made with astonishing regularity. It is surprising, therefore, that so many who have written on the Spanish period of Texas history, have been satisfied to give general statements concerning this extremely interesting subject. Nothing gives a better idea of the effect upon the population of the economic policy adopted during the last decade of the eighteenth century than these figures, nor is there any fact more significant.

At the close of 1783 a long and detailed census report of the province was made. There were at this time 1,248 persons living in the Presidio de San Antonio and the Villa de San Fernando, of whom 21 were slaves. In Mission San José there were 128 neophytes; in San Juan Capistrano, 99; in Espada, 96; in Concepción, 87; and in Valero, 144. In the Presidio of Nuestra Señora de Loreto at La Bahía there were 454 persons, of whom one was a slave. At the Mission of Espíritu Santo there were 214 Indians. The recently established settlement of Nuestra Señora del Pilar de Bucareli, now at the old site of the mission of the Nacogdoches, had 349 persons, of whom 14 were slaves. These figures give a total population of 2,819 in the three centers of Spanish power in Texas. Of this number, 1,577 were classed as Spaniards; 677, as Indians; 125, as mestizos (Spanish-Indian); 404, as color *quebrado* (mulattoes); and 36, as slaves.[41]

We have another detailed census report, that of San Antonio for 1786. It shows a considerable decrease in population. The total number of inhabitants in the Presidio de San Antonio and Villa de San Fernando was then only 975. In mission San José there were 189 Indians; in Capistrano, 110; in Espada, 144; in Concepción, 104; and in Valero, 126. This gave San Antonio a total of 1,648, not counting 15 slaves. Of this number, 707 were classed as Spaniards; 479, as Indians; 167, as mestizos; and 288, as mulattoes. Present were one secular priest and six mission-

---

[41]Estado que manifiesta el número de Vasallos y Habitantes que tiene el Rey en esta Jurisdicción de la Provincia de los Texas, 1783. *Béxar Archives,* University of Texas.

SECULARIZATION OF MISSION SAN JOSÉ Y SAN MIGUEL DE AGUAYO

aries. There were 790 married persons, 74 widows and widowers, and 203 bachelors.[42]

The report, made in 1787 for the Presidio of Nuestra Señora de Loreto at La Bahía and the missions there, shows that there were 429 Spaniards, 103 Indians, 13 mestizos, 45 mulattoes, and 1 slave, making a total of 591.[43] Like the report for San Antonio, this one revealed a decided drop when compared to the total of 668 reported in 1783.

A special report on the missions in San Antonio was made in December, 1788. It indicated that Valero had at that time 45 Indians; Concepción, 51; San José, 114; San Juan Capistrano, 34; Espada, 46; and Espíritu Santo, 82. But the number of neophytes varied considerably during the closing years of the missions. In December, 1789, the general census taken showed Valero had 121; Concepción, 74; San José, 198; Capistrano, 80; and Espada, 93.[44]

In the report for 1789, the population of the Presidio de San Antonio and the Villa de San Fernando also disclosed a marked increase since 1786. There were 1,279 persons, of whom 546 were men, 431 were women, 152 boys, and 150 girls. Of these 961 were Spaniards. There were 1,028 married, and 80 widows and widowers. One secular priest ministered to the spiritual wants of the Presidio and Villa, and six regulars looked after the missions.[45]

The following year, however, the population of this, the most important center in Texas, for some inexplicable reason had decreased to 1,001; of whom there were 271 men, 310 women, 220 boys, and 200 girls. The missions, too, had lost considerable numbers of neophytes. Valero had 48 persons living in the old mission; Concepción, 47; San José, 144; Capistrano, 21; and Espada, 46. Analyzing the report by classes there were 780 Spaniards, 269 Indians, 30 mestizos, 324 mulattoes, and 11 slaves.[46]

The government asked for a special report on the number of foreigners living in Texas in 1792. This shows that there were 31 in San Antonio, 8 in La Bahía, and 86 in Nacogdoches. Their description and names are given in detail, as well as their nationality and place of origin.

---

[42]Estado que manifiesta el numero de vasallos en el Presidio de San Antonio y Villa de San Fernando, 1786. *Nacogdoches Archives,* Vol. VI, pp. 85-86.

[43]*Nacogdoches Archives,* Vol. VI, pp. 99-100.

[44]Census reports in *Nacogdoches Archives,* Vol. VI, pp. 103; 121-122.

[45]Census reports, *Nacogdoches Archives,* Vol. VI, pp. 121-122.

[46]*Ibid.,* Vol. VI, pp. 153-154.

Frenchmen predominated, although it is of interest to note that there were a few Englishmen among them at this early date.[47]

Mission Rosario, near the presidio at La Bahía, was abandoned for a few years, but in 1788 an effort was made to reëstablish it. By July, 1790, it had progressed slightly. On July 2 of that year the missionary reported that there were 45 Indians living in the mission and that 79 others were expected to return in October. These had gone away on account of lack of food. When the crops were harvested and some of the mission cattle were rounded up in the fall, there would be sufficient supplies to enable these Indians to come to live permanently in the mission.[48] By 1794, Mission Rosario had 139 neophytes registered. Of this number 100 had been Christianized and civilized, and 39 were still receiving instruction when Governor Muñoz visited the mission.[49] At the same time Mission Espíritu Santo reported it had 35 Jaranames, 19 Tamiques, 18 Parantones, 12 Prietos, 9 Brazos Largos (Long arms), 6 Vende Flechas (Arrow Peddlers), and 12 Campusas, a total of 111.[50]

The captain of the Presidio of Nuestra Señora de Loreto complained on August 26, 1791, that the presidio chapel was in dire need of more decent articles for the church and solicited from the viceroy one red and one white set of vestments for the celebration of Mass. The request was approved by Viceroy Revillagigedo, who ordered that the vestments should be bought by the royal treasurer and sent to La Bahía. By the end of the year the presidial chapel had received the two vestments which cost one hundred and seven *pesos*.[51]

---

[47]*Ibid.*, Vol. VI, pp. 230-234.

[48]*Nacogdoches Archives*, Vol. VI, pp. 140-145.

[49]Report on Mission Rosario, September 26, 1794. *Saltillo Archives*, Vol. VI, pp. 203-204.

[50]Report on Mission Espíritu Santo. *Saltillo Archives*, Vol. VI, pp. 199-202.

[51]Expediente relativo a ornamentos para la capilla del Presidio de la Bahía, 1791. *Saltillo Archives*, Vol. V, pp. 67-70.

CHAPTER II

The Secularization of the Missions

Spanish officials ever since 1778 had been contemplating drastic changes in the mission system of New Spain. The missions in the northern Interior Provinces of Coahuila, Nuevo Santander, and Texas had been a constant drain on the royal treasury. Contrary to the general provisions of the Laws of the Indies, and to the practice observed in the more populated regions of Mexico, the ten-year period had been prolonged in Texas to more than half a century. The usual practice was to distribute equitably among the neophytes the wealth (surplus products) accumulated during the ten years. The church and the priests' quarters were turned over to the ordinary with all their ornaments, vestments, sacred vessels, and other property. The bishop appointed a parish priest, the mission as such disappeared, and a new self-supporting community came into being.

But many new factors, unknown to the missionaries who worked in the thickly populated valley of Mexico, and incomprehensible to authorities in Mexico and Spain, conspired to delay indefinitely, so it seemed, the attainment of the desired goal in Texas. These factors slowed down the process of secularization by constantly maintaining the mission in a primitive stage through the continual renewal of the membership of the neophytes or mission Indians. The nomadic character of the natives, their cruder civilization, their more barbarous nature, and the presence of European rivals of Spain amongst them, such as the French and English traders, seriously complicated the task and in a large measure defeated the purpose of the missionaries, whose influence was restricted to those who came under their direct care. While it was true that local officers realized these facts, impatience with a situation that seemed to prolong itself indefinitely at a time when every effort was being directed towards the increase of royal revenues changed into open disgust.

By an incongruous twist of fate the actual secularization of the missions in Texas was accelerated and brought about by the efforts of a zealous son of the old College of Zacatecas, founded by the saintly Margil de Jesús. In his zeal to spread the faith and reach new tribes, this follower of Margil advocated the secularization of Valero and the reduction of the other four missions in San Antonio to two. He was thus inadvertently responsible for opening the floodgates that were to sweep away the Spanish mission system in Texas, waste the reserves built up during more than half a century of systematic and painstaking effort, reserves which might have been utilized for its settlement, but gave an unexpected opportunity to the ambitious pioneers of the north to penetrate the vast province. The flotsam of the wreck was to attract the hungry sea gulls and birds of prey.

Proposals for secularization of San Antonio missions. When Father Fray Manuel Silva was elected commissary and prefect of the missions of the College of Zacatecas in 1790, he undertook a personal inspection that brought him to Texas. Aroused by a desire to convert the wild coastal tribes who had resisted all missionary endeavors, he conceived a grandiose plan that included the establishment of a new mission near the Presidio of La Bahía and a line of similar establishments from the mouth of the Colorado to the distant villages of the Taovayas.[1]

Early in 1792 Father Silva went to Mexico and presented a long memorial to the viceroy concerning the new mission and others which he intended to found for the Karankawa and Tawakoni Indians on the Colorado and the Taovayas on the Red River. He explained that by establishing the proposed missions with the proper military guard, numerous tribes along the entire Gulf coast and the rivers that flowed into it would be brought under control, and the work of evangelization eventually would be extended to the fierce Comanches. In order to save additional expense to the royal treasury, he proposed that the old mission of Valero be secularized, that the four missions of Nuestra Señora de la Concepción, San Juan Capistrano, San José, and San Francisco de la Espada be reorganized as two, and that the two missionaries assigned to the new settlement of Nuestra Señora del Pilar at Nacogdoches be released and the spiritual administration be turned over to a secular priest. These measures would make available six missionaries for the new establishments without additional expense to the royal treasury.[2]

Objections to plan of Father Silva. Fray José Mariano de los Reyes, who had dedicated much time to the study of the missions of New Spain, and who had labored in Texas, was the first to be consulted. He objected

---

[1]Petition of Fray Manuel de Silva to the King, October 10, 1793. *A. G. I., Audiencia de Guadalajara,* 104-1-1 (Dunn Transcripts, 1790-1793, pp. 164-169).

[2]Memorial to the Viceroy, March 13, 1792, summarized in letter of Galindo Navarro to Commandant General Nava, June 26, 1794. *A. G. I., Audiencia de Guadalajara,* 104-1-1 (Dunn Transcripts, 1794-1798, pp. 14-15).

at once to the location chosen for the first new mission on the coast. Father Reyes doubted seriously the practicability of the proposed conversion of the Tawakonis by the establishment of a new mission on the Colorado. These Indians, he claimed, were as faithless and disinclined to accept Christianity as the Lipan-Apaches with whom they had the closest ties. The Tawakonis and Taovayas lived too near the French and the settlement of Nacogdoches. The proximity to and association with French and Spanish traders had vitiated them. There was little hope for successful missionary activity among them. The Comanches could, he conceded, be Christianized, but the task would require much time and considerable expense.[3]

Opinion of Count of Sierra Gorda. At this time the Count of Sierra Gorda was in San Antonio, temporarily acting as governor of the province while certain charges brought against Governor Manuel Muñoz were being investigated. The viceroy, at the suggestion of the *fiscal,* sent both the memorial of Father Silva and the objections of Father Reyes to the governor *ad interim* whose intimate acquaintance with frontier conditions in Nuevo Santander and Texas qualified him to give an authoritative opinion. After a careful study of the two proposals, the Count rendered a detailed report which became the basis for the subsequent action taken by the viceroy.

He favored the proposal of Father Silva respecting the site chosen for Refugio Mission at or near the confluence of the San Antonio and the Guadalupe rivers. If the new establishment was intended for the Karankawa Indians as indicated, no better location could be found, because this area had been the native habitat of these Indians for many years.[4]

Plans for secularization of Mission San Antonio de Valero. Father Silva in his memorial to the viceroy had formally expressed his willingness to give up Mission Valero, one of those placed under the care of the College of Zacatecas, and had agreed to the reduction of the other four to two. He did not, however, suggest the manner in which Valero was to be secularized, nor how the reduction of the other four was to be accomplished. As soon as his memorial was referred to the Count of Sierra Gorda, Father Silva immediately seized the oppor-

---

[3]Plan of Fray José Mariano de los Reyes, summarized in report of Conde de Sierra Gorda, September 7, 1792. *Nacogdoches Archives,* Vol. VI, pp. 235-243.

[4]Conde de Sierra Gorda to the Viceroy, September 7, 1792. *Saltillo Archives,* Vol. V, pp. 227-234.

tunity to endorse the secularization of the old mission. He agreed that it should be turned over to a secular, its property divided among the neophytes, and the residue among the former settlers of Los Adaes who were still in San Antonio. He pointed out that the houses of the old mission were not more than eighty *varas* from the Villa de San Fernando, for they were separated from the latter by only the river. These houses should be incorporated with the Villa, the streets of which should be extended through into the new addition.

The mission Indians, except for a few brought in recently who were still receiving instructions, had not only been thoroughly Christianized and civilized, but also had intermarried in a good many instances with the neighboring settlers.[5]

Conditions at La Villita. The Count of Sierra Gorda mentioned the fact that adjacent to Mission Valero and just outside the Villa de San Fernando, there had grown up a fairly large settlement of families generally called *agregados* (squatters). It was with these that many of the mission Indians had intermarried.[6] This is one of the earliest concrete references to the origin and development of La Villita which eventually came to form an important part of San Fernando and present San Antonio.

Returning to the matter of the disposition of the neophytes and the property of the mission, he suggested that the Indians who were still receiving instruction could be moved to San José. The other neophytes should each be given a yoke of oxen, a cow with a calf, a plow, a rake, a hoe, a parcel of land sufficiently large to plant four bushels of seed, a share of the corn, beans, and other products now stored in the common warehouse, and a house. Since the number of Indians was relatively small, there would be a surplus of supplies and land, as well as of available houses, remaining even after each member of the mission community received his share and provisions for a year. The acting governor proposed that any stock and all the supplies left over in the warehouse could be used to aid in founding the new mission or missions proposed by Father Silva. The houses and farm lands not needed by the neophytes could be distributed among the destitute families which had abandoned their homes at Los Adaes in 1772 by royal decree and were still living in San Antonio.

---

[5]Conde de Sierra Gorda to the Viceroy, September 27, 1792. *Saltillo Archives,* Vol. V, pp. 227-234.
  [6]*Ibid.*

The Count had evidently given some study to this question, for he explained that there still were forty-five families by actual count. These had repeatedly requested that they be given a portion of the lands of the old mission, and Hugo Oconor in fact had authorized and ordered the distribution. Governor Ripperdá had taken steps to appoint Simón de Arocha to carry out the secularization of the mission at the time, but for some reason or other the order was not executed. Since then the petitions of the *Adaesanos* for land on which to start life anew, had been refused for lack of available property. But the proposed secularization of Mission Valero would release enough arable land to meet all needs. He suggested, therefore, that after the Indians of the mission were given first choice, the remainder should be distributed among the *Adaesanos* by giving each adult male enough land for the cultivation of half a *fanega* (about a bushel) of seed.[7]

The missionaries at Nacogdoches. When Ibarbo took his settlers to the abandoned mission of Nacogdoches, he had asked the crown to furnish a missionary at royal expense to minister to the settlers, for which he held out as an inducement the possibility of attracting the former neophytes. Father Silva proposed that the two missionaries assigned to the post as the result of Ibarbo's petition be released and that a parish priest be appointed in their place, alleging that there was little or no hope of congregating the Indians. To this the Count of Sierra Gorda took objection. He pointed out that the Nacogdoches, Ais, and Tejas lived close to the new settlement, and being allies among themselves and friends of the Spaniards, they should be attracted by missionary endeavors to return to their former life. Far from removing the missionaries at the settlement of Nuestra Señora del Pilar de Nacogdoches, this post should have two or three more *Padres* from San Antonio, after the other four missions had been reorganized as two.

The Tawakonis did not live on the Colorado, he stated, but they had two pueblos on the Brazos River, some seventy-eight leagues from Nacogdoches, and ninety-two from San Antonio. They could be reached more easily from the new settlement than from the old. This was another reason for reënforcing rather than suppressing the missionary establishment at that place.[8]

---

[7]Conde de Sierra Gorda to the Viceroy, September 7, 1792. *Saltillo Archives,* Vol. V, pp. 227-234. For a detailed account of the first proposal and plan for the secularization of Mission Valero see Vol. IV, Chapter IX.

[8]*Ibid., Saltillo Archives,* Vol. V, pp. 227-234.

Approval of recommendations of Sierra Gorda. The report was sent to the *fiscal,* who, on November 13, suggested the whole matter be referred to a *Junta Superior* (Superior Council). The two plans proposed and the report of the Count of Sierra Gorda were fully discussed on December 22, at which time the Council voted that no change be made in regard to Nacogdoches, but that orders be issued for the secularization of Mission Valero in accordance with the suggestions of Sierra Gorda, and that the other four missions be reduced to two.[9] The corresponding orders were accordingly issued on January 9 and 24, 1793. While it was the intention that only Mission Valero be turned over to the ordinary and that the other four missions be consolidated as two, the execution of the decree carried the process to its inevitable end, the complete secularization of all the San Antonio missions. Copies of the decree were sent to the bishop of Monterrey, to the governor of Texas, and to the president of the missions at San Antonio.

The suppression of Mission Valero. The order of the viceroy was received by Governor Muñoz at La Bahía, where he had gone after his return to Texas. There he issued a proclamation on February 23, 1793, commanding the immediate execution of the viceregal decree just received and giving instructions as to the manner in which all property was to be listed, how it was to be distributed, and what was to be done with what remained after the mission Indians were given their share.[10]

On April 11, 1793, Governor Muñoz summoned Fray José Francisco López, president of the missions in San Antonio under the administration of the College of Zacatecas, and informed him officially of the decree concerning the secularization of Mission San Antonio de Valero (present Alamo). He was accordingly instructed to make an inventory of all the sacred vessels, ornaments, vestments, and other church property, and to give each Indian a yoke of oxen, a plow, a harrow, a hoe, an axe, and a milk cow with a calf. The governor, aided by Pedro Huizar, the surveyor, would take care of the distribution of the land.[11]

Without loss of time, Father López appointed Fray José Francisco Lozano, missionary of Valero, to proceed at once with the distribution of supplies, implements, and stock to the neophytes. This took place that

---

[9]Galindo Navarro to Commandant General Nava, June 26, 1794. *A. G. I., Audiencia de Guadalajara,* 104-1-1. (Dunn Transcripts, 1794-1798, pp. 14-33.)

[10]Auto del Gobernador Manuel Muñoz, February 23, 1793. *Saltillo Archives,* Vol. V, p. 227.

[11]Auto del Gobernador, April 11, 1793. *Saltillo Archives,* Vol. V, pp. 234-236.

same day. The governor and legal representative of the mission Indians, Esmeregildo Puente, brought all the Indians who were then living at the mission before Fray Lozano who gave each family its share. It may be well to give the entire list and the goods received by each, since the actual record of the secularization has never before been made public. Each Indian family, widower, and bachelor, received a pair of oxen, a plow, a harrow, a hoe, and a cow with a calf. From the corn in the granary, the following distributions were made:

Urbano, his wife, and two daughters were allowed thirteen bushels of corn for a period of six and a half months.

Juan de Dios, his wife, an adult daughter, and two minors were given eighteen bushels of corn.

José Miguel, his wife, and two sons were allotted thirteen bushels of corn.

Juan José and wife were apportioned nine bushels.

Esmeregildo Puente, his wife, and one daughter took thirteen bushels.

José Joaquín, his wife, and one young daughter received eleven bushels.

Domingo and his wife were given nine bushels of corn.

Manuel, his wife, and an orphan boy were allotted thirteen bushels.

Dolores, widow with three children, was assigned eight and a half bushels of corn besides the regular equipment.

Anselmo, his wife, and three children were given fifteen bushels of corn.

Mateo, widower, received four and a half bushels of corn.

Bernardo, bachelor, was granted four and a half bushels of corn.

Francisco, bachelor, received four and a half bushels of corn.

José Agustín, bachelor, was given four and a half bushels of corn.[12]

Thus thirty-nine persons, including men, women and children, received rations from the granary of Mission Valero intended for their support until the new crop was harvested. The Indian governor, Esmeregildo Puente, witnessed the distribution and signed a certified receipt for the mission Indians. But that same day he filed a formal protest, alleging that the corn allowed the mission Indians was inadequate for their maintenance until the next harvest because, due to the severity of the winter, the fields had not been planted at the usual time. This meant that the sowing would not take place now until late in November. Furthermore, the corn given each family would suffer greater loss from rats,

---

[12]Autos sobre secularizatión, *Saltillo Archives*, Vol. V, pp. 237-239.

mice, and other pests than if kept in a common granary and rationed weekly. In view of these circumstances, he requested Governor Muñoz to instruct the missionary to give each family four and a half additional bushels of corn, which amounted to forty-two bushels. He also requested a crowbar and six axes.

Governor Muñoz readily agreed to the request and ordered Fray López to give the neophytes the corn and implements solicited and any other supplies they might need. Accordingly, on April 13, Father López gave the former mission Indians forty-two bushels of corn, three and a half bushels of beans, three and a half bushels of salt, a crowbar, six axes, two carts, two yoke of oxen, and eleven horses.[13]

Distribution of the land. In accord with the decree of January 9, Governor Muñoz took immediate steps to subdivide the farm lands of Mission Valero. On April 12, he went to the *Labor de Abajo* (Lower Farm), where Esmeregildo Puente, the Indian governor and legal representative of the mission Indians, met him by appointment. With Puente were Urbano, Juan de Dios, José Miguel, Juan José, José Joaquín, Domingo, Manuel, Anselmo, Mateo, Bernardino, Francisco, and José Agustín to whom the lands were to be assigned. Pedro Huizar, the official surveyor, accompanied Muñoz. They proceeded to divide the farm into equal tracts, each suitable for the planting of two bushels of seed. In addition to the tracts for these twelve, another tract was surveyed for Dolores, the widow. The distribution having been satisfactorily completed, and there being considerable land left over, Vicente Amador, resident of the Villa de San Fernando, and Pedro Huizar, the surveyor, formally requested for themselves a tract of land, similar to those assigned the mission Indians. The Indians were asked if they had any objections, and replied that they did not; whereupon the governor granted their request.[14] The survey and distribution were witnessed by the two governors, Pedro Huizar, Manuel Arocha, *alcalde* of the Villa de San Fernando, and Luiz M. Menchaca, commander of the Presidio of San Antonio de Béjar.

Aid for the founding of Mission Refugio. It will be remembered that the Count of Sierra Gorda had recommended that after the neophytes of Valero had received a fair share of the mission property and supplies, the residue was to be used in part to help found the new mission proposed

[13]*Ibid., Saltillo Archives,* Vol. V, pp. 241-242.
[14]*Ibid.,* pp. 239-241.

by Father Silva. On April 15 Governor Muñoz acknowledged the receipt of twenty-seven milk cows, twenty-two heifers one year old, seventeen bull calves one-year old, two other bull calves, eighteen heifers, and twenty-six oxen, a total of one hundred twelve head intended for the new mission. At the same time he received ten saddle horses which were turned over to Corporal Facundo Mansolo to be taken to Refugio where Father José Mariano Garza, left in charge by Father Silva, was to sign a receipt. In the granary there were at this time two hundred fifty bushels of corn on the cob, five bushels of beans, and six bushels of salt.[15]

Church property. On April 23 Governor Muñoz proceeded to make an inventory of the property in the old chapel of the Mission of San Antonio de Valero founded in 1718 by Father Olivares. In this task he was assisted by Fathers Fray José Francisco López and Fray José Mariano Garza, both of the College of Zacatecas. In the sacristy were found one complete set of somewhat worn vestments of black velvet, trimmed with silver braid and lined with black; one white set embroidered with flowers of various colors, trimmed with gold braid and lined with pink silk; another of red chintz, with imitation gold braid, and the lining worn; the fourth of red damask, trimmed with silver braid; one of white damask, trimmed with gold braid, and lined; a green satin set, trimmed with gold braid, and lined with red cloth; a seventh of purple damask, trimmed with fine gold braid and lined with red cloth; and three complete sets of vestments, red, white, and green, brought back from the Mission of Nuestra Señora de Guadalupe de Nacogdoches. There was one cope of white chintz with red embroidered flowers, and fine gold braid trimmings, lined with purple cloth; two purple altar veils for Passion Week; a black velvet tunic and mantle with silver trimmings for the image of Our Lady of Sorrows; another of blue satin; a string of imitation pearls; three large brass crosses and a pallium.

The linen consisted of fourteen albs, a set of white altar cloths embroidered with red silk, six sets of plain white altar cloths, and a good supply of the necessary cloths, towels, and other linen.

The missal was bound in red velvet and had silver clasps. There were a gold monstrance, two chalices with their patens, one gold and one silver; two ciboria of the same metals; two sets of cruets with their corresponding trays, one of glass and the other of silver; one set of

---

[15]Auto del Gobernador, April 15, 1793. *Saltillo Archives*, pp. 242-243.

altar bells, one censer, six candlesticks, and a silver cross. The weight of all the silver artefacts found in use was estimated at one hundred twenty-two pounds. In addition to the silver listed, there were numerous brass and copper objects such as candlesticks, processional crosses, censers, bells, and water fonts. The furniture was likewise carefully listed, but space does not permit its inclusion.

Condition of the church and buildings of the mission. The following day Governor Muñoz appointed Antonio Salazar, master mason, and Pedro Huizar, carpenter, to make a report on the buildings of the mission. Vicente Amador and Joaquín Flores, residents and officers of the Cabildo of the Villa de San Fernando, assisted them. The home of the missionary was found to be a solidly built stone house, measuring twenty-two and three-quarters by twenty-two and one-half *varas*. The north and the south wings were both two stories high, and divided by a hall. Each wing had five rooms which served as cells, each cell being five *varas* by four. These two tiers of cells were in need of repair, because the flat roof was full of holes. The west wing also had a second story and a corridor. On the first floor there were an office, and four rooms, longer than those described, and a small room at the base of the stairway. On the second story were three cells. The roofs were partly rotted and needed repairs.

In the middle of the patio there was a well with its stone superstructure, arch, and bucket. On the east side of the irregular rectangle of the mission ran a wall from north to south one hundred and seventy-five *varas* long. The south wall ran east and west for fifty-eight *varas*. Both walls were three *varas* high and three-quarters of a *vara* thick, made of stone, adobe, and mud. Half the north wall was in ruins. The main gate that led to the plaza through the south wall measured five *varas* in width and four in height. Within the enclosure completed by the church and mission buildings were the houses of the neophytes. Adjoining the *Padres'* quarters was a building thirty *varas* long, five wide, and seven high, with adobe floor. This was used as the barn. The roof of this storehouse was in very poor condition, for only the beams were sound. A small rampart with a one-pound cannon stood near the entrance of the *Padres'* house. There was also a large *jacal* built of mud and willow wands with a straw roof, which was likewise being used as a storehouse at this time. Most of the Indian quarters faced the archway along the western wing. Of these, only twelve were habitable, for the others were in ruins.

The church. This had not been completed. It was one hundred *varas* long and nine wide, with a transept. The type of architecture was Tuscan. The domed roof rested upon groups of columns. The group of columns in the presbytery had been completed and three others almost finished. The baptistry lacked only the doors. The central façade was a showy and impressive piece of Tuscan architecture. The first group of sculptured figures consisting of two stone statues of St. Francis and St. Dominic, was completed.

The sacristy. This was twelve *varas* long, five high, and five wide. At this time it was being used as the church. It too had a domed roof. The walls, though not plastered, had been neatly whitewashed. There were two doors with carved stone frames. One of these led into an adjoining room eight and two-thirds *varas* by seven and two-thirds, with a wooden roof and cedar rafters. This room had a door on the north side and one on the east and two windows facing south and west. The doors had iron hooks and eyes. Its roof, like that of the rest of the building, was in urgent need of repairs.[16]

Statues and paintings. On April 24, the inventory of the statues, paintings, and altars was made. On one of the side altars, in a glass case, was a statue of Saint Anthony holding the child Jesus in his arms. The Child wore a crown of silver. Over the main altar hung a large cross, one and a third *varas* long. On one side of the altar was a statue of the Nazarene in a purple tunic, bearing His cross. On the opposite side was a statue, three-quarter size, of Saint Joseph, with a silver crown and staff and the child Jesus standing by his side. There was also a statue of Our Lady of Sorrows. In the adjoining room, which served as the sacristy, was another three-quarter statue of Saint Anthony. On a post outside the building were a large bell in good condition, and two others that were cracked. There were also five thousand five hundred new shingles, eighteen hewn logs, and one hundred fifty cedar rafters intended for the repairs of the roofs.[17]

Lipan Indians refuse to be moved. Up to this time no difficulty had been encountered in executing the orders of the viceroy in regard to the suppression of Mission Valero. But when Chief Mariano of the Lipan nation was summoned by Governor Muñoz and Father Fray José

---

[16]Expediente sobre el recibo de los vasos sagrados, y demás utensilios de la Mision de San Antonio Valero. *Saltillo Archives*, Vol. V, pp. 244-252.

[17]*Ibid., Saltillo Archives*, Vol. V, pp. 252-253.

Francisco López and was told that he and his seventeen followers now at Valero were to be moved to Mission San José, as recommended by Count de Sierra Gorda, the chief replied that he and his people preferred to remain where they were. "It was explained to him with all clearness," declared the governor, "how they would be much better taken care of at San José." Chief Mariano's only reply was that he wanted to stay in Valero where he had always lived and where many of his relatives were buried. This answer was repeated individually by the other seventeen Lipans. The governor had no choice but to allow them to remain until he had consulted the viceroy.[18]

Decree for secularization of all missions. Before the interrupted suppression of San Antonio de Valero could be completed, there came a new decree ordering the secularization of all the missions in Texas. The previous order had affected only Valero, but the new decree applied to all. The matter had finally been decided by the king's council. The various recommendations of short-sighted officials and disgruntled or overzealous missionaries had at last borne fruit.

The decree of April 10, 1794, issued by Pedro Nava as commandant general of the Interior Provinces, put an end to the old missions in Texas and set up a new system for the administration of the communal property of the mission Indians. It provided that in all the mission pueblos in the Interior Provinces, which had existed more than ten years, the old system of administering the temporal property of the neophytes was to be abolished. Only in the case of missions founded within less than ten years was the communal property to continue to be administered by the missionaries. From the date of publication of the new regulations, every mission Indian was henceforth to enjoy all the liberty, freedom, and privileges granted by Spanish laws to Spaniards and *gente de razón* (beings endowed with reason). They were individually to take care of their own cattle, cultivate and plant their own lands, enjoy the returns of their crops, engage freely in trade, pursue the work they preferred, and seek gainful employment as laborers to provide for the needs and care of their families. But the justices and other public officials were to exercise particular zeal to prevent them from falling into idle habits or evil ways and to keep them from indulging in drunkenness and other excesses to which they were prone.[19]

[18]Autos del Gobernador, April 24, 1793. *Saltillo Archives*, Vol. V, pp. 253-254.
[19]Decreto de secularización del Comandante General Don Pedro Nava, April 10, 1794. *Saltillo Archives*, Vol. VI, pp. 99-106.

The new administrative officers, the *justicias* (justices), were given all the powers formerly exercised by the missionaries in supervising the natives and in protecting their interests. The neophytes came to enjoy much less of the theoretical liberty and freedom so loudly proclaimed by the edict under the new guardians. The missionaries had a sincere interest in the welfare of their wards whom they could not help loving as their own children. The new officers entrusted with this duty lacked, and could never come to have such affection. The Spaniards in the vicinity of the missions had long awaited this opportunity to exploit the unwary neophytes.

But let us return to the provisions of the edict. The justices were to watch carefully that the Indians were to be given a fair price for their products and goods, and that when they contracted to work as laborers for a specified wage, they were to be paid in cash as stipulated, without shortchanging them. But if the Indians were willing to receive a part of their wages in kind, the justices were to allow them their choice, and insist that the goods given them be of good quality and at the current market price. They were to see to it that no gamblers or peddlers entered the secularized pueblos, and that wine and liquor peddlers did not ply their trade among the natives. It was pointed out that the sale of intoxicants not only encouraged drunkenness but led to the sale of the Indians' products, cattle, and goods for ridiculously low prices.

From the best and most fertile lands near the mission pueblos, eight *suertes* (plats), four hundred by two hundred *varas* each, were to be surveyed and set aside for the common use of the Indians, in which each might plant his corn in accord with the provisions of Law 31, Title 4, Book 6 of the Law of the Indies, ordered to be observed by Article 44 of the Ordinances of the Intendencies. Two or three additional plats of the size indicated, or as many as might be deemed advisable, were at the same time to be surveyed and set aside to provide for the future needs of the Indian community.

In addition to the communal lands for the benefit of each pueblo, similar plats were to be surveyed and assigned to each family. In the case of large families, if one plat was insufficient, two might be allowed.

Each Indian was to receive title to the land assigned him, setting forth clearly the bounds and limits of his property. This service was to be performed free of cost in the name of the king. The Indians could not, for any reason, sell, alienate, dispose of, or mortgage in any manner the lands assigned them. Furthermore, the grant carried with it the obligation to make productive the lands received. Any Indian who failed to cultivate his property for a period of two years lost title to it. Such land could then be granted to someone more industrious.

With the exception of the governors, the chiefs, and the *alcaldes,* all other members of the Indian pueblos formerly in missions, were obliged to labor in the common fields for a stated period of time each year without pay.

In the administration of communal property, the provisions of the Ordinances for Intendencies, article 28 and the following, were to be observed.

All missionaries and parish priests in Indian communities were to be formally released from the administration of temporal property, which henceforth was to be under the jurisdiction of the royal justices appointed for that purpose. Upon receipt of the new regulations, the missionaries were to proceed without delay to the formal delivery by inventory of all communal property held and administered for the benefit of the neophytes.[20]

Useless warning. The decree was sent to Governor Muñoz, as well as to the bishop of Nuevo León and all the other officials of the Interior Provinces. Wisely and with justified apprehension the bishop pointed out the serious consequences that might result from the great powers given to the justices by the new regulations. On May 11 he wrote to the commandant general setting forth his opinion. The bishop, while granting that the justices selected to guard and protect the interests of the natives proved to be wise and honest men, and charitably inclined, asserted that the powers given them were such that without some check or other means of holding them responsible, grave abuses were inevitable. The paymasters of presidial troops, who were given an adequate salary, made bond and were under constant supervision; they were, nevertheless, frequently found guilty of embezzlement. Even officers of the royal treasury had, in recent years, been found guilty of forgery. What could be expected of the justices placed in charge of the temporal goods of Indian pueblos, far removed from any supervision, assigned no salary for their services, and not required to make bond? How could they be expected to dedicate their full time to the supervision of the labor of the Indians in the field and to the sale of

---

[20]Decreto de secularización del Comandante General Pedro Nava, April 10, 1794. *Saltillo Archives,* Vol. VI, pp. 99-106.

their products, when they themselves had to work for a living? The missionaries lived with the Indians, they had interests in common, and had no other obligations to meet. The justices had families of their own to provide for and would have to neglect their duties toward the Indians unless an adequate salary or compensation was granted them. The temptation to profit from their position would in all probability prove too great for the inherent weakness of human nature.

He remonstrated that the usual ten-year limit for secularization should not be applied to the missions of the Interior Provinces. Ten years were not sufficient to teach the wild Indians of Texas the habits of industry and self-control. In that time they could not learn to be self-supporting, nor could a surplus be accumulated by the common labor of the neophytes to permit each Indian to become a self-supporting individual. It was a grave mistake to think that the surplus accumulated by the missions was idle wealth. The supply of food and clothes stored by the mission was indispensable as a reserve in lean years and as a constant inducement to attract new converts. "It is always necessary," he declared, "to provide for the widows, the invalids, and the orphans of each mission. But in order to attract and hold the new converts, the goods and supplies themselves are a powerful inducement, constituting a guarantee that they will be fed."[21]

The opinion of the bishop in the case was entirely disinterested. It is to be kept in mind that he would receive no direct revenue from the mission pueblos as long as these were under the administration of the missionaries. Once secularized, each pueblo became a parish under a secular priest. Had selfish motives dictated the letter of the bishop of Nuevo León, he would have heartily endorsed the plan for their immediate secularization.

Governor Muñoz pleads for time. On June 25, 1794, the governor wrote the commandant general that he would proceed to put in effect the decree of secularization as soon as circumstances permitted him to carry out its provisions. A sense of duty, he felt, constrained him to explain the difficulties confronting him at this time.

In the first place, the condition of the missions was such that it made their secularization almost impossible. San Francisco de la Espada had only fifteen Indians; San Juan Capistrano, eleven; San José, twenty;

---

[21]Bishop of Nuevo León to Pedro Nava, May 11, 1794. *Saltillo Archives,* Vol. VI, pp. 80-84.

and Concepción, thirteen. These numbers included the sick and aged. The property held was as meager as the number of Indians left. Espada had eight yoke of oxen, one cow, five horses, about thirteen hundred sheep, and six bushels of corn planted. Capistrano had only two yoke of oxen of its own, having to borrow six more yoke from Concepción to plant its crop. It had thirty-seven cows, twelve horses, and a small field of corn. San José owned twelve yoke of oxen, thirty head of cattle, forty horses and mares, and ten bushels of corn planted. Concepción had nine yoke of oxen, about one hundred head of cattle, and eight bushels of corn planted in the fields. The governor further explained that he had obtained this information not from the missionaries, but from mission overseers.

There was one other consideration that made it advisable to postpone the secularization of the missions until after the crops had been harvested. Espada and San José, promising to pay after the harvest, had purchased supplies on credit from the presidio and from some of the merchants of the Villa de San Fernando. If the entire mission property was distributed now, the creditors would be unable to collect.[22]

Secularization of Mission San Francisco de la Espada. While pleading for time, the governor took steps, nevertheless, to comply with the orders received. The same day on which he wrote to Nava, he requested the new president of the missions, Father Fray José Mariano Cárdenas, to instruct the missionaries under his jurisdiction to make the necessary inventories for turning over all temporal property to the Indians of the respective missions as ordered by the commandant general. He set July 11 as the date for putting the decree into execution and stated that the secularization of the remaining missions would begin with San Francisco de la Espada.[23]

Father Cárdenas had previously received a copy of the decree directly from Nava. He wrote to the commandant general on July 6, assuring him that the news of the decision taken would please Father Fray Ignacio María Lava, guardian of the College of Zacatecas, since the college had been anxious for many years to be relieved of the responsibility of the temporal administration which he had offered to surrender when the Caballero de Croix was in Texas in 1778. "If I may speak

---

[22]Governor Manuel Muñoz to Pedro Nava, June 25, 1794. *Saltillo Archives,* Vol. VI, pp. 85-87.

[23]Governor Muñoz to Fray José Mariano Cárdenas, June 25, 1794. *Saltillo Archives,* Vol. VI, pp. 106-109.

frankly," he said, "I can not praise sufficiently the justness, the fairness, and the wisdom of the measure." He added that all the missionaries had been duly informed of its provisions and instructed to carry them out as soon as the governor was ready to effect the formal transfer of all mission property.

Considering that the welfare of the Indians was the prime motive for secularization, Father Cárdenas asked permission to make a recommendation with regard to Mission Espíritu Santo. Although it was true that the mission had been founded many years ago, the neophytes now living there were still in a rather wild stage and totally incapable of administering their property individually. To divide among them the temporal goods of the mission would be to squander its resources uselessly, because these Indians, if left alone, would revert to savagery. The reason for this state of affairs was that those now in the mission had lived as apostates among the Tawakoni for many years, and had been brought back only three years previously. "I call the attention of your lordship to these facts," he declared, "in case you wish to make an exception in this instance, preventing thereby the loss of their souls."[24]

On July 11, 1794, Governor Muñoz went to Mission San Francisco de la Espada and was met there by Father Fray Pedro Noreña, minister in charge, and by José Lázaro de los Santos, the newly appointed *justicia*. He ordered that all the mission Indians be summoned and that the decree of the commandant general be read and explained to them. Fifteen neophytes, including three who were old and disabled, were brought. They were the Indian governor, Blas Torres, José Tejada, Tomás Ganzábal, Patricio Codallos, Miguel Codallos, Mariano Díaz, Esteban Galindo, Emeterio Espinosa, Cosme Ceballos, Juan de Dios Montes, Antonio Villegas, Juan Eustaquio Tejada, José Miguel Conti, Jorge Pinilla, and Francisco Antonio Pinto. Upon hearing the terms of the decree of secularization, they declared they were ready to receive their share of the mission property and to administer and increase it. The governor had his doubts as to the ability of these Indians to carry out their promise, as he honestly and frankly expressed his opinion in the record. "The governor is of the opinion," he wrote, "that the fifteen Indians are incapable of fulfilling their promise with regard to the administration and increase of their individual property." Pedro Huizar,

---

[24]Fray José Mariano de Cárdenas to Pedro Nava, July 6, 1794. *Saltillo Archives*, Vol. VI, pp. 91-93.

the surveyor, was instructed to proceed with the survey and division of
the mission lands, but nothing more was done this day.

On July 12, the actual survey and distribution took place, witnessed
by the two governors, the new *justicia,* and Fray Noreña. Eight plats,
four hundred by two hundred *varas* each, were first surveyed and set
aside as communal lands of the mission pueblo. Then fifteen other plats
were surveyed, each three hundred by two hundred *varas,* one of which
was assigned to each mission Indian. They were then told that any lands
which they could not cultivate should be rented to the Spaniards with
the consent of *Justicia* José Lázaro de los Santos. It was further explained
to them that the woods and pasture lands of the mission were now theirs,
and that they should demand rent from any person who used them for
his private stock and cattle.

In addition to the communal lands assigned the new pueblo and the
individual farms granted to each Indian, they also were given on this
day eight yoke of oxen fully equipped, eleven plows, nine harrows, and
four hoes with handles; twenty-five pounds of iron, three pounds of
steel; three crowbars, five axes, one bucksaw, a handsaw, an English
saw, a compass, four bits, a pair of beam scales, a brass scale, a small
brass frame; two one-pound cannon weighing two hundred fifty-six
pounds, and ninety-eight pounds of lead; fifteen pairs of shears, eight
hundred seventy-five pounds of wood, and two looms complete with their
respective combs, cards, spinning wheels, and shuttles; a mare and three
horses, three mules, and nine sets of harness, a cow with a calf, and
eleven hundred fifty head of sheep.

The two hundred seven sheep and their lambs were not divided among
the Indians but left to be cared for as a flock by Joaquín Lerma who
agreed to tend them. The Indian governor and the others agreed to pay
Lerma eight *pesos,* two bushels of corn, and a *peso* and a half of cigarettes
each month for his services. These were to be paid after the sheep had
been sheared.

Having completed the delivery of all the mission property to the
neophytes, Governor Muñoz reviewed for them again the new method
they were to follow in the administration of their individual property,
the cultivation of their lands, and the disposal of the crops raised. They
replied that they understood their duties and would consult with the
new *justicia* to solve all the problems that might arise. Governor Muñoz
further explained to them that the plat of land called *"jardín,"* and

surveyed for the secular priest who was to look after their spiritual welfare, was to be cultivated at his own expense.[25]

Secularization of Mission San Juan Capistrano. Without loss of time Governor Muñoz went to Mission San Juan Capistrano on July 14 and requested Fray José Mariano Cárdenas, who was temporarily in charge during the absence of Father Fray José Ramón Tejada, to proceed at once with the transfer of all temporal property to the neophytes. With him came José Gil, the newly appointed *justicia.* Father Cárdenas immediately summoned the Indian governor, José Cayetano Valle, who brought with him all the neophytes of the mission. These were José Díaz, Matías Jiménez, José María Rivera, Marcelino Castañeda, Antonio Bustillos, José Ventura Quiñones, Matías Prado, Salvador Flores, Luís Bustamante, Conrado Riveras, and Mariano Tejada. The decree of secularization was read to them, and Pedro Huizar was ordered to proceed at once with the survey and subdivision of the mission lands.

Eight plats, two hundred *varas* by four hundred, of the best lands nearest the mission were set aside as the communal farm. The bounds and limits were carefully marked. Then the surveyor measured off twelve plats, two hundred *varas* by one hundred, which were assigned individually to the twelve Indians listed for their own use and their families'. Of the field adjacent to the main *labor* (farm), planted with sugar cane in forty-seven rows, three additional sections of the same size were surveyed and marked. These were assigned to the mission Indians for common use and the crop gathered therefrom was to be apportioned among themselves. They agreed that after the sugar cane was harvested, the three plats would be rented and the proceeds, as with the communal lands, were to be used for the benefit of the pueblo.

Having received the lands, they returned to the mission where the following property was turned over to them: Two crowbars of twenty-five pounds weight, six hoes with handles, and two axes, two large bits and a small one, one large and one small hacksaw, and an English saw, two chisels, a small hammer, two trowels, one large and two small beam scales; a wooden bushel measure, a peck measure; a weaving loom, a loom and shuttle spindle and two combs; one harrow and four plow-

---

[25]Inventario de los bienes de Temporalidad de la Mision de Sn. Franco. de la Espada Provincia de los Texas. Entregados con arreglo á orden del señor comandante general de estas Provincias Ynternas de Nueva España Briger. Dn. Pedro Nava a los Yndios de ella por el Governador Dn. Manuel Muñoz. *Saltillo Archives,* Vol. VI, pp. 99-117.

shares, weighing nineteen pounds, seven plows with their yoke and harness; one cart, two extra cart wheels; a mule, a mare and two horses, and four yoke of oxen; two branding irons; one iron cannon and three one-pound balls. There were fifty-five head of cattle, of which twenty-two were cows, twenty-two yearlings, and eleven calves. The Indian governor and the other twelve neophytes each took four, and the remaining three cows with their calves were left for the use of the new parish priest when he would come.

The pasture lands, a field planted in sugar cane, and the crop from four bushels of corn that had been planted but not yet harvested, were assigned to the neophytes also, but with the understanding that they were to distribute the harvest equally among themselves and use the pasture in common for their stock and cattle. Out of the income derived from these fields the Indians were to provide for the needs of the orphans, the widows, the disabled, and the sick.

Governor Muñoz explained to them their new status, their duties and obligations, and the relation that existed now between them and José Gil, the Spanish *justicia* appointed to look after their interests. They were told, also, that before going to work, they were to continue to attend church and hear Mass as good Christians should.[26] Not much was to be expected from the new *justicia* who had to have his son sign his name for him.

Secularization of Mission San José. The governor next went to Mission San José de San Miguel de Aguayo on July 16, and requested Father Fray José Manuel Pedrajo, the priest in charge, to summon all the neophytes and proceed to turn over to them all the temporal property of the mission in the presence of José Herrera, the *justicia* just appointed guardian of the Indians. Father Pedrajo immediately complied with the request, and a detailed list of the neophytes, who were much more numerous than in the two previous instances, was carefully made. This list shows that there were at San José twenty-seven men, twenty-six women, eleven boys, and fourteen girls, who were Christianized, and fifteen who had come to the mission recently and were still receiving instruction, a total of ninety-six persons.

---

[26]Ynventario de los bienes de temporalidad de la Misión de Sn. Juan Capistrano Provincia de los Texas Entregados con arreglo á orden del señor comandante general de estas Provincias Ynternas de Nueva España Briger. Dn. Pedro de Nava. A los Yndios de ella por el Governador Dn. Manuel Muñoz. *Saltillo Archives*, Vol. VI, pp. 119-134.

The survey and subdivision of the farm lands for San José took longer than for the other missions. Pedro Huizar reported on July 22, however, that he had completed the task. The following day Governor Muñoz, Father Pedrajo, Huizar, Herrera, and twenty-eight others, heads of families and bachelors, went to the lands surveyed for the formal assignment. The plats, it is to be noted, were larger than those of the two previously secularized missions, for these were two hundred by three hundred *varas* each. After giving each Christian Indian one plat, Governor Muñoz granted to the six heads of the gentile Indians, who were still under instruction, two similar plats which would enable them to acquire habits of industry. For the communal lands, eight plats were set aside, each one four hundred by two hundred *varas*.

The governor and the other officials then returned to the mission where the rest of the property was distributed to the neophytes. This consisted of sixteen plows, eight harrows, and two plowshares weighing sixty-two pounds; six hoes, seven axes, one chisel, two crowbars weighing twenty-four pounds; four bucksaws, one handsaw, an English saw, eighteen adzes, and fifty-two pairs of shears. The mission had fourteen yoke of oxen, thirteen yoke of young bullocks partially trained to work, and thirty-four milk cows with their calves. One cow was given to each Indian and to Fermín Ramírez who had married a Creole woman and had left the mission pueblo but returned to claim his share; the other six were given to the gentile Indians in the mission. Twenty-seven horses belonged to the mission, likewise seven mares, of which five were given to the gentile Indians. The field planted with two bushels of corn was almost ready to harvest, and another field with seven bushels would be harvested later; four fields were planted with sugar cane in one hundred eight rows. The granary contained ninety *cargas* (sacks) of wheat, calculated to be about five hundred forty bushels. Included in the list were a branding iron, three looms fully equipped, five pairs of carders, and twenty-three *arrobas* (five hundred seventy-five pounds) of raw wool. Two droves of mares, each of forty-five head, and a stallion, were in the inventory. A completely equipped blacksmith shop with its bellows, anvils, hammers, tongs, files, and other tools were mentioned. There were other miscellaneous articles, such as a mason's hammer, two stone picks, a bushel measure and a peck measure, a plane, a large bit, and a large wooden tool box with two latches.

They were also given the deed to eleven *sitios* of land which had been purchased by the mission on November 22, 1766, from Francisco

Antonio de Echevarría. It was explained that the pasture lands on León Creek belonged to them also, as well as all branded cattle and stock found therein. But if any unbranded livestock was caught or killed, their number was to be reported to the governor for the payment of the fee exacted by His Majesty.

Father Pedrajo declared that there were some debts owed the mission by various individuals and that he would prepare a detailed report of these assets, so that the new *justicia* might take steps to collect them. He added that there were in Reynosa thirty-two horses and one mule which belonged to Mission San José. These were to be brought back by Felipe Neri Montoya who had already gone for them.

The neophytes were given possession also of the granary, a stone building forty *varas* long and eight wide, with a domed roof and two doors. There were, besides this structure, the carpenter shop with its triple arch *corredor,* a workshop, and fifty-four dwellings. Six of the latter were in ruins, but the others were in fairly good condition. Most of them had doors and windows.[27]

Misgivings concerning La Bahía Missions. While waiting for the completion of the survey and division of the San José mission, Governor Muñoz reported to the commandant general the secularization of San Juan Capistrano and La Espada. At the same time Muñoz called his attention to the fact that there were three men and five women at San José who were not civilized or capable of administering their own affairs. These eight Indians had many relatives on the coast who might come to join them. The governor wanted to know what he should do with them. In the meantime, while awaiting the decision, he would assign them sufficient property to insure their livelihood under the supervision of the missionary.

It is of interest to note that he also informed Nava at this time that there was a group of Indians at Reynosa who had expressed a desire to join Mission San José. In view of the circumstances, he had sent an Indian and a Spaniard to inform them of the secularization and to find out if they still contemplated coming. Should they decide to come, the governor assured Nava he would take such steps as were necessary to provide for them until he received instructions.

---

[27]Ynventario de los bienes de Temporalidad de la Misión de S. S. José, Provincia de Texas, Entregados con arreglo á orden del señor comandante general de estas Provincias Ynternas de N. E. Briger. Dn. Pedro de Nava a los Yndios de ella por el Governador Dn. Manuel Muñoz. *Saltillo Archives*, Vol. VI, pp. 135-157.

Conditions somewhat analogous existed in Missions Espíritu Santo and Rosario at La Bahía. The Jaraname Indians now at Espíritu Santo were mostly apostates, who recently had been induced by the zealous Fray José Mariano Garza to return to the mission. He had penetrated the country of the Tawakoni where the apostates had taken refuge and had persuaded them to return. Many of their relatives still lived among the Tawakoni. They had not had time to become good Christians or to acquire the restraint necessary to administer their own affairs. There was danger that once they had squandered the goods and property of the mission, they would soon return to their former apostasy and join their old friends, the Tawakoni.

Because of these considerations, the governor did not transmit the order for secularization to the captain of that presidio. He decided to wait until he had finished in San Antonio so that he could go to Espíritu Santo in person, and take with him Fray José Mariano Cárdenas who had labored among the Jaranames before and who understood their language. It was his intention to ascertain the desire of the Indians and their degree of civilization before putting the orders of the commandant general into execution.[28]

Secularization of Mission Nuestra Señora de la Concepción. On July 31, Governor Muñoz requested Father Fray José María Camarena to turn over all mission property to his former neophytes, as provided by the decree of secularization. Father Camarena immediately summoned the Indian governor, Salvador de Soto, and instructed him to bring all the mission Indians. These were then presented to Governor Muñoz, who ordered that a list of their names be made by *Justicia* Pedro Huizar, the surveyor. The Indians present were Salvador de Soto, Felix Castillo, Francisco Hernández, Jacobo Pintado, Lorenzo Villegas, Manuel Pintado, Cecilio de Armas, Melchor Villegas, Javier Camacho, José Manuel Cuevas, Julián Paredes, Ventura Villegas, Juan Antonio Corbera, Francisco Coronado, José Guadalupe, Mariano Pintado, María Rosa Cuevas, Juana Francisca, Gertrudes Cuevas, Magdalena Menchaca, Viviana Paredes, Gertrudes, Petra Villegas, Antonio Tampila, María Vicenta Hernández, Catalina Gutiérrez, Isabel de la Encina, María Susana Tampila, Serafina Andrade, Serafina Micheas, Gertrudes de Armas, a total of sixteen men and fifteen women. To this list should be added one boy and six girls, bringing the grand total to thirty-eight persons. Muñoz issued

---

[28]Governor Manuel Muñoz to Pedro Nava, July 18, 1794. *Saltillo Archives*, Vol. VI, pp. 88-90.

instructions for the immediate survey of the mission lands, but it being late in the day the actual distribution was postponed until the next morning. Eight plats, four hundred by two hundred *varas* each, were duly marked off and set aside as common lands for the benefit of the new pueblo. They then proceeded to stake off eighteen plats, three hundred by two hundred *varas* each, which were assigned in the following manner: sixteen were given to as many mission Indians; one to a former Spanish overseer of the mission, Javier Longoria, who agreed to continue to supervise the sowing of the crops; and one to Pedro Huizar, the new *justicia*, to cultivate or rent for his benefit and his family's in lieu of a salary for his services.

After returning to the mission, the secularized Indians received all the other property formerly owned by the community. This consisted of a farm planted with eight bushels of corn, two cotton fields, a farm with ten pecks of beans; eighteen yoke of oxen, one hundred twenty-eight cows with their calves, placed under the care of a herder who was to be paid for his services out of the community funds of the pueblo; eleven saddle horses, eleven mares, with a stallion and a jack, five mules with pack equipment, thirteen horses bearing the mission brand. All this was distributed equitably among the neophytes. Any unbranded cattle caught or slaughtered were to be reported to Governor Muñoz for the payment of the royal fee.[29] The San Antonio missions as an institution of the Spanish frontier had passed away.

Labor on public works, primary schools, and churches. Now that the missions were secularized, and the communal property was distributed, several matters remained to be settled. On June 14 the commandant general wrote Governor Muñoz asking him to state his opinion regarding the extent to which the former neophytes could be expected to render personal service in the construction or repair of churches or the priests' quarters and the building and maintenance of primary schools in their respective pueblos.

Nava seems to have had a special desire to keep the Indians, now being set free from the tutelage of the missionaries, from doing any work whatever for the *Padres*. Without awaiting the reply of Governor

---

[29]Ynventario de los bienes de Temporalidad de la Misión de la Purísima Concepción Entregados á los Yndios de ella consiguiente á orden del Señor Comandante General Briger. Dn. Pedro de Nava de 10 de abril de este corriente año. Comunicada al Governador de esta Provincia de los Texas. The Corl. Dn. Manuel Muñoz, 1794. *Saltillo Archives*, Vol. VI, pp. 158-178.

Muñoz, he, on July 14, wrote Father Cárdenas, president of the Zacatecan missions, and actually instructed him that the former mission Indians were not to be required to render any service in the construction, completion or repair of parish churches or ministers' quarters. Furthermore, they were not to contribute their labor for the construction, maintenance, or repair of the primary school buildings. If they agreed to work on any of these projects, the previous consent of the commandant general was required.

Father Cárdenas replied on July 20 that he had taken due notice of the new regulations concerning the labor of natives on public works and had issued instructions to all the missionaries accordingly.[30]

To Nava's request for an opinion, Governor Muñoz replied on August 14. He explained that the material resources of the Indians were very limited, as proved by the records of the distribution of the mission property. Nevertheless, the natives were morally bound as parishioners to contribute to the maintenance and repair of their churches, the curates' homes, and their schools. They could either render personal labor in the repair of these buildings or pay out of the communal funds of the new pueblos an amount equivalent to the value of the labor. These funds were the result of communal labor on the common lands (*ejidos*) and were intended for meeting debts incurred in procuring common benefits to the pueblos. He pointed out that this was even provided by the Laws of the Indies in Book 6, Title 4, Law 6.

With regard to a primary teacher, Governor Muñoz was of the opinion that this essential expense should be met also out of the funds of the community treasury. At this time the number of children in the pueblos of the four secularized missions was small and there was no pressing need for primary schools. Nevertheless, in drawing up regulations defining the economic obligations of the common funds of the new pueblos, the governor thought it would be wise to include an adequate amount for the payment of primary school teachers.[31]

With characteristic deliberation, the points brought up by Governor Muñoz, as well as other matters by different officials, were referred to the mature judgment of the *Asesor* (legal advisor) of the Provincias Internas, who after more than two years finally rendered a long and

---

[30]Fray José Mariano Cárdenas to Pedro Nava, July 20, 1794. *Saltillo Archives*, Vol. VI, p. 94.

[31]Manuel Muñoz to Pedro Nava, August 14, 1794. *Saltillo Archives*, Vol. VI, pp. 183-187.

detailed opinion on all the questions raised. Galindo Navarro, the *Asesor*, believed that the repair and maintenance of the parish churches and priests' houses should be paid for out of the church treasury. However, if the revenue derived by the priests in charge of the new pueblos was not sufficient to take care of these essential obligations, a moderate sum for the necessary repairs might be taken each year from the *fondos comunes* (community funds). The same source might be drawn from for the indispensable sums to purchase flour and wine for the celebration of the Holy Sacrifice of the Mass, wax candles, and altar linens. But in the case of extensive repairs or the construction of additions to either the churches or the priests' quarters, neither should be undertaken without a special permit from the commandant general, authorizing the use of native labor for the purpose.

Navarro completely ignored the question concerning the payment of primary teachers and the construction of schools. Perhaps he thought that the parish priest was supposed to teach the children, and that since their number was small, the priest's house in each pueblo was adequate to take care of the children for some time without additional expense to the recently secularized natives.[32] The commandant general finally approved the recommendations of Navarro and issued a formal decree to that effect.[33]

Attempt to secure salaries for justicias. On August 4, 1794, Governor Muñoz, apparently following a suggestion previously made by the bishop of Nuevo León, recommended to the commandant general that the new justices, who were to have general supervision of the secularized Indians and to help them administer their temporalities, should be assigned a salary which would enable them to devote more time to this important office. He explained that he had given each one of them a plat of land equal to that assigned to each Indian family. Ever since the property had been allotted to the natives, they had shown diligence in attending to their own affairs, and the justices had been most zealous in the performance of their duties. But the governor expressed a fear that they might lose interest after the novelty of their office had worn off. He thought it would be advisable to determine the exact salary to be paid them out of the community funds of each pueblo, or to allow them

---

[32]Galindo Navarro to Pedro Nava, May 10, 1793. *Saltillo Archives*, Vol. VI, pp. 220-225.

[33]Pedro Nava to Manuel Muñoz, May 24, 1794. *Saltillo Archives*, Vol. VI, pp. 228-229.

a percentage on the net proceeds from the crops harvested and marketed through their efforts.[34]

This matter was carefully considered by the officials of the Internal Provinces. Navarro declared that, in his opinion, the decree of April 10, 1794, clearly defined the duties of the justices and that the acceptance of the office carried with it the obligation to look after the interests of the Indians, to supervise their work, and to induce them to increase their temporalities without expecting any emolument. Under the circumstances there was no reason for granting a salary or a percentage from the sale of the products raised by the secularized Indians.[35]

Nava took the matter under consideration. He decided that although there was no provision for a salary or a commission for the faithful performance of duty by the new justices, nevertheless their zeal should be rewarded and encouraged. He instructed Muñoz, therefore, to give the justices one or even two additional plats as a reward for diligently fulfilling their duties. These grants should be made judiciously in order that they might stimulate the pride of the new officers in their honest administration of the temporalities of the secularized pueblos.[36]

The settlement of mission debts. When San José was secularized, Fray José Manuel Pedrajo stated that there were certain sums which private individuals owed the mission, as well as other moneys owed by the mission to its creditors. He promised at that time to render a complete and detailed account of the assets and liabilities. On August 4, 1794, Governor Muñoz reported that this matter was still pending, and on the 17th of the same month he again informed Nava of this unfinished business and asked for instructions.[37]

Nava had written Governor Muñoz on July 29 about the collection of a bill for goods advanced to San José Mission by the commissary of the Presidio of San Antonio, and asked for details about this transaction, of which he evidently disapproved. Muñoz replied on October 24 that the bill amounted to four hundred fifty-eight *pesos*, that it was

---

[34]Manuel Muñoz to Pedro Nava, August 4, 1794. *Saltillo Archives,* Vol. VI, pp. 179-181.

[35]Galindo Navarro to Pedro Nava, May 10, 1797. *Saltillo Archives,* Vol. VI, pp. 220-225.

[36]Pedro Nava to Manuel Muñoz, May 24, 1797; Navarro to Pedro Nava, May 10, 1797. *Saltillo Archives,* Vol. VI, pp. 228-229; 220-225.

[37]Muñoz to Nava, August 4, 1794; same to same, August 17, 1794. *Saltillo Archives,* Vol. VI, pp. 179-181; 188-189.

for goods advanced to the missionary, consisting chiefly of tobacco, grain, and clothes for the mission Indians. Muñoz continued that there was no written record of the transaction because it was a verbal agreement between the minister and the commissary, whereby the missionary agreed to pay for the goods with grain after the crops had been harvested. But the matter was now settled. The amount had been collected from fifteen individuals who were debtors of the mission and the sum turned over to the paymaster at the presidio.[38]

The promised account of all the money due to, or possessed, by Mission San José was finally turned over to the governor by Father Pedrajo on June 12, 1795. The embarrassed *Padre* explained that the long delay in fulfilling his promise concerning a matter of such importance was not due entirely to neglect or procrastination on his part. Immediately after the secularization of San José on July 30, he had been ordered by the new president of the missions to go without delay to Refugio as assistant to the resident missionary. He had been engaged at the time in the revision of the accounts of San José from 1761 on, and so had asked to be permitted to finish his report before leaving for Refugio. But Fray Cárdenas, promising he would finish the task, had urged him to go. However, when in June, 1795, he returned to San Antonio on business for Refugio, he found, much to his amazement, that the report he had started was exactly as he had left it. He had made haste to finish it and now sent it with his apologies.[39]

This interesting account is significant in that it discloses the amounts advanced by the missions to private individuals for the promotion of trade and industry. It reveals the mission playing an unsuspected role on the Spanish frontier. Here is another service rendered by the mission in the development of civil settlements. Although the list is long, it deserves to be included in the present history for its economic significance. Juan José Flores, heading the group, had obtained from the mission 2,533.75 *pesos*. The well-known French trader, Nicholas Lamathe, who became an important Indian agent for the Spanish officials after the cession of Louisiana, borrowed from the mission in cash, products, cattle, and horses, 1,385.50 *pesos;* Vicente Flores, 122.00; Pedro Montalvo, 82.75; Vicente Bocanegra, 283.50; Ignacio Mireles, 30.00; Julían de Arocha, 23.75; José Luís Salazar, 49.00; José F. Ramón, 13.00; Ignacio Calvillo,

---

[38]Manuel Muñoz to Pedro Nava. *Saltillo Archives,* Vol. VI, pp. 196-198.

[39]Fray José Manuel Pedrajo to Manuel Muñoz, June 12, 1795. *Saltillo Archives,* Vol. VI, pp. 216-217.

13.75; Marcos Jaime, 62.25; Manuel Martínez, 24.00; José Antonio Esqui-
vel, 13.00; Simón de Arocha, 15.87; María Gertrudis Cantuna, 63.00; Juan
José Sánchez, 37.00; Joaquín Jaime, 32.37; Francisco Pérez, 4.00; Juan
Antonio Urrutia, 16.00; Pedro Sambrano, 39.50; Francisco Rodríguez
Montemayor, 66.50; Felipe Nerí Montoya, 307.50; Francisco Arocha,
37.00; Juan Antonio Díaz, 40.50; Mateo Rodríguez, 7.00; José Andrés
Hernández, 3.75; Francisco de los Santos Coy, 8.00; José Xavier
Menchaca, 165.12; Francisco Xavier Longoria, 63.00; José Antonio
Chirino (of Nacogdoches), 1.25; Pablo de los Santos, 123.00; Fernando
Benítez (soldier), 24.00; Pedro Nuncio (Saltillo), 56.12; José Zaragoza,
15.00; Fernando Arocha, 15.00; Joaquín Leal, 23.12; Cristóbal de los
Santos, 39.12; José Antonio Bustillos (estate), 211.37. The total due
San José by its debtors was 6,118.75 *pesos*.[40]

The books of the mission showed that the liabilities incurred in recent
years were as follows:

> To Angel Navarro (merchant)..............................$ 745.00
> To Joaquín Flores 53.00
> To Domingo de Otón (merchant in La Bahía)......... 1,432.00
>
> _____
>
>   Total...$2,230.00

Fray Pedrajo turned over a complete record of the accounts to Governor Muñoz who sent them to the commandant general on June 15.[41]

Not until two years later did Muñoz receive instructions respecting the
final settlement of the accounts of San José. Nava informed him that
he was to proceed with the collection of all moneys due the mission. But
in collecting he was to use no harsh measures, and was to allow the
debtors or their representatives the necessary time to settle their accounts.
After he had collected the debt of 6,118.75 *pesos*, he was to call the
creditors to make them substantiate their claims by showing what goods
were sold to the mission and verifying the use to which the goods or
supplies were put, before paying the 2,230.00 *pesos* claimed.[42]

_____

[40]Relación de lo que adeudan á esta Misión de Sor. Sn. José . . ., June 5, 1795.
Saltillo Archives, Vol. VI, pp. 209-214.

[41]Relación de las cantidades que deve la Misión de Sr. Sn. José de Sn. Miguel
de Aguayo . . ., June 5, 1795; Manuel Muñoz to Pedro Nava, June 15, 1795.
Saltillo Archives, Vol. VI, pp. 215; 217-218; 219-220.

[42]Pedro Nava to Manuel Muñoz, May 24, 1797. *Saltillo Archives*, Vol. VI,
pp. 232-233. In this decree the commandant general approved the recommendations
of Galindo Navarro, the *Asesor*, and ordered a copy added to his decree. See
Navarro to Pedro Nava, May 10, 1797. *Ibid.*, pp. 220-225.

At the time that a decision was rendered on the settlement of the debts of Mission San José, final instructions were also issued with regard to the three men and five women at the mission who were still under instruction. They were to be permitted to remain at San José. Provision for them was to be made out of the proceeds of the property and land assigned to them, which, until further instructions from the governor, was to be administered by the missionary or parish priest in charge of the secularized mission pueblo.[43]

The secularization of the missions at La Bahía. Governor Muñoz had expressed doubts concerning the practicability of putting into effect the decree of secularization of April 10 in the missions at La Bahía. On September 11, 1794, he informed Nava that he was leaving San Antonio for La Bahía where he intended to put the Jaraname Indians of Mission Espíritu Santo in possession of the communal property, provided that they were qualified to assume charge of its administration.[44] Upon his arrival, he requested Fray Juan José Aguilar, the resident missionary, to assemble all the Indians of the mission. There were forty-one Jaranames, twenty-four Tamiques, twenty-one Parantones, twelve Prietos, nine Brazos Largos, six Vende Flechas, and twelve Cumpusas, a total of one hundred twenty-five. Governor Muñoz saw them and talked to them. Only a few understood Spanish and fewer still could speak it. The *Padre* explained that these various Indians were in fact all Jaranames, belonging to the same stock and speaking the same language. After questioning them, the governor was convinced that they were incapable of managing their own affairs. In his opinion they were as helpless as children. They had not yet learned to work. On October 13 he formally reported to the commandant general in Chihuahua that in view of the state of the natives, he had not carried out the secularization of the mission as ordered by the decree of April 10, 1794, but that he would await further instructions in the hope that an exception would be made in this instance.[45]

---

[43]*Ibid.*, pp. 220-225.

[44]Manuel Muñoz to Pedro de Nava, September 21, 1794. *Saltillo Archives*, Vol. VI, pp. 190-191.

[45]Manuel Muñoz to Pedro de Nava, October 13, 1794. *Saltillo Archives*, Vol. VI, pp. 193-195. At this time he sent also a detailed list with the names, age, and sex of each Indian in the mission. See Relación de los Yndios de la Misión del Espíritu Santo dependiente del Presidio de la Bahía y ál Govierno de la Provincia de Texas de las Naciones Jaranames y demas que se expresan. *Ibid.*, Vol. VI, pp. 199-202.

Mission Rosario. While at La Bahía, Muñoz also inspected Mission Nuestra Señora del Rosario. Here Fray José Francisco Jaudenes presented the neophytes to the governor. There were one hundred thirty-nine, of whom only eight were old Christians; the rest, with the exception of thirty-six who had just joined the mission, had been at Rosario only about three years.[46] These Indians belonged chiefly to the Karankawa and the Copano nations and could not speak Spanish. They were incompetent to manage the temporal property of the mission.

The governor informed Nava on October 25, that as in the case of Espíritu Santo Mission, it was impossible to put into effect at Rosario the decree of April 10. He explained that to comply with the decree would result in the return of the Jaranames to the Arkokisas and to savagery. These missions had extensive farms, but their cultivation required more work and skill than those of San Antonio because there was no irrigation. Furthermore, they owned extensive herds of cattle which were at this time roaming wild in the woods. Under the direction of the missionaries some of these would be rounded up.[47]

The commandant general referred this matter, as well as all the others in connection with the secularization of the missions in Texas, to the *Asesor.* Almost three years elapsed before a decision was reached. Finally, on May 10, 1797, Navarro, recommended that in view of the circumstances, the backward state of the Indians in Missions Espíritu Santo and Rosario, an exception should be made and that the missionaries should be allowed to continue in charge of the administration of their temporalities for a period of five more years. But during this period the missionaries were to be required to make to the governor a careful and detailed report of all the income and all the expenses of the missions under their care. At the expiration of the five-year period, the governor was to render an account to the commandant general on the actual progress made by the Indians and on the material improvements so that the latter might be in a position to decide intelligently the future policy.[48]

---

[46]Estado que manifiesta el que tiene esta Misión de Nuestra Señora del Rosario segun existen sus indivíduos hoy 26 de Septiembre de 1794. *Saltillo Archives,* Vol. VI, pp. 203-204.

[47]Manuel Muñoz to Pedro Nava, October 13, 1794; October 25, 1794. *Saltillo Archives,* Vol. VI, pp. 193-195; 205-208.

[48]Galindo Navarro to Pedro Nava, May 10, 1797. *Saltillo Archives,* Vol. VI, pp. 220-225.

Nava approved the recommendations and instructed Governor Muñoz and Bishop Andrés Llanos y Valdez, of Nuevo León, that the Mission of Espíritu Santo and Mission Rosario were to be exempted from the provisions of the decree of April 10 for a period of five years. The time was to be counted from the date of publication of the exemption in the respective missions. The governor was further ordered to inform the missionaries of their duty to report each year to him in order that at the end of the period of grace, he might, in turn, make his report to the commandant general.[49]

The San Antonio missions had ceased to exist as such. Those at La Bahía had been given a brief respite with peremptory orders to speed up the process of Christianization and civilization of the indifferent natives. But the processes of civilization cannot be hurried at will. These missions, with the new one of Refugio, treated in the subsequent chapter, were to linger on for a few years. The work of the Franciscan missionaries was not yet finished.

---

[49]Pedro Nava to Manuel Muñoz, May 24, 1797; Pedro Nava to Andrés Llanos y Valdez, same date. *Saltillo Archives*, Vol. VI, pp. 232-233; 230-231.

CHAPTER III

The Founding of Mission Nuestra Señora del Refugio

At the very time the missions of San Antonio were being secularized, the sons of the College of Nuestra Señora de Guadalupe of Zacatecas were fervently occupied in establishing a new outpost to civilize and convert the fierce coastal tribe of the Karankawas in the vicinity of Matagorda Bay. The diligent efforts of Captain Manuel de Espadas at La Bahía had succeeded in bringing back to Mission Rosario many of the apostate Jaranames. "No sooner had Rosario been placed again in operation," declares Dunn, "than a movement began which was to result in the founding of the last of the Texas missions during the Spanish regime, that of Nuestra Señora del Refugio or Our Lady of Refugio."[1] This was not, however, due entirely to the influence of the revered memory of Fray Antonio Margil de Jesús. Rather it was the result of a series of circumstances which culminated in this "the final outburst of missionary zeal in provincial Texas . . . one of the last flickers of ebbing Spanish energy and initiative on the northeastern frontier of New Spain."

Renewed interest in the coastal region. To understand the conditions that brought about the founding of Refugio, a summary of the situation at that time is necessary. One year before Fray Manuel de Silva's untiring efforts resulted in the founding of the new mission, the king of Spain issued instructions to the viceroy to investigate the possibilities of establishing closer trade relations between the provinces of Louisiana and Texas by opening a port on the Gulf coast. He also inquired if it might not be well to extend the boundary of Louisiana to Río Sabinas.[2] The interest in bringing about closer ties between the two provinces,

---

[1]Dunn, W. E., "The Founding of Nuestra Señora del Refugio, the last Spanish Mission in Texas," *The Quarterly*, XXV, 176. Up to the present, this article constitutes the only detailed study of this mission available. There is one other very brief account by Bolton, "The Beginnings of Mission Nuestra Señora del Refugio," *The Quarterly*, XIX, 400-404.

[2]King to the Viceroy of New Spain, November 1, 1789. *A. G. I., Audiencia de México*, 96-2-12 (Dunn Transcripts, 1787-1791, pp. 55-56); Viceroy Revillagigedo to Antonio Porlier, April 27, 1791. *A. G. I., Audiencia de México*, 89-6-14 (Dunn Transcripts, 1787-1791, pp. 178-181).

a marked departure from the traditional policy of Spain, was the result
not of liberalism on the part of the king, but of a growing fear of attack
by either the English or the Americans. The frontier of the Spanish
possessions in America and of the now independent and aggressive
English colonies had at last met. The onward rush to the West had
brought the Americans to the banks of the Mississippi.

The viceroy warned the king that the establishment of communication
between the two provinces and the extension of the boundary of the
Province of Louisiana would entail considerable expense.[3]

Three years later, with hostilities about to break out between Spain
and France in which England might become involved, the viceroy took
up the matter again. He considered as impractical the whole plan of
opening a port on the Texas coast and of encouraging trade between
the two provinces. "This great project, as well as other similar ones,
proposed by the first commandant of the Interior Provinces and the
Viceroy Conde de Gálvez," he declared, "are praiseworthy undertakings,
but they require many years and imply infinite combinations." The
proximity of aggressive neighbors made its realization impossible. The
time was not opportune for undertaking new settlements. There could
be no objection to the extension of the boundary of Louisiana to the
Sabine River, since both provinces were Spanish possessions. But before
the jurisdiction was extended, it would be highly advisable to appoint
a capable person to make a survey and draw maps of the areas involved
in order to determine the best policy to be adopted in view of the
obvious danger of attack. He had begun to take steps to carry out the
survey, but before he was able to complete the necessary preparations,
the commandant of the Interior Provinces was declared completely
independent of the viceroy. He consequently sent to him all the documents and maps relative to the subject.

He was of the opinion, however, that given the circumstances that
now prevailed, no innovation should be made in regard to the commercial
relations between the two provinces; that all trade between Texas and
Louisiana should cease; and that traders from Louisiana should be
prohibited from entering Texas under heavy penalties. Furthermore, in
order to put an end to illicit trade and contraband, it might be advisable
to abandon Nacogdoches which now served as a half-way station and a
safe hiding place for smuggled goods. If this post was not to be aban-

---

[3]Viceroy Revillagigedo to Antonio Porlier, April 27, 1791. *A. G. I., Audiencia
de México*, 89-6-14 (Dunn Transcripts, 1787-1791, pp. 178-187).

doned, an adequate garrison should be placed there to enforce the law strictly, to defend the province in case of attack, and to keep a watch on all hostile movements.[4]

Interest in the status of the missions. The mission, being a frontier institution designed to Christianize and civilize the natives on the ever widening periphery of New Spain and to serve as an outpost to reënforce the frontier against surprise attacks or insidious penetrations by foreigners among the Indian nations, naturally became an object of concern for the king and his officers in the closing years of the eighteenth century. As early as 1784, Charles III issued an order to the viceroy instructing him to prepare a simple, accurate, and clear report on the actual condition of the missions of New Spain, and to compare the present status with that at the time of the expulsion of the Jesuits (1767), and to make suggestions for its improvement.[5]

Viceroy Matías de Gálvez, in June of the same year, ordered the collection of the necessary data, but the individual reports from the numerous frontier officers and mission establishments came in slowly and not always so fully and clearly as desired. Three years thus elapsed. On March 21, 1787, a royal *cédula* was sent to the viceroy repeating the request for an immediate report on the general condition of the missions. It included instructions to make a similar report every two or three years in the future in order that the Council of the Indies might be informed as to the progress or lack of progress made by this important frontier institution.[6]

Before the required information was at last compiled by the industrious and painstaking secretary of the viceroyalty, Antonio Bonilla, many changes in the administrative system of the missions had taken place. The interest shown by the crown had called forth numerous plans and suggestions, some quite fantastic, for the improvement and expansion of missionary activity on the one hand, and for the complete abolition of the system on the other. The effect of these conflicting reports and suggestions upon the missions in Texas has already been noted in the previous chapter.

---

[4]Viceroy Revillagigedo to Diego de Godorqui, April 30, 1793. *A. G. I., Audiencia de México,* 96-2-12 (Dunn Transcripts, 1787-1791, pp. 48-53).

[5]Real Orden de Enero 31, 1784. *A. G. I., Indiferente General,* 154-7-14, pp. 1-2.

[6]Copia del Informe General instruydo en cumplimiento de el Orden de 31 de Eno. de 1784 Sobre las Misiones del Reyno de Nueva España . . . *A. G. I., Indiferente General,* 154-7-14, pp. 3-4.

Father Silva's proposal for new missions. It is in view of these antecedents that the proposal of Father Fray Manuel de Silva, commissary general and prefect of the College of Nuestra Señora de Guadalupe of Zacatecas, which resulted eventually in the founding of Mission Nuestra Señora del Refugio, should be considered. Truthfully has Bolton said: "The founding of the mission of Nuestra Señora del Refugio was closely connected with plans for Texas of great breadth and importance; or, it might be said, its founding was the slender outcome of these larger plans, which had to be set aside by force of untoward circumstances.[7]

Missionary rivalry. Throughout the colonial period there existed a healthful rivalry between the members of different religious orders as well as among those of the same order. Political considerations had focused the attention of Spanish officials on Texas, and this new interest had aroused likewise the ambitions of the Franciscans who saw in the situation an opportunity to attempt the realization of Fray Antonio Margil de Jesús' dream, the conversion of the fierce tribes of the north. Hoping to steal a march on their brethren, the friars of the College of Pachuca presented a petition to the viceroy for permission to undertake missionary work among the natives of north Texas. The news of this plan to enter Texas reached the College of Nuestra Señora de Guadalupe of Zacatecas early in 1790. Immediately, the strongest sense of emulation was aroused, not untinged with a feeling of just resentment. Zacatecan missionaries had gone to Texas with the first *entradas* and they had labored incessantly from that time on for the conversion of the natives. The sons of the College of Zacatecas had not abandoned the field. They had, in fact, taken over the missions administered by the College of La Santa Cruz de Querétaro, which the latter house had given up for those in California. The College of Pachuca would be an interloper if it came into a field won by the labors of Zacatecan friars.[8]

The *Discretorio* of the College of Zacatecas had several meetings to discuss the policy to be adopted. It was finally decided that Fray Manuel de Silva[9] should undertake a survey of the missions in

---

[7]Bolton, H. E., "The Beginnings of Mission Nuestra Señora del Refugio," *The Quarterly*, Texas Historical Association, XIX, 401.

[8]*Ibid.*, XIX, 401.

[9]The documents used by the writer give his name as Manuel de Silva, but Bolton, *op. cit.*, gives it as it as Manuel Julio de Silva. *Cf.* Dunn, W. E., "The Founding of Nuestra Señora del Refugio," *The Quarterly*, XXV, 176.

Texas and outline a program for the conversion of the Tawakonis, Kichais, Taguayas (Taovayas), Tonkawas, Comanches, and other northern tribes, which up to this time had never been brought under missionary influence.[10]

"Father Silva," says Dunn, "had worked for many years in the missions of New Spain, and was one of the most capable of the many sincere and zealous priests who endeavored to spread the doctrines of Christianity among the native tribes." He had just been elected commissary and prefect of the College of Zacatecas in August, 1790, and he was anxious to set out on a task that had long fascinated him. He gladly accepted the decision of the *Discretorio* and lost no time in preparing for his departure. He wisely chose as his companion a veteran in the missionary field, Father Fray José Francisco Mariano Garza, who had taken an active part in the founding of Nuestra Señora del Pilar de Bucareli on the Trinity, and who had later served for a while at Nacogdoches. He knew conditions in Texas and was well acquainted with the northern tribes. Governor Muñoz, in a private report to the viceroy, declared that Father Garza was a native of Linares, who had been a missionary for twenty-seven years, had been teacher of sacred theology and a member of the *Discretorio* of the College of Zacatecas. He had served twelve years in Texas, particularly among the Jaranames and Karankawas on the coast and had been president of the San Antonio missions.[11]

Fathers Silva and Garza set out for Texas. Early in November the two missionaries were ready to start on their ambitious undertaking. Travelling by different routes to enable the commissary and prefect to visit some of the Franciscan houses on the way, they met, on January 1, 1791, at Boca de Leones where the College had a hospice.[12] They now proceeded together to San Antonio where they arrived within a week's time. Father Silva was amazed at the deplorable condition in which he found the once opulent missions of San Antonio. The number

---

[10]Bolton, *op. cit.*, XIX, 401.

[11]Dunn, *op. cit.*, XXV, 176-177; Bolton, *op. cit.*, XIX, 401; Manuel Muñoz to Viceroy Revillagigedo, February 13, 1792. *Nacogdoches Archives*, Vol. VII, pp. 181-182.

[12]Bolton, *op. cit.*, XIX, 401. The brief account given by Bolton gives no references to any specific sources used by him, but he states that "it is based on considerable manuscript material in my possession." Dunn's account, to which frequent reference is made also, is fully documented, but he does not give the date of departure.

of Indians under instruction, or Christianized, was inadequate for the proper cultivation of the extensive lands of the missions and insufficient to carry on the multiple activities of this once flourishing establishment, with its looms now idle, and shops abandoned. But the enthusiastic missionary would neither be discouraged nor would he spread the alarm by making known the conditions he found.[13] The reports of Governor Muñoz, two years later, when the order for secularization was put in effect, disclosed the true condition of affairs, the causes for which have been previously discussed in the present volume.

Modification of original plan. It had been the main purpose of Father Silva and his companion to visit the northern tribes and to make plans for their conversion. When they manifested their desire to the governor of Texas, he informed them that at this time they could not carry out their proposed visit, because all communication with the northern tribes had been suspended on account of the vigorous campaign being waged by the commandant of the Eastern Interior Provinces, Colonel Ugalde, against the Lipan-Apaches.[14] Here was a turn of affairs that had not been foreseen. But Father Silva was consumed by a desire to undertake a heroic task in his mature years and to accomplish something that should shed legitimate glory upon the College of Zacatecas and its devoted sons. He listened with interest to the reports of recent depredations by the Karankawas and other coastal tribes in the vicinity of Matagorda Bay. These Indians had consistently refused to be Christianized and civilized. Mission Rosario had just been reëstablished and by dint of strenuous efforts on the part of its missionaries and the commander of La Bahía (Goliad), some of the Karankawas and Jaranames had been induced to enter mission life. "Knowing the long continued and fruitless efforts of the royal government to pacify the coastal region, Father Silva concluded that he could not find a more laudable or more useful thing than the conversion of the unruly Karankawas."[15]

Early labors of Father Silva among the coastal tribes. Having made up his mind, Father Silva, accompanied by Father Garza, went to La Bahía, where he arrived early in February. His first step was to send

---

[13]Governor Manuel Muñoz to Commandant General Pedro Nava, January 26, 1795. *A. G. I., Audiencia de Guadalajara,* 104-1-1 (Dunn Transcripts, 1794-98, pp. 42-46).

[14]Bolton, *op. cit.,* XIX, 401-402.

[15]Dunn, "The Founding of Nuestra Señora del Refugio," *The Quarterly,* XXV, 177.

some of the converted Indians, now living at Mission Rosario, to visit among their kinsmen, and to assure them that the Spaniards desired to be their friends. The mission of the peace emissaries proved successful. Within a few days Indians began to visit the presidio, and were convinced of the friendship of the Spaniards by the frank hospitality extended to them.

On March 31, 1791, a Karankawa chief named Frazada Pinta (Spotted Blanket) came to Mission Rosario and was so highly impressed by the cordial treatment shown him, that on taking leave he promised Father Silva he would return within ten days and bring an escort to conduct the good missionary to visit his people. Before the ten days were up, Chief Frazada Pinta was back with twenty-four stalwart warriors. Father Silva was overjoyed. On April 10 he set out with his host, taking with him five soldiers and two mission Indians in addition to the twenty-four warriors brought by the chief.[16]

Two days later they arrived at the village of Chief Frazada Pinta, a settlement of considerable size. The shrewd friar said nothing to the natives about founding a mission for them, nor did he hint or suggest that they ought to join a mission. He devoted himself to making friends, distributing gifts of small value and talking to all the Indians. When after a few days he was departing, the Indians asked him to come again, and assured him that they would always welcome the *Padres* even if they were at war with the presidio at La Bahía.

Before returning to the presidio, Father Silva went to another village, whose chief was Llano Grande (Great Plain). He was cordially received by the natives. He noticed that among the followers of Llano Grande there were several apostates from Mission Rosario. He convinced them that they should return to the mission and took them with him when he departed. Chief Llano Grande and his people invited Father Silva to visit them again and the happy missionary was only too glad to promise them an early return.[17]

Father Silva temporarily called away. Shortly after his return, the new prefect received orders from Fray Manuel María Truxillo, commissary general of missions in the Indies, to preside over the chapter meeting to be held in October by the Province of Zacatecas. Much to his regret, he found himself obliged to abandon his labors in Texas for

---

[16]Bolton, *op. cit.*, XIX, 402.
[17]*Ibid.*, XIX, 402.

the time being. But his absence did not halt the work started among the coastal tribes. Father Fray José Mariano Garza, who had in the meantime been appointed chaplain of Presidio Espíritu Santo, was assigned to continue the work of conversion among the Karankawa and the other coastal tribes. He was duly instructed to maintain the closest and most friendly relations with the military and civil authorities of Texas and particularly with Governor Muñoz, whose coöperation was to be enlisted in the new enterprise. Harmony between the ecclesiastics and the military was essential for the success of the contemplated conversion of the coastal tribes. Frictions between them had too often resulted in the failure of missionary endeavors. Father Garza was to keep Father Silva informed of developments.[18]

Early labors of Father Garza among the coastal Indians. Father Garza proved a wise choice, for his long experience in Texas, his acquaintance with the coastal and northern tribes, and his own zeal, guaranteed the successful prosecution of the work so enthusiastically begun by Fray Silva. Early in May, 1791, shortly after the departure of Father Silva, a party of Jaraname apostates from Missions Espíritu Santo and Rosario paid a visit to Father Garza and expressed their willingness and that of their kinsmen, now living on the San Xavier (San Gabriel), to return to mission life if the missionary would go with them to their *ranchería*. Father Garza immediately saw an opportunity to bring back a large group of apostates and to revisit the friendly coastal tribes. He could, at the same time, reconnoiter the country of the Karankawas, the Copanos, and the Guapites along San Bernardo Bay and try to determine a suitable location for the mission on which his superior had set his heart. He consequently requested permission from Governor Muñoz to make the trip. He gladly granted it and gave the missionary an adequate escort.

Setting out from La Bahía, Father Garza first visited the coast and then went to the San Xavier where he persuaded twenty-three men, fourteen women, and twenty-one children to return to Mission Rosario. During his visit to the coast, he selected the most likely site for a mission. This was located at the confluence of the Guadalupe and the San Antonio, a few miles from the coast. The Indians were still friendly

---

[18]Memorial of Fray Manuel de Silva, March 7, 1793; Fray Juan de Moya to Antonio Ventura de Toranco, February 11, 1794. *A. G. I., Audiencia de Guadalajara*, 104-1-1 (Dunn Transcripts, 1790-1793, pp. 164-169; 1794-1798, pp. 1-4); also Dunn, *The Quarterly*, XXV, 128.

and interested. In his report to the viceroy, Father Garza for the first time gave the name of the contemplated mission as Nuestra Señora del Refugio.[19] This may have been suggested by the location chosen, or by the proximity to the island near the mouth of the river, where the Indians were in the habit of taking refuge.[20]

Following the policy of Father Silva, he said nothing to the natives concerning the advisability of their joining a mission. Father Garza seems to have made several visits to the coast during the summer of 1791, but he waited patiently for the Indians to take the initiative. He wrote a long letter to Governor Muñoz on August 17, giving him an account of his visits and the favorable reception. He expressed his hope of success and assured the governor it would not be long before the Karankawas would want a mission in their lands.[21]

Request for mission. On October 24 the faithful missionary found his hopes realized. Upon his return from the coast to Rosario with fifty-two apostates, he found a delegation headed by Chief Frazada Pinta waiting for him. They had come to ask him to go with them to their *ranchería*. Before he could set out, another delegation sent by Chief Llano Grande arrived in Rosario with a similar request. By October 28 he was in the village of Frazada Pinta, where one hundred twenty-four persons had gathered to welcome him. They told him that they wanted a mission established in their own country in order that they might not be obliged to leave the coast. Elated at the request, Father Garza went on to the village of Chief Llano Grande where one hundred eighty-six Indians had congregated to solicit a mission for their people. This was on the site previously visited by Father Garza and chosen as the best suited for the purpose, at the confluence of the Guadalupe and San Antonio rivers, some eight miles from the coast. One of the chiefs said to the missionary, "If you build a mission at the mouth of the Guadalupe, the whole coast is yours."[22]

---

[19]Pedro Nava to the King, November 11, 1794; Manuel Muñoz to Pedro Nava, January 26, 1795. *A. G. I., Audiencia de Guadalajara,* 104-1-1 (Dunn Transcripts, pp. 51-62; 42-46).

[20]The place chosen is referred to in the documents as Cayo del Refugio, Caballo del Refugio, and Nuestra Señora del Refugio. *Cayo* means "islet," or "small island." Caballo is evidently a corruption of the word. It was perpetuated, however, in the neighboring Caballo Pass. Bolton states Garza visited and named the site on July 17, 1791. Bolton, *op. cit.,* XIX, 402.

[21]Manuel Muñoz to Pedro Nava, January 26, 1795. *A. G. I., Audiencia de Guadalajara,* 104-1-1 (Dunn Transcripts, 1794-98, pp. 47-50).

[22]Dunn, "The Founding of Mission Refugio," *The Quarterly,* XXV, 172-179.

Father Garza assured the Indians that he would try to fulfill their request, explaining to them he would have to take up the matter with the *Capitán Grande,* the viceroy, and promised them he would return as soon as possible. He hurried back to Espíritu Santo to write a full account of the circumstances to Father Silva. At the same time he requested permission from and solicited the support of Governor Muñoz. He again pointed out that the location called Cayo del Refugio, previously chosen, was the best site for the contemplated mission, because it was where the Karankawas habitually camped the greater part of the year. Captain Juan Cortés, the new commander at La Bahía, verified the report of Father Garza on November 8, stating that the number of Karankawas who had solicited the mission and who were ready to join it was one hundred eighty-six. Governor Muñoz, without awaiting further details, transmitted the request to the viceroy on November 20, with his full approval of the project.[23] At this time the Province of Texas was not under the jurisdiction of the commandant of the newly created Interior Provinces, but directly under that of the viceroy.

Prompt approval by viceroy. With incredible speed, the viceroy approved the plan for the proposed mission at the place called Refugio on December 31, 1791. Having consulted Ramón de Posada, the *Fiscal de Real Hacienda,* he instructed Father Garza to proceed with the construction of the necessary buildings and to secure the things and supplies necessary for divine service. At the same time Governor Muñoz was authorized to furnish the essential supplies for the establishment of the mission. The orders were formally transmitted by viceregal decree on January 4, 1792. Only one missionary was assigned to Refugio, who was to draw his salary from the royal treasury at San Luis Potosí.[24]

Unexpected delays. Ignorant of the success with which the efforts of Father Garza had met both among the Indians and before the viceroy, Father Silva arrived in Mexico from Zacatecas early in March and prepared a long memorial in support of his cherished project. While the report and petition were dated March 10, 1791, they were not presented to the viceroy until March 13. Father Silva explained in detail

---

[23]Pedro Nava to the King, November 6, 1794. *A. G. I., Audiencia de Guadalajara,* 104-1-1 (Dunn Transcripts, 1794-98, pp. 51-62). Bolton gives the date as November 22, 1791, *op. cit.,* XIX, 403.

[24]Nava to the King, November 11, 1796. *Ibid.,* pp. 51-52; also Galindo Navarro to Pedro Nava, June 26, 1794. *A. G. I., Audiencia de Guadalajara,* 104-1-1 (Dunn Transcripts, 1794-98, pp. 14-33).

the great advantages of establishing a mission at the site called Refugio. Located at the confluence of the Guadalupe and San Antonio rivers, it would make safe communication possible between Matagorda Bay and Espíritu Santo and give access to many inland points in the province. This mission, together with Mission Nuestra Señora del Rosario, would protect the entire coastal region against transgression by foreign traders and Indian agents as far as the Colorado River. The work of conversion and civilization could thus be extended to other branches of the Karankawas, as well as to the Cocos, the Arkokisas, the Tawakonis, the Tawash, and the feared Comanches.

It was in this memorial that Father Silva, carried away by his enthusiasm for the contemplated reduction of tribes never before brought under the influence of the missionaries, innocently proposed the secularization of Mission Valero and the suppression of two of the other four missions in San Antonio.[25] The idea that prompted the proposal was to relieve some missionaries assigned to these missions so that they might take charge of the ones contemplated for the coastal tribes, and thus save additional expense to the royal treasury.

Far from expediting the launching of the new enterprise and the establishment of Mission Refugio, it delayed the execution of the decree of January 4, 1792, for more than a year. His astounding proposals were referred to the *fiscal,* who, aroused by the far-reaching effect of the measure suggested, recommended on March 27, 1792, that Father Silva be informed of the action taken on January 4 concerning Mission Refugio, and that his proposal be sent to the Count of Sierra Gorda and to Fray José Mariano Reyes with a request for an opinion. The latter soon replied, raising objections to the site selected by Father Garza and suggesting that the mouth of the Nueces River offered greater advantages.

Determining amount of royal aid. In view of the numerous questions raised by the memorial of Father Silva, the *fiscal* rendered a supplementary opinion on May 21, 1792, as to the amount that should be contributed by the royal treasury for the founding of Mission Refugio. Citing as a precedent the regulations adopted for the missions of California, he recommended that one thousand *pesos* be allowed for the equipment of the new mission; that the older missions in San Antonio render such aid as they could give; and that Father Silva and the

---

[25]See the preceding chapter, pp. 35-36.

officers of the royal treasury agree on the cost of the essential sacred vessels, vestments, and other articles for the divine service. The recommendations were approved on June 2 by a *Junta Superior*.[26]

Upon being informed of the action taken by the *Junta*, Father Silva protested on June 28 that the amount allowed by the *fiscal* for the establishment of Mission Refugio was inadequate; that the regulations adopted for the missions in California were not applicable to Texas, where conditions were very different; and that the older establishments were unable at this time to furnish any aid. He concluded by soliciting more liberal support for the new mission. When the matter was referred to the *Tribunal de Cuentas* (Tribunal of Accounts), this body sustained the plea of Father Silva. It explained that in 1764, when missions were established in Nuevo Santander, the royal treasury had furnished not only everything necessary for religious ceremonies but also the sum of ten thousand *pesos* for San Agustín de Laredo and similar amounts for others. The *Tribunal* further stated that in 1758 the royal treasury furnished seven thousand *pesos* as the initial expense for the new Mission of Rosario at La Bahía, and later supplemented this amount with four thousand one hundred two *pesos* to complete its establishment.

Confronted with these facts, the *Junta Superior* recommended on August 31, 1792, that Father Silva consult treasury officials respecting the expenditure of the one thousand *pesos* already allotted, and that he, together with the governor of Texas, determine the additional amount necessary for erecting a church and the other buildings. The figure agreed upon would be paid by the treasurer of San Luis Potosí, after it had been endorsed by the governor of the province.[27]

Father Garza's estimate of expenditure. The matter became complicated because of slow communications. Furthermore, Father Silva, in Mexico, was able to follow more closely the development of the plans of the viceregal officials, whereas Father Garza, in Texas, was closer to the actual field of missionary endeavor. Shortly after the decree of January 4 was received by the governor, Father Garza, ignorant of Father Silva's memorial and its consequences, prepared a detailed estimate of the necessary expenses for the projected mission. He computed

---

[26]Pedro Nava to the King, November 6, 1794. *A. G. I., Audiencia de Guadalajara*, 104-1-1 (Dunn Transcripts, 1794-98, pp. 52-54).

[27]Galindo Navarro to Pedro Nava, June 26, 1794; Pedro Nava to the King, November 6, 1794. *A. G. I., Audiencia de Guadalajara*, 104-1-1 (Dunn Transcripts, 1794-1798, pp. 16-17; 54-56).

the cost of the church, the priest's lodging, the storeroom, and stockade, all to be built of timber, at one thousand *pesos;* the vestments, sacred vessels, baptismal font and other necessities for administering the sacraments at six hundred fifty-two *pesos;* four hundred fifty cows with calves, twenty-two hundred fifty *pesos;* corn to feed the Indians until the first crop was harvested, three hundred *pesos;* clothing, tobacco, farm implements, kitchen utensils, twenty-five horses, trinkets for gifts, and wages for servant help during the first year, twenty-four hundred eighteen *pesos,* a total of six thousand six hundred ten *pesos.*[28] At the same time he explained that the Indians to be congregated were wild and untrained, incapable of tending the stock or planting the new crop. He suggested, therefore, that the soldiers assigned to guard the mission be instructed to assist the missionaries in tending the cattle and in teaching the Indians how to till the soil and how to plant and harvest the crops. Their services would save the expense of employing civilians to do this work during the first year.

The *fiscal* was shocked at this last suggestion. On May 2, 1792, he declared that those duties were incompatible with the dignity of the soldiers, and should be performed by civilians.[29]

In the meantime Father Garza had returned in August, 1792, to the coast, where he found two hundred eight Indians gathered at Muelle Viejo (Old Wharf). This seems to have been at or near the village of Chief Llano Grande, and possibly derived its name from a common landing place used by the Karankawas at or near the mouth of the Guadalupe River. The location was probably near the present site of Tivoli. He informed the natives of what had taken place and assured them he would soon return to establish the desired mission for them. In December, Father López, president of the missions in San Antonio, called Father Garza and urged him to carry out the establishment of the mission in accord with the viceregal decree of January 4, 1792. Father Garza requested Governor Muñoz to accompany him to select the site for the formal establishment, and the two undertook the preliminary survey.

---

[28]Memoria de lo que por ahora se juzga precisamente necesario para la nueva fundación del Refugio presentada por Fray José Francisco Garza. *A. G. I., Audiencia de Guadalajara,* 104-1-1 (Dunn Transcripts, 1794-1798, pp. 183-186).

[29]*Ibid., A. G. I., Audiencia de Guadalajara,* 104-1-1 (Dunn Transcripts, 1790-93, pp. 183-190); Galindo Navarro to Pedro Nava, June 26, 1794, (Dunn Transcripts, 1794-98, pp. 15-16).

Early in January they set out for Espíritu Santo. They proceeded to Muelle Viejo, accompanied by Father Fray Mariano Velasco who had been appointed to take care of the new mission until Father Silva returned from Mexico. Upon their arrival they found only one hundred thirty-eight Indians still waiting; the others had gone hunting food.[30]

The formal founding of Mission Refugio. After the inspection of several sites, it was decided to establish the mission at Muelle Viejo, near the mouth of the Guadalupe. The confusion that has existed as to the actual date of the founding can now be dispelled. Here are the facts drawn from the documentary sources. The governor, anxious to return to San Antonio, desired the ceremony to take place on February 2, but Fathers Garza and Velasco wished to postpone it until the 4th. At the insistence of the governor a compromise was reached and the 3rd was agreed upon as the date. But a severe storm during the night of the second made it impossible to carry out the ceremony as scheduled. Thus, because of the inclement weather, the formal founding was delayed until February 4. Father Mariano Velasco was placed in charge of the new mission in a ceremony witnessed by the one hundred thirty-eight Karankawas who agreed to be congregated.[31]

The beginnings of Mission Refugio were beset with hardships which reveal the difficulties which the missionaries had to put up with even at this late date.[32] On February 24 Father Garza wrote Governor Muñoz that it was very difficult to keep the Indians in the new mission without the essential food. Lack of food had already forced a large number to go hunting game. He estimated that to feed the one hundred thirty-eight Indians of the mission, he needed at least eight bushels of corn and eight beeves a week, a total of four hundred sixteen bushels of corn

---

[30]Bolton, *op. cit., The Quarterly,* XIX, 403. *Cf.* Dunn, *op. cit., The Quarterly,* XXV, 181.

[31]Bolton, *op. cit., The Quarterly,* XIX, 403; Pedro Nava to the Viceroy, November 6, 1794. *A. G. I., Audiencia de Guadalajara,* 104-1-1 (Dunn Transcripts, 1794-98, p. 67). Governor Muñoz, in a subsequent report made two years after the founding took place, stated that the ceremony was on February 8. He was writing from memory and probably mistook the date of his official report of that date for that of the founding (Muñoz to Nava, January 26, 1795, *ibid.,* p. 43). The actual date is confirmed in a letter of Father Garza to Governor Muñoz, written on February 24, 1793, in which the missionary requested reimbursement for the expenses of maintaining the Indians at the new mission from February 5 to date. *(Béxar Archives).*

[32]The only two monographs on the establishment of the mission are those of Bolton and Dunn to which reference has been made. The details of the hardships are not given in either.

and as many beeves for a year. He suggested as a remedy that one thousand head of cattle be secured at once. These could be bought for four thousand *pesos*. The Indians could learn to tend them, and while obtaining their meat supply, they could at the same time build up a herd that would make them self-supporting after the first year. He pointed out that hunger does not wait. Food was more important for the success of the mission than the church, buildings, ornaments, and sacred vestments. The Indians could live in temporary shelters, services could be held under a tree, but all the natives had to be fed each day.[33] On March 12, the governor personally took a train of such supplies as he could spare, and a guard of fourteen men from San Antonio, under Sergeant Mariano Rodríguez, to help Fathers Garza and Velasco.[34]

Instructions given to Rodríguez. The soldiers were not to be employed in hunting to supply meat except in case of extreme necessity. In that case they were to accompany the Indians designated by the missionary. They were not to take the wild cattle on the lands of Mission Espíritu Santo. The first duty of Rodríguez and his men, however, was to construct a strong stockade and build a *chamacuero* (cow pen). They were to assist in the construction and repair of the church and the *Padre's* house. The quarters for the mission guard were to be erected on the location designated by the missionary. Intimacy with the Indians was to be avoided and the highest moral conduct observed. The soldiers were to attend prayers daily in order to set a good example to the Indians, but a mounted sentinel was always to be left at the door of the church to guard against surprise attacks. Likewise, a mounted guard should be maintained at headquarters. Two horses were to be kept saddled at all times for any emergency. Rodríguez was further instructed not to send messengers to San Antonio, but to communicate with the governor through the commander at Espíritu Santo.[35]

Early trials and tribulations. A diary kept by Rodríguez during his stay at Refugio gives an intimate view of life at the new mission during its first three months. Governor Muñoz who had brought the guard and the supplies, left on March 15, after seeing work on the stockade begun two days before. The day after the governor departed, twenty-three

---

[33]Father Garza to Muñoz, February 24, 1793. *Béxar Archives.*

[34]Muñoz to the Viceroy, March 12, 1793. *Béxar Archives.*

[35]Ynstruccion y Orden a qe. se deve arreglar el Sargento Mariano Rodríguez en esta Nueba Mision de Ntra. Señora del Refugio, con los catorce hombres de Tropa de la Rl. Compañia de Sn. Antonio de Béxar. *Béxar Archives.*

Indians, dissatisfied with the meager rations, abandoned the mission. On March 18 a new thatch roof was placed on the rude structure that served as the first church, and on the following day ten Indians and four soldiers went to hunt wild cattle, because there was no meat at the mission. They returned on March 22 with nine beeves. Chief Frazada Pinta, who was to cause much worry, came on March 26 to inquire whether or not a good supply of food had been received. He had not been present at the founding, and his principal concern now was how much there was for himself and his seventy warriors to eat. They stayed for a few days and attended services on Holy Thursday and Good Friday, which came on March 28 and 29. On Saturday the garrison began cutting timber for the stockade, while most of the Indians looked on.

On April 2 Father Velasco and Rodríguez attempted to explore the bay. The Indians had agreed to take them. When the two came to the canoe, a group of Karankawas sat sullenly on the shore. When asked to get in and paddle, they merely grunted. The *Padre* tried to set them an example and, smiling good-naturedly, stepped into the canoe, almost capsizing it. The Indians laughed but offered no help. Both Rodríguez and Velasco were unaccustomed to canoes, so they were obliged to give up the trip. The Indians insolently leered and jeered at them.

Captain Cortés from La Bahía visited the mission the following day and was shocked by the lack of food. He ordered Rodríguez to cross the Guadalupe to get some beeves, even if they belonged to the herds of Mission Espíritu Santo. This order gave the soldiers and the faithful Indians a welcomed relief. A few days after Cortés' departure, the erection of the stockade was begun on April 9. It was high time. The Indians were becoming sullen and impudent. They were disgruntled because of the food shortage and the absence of presents. When urged by Father Velasco on April 28 to help the soldiers, after he had reprimanded them for killing some cattle without permission, they threatingly took up their bows and arrows and menaced the *Padre*. Order was restored by the timely interference of the guards, but no adequate punishment could be inflicted.

On May 6 a tropical storm and severe rains destroyed the flimsy church and the wretched huts of the Indians and soldiers alike. The stockade, built at the cost of so many hardships, was partly washed away. Four days later, an insolent Indian called El Surdo (Lefty), after openly insulting Father Velasco, took the *Padre's* horse and brazenly rode away. On the way out, he attacked and wounded a muleteer who was bringing much needed supplies.[36]

Little wonder that Father Velasco contemplated abandoning the project until adequate means were available for the successful operation of the mission. "Might it not be better," he asked, "to allow them all to go away than to see them drift away without consent?"[37] The governor, it must be said, did everything in his power to remedy the situation. Upon his return to San Antonio on March 23, he had sent one hundred thirty-six *fanegas* of corn (272 bushels), and authorized the purchase of some bulls for slaughter. These were to be bought at ten *reales* a head from Mission Espíritu Santo. He also secured a mule from each of the San Antonio missions to carry supplies, and obtained several yoke of oxen from Father Cárdenas to be used for sowing a crop at Refugio.[38]

Progress was being made. Father Garza, who went to Refugio on May 11, found the stockade had been repaired and finished. The north wall was 82 *varas* long, the south 68, the east 38, and the west 49, to form an irregular quadrilateral figure with 980 posts, and with a gate on the south side. The church and the other buildings were much in the same condition and afforded scanty shelter. The *chamacuero* (cow pen) had been completed and was capable of retaining perhaps 600 head of cattle. The Indians at the mission were still firm in their determination to become Christians. On May 14, Father Garza gathered the natives, young and old, at the foot of a large rustic cross set up on the consecrated burial ground, and began formal instruction in catechism. The *Padre's* heart was warmed by the spontaneous response, and he praised the good example set by the soldiers. Within a week the Indians had learned the *Pater Noster* and were making progress with the *Ave Maria*. Father Garza urged the governor—until respect for authority was established—to increase the guard to twenty-five or thirty men to prevent insults.[39]

The unhealthful climate proved a serious handicap. Colds, chills, fever, and malaria prevented both the soldiers and the Indians from building the houses, clearing the fields, and planting the crops. The governor inquired about the cause of the sickness, and Captain Cortés replied

---

[36]*Diario* kept by Mariano Rodríguez, March 13-May 23, 1793. *Béxar Archives.*

[37]Father Garza to Muñoz, April 1, 1793. *Béxar Archives.*

[38]Muñoz to Juan Cortés, March 23, 1793. *Béxar Archives.*

[39]Garza to Manuel Muñoz, May 17, 1793; Juan Cortés to Manuel Muñoz, May 6, 1793. *Béxar Archives.*

that it was not known, but that the garrison at La Bahía was similarly afflicted. Fourteen soldiers and several families at Espíritu Santo also were sick. Before the end of the summer, Sergeant Rodríguez, the first commander of the mission guards, died at Refugio. During an exploration trip to the coast and the neighboring islands, Captain Cortés discovered the probable cause of the illness. In his report he declared that the swarms of mosquitoes and sand flies were incredible and that they set the skin afire with their stinging bites.[40]

The sickness and inadequate food supply reduced the number of natives to ninety, but the missionaries were satisfied with and made no effort to increase the number because, in their present plight, it would only multiply their difficulties. Chief Frazada Pinta reappeared on June 8 with twelve families and offered to join the mission; sixteen Indians from the Colorado arrived in July and expressed their desire to stay and send for their families. The *Padres* treated all the visitors kindly but explained that no more could be admitted at the time. They assured the Indians that word would be sent them as soon as the mission received the supplies necessary to take care of them.[41]

Work on the mission building had to be continued in spite of reduced numbers, and a start had to be made on sowing crops to provide for the winter. The lack of adequate materials, however, delayed the work. The soil was not suitable for adobes, for it contained too much sand and broken shells, and consequently lacked the cohesive qualities essential for sun-dried brick. An effort was made to mix the mud with Spanish moss and hay, but even this device gave the adobe no consistency. Cedar was abundant on the northern bank of the mouth of the Guadalupe, but there were transportation difficulties to overcome. By the end of June considerable timber, nevertheless, had been gathered and three hundred adobes had been made. The next month the number was increased to seven hundred. The soldiers were of some assistance, but carpenters and masons were needed to speed up construction, and experienced farmers to teach the natives how to plant and to tend the stock. Father Garza requested skilled laborers, and Governor Muñoz replied that they could

---

[40]Garza to Muñoz, June 17, 1793; Muñoz to Juan Cortés, June 7, 1793; Cortés to Muñoz, July 13, 1793; Muñoz to Juan José Farías, September 13, 1793; and Juan Cortés to Muñoz, August 23, 1793. *Béxar Archives.*

[41]Garza to Muñoz, June 17, 1793; July 21, 1793. *Béxar Archives.*

be hired but that they demanded wages starting from the day they left San Antonio.[42]

Tuna time (prickly pear season) was an irresistible temptation to the Karankawas to leave Refugio that first summer. Likewise, were fishing and surf bathing on the neighboring islands. On June 29 they asked the missionary for permission to go to Toboso, Copano, and Aránzazu (Aransas Pass) islands. Father Garza wisely observed that it was not possible to confine suddenly to a sedentary life those who had roamed all their days. Seventy-four happy Indians left the mission. Only twenty-four stayed behind to help the soldiers.[43]

The country and coast near Refugio. Captain Cortés undertook an inspection of the new mission at the end of July. Setting out from Presidio de la Bahía with a corporal and three soldiers, he first went to the Rancho de la Misión del Refugio, the pasture chosen for the cattle and stock. This was on the north bank of the Guadalupe, almost at its mouth, bordering on an inlet bay of brackish water, very likely present Mission Bay. Cortés noted along the lake front lime rock which he suggested might be used for building Refugio Mission. The stone could be transported in canoes. He estimated the distance from the ranch to the lake as one-quarter league. On August 2 he went to a point opposite an island called Toboso. It took one and one-half hours to row across on the following day. The water was shallow, and Cortés observed that at low tide it could be crossed on horseback or even on foot. But the numerous oyster shells cut the horses' hoofs badly. He described the island as small, and devoid of vegetation and hiding places. Near the place of landing there were a few clumps of trees and bushes that should be cut down to prevent the natives from using them to hinder landing parties.

From Toboso Island he went to Matagorda Bay, landing probably near present Port O'Connor. He noted that the bar was too shallow to permit ships to enter and that the bay itself was not very deep. Landing was possible only by casting anchor about a quarter of a league out at sea. The new Mission of Refugio could be reached by water from the bay in a canoe, but the trip would take about a day. Along the beach he found no trace of shipwrecks or timber. There

---

[42]Garza to Muñoz, June 17, 1793; same to same, July 21, 1793; Juan Cortés to Muñoz, May 6, and July 13, 1793. *Béxar Archives.*

[43]Garza to Muñoz, July 21, 1793. *Béxar Archives.*

were a few corn stalks and old tree trunks probably brought down by
the river in times of flood. Before returning to Refugio Mission he
explored the coast line of the bay and the mouths of the Guadalupe
and the San Antonio, and noted the abundance of cedar along the
north bank of the former.[44]

Return of Father Silva. Governor Muñoz received a letter on August
8 from Father Silva asking for an escort of three to five soldiers to
accompany him from Laredo to Mission Refugio. The friar explained
he had just arrived with a train of supplies and that he was anxious
to visit the mission. He wanted the soldiers to meet him at the crossing
of the Nueces near its mouth, probably modern Calallen. He promised
the governor to pay him a visit in San Antonio after he had taken the
supplies to Refugio. Although the requested escort was not sent, Father
Silva went on to Mission Rosario where he left the train of supplies
for safe-keeping while he visited Refugio. But ill-luck seems to have pursued his every step. Shortly after his arrival a terrific storm almost swept
the mission away. Father Silva described to Governor Muñoz the difficulty he experienced in preventing the sacred vessels, the statues, and
the vestments he brought from being lost. He deplored the absence of
a substantial church and urged the necessity of erecting one. Fathers
Velasco and Garza welcomed their superior with such enthusiasm as
their sad plight permitted. Father Garza soon after asked permission to
retire to his college. The privations, the unhealthful climate, and the
long years of service in the coastal region had completely undermined
his strong constitution and he was suffering from chills and fever.
Governor Muñoz granted the request and Father Garza retired to
Zacatecas where he lived only a few months more.[45]

Father Silva brought twenty-four hundred eighty-seven *pesos'* worth
of implements, supplies, and church goods purchased with the money
granted for expenses in the establishment of the new mission.[46]

Appeal to the king. A change in the organization of the Interior
Provinces gave him the opportunity to appeal directly to the king in

---

[44]Juan Cortés to Manuel Muñoz, August 23, 1793. *Béxar Archives.*

[45]Manuel Silva to Manuel Muñoz, August 8, 1793; September 3, 1793; José
Mariano Garza to Manuel Muñoz, September 11, 1793; Muñoz to Garza, September
12, 1793. *Béxar Archives.*

[46]Pedro Nava to the Viceroy, November 6, 1794. *A. G. I., Audiencia de Guadalajara,* 104-1-1 (Dunn Transcripts, 1790-1798, p. 57).

behalf of his project. By the royal decrees of November 23 and 24, 1792, the Provinces of Coahuila and Texas, left under the immediate jurisdiction of the viceroy when the Interior Provinces were first organized under the independent administration of the commandant general, were added to the jurisdiction of the latter official. Early in 1793, Father Silva was informed by the viceroy of the change. It was this news that hastened his departure for Texas with the intention of calling upon the new commander.

But before leaving Mexico City, he addressed a formal memorial to the king on March 7, 1793, soliciting royal support for his enterprise. He recounted his experiences in Texas, how he had contacted the Karankawas, the Guapites, and the Copanos, and how he had won their friendship and confidence. He explained that these tribes and many others had agreed to congregate in missions and had, in fact, earnestly requested instruction in the faith. Their conversion, he argued, would lead to the reduction of other tribes in central and north Texas. The viceroy had authorized the establishment of only one mission on San Bernardo Bay and this had already been founded. One missionary had been assigned to care for the numerous natives who came daily. The amount of money appropriated for its development was inadequate. With only one mission and one missionary and the meager resources furnished, it was impossible to expand the work of conversion to the adjacent tribes.

Father Silva described vividly the possibilities of his original missionary plan. Only eighty leagues up the coast from the new mission were the Arkokisas who ardently desired instruction in the faith. From their lands the missionaries could reach the Tawakoni and the Taovayas. These nations had numerous pueblos, some of which had, perhaps, more than a thousand inhabitants. All these Indians desired instruction and sought baptism, but they were reluctant, he explained, to abandon their lands and homes to join the missions in San Antonio. They desired missions in their own land. It was through them that the distant Comanches might be brought into the faith.[47] But he either did not know, or he forgot to mention that Mission Nuestra Señora de la Luz had been established in the country of the Arkokisas and abandoned at the

---

[47]Fray Manuel Silva, Comisario y Prefecto de Misiones de los Colegios Observantes de America Septentrional, e hijo de el de Ntra. Sra. de Guadalupe de Zacatecas [to the King]. March 7, 1793; Father Silva to the Secretary of the Council of the Indies, March 18, 1793. *A. G. I., Audiencia de Guadalajara,* 104-1-1 (Dunn Transcripts, 1790-93, pp. 164-169; 162-163).

recommendation of the Marqués de Rubí on account of the indifference of the natives.

When he finally arrived in Texas again, the deplorable conditions he found at Refugio did not discourage him. They only increased his determination to secure the material support needed for the success of the enterprise. He and his successors at Refugio never doubted for a moment the sincerity of the natives in their desire to become Christians. Confident that the king would support his project, he decided that since the viceroy had no longer jurisdiction in the matter, he would now appeal to the governor, and through him to the commandant general for additional funds to carry out the program along the ambitious lines of his original plan.

Accordingly, on September 21, 1793, he made formal request to the governor for four thousand *pesos*. With this sum he obligated himself to erect a permanent church, quarters for the missionaries, and all other necessary buildings, such as a granary and shops; to secure one thousand cows with calves, fifty mares, twenty yoke of oxen, twenty-five horses, and the mules required for the mission. He explained that if the four thousand *pesos* were granted, he would not expect another cent from the royal treasury other than the appropriation for the corn and beef consumed by the neophytes during the first year. Father Garza had originally estimated the cost would be thirteen thousand, he declared, but in view of the materials already gathered and the start made, Father Silva felt confident that the sum indicated in his petition would suffice. He urged the prompt approval of the expenditure to insure the success of the enterprise.[48]

Unsuitable nature of original location. Nine months were to elapse before action was taken on the new petition of Silva. In the meantime, both missionaries and civil officials became convinced that the site chosen at Muelle Viejo, also called Cayo del Refugio, which appears to have been a short distance from Mission Bay in Calhoun County, was unsuitable.

Corporal Juan José Farías had succeeded Rodríguez as commander of the mission guard. On September 13 Governor Muñoz sent José Manuel Castro with a detachment of troops to relieve the soldiers at Refugio, many of whom had been sick. Castro arrived on September 18. He found

---

[48]Muñoz to Pedro Nava, January 26, 1793; Pedro Nava to the Viceroy, November 6, 1794. *A. G. I., Audiencia de Guadalajara*, 104-1-1 (Dunn Transcripts, 1794-1798, pp. 43-44; 56-57); Manuel Silva to Muñoz, September 21, 1793. *Béxar Archives.*

the stockade around the mission had been completed. The church was a *jacal* of timber with a *tule* (swamp grass) roof. The *Padre's* residence was a similar structure. The headquarters for the troops was a *jacal*, seventeen *varas* in length covered with a straw roof. A smaller *jacal*, six and a half *varas* long, served as the administrative office, storeroom, and library. How justly this may be called the first library in Texas is questionable, but in his report, Castro so designated it. There were two other similar huts for the Indians. Such was the physical plant at this time. Pedro José Salinas and José Raymundo Díaz, who had been sentenced in San Antonio to four years of labor on public works, were sent with Castro to help build the mission.[49]

Farías had built the stockade, two additional thatched huts, each thirteen and a half *varas* long; made 1,900 adobes; cut 32 boards of seasoned timber; and hewed 21 cedar beams. But sickness constantly hindered progress. There were one hundred twenty-five natives at the mission, of whom forty-one were warriors. Many of them, however, were sick. Fathers Velasco and Silva were also sick at the time, and on an average from four to six of the small guard of sixteen men were always on sick leave. The Indians were quiet, gentle as a rule, but incapable and indolent by nature. It became necessary to employ three laymen to teach the natives how to tend the stock. These were paid five *reales* (60 cents) a day. The overseer received six *reales*. The natives began to clamor for clothes and more food as winter approached. The soldiers turned to the semi-wild cattle of Mission Rosario that roamed beyond the Guadalupe, but Fray José de Cárdenas, who was himself having diffi-culty keeping his Indians in the mission, protested. The guards, too, were becoming unruly under such adverse conditions.[50]

On November 20, Governor Muñoz informed Father Silva that the mission bells, ornaments, vestments, and other supplies had arrived in San Antonio and would be sent to Refugio soon. These were delivered to Father Silva early in December at Rosario where he was staying because of illness. Father Velasco was there, also, seriously ill. At the new mission was Father Francisco Puelles, sent from Rosario to take care of the Indians until the other two had recovered. The train master

[49]Muñoz to Juan José Farías, September 13, 1793; Noticia de lo que corresponde a dha. mición entregada por el cavo Juan José Farías a José Manuel Castro . . . . *Béxar Archives.*

[50]Fray José Luis Mariano Cárdenas to Manuel Muñoz, October 31, 1793; Juan José Farías to Governor Muñoz, October 22, 1793; Fray Manuel Silva to Governor Muñoz, November 1, 1793.

presented a bill for transporting the goods, but Father Silva refused to pay the freight, because the train, he claimed, should have been sent at royal expense.[51]

The series of Indian protests which took place at the new mission reveal the evil temper of the prospective converts. Alleging that the lean meat being given them was the cause of much of their illness, they left in a group late in November, and stayed away two days, according to Fray Puelles. The friar did not blame them. The last bull killed looked sick and was all skin and bones. He blamed the soldiers, for he suspected them of taking the better stock for themselves. They had reported one hundred thirty head of the mission herd as lost. Private trading and gambling were common between soldiers and natives, he declared, and the Indians were unable to keep anything.

By June, 1794, the mission was practically abandoned. The hostility of Frazada Pinta and his followers, who had never joined the mission, became unbearable. A band of Indians on June 4 attacked five soldiers and twenty-three natives who were guarding the cattle, and drove them from the ranch. The next day they entered the mission itself, killed a horse, broke with a hammer the lock on the storehouse, and took a bundle of hatchets and one of *comales* (flat cooking pans), sacked the *Padre's* house, drank the wine kept for Mass, stole the brown sugar and chocolate, as well as the cigarettes and ribbons, broke the glass bottles, and scattered the mission records to the four winds. Not satisfied, they wantonly killed two milk cows and one calf before they left. The governor, when he heard of it, asked where the *Padre* was at the time of the attack. He was told that Father Puelles, who was still looking after Refugio, was away trying to persuade some of the mission Indians to return.[52]

Removal of Mission Refugio. It will be remembered that Father Silva appealed through Governor Muñoz early in September to Pedro Nava, commandant of the Interior Provinces at Chihuahua, for help to establish the mission on a firmer basis. In the meantime, while waiting impatiently for relief, he repeatedly asked the governor to allow him to go to Chihuahua to plead the cause of Refugio. In his letters, he raised questions pertaining to the need of more missionaries, the advisability of moving to a better location, the need of establishing a civil

---

[51]Fray Manuel Silva to Governor Muñoz, November 20, and December 12, 1793.

[52]Fray Manuel Silva to Governor Manuel Muñoz, December 12, 1793; Muñoz to Juan Cortés, May 16, 1794; José Antonio Cadena to Muñoz, June 8, 1794; Muñoz to Juan Cortés, June 10, 1794. *Béxar Archives.*

settlement in connection with the mission, the increase of the Refugio garrison to twenty-five or thirty men, and the amount of money needed to complete the establishment.[53]

Early in May, 1794, Father Silva, who had by now fully recovered from his illness, went to Chihuahua and interviewed the commandant general.[54] Nava, unwilling to make a hasty decision, referred the whole matter to his *auditor*, the able Galindo Navarro, who in a detailed report made on June 26, 1794, discussed the questions raised by the enthusiastic missionary and recommended the course of action to be followed in each case.

Taking them one by one, he reviewed first the general policy regarding the number of missionaries for new missions. He cited the regulations drawn on December 14, 1780, by Fray Manuel de la Vega and approved by the Council of the Indies on February 15, 1781, which provided for the appointment of two for each mission; but he pointed out that this provision was not observed in the establishment of missions in California, where only one was allowed. He concluded, however, that in view of special circumstances in Texas, it might be best that Refugio Mission be given two missionaries during the first few years.

The question of the removal to a more suitable and healthful location did not seem to present serious difficulties, declared Navarro. Governor Muñoz and Father Silva, as well as Father Reyes and the Count of Sierra Gorda before them, were agreed on the unhealthful character of the present site. The Count of Sierra Gorda had suggested in the very beginning the mouth of the Nueces (Corpus Christi) as more suitable. This suggestion had been deemed inadvisable then because of the danger of attack by Lipans. In view of the circumstances reported now, the *auditor* was inclined to think it might be best that it be moved to a site as near as possible to La Bahía, that the exact location be determined after a careful survey and investigation was undertaken by Governor Muñoz, Father Silva, and other persons experienced in such matters. The removal from the original location would involve little or no additional expense, he explained, because no permanent buildings had been erected and the stockade put up was only temporary.

---

[53]Silva to Muñoz, December 12, December 19, 1793; January 3, 1794. *Béxar Archives.*

[54]El Comandante Gral. de Provincias Ynternas de N. E. Ynforma sobre el estado de la misión del Refugio . . . November 11, 1794. *A. G. I., Audiencia de Guadalajara,* 104-1-1 (Dunn Transcripts, 1794-98, pp. 51-62).

The matter of establishing a civil settlement in connection with the mission had not been a part of the original plans. But the idea was highly commendable, Navarro observed. The coastal Indians were known to be fickle. The experience of Missions Espíritu Santo and Rosario bore eloquent testimony to that fact. Consequently, a civil settlement would provide a permanent nucleus and set a good example to the natives. But this should be located at least one league from the mission itself.

Father Garza had suggested before leaving, that the garrison be increased to thirty men. Father Silva was of the same opinion. Navarro was careful not to commit himself as to the number, and left the matter for the commandant general to determine, but he declared that regardless of the size of the guard decided upon, the garrison should not be required to do menial work as in the past. Such labors were unworthy of soldiers and caused the Indians to lose respect for them. If a civil settlement was decided upon, married soldiers should be offered lands on which to settle in the community upon the expiration of their term of enlistment.

The question of expenses for the permanent and firm establishment was of great importance, Navarro agreed. He pointed out that the original estimate made by Father Garza was 6,610 *pesos,* according to the record.[55] Father Silva, however, had requested only 4,000, declaring that if this amount was granted, it would suffice to place the mission on a self-supporting basis. Under the circumstances, the request of Father Silva was reasonable, commented Navarro.[56]

Pedro Nava, the commandant general, approved the recommendations made by the *auditor* and instructed Governor Muñoz on July 5, 1794, that the mission might be moved to such a location as would be deemed more suitable; that officials in Texas were to give all possible aid to the missionaries in order to enable them to feed, clothe, and instruct the Indians of Refugio; and that two missionaries were to be assigned to the new mission for a period of three years. He was informed that the royal treasury at Saltillo was to pay 4,000 *pesos* to Domingo Otón, *síndico,* who was to hold the money at the disposal of Father Silva; that the guard of the mission was to be reduced to eight or ten men, including a corporal, who were not to work on the construction of mission

[55]Memoria de lo que por ahora se juzga precisamente necesario para la nueva fundación del Refugio. Undated, *A. G. I., Audiencia de Guadalajara,* 104-1-1 (Dunn Transcripts, 1790-93, pp. 183-186).

[56]Galindo Navarro to Pedro Nava, June 26, 1794. *A. G. A., Audiencia de Guadalajara,* 104-1-1 (Dunn Transcripts, 1754-98, pp. 14-33).

buildings or in tilling the soil; that the missionaries of Refugio were to be allowed from two to four soldiers as an escort when going after runaway natives, but that soldiers should never be sent alone on such errands. Lastly, the governor was told that the establishment of a civil settlement was authorized for whatever new location was chosen, settlers for which might be recruited in Coahuila, Nuevo León, and Nuevo Santander with the consent of the respective governors.[57] The instructions were received in San Antonio on August 15, but measures to carry them out had to be temporarily postponed.

Selecting the new site.   When the orders of Nava arrived, Fray Silva had not returned from Chihuahua. It seems he first went to Saltillo to purchase some needed supplies. Governor Muñoz, worried over the change in policy outlined in the new instructions, asked Nava who was to pay for the meat and corn supplied by La Bahía and San Antonio since February 4, 1793, the date of the founding. The original order of the viceroy had stipulated that payment would be made at San Luis Potosí. During this period, four hundred ninety-four *fanegas* of corn (more than one thousand bushels) had been sent to the mission. These cost nine hundred eighty-eight *pesos,* besides five hundred seventy-four *pesos* for drayage.[58]

Father Silva was back in San Antonio late in October or early in November. In company with Governor Muñoz, he undertook the selection of a new site.[59] The governor reported on November 7 that they first explored the Guadalupe, and found that the spring said to be near its mouth was a fresh water lake formed by rain. No location suitable for the permanent establishment of the mission was found in the vicinity. They then carefully examined the lower San Antonio to its mouth, the bay, and the site of Rancho del Refugio. No place was found where irrigation was practical. There were a few wooded areas and some places where rock was available in this region, the pasture lands were good, but the consensus of opinion was against a permanent establishment here. The party next visited the Paso del Apache, a crossing on the San Antonio just below Missions Espíritu Santo and Rosario. This site,

---

[57]Pedro Nava to Governor Muñoz, July 5, 1794. *Béxar Archives.*

[58]Governor Muñoz to Nava, August 18, 1794. *Béxar Archives.*

[59]Dunn, who has to date written the fullest account, speaking of this incident, says: "No details are available to the writer in regard to the removal." *The Quarterly,* XXV, 183. The account given here is based on materials used for the first time.

suggested by Chief Llano Grande of the Karankawas, was too near La Bahía. Its permanent occupation close to the new mission might prove prejudicial to the interests of the Jaranames already congregated in Rosario.[60]

The party had made a careful examination likewise of the mouth of the Nueces River and Corpus Christi Bay, and experienced considerable discomfort from high winds and adverse weather on account of the season of the year. They had gone then to the Rancho de Santa Gertrudis where Juan Barrera, the tithe collector, kept his cattle herds; this place was known also as Cayo de Aránzazu and was probably in the vicinity of modern Aransas Pass, several miles to the north. Governor Muñoz was strongly impressed by the location, but Father Silva was not entirely satisfied. The governor had to return to San Antonio before he could inspect the last site suggested, known as Santa Dorotea. This was done by Captain Cortés and Father Silva. It was about three or four leagues from La Bahía on the San Antonio, probably near present Charco.[61]

A few faithful Karankawas were still at Rancho del Refugio, the original location of the mission. Governor Muñoz instructed Father Silva to inform them of the decision to move to either Santa Gertrudis or Santa Dorotea. But Chief Llano Grande, to whose loyalty and sincerity the small measure of success attained was due, had died early in November, 1794. His brother was asked, therefore, to go into the woods to inform those who had gone to hunt, of the projected removal of the mission.[62] At the same time, Governor Muñoz wrote Captain Cortés that the reëstablishment of the mission on whichever of the two sites was chosen by Father Silva should not be delayed. Cortés was instructed to put the missionary and the Indians in possession at the new location, to furnish them corn and meat in quantities proportionate to their number, and to report how many joined the mission.[63]

Reëstablishment at present Refugio. After a second visit, Father Silva decided on a site near the Rancho de Santa Gertrudis, also known as Aránzazu. This was in the vicinity of Refugio, where the mission was formally reëstablished on January 8, and possession of the lands given to the Indians on January 10, 1795, in the name of the king by Captain

---

[60]Governor Muñoz to Pedro Nava, November 7, 1794. *Béxar Archives.*

[61]Governor Muñoz to Nava, November 30, 1794. *Béxar Archives.*

[62]Muñoz to Nava, November 7 and November 30, 1794. *Béxar Archives.*

[63]Governor Muñoz to Captain Juan Cortés, December 7, 1794. *Béxar Archives.*

Cortés. There were forty-three Indians present. All property that could be moved from the original location had been brought by Father Silva and the Indians. The long caravan of cattle, carts, and natives finally reached the new site on January 8. On one of the carts had been loaded the new hand-carved doors for the mission chapel and the bells that had come from distant Mexico, while the pots, the rude furniture, and such supplies as there were, had been loaded on other carts and mules. On a broad plain, not far from the new site, the cart with the bells and doors broke down and had to be left until the weather permitted its rescue from the mire. There were no other mishaps.[64] The site chosen was approved by Nava on February 26, as well as the arrangements made by Governor Muñoz to supply the mission with food from La Bahía.[65]

Slow growth and development. Almost in the same breath, Father Silva reported both the reëstablishment at Santa Gertrudis and the urgent need of food. Cattle sufficient to feed the Indians for a year would have to be supplied at once to save the mission herd. The success of the entire enterprise would otherwise be endangered. He suggested that fourteen hundred and fifty-two *pesos* be turned over to him out of the Mesteña Fund in San Antonio to buy the necessary stock in Nuevo Santander.[66] Nava immediately sensed an inordinate desire on the part of Father Silva to handle money and to manage everything. He consequently instructed Governor Muñoz not to accept the proposal. He warned that only the Indians actually living in the mission were to be fed. Those who came merely to get supplies in order to return to the coast were to be told that they had to stay in the mission if they wanted to be fed. Cattle were not to be brought from outside the province.[67]

The governor did his best to provide for the immediate needs of the mission. On April 22 Father Silva acknowledged receipt of two hundred twenty-seven bulls sent from La Bahía to be slaughtered for the hungry Indians at the mission. Seemingly it was agreed that three hundred sixty-six bulls would suffice for the first year. One hundred thirty-three more were delivered on May 10 to bring the total received to six less than the number upon which they had agreed. A few days later the

---

[64]Fray Manuel Silva to Governor Muñoz, January 12, 1795; Juan Cortés to Muñoz, January 16, 1795; Muñoz to Pedro Nava, January 26, 1795. *Béxar Archives.*

[65]Pedro Nava to Manuel Muñoz, February 26, 1795. *Béxar Archives.*

[66]Manuel Silva to Muñoz, January 12, 1795. *Béxar Archives.*

[67]Pedro Nava to Muñoz, February 26, 1795. *Béxar Archives.*

shortage was more than made up when Captain Juan Cortés of La Bahía turned over to the new mission thirty-nine more, brought by Felipe Flores.[68] This number was sufficient to supply more than one bull a day, which, considering the number of Indians congregated, between forty and fifty, should have been enough to provide a reasonable amount of meat for each person.

Securing laborers and teachers. Father Silva had agreed to erect permanent buildings and complete the physical plant of the mission. As early as May, 1795, he sent Fray José Manuel Pedrajo to San Antonio to hire skilled laborers. He asked the governor's coöperation and assured him the workmen who agreed to come would be paid current salaries in cash and given the best treatment possible.[69] But tradesmen such as carpenters, masons, cabinet-makers, and blacksmiths were not easily available even in San Antonio. After a month of searching, Father Pedrajo found one carpenter and a possible violin instructor, an Indian, who might prove very useful in training the neophytes to play and sing in the choir.[70] He was José, of Mission San Juan Capistrano. Father Silva assured the governor that the violinist would be most useful in the organization of a choir. There was a real need for music during the Sunday services. Furthermore, the Indian, José, was kinsman of some of those in Refugio and would therefore be welcomed.[71]

The first carpenter engaged to go to Refugio was named Losoya. Father Silva was elated at the prospect of securing the services of a skilled craftsman to teach his trade to the mission Indians. But, for some reason, Losoya did not arrive. Father Silva asked the governor in August to inquire from Father Zambrano, parish priest in San Antonio, concerning the probable cause of delay. In September, he gave up hope and sent word to Losoya that he need not come.[72]

Not until the first week in August did Guadalupe Cerda and Juan José Garza, a foreman and a carpenter respectively, arrive in Refugio. But Garza had an affliction in one eye, which became serious and prevented him from working. In disgust, Father Silva sent Fray Francisco

---

[68]Fray Manuel Silva to Governor Muñoz, April 22, May 10, 1795; Juan Cortés to Manuel Muñoz, May 16, 1795. *Béxar Archives.*

[69]Fray Silva to Governor Muñoz, May 18, 1795. *Béxar Archives.*

[70]Fray Silva to Governor Muñoz, June 23, 1795. *Béxar Archives.*

[71]Fray Silva to Muñoz, June 29, 1795. *Béxar Archives.*

[72]Fray Silva to Muñoz, June 29, August 22, and September 27, 1795. *Béxar Archives.*

MISSION NUESTRA SEÑORA DEL REFUGIO, DRAWN FROM A PICTURE OF THE ORIGINAL MISSION

Puelles in September, 1795, to recruit laborers in Boca de Leones, Monclova (Tlascala de Monclova) and Revilla. Before the end of the month, José Nájera, a carpenter by trade, arrived with Fray Puelles and began to work. He knew his trade and was satisfied with room and board. The first products of his labor at Refugio were two benches, three chairs, a table, and an altar. He started the doors for the new chapel that was being built of adobe.[73]

But the rush season stopped all work on buildings. The corn, planted with much difficulty and delayed by prolonged droughts, was ready for harvesting. The *Padre* estimated the yield at two hundred *fanegas* (four hundred bushels). The Indians who had gone to the coast returned on September 22, and everybody was busy harvesting.[74]

By January, 1796, the need for a blacksmith at Refugio had become urgent. But the only one in San Antonio who was willing to go, was being detained by his debtors. Father Silva appealed to the governor to permit the blacksmith to spend a month and a half in Refugio. He could work off his debts after his return, the *Padre* explained. Father Silva was disgusted with the difficulties experienced in securing and managing labor. He assured the governor that of several workmen who had come to the mission, only three earned their salary. The others had proved a constant source of trouble.[75]

But in spite of grumblings and apparently needless delays, a new adobe church had been completed, and the natives had been initiated not only in the fundamental teachings of Christianity but also in the various trades and the habit of daily labor. The poor quality of the soil for making adobes was perhaps responsible for the collapse of one of the wings of the new church. When Captain Cortés visited the mission in February, 1796, he found the Indians repairing the damage.[76]

By March, an additional adobe structure to serve as quarters for the *Padres,* storeroom and shop, had been finished. It was duly dedicated and blessed during Holy Week. Many Indians from Mission Rosario attended the ceremony. The *Padre* complained, however, that these neighbors were a nuisance. That this was true will be seen in the course of this chapter. He likewise complained that a carpenter named José María Uraga had left without notifying him. He had made seventy-

---

[73]Fray Silva to Governor Muñoz, September 9, and 27, 1795. *Béxar Archives.*
[74]*Ibid., Béxar Archives.*
[75]Fray Silva to Governor Muñoz, January 12, 1796. *Béxar Archives.*
[76]Captain Cortés to Governor Muñoz, February 13, 1796. *Béxar Archives.*

nine beams, ninety-one boards, one thousand sixty shingles, and several carts in a little less than a year at the mission. The *Padre* was glad he had gone. He said Uraga was a slow and poor worker. The same was true of a man named Joaquín Jaime, who left owing the *Padre* twenty-two *pesos*. He had asked permission to go to work at Presidio de la Bahía, but had gone to San Antonio instead. Father Silva hoped he would never return. There was also a pottery maker, brought to teach the Indians his trade, but his work seemed unsatisfactory to Father Silva.[77]

The legal status of Refugio. Mission Refugio up to the end of 1796 was under the personal administration of Father Manuel Silva who had conceived the idea of its establishment and secured its approval. He was the sole sponsor and the only one responsible for the enterprise. The *Discretorio* and the guardian of the College of Zacatecas had not been consulted. The moneys granted first by the viceroy and later by the commandant general were turned over not to the College but to Father Silva. The governor had been instructed to deal directly in all matters with Father Silva. The status of Refugio, therefore, was unique.

The appeal made to the king in 1793 started an investigation of this unusual one-man enterprise. The royal *fiscal* requested further information from the commissary general of the Franciscans in Spain concerning Fray Manuel Silva and his plan.[78] Fray Juan Moya replied on February 11, 1794, that the plan itself appeared worthy of support, if its practicability was borne out by more concrete evidence. He expressed some doubts about Fray Silva's sincerity and dependability. He pointed out that, judging from the information at his disposal, it appeared to him that Father Silva had gone to Texas first in 1790; that after starting the promotion of the new mission, he had been called to preside at a chapter meeting held at Pachuca on October 29, 1791; but that he should have returned shortly thereafter to Zacatecas and then to his mission in Texas. But in March, 1793, he was still in Pachuca, near Mexico City, where he wrote his memorial to the king. In his appeal to the king he stated that he had petitioned the viceroy for aid, but gave no details as to the action taken, the extent of aid granted, or the actual progress made. In view of the facts available, Moya hesitated to endorse the

---

[77]Fray Silva to Governor Muñoz, March 27, 1796; Fray Antonio de Jesús Garabito to Manuel Muñoz, June 4, 1797. *Béxar Archives.*

[78]Dictamen del Real Fiscal. *A. G. I., Audiencia de Guadalajara*, 104-1-1 (Dunn Transcripts, 1794-1798, pp. 181-182).

request for additional funds.[79] The royal *fiscal* promptly advised the Council of the Indies that under the circumstances, the viceroy, the bishop of Guadalajara, and the commandant general should be requested to report on the proposal and the character of Fray Silva.[80]

The viceroy, Marquis de Branciforte, replied that the request had originally been made to Viceroy Revillagigedo, that in the meantime the Province of Texas had been removed from his jurisdiction and placed under that of the commandant general of the Interior Provinces. Consequently, he was unable to give any additional information. Pedro Nava referred the inquiry to Governor Muñoz, who on January 26, 1795, made an extensive reply explaining the attitude of the various Indian nations to the establishment of missions in the area designated by Father Silva.[81]

After recounting in detail the circumstances attendant upon the founding of Mission Refugio, Governor Muñoz discussed the plan for the establishment of missions among the Arkokisas, Tawakonis, and Taovayas. He pointed out that he had come in contact with these nations since taking over the government from Martínez Pacheco in 1790. His impression was that they did not desire missions. With regard to the Arkokisas, Fathers Fray José Mariano Garza and Fray José Mariano Reyes had spent many years trying to persuade them to live in a mission, but they had found that these natives were interested not in conversion but in gifts. Just recently sixty-one Tawakonis had visited San Antonio. When asked if they desired to be reduced to mission life, they replied that they were "all right as they were." Father Silva had said he could place them in a mission if he had twelve thousand *pesos* to do it with; but, when Governor Muñoz offered to give him the money, Silva had pleaded lack of time. Muñoz concluded his report with the interesting observation that the Talapousas and Alpames (Alabamas) were beginning to drive the Ais and their friends westward.[82] When this information was eventually received by the Council of the Indies, it was decided that there was no justification for the establishment of any more missions

---

[79]Juan de Moya to Antonio Ventura de Taranco, February 11, 1794. *Ibid.*, pp. 1-4.

[80]Antonio Ventura de Taranco to the Council, March 17, 1794. *A. G. I., Audiencia de Guadalajara,* 104-1-1 (Dunn Transcripts, 1794-1798, pp. 11-13).

[81]Marqués de Branciforte to Antonio Ventura Taranco, September 30, 1794; Pedro Nava to Manuel Muñoz, November 29, 1794. *A. G. I., Audiencia de Guadalajara,* 104-1-1 (Dunn Transcripts, 1794-1798, pp. 34-36; 40-41).

[82]Governor Muñoz to Pedro Nava, January 26, 1795. *A. G. I., Audiencia de Guadalajara,* 104-1-1 (Dunn Transcripts, 1794-1798, pp. 47-50).

along the coast. But by this time, Father Silva's enthusiasm had been chilled by cold reality, and he was ready to retire, broken both in health and spirit.

Retirement of Father Silva. By August, 1796, Father Silva was seriously contemplating giving up the enterprise. He was sick, practically an invalid. He had lost the use of his left hand, and inflammatory rheumatism had stiffened his knees so much that he could not bend them. He wrote Fray Francisco Gomarra, guardian of the College of Zacatecas, that he would have to leave soon for treatment and that he was about to turn over the administration of Mission Refugio to the College. On August 16, Fray Gomarra warned Father Silva not to leave Texas without making the necessary arrangements with the commandant general for the legal transfer of the mission.[83]

But Father Silva had always been impulsive and, once he had made up his mind, he was in the habit of translating his decision into immediate action. On September 8, 1796, he informed Father Fray José Antonio Mariano Garavito, who was still convalescing from a serious attack of malaria fever, that he was turning over the mission to him and his assistant, Fray José Mariano Sáenz, as representatives of the College of Nuestra Señora de Guadalupe of Zacatecas, who would henceforth be responsible for its administration. In vain did Fray Garavito remonstrate that he did not have the authority to assume the responsibility and that the act had to be approved first by the *Discretorio* of the College and the commandant general of the Interior Provinces. He handed to his amazed companions inventories of the mission property, a financial report which showed there were no outstanding debts, and summoned the Indians to ask them if they had any objections to being administered henceforth by the College. The surprised and uncomprehending Indians replied in the negative. He left that same day for La Bahía, assuring Fray Garavito and Fray Sáenz that his sickness brooked no delay, that in due time he would inform the governor, the commandant general, and the guardian of the College and get their approval for the transfer.[84]

From La Bahía, he informed Governor Muñoz of the transfer and

---

[83]Francisco Gomarra to Pedro Nava, November 7, 1796; Fray Silva to the *Discretorio* of the College of Zacatecas, September 11, 1796. *Béxar Archives.*

[84]Manuel Silva to Manuel Muñoz, September 13; same to the *Discretorio* of Zacatecas, September 11, 1796; José Garavito to Francisco Gomarra, September 23, 1796. *Béxar Archives.*

explained that it was imperative for him to leave in order to take the sulphur baths at a health resort near Monterrey. He had not asked the governor to come to Refugio to witness the transfer out of consideration for that official's poor health. Muñoz had been seriously ill for some time. Silva sent him copies of the inventories and a report of the transfer, with a request that these be sent to the commandant general.[85] To the *Discretorio,* he explained that his poor health had forced him to turn the mission over to the College. He assured the College there were no debts outstanding, that Fray Domingo Otón, *síndico* at Saltillo, still had a balance of one hundred fifty *pesos* from the original four thousand granted by Nava; that two hundred seven *pesos* had been paid to the servants employed at the mission to work during the rest of the year, which would preclude additional expenses; and that in addition to the four hundred *pesos* due Fray Garavito by the royal treasury for the previous year, nine hundred more would soon be due as allowance for the present year. These should be sufficient to meet all the obligations of the mission. But Father Garavito, in his report to Guardian Gomarra, declared that Fray Silva had not given him an account of the finances, but had only stated that he had received four thousand *pesos* from Nava, although he had been obliged to spend much more out of alms received from friends.[86]

The College of Zacatecas takes over Mission Refugio. The news of the unauthorized transfer of the mission by Fray Silva came as a distinct surprise to the commandant general. When Guardian Gomarra informed him of the impending departure of Fray Silva on account of his health, and intimated his probable abandonment of Mission Refugio, Nava wrote Governor Muñoz that no information had been received concerning the progress made by the mission since October, 1795, and reminded him that an annual report should have been made. He wrote Fray Gomarra at the same time that if Father Silva had to retire, the College should assume the administration of the mission, as had been done with the other missions in Texas. But in this instance, Father Silva should be required to make a full report of all the expenses incurred, and the transfer should be made through the governor.[87]

---

[85]Manuel Silva to Manuel Muñoz, September 13, 1796. *Béxar Archives.*

[86]Manuel Silva to the *Discretorio* of Zacatecas, September 11, 1796; Garavito to Francisco Gomarra, September 23, 1796. *Béxar Archives.*

[87]Francisco Gomarra to Pedro Nava, September 26, 1795; Nava to Manuel Muñoz, October 18, 1796; same to Francisco Gomarra, October 18, 1796. *Béxar Archives.*

Fray José Mariano Cárdenas was the president of the Texas missions at this time. To him Gomarra wrote immediately, instructing him to receive Mission Refugio from Governor Muñoz, since the *Discretorio* had agreed to assume its administration. If Father Silva were still in Texas, he should be requested to make a report on the finances of the mission. Copies of the terms of the transfer and the inventories of all mission property were to be sent to the College.[88] But Father Silva had already departed, and Governor Muñoz was unable to go to Refugio, because he was ill himself. Captain Cortés, therefore, at the request of the governor, confirmed the transfer, and Refugio became a Zacatecan mission. The *Discretorio*, composed of Fathers Ignacio María Laba, José Mariano Rojo, Francisco Gomarra, José Antonio Alcocer, Juan Bautista Larondo, and José Ramón Texada, acknowledged their appreciation to Father Silva for his sacrifices, and his personal interest in founding the mission, and expressed deep regret for his affliction.[89]

Settling the debts of Refugio Mission. In spite of the avowed assurances of Silva that there were no debts outstanding, Captain Juan Bautista Elguezábal found, upon conducting an inspection of La Bahía in 1797, that Mission Refugio owed Presidio Nuestra Señora de Loreto one thousand fifty-five *pesos*. Nava was incensed to learn that this debt for supplies had not been paid. He wrote Muñoz to remind him that Father Silva had agreed to put the mission on a self-supporting basis with the four thousand *pesos* granted to him, and that when he turned it over to Fathers Garavito and Sáenz on September 8, 1796, he had declared there were no debts outstanding. Father Cárdenas, president of the missions, was to be informed, therefore, that the money due the presidio at La Bahía would have to be paid.[90] On January 19, 1798, Nava wrote Captain Elguezábal again to inform him that he had instructed Father Cárdenas to order Mission Refugio to settle the account without delay. If no settlement was made within eight days, Elguezábal was to proceed to the confiscation of such property as was not needed for the maintenance of the Indians.[91] In this manner the accounts contracted by Father Silva were finally settled.

---

[88]Francisco Gomarra to José Mariano Cárdenas, October 31, 1796. *Béxar Archives.*

[89]Discretorio del Colegio de Zacatecas to Manuel Silva, November 7, 1796. *Béxar Archives.*

[90]Nava to Manuel Muñoz, August 4, 1797. *Béxar Archives.*

[91]Nava to Elguezábal, January 19, 1798. *Béxar Archives.*

Relations between the Indians of Refugio and Rosario. When the mission was moved to Santa Gertrudis, it was reëstablished with only forty-three Indians. A little over a month later, on February 21, 1795, a party of thirty-two more arrived. By the end of October, when the first report on the progress made was sent to Governor Muñoz, there were eighty-two Indians, but twenty-six of them had gone to the coast with the permission of the *Padre* to visit relatives and induce them to join the mission. The missionary complained that the natives were unaccustomed to labor and that there was no way in which they could be induced to exert themselves for long.[92]

Most of the Indians at Refugio were Karankawas, but their number was not large. Mission Rosario, under the administration of Father Francisco Jaudenes, was experiencing great difficulty in keeping its neophytes fed and clothed. Early in 1797, Fray Jaudenes, unable to care for the Cocos and Karankawas in his mission, suggested that they be temporarily placed in Refugio. Captain Juan Bautista Elguezábal, who was at La Bahía at this time making an inspection, interviewed the chiefs of the two nations to ascertain if they preferred to be sent to San Antonio, where they could be cared for better. The Karankawa chief, Zertuche, the Coco chief, Pedro Jaspe, and several other leaders of the mission Indians of Rosario told Elguezábal that they did not want to go to San Antonio because it was too far from their lands and too many Comanches frequented the place. They preferred to live at Refugio, the place Father Jaudenes had suggested. The climate was more agreeable and they would be closer to the coast and farther from the Comanches. When told the Comanches would not bother them because they were now the friends of the Spaniards, the Karankawas and Cocos of Rosario refused to believe it.

Father Garavito frankly opposed transferring the Rosario Indians to Refugio, and objected on the score that the Refugio Indians would be hostile to the newcomers. The chiefs replied that they were all one people, that they spoke the same language and belonged to the same nations. Elguezábal consented to the transfer and asked Father Garavito to make a report on the number of Indians at Refugio, designating the nation and number of the old residents and of the newcomers. On June 30, 1797, he reported that there were seventy-two Karankawas who belonged to Mission

---

[92]Cortés to Manuel Muñoz, February 21, 1795; Manuel Silva to Manuel Muñoz, September 30, 1795; Manuel Muñoz to Pedro Nava, October 26, 1795. *Béxar Archives.*

Refugio. From Rosario had come forty-seven Karankawas and fifty-two Cocos. The total number at Refugio now was one hundred seventy-five.[93]

The arrangement proved to be decidedly unsatisfactory. In February, 1798, Father Garavito remonstrated that he could not continue to care for the Indians of Rosario indefinitely. It was unfair to expect him to keep up the neophytes of the two missions, particularly since one missionary had been removed, and the annual allowance, consequently, reduced to four hundred fifty *pesos*. Refugio Mission could and would supply meat for the maintenance of the Rosario Indians, but it could not supply corn and other farm products, because it did not have them. The crops had been lost on account of the drought. The Rosario Indians knew how to plant, but they refused to help or harvest at Refugio. This attitude set a bad example to the others. In spite of the fact that they were of the same nations and spoke a common tongue, they did not get along together. If the present arrangement was continued it would inevitably result in the ruin of both missions.

At about the same time Elguezábal wrote the governor that the continual failure of the crops at Espíritu Santo and Rosario was the reason for the prolonged stay of the Rosario Indians at Refugio. There was only one solution: the construction of irrigation canals to insure the successful cultivation of their farms. While such a project was expensive, nevertheless the money could be secured either by a collection taken up by the missionaries in the more prosperous *Reales de Minas* (mining towns) or, as a last resort, by a grant from the royal treasury. The benefits would more than offset the initial expense. Elguezábal pointed out that an advantageous source of revenue for these impoverished missions might result from permitting them to exchange their surplus cattle for the wild horses of Nuevo Santander at a convenient place. He suggested Laredo as a possible center of exchange. If a date was designated on which the mission could, each year, send the cattle to the appointed place, this trade might prove an important source of revenue. He concluded by declaring that the three missions in the vicinity of the presidio of La Bahía were important for the control of the coastal tribes and merited more consideration. The funds at their disposal were inadequate.[94]

---

[93]Fray José Antonio de Jesús Garavito to Juan Bautista Elguezábal, June 30, 1797; Juan Bautista Elguezábal to Manuel Muñoz, July 3, 1797. *Béxar Archives.*

[94]José Antonio de Jesús Garavito, February 3, 1798; Juan Bautista Elguezábal to Manuel Muñoz, February 4, 1798. *Béxar Archives.*

A month later, in March, 1798, Father Garavito informed the authorities that the Rosario Indians could not remain much longer as guests at Refugio. He related that when the regular neophytes of his mission were about to set out for a short vacation on the coast, their chief told him, "Let the Rosario Indians eat our cattle while we are gone to fish. We hope their children will have to go and hunt for food in the woods when the cattle are gone." The *Padre* complained that the unwelcome guests committed many abuses, were insolent, and refused to help the others. Their presence was demoralizing the neophytes of Refugio, who could not understand the reason that their visitors enjoyed so many privileges. He could not understand the insistence of the commandant general on this unnatural and prejudicial arrangement. It did not help the Rosario Indians very much and was completely ruining Refugio. He warned that he would not be responsible for the consequences. Elguezábal seems not to have understood the attitude of Father Garavito and attributed his objections to a lack of coöperation. Governor Muñoz was puzzled by the contradictory reports of the missionary and the captain at La Bahía, and regretted that his continued illness prevented him from personally investigating the true state of affairs.[95] It was almost a year before the Rosario Indians were finally returned to their mission.

Indian hostilities and depredations at Refugio. Let it not be thought that the Rosario-Refugio tilt was the only incident which disturbed the peace and harmony of Mission Refugio. The enmity between the neophytes of the two missions went back to the very reëstablishment at Santa Gertrudis. Shortly before, a Coco named Chepillo, who was an apostate from Rosario living with the Guapites and the Copanos after killing a soldier, came to Refugio while the mission was still at its original location. He sent his squaw to talk to the *Padre* in his behalf, but became panicky and left without waiting for a reply. Two months later he returned, and Father Silva offered to forget the past if he would give up his evil ways and join the mission. He promised to reform, but three days later, in company with several other Rosario Indians, he killed the fattest cow of the Refugio herd and insolently brought the ill-gotten prize to the mission. When reprimanded by Father Silva, he flew into a rage and even threatened the *Padre*. Chepillo gave trouble to the mission and La Bahía for six years. He became the leader of a

---

[95] José Antonio de Jesús Garavito to Juan Bautista Elguezábal, March 25, 1798; Elguezábal to Manuel Muñoz, March 28, 1798; Muñoz to Elguezábal, April 3, 1798. *Béxar Archives.*

band of marauding Indians. After he had been at last captured in April, 1801, he attempted to escape while being led to the presidio at La Bahía, wounded a sergeant and a soldier, and almost succeeded in escaping before he was shot in the resultant scuffle.[96]

Chief Frazada Pinta, who it will be remembered did not join the mission, was a constant source of worry. He, accompanied by a band of braves, would visit the mission at irregular intervals. He was always on the point of joining and he always promised that upon his return from the present hunting trip he and his people would settle down. His visits were preceded or followed by the disappearance of the choice stock from the mission herd and the loss of numerous trifles. In time he became openly hostile. On July 18, 1797, a soldier from Refugio reported at La Bahía that the night before Chief Frazada Pinta and his party had attacked the mission herd, killed a servant, wounded another, and escaped. *Alférez* José Antonio Cadena was sent with four men to investigate the case. He reported that, judging from the tracks, the attacking party consisted of twelve or fourteen men, and that they had taken refuge on the neighboring coast islands. Almost a year later Captain José Miguel del Moral from La Bahía went to Refugio to investigate another attack by Frazada Pinta. Upon his arrival, on June 20, 1798, he found that fourteen Indians, Karankawas of Frazada Pinta's tribe, had executed a raid and fled immediately with their loot to their chief's inaccessible *ranchería*, known as Vergantín.

Another Karankawa chief from Rosario named Zertuche also committed numerous depredations on Refugio. Father Garavito wrote José Miguel del Moral at La Bahía that Zertuche was "the worst Indian living under the sun." He was absolutely faithless and treacherous. He had recently killed two cows in sight of the mission but denied it. Angered at the accusation of an act which was witnessed by everybody, he ran away and took with him the *Padre's* mare from the corral.[97]

The Comanches, while maintaining peace with the Spaniards after a fashion, did not respect in the least their enemies who, like themselves, were Spanish allies. For some time they had been making incursions into the area south of San Antonio pursuing their enemies as far as

---

[96]Manuel Silva to Manuel Muñoz, January 28, 1795; Governor Muñoz to Francisco Xavier Uranga, April 4, 1801. *Béxar Archives.*

[97]Captain of La Bahía to Muñoz, July 20, 1797; José Miguel del Moral to Muñoz, June 21, 1798; Garavito to José Miguel del Moral, October 27, 1798. *Béxar Archives.*

the coast. In October, 1797, a party of Comanches raided the cattle ranch of Mission Refugio and drove off two herds. Lieutenant Amangual from La Bahía was sent in pursuit, but they outdistanced him. Intimidated by these fierce fighters, many of the mission Indians in Refugio, as well as in Espíritu Santo and Rosario, began to take refuge in the inaccessible marshes, lakes, and islands along the neighboring coast whenever an attack or raid was rumored.[98]

Pedro Nava, the commandant general of the Interior Provinces, disapproved of the frequent abandonment of the missions by the Indians. He argued, and with much justification, that if the natives were allowed to leave to hunt for food, or protection, or pleasure, they could not be Christianized and trained in the habits and customs of civilized man. He urged the missionaries not to permit the neophytes to leave their missions on any pretext. At the same time he gave strict instructions to all officials in Texas to keep the missions supplied, and to furnish them with adequate protection in order that the natives congregated should have no excuse for leaving.[99]

Relations with the military to 1801. Except for an occasional complaint,[100] the first two years of Mission Refugio at its permanent location were remarkably free from friction with military officials. Trouble with the Indians during this same period was also slight. The commandant general consequently instructed Muñoz to reduce the mission guards from ten to five. Nava was a firm believer in discipline and he thought that soldiers detailed to mission duty and to the protection of presidial stock became lax in the observance of military duties. He desired the largest and most efficient number of soldiers to be available at a moment's notice in the presidios.[101]

Two years later Fray Garavito protested against the quartering of troops among the neophytes. He had been looking over the early instructions for the establishment of Refugio and decided that the soldiers should be stationed outside the mission stockade. They had of late become too familiar with the natives. Fray Garavito attributed their desire to live within the enclosure to laziness and to their pro-

---

[98]Governor Muñoz to Elguezábal, October 17, 1797; Garavito to José Miguel del Moral, October 13, 1798. *Béxar Archives.*

[99]Juan Bautista Elguezábal to Muñoz, January 17, 1798; Elguezábal to Garavito, February 1, 1798. *Béxar Archives.*

[100]Silva to Muñoz, June 22, 1796. *Béxar Archives.*

[101]Pedro Nava to Manuel Muñoz, June 7, 1797. *Béxar Archives.*

pensity for promiscuity. When Captain Del Moral at La Bahía received the protest, he replied that the soldiers were not lazy; that they had, in fact, built the stockade; that they had always conducted themselves with decency, and that from the earliest times of the foundation they had always been permitted to reside within the stockade.[102] He wrote an indignant dissent to Governor Muñoz and threatened to withdraw the guards altogether. But the governor advised moderation, Fray Garavito relented, and the rift ended.

The reduced number of troops at the mission, however, proved painfully inadequate during the closing years of the century. Comanche raids, fear of foreign agents among the natives along the coast, and the internal dissensions of the Cocos and Karankawas compelled the governor to increase the guard from five to fifteen men.[103]

The missionaries at Refugio. After Father Garza had left, and just before the mission was moved to Santa Gertrudis, Fray José Manuel Pedrajo was sent to assist Father Silva. He was present at the removal and he claimed to have set out from Zacatecas for Texas on November 15, 1794. But the climate proved too unhealthful for Father Pedrajo, forcing him to leave Refugio on June 23. Six days later he left San Antonio to return to his college.[104] He was replaced by Father Francisco Puelles, who was temporarily relieved of his duties at Mission Espíritu Santo. He served but a short time, only until the new missionary arrived.

Fray Antonio Mariano José Garavito was ordered to go to Refugio on December 29, 1794. He appears to have arrived in Texas just as the mission was being moved. Shortly afterwards, he assumed his duties and served until 1801, assisted at various times by other missionaries.[105] It is to be remembered that originally only one missionary was authorized, but as the result of the appeals of Father Silva, an assistant was granted for three years. The regulation went into effect at the time of the reëstablishment of Refugio in January, 1795. When in June, 1799, Father Cárdenas, president of the missions in San Antonio, requested payment of the salaries for the two missionaries at Refugio, Nava reminded the governor that the three-year period had expired and that

---

[102]Garavito to Del Moral, March 12, 1799; Del Moral to Muñoz, March 13, 1799. *Béxar Archives.*

[103]Governor to Uranga, April 28, 1801. *Béxar Archives.*

[104]Muñoz to Silva, February 20, 1795; José Manuel Pedrajo to Muñoz, June 28, 1795. *Béxar Archives.*

[105]Certification of Governor Muñoz, February 12, 1796. *Béxar Archives.*

only one missionary should now be assigned to Refugio. In spite of protests, however, two missionaries continued their labors at Refugio for some time.[106]

Refugio does its bit for king and country.   The troublous times that followed the establishment of the first French Republic in 1793, plunged Spain into war. It was not unusual for the king to call upon all loyal subjects to aid in the successful prosecution of a war by making liberal contributions. When such a call as this came in the fall of 1798 to the distant outpost of Spain in Texas, Mission Refugio responded enthusiastically. Father Garavito pledged one hundred cows which were accepted and sold at auction by Captain Del Moral at La Bahía. He obtained ten *pesos* a head for eighty-nine, and six *pesos* each for the remaining eleven, a total of nine hundred fifty-six *pesos* for the war fund, a sum more than three times the amount contributed by the garrison and scattered settlers of La Bahía. Both Nava and Muñoz acknowledged receipt of the liberal donation.[107]

---

[106]Nava to Muñoz, June 15, 1799. *Béxar Archives.*

[107]J. M. del Moral to Muñoz, January 23, and February 4, 1799; Nava to Muñoz, February 19; Del Moral to Muñoz, March 17, 1799. *Béxar Archives.*

CHAPTER IV

LAST ATTEMPTS AT MISSIONARY CONTROL OF INDIANS, 1783-1801

The control of the native tribes grew in importance as the eighteenth century was drawing to a close. The urgent need of winning their friendship and support in order to block effectively the westward march of the Anglo-American pioneer admitted of no delay. Faith in the old and tried frontier mission system had been seriously shaken by its retarded achievements but not altogether lost. The Refugio Mission undertaken so late in the period demonstrates the truth of this assertion. Officials, however, were growing desperate in the face of the unmistakable signs of the approaching storm. The Indian hordes which raided the weakened outposts were like the leaves of the forest swept by the whirl-wind. The cession of Louisiana to Spain had momentarily lulled the fears of Spanish authorities in Texas and transferred interest to the more eastern frontier. But the realization that Louisiana had, in fact, brought the danger of foreign aggression closer home and made it a reality, came as a rude awakening that caused the frantic governors to make strong pleas to the commandant general and the viceroy for the help which was granted too late. The policy of conciliation and appease-ment was given one last trial, and the king was almost fooled into supporting one more scheme for the conversion of all the natives of Texas before the missionary system was abandoned to a slow and lingering death. Hope for the salvation of Texas and of the whole of New Spain was to be transferred to colonization and military prowess.

When the new commandant general, Felipe Neve, took charge of the Internal Provinces, Sonora, Nueva Vizcaya, Coahuila, and Texas, he wrote the stern *Visitador,* José de Gálvez, that the military force posted in Texas was woefully inadequate to protect the miserable settlers of this wretched province even against the Indians, let alone against foreign attack. There were fifty-six men at San Antonio de Béjar and ninety-six at La Bahía, with an irregular force of thirty men at Nacogdoches. Fortunately the numerous and warlike nations of the north were in general friendly. But the depraved and thieving Apaches were a drain on the slender resources of the settlers and the missions. These Indians, like leeches, were sucking the lifeblood of the province. Kindness and fairness were lost on such perfidious savages. A war of extermination was the only solution. It would teach the survivors and the other natives to respect the Spaniards.[1]

Before a war could be undertaken, more troops would have to be sent to Texas from the other provinces; coöperation between the commanders in New Mexico, Coahuila, Santander, and Texas assured; and the friendship and support of the nations of the north secured. He deplored the existing conditions in the organization of the military forces and the lack of care and of equipment in the entire commandancy under his jurisdiction. There was only one royal hospital located in Durango to attend to the needs of the Interior Provinces. Both the officers and the soldiers lacked proper medical attention for the treatment of wounds and the numerous ailments which a life of exposure on the frontier entailed. The establishment of many more hospitals, distributed among the provinces would prevent the spread of epidemics, save considerable expense in the treatment of disabled veterans, who were practically invalids, save many lives by the proper care of the wounded, and prove of inestimable value in the control of smallpox and other infectious diseases among the Indians.[2]

The attempted suppression of the Province of Texas. But neither Neve's appeal nor the continued complaints of the authorities in Texas seem to have aroused officials in Spain to a realization of the menace that threatened Spanish interests in Texas. Convinced that this remote outpost was now an interior province, the king decided that there was little need or justification for the maintenance of a governor in San Antonio. The astonishment of the commandant of the Interior Provinces of the East may be imagined at the receipt of a royal order dated June 19, 1788, transmitted by Viceroy Flores, suppressing the office of governor of Texas and instructing Juan Ugalde to entrust the administration to the captain of the Presidio de San Antonio. Viceroy Flores recommended, however, that Captain Rafael Martínez Pacheco continue as governor *ad interim* until new orders were received, showing that even the viceroy could not believe this radical change was intended to be permanent.[3]

Ugalde lost no time in interceding with the viceroy for the repeal of

---

[1]El Comdt. Gral. Don Felipe Neve hace relación concisa y exacta del estado en que ha encontrado las Prov. Int. y la divide en los 4 ramos, Justicia, Policia, Hacienda, y Guerra. *A. G. I., Audiencia de Guadalajara,* 1783. 103-4-10, pp. 1-60.

[2]*Ibid.,* pp. 1-60.

[3]Viceroy Flores to Juan Ugalde, September 30, 1788. *A. G. M., Historia,* Vol. 93, p. 2.

the order. He emphatically stated that the importance of Texas had never been fully realized. The unfavorable reports of officials, who did not understand the significance of this frontier outpost of Spanish power in America, had given the king and his advisors an erroneous impression, gathered from the insignificant gains made in population, the absence of revenues, and the retarded progress of the missions. It was true that in the vast province there were only three settlements and six missions still in operation, with a total of two thousand five hundred twenty-two persons in all. Many poor *Alcaldías* had a much larger population. But Texas had rich and fertile fields and large rivers capable of great development, and countless Indian nations who were potential enemies and whose friendship had to be courted and maintained. The vigilance and care of a zealous governor was indispensable to the preservation of the province. The suppression of this office might result in the loss of the province, an irreparable misfortune.

The mistaken policy adopted after the visit of Rubí had resulted in the abandonment of Los Adaes, the mission of the Arkokisas on the Gulf coast, and of Nacogdoches, Ugalde pointed out. Fortunately this last outpost, located more than one hundred fifty miles from San Antonio, had been reoccupied and was precariously held by a group of determined settlers. But the abandonment of La Bahía and Nacogdoches itself was again being advocated and there was added now the suppression of the governorship, the reduction of the occupied area to San Antonio and its placement under the protection of a presidial company and one captain. Carrying out these recommendations would be equivalent to the abandonment of the entire province. Instead of this short-sighted policy, La Bahía and Nacogdoches should be reënforced, the mission for the Arkokisas reëstablished, San Antonio fortified, and the settlement of the entire province encouraged.

With surprising foresight, Ugalde declared that the military importance of the Provinces of Sonora, Nueva Vizcaya, Coahuila, Nuevo León, and Santander was insignificant as compared to that of Texas. Here were more Indian nations than in the other four. Texas was more exposed to foreign aggression and its natives were more amenable to the influence of foreign agents. The cultivation of peace with the Comanches, the Taovayas, and all the other northern tribes was more important now than ever. For this, if for no other reason, the governorship should not be suppressed. There were four governors in the commandancy-general of the East. If any was to be suppressed, it should be the least important,

MILITARY PLAZA, SHOWING HITCHING POSTS IN REAR OF OLD SAN FERNANDO

Courtesy of Fred C. Chabot.   (*With the Makers of San Antonio*, p. 110)

Coahuila. Nuevo León might also be suppressed, if necessary, but never those of Santander and Texas, the coast line of which extended from the Sabine River to Tampico. He sent to the viceroy a map of the coast line and sketches of the course of several of the more important rivers.[4]

The commandant general concluded by urging that the office of governor of Texas be not suppressed, that measures be taken immediately for rebuilding the fortifications and constructing an irrigation system to encourage settlement at La Bahía; and that similar improvements be undertaken at Nacogdoches. In order to improve conditions at the last named post and stimulate settlement, he recommended the removal of its commander, Antonio Gil Ibarbo, whom he suspected of permitting French and English traders to enter the province. But the most important consideration, he asserted, was the control of the numerous and warlike nations of the north, who would be emboldened beyond measure should the province be abandoned and its governor removed. "If the Indians held in check in Texas are permitted to reach the frontiers of Coahuila and Nuevo Santander [unhindered]," he declared, "they will sweep across the Río Grande of the North and, swollen with the insolence of victory, they will carry the war to the very heart of the kingdom of New Spain. These things and much more will the Indians of the north dare, should they succeed in driving the Spaniards from the Province of Texas."[5]

The commander of the Interior Provinces of the East enjoyed the well-earned reputation of being one of the most loyal servants of the king and one of the most determined Indian fighters on the northeastern frontier. His vigorous and earnest representation convinced the viceroy of the necessity of maintaining the office of governor in Texas and of the advisability of strengthening the Spanish outposts in the province. Thus was a measure tantamount to the complete abandonment of Texas averted and the realization of the importance of the Indian problem brought strongly to the attention of the viceroy.[6]

Changes in Indian policy and conditions in Texas. Ugalde was engaged in a campaign against the Apaches at the very time he wrote to the viceroy. Shortly thereafter he penetrated into the area of present

---

[4]These maps would prove of considerable interest if found. They probably are in the vast archives of Mexico City.

[5]Juan Ugalde to Manuel Antonio Flores, October 30, 1788. *A. G. M., Historia*, Vol. 93, pp. 3-11.

[6]Manuel Antonio Flores to Juan Ugalde, February 3, 1789. *A. G. M., Historia*, Vol. 93, pp. 12-13.

Uvalde County (named thus in his honor but incorrectly spelled) and inflicted serious defeats upon the perfidious enemy. The Spaniards had decided to make the Lipan-Apaches have a wholesome respect for Spanish authority, to court the friendship of the Indians of the north, and to reorganize the mission system. The king called for detailed information on the general conditions that prevailed in the Interior Provinces, and the reports of Ugalde and other officials were sent. The Count of Sierra Gorda recounted the occurrences in Nuevo Santander, whose settlements along the Río Grande from Laredo to the mouth of the river have come to form part of present Texas. He explained that, as a matter of fact, Laredo was east of the river. The Lipan-Apaches were a constant menace to this outpost, and were now in the habit of extending their raids to Revilla, Mier, Camargo, and Reynosa. Early in February, 1792, Chief Zapato Zas had led a party of Apaches as far as Reynosa where they had killed a mission Indian and wounded another, and succeeded in driving away a considerable number of cattle. Detachments from Camargo and Revilla set out in pursuit under Captain Bustamante, crossed the river into Texas, and overtook the marauders at Palo Blanco, killed Chief Zapato Zas and fifteen of his followers, and recovered a part of the loot. The Count of Sierra Gorda at about the same time had himself followed the tracks of another raiding party that led him to the mouth of the Nueces River, but he had not been so fortunate as Bustamante in overtaking the raiders. He remarked that in addition to the raids, the entire province of Nuevo Santander had recently suffered an epidemic of smallpox, during which almost two thousand persons had died.[7]

But it is in the summary report of Viceroy Branciforte that a picture of the missionary situation throughout New Spain in 1795 is to be found. We take from it the data pertaining to all the missions in operation at that time within the present jurisdiction of Texas. At the southernmost point was Reynosa. Here there was a mission, which, although located on the Mexican side of the river, ministered to the Indians in what is today Texas in a *Visita* established for this purpose. One missionary looked after the Indians without charge to the royal treasury.

Twelve leagues above Reynosa was Camargo where a similar mission and a Texas *Visita* were being administered by another missionary from the College of Zacatecas without expense to the king.

Laredo had no mission but a regularly established parish with a priest,

[7]Conde de Sierra Gorda to the King, December 30, 1792. *A. G. I., Audiencia de México*, 98-6-23 (Dunn Transcripts, 1792-1799, pp. 50-58).

who looked after the spiritual needs of the settlers and those Indians who came to the settlement. A few miles south of Laredo was the Hacienda de Dolores where a *Visita* was maintained.

Although the missions had been secularized, four Franciscan missionaries were still taking care of the uninstructed Indians of Concepción, Capistrano, San José, and San Francisco in San Antonio. These *Padres* were each paid four hundred fifty *pesos* annually by the royal treasurer.

In the vicinity of La Bahía, dependent upon its garrison for protection, there were three missions: Espíritu Santo, Rosario, and Refugio, where four *Padres* from Zacatecas resided and received the usual stipend from the king's bounty.

Nacogdoches had two *Padres,* one to look after the settlers and one to care for the Indians.

The president of the Texas missions resided in San Antonio and was paid annually by the royal treasurer the same salary received by the missionaries. The viceroy remarked that the maintenance of missionary activities in San Antonio, Nacogdoches, and La Bahía cost the king forty-five hundred *pesos,* and that there were five hundred seventy-three mission Indians, on whose farms sugar cane, corn, beans, cotton, and other products were raised.

In El Paso, Isleta alone seems to have been still operated by a missionary who received only three hundred thirty *pesos*. At La Junta (modern Presidio) there were still two missions: San Antonio de Julimes and Santa Cruz de Tapacolines, each with a missionary who was paid two hundred fifty *pesos*.[8]

Mission administration after secularization. After the execution of the viceregal order of April 10, 1794, the bulk of the property of the missions in San Antonio was distributed among the neophytes.[9] But it will be remembered that in several of the missions there were groups of Indians who had recently been taken in, and had not yet reached that stage of development which would enable them to look after their own interests. It was to care for these persons that four missionaries were permitted to continue their labors in San Antonio. But the former inmates who had received their share of the communal property and wealth were no longer to enjoy the free administration of the sacraments

---

[8]Marqués de Branciforte to Eugenio Llaguero, January 15, 1795. *A. G. I., Audiencia de México,* 88-1-15 (Dunn Transcripts, 1792-1799, pp. 107-128).

[9]For details see Chapter II of this volume.

and the other services of the *Padres*. Commandant General Pedro Nava reminded the governor that the secularized neophytes were to contribute individually hereafter for such services. They were to understand that they were no longer charges of the king. They were now independent members of the new parishes created by secularization. The same was true with regard to the maintenance and repair of the church and other buildings in each of the new parishes. All these expenses were to be paid hereafter out of profits derived from the products raised on the communal lands set aside for that purpose. The religious were excused from the administration of all temporalities in order that they might dedicate themselves entirely to the spiritual and moral welfare of the natives still under instruction.[10]

The missionaries, relieved from the temporal responsibility, continued to instruct the remaining neophytes not only in religion but also in their civil duties in order to fit them to become citizens and to exercise the right of suffrage. For example, on January 1, 1796, Father José Cárdenas, president of the missions, informed the governor that the annual election of officers for the Indian pueblo of Mission San José and Mission Concepción had been held under the supervision of their respective missionaries. Each mission had its native governor and *alcalde,* who had charge of the affairs of the mission Indians. At this time, José Antonio Bustillos was elected governor and José Núñez, *alcalde* of San José; and Felix del Castillo and Lorenzo Villegas, governor and *alcalde* respectively of Mission Concepción. It was the duty and privilege of Governor Muñoz to install the new officers and invest them with the insignia of their office. Two years later, the election held at San José placed the responsibility of the respective offices on Fermín Ramírez and Francisco Xavier.[11]

Indian hostilities. The efforts of Ugalde and others to annihilate or reduce to submission the Lipan-Apaches and to win the support of the Comanches and the Indians of the north were not entirely successful and the hostilities of both groups harassed not only the settlements in Texas but also those in Coahuila and the whole Río Grande area as well. Early in 1795, a band of six Comanches slipped into the vicinity of San Juan Bautista and drove off a herd of cattle from the missions. A group of

---

[10]Pedro Nava to Manuel Muñoz, July 18, 1795; also his letter of May 24, 1797. *Béxar Archives.*

[11]José Mariano Cárdenas to Manuel Muñoz, January 1, 1796, and January 1, 1798. *Béxar Archives.*

Lipans set out after them, followed the marauders to the San Sabá Canyon, surprised them, and restored the stolen cattle to their mission.[12]

On April 13, 1795, a train of supplies, escorted by a corporal and three soldiers, started from La Bahía for Nacogdoches. The guards were given instructions to accompany the train which was to follow the lower road as far as the crossing on the Colorado. As the train proceeded unsuspectingly along the well-known route, they were suddenly attacked at La Navidad crossing by a group of about forty Tonkawas who took almost everything from the astonished Spaniards, leaving them only their mounts. The stranded party sent an urgent request for relief to La Bahía. The commander sent four men, all he could spare, and informed Governor Muñoz that he had just learned from other Indians that the entire Tonkawa nation was encamped at this time a short distance above the Colorado River crossing and that a French trader was with them. He feared that a second attack might be made on the train waiting at La Navidad to wipe out all evidence, and urgently requested reënforcements from San Antonio. In the train were a number of La Bahía settlers who had taken advantage of the opportunity to go to Nacogdoches to visit friends and to trade.[13] The four men sent to La Navidad crossing had been instructed to join the others from San Antonio and to go as far as the Trinity.[14]

The warning sent by Lieutenant Bernardo Fernández of Nacogdoches in August of the same year was more alarming. He had recently learned from a licensed trader, accredited to the country of the Tawakoni, that the Comanches were planning a meeting of their braves on the San Andrés River to undertake an extensive raid on San Antonio and La Bahía itself, ostensibly while on a campaign against the Lipan-Apaches. When Cortés was questioned by Governor Muñoz, he replied that he did not believe the Comanches would penetrate that far down the coast and that precautions should be restricted to the San Antonio area.[15]

The Comanches had made peace with the Spaniards and were friendly in a passive way. But they insisted that their peace did not extend to those Indians who, though friends of the Spaniards, were the traditional enemies of their nation. Consequently, when they visited Spanish settle-

---

[12]Pedro Nava to Manuel Muñoz, January 27, 1795. *Béxar Archives.*

[13]Juan Cortés to Manuel Muñoz, April 22, 1795. *Béxar Archives.*

[14]Juan Cortés to Muñoz, April 24, 1795. *Béxar Archives.*

[15]Muñoz to Cortés, August 10, 1795; Cortés to Muñoz, August 8, 1795. *Béxar Archives.*

ments and found Lipan-Apaches living in the missions, they invariably committed outrages that involved the property of friend and foe alike. Chief Chamanquequera visited Laredo in May, 1795, and after paying his respects to the commander, he and his followers drove off thirty head of cattle. The governor of Coahuila protested to the commander general who wrote Governor Muñoz to call a meeting of the Comanche chiefs in San Antonio and explain to them that they had to respect Spanish and mission property. He was to warn them that such actions were a violation of their pledges.[16]

Conditions, however, did not improve. The Comanches and other northern tribes, who now visited San Antonio frequently as friends, picked up and carried off all the property they could lay their hands on, not excepting the horses and cattle of the inhabitants of the old settlement. The prominent citizens formally protested on September 22, 1796, declaring that the continued thefts committed by the new friends of the Spaniards were becoming unbearable. Neither cattle nor horses were safe in the vicinity of San Antonio. The vigilance exercised against enemies had been relaxed, but the new friends were not responding to the trust placed in them. The abuses committed almost invariably by departing groups had infuriated the peaceful settlers and they expressed their determination to put a stop to them. They recommended that the Comanches and all northern tribes be told that in the future single members or small and irresponsible groups who came unaccompanied by a chief would not be permitted to visit in the city. Furthermore, the Indians were to be told that those who strayed from larger parties for the purpose of committing depredations wantonly would be treated as enemies by the settlers.[17] The governor deplored the losses sustained by the citizens as a result of the new policy of appeasement, recommended patience and moderation, and assured them that he would, by all the means in his power, impress upon the chiefs of the new friends from the north the need of putting an end to such reprehensible practices by irresponsible members of their tribes.

A little earlier, in the summer of 1796, the commandant general had become apprehensive. Rumors, not unconfirmed, had reached him that the Lipan-Apaches, who had recently been forced to make a solemn peace

---

[16]Pedro Nava to Manuel Muñoz, June 4, 1795. *Béxar Archives.*

[17]Representación de Salvador Rodríguez, Vicente Amador, Luis Menchaca, Joaquín Leal, José Antonio Saucedo, José Hernández, Feliz Ruiz, and Manuel Derbón. September 22, 1796; reply of Governor Muñoz, same date. *Béxar Archives.*

to save themselves from complete annihilation, were about to conclude an alliance with the Mescaleros. This tribe belonged to the same stock, spoke a similar language, and dressed in the same manner, but its members were inflicting severe damage on the frontier outposts of New Mexico and Nueva Vizcaya. Nava suggested that the Lipans in Texas be kept under the closest surveillance, as their relations with the Mescaleros were a violation of their plighted word. Because of the similarity in language and dress, they were not to be allowed to enter the presidios unless they first proved their identity.[18]

The Indian situation was further complicated by the appearance of new tribes upon the northeastern Texas frontier, such as the Iowas and the Choctaws, who were being relentlessly driven westward by the advance of the Anglo-American pioneer in his march to the Mississippi and beyond. Members of the old Assinai Confederacy, who had befriended in their way the Spaniards ever since their expedition in search of La Salle in 1689, resented and feared the newcomers. A group of Cadodachos (Caddo stock) headed by their chief, now old and blind, and several members of the greatly reduced tribe of Nacogdochitos came to plead for their people. News had come through José del Moral of the new settlement of Opelousas, that a group of two hundred fifty Choctaws were making ready to attack the Cadodachos and to occupy their lands.[19] The Choctaws, the Iowas, and the Huasas (pronounced Wasas) were beginning to push out the weakened tribes of northeastern Texas and the Spaniards were helpless to stop by force the onward march of these natives, who were in turn being driven from their happy hunting grounds by the advance of the ruthless Anglo-American pioneer.

Attacks upon Coahuila by Texas Comanches. One of the first acts of Lieutenant-colonel Antonio Cordero, distinguished official of the Interior Provinces, when he took charge of the government of Coahuila after the death of Governor Juan Gutiérrez, was to report the theft of three hundred head of cattle from Mission San Bernardo, near San Juan Bautista, by a band of Comanches on February 21 and 24, 1797. A detachment of soldiers and mission Indians were sent in pursuit, the raiders were fortunately overtaken in the vicinity of the old mission of San Sabá, and a large part of the cattle recovered. The San Sabá Canyon had become, it seems, a favorite rendezvous for marauding bands

---

[18]Pedro Nava to Manuel Muñoz, July 16, 1796. *Béxar Archives.*

[19]José María Guadiana to Manuel Muñoz, Nacogdoches, October 23, 1796. *Béxar Archives.*

of Comanches. Not satisfied, Cordero had sent Lieutenant Antonio Toledo to protest formally to the Comanche chiefs living in San Sabá Canyon against the repetition of these outrages by irresponsible young warriors. It had already become a common practice for the Comanche chiefs to excuse these depredations by explaining that they were the unauthorized actions of independent and irrepressive young warriors who grew restless under prolonged peace. Pedro Nava wrote Governor Muñoz, therefore, suggesting that he impress upon all Comanche chiefs who visited in San Antonio that the Spaniards would henceforth hold them responsible for the action of their young warriors and that unless they were restrained effectively, the Spaniards would have to retaliate by discontinuing the distribution of gifts.[20]

These instructions were emphatically repeated by the commandant general in May, 1798, and made known not only to the Comanches but also to all the northern tribes. The occasion for this repetition in much more stringent terms was a second report of Governor Cordero of Coahuila in which he informed Nava that the depredations by desultory bands of Comanches all along the Río Grande from San Juan Bautista to Laredo had continued in spite of protests. He had, consequently commissioned Captain José Menchaca, of the Presidio de Agua Verde, to go to San Antonio with one hundred twenty-one men to demand restoration of stolen property from such Comanche chiefs as were there and to proceed to the *rancherías* of the Comanche chiefs, as well as to those of all northern tribes, to make a similar request for the return of stolen horses and cattle.[21]

Spanish officials, fully aware of the inadequate force at their disposal to command obedience or respect from the numerous Indian nations, whose actual strength was unknown, were obliged to be cautious. This wariness, excessive at times, perhaps, was misunderstood by the insolent and simple-minded natives, whose primitive processes confused it, as many others have, with cowardice or lack of spirit. But the fact is that the officials realized clearly that they, like an animal trainer in a cage of roaring lions, were unable either to abandon their precarious position, or permanently appease the hunger of their wards for gifts, or command the means to reduce them to impotency. This explains the half-hearted approval of the aggressive policy adopted by Governor Cordero in Coahuila. Nava approved his actions in principle but pointed out that

---

[20] Pedro Nava to Manuel Muñoz, April 4, 1797. *Béxar Archives*.
[21] Pedro Nava to Manuel Muñoz, May 24, 1798. *Béxar Archives*.

the sending of Menchaca with one hundred twenty men into the country of the Comanches and the Indians of the north to make a concrete demand for restitution of stolen property was extremely dangerous. What if Captain Menchaca found stolen horses and cattle in a *ranchería* and the chief refused to restore them? If his authority was defied, what then? Was it prudent to force the issue when no more than one hundred twenty men could be sent against the natives?

He then expressed his conviction that the number of raiders responsible for recent depredations was small, and that the extent of the loss suffered and the damages inflicted could have been reduced by greater vigilance and more caution on the part of the commander, the soldiers, and the citizens. The Spaniards themselves were in a large part responsible for the losses suffered. Was it fair for them to complain so loudly and to implore the coöperation of the chiefs in recovering what they had lost largely through their own carelessness? For the Spaniards, moreover, while nominally at peace, to penetrate Indian territory with an armed force, Nava observed, might justly be interpreted by the natives as a hostile act or as an indication of a suspicious move being contemplated against them. In short, the governor of Coahuila had been hasty in his action and Nava hoped only that no evil effects might follow.[22]

Governor Muñoz, of Texas, a more mature and experienced officer in the ways of the northern frontier, shared the fears of the commandant general. He was much relieved when he learned in July that Captain Menchaca had avoided what might have become an embarrassing situation by retiring from San Sabá to Agua Verde without pushing the issue with the Comanche chiefs. He wrote Nava that the action was most prudent.[23]

Trade relations with the Indians, 1795-1800. While trying to restrain the irresponsible bands of Comanches and treacherous Lipan-Apaches in the south and west, officials attempted to develop closer trade relations with the nations of the north along the northeastern frontier, and to guard jealously against the penetration of obnoxious foreign agents among them either along the coast or from the settlements above Natchitoches. In the spring of 1795, the old chief of the Tawakoni, named Quiscat, accompanied by a group of Kichai and Wichitas, visited Nacogdoches to request that an accredited Spanish trading agent be

---

[22]Pedro Nava to Antonio Cordero, May 29, 1798.
[23]Pedro Nava to Manuel Muñoz, July 10, and July 24, 1798. *Béxar Archives.*

sent their people. Lieutenant Bernardo Fernández promptly transmitted the petition to Muñoz, who appointed Juan José Bueno and Francisco Villalpando to supply the trading needs of these friendly nations. It was high time. Chief Quiscat had explained that two French agents and several Spaniards without the proper papers had been selling prohibited goods. He promised to catch them if they came again and to send them to Nacogdoches for examination.[24]

The unauthorized traders from Louisiana and some adventurous English and American pioneers found traffic in arms and ammunition a very profitable business and extended their activities from the upper Red and Mississippi rivers to the Gulf coast. Fernández, of Nacogdoches, complained that the Arkokisas, the Cocos, and even the Karankawas now had an unusually large number of arms and great quantities of ammunition, and he warned that these were being sold to them by traders from the new posts of Rapide and Opelousas. Governor Muñoz recommended that Fernández report these violations to the governor of Louisiana and invite the coöperation of the commander at Natchitoches in checking the illicit trade. He regretted that at this time (1796) he was very much occupied with the problem created in the west by the alliance of the Mescaleros and the Apaches and deplored his inability to give more effective aid to the distant post of Nacogdoches. He expressed deep concern, however, at the increasing difficulty of subduing the coastal tribes which were receiving a steady supply of arms and ammunition. Friendship between them and the northern tribes should be discouraged.[25]

The Spaniards found out the source of supply early in 1797. Traders who returned to Nacogdoches from the Tawakoni, the Tonkawa, and the Kichai reported that these Indians obtained their arms and ammunition from the Huasas to whom they gave their horses and cattle in exchange. The Huasas, in turn, took the horses and cattle to trade with the Anglo-Americans for the prohibited arms, powder, and lead. This was more serious than a mere violation of the trade monopoly of Spain. Governor Muñoz was much worried. He advised that more vigilance be exercised and the details of this dangerous but lucrative trade be ascertained. In the meantime the northern Indians of Texas were to be treated with great kindness and tact in order not to antagonize them.[26]

---

[24]Nava to Muñoz, July 8, 1795. *Béxar Archives.*

[25]Manuel Muñoz, to Bernardo Fernández, September 25, 1796. *Béxar Archives.*

[26]Manuel Muñoz to José María Guadiana, April 25, 1797. *Béxar Archives.*

Needless and futile were these suggestions of the governor. José María Guadiana, the commander at Nacogdoches, could no more increase the vigilance with the force at his command than the average indigent tubercular patient can afford eggs, meat, milk, sunshine, and rest.

When Guadiana attempted to carry out the governor's instructions, he found an even more alarming condition existed among the coastal tribes. Having heard that strangers frequented the Arkokisas, he sent Bernabé del Río, an experienced soldier, with two others to visit and reconnoiter the coastal area from the mouth of the Trinity to the Neches and the Sabine. Three men were all he could spare. They learned from the Arkokisas that a French trader had established his quarters just beyond the Sabine, but Del Río was unable to proceed as far as this river. The party observed that there were Cocos and Karankawas living among the Arkokisas, many of whom were apostates from Refugio and Rosario Missions. They were, moreover, agents of the renegade chief, Frazada Pinta, who had come to invite the Arkokisas to join him in an attack on Refugio. They held out to their prospective allies the ease with which the herds of the new mission could be driven off. The three soldiers learned that Indians from different tribes were gathering near the crossing on the Colorado and also in an area between the Brazos and the San Jacinto for the attack. Chief Frazada Pinta was sick, but other chiefs would lead the hordes if he should die.[27] The implication of the effect of the abundant supply of arms and ammunition and of the contact with foreign traders is plainly revealed in the development of such a situation as this.

But it was not until a year later that some of the fears of the commandant general were realized. On August 14, 1799, there arrived in the country of the Tejas, near Nacogdoches, nine settlers from the Arkansas, subjects of Louisiana, accompanied by twenty Indians from the north. They brought considerable merchandise for trade without a permit of any kind. At about the same time, ten Louisianians, mostly English traders, accompanied by Cherokees, Chickasaws, and Arkansas penetrated to the villages of the Taovayas and the Comanches on Red River with a large supply of guns, powder, and lead to be offered in exchange for horses. Lieutenant Del Moral set out from Nacogdoches with twenty-two men to order the intruders out. When he arrived in the country of the Taovayas, great was his surprise to find that these Indians and the Comanches supported the intruders, warned him not to

---

[27] José María Guadiana to Manuel Muñoz, October 23, 1798. *Béxar Archives.*

molest them, and prepared to resist any attempt to arrest them. Del Moral was powerless to enforce his demand or to carry out his purpose. He had to return to Nacogdoches and make a lame excuse for his futile trip.

When Nava heard of the incident, he reprimanded the zealous commander for his hasty action. The attempt to drive the traders out with such a small force was a serious mistake. It would have been wiser to have allowed the traders to withdraw peaceably and then to warn the Indians against such trade, threatening to discontinue the annual gifts and to suspend all relations with them. The forced retirement of Del Moral had only served to reveal to friends and foes alike the inability to enforce the law. Such an exhibition of weakness, Nava feared, would result in the loss of the little respect the Indian allies had for the Spaniards.

Repetition of the incident was to be avoided by a stricter enforcement of the law prohibiting the entrance of foreigners. This end might be more effectively attained through the coöperation of the commander at Natchitoches and the governor of Louisiana himself, through whose province they had to pass first. The soldiers at Nacogdoches were advised to make more frequent visits to the country of the friendly northern nations to cultivate their friendship. Their support of the intruders was attributed by Nava to dissatisfaction with the Spaniards. Such dissatisfaction, he went on to elucidate, was perhaps traceable to indiscretion and lack of tact which had been turned to good account by the foreign traders in order to set the natives against the Spaniards. Lastly, trading horses for ammunition and guns should be stopped by all means.[28]

The problem presented by the obnoxious trade in arms was carefully considered and analyzed in an effort to find a solution. The Comanches who came to San Antonio were adroitly questioned. It was learned that Chief El Tuerto and others were the principal participants in the arms and munition trade with the Taovayas who were supplied by foreigners. The occasion for the penetration was not primarily a desire to trade in arms alone, but to supply the Indians of the north with many articles they had formerly obtained from the Spaniards whose European markets had been closed by the war. The inability of Spanish trading agents to meet the demand had made the natives grow cold and to turn to the

---

[28]Pedro Nava to Manuel Muñoz, September 18, 1799. *Béxar Archives.*

foreign intruders to satisfy their needs. This was the frank opinion of Spanish officials.[29]

In order to regain or retain their friendship, Nava recommended the distribution of annual gifts with greater regularity. He even raised the question as to whether the dispersion would be more acceptable to the northern Indians at Nacogdoches than at San Antonio. It would save them a long trip, he suggested. But he did not realize that the wily Indians preferred to have an excuse to travel inland in order to steal from the Spanish settlers and the missions, for they knew that the officials would only remonstrate and take no action.[30]

The Taovayas and the Tawakoni responded to the advances made by the Spaniards to win their favor and support. Four of their chiefs, accompanied by twenty warriors, visited Nacogdoches and solemnly assured the commander they would not trade any longer either with French or English agents. Should any enter their country, they would capture and bring them with their goods to Nacogdoches.[31] As a matter of fact, on October 2, 1799, the Tawakoni Indians did capture a certain Pedro Engle and two companions, who were taken to Del Moral.[32]

The firm but friendly policy adopted by Spanish officials brought protestations of loyalty and a desire of friendship from the erring Comanches, but even as they made the promises they violated their word. Early in December, 1799, a party of seventy-eight Comanches, led by three well-known chiefs, El Tuerto, Zoquiné, and Blancón visited the governor in San Antonio and assured him their people wanted to be friends and would not do anything to displease the Spaniards any more.[33] It is to be remembered that El Tuerto and Zoquiné were known to be instrumental in the exchange of horses for guns and ammunition carried on by illicit traders.

The elation over their promises still warmed the heart of Elguezábal, acting governor, when he heard a few days later that this same party had left from San Antonio for Laredo, where they had stolen forty-nine horses. Commandant General Nava wrote him in no uncertain terms that these Indians must be made to understand that they had to keep

---

[29]Pedro Nava to Manuel Muñoz, October 1, 1799. *Béxar Archives.*

[30]*Ibid.*

[31]José Miguel del Moral to Governor Elguezábal, October 28, 1799. *Béxar Archives.*

[32]Pedro Nava to Elguezábal, October 29, and December 24, 1799. *Béxar Archives.*

[33]Pedro Nava to Elguezábal, Governor *ad interim,* December 25, 1799. *Béxar Archives.*

their word. If they persisted in committing abuses, all gifts to their people were to be suspended, and they were to be treated as enemies.[34]

In the spring of 1800, a large group of Comanches, two hundred and eighty warriors, all bedecked in war paint, arrived in San Antonio. The fears of the settlers were allayed by the assurance that they were not going to molest Spaniards. They explained that they were engaged in a campaign against the Lipans. Chief Soxas, well-known Comanche leader in northeast Texas, informed the governor that his people preferred to come to San Antonio for their gifts rather than wait for them at Nacogdoches.[35]

The policy of appeasement and its cost. Unable to reduce the various tribes in Texas by force, the Spaniards were obliged to adopt a policy of appeasement. There was only one way in which to keep the natives from stealing and raiding the settlements: giving them in a reasonable amount the goods they coveted. There was no other choice. But such a policy is always fatal. The recipient of favors, convinced of the impotency of the donor to refuse, becomes emboldened and constantly increases his demands; mutual respect is lost; insolence replaces gratitude; and the result is deeply rooted hatred rather than friendship between the parties.

An idea of the goods desired by the natives and the amount generally consumed, may be obtained in part from a list prepared by Bernardino Fernández, Indian agent of Nacogdoches. On January 16, 1795, he received in San Antonio for distribution among the northern tribes: three bolts of blue and red cloth, eighteen blankets (six fine and twelve common), four uniforms (two red and two blue) trimmed with braid for Indian chiefs, one hundred forty-seven *varas* of ribbon of various colors, eight pounds of vermilion, eight bundles of tobacco (about fifty pounds each), six dozen knives, one thousand needles, one hundred eight pairs of scissors, twelve hoes, one hundred awls, twelve large axes, twelve hatchets, twenty-four small bells, fifty-four mirrors, forty-two dozen jingles, four bundles of beads (all colors), seven pounds steel wire, one pound gold wire, one hundred combs, twelve rifles, seventy-five pounds powder, one hundred fifty pounds of lead bullets, one hundred flints for gunlocks, one hundred gun rods, and seven bundles of burlap sacks. It is to be noted that flints for guns, powder, and lead were included. The

---

[34]*Ibid.*

[35]Pedro Nava to Governor Elguezábal, April 14, 1800. *Béxar Archives.*

trade in these articles had been strictly prohibited in the past, but the Spaniards had come to realize that if they did not supply the natives with these things, foreigners would. Furthermore, the Indians became dissatisfied with the Spanish agents for not bringing them these supplies.[36] José Gil Morín, agent for the Tawakonis, received from the governor of San Antonio for Chief Quiscat four pounds of powder, eight pounds of lead, eight bundles of tobacco, one and one-half *varas* of blue woolen cloth, two mirrors, and four pounds of red paint.[37]

An idea of the number of Indians who came to San Antonio in 1795 to receive gifts may be obtained from a report for the months of May, June, July, and August. During these four months one thousand two hundred sixty-one Indians of the Comanche, the Tonkawa, the Tawakoni, the Taovaya, and the Wichita nations came.[38] More detailed and complete are the statistics kept for the year 1796. From January 1 to April 30, there came to San Antonio eight hundred forty-three Comanches, Tonkawas, Tawakonis, and Lipans. They were all received as friends and entertained at the expense of the governor. The cost of entertainment and the gifts distributed was six hundred one *pesos*. From May 1 to August 31, the number of visitors was eleven hundred fifty-nine and included Comanches, Tawakonis, and Lipans. The cost of entertainment was six hundred twenty *pesos*. From September 1 to December 31, six hundred thirty-nine Indians, Comanches, Lipans, Tonkawas, Tejas, and Wichitas, were provided with gifts. The number was much smaller than in the previous three months, but the cost was almost twice as much, having amounted to eleven hundred eighty-eight *pesos*. In summarizing the cost of entertainment of Indian allies in San Antonio, we find that twenty-six hundred forty-one Indians visited the governor, that they represented six different nations, and that it cost twenty-six hundred nine *pesos*.[39]

The number varied slightly, but the nations represented by the visitors increased. By 1797 we find Huasas, Aguagues (Iowas), and Wichitas frequenting San Antonio with other northern tribes to receive gifts. The cost of entertainment and gifts, according to the figures for the years 1795 to 1800, averaged about one *peso* per person. On March 12, 1800,

---

[36]List of goods received by Bernardino Fernández, Indian agent of Nacogdoches, January 16, 1795. *Béxar Archives.*

[37]List of goods for Chief Quiscat, March 13, 1795. *Béxar Archives.*

[38]Lista de tribus, August 1, 1795. *Béxar Archives.*

[39]Reports of Indian nations and expenses of entertainment in San Antonio, 1796. *Béxar Archives.*

Chief Soxas of the Comanches came with forty women and eleven children for the gifts to his tribe. It is interesting to note that while his companions were all women, they received as presents guns, knives, scissors, hatchets, a little cloth, tobacco, and war paint.[40] In a summary report made on May 1, 1800, at the request of the commandant general, the governor declared that from January 1, 1794, to July 27, 1799, the total expenses of entertaining friendly allies in San Antonio had been eighty-eight hundred forty-nine *pesos*. Of this amount thirty-one hundred eight *pesos* were paid out of the Mesteña Fund. This was the fund created by the collection of a fifty-cent impost on each wild cow or bull killed or caught and on every wild horse taken. The balance was paid by the royal treasury of San Luis Potosí.[41] During 1800 the governor entertained one thousand nine hundred seventy-three Indians at a cost of nine hundred fifty-six *pesos,* and in 1801 the expense was almost identical, although the number of Indians was not so large.[42]

By this time the difficulty of obtaining many of the goods needed for gifts and trade with the friendly nations had become so great that the governor received orders from Nava to secure these goods from New Orleans. A Mr. Gilbert Leonard sent a typical consignment of merchandise to Nacogdoches on June 26, 1800, that will serve to illustrate the supplies obtained from New Orleans for the Indian trade, their cost, and the cost of transportation. The shipment included one hundred English rifles (note the make) that cost eight *pesos* each, much cheaper than those brought from Spain or France at that time. There were one hundred dozen knives of medium size; thirty dozen with horn handles; sixty dozen scissors; sixty hatchets; fifty dozen combs; fifty pounds of copper wire, intended for beaded necklaces and other ornaments; fifty pounds of beads; thirty dozen small mirrors; sixty-two copper kettles; sixty dozen jingle bells; and twenty pair of short trousers, trimmed with braid and with buckles. The invoice amounted to 3,194.50 *pesos*. The expense of transportation from New Orleans to Nacogdoches was 148.00 *pesos*.[43]

Tawakonis propose settlement of Colorado, 1796. It is during this period that Indian nations began to request permission to move from

---

[40]Gifts to Chief Soxas, March 12, 1800. *Béxar Archives.*

[41]Lista de gastos erogados . . ., May 1, 1800. *Béxar Archives.*

[42]Lista de gastos erogados . . ., December 31, 1800. *Béxar Archives.*

[43]List of merchandise sent by Gilbert Leonard to Nacogdoches, June 26, 1800. *Béxar Archives.*

their former habitat to more desirable locations or to enter the Province of Texas. It is another manifestation of the effect of the westward and southward advance of the Anglo-American pioneer, who, exercising undue pressure on the native population, forced it to move into the interior of Texas and to seek homes in New Spain beyond the Río Grande. One of the first instances of this phenomenon is that of a delegation of Tawakoni Indians, headed by the son of Chief Quiscat, who presented themselves to the Count of Sierra Gorda at Laredo in October, 1796, and requested permission to go to Mexico City to interview the viceroy. When asked the purpose of the visit, they explained that their people wanted to establish a pueblo on the Colorado River. The Count of Sierra Gorda was both surprised and pleased at such a novel request and assured the Indians he would be glad to grant them an escort.[44] It is not clear whether this group set out shortly thereafter, or stayed in Laredo until the spring. But on March 1, 1797, Captain José Ramón Díaz Bustamante, of Laredo, informed Governor Muñoz that he had detailed a corporal and twelve soldiers to escort a party of thirteen Tawakonis who were going to Mexico to see the viceroy.[45] It is doubtful whether the Indians understood what they were doing, and there is a suspicion that the wily natives might have used this means as a ruse to penetrate into the interior of New Spain in order to learn more about the resources and defences of the Spanish settlements. But similar delegations came from time to time and the practice continued until after the days of Spanish domination in Mexico.

Last attempt to refound the mission of the Orcoquisacs (Arkokisas), 1788-1792. But while faith in the efficacy of the mission as an agency in the control of the native population of Texas was rapidly waning with the closing years of the eighteenth century, it was not yet entirely lost or dead. It is to be remembered that one of the consequences of the recommendations of the Marqués de Rubí had been the abandonment of the ill-fated Mission of Nuestra Señora de la Luz in the vicinity of the mouth of the Trinity, at or near modern Liberty. These Indians had continued to frequent La Bahía and to bemoan the abandonment of their own mission, now and then going even to San Antonio to complain. While their sincerity may be questionable, nevertheless their demands and supplications for refounding the mission always found a

---

[44]Count of Sierra Gorda to Governor Manuel Muñoz, October 23, 1796. *Béxar Archives.*

[45]José Ramón Díaz Bustamante to Manuel Muñoz, March 1, 1797. *Béxar Archives.*

responsive cord in the heart of the missionaries. When in 1788, Rafael Martínez Pacheco, the former commander of the presidio established to protect the mission, came to San Antonio as governor *ad interim,* he naturally listened with unfeigned interest to the pleadings for its reëstablishment.

On September 8, 1788, an Orcoquisac chief, fourteen Atacapas, and one Coco came to San Antonio for their annual gifts and remained four days. Martínez Pacheco and the Indians were equally surprised at their chance meeting, and they talked of the days at the old mission of the Orcoquisacs. They assured Pacheco that all the coastal tribes in the vicinity of the mouth of the Trinity were anxious for the return of the *Padres* and the Spaniards. Martínez Pacheco wrote Colonel Juan Ugalde, declaring to the commandant that he knew these Indians personally and could vouch for them. In his opinion, their request deserved serious consideration. He had lived among them for years and was convinced of the importance of refounding the mission so hastily abolished.[46]

At this same time there was a zealous missionary living in San Antonio, who had also been among the Orcoquisacs, knew them, and loved them. This was Father Fray José Mariano Reyes, now in charge of Mission San Juan Capistrano. He explained to Governor Martínez Pacheco how these Indians, after their visit with him, stopped to see him. They had begged and entreated him to go back with them, saying that their people cried for the *Padres* when they died, and that since the missionaries had gone away, the dead were left to be eaten by the wolves and the coyotes. When they saw their pleadings were in vain, they threatened to kidnap their old friend and take him back to the Trinity. Father Reyes patiently explained to them that he was anxious to go, but that he could not undertake to visit their pueblos or to reëstablish the mission without the consent of the governor. He advised them to go back peaceably and promised he would visit them soon if he was allowed to do so.[47] He lost no time in requesting the desired permission. Martínez Pacheco, who was thoroughly in sympathy, replied immediately that he would intercede both with the president of the missions in San Antonio and the commandant general in Chihuahua. He asked Father Reyes to tell the Indians in the mean-

---

[46]Rafael Martínez Pacheco to Juan Ugalde, September 15, 1788. *A. G. M., Historia,* Vol. 93, p. 14.

[47]José Mariano Reyes to Rafael Martínez Pacheco, September 13, 1788. *A. G. M., Historia,* Vol. 93, pp. 15-16.

time that he would be ready to accompany them the next time they came to San Antonio.[48]

Father Reyes had lost his heart years before to these simple Indians. Seeing that no action was taken and growing impatient, he decided to appeal directly to the energetic commandant general. On October 30, he wrote to Juan Ugalde, giving him the details of the recent visit and recounting his experiences with these Indians. On September 8, a group of thirty-one natives from the Arkokisa, Atacapa, Coco, and Bidais nations had come to San Juan Capistrano Mission to look for him. Not finding him, they went on to the presidio, thinking the *Padre* had gone there. But Father Reyes was at Mission Espada at the time, helping the missionaries who were sick. On their return, the natives stopped again at San Juan Capistrano. In their childish way they upbraided Father Reyes for not having kept his word to return to Mission Nuestra Señora de la Luz as he had promised years before when he left. They assured the delighted missionary that their people had missed him very much and were literally crying for his return.

Father Reyes suggested that they ought to go to the *Padres* at Nacogdoches for spiritual ministration and explained to them that two missionaries were there for that purpose. Nacogdoches was much nearer to their pueblos than was San Antonio. But the Indians replied that they did not want to go to Nacogdoches, that they wanted a mission in their own country, and that Gil Ibarbo made many promises to them but did not keep them. In vain did Father Reyes urge them to appeal directly to the governor or to the president of the missions. The Indians replied that they had appealed to Governor Cabello, but he had put them off with promises. When they had asked Agustín Falcón, the former president of the missions, he had refused to believe in their sincerity.

It was then that Father Reyes had undertaken to intercede for them with the governor, and assured the delegates that after he had received that official's reply, he would go with them when they returned in the spring.

He recounted how he had spent eight months among them when he was in charge of Mission Nuestra Señora de la Luz and how his reports and suggestions for the improvement of conditions had been ignored. He reminded the commandant general that the failure of the enterprise had not been due to the indifference of the natives, but to the rivalry of the officers charged with the protection of the mission. It had been

---

[48]Martínez Pacheco to Reyes, September 13, 1788. *Ibid.*, p. 17.

alleged that the Indians refused to come to live in the mission, but the truth of the matter was that there never were sufficient supplies available to support and keep them in the mission. Much of the missionary's time, furthermore, was taken up by his duties to the garrison, leaving him very little opportunity to work among the natives. The French traders who frequented this area at that time had much more to offer them than the Spanish presidio and the missionary, but he was convinced that the natives were well-disposed towards the Spaniards and that they were sincere in their desire to embrace Christianity.

Father Reyes took advantage of the opportunity to state the reasons for the reëstablishment of the mission. Louisiana was now a Spanish province. The French traders would no longer work among the natives to set them against the Spaniards; consequently the missionaries would be able to teach them. The site proposed by the Indians at Atascosito was not surrounded by marshes and there were no swarms of mosquitoes and other pests as at the original location. The Indians wanted to become Christians. Their sincerity could not be doubted. As an illustration of their faith, he cited the instance of the epidemic that desolated the country shortly after Bucareli was established. At that time a group of Bidais and Tonkawas asked Father José Mariano Garza to permit them to take the statue of Our Lady del Pilar to their pueblos. With great reverence the sacred image was carried in a solemn procession by the natives. Conditions were more favorable now than at any other time to convert the native tribes of the coast to Christianity, bring them under the permanent influence of Spain, and prevent the intrusion of foreigners into this dangerous zone.

Father Reyes was old and growing feeble. He was contemplating his return to the College of Zacatecas for a well-earned rest. But he assured the commandant general that after the recent visit of his old friends he had changed his mind and decided to sacrifice the comfort of the College in his declining years. He would wait until spring, hoping that the desired permission to visit among the Arkokisas would be granted. He expressed an ardent hope that the mission would be reëstablished, and that, if this decision was reached, the officials would undertake to make available to the missionaries supplies in sufficient quantity to assure the success of the enterprise. He estimated the cost would amount to eight thousand *pesos*. The last time he had been to the country of the Arkokisas he had risked his life for lack of proper protection and had endured sickness and privations from the effects of which he was still suffering; nevertheless he was ready to brave the same hardships for the privilege of carrying the comforts of religion to these Indians who still cried out for it.[49]

Ugalde was impressed with the sincerity of the plea of Father Reyes and the recommendations of Governor Martínez Pacheco. He wrote to Viceroy Flores to acquaint him with the circumstances of the request to reëstablish the mission of the Arkokisas. He explained to the new viceroy that the mission had been abandoned primarily as the result of the new regulations for presidios issued by the king on September 30, 1772. The petition of the delegation of Orcoquisacs, Atacapas, Bidais, and Cocos had been unsolicited and was endorsed by both Father Reyes and Governor Martínez Pacheco, who knew the petitioners and had lived among them.

With characteristic caution, Ugalde was unwilling to recommend, however, that the reëstablishment be undertaken without further investigation to ascertain the true attitude of the natives. He suggested, therefore, that Father Reyes be assigned to Nacogdoches in place of one of the two missionaries now at that post in order that from that place he could determine better the sincerity of the petitioners. This was essential before a decision was made. He recommended that if his suggestion was followed, Father Reyes be allowed five hundred *pesos* to purchase and transport to Nacogdoches such supplies and gifts as he might deem advisable to win the good will of the natives.[50]

When the *fiscal* was consulted in due time, he summed up the situation in these words: "It is not wise to waste the resources of the royal treasury without reasonable assurance of fruitful results, but it is equally unfair to ignore a petition, made perhaps in good faith, which may result in the spread of our religion and of the confines of the State." The suggestion made by Ugalde seemed reasonable. It would involve the expenditure of only five hundred *pesos*. The viceroy was of the same opinion, but financial disbursements, no matter how insignificant, had to be approved by the *Junta Superior de Real Hacienda* (Superior Council of Finance). Consequently, he ordered that the question be submitted for its consideration.[51] The *Junta* finally approved the recommendation and

---

[49]José Mariano Reyes to Juan Ugalde, October 30, 1788. *A. G. M., Historia,* Vol. 93, pp. 18-24.

[50]Juan Ugalde to Viceroy Flores, December 9, 1788. *A. G. M., Historia,* Vol. 93, pp. 25-27.

[51]Dictamen Fiscal, February 10, 1789; Auto del Virrey, February 19, 1789. *A. G. M., Historia,* Vol. 93, pp. 29-30.

authorized the expenditure on April 15, 1789, and six days later the viceroy ordered that the plan suggested by Ugalde be carried out.[52]

The official hurdles had been cleared and it looked as if a start towards the ultimate reëstablishment of Mission Nuestra Señora de la Luz would now be made. But months passed and viceregal officials heard no more about it. The question of the control of the coastal tribes had, however, grown in importance. The new viceroy, Revillagigedo, inquired anxiously from Ugalde what had become of the project for the reëstablishment of the abandoned coastal mission. The old story of native fickleness was the answer. Ugalde informed Revillagigedo in September, 1790, that upon receipt of the instructions from Viceroy Flores, Father Reyes had made preparations to visit the Arkokisas and to take charge of his new post at Nacogdoches. But it had been thought best to wait for the promised return of the delegation in the spring of 1789. In vain did Father Reyes await the return of his friends to take him back as they had promised. Hope turned into despair, and the plan was abandoned. The failure of the natives to return for the missionary was proof incontestable of their insincerity, Ugalde observed.[53]

The new viceroy was a methodical and energetic man. He fully realized the importance of the distant frontier in Texas. He inquired from the new governor, Don Manuel Muñoz, an experienced and zealous servant of the king, if the Indians had made any further efforts to secure missionaries or requested the reëstablishment of a mission and presidio in their lands. He was puzzled by the report of Ugalde and wished to verify the facts. He asked Muñoz, furthermore, that if their petitions were renewed, to tell him confidentially what the advantages of such an establishment were, what the distance to the new site was from San Antonio and from Nacogdoches, and how the Indians could be kept from abandoning the mission if refounded.[54]

Governor Muñoz made inquiries, and replied that the Orcoquisacs and their friends had not repeated their request for a mission in their country. Father Reyes, who was still in San Antonio, had told him that he was convinced the Indians had lost interest in the enterprise and did not

---

[52] Junta Superior de Real Hacienda, April 15; Decreto, April 21, 1789. *Ibid.*, pp. 31-32.

[53] Juan Ugalde to Viceroy Revillagigedo, September 21, 1790. *A. G. M., Historia*, Vol. 93, pp. 43-44.

[54] Revillagigedo to Manuel Muñoz, December 10, 1790. *A. G. M., Historia*, Vol. 93, pp. 49-50.

want to live in pueblos or receive instruction in the faith.[55] One can imagine the pain which such a confession must have caused the old and disillusioned missionary.

The final epitaph of the Orcoquisac venture was written in 1792 by the new commandant general, Ramón de Castro. When asked again by the viceroy what the prospects were, he replied that the enterprise should be dropped in view of the indifference of the natives which reflected their loss of interest in mission life.[56] The mission as a frontier institution capable of coping with the conditions that now existed in Texas was being fatally discredited. It was not the agency for controlling such Indian tribes as it had to deal with on the northeastern frontier of New Spain. It had not been designed for that purpose, nor could it be adjusted to meet the new situation without considerable military aid. The real attitude of the Indians of the north in regard to the mission system was clearly and emphatically stated by Governor Muñoz in 1795, in response to a new inquiry made in connection with the request of Father Silva for additional funds to extend the missionary activities of Mission Refugio to other tribes along the coast and to the northern Indians themselves. He declared that the northern nations were not inclined to mission life; that if they ever sought the security of the missions and agreed to recognize their authority, they would have to be driven to it by the cruelty and superior numbers of their enemies. With remarkable insight, he assured the commandant general that these proud Indians would be compelled to seek refuge in the missions and the Spanish presidios, however, when the Americans penetrated their lands and forced them to retreat before their resistless advance, as the Ais were even now being forced by the Talapousas and the Alabamas.[57]

The Ais Indians seek refuge in Spanish settlements. The Ais and the Bidais, who for more than a century had lived in the vicinity of Los Adaes and Natchitoches, found themselves hard-pushed by the Talapousas and Alabamas at the close of the century. Antonio Leal, Spanish agent in Natchitoches, reported to Governor Muñoz in January, 1795, that a group of ninety Ais had journeyed with him from Natchitoches to the Trinity River and had asked him to request permission to

---

[55]Manuel Muñoz to Revillagigedo, February 9, 1791. *A. G. M., Historia,* Vol. 93, pp. 54-55.

[56]Ramón de Castro to Revillagigedo, May 15, 1792. *A. G. M., Historia,* Vol. 93, pp. 71-79.

[57]Manuel Muñoz to Pedro Nava, January 26, 1795. *Béxar Archives.*

move to San Antonio or some other Spanish settlement, where they could be established in a mission. They explained that the foreign Indian tribes were harassing them and that American traders were supplying their enemies with arms. They would wait at the Trinity for the reply of the governor.[58]

Governor Muñoz welcomed the proposal and immediately sent Lieutenant Bernardo Fernández, an Indian interpreter, to urge the Ais and their friends from East Texas to come to live in the San Antonio missions. He was to assure them that if they wanted to settle on the lands of the now secularized San Antonio missions an escort would be sent to bring them from the Trinity and the necessary supplies for the trip and their maintenance for a year would be furnished.[59]

When the commandant general was informed of the proposal and the reply, he approved the action taken, but warned that the Ais should be made to understand clearly that they were to be settled in San Antonio and that they were to submit to mission regulations. Upon their arrival they were to be distributed among the old missions in order to keep expenses down to a minimum. They could raise crops on the lands already cultivated and save considerable expense in supplying the necessary food for their maintenance. The governor was asked to make a rough estimate of the number of oxen, plows, tools, and other essentials for the newcomers and submit it to Nava, but he was not to buy anything until formal approval was given to the plan.[60]

Antonio Leal took the message back to the waiting Ais and urged them to come to San Antonio, in accordance with their expressed desire. It seems that the Indians were not so enthusiastic about the plan proposed as were the Spanish officials. They reluctantly set out for San Antonio with Leal late in the spring and went as far as the Navasota. They were accompanied by several Bidais and Chief Flechado. It was now flood season and the rivers were impassable. The group camped on the Navasota, and Leal reported that they were waiting for the floods to subside to continue their journey. He explained that what the Indians wanted was not to settle in San Antonio, but to have a mission established for their people on the Trinity, and a presidio of about fifty men to protect them.

------

[58]Manuel Muñoz to Pedro Nava, January 31, 1795. *Béxar Archives.*
[59]*Ibid.*
[60]Pedro Nava to Manuel Muñoz, February 26, and May 5, 1795. *Béxar Archives.*

When Nava was informed of the new request, he replied that the proposal was unacceptable, because it involved too much expense. According to the report of the Indians making the request, there were only twenty men, twenty-two women, and forty-eight children. To assure their protection, they were asking for a garrison of fifty men and two missionaries. The expense that this would involve was not justified by the reduction of only ninety persons to mission life.[61]

On July 22, a group of the Ais came to San Antonio with Leal. With them came some Bidais also. They were asked to remain and were promised lands and spiritual care. They replied they did not want to be so far from their former home. They said that if a mission could not be founded for them on the Trinity, they would be willing to come as far as the Brazos. All efforts to persuade them to come to stay in San Antonio proved futile and the band left the following day. When Nava was informed of the visit, he replied that it was impossible to grant the request.[62]

The grandiose plan of Fray José Alberola.   Puzzled officials both in New Spain and Spain were still worrying about the solution of the Indian problem in the remote frontier provinces of Texas and New Mexico. It was becoming more urgent than ever to solve the problems in these two provinces if foreign infiltration was to be checked. An unknown friar of the College of Zacatecas named José Alberola submitted a plan at this critical moment which sounded practical and promised a solution. He boldly asserted that he was ready to convert and civilize all the Indians of the north without expense to the royal treasury. He declared that for years he had been studying the methods employed by other European nations for the control of the Indian tribes within their possessions in America, and had noted how, in spite of similar difficulties, they had succeeded where the Spaniards had failed. It was imperative, he said, to view the situation realistically, to awaken to the facts, and to adopt a change in policy.

Still speaking in generalities, Alberola went on to state that he proposed to use no soldiers in his plan, that he was going to depend entirely on the strength of the Gospel, the binding ties of genuine friendship, the compelling force of love and kindness. Patience and understanding would replace harshness. He would establish large cattle

---

[61]Pedro Nava to Manuel Muñoz, July 15, 1795. *Béxar Archives.*
[62]Pedro Nava to Manuel Muñoz, August 26, 1795. *Béxar Archives.*

ranches, *haciendas,* and settlements in which the Indians and the Spaniards would live in perfect harmony, have friendly intercourse daily, and
learn to love and respect each other by working together and mingling
freely for the benefit of all. He would choose the sites for the new
establishments with care, picking out the numerous fertile valleys, the
banks of the beautiful and large rivers, and the bays that offered the
best facilities for the promotion of maritime trade. To carry out his
plan, he would have to be given full control of its execution. When the
work was completed—the Indians reduced to Christianity, the country
settled, and prosperity established—he would turn everything over to
government officials to administer. He estimated that it would take from
six to ten years to accomplish the many desirable ends he had so
glowingly outlined. The only concrete proposal was that he would need
an allowance of four thousand *pesos* a year for himself during the
time he was putting the plan into execution and two thousand *pesos*
for an assistant, who would also act as secretary. He intended to begin
the reduction of the Indians with the Apaches.[63]

The plan was certainly attractive, but it is strange that it should not
have been discarded at once as impractical. But a drowning man always
clutches at a straw and the Spanish authorities were rapidly growing
desperate. Fantastic as the plan was, it was referred to the *fiscal* for
an opinion. This official, who was generally an experienced and matter-
of-fact individual, expressed doubt and suggested the matter be referred
to the assessor general, since it involved an outlay of six thousand *pesos*
a year, in spite of the assurance of Alberola that the plan would involve
no expense to the royal treasury. The higher official replied on August 12
that before a decision could be made, it was necessary for Fray Alberola
to submit a more detailed report of how he intended to accomplish the
highly laudable results he promised. The viceroy approved the recommendation and Fray Alberola was requested to state concretely how he
was to put his plan in operation.[64]

Fray Alberola now declared that he was a native of a small villa in
Valencia and that he had long been interested in the problem of Indian
control in the Spanish dominions. After restating his original plan, he
pointed out that the expense involved in its execution would be nothing

---

[63]José Alberola to the Secretary of State, February 6, 1800. *A. G. I., Papeles de
Estado, México, Leg. 10, Núm. 113* (Dunn Transcripts, 1795-1817, pp. 45-47).

[64]Consulta del Fiscal Asesor General, August 4, and 12, 1800; Auto del virrey,
August 12, 1800. *Ibid.,* pp. 48-50.

compared to what was being spent on the missions of California. Joaquín Dongo, he declared, had left an endowment of 500,000 *pesos* for those missions. If something similar could be done for the missions in Texas, the Indian problem would be solved without difficulty.

In order to carry out his plan it would be necessary to set aside at least ten thousand *pesos* a year for supplies needed by the Indians and the settlers to establish themselves in their new homes. To induce settlers to move to the new lands, the inhabitants of Coahuila, New Mexico, and Texas should be offered a ten-year exemption from all taxes, and the enjoyment of free trade. In addition to the ten thousand *pesos* a year for supplies, Fray Alberola now increased the sum for himself to eight thousand, and requested a proportional allowance for two assistants and a separate secretary.[65] There was very little concrete detail in the second exposition other than the statement in regard to the expense for supplies and the increase in his personal salary and that of two assistants and a secretary. The suggestion for exemption from taxes and for free trade was to arouse the concern of the officials.

As months passed and Fray Alberola received no reply, he decided to write to the viceroy a personal letter to solicit his coöperation in expediting the execution of a plan that would prove so beneficial to the interests of the king. He explained that he did not appeal to the commandant general of the Interior Provinces, because he was convinced that official was prejudiced against the missions. He was responsible for the order that resulted in their secularization in Texas. He would not understand the purpose of the plan proposed now. Alberola hinted that he dared not say more in the letter, and asked that he be allowed to tell his excellency verbally many things that could not be committed to writing.[66]

The insinuations against the commandant general only increased the misgivings of the viceregal advisors. The *fiscal* recommended on September 16, 1801, that Fray Alberola be asked to outline fully the details of his plan, that the report be in writing, and that he be informed that his personal appearance in Mexico City at this time was unnecessary. The assessor general was of the same opinion, and the viceroy, accepting

---

[65] José María Alberola to Felix Berenguer de Marquina, viceroy, April 17, 1801. *Ibid.*, 50-56.
[66] Alberola to the Viceroy, August 21, 1801. *Ibid.*, pp. 56-58.

their recommendations, informed Alberola on September 22 in a curt little note of the decision reached.[67]

In his third report, Fray Alberola explained to the viceroy that the bases of his plan were love, kindness, and understanding in dealing with the natives. The new establishments were to be formed with Indian and Spanish settlements, in which the Indians would not be set aside and apart from the Europeans. This practice was responsible for the persistence of idolatrous practices among the natives of New Mexico after so many years, he asserted. The frequent absence of missionaries and the habit of settlers leaving the settlements at will was the reason for numerous failures in the progress of the missions. In the area which he planned to colonize and convert, neither the missionaries nor the settlers were to be permitted to leave without the permission of the commissioner. Both the settlers and the missionaries were going to have to set an example of industry to the natives by performing their tasks daily. This was essential to the success of any plan designed to train the natives in the customs and habits of civilized men while instructing them in the principles of the Christian faith.

He singled out for an example the success of Mission San José in San Antonio, and he attributed this in a large measure to the character of the missionary in charge during its later years, Fray Francisco Pedrajo. Through love and understanding, he had succeeded in establishing looms that produced cloth and blankets as good as those of Querétaro, he had built a flour mill, and he had improved the products of the mission farm. More missionaries like Pedrajo were needed, he assured the viceroy.

After due consideration, Alberola decided that to put his plan in operation he would need soldiers to protect the new establishments during the first few years. Troops were needed to inspire respect. Father Silva had required them for the establishment of Refugio. The older Indians could not be converted. He recalled an anecdote told him by Father Silva. In talking to Chief Soxas, the missionary had been told that it was a waste of time to attempt to convert old men like him. They were too old to learn the new religion. The missionaries should baptize all the children under fourteen and make them live in the missions. The older ones should receive baptism only when dying. In that way, after

---

[67]Consultas del Fiscal y Asesor, September 16, and 19, 1801; Auto del virrey, September 22, 1801. *A. G. I., Papeles de Estado, México, Leg. 10, Núm. 113* (Dunn Transcripts, 1795-1817, pp. 56-60).

all the old Indians had died, the young ones would all be Christians. It was his intention, Alberola averred, to follow this good advice of the aged chief.

He explained that the chief agency in controlling the Indians and in civilizing and Christianizing them was still to be the mission. In the new enterprise the natives were to be under the instruction of missionaries. The Indians of the north favored mission life and had always requested the establishment of missions in their own lands. Recently a group of Tawakoni had come to Mexico from Laredo to solicit a mission. The Cocos, the Orcoquisacs (Arkokisas), the Karankawas, the Adais, the Ais, the Bidais, and many others wanted missions and all would work and keep their word, if they were treated more kindly and given the proper leadership.

To inject a compelling consideration, Alberola referred to the recent Nolan affair, his death, and the arrest of his companions. Alberola's enterprise was designed to prevent a repetition of such incidents. When his plan was put in operation, the penetration of Americans and Englishmen into Spanish territory would be impossible.

After his long introduction and endless circumlocutions, he finally stated what he expected in order to carry out his plan. In doing so he revealed more of the details. The viceroy was first to guarantee the free emigration of families from the settled districts of Coahuila, New Mexico, Texas, and other neighboring provinces into the new lands which he was to open to colonization, in order that settlers might not be hindered from moving if they so desired. All those transferring to the new establishments were to enjoy all the privileges granted to first settlers by the Laws of the Indies. In the second place, he would expect, for the duration of the project, an appropriation of seventy thousand *pesos* a year which were to be placed at his disposal. This money was to be used for transporting the families, for purchasing gifts for the Indians, for constructing public buildings and storehouses, and for securing tools, furnishings, seeds, implements, and cattle. He, as commissioner of the new enterprise, would keep a careful account of all expenditures and make a report each year of how the money was spent.

Although in the original project he had declared that he would need only one assistant and secretary, by now his official family had been considerably enlarged. He requested the appointment of Juan Bautista Blanes as surveyor, with a salary of fifteen hundred *pesos,* and of Bernardo Portugal as his secretary with a salary of one thousand *pesos.*

He also needed an assistant to whom a salary of five thousand *pesos* should be assigned. He inadvertently stated that Blanes, the surveyor, resided in Mexico City.

The military aid solicited for the execution of his plan was by now equally increased. He requested two companies of seventy-five men each, with the corresponding officers, all to be placed under his immediate command and jurisdiction. He suggested that Diego Menchaca, who lived in San Fernando (Nuevo Santander), and José Bustamante y Berroterán, now at Laredo, be given the command of the two companies, both being experienced and reliable frontier captains. He would need a physician and two chaplains to attend him and the troops. He modestly declared that he was not asking any salary for himself, but that he left it to the generosity of His Majesty to reward him as his services might merit. He expected his travelling expenses to be paid by the royal treasury, however, and wanted to be authorized to draw upon it as need arose.[68]

The shock of such an ambitious and foolhardy plan upon the astounded *fiscal* can well be imagined. Only a madman or one totally ignorant could have conceived such an involved, impractical, and impossible scheme. The irate official promptly informed the viceroy that the plan, as detailed by Alberola in his last report, was inordinately ambitious, ambiguous, and absurd, filled with contradictions, and ridiculous in its requests. The commandant general of the Interior Provinces should be consulted at once, the bishops of Sonora and Nuevo León be asked to give their opinion, and the guardian of the College of Zacatecas requested to give a confidential report on the character of Fray José María Alberola. This was the identical opinion of the *Fiscal de Hacienda* (Royal Advocate of the Treasury).[69]

The unraveling of the hoax. The suggestions of the *Fiscales* were followed and the first to report was the guardian of the College of Zacatecas, Fray Ignacio del Río. He was as surprised as the *Fiscales* had been to learn that a friar of his college had made such absurd requests from the viceroy. He declared that Fray José María Alberola was a lay brother who had been in the order nine years, and who was now thirty-five years of age. Before joining the Franciscans, he had

---

[68]José María Alberola to Felix Berenguer de Marquina, October 17, 1801. *A. G. I., Papeles de Estado, México, Legajo 10, Núm. 113* (Dunn Transcripts, 1795-1817, pp. 60-79).

[69]Consulta del fiscal, October 29, 1801. *Ibid.*, pp. 78-79.

been a sergeant in the palace guards in Mexico City. His private life before entering the order had not been particularly noted for virtue. After he joined the order he had shown no special ability. The guardian was convinced that Alberola was not the author of the memorials sent to the king and the viceroy, because the friar could not write anything but his name. Furthermore, he declared that the memorials were not in the handwriting of any member of the College, for he had compared the calligraphy in them with the writing of the different members.

Fray Alberola had never seen an Indian of the north nor had he had any experience in dealing with natives. He had not left the College more than once or twice, when he had been granted permission to take the baths near Mexico City. He had accompanied the bishop of Sonora as a personal attendant once and had been away a year with him. On his return, he had asked to be permitted to remain in the convent of Guadalajara, but shortly afterwards he changed his mind and begged to return to Zacatecas, where he was the cook. The report of Guardian Ignacio del Río was signed by five members of the *Discretorio,* Fray Ignacio María Labaex, Fray Juan José Aguilar, Fray José Ramón Tejada, Fray Mariano Velasco, and Fray José María García.[70]

In view of the report of the guardian of the College of Zacatecas, the *Fiscales* recommended to the viceroy that since it was proved that Alberola could not be the author of the memorials, it would be well to commission Fray Manuel Clavijo, residing in Zacatecas, to summon Bernardo de Portugal, mentioned in the plans presented, for questioning. The recommendation made on January 21, 1802, was immediately ordered carried into execution, and on January 25, Clavijo carefully interrogated Portugal. Confronted first with the original memorials, Portugal admitted readily that they were in his handwriting. He explained that the ideas were not his, however, because all he had done was to reduce to writing what Fray Alberola had dictated, leaving out many unnecessary repetitions. He was then asked to produce the rough drafts. He replied that he had torn them to pieces with the exception of a few pages which were still in possession of Fray Alberola. He added that the first memorial, which had been sent directly to the Secretary of the King to be presented to His Majesty, had not been written by him. Questioned as to who had written the first plan, he answered he did not know. He declared that he had received no pay for writing the subsequent memo-

---

[70]Fray Ignacio del Río, Guardian of Zacatecas, to Viceroy Felix Berenguer de Marquina, December 23, 1801. *Ibid.,* pp. 79-90.

rials and letters, that he had done this for Alberola, because he was
indebted to him for past services. Portugal was an officer in the custom-
house of Zacatecas.[71]

When the *fiscal* looked over the testimony obtained by Clavijo, he
rendered an opinion that the evidence thus far received showed clearly
that the whole Alberola plan had been drawn up by an impostor; that
the real author was Portugal in spite of his denials; and that Fray
Alberola had been merely an instrument in the scheme devised by the
ambitious intriguer. In view of these facts, it was not necessary to
continue the investigation. The *fiscal* thought it best to drop the whole
matter and to inform the king of the result of the measures taken to
determine the validity of the proposal which had unjustly occupied the
attention of His Majesty and of government officials.[72]

Viceroy Marquina reported the whole matter to the king on May 27,
1802. He pointed out that the suspicions of the *Fiscales* had been aroused
by the second statement of Alberola; that when in the third report, he
had made such absurd requests as permission for free trade, complete
control of all administrative, religious, and military matters in the area
to be settled, the right to reward merit and to punish misconduct they
had been seriously alarmed; and that when they learned that he sought
what was equivalent to more than one hundred thousand *pesos* a year, they
had become convinced of the absurdity of the whole plan. In view of these
circumstances, the viceroy apologized for having permitted such a hoax
to be perpetrated and assured the king all further action in the matter
would be dropped.[73]

This plan completely discredited the mission system. In the future,
officials in New Spain and in Spain itself turned to colonization as the
solution of the problem of holding the vast frontier of Texas and New
Mexico against the advance of the American pioneers, who, since 1795,[74]
had obtained the right of navigation on the Mississippi and had begun
to penetrate into the Spanish territory occupied by that numerous group
of Indian tribes generally designated by the Spaniards as the Indians
of the north.

---

[71]Investigation conducted by Manuel Clavijo, January 25, 1802. *Ibid.*, pp. 90-93.

[72]Dictamen del Fiscal, January 31, 1802. *Ibid.*, p. 93.

[73]Felix Berenguer de Marquina to Pedro Ceballos, May 27, 1802. *A. G. I.*,
Papeles de Estado, México, Leg. 10, Núm. 113 (Dunn Transcripts, 1795-1817, pp.
41-43).

[74]Treaty between the United States and Spain signed on October 20, 1795. It
defined the boundary and provided for the free navigation of the Mississippi River.
Fortier, *History of Louisiana*, Vol. 2, 162-163.

CHAPTER V

COMMUNICATIONS BETWEEN SANTA FE AND SAN ANTONIO*

Like two isolated bastions on the far-flung northern frontier of New Spain stood Santa Fe and San Antonio, guarding jealously but somewhat ineffectively the vast dominion of Spain in North America against foreign encroachments. Advanced posts had been set up in East Texas from San Antonio to check the French of lower Louisiana, and similar tentacles spread to the north and east of Santa Fe. But the enterprising fur traders, who followed the waterways, had by 1750 penetrated to the distant capital of New Mexico by ascending the Mississippi, the Red, the Canadian, and the Arkansas rivers. The far-sighted and shrewd advisor of the viceroy, the Marqués de Altamira, urged in 1751 that steps be taken to establish direct communication between the two main outposts as an indispensable measure in the defence of the northern frontier. In the mountains and valleys of the intervening country lived numerous native tribes and nations who had gradually become known to the Spaniards, partly through the efforts of the missionaries, partly through trade relations, and partly through the preying activities of hostile tribes. In search of neophytes and converts, or in pursuit of marauding tribes the country had been entered at various times and irregularly explored, now from one point and now from another.

But until well past the last half of the eighteenth century, officials and travellers alike who wished to visit San Antonio had to make a long, unpleasant, and dangerous detour by way of El Paso to Nueva Vizcaya, hence to Monclova or San Juan Bautista in Coahuila, to enter the Province of Texas and eventually reach San Antonio. Several hundred miles of equally dangerous and unsettled country had still to be traversed to reach the lonely outpost of Los Adaes, opposite the thriving and bustling French post of Natchitoches. Spanish officials fully realized the importance of establishing direct communication between Texas and New Mexico. This consideration was one of the determining factors in the founding of San Sabá in 1757. It was earnestly hoped that the new mission center and outpost would eventually form a basis for direct communication and commerce between the two provinces. But to the hardships

---

*This chapter was originally read as a paper before the Texas Geographic Society and has been published in the *Texas Geographic Magazine.* Vol. 5, No. 1.

of the irregular and little known terrain, was added the more formidable obstacle of the hostility of the powerful Comanches, who, in pursuit of their traditional Apache enemies, had penetrated and occupied a great portion of the intervening country.

Effect of the westward advance of the French and the English. The importance of establishing the desired communication, formally urged by Altamira in 1751, became daily more apparent as a result of the relentless advance westward of the French and the English. That this fear was not a figment of the imagination was amply proved by the destruction of the San Sabá Mission in 1758 by allied northern tribes armed with English rifles, and possibly instigated by French traders and leaders. When Colonel Ortiz Parrilla undertook his unsuccessful expedition against these tribes, he captured three Frenchmen at a Tawakoni village, who admitted before witnesses that they had been instructed to accompany the Indians in their attack on San Sabá. Governor Tomás Vélez Cachupín of New Mexico arrested at almost the same time a group of French traders who had penetrated almost to Santa Fe. Indian captives from the Taovayas told how strange white men who were neither French nor Spanish came frequently to their village, modern Spanish Fort, and traded guns and ammunition for horses, mules, and hides. Father José de Calahorra warned at this same time that Quebec had recently been taken by the English, who, it was said, had set out for the country of the Illinois with a force of five thousand men. Calahorra was a missionary at Nacogdoches. He wisely pointed out that the Illinois flowed into the Mississippi which led directly to New Orleans.[1]

It was this same Father Calahorra who, while among the Tawakoni and the Taovayas on Red River, learned from them that New Mexico was only a fifteen days' journey from their villages. They offered to escort him, if he wanted to go to see the other Spaniards, thereby revealing that these natives were accustomed to visit the remote province. North of the Taovayas, they explained, lived the Seautos (Sioux), known also as Apache Pelones (Short-haired Apaches) because of the manner in which they wore their hair. French traders from a fort on

---

[1]José Calahorra to Angel Martos y Navarrete, May 27, 1760. *A. G. I., Audiencia de México,* 92-6-22; Diego Ortiz Parrilla to the Viceroy, November 8, 1760. *A. G. M., Historia,* Vol. 84, pt. 1, pp. 100-117; Consulta de Diego Ortiz Parrilla, November 18, 1760. *A. G. I., Audiencia de México,* 92-6-22.

the Arkansas had established five trading posts in the country between the Taovaya village and New Mexico.[2]

Truly did Captain Felipe de Rábago y Terán declare in 1761 that the Presidio of San Luis de las Amarillas was the bulwark of four provinces: Texas, New Mexico, Nueva Vizcaya (Chihuahua), and Coahuila. Los Adaes, the remote capital of Texas, was two hundred and twenty-five leagues to the northeast; San Antonio, the strongest post in Texas, was seventy leagues to the southeast; the old Presidio of San Juan Bautista was one hundred and twenty leagues to the southwest; the new Presidio at La Junta, where the Mexican Conchos River enters the Río Grande, was one hundred and fifty leagues to the northwest; and New Mexico was to the north, but no one knew how far.[3]

Early efforts to find a route from San Sabá to New Mexico. On his own initiative, Rábago y Terán undertook the blazing of a trail to New Mexico in the spring and summer of 1761. A detachment of forty men set out from present Menard and went west to the headwaters of the Texas Concho, passing by or near modern San Angelo. They appear to have struck the Pecos River in the vicinity of present McCamey. They ascended the Pecos perhaps to the present site of Pecos, Texas, where they found a large Indian settlement. The river, they declared, flowed across apparently endless plains and was about eighteen *varas* wide and almost two *varas* deep. The country along the river was more or less flat but two ranges of mountains were discernible to the west.[4]

The Presidio of San Sabá and its energetic commander had been instrumental in the creation of interest and the stimulation of efforts in establishing direct communication between Texas and New Mexico. But when, in 1767, the austere and grim inspector of the frontier outposts, the Marqués de Rubí, finished his visit to the first line of defence of Spain in America, he returned thoroughly convinced of the uselessness of maintaining San Sabá in the midst of the vast and boundless expanse of West Texas. With characteristic incisiveness, he declared, "It affords as much protection to the interests of His Majesty in New Spain as a

---

[2]Diario del Viage que hizo Fray Joseph de Calahorra. *A. G. I., Audiencia de México,* 92-6-22, pt. 2, pp. 106-110; Calahorra to Martos y Navarrete, October 18, 1766.

[3]Rábago y Terán to the Viceroy, March 2, 1761. *A. G. I., Audiencia de México,* 91-3-3, pp. 15-25.

[4]Rábago y Terán to the Viceroy, July 12, 1761. *A. G. M., Historia,* Vol. 94, pp. 12-15.

ship anchored in mid-Atlantic would afford in preventing foreign trade with America."[5]

Effect of the cession of Louisiana. The inspection of the frontier presidios by the Marqués de Rubí in 1766-1767 was only one of the consequences of the unsolicited and unexpected cession of Louisiana to Spain in a grand gesture of feigned generosity by the king of France. The excitable French neighbors along the eastern frontiers of Texas and New Mexico were now replaced by the implacable, grasping, and unscrupulous English. Texas and New Mexico ceased to be frontiers and became interior provinces. Heretofore, the chief justification for their military occupation, their settlement, and the conversion of the Indians had been the defence and protection of Spain's colonial empire against the French. A complete reorganization of the Province of Texas in particular was a logical and inevitable sequence to the Treaty of Fontainebleau. Equally important and essential to the safeguard of Spain's interests was the control of the Indian nations that roamed the trackless expanse bounded by a line drawn from Santa Fé to St. Louis, hence to Natchitoches, Nacogdoches, San Antonio, and back to the starting point. This control implied the inevitable establishment of routes of communication between these points to maintain closer relations between them and the natives.

Prior to the cession of Louisiana, foreign fur traders had been the greatest menace to Spanish interests in the northern provinces. French traders had very early acquired practical control over the Indian tribes along the Mississippi and its western tributaries. It was the fear of the extension of their influence that had caused Spanish authorities to maintain the costly but ineffective line of presidios and missions along the entire northeastern frontier. Unlike the English, the French traders, advancing no political claims, had been satisfied with the right to carry on their business undisturbed. But Spain was fully aware that the English pioneer, once he penetrated a new area in the pursuit of trade with the natives, was not satisfied until political sovereignty was established over the new territory. If Spain had feared the French, she had much more reason to fear the English who would influence to a far greater extent the tribes ranged along the Mississippi and the easily accessible Missouri.[6] Thus the friendship and good will of the Indian nations became the paramount objective in the struggle for supremacy over the extensive

---

[5]Inspection of Presidio de San Sabá by the Marqués de Rubí, July 27-August 4, 1767. *A. G. I., Audiencia de Guadalajara,* 104-6-13 (1767), pp. 197-203.

[6]Bolton, *Athanase de Mézières,* I, 19.

plains, the rich valleys, and the rolling hills that lay between the Mississippi and the distant outposts of the weakly held line of defence of New Mexico and Texas. The wisdom of abandoning the eastern establishments in Texas is seriously to be questioned when the matter is viewed in this light.

Effect of the attainment of independence by the American colonies. Far from lessening the growing uneasiness of Spanish officials, the attainment of independence by the struggling English colonies was the determining factor in the search for a more direct route between the distant outposts in New Mexico, Texas, and the Mississippi. Juan Gasiot, a French Indian agent, called the attention of the commandant general of the Interior Provinces, Felipe de Neve, to the serious danger threatening Spanish interests west of the Mississippi, now that the war against England was ended. "It is necessary to keep in mind," he declared, "that a new independent power exists now on this continent, founded by an active, industrious, and aggressive people. With its citizens free from the war sustained for many years against the mother country, from which they have at last succeeded in obtaining independence, this power is already directing its energies to the welfare of its people that they may be respected in the future. These men, freed from the hardships of war that have engaged them so long, will turn their industrious genius to agriculture, the arts, and commerce." The inevitable development of this new and vigorous nation, Gasiot warned, would prove a constant menace to Spain's dominions in America. Spain should lose no time, therefore, in consolidating and reënforcing its defences against the relentless westward sweep of its advance. Texas, Coahuila, and New Mexico stood directly in the path of the westward march and should receive attention first. "If we fail to do so," Gasiot exclaimed with remarkable foresight, "we will see the citizens of the United States of America, lured by the advantages offered by the uncontrolled Indians in the territories lying between their frontiers and our provinces of New Mexico and Texas, make frequent incursions in order to establish trade with the natives. Thus the natives will become attached to them by bonds of interest. The trail blazers will next establish forts among them and continue to advance in this manner until they reach the limits of our borders, where they will have to be stopped. But by that time they will have become irresistible, drawing great strength from their new acquisitions and the establishment of alliances with numerous Indian nations." He concluded by stating that in order to forestall this impending danger, immediate steps should be taken to win the support of the Indians in the intervening area, and to increase the resources for resistance by the development of trade with the natives. It was true that there was gold in the country of the Taovayas and the Comanches, and it was known that all the natives in this vast area had valuable hides and pelts. The country occupied by the Taovayas, Tawakonis, Wichitas, Iscanis, Quitseys, and the Comanches offered easy access to the Province of Louisiana from New Mexico and Texas. Once their friendship was won and the bonds of good will were strengthened by the intimate relations of trade, foreigners could effectively be kept out of the three provinces. Kind and fair treatment would win the friendship of these warlike nations and trade would develop ties of interest that would strengthen their attachment.[7]

Exploration of route from San Antonio to Santa Fé by Pedro Vial, 1786-1787. When in the fall of 1786 Pierre Vial, a Frenchman, who had traded among the northern Indians in the vicinity of Natchitoches and up Red River as far as the Taovayas, was in San Antonio, Governor Cabello decided to utilize him for his long cherished project of finding the most direct route to Santa Fe. Vial was particularly well suited for the task, being a good woodsman, thoroughly versed in the ways of the outdoors, and familiar with many of the different tribes of the north. He was destined to traverse the country between New Mexico, Texas, and Louisiana several times during the next few years. Governor Cabello instructed him to set out from San Antonio in company with Cristóbal de los Santos, a citizen of the Villa de San Fernando, to find as direct a route as possible to Santa Fe. He was to keep a careful diary of the distances and direction of travel day by day, noting the character of the country, the rivers and streams crossed, the direction in which they flowed, and any other details deemed pertinent. He was likewise to note the Indian tribes and nations he met, the size of the *rancherías,* the number of warriors of each, their customs, and their habits. To all he was to explain that the Spaniards and the French were one now, and he was to try to win their friendship and good will for Spain.

Armed with his instructions and a letter for the commander of Santa Fe, Vial and his companion left San Antonio on October 4, 1786. The first day they halted at Los Canales (The Canals), probably irrigation ditches near the headwaters of the San Antonio River. Continuing to

---

[7]Juan Gasiot to Felipe de Neve, October 9, 1783. *San Francisco el Grande Archives,* XXXIII, pp. 151-162.

the north, they travelled eight leagues to the Guadalupe, crossing it just below modern Spring Branch. Here they suffered their first accident, losing a horse loaded with supplies in crossing. Two days later, still going north, they crossed a river which they called Chanas (Llano), after travelling, according to their record, twelve leagues. It seems more probable that the river was not the Llano but the Colorado which they crossed at or near present Marble Falls, a short distance below the point where the Llano joins the latter stream. Still going north, they again crossed the Colorado in the vicinity of present Tow. Vial was ill, but they continued along the river for five leagues during the next day. By October 11 they came to the point where the San Saba River joins the Colorado. Here they evidently abandoned the river in order to continue their northern course; and, after travelling fifteen leagues during the next three days, they came to a small stream which probably was Leon River. In crossing it, near Gustine, Vial, who had grown steadily worse, fell from his horse and was senseless for several hours. When he regained consciousness, his companion, Cristóbal de los Santos, alarmed by his condition, asked him for a statement in writing that might serve to prove the cause of death in the event that he should die. Vial reassured Santos that he would not die. He decided, however, to change his course and proceed directly to the pueblo of the Tawakoni for treatment. He seems to have visited the pueblo before, and he was of the opinion it was not far away.[8]

Detour to Tawakoni villages. Although the diary states that the general direction of his march from October 15 to October 29 was north, this is an error which may be attributed to the copyist or to Vial's sickness. He clearly stated on the 14th that he was changing his course; he had to change it if he was to go to the Tawakoni villages on the Brazos which were almost due east from his camp.

---

[8]The details of Vial's first attempt to find a direct route to Santa Fé are taken from *Diario que por la gracia de Dios comienzo (yo Pedro Vial) á hacer desde este Presidio de Sn. Antonio de Béjar, hasta arribar al de la Capital Villa de Santa Fe por comision de mi Governador Dn. Domingo Cavello, Governador de la Provincia de los Texas, con expresion de las jornadas desde el día 4 de Octubre de 1787.* [1786.] *A. G. M., Historia,* Vol. 43, document 14. Copies of the same diary are found also in *Historia,* Vol. 52, document 17, and in *Historia,* Vol. 62, document 2. All references are to the diary in *Historia,* Vol. 43, photostat copies of which are in the University of New Mexico. This expedition as well as those of José Mares to San Antonio and back by way of Natchitoches and San Antonio are very briefly summarized in Bolton, *Texas in the Middle Eighteenth Century,* 127-133.

In search of the Tawakoni, he halted on October 17, after travelling eighteen leagues to the east, and stayed in camp a day. Resuming his march, he crossed several tributaries of the west branch of the Brazos and once came upon tracks of Indians on the hunt, before he arrived, on October 24, in a deserted Tawakoni pueblo six leagues west of the main stream of the Brazos. Here he stopped to rest again. Continuing his march, he next arrived at the Quiscat pueblo of the Tawakonis in the vicinity of Waco. He had travelled approximately fifty leagues over an irregular route going either by Hamilton, Cranfill's Gap, and Clifton or by Hamilton and Gatesville to Waco. The village was not on the Brazos but on a small stream, perhaps the Bosque, that flowed into the river.

Vial and his companion were welcomed by Chief Quiscat. The Tawakonis were surprised to see the visitors and inquired of them where they were going. Vial said he was on the way to visit the Comanches and to find a way to Santa Fe. The Indians were apprehensive that they might be held responsible for the recent depredations committed in San Antonio by the Taovayas and asked the newcomers what they knew. Vial explained that he was in San Antonio when the Taovaya chief and a band of Wichitas stole a drove of horses; that at first the Spaniards thought the marauders were Apaches; but that the next night they doubled the sentinels, and shot one of the robbers. The captain of the presidio had asked Vial to identify the nation of the victim and he had satisfied himself that the Indian was a Taovaya.

Much relieved by the information, the Tawakoni chiefs emphatically disclaimed all participation in recent raids and assured Vial they had maintained the peace negotiated with the Spaniards. It is of interest to note that these Indians told Vial of the visits of De Mézières to their villages more than twenty years before and related how they had, in turn, visited San Antonio to make peace with the Spaniards, and how Governor Ripperdá had given their chief a suit of clothes and a medal. The faithfulness with which these events were narrated is indicative of the deep impression made upon them by De Mézières and of the preservation, through tradition, of events among the Indian nations of the north. Vial did not know of De Mézières and what he set down in his diary is what the Indians told him.

Chief Quiscat was glad to permit the medicine man of the tribe to treat Vial who was very sick when he arrived on October 20. He remained in the village until December 15, by which time he had fully recovered and was ready to resume his journey to Santa Fe.

Visit with the Taovayas and Wichitas. Setting out from the Quiscat village of the Tawakonis in the vicinity of Waco on December 15, Vial and his companion followed the river in a general northwestern direction until December 21, when they observed a smoke signal. They had travelled thirty-six leagues or approximately ninety miles. This places them in or near Dennis. They made a counter signal and were soon met at the river by two Wichitas and a Spanish captive named Juan de la Cruz. Conversation disclosed that these Indians belonged to the band that had raided San Antonio.

Vial and his companion took a more northerly course in order to visit the pueblos of the Taovayas and Wichitas. On Christmas day they crossed a river, which probably was the Trinity, at or near Bridgeport; and, on December 28, after travelling thirty-six leagues, they arrived in the pueblos of the Taovayas on Red River in the vicinity of modern Spanish Fort.

The arrival of the visitors created considerable interest and the chiefs of the Taovayas and Wichita villages gathered at the house of Chief Corichín to inquire about the fate of those who had recently gone to San Antonio to steal horses. Vial told them the truth, and upbraided them for their failure to observe the peace. The chiefs brought out a peace pipe, and after solemnly smoking it, assured Vial that the raiders were irresponsible young warriors; that the chiefs were the friends of the Spaniards; and that, because they wanted peace, they were sorry for the misdeeds of the young men. Vial remained in the house of Chief Corichín until January 5, 1787.

Visit with the Comanches on Red River. While in the village of the Taovayas, a delegation of six Comanches came to guide Vial to their village. Setting out on January 6, in company with his guides, he went west for twelve leagues and came to the village of Chief Zoquiné, where he arrived on January 11. This must have been in the vicinity of modern Byers.

Chief Zoquiné was a good friend of the Spaniards and was genuinely happy to see Vial and Santos. A peace smoke was held and Vial explained the purpose of his exploration, assuring the Comanches that the Spaniards in both Santa Fe and Texas were their friends. Chief Zoquiné attempted to persuade the travellers to stay with his people until the spring, when he would guide them to their destination. They discussed also the reëstablishment of the Mission and Presidio of San Sabá for the Comanches either at the old site or on the Pedernales.

Vial decided to go on, and promised to take up the matter of San Sabá with the *Tata Grande* (Big Father) in San Antonio upon his return to Texas. He remained a few more days, however, with Chief Zoquiné before resuming his journey on January 17. He took a westward course and, travelling slowly on account of the cold, he made about twelve leagues during the next three days. He was now at or near modern Clara or Burkburnett. Here he established winter quarters and stayed until March 4.

Chief Zoquiné and some of his followers accompanied Vial and his companion when they resumed their march in the spring. They again went almost due west, leaving the main stream of the Colorado and following for a while Pease River to the vicinity of Coleyville, in Cottle County, where they camped on April 7, after travelling about forty-eight leagues and passing probably through modern Vernon and Medicine Mound. Here they were overtaken by two Comanches who declared that three of their friends had just returned from San Antonio and brought word that the captain of Santa Fe had written to the commander in Texas to kill all the Comanches, and that Vial had deceived them and was leading them to New Mexico in order that they might all be killed. Chief Zoquiné said that he did not believe a word of it, and would continue to accompany his friends. His firmness saved Vial and his companion, and the journey was resumed after a four-day halt.

By May 11 they had travelled approximately fifty-two leagues to the northwest, halting frequently to hunt buffalo. According to the diary they went eight leagues west from Coleyville, then turned north for three leagues, and then nineteen leagues to the west; this course would take them to the vicinity of Whitefield and Kress. Here they turned north for twenty-two leagues to a large river they thought was the Red, and so named it, but it was the South Canadian which they struck north of Amarillo, after passing by the site of the city of this name. They now followed the river west for a distance of thirty-five leagues and came to a *ranchería* of Tupos seemingly in the vicinity of present Logan, New Mexico. The chief welcomed Vial and showed him a Spanish flag that had been given him by the captain of Santa Fe. The party rested for a day and went on to the neighboring *ranchería* of the Tumparías, located on the same river two leagues beyond. They found these Indians equally friendly. They continued their journey westward, inclining slightly to the north, and, after going seventy leagues, arrived on May 25 in the old pueblo of Pecos. The next day Vial and his companion went on to Santa Fé, where Vial delivered the letters to the governor, together with a diary and a map of the route followed. Vial had travelled a total of 459 leagues, more than 1,100 miles, from San Antonio to Santa Fé by way of the Taovaya villages on Red River. But this route was far from being direct.

Governor Fernando de la Concha of New Mexico was as anxious as Governor Cabello of Texas to discover a direct route of communication between the two provinces. Shortly after the arrival of Vial, he consequently commissioned Corporal José Mares to undertake a similar expedition with instructions to follow a more direct route from Santa Fe to San Antonio.[9]

The expedition of José Mares from Santa Fe to San Antonio, 1787. José Mares, accompanied by Cristóbal de los Santos who had gone to Santa Fe with Vial, and by Alejandro Martín, a Comanche interpreter from New Mexico, set out on July 31, 1787, and following a southeastern course to the Pecos River, crossed this stream and turned east to Bernal; they reverted to the southeast and camped on Gallinas River on August 2, probably at or near Lourdes. The next day they went south for seven leagues, possibly to modern Chaparito, where they turned east. During the following three days they travelled thirty-four leagues eastward, probably along the southern tributaries of the South Canadian, to a point east of Tucumcari, where they met a band of Comanches who had had a battle with the Apaches to the south, in which they had killed five and captured thirty.

Mares and his companions continued east four more leagues, approximately ten miles, and then turned south probably in the vicinity of modern San Jon; continuing in this direction and passing by Cameron and Grady, they reached Blanco River (Creek) on August 9. They pro-

---

[9] *Por el Nombre de Dios Todopoderoso, y de la Santísima Virgen Maria mi Señora del Rosario Conquistadora del Reyno, y la Provincia del Nuevo México concevida en gracia Amen. Yo el cavo José Mares Ymbalido del Rl. Presidio de la Capital Villa de Santa Fé, hago este derrotero para inteligencia, y conocimiento del tránsito que comienzo a hacer para el Presidio de San Antonio de Béjar, hoy el día 31 ultimo del mes de Julio del presente año de mil setecientos ochenta y siete.* The copy used in this study is in *A. G. M., Historia*, Vol. 43, document 4. But the original is in the *Béxar Archives*, now in the University of Texas. This was compared with the copy in *Historia*, Vol. 43, used in the present study.

ceeded in a general eastern direction across plains, noting the numerous lakes in the area between Rhea (they had entered Texas just above it) and Dimmit. In the vicinity of Tulia they came upon a *rancheria* of Comanches, where they met Chiefs Zoquinatoya and Tazaquipi. On August 11 they visited the *rancheria* of Chief Nocay, which they found some nine leagues to the east.

Across the plains for a distance of thirty-four leagues they followed an almost due east course, slightly inclined to the south, and on August 22 came upon two *rancherias* not far apart on Prairie Dog Town Creek, in the vicinity of present Quanah, in Hardeman County, which Mares called San Marcos. Mares turned south, and on August 28 after going nine leagues, came upon a river which he called the River of the Taovayas, and noted the water was "very red." This stream was not Red River as may be supposed, but North Pease River which Mares and his party must have struck slightly west of Vernon. From here he continued almost due east for a distance of sixty-six leagues, and arrived at the villages of the Taovayas on September 5.

Visit with the Taovayas. Mares was warmly welcomed by these Indians who, since the time of the visit of De Mézières, had been on the most friendly terms with the Spaniards. He found that two of the pueblos were on the north side of Red River and one on the south, in the vicinity of modern Spanish Fort. The first had twenty-three houses, the second had forty, and the third, which was on the south side of the river, close to present Farmers' Creek, had twenty-seven.

Route followed from the Taovayas to San Antonio. After a four-day visit Mares and his companions set out to the south, crossed a dry ravine, and, after going three leagues, camped on high ground near two small mesas. Here the French had long maintained a trading post to deal with the Comanches. Southwest of Spanish Fort there is today a site called Belcherv, highest point in the vicinity with an elevation of 981 feet, and to the southeast of Spanish Fort is a place known to this day as Illinois Bend, both mute evidence of the activity of French traders from the Illinois and the Arkansas in this area.

Striking out across plains and intervening ravines in a general southern direction, slightly inclined to the west, Mares made thirteen leagues in two days and came to a Comanche *rancheria* located in a deep and densely wooded ravine. This probably was between Saloma and Sunset. He turned to the west at this point and went nine leagues across prairies to a large river which he called the Brazos, but which was in reality West Fork, one of the streams constituting the headwaters of the Trinity. He must have come upon West Fork in the vicinity of Jacksboro.

From Jacksboro he continued generally to the south, at times inclining to the west, and after travelling forty-six leagues over heavily wooded areas, crossing many small streams and some open country, he came to a river which he called the Pedernales. This cannot possibly be the Pedernales of today, because to reach this stream, he would have had to cross the Colorado, the San Saba, and the Llano and to have travelled a much longer distance than forty-six leagues. The river he called Pedernales probably is one of the streams that form the upper waters of Leon River which he seems to have struck at or near present Comanche, as is apparent from the distance covered and the general direction followed until September 21. He noted that the stream was heavily wooded and flowed eastward.

In the same general direction, but inclining too far to the west, Mares went forty-two leagues before reaching a large river of reddish water which he called San Rafael del Colorado. In the course of the march he had at times to meander considerably. It seems, therefore, that the river was the Colorado which he crossed in the vicinity of modern Waldrip. He changed his course to the south, and at or near modern Brady, crossed Brady Creek which he called San Miguel, and about ten miles beyond, in the vicinity of present San Saba, he reached the San Saba River which he erroneously called the Chanas (Llano). He continued almost due south, and, at or near Mason, crossed the Llano on October 1, mistaking it for the San Saba. He made special mention of its beauty. He proceeded south and crossed the Guadalupe on October 7 near Kerrville, where he seems to have begun following the route of the present highway via Bandera to San Antonio where he arrived on October 8, and reported to the governor who was now Rafael Martínez Pacheco.[10]

Mares had traversed 373 leagues, or approximately 932 miles, but, like Vial before him, he had failed to follow a direct route. Either his Indian guides wished to go by the popular and well-known pueblos of the Taovayas, or Mares himself desired to visit them on this occasion. The route to the Taovaya villages was fairly direct, but from the Taovayas to San Antonio his guides led him in a roundabout way, going too far west. In reporting the arrival of Mares to San Antonio, Governor Martínez Pacheco explained that Cristóbal de los Santos had reached San

---

[10] *Diario* of José Mares. *A. G. M., Historia*, Vol. 43, document 13.

Antonio a day before Mares, and that he had come with two Comanches. When Mares arrived on the following day, October 8, 1787, there came with him four chiefs, thirty-eight braves, twenty-three women, and six children, all from the *rancherías* of the eastern Comanches. Among them was Chief Sofais, who claimed he had accompanied Vial in January on his trip from the Comanche *rancherías* to Santa Fe. He now offered to lead a party by a more direct route back to New Mexico. But with winter approaching, Martínez Pacheco thought it might be best to wait until spring or summer before Mares undertook the return trip in company with Chief Sofais.[11]

Expedition of José Mares from San Antonio to Santa Fe, 1788. But something made Governor Martínez Pacheco change his mind. Perhaps Mares was anxious to return to Santa Fe. Whatever the cause, José Mares was ready to start back by January, 1788, in the very middle of winter, to try to discover a more direct route from Texas to New Mexico. Guided by a group of friendly Comanches who were headed by Chief Sofais, he started from San Antonio on January 18, 1788, to go as far as a creek which he called Novillo, located about three leagues north of San Antonio.[12] This was the upper branch of Salado Creek. Continuing north, he crossed the Cibolo ten miles beyond and came upon the Guadalupe about two miles west of modern Spring Branch, just below the point where Curry Creek joins the Guadalupe River. He now went over the hills to the Blanco River where he noted an Indian trail in the vicinity of the present city of that name, and after making a short offset to the west, he resumed his northern course to the Pedernales which he crossed at or very near modern Hye. Here he started north to a creek (Grape Creek), and after travelling about six more leagues he crossed a stream which he called the San Gabriel. This was not the San Gabriel of today, because to have reached it, Mares would have had to cross the Colorado first, and to have travelled much further. The stream which he crossed in the vicinity of Click was our Sandy Creek. He noted that it was

---

[11]Rafael Martínez Pacheco to Juan de Ugalde, October 20, 1787. *Spanish Archives of Texas*, University of Texas, Austin.

[12]*Derrotero y diario que corresponde al número de Leguas que hay desde la Capital de San Antonio de Béjar Provincia de los Texas hasta la de Santa Fé del Nuevo México, que hago Yo José Mares, cabo Ymbalido de la Compañia de ella por los terrenos que me conducen los Yndios Amigos Comanches, para descubrir camino de derechura. A. G. M., Historia*, Vol. 43, document 16. Copies also in *Historia*, Vol. 52, document 17, and in *Historia*, Vol. 62, document 6.

heavily wooded and flowed east. He camped on present Honey Creek, a few miles northeast of Oxford.

On January 22, shortly after leaving Honey Creek, Mares and his party came to the Chanas River (Llano) which they probably struck at or near Llano, considering the general direction of their travel and the distance covered. It is interesting to note that the party here met Lieutenant Curbelo from the garrison of San Antonio, who was out on a private trading expedition. They spent the rest of the day with Curbelo. When they resumed their march, the party proceeded more slowly. They camped somewhere on Buffalo Creek not far from modern Cherokee. Here they met a group of Indians who apparently were either Apaches or Taovayas, and had with them a Spanish captive. Mares had been instructed by Governor Pacheco to buy any captives with whom he might come in contact. He accordingly bargained with the wily Indians and succeeded in ransoming the captive for eight horses.

From the San Saba to the Colorado. On January 27 Mares and his companion started over relatively rough country, through heavy woods, crossed a relatively high mesa and a plain, and, after travelling fourteen leagues, reached the San Saba somewhere in the vicinity of Algarita, several miles west of the present city of San Saba. Shortly after crossing the river, he turned west for three leagues and camped in a dry ravine, probably at or near modern Richland Springs. The weather was getting bitter cold. On January 28 they again turned north by west and travelled seven leagues to a creek almost filled with snow, in the vicinity of Placid. The next day, inclining more towards the north, they went seven leagues more and reached the Colorado at or near Fife.

From the Colorado to the Rancheria de Comanches. Mares and his friend followed the Colorado to the west for four leagues, then turned north for nine leagues. Here, on February 1, they discovered a wide buffalo trail which they followed for five leagues in a general northern direction. For the next three days they kept almost due north, slightly inclined to the west, and after covering twenty-four more leagues arrived at a Comanche *rancheria* located in a ravine.

From the direction of travel and the distance covered, Mares and his party must have passed by the sites of Santa Anna and Coleman, and due north through Baird to the headwaters of the Clear Fork of the Brazos. The *rancheria* probably was in the vicinity of present Lueders. They were now on the great plains. The weather was severe, yet Mares pushed on for five days, going west and northwest for sixteen leagues. On February 11 he camped near two small mesas on the banks of a stream that flowed east. It seems that he established his winter quarters in the vicinity of present Hamlin, perhaps some six or eight miles due north, on Double Mountain Fork, another one of the streams that form the upper waters of the Brazos. Here he decided to stay until spring.

From the Double Mountain Fork to the Comanche rancherías in Briscoe County. On March 6 Mares resumed his journey. He took an almost due north course, with a slight inclination to the west. He was now on the high plains of northwest Texas. After going some twenty leagues on March 16 and crossing several creeks and ravines, some with salt water, he came to a fairly large river which he thought was the Brazos. This was in all probability the South Fork of the Wichita River, which he crossed at or near Guthrie, a few miles east of the present road between Dickens and Matador, and continuing through Quitaque, he came upon the first of the Comanche *rancherías* on Prairie Dog Town Fork in Briscoe County, perhaps at the entrance to the relatively deep canyon of this stream. It seems the Comanches chose the canyons or deep ravines for their *rancherías* in the great plains, because they could be less easily detected by enemies in a country where observers can see as far as the eye can reach, and because the canyons and ravines afforded protection against biting northers, as they swept across the plains. Three leagues beyond the first *ranchería* there was another. Here the chief gave Mares two young boys to accompany him to Santa Fe. Mares spent almost two weeks with the Comanches before resuming his journey. On April 6 he set out again, and going north, came to a river which he called Sangre de Cristo. This was the South Salt Fork of the Red River which he crossed in the vicinity of Ashtola.

From the headwaters of the Red River to Santa Fe. He now turned west and after crossing some mesas and plains for thirteen leagues, probably to present Lita, then turning north for ten leagues, he reached Amarillo Creek, just about where modern Amarillo is; and reverting west across the plains, he arrived at Río Blanco in New Mexico on April 13. He ascended this small stream to its source, in the vicinity of Frio. Ten more leagues west brought him to a point somewhere between West and Ima. Then passing east of Sierra de la Luz, he resumed his westward course to Gallinas River on April 23 in the vicinity of Lourdes; thence he

Mapa tranzitau

en S.ta Jaf

villa
precidio
pueblo de los
yndios
fuerte

los cacos

? de rivera

Nueba orlean

p.to de la
baliza

made his way to Bernal Canyon, crossed the Pecos to the pueblo of the same name, and on April 27 arrived at Santa Fe.[13]

He had travelled a total of 325 leagues, or some 710 miles, and had taken a much more direct route than the one followed by Vial in 1786, or by himself on the way to San Antonio. The route touched those of the two previous explorations, or came very near to them at some point. The location of the Comanche *rancherías* at the headwaters of the Brazos in the vicinity of Hamlin and at the entrance to Palo Duro Canyon near Ashtola is of interest. Gradually more detailed knowledge concerning the country and the extent of the ground over which the various northern tribes ranged was being acquired.

The expedition to the Jumanos and the exploration of a route from Santa Fe to Natchitoches, 1788-1789. The return of Mares from San Antonio seems to have aroused still further the interest of officials to learn more about the native tribes and the country that lay between Santa Fe and the friendly Jumanos, Natchitoches, and the capital of Texas. The desire to strengthen the relations with the Indian nations of the north, and to establish definite lines of communication with Natchitoches and San Antonio prompted Governor Fernando de la Concha of New Mexico to organize a new expedition in June, 1788, two months after the return of Mares.

Pedro Vial, who had recently traversed the route from the pueblos of the Taovayas on Red River to Santa Fe and who had previously frequented them from his former residence in Natchitoches, was commissioned to discover the most direct route from New Mexico to the distant outpost. From Natchitoches he was to undertake a similar exploration to determine the shortest route to San Antonio, and to ascertain the attitude of the native tribes towards the Spaniards throughout the country visited in the course of his explorations. From San Antonio he was to return to Santa Fe to verify the routes previously followed by himself with Mares, and by Mares alone. He was consequently given letters for the commanders of the posts he was to visit, requesting them to extend to him whatever aid he needed for the execution of his commission.[14]

---

[13]The details summarized are from the *Derrotero y diario . . . desde la Capital de San Antonio de Béjar . . . hasta la de Santa Fé . . . que hago Yo José Mares.* A. G. M., *Historia*, Vol. 43, document 16. Location of other copies has been indicated in the preceding note. The date of his arrival is erroneously given as April 17, 1788, by Bolton. *Cf. Texas in the Middle Eighteenth Century*, 130.

[14]*Derrotero, Diario y Calculación de leaguas, que en descubrimiento por derecho desde esta Provincia del Nuevo México hasta el Fuerte de Natchitoches y la de*

With him were to go Francisco Xavier Fragoso who was to keep a careful diary; three natives of New Mexico, José María Romero, possibly a brother of the Romero who had been sent in 1763 to San Sabá, Gregorio Leiva, and Juan Lucero; and Santiago Fernández, commander of a squad of soldiers who were to escort the party as far as the Jumanos. Fernández, in addition to escorting Vial, was to foster the friendship of all the Indians visited, particularly the Jumanos to whom he carried especial gifts and greetings.[15]

The two travelled together as far as the Jumano pueblos, which from the description appear to be the Taovaya villages, but which Fernández asserted were on a river which he called the Blanco, contrary to the established name of the Red River, known to the Spaniards as well as the French by this time. But let us follow the explorers on their journey.

Vial-Fernández expedition to the Jumanos. On June 24, 1788, they set out from Santa Fé, and following the regular road, went to Pecos pueblo. Here they turned to the south, keeping a mesa on their right, crossed the Pecos at the usual place and camped at Bernal. They now took an easterly course and crossed the Gallinas River at or near Lourdes, and the next day, after going some twenty leagues from Bernal, they camped at a spring in the midst of a grove of cottonwoods, which they called Pajarito. This was very likely at or near present Garita, on one of the small streams flowing into the New Mexico Conchos which in turn flows into the South Canadian. They spent a day at the spring to rest after crossing the mountains, and resumed their march on June 29. The next two days they went over some plains and mesas and on June 30 they camped on Mesa Tucumcari, probably near Montoya. Three leagues beyond, to the east, they came upon a Comanche *ranchería* in a ravine.

---

los Texas de orden superior voy a practicar en compañia de Dn. Pedro Vial, comisionado a este propósito, yo el abajo y a lo último firmado (Francisco Xavier Fragoso). *Villa de Santa Fé veinte y quatro de junio mil setecientos ochenta y ocho. A. G. M., Historia,* Vol. 43, document 17. Copies also in *Historia,* Vol. 52, document 17, and *Historia,* Vol. 62, document 7. There is an abbreviated copy of this diary in the Land Office, Austin, Texas, which covers the journey only from Santa Fé to San Antonio by way of Natchitoches, ending with the entry for November 18, and omitting descriptions of places visited.

[15]*Derrotero, diario y calendario de leguas que hago Yo el abajo firmado* (Santiago Fernández) *en descubrimiento desde esta de Santa Fé a los Pueblos de Jumanos por orden Superior del Sr. Governador Dn. Fernando de la Concha, a condución y guia de Pedro Vial, y es como siguen.* Santa Fé, December 17, 1788. *A. G. M., Historia,* Vol. 43, document 15. Copies also in *Historia,* Vol. 52, document 14, and in *Historia,* Vol. 62, document 5. Date erroneously given as December 16. *Cf.* Bolton, *Texas in the Middle Eighteenth Century,* 131, n. 45.

It had fifty-six tepees and was ruled over by Chief Naisaras. The Indians invited the travellers to rest and to smoke the pipe. When told they were going to the Jumanos, the Comanches assured them they were travelling in the right direction. Several of the Indians offered to accompany them for a short distance, and together they went on to three other *rancherías* located in the vicinity, towards the east, at intervals of two or three leagues.[16] They evidently passed north of present Tucumcari, as they distinctly stated that they kept a high, black mesa to the right or south of their line of march, and fairly wide plains to the left or north.

Continuing east, they seem to have followed the present road by way of San Jon, through Baird to Glenrio, at which point they crossed into present Texas and came into the high plains. On July 3 they travelled over plains so flat and devoid of trees that Fragoso wrote, "They are so vast that not a hill or mesa was discernible as far as the eye could see." That day they passed thirteen lakes and came to the source of Blanco River.[17] They had covered approximately sixty-five miles since leaving Glenrio. From the description of the country and the reference to the lakes, it is easy to identify the route followed. They came slightly south of the present road to Amarillo, passing by the numerous lakes found to the southwest of this city and in the vicinity of present Canyon, struck the Prairie Dog Town Fork of the Red River which they called the Blanco River.

They continued along this stream through Palo Duro Canyon for two days, and came to a small Comanche *ranchería* of four tents, where they saw many horses. This was the same *ranchería* visited by Mares at the eastern extremity of the canyon in Briscoe County, a few miles north of Silverton. They passed the eastern end of Tule Creek during the second day. By following Prairie Dog Town Fork eastward, they seem to have arrived in the vicinity of Estelline by July 8. They noted that by now the river had become very wide, almost a gunshot in width, and that the hills began to flatten out. On July 9 they halted briefly at another Comanche *ranchería* of fourteen tents, located along what they called the Río Blanco, the same stream they had been following. This was probably between modern Quanah and Eldorado. Chief Pachinacazen welcomed the visitors, and they had a peace smoke before resuming the

---

[16]Fragoso and Fernández kept separate diaries. The details summarized are found under the respective entry under July 1 of the two diaries previously cited.

[17]Fragoso, *Derrotero, diario y calculación*, entry for July 3, 1788. It is interesting to compare this description with that of Coronado's march across the plains.

journey. The Comanches assured them they were on the right road and that all they had to do was to follow the river.[18]

Still in an easterly direction and following the river valley, they came to another *ranchería* of Comanches on July 11, who again reassured the travellers they were going in the right direction. This must have been in the vicinity of Vernon. The next day they crossed the Red River to the north bank and saw a range of mountains far to the north. They were probably near present Grandfield; and the mountains seen in the distance were the Wichita Mountains in Comanche County, Oklahoma. They crossed Coche Creek near Taylor, Oklahoma, and Beaver Creek in the vicinity of Ryan, indicating in the diaries that both streams flowed into the Blanco River (Red) from the north. They inclined to the south on July 15 and crossed the river, noting the Little Wichita which joins the Red from the south. They soon came to a wide Comanche trail where they were met by three chiefs, Zoquacante, Cochi, and Pisinape, who took them to their *ranchería* on the river. This was the largest Fernández had seen, consisting of three hundred seventy-two tents. The probable location was in the vicinity of Fleetwood, not far from Ryan, Oklahoma. At this *ranchería* Fernández left a number of his tired mounts to be cared for until the return from his visit to the Jumanos.[19] Chief Sofa (Sofais), who had guided Vial to Santa Fé and who had gone to San Antonio with Mares, now accompanied the party to the Jumano villages (Taovayas).[20] During the next five days they went north fourteen leagues, then east for almost the same distance, then south for thirteen leagues and again turning east, crossed the Red River and arrived at the first of the Jumano or Taovaya pueblos on the Red River, north of modern Spanish Fort and in the vicinity of Grady and Belleville in Oklahoma. The Indians seemed pleased at the visit and inquired what was the occasion of their coming. Fernández explained they had come to see them, and to accompany the explorer, Pedro Vial, on his way to Natchitoches.

The first pueblo had seventeen houses, made of straw or grass. The other two pueblos, Fernández estimated, were approximately of the same size. The river flowed near by and separated two of them from the other.

---

[18]Fragoso, *op. cit.*, entry for July 9. *Cf.* Fernández, *Derrotero, diario y calendario*, entry for July 9.

[19]Fernández, *Derrotero, diario y calendario* . . ., entry for July 15. *Cf.* Fragoso, *Derrotero, diario y Calculación*, for same date and July 16.

[20]Fernández consistently called them Jumanos, but Fragoso, who kept the diary for Vial and who knew the Indians well, clearly stated that they went to visit the Taovaya pueblos. See Fragoso, *Derrotero*, entry for July 20.

They were located about one-half league apart. The Indians cultivated the land and had irrigated farms on which they raised corn, beans, watermelons, and pumpkins. Both Fernández and Vial stayed in the villages until July 24, when the captain took leave of Vial and, guided by Sofais, departed for New Mexico.[21]

Return route of Fernández to Santa Fe. Before continuing east to Natchitoches and hence to San Antonio, let us follow Fernández on his return trip. Guided by Chief Sofais, the little cavalry troop set out due west from the pueblos of the Taovayas by a more direct route than the one previously followed. They went seven leagues, probably to the vicinity of Fleetwood, then turned due north for twelve leagues, and on July 26 turned west and arrived at the Comanche *rancherías* at or near the point where Beaver Creek enters the Red River near present Ryan. It was at this *ranchería* that Fernández and his men had left their tired horses. He returned the animals lent him and took those he had left on his march east. On July 28 the journey was resumed. Fernández and his men followed a westward course with a slight inclination to the north, keeping generally close to the Red River. He must have crossed the Wichita above Witchita Falls, and, retracing in part the route followed before, passed by or near Electra, Vernon, and Childress to arrive at Estelline, or in its vicinity. Here he began following Prairie Dog Town Fork through Palo Duro Canyon to the site of modern Canyon, and going across the plains, he made his way to the Comanche *rancherías* in the vicinity of Tucumcari. Following the well-established route, he now continued to the Gallinas River which he crossed near Chapelle, hence to the old pueblo of Pecos, then to Santa Fé, where he arrived August 17, 1788. He had made the return trip in twenty-four days. According to his diary, he travelled 255 leagues on the way out to the Jumano pueblos, or approximately 637 miles. On his return trip, by following a more direct course, he covered 243 leagues, or about 610 miles, making a total of approximately 1,250 miles in all.[22]

Vial's route from Los Jumanos to Natchitoches. But let us return to Vial who remained in the pueblos of the Taovayas. On July 25 he set

---

[21]Fernández, *Derrotero, diario y calendario*, entry for July 20-23, and Fragoso, *Derrotero, diario y calculación*, same dates.

[22]Fernández, *Derrotero, diario y calendario. A. G. M., Historia*, Vol. 43. It should be noted that while the diary ends with the entry for August 17, 1788, it was signed and dated by him on December 17. Perhaps the latter date indicates the time when he made his report to the governor and when he turned over the diary to this official.

out and travelled eastward only about three miles. During the next three days he proceeded south for a short distance and then almost due east. On July 30 shortly after entering the timber belt, known to Vial and the Spaniards as Monte Grande, he camped all day. He had made about twenty leagues, or approximately fifty miles, from the pueblos of the Taovayas.

He was now at or near Gainesville. This assumption is confirmed by the fact that the next day, July 31, after turning east, he crossed a small stream which ran south and which he was told was the Trinity.[23] It was the headwaters of Elm Creek which rises almost due north of Gainesville, and flows through the eastern section of that city today. Changing his course to the southeast, he kept steadily in this direction, first through a heavy wood, then over wide plains, until August 6, when he came to another heavily timbered area which he called the Natchitoches Woods. He halted and camped on a small stream. He had travelled thirty-three leagues, or seventy-five miles. This would place him at or near present Greenville. The stream on which he camped was probably modern Cowleech Fork which forms part of the headwaters of the Sabine River. Vial called the stream San Diego. The woods, Vial noted, were chiefly cedar, pecan, oak, and sabine.

Vial turned due south at this point and, after going eight leagues, camped the second day on a lake which he called Whetstone, and on August 9 came to the Sabine River, a few miles east of Terrell, having noted alligators in the shallow lakes and marshes just above this area. Here he changed his course again; and proceeding southeast, he arrived on August 12 at the pueblo of the Nadacos. He had travelled about twenty-five leagues, or approximately sixty-two miles. Given the direction of his march and the distance covered, the pueblo reached by Vial probably was in or near present Winona near the Sabine. The pueblo consisted of some fourteen or fifteen houses, rather large, and made of grass.[24] The next two days he continued almost due east, with a slight inclination to the south, and on August arrived at one of the ranches of the Bidais, located about twenty miles from the Nadacos, probably in the vicinity of Gladewater. During the next two days Vial passed by two ranches owned by Frenchmen, Atanacio and Cadelafita. Might this be a relative of the notorious Lafitte of later times? Vial enjoyed the hospitality of the latter and stayed for two days. On August 19 he continued southeast

---

[23]Vial, *Derrotero, diario y calculación*, entries for July 29-31.
[24]*Ibid.*, entry for August 12.

and halted at a ranch owned by an Englishman. This was probably in the vicinity of modern Logansport, or perhaps Mansfield, Louisiana. "We could not understand his conversation, nor could he understand ours, but he treated us with generous hospitality," wrote Fragoso in his diary.[25] The next day Vial and his companion arrived in Natchitoches.

Description of Natchitoches by Vial. The fort and town were located in a pleasant but not too extensive valley, and formed an imposing settlement with a population estimated by Fragoso and Vial to be three thousand souls. The settlers were mostly French, although there was a goodly intermixture of English. There were many negroes, the majority of whom were slaves; a few were free and owned property. The houses, built of timber, were large and revealed good taste. They flanked both banks of the river which flowed through the town. On its broad and deep waters were many canoes and boats of different kinds used by the inhabitants in going to New Orleans and in trading with the settlers and the natives up and down the river. The commander of the fort was Louis Blanc, to whom Vial and Fragoso delivered their dispatches and the report of the trip from Santa Fé. He welcomed them with characteristic French hospitality, gave them lodgings, and looked after all their wants during the next ten days.[26]

Route from Natchitoches to San Antonio. On August 30 Vial and his companions bade farewell to the commander of Natchitoches and set out westward for the Province of Texas. After going a short distance, they inclined a quarter south and continuing in this direction through woods and rolling country, crossed the Sabine on September 1, probably near present Isla, not far from Milam, and camped that night at a place called Patrón which, according to the diarist, was a well-known landmark. They had travelled approximately fifty miles from Natchitoches. If they passed by the old site of Los Adaes no mention of the fact was made.

After crossing the Sabine, they followed an almost due west course, passing on September 2 a ranch called Lobanillo, where they found several Spaniards from Nacogdoches who had settled there. This was the site of Gil Ibarbo's ranch. They crossed a stream called Río de los Ais, evidently Ayish Bayou, and camped on another ranch called Atoyaque, probably in modern Attoyac. The route followed must have taken them by San Augustine. On September 3 they passed by Atascoso ranch,

---

[25]*Ibid.*, entry for August 19.

[26]Fragoso, *Derretero, diario y calculación* . . ., entry for August 20-30, 1788.

probably at Tuscosso Creek, where they found some Spaniards from Nacogdoches had settled. This old ranch was probably a mile or two west of present Swift. At sundown they arrived in Nacogdoches.

Description of Nacogdoches. The town was located in the middle of a wood of various kinds of trees and consisted of eighty or ninety houses, mostly of timber. The population was made up of Spaniards and Frenchmen, some two hundred fifty persons. Here Vial and his companions were welcomed by Lieutenant-governor Gil Ibarbo. Either because of their fatigue or their journey through the woods and swamps, the party was stricken with chills and fever. All but Vial were confined to bed, and it was not until October 23 that they were sufficiently recovered to make preparations to continue their journey.[27]

From Nacogdoches to the Brazos. On October 24 the party resumed their westward march and by October 26 had crossed the Neches and halted at San Pedro. This was probably on the creek of this name at or near modern Weches. They identified Loco Creek which they crossed almost at the point where it flows into the Angelina. Continuing southwest from Weches and after travelling fifteen leagues, or some thirty-five miles, they camped on October 28 at the old site of the Bucareli settlement just south or west of the Trinity River. This probably was a few miles north of Midway and just south of Lucy Womack State Park in Madison County.[28]

From old Bucareli they went west possibly to present Madisonville and then turned south for almost forty or fifty miles before reaching a place which significantly enough they called Corpus Christi, probably where De León and Massanet celebrated this feast a hundred years before. This was at or near Navasota. About fifteen miles beyond, he crossed the Bayou on November 1, in the vicinity of Clay. Five days later, on November 6, after going some seventy miles in a general southwestern direction, he crossed the Colorado at or near La Grange. He observed that he was off his regular route. Turning slightly more to the west for some fifty miles, he came to the Guadalupe in the vicinity of Gonzalez. On his way to San Antonio, he passed three ranches, El Carrizo, Ratón, and Chayopines. He arrived at his destination on November 18.

---

[27] *Ibid.*, entry for September 23-24.

[28] Bolton has placed the location of Bucareli in Madison County at the old Robbins' Ferry. *Cf.* Bolton, *Texas in the Middle Eighteenth Century,* 406.

Description of San Antonio. Vial and his companions were received by Governor Martínez Pacheco. The presidio, wrote Fragoso, was located in the middle of the Villa de San Fernando. There were some seven hundred persons living in the Villa. The houses were for the most part of wood, but there were a few of stone and mortar, built with taste. Along the river they noticed there were five missions. The stream had its source in a spring about half a league to the north of the Villa.

Soon after their arrival, the entire party again fell sick with chills and fever and were in a serious condition until February, 1789. Although out of danger after this date, they felt too weak to continue to Santa Fe. By June they were finally ready to complete the last lap of their journey.[29]

Vial's return trip to Santa Fe. Guided by four Comanches, Fragoso left on June 25 for the headwaters of the San Antonio. Vial stayed in San Fernando conferring with the governor. Following the same route Mares had taken, Fragoso crossed the Guadalupe near Spring Branch on June 25, and waited the next day for Vial who, with a corporal and eight soldiers, joined him. These were to escort the explorers as far as the Colorado. Together they now continued along the same route of Mares to the Pedernales which they crossed near Hye, but here they inclined slightly to the east and came to the Colorado a few miles south of Kingsland. Vial noted that at the crossing the river was deep but narrow. They followed the river north along its eastern bank and at the end of the day the corporal and his soldiers left Vial and Fragoso with their Comanche guides to continue their journey.[30]

For sixteen leagues they followed the Colorado closely, going almost due north, but in the vicinity of Bend, because the river turns more to the west, they abandoned the river route and struck due north for twenty-three leagues, until July 13, when they came upon a band of young Comanche braves who were on the warpath against the Apaches. One of the four guides could not resist the temptation to join the warriors. From the distance and direction of travel it probably was in the vicinity of Comanche and Dublin. Continuing north, they came upon a *ranchería* which Fragoso called Jumanos. This was eighteen leagues from their last stop and probably was near Stephenville. Still going north, perhaps

---

[29]Fragoso, *Derrotero, diario y calculación* . . ., entries for November 18-June 25, 1789. The copy of this diary in the Texas Land Office omits this description, as well as those of Nacogdoches and Natchitoches.

[30]*Ibid.,* entries June 25-July 5.

slightly east, they recognized the Brazos which they crossed not far from Mineral Wells.

Here he began following the Brazos upstream to the vicinity of Graham, and continued to or near Seymour. He remarked on the saltiness of the stream which was no other than Salt Fork. He changed direction to the northwest to the Wichita River, finally reaching Pease River which he confused with the Red. He now made his way to the Blanco River in New Mexico, where he camped on August 5, 1789, on the same spot as before. He continued along the well-established route to Santa Fe by way of Chapelle and Pecos pueblo for eighty leagues, and arrived at home on August 20.

With Fragoso and his guides, Vial had accomplished a remarkable exploration without the loss of a single man. He had travelled 361 leagues from Santa Fe to Natchitoches, 51 to Nacogdoches, 154 to San Antonio, and 348 back to Santa Fe to complete the circle, a total of 914 leagues, or approximately 2,295 miles.[31] He had visited many Indian pueblos in the vast area explored; he had found everywhere an abundance of wild game, fruits, and nuts; he had made an accurate map[32] of the road to Natchitoches; and he had followed a route that was probably the shortest and most practical in connecting all these points. The route was, in fact, followed subsequently. These expeditions of Vial, Mares, Fernández, and Fragoso are significant not only because they blazed the way, but also because they afford us detailed geographic and ethnological information. They reveal the general distribution of Indian tribes in Texas at the close of the eighteenth century, the relations existing among them, and their habits and customs. The dangers braved by these explorers are comparable to those of Lewis and Clark, and the fund of information obtained is no less important. They prepared in great part the way for future penetrations of the vast area between the remote Provinces of New Mexico and Texas and the no less remote fringes of Spanish dominions in the hitherto unexplored regions of the north and east.

---

[31]*Ibid.*, July 28-August 20.

[32]Bolton, *op. cit.*, reproduces the map opposite p. 126.

CHAPTER VI

PREPARING TO WEATHER THE STORM, 1790-1800

With communication established between distant Santa Fe, St. Louis, Natchez, Natchitoches, Nacogdoches, and San Antonio, Spanish officials turned their attention to other measures of defence. The new policy—appeasement of the native tribes at all costs—discussed in a previous chapter,[1] revealed the urgency of strengthening Spain's weak hold on her far-flung northern frontier against the impact of the American pioneer. Texas assumed an importance not equalled by any of the Interior Provinces in the approaching struggle for supremacy. The necessity of connecting Texas with Louisiana, as well as with the other provinces of New Spain, by stronger economic ties, occupied the attention of officials in the closing years of the century. This interest, in addition to the growing pressure of the English and the Americans upon Louisiana, and the instability of ancient monarchies in Europe resulting from the profound changes brought about by the advance of the French Revolution, combined to arouse the Spaniards in the Interior Provinces to desperate efforts to prepare against the approaching storm.

The question of the Louisiana frontier. The boundary between Texas and Louisiana had never been clearly defined prior to the unsolicited cession of the French province. Subsequent to its acquisition, the boundary ceased for a few years to be a matter of great importance, but gained considerably in significance towards the last decade of the eighteenth century. In February, 1790, the viceroy had recommended that a careful exploration of the coast line from San Bernardo Bay to the mouth of the Mississippi be undertaken, and that a commission be appointed to determine the boundary between the two provinces. The purpose was to extend the limits of Louisiana to the Sabine River, and to open a port on the Texas coast for trade. The king, who was deeply interested in the encouragement of trade as a source of royal revenue, readily assented and issued orders for the recommendation to be carried out. But Viceroy Revillagigedo replied in April, 1791, that he had suspended the execution of the order to acquaint His Majesty with the facts involved. He explained that the undertaking would require that commissioners be sent

---

[1]See Chapter IV.

from Mexico to distant Natchitoches, a post that was more than five hundred leagues away; he added that the character of the country was such that all supplies needed by the commission would have to be shipped over that distance; and that, under the circumstances, it would probably cost more than ten thousand *pesos*.[2]

The thoroughness of the investigation planned may be deduced from the set of instructions submitted by the viceroy. The commissioner and his assistant, accompanied by an adequate escort, were to proceed by way of San Luis Potosí to Saltillo, and thence to Monclova. The soldiers from Saltillo were to return to their post, for they were to be replaced by a similar escort from each successive post visited. The itinerary to be followed was to take them first to San Antonio, hence to La Bahía, the Trinity, Nacogdoches, the Sabine, and Natchitoches. They were to keep a careful diary from the day they left Saltillo, noting the distances between places, the direction of travel, the state of the missions visited, the number and condition of the ranches and *haciendas,* the state of the presidios and their garrisons, the development of the civil settlements, and the nature of the agricultural and grazing areas, indicating how these could be improved. This information was to be forwarded from each of the principal points visited.

While in La Bahía the commission was to make a careful survey of San Bernardo Bay and the adjacent islands, the home lands of the Karankawas and other coastal Indians. They were to observe carefully the number, the customs, and general character of the various natives. The findings of the explorations were to be set down on maps and drawings to show the location of the islands, the presidios, the missions, and the chief physical characteristics of the country between San Antonio and La Bahía.

From La Bahía the commission was to go overland to the Trinity River by the lower road and follow that stream to its mouth, where a similar reconnaissance of the coast was to be conducted. A special report was to be made on the port that had been discovered and named Galvestown by José Antonio Evia.

After making similar notations on Nacogdoches, they were to explore the course of the Sabine River and the location of the abandoned site of Los Adaes; they were, likewise, to determine the distance between that old post and Natchitoches, and report on the character of the

---

[2]Viceroy Revillagigedo to Antonio Porlier, April 27, 1791. *A. G. I., Audiencia de México,* 89-6-14 (Dunn Transcripts, 1787-1791, pp. 178-181).

Tawakonis, the Taovayas, and all the Indian tribes along Red River, making maps and drawings of all places visited.[3] The expenditure involved in executing the order, however, so discouraged the king that the formal exploration was abandoned for the time being.

But interest continued in the question of opening trade between the two provinces and in the extension of the limits of Louisiana. Late in 1792, Diego de Gardoqui, Secretary of the King, again requested the opinion of Revillagigedo on the subject. The viceroy replied in April, 1793, that the original suggestion had been made by the Caballero de Croix and taken up by Viceroy Gálvez. In the opinion of Revillagigedo, the plan for trade and closer relations between the Interior Provinces and Louisiana was impractical. The extension of the boundary he considered a domestic problem. He reminded the king, however, that if the plan was to be carried out, it should be preceded by a careful survey—such as he had suggested before. In view of his subsequent experience, he now believed that communication and trade between Texas and Louisiana should not be encouraged, but rather discouraged and perhaps prohibited altogether. He suspected officials and private individuals in Texas were anxious for such trade because they anticipated great profits, largely from smuggling. He now recommended, therefore, that all communication between the two provinces be suspended; that neither transients nor settlers be allowed to enter Texas; and that, in order to make the new restrictions effective, Nacogdoches be abandoned. This post, in his opinion, served merely as a half-way station for intruders, smugglers, and other undesirables. If the settlement was to be maintained, a strong garrison should be stationed there, adequate to make the authority of Spain respected, to check invasion, to stop illegal traffic, and to give timely warning in case of serious danger.[4] In view of the circumstances, the king gave up the idea of the survey. He decided to maintain the existing relations between the two provinces. The proposed garrison at Nacogdoches was out of the question because of the expense involved.[5]

Illicit trade and the attempted removal of Ibarbo. Ever since the reoccupation of Nacogdoches, Gil Ibarbo had been suspected of ulterior motives. Both he and Governor Ripperdá had been charged with smuggling. The suspicion persisted. Anxious to ascertain the true state of

---

[3]Instrucciones para los comisionados. *Ibid.*, pp. 182-187.

[4]Revillagigedo to Diego Gardoqui, April 30, 1793. *A. G. I., Audiencia de México*, 96-2-12 (Dunn Transcripts, 1787-1791, pp. 48-53).

[5]The King to Viceroy Revillagigedo, September 21, 1793. *Ibid.*, p. 54.

affairs and to put an end to all trade with Louisiana, the viceroy requested Juan Ugalde to order the governor to institute a secret investigation. Martínez Pacheco, governor *ad interim*, explained that, although he was convinced of the guilt of Ibarbo, he dared not carry out the instructions at this time because of the many friends of the commander of Nacogdoches and the fear that the investigation might incite the Indians to rebellion.[6] The influence of Ibarbo over the natives had been recognized by Ripperdá and Croix before. Martínez Pacheco suggested a more diplomatic way of removing the enterprising pioneer. He could be summoned for a personal interview and not be permitted to return. But Ugalde, experienced in the ways of the frontier and the character of the natives, decided to postpone the investigation until he could attend to the matter in person.[7]

The *fiscal*, however, unacquainted with conditions in distant Nacogdoches, urged that formal judicial proceedings be instituted without delay. Equally unacquainted with the antecedents of Ibarbo, he raised the perennial questions of who had appointed him lieutenant-governor, how much salary he was receiving, how long he had been residing in Nacogdoches, and how much property he owned.[8] The facts are that it was Governor Cabello who first referred to Ibarbo as "Captain of Militia and Lieutenant-governor of Nacogdoches" in a letter to Croix late in December, 1779, and who notified Ibarbo on March 11, 1780, that a salary of five hundred *pesos* had been assigned to him.[9] When informed of the circumstances, the *fiscal* recommended that the new governor, Don Manuel Muñoz, an officer of known integrity, be instructed to undertake the secret investigation.[10]

The new viceroy, acting upon the recommendations of the *fiscal* and the reports of Ugalde, instructed Governor Muñoz to investigate secretly the charges against Ibarbo and to report his opinion on the advisability of maintaining Nacogdoches. Ugalde, who seems to have conceived a deep hatred for Ibarbo, had charged that he was incapable as an administrator, that he engaged in illicit trade and was responsible for the

---

[6]Rafael Martínez Pacheco to Juan Ugalde, March 9, 1789. *A. G. M., Historia,* Vol. 93, pp. 34-35.

[7]Juan Ugalde to Manuel Flores, April 18, 1789. *Ibid.,* pp. 35-37.

[8]Dictamen Fiscal, May 28, 1789. *A. G. M., Historia,* Vol. 93, p. 39.

[9]Domingo Cabello to Teodoro de Croix, December 17, 1799; Cabello to Gil Ibarbo, March 11, 1780. *Béxar Archives.* Ibarbo presented a copy of the letter shortly after this inquiry as proof of his official appointment.

[10]Dictamen Fiscal, November 22, 1790. *A. G. M., Historia,* Vol. 93, pp. 46-47.

constant sale of cattle and horses in the Province of Louisiana; that he maintained relations with unauthorized French and English traders; and, lastly, that he was a mulatto.[11] Muñoz sent a certain Gaspar de Verazady to Nacogdoches with a permit to purchase buffalo hides and tongues, but with secret instructions to investigate the activities of Ibarbo. Muñoz wrote the viceroy that he would later go in person to institute formal proceedings against Ibarbo if the evidence justified the action. He explained that Nacogdoches was about one hundred fifty leagues from San Antonio and that the natives in East Texas appeared to have secured arms and ammunition at that post contrary to existing regulations, but from San Antonio it was impossible to stop this illicit traffic.[12]

Before the investigation proceeded further, Revillagigedo instructed the governor to suspend all action until Ramón Castro, the recently appointed commander of the Eastern Interior Provinces, took charge. Muñoz was to report the findings of Verazady to Castro before continuing with the investigation.[13] The repeated investigations of the illicit trade at Nacogdoches had convinced officials of the necessity of taking radical measures. Here are to be found the reasons for the recommendations of Revillagigedo that Nacogdoches be either abandoned or reënforced.

Extent of Nacogdoches jurisdiction. The zeal of Father Bernardino Vallejo, veteran missionary, reveals the extent of French and English infiltration and of the jurisdiction of Nacogdoches in 1797. In February of this year, he complained to José María Guadiana, the commander of the garrison, that ever since his arrival over a year ago, he had experienced considerable difficulty in making the settlers living east of the Sabine River comply with their religious duties. When asked why they did not come to Nacogdoches, they replied that they were in the jurisdiction of Natchitoches, Province of Louisiana. With the approach of Lent, Father Vallejo was anxious to secure an official list of the residents within the jurisdiction of Nacogdoches who were living east of the Sabine in order to get them to make their Easter duty. He pointed out that most of them were French, but that among them were several English settlers who he strongly suspected were not Catholics, and had

---

[11]Revillagigedo to Muñoz, December 10, 1790. *A. G. M., Historia*, Vol. 93, pp. 51-53.

[12]Manuel Muñoz to Revillagigedo, March 10, 1791. *Ibid.*, pp. 56-58.

[13]Revillagigedo to Muñoz, April 13, 1791. *Ibid.*, pp. 59-60.

entered the province without permission. It was important, the friar declared, to determine their status and religion.[14]

Guadiana promptly furnished him a list of persons living east of the Sabine River, explaining that he had prepared it with the aid of the oldest settlers of the abandoned post of Los Adaes, who had assured him that the jurisdiction of Nacogdoches extended to the old limits of Los Adaes. He asked the *Padre* to make further inquiries from officials in San Antonio concerning this matter, as he was anxious to know if the actual limits between the two provinces had been defined. He hoped Vallejo would check the list and urge the settlers to perform their Easter duty as all subjects of His Catholic Majesty were expected to.[15] The list included Pablo Lafitte and Andrés Valentín, on Arroyo Piedras; José Gaviña, on Llano de las Cebollas; Pedro Dolet and Antonio Dubois, on Arroyo Cristal; Francisco Prudhome, in the Adaes Pueblo; Francisco Morban, on Arroyo Durazno; the widow Tutin, on Arroyo Tepalcate; Manuel Prudhome and Morfil, on Arroyo Hondo; Rouguier, on Adaes Lake; Francisco Rouguier, on Laguna Purita; José Piernas, on the ranch of Santa María de Adelaida; and Sam, the Englishman, on Arroyo de San Francisco.[16] While the list is evidently not complete, judging from the statement of Father Vallejo, still it is of interest. Guadiana inquired from Governor Muñoz concerning the boundary between Texas and Louisiana, but the governor failed to answer, for there was no definition in the archives of San Antonio.[17]

Before the end of the year the assistant of Father Vallejo suffered a nervous breakdown. Father Pedro Portugal appears to have become deranged on May 7. He was kept under surveillance for a day or two, but finding his condition did not improve, Father Vallejo decided it would be best to send him to San José. Guadiana furnished an escort of five soldiers and a corporal, and Father Vallejo appointed José de la Vega, notary public, to look after the sick missionary while on the road.[18]

Reënforcement and improvements at La Bahía. Turning to La Bahía, we find that, as a result of the recommendations of Ugalde, a determined

---

[14]Bernardino Vallejo to José María Guadiana, February 20, 1797. *Béxar Archives*.

[15]José María Guadiana to Bernardino Vallejo, February 26, 1797. *Béxar Archives*.

[16]Relación de los Ranchos y Habitantes pertenecientes a esta Jurisdicción de Nacogdoches que se Hallan Situados en la Parte Oriental del R. de Sabinas, February 26, 1797. *Béxar Archives*.

[17]Guadiana to Muñoz, February 28, 1797. *Béxar Archives*.

[18]Guadiana to Muñoz, May 9, 1797. *Béxar Archives*.

effort to improve the fortifications of this outpost on the Gulf coast was made. When Revillagigedo assumed his duties as viceroy, he gave serious consideration to many of the suggestions made by the able frontier commander of the Interior Provinces. He, consequently, requested Muñoz to make a formal report on the practicability of irrigating the lands in the vicinity of La Bahía, the cost of such an improvement, and an estimate of the repairs needed to put the presidio in condition to withstand attack.[19]

Report of Pedro Huizar.   The governor appointed Pedro Huizar to go to La Bahía to make a careful study of the needs of the presidio and the possibility and cost of irrigating the lands at the post, or in its vicinity. It seems that Angel Anglino and Francisco Araujo, an engineer, had previously made a survey and had recommended the digging of an irrigation ditch at several locations. Huizar proceeded to investigate the places designated, and carefully explored and surveyed the sites suggested on Garcitas Creek, Palitos Blancos, Islitas, Mission Rosario, and Babillas. He reported to the governor that the missionaries of Mission Espíritu Santo had attempted to dig an irrigation ditch at Garcitas, but had been forced to abandon it as impractical. A similar attempt had been made at Babillas Creek, where he examined the remains of the dam that had been attempted and some old wells dug for the same purpose. He estimated that the cost of completing the dam would be prohibitive and concluded that the character of the stream and the sandy soil made the project impossible. The San Antonio River at La Bahía flowed three and one-half *varas* below its banks; the general character of the surrounding country was sandy and the water of the river not abundant. These factors made irrigation at this point equally impractical. The suggestion of Araujo for the construction of an aqueduct to supply La Bahía with water from Palitos Blancos was not feasible, according to Huizar.[20]

Needs of the presidio.   At about the same time, Manuel Espadas, the commander *ad interim* of the Presidio of Nuestra Señora del Pilar, made a detailed report on the condition of the post and its needs. In his opinion the presidio should be completely rebuilt of limestone. This material was available a short distance from La Bahía. The stone, too,

---

[19]Revillagigedo to Muñoz, December 10, 1790. *A. G. M., Historia,* Vol. 93, p. 48.

[20]Pedro de Huizar to Manuel Muñoz, March 4, 1791. *A. G. M., Historia,* Vol. 93, pp. 65-66. Transmitted by Muñoz to the viceroy on March 26. *Ibid.,* p. 67.

could be converted into the lime necessary for the mortar. White sand, though not of the best quality, could also be obtained in the vicinity, and there was an abundance of cedar wood which would make excellent beams and rafters. All the water needed for the use of the garrison, as well as such as might be needed in the construction of a new presidio, had to be brought in carts or barrels rolled up the bank by the men. The soldiers could help with the work of construction but they knew nothing about masonry. There were no tools, such as crowbars, hatchets, trowels, and other implements needed for construction work. But most of these could be made by the blacksmith if he was provided with the iron. He concluded by pointing out that the materials required for the reconstruction of the presidio were available, that the garrison could furnish the unskilled labor, but that artisans would have to be brought, and that only a few minor materials, such as iron, would have to be secured abroad. He estimated that the cost of the labor and supplies needed to rebuild the presidio would probably be about twenty-five hundred *pesos*.[21] This report and that of Huizar were sent by Muñoz to the viceroy for his information.

When the viceroy consulted Ramón Castro, the recently appointed commander of the Eastern Interior Provinces, he replied that in spite of the difficulties pointed out by Huizar and the expense of the undertaking, the irrigation project for La Bahía should be attempted. Castro deemed the project essential for the development and welfare of the settlement and the presidio at La Bahía. Only in this way could crops be assured. He fully agreed with the opinion that the enterprise would require a considerable outlay by the royal treasury, but he believed it would be a wise investment.

With regard to the presidio, he was even more emphatic. He pointed out that La Bahía was more than fifty leagues from San Antonio, that it was the only outpost for the entire Gulf coast from the mouth of the Río Grande to the Mississippi, and that, as such, it should be reënforced. The present presidio was on a high bluff, about a cannon-shot's distance from the San Antonio River, and dominating the surrounding country. But the building had been poorly planned and constructed. The cannons were placed at the corners of the quadrangle. Unwittingly, however, the soldiers and settlers had subsequently built their houses outside the

---

[21]Manuel de Espadas to Muñoz, March 10, 1791. *A. G. M., Historia*, Vol. 93, pp. 61-62. Also Calculo prudencial que forma el Comdte. Into. de la Bahía de Esptu. Santo, Don Manuel Espadas. *Ibid.*, p. 62.

quadrangular wall and directly in the line of fire. If attacked, the defenders would have to fire across the outlying buildings, and thereby cause considerable damage to their own property and that of the settlers. The present wall, moreover, had been so poorly constructed that it was now in ruins. He suggested, therefore, that a larger enclosure be built of solid rock, and that all the settlers and families be ordered to build their homes within the new walls. The expense of reconstruction would be more than offset by the savings in the cost of frequent repairs that were now required at relatively short intervals. Furthermore, if rebuilt along the lines proposed, it would afford greater protection and security to the settlers and be in condition to repel attacks. He warned that the latter possibility was not so remote as might be thought. The estimate of Captain Espadas was reasonable and the oxen needed for hauling the required materials could be secured in San Antonio. The carts could be built in La Bahía at royal expense.[22]

Fiscal Posada approved the recommendations of the commandant general and declared that the estimate of the expense involved was not excessive. The viceroy submitted the question of the reconstruction of the presidio and the building of an irrigation system to the *Junta Superior de Hacienda* (Superior Finance Council), which rendered a report on July 13, 1792. The *Junta* was of the opinion that the irrigation project was not practical, but it approved the reconstruction of the presidio, and authorized the expenditure of the twenty-five hundred *pesos* as suggested by Espadas and Castro. Revillagigedo issued the necessary order on November 1, instructing Governor Muñoz to draw on the intendent of San Luis Potosí for the amount authorized by the *Junta*. If this appropriation was found inadequate to complete the work, the governor was to submit for approval the additional needs. He was requested to keep an accurate account of all expenses incurred for the undertaking.[23]

Cannons at La Bahía and Nacogdoches. Captain Juan Cortés reported in January, 1795, that there were eight cannons at La Bahía, twelve and sixteen-pounders, all of which were well mounted and in good condition. Unfortunately, however, there was not a single soldier in the garrison who

---

[22]Ramón de Castro to Viceroy Revillagigedo, May 15, 1792. *A. G. M., Historia,* Vol. 93, pp. 71-79.

[23]Dictamen del Fiscal Posada, June 26, 1792; Junta Superior de Real Hacienda, July 13, 1792; Auto del Virrey, November 1, 1792. *A. G. M., Historia,* Vol. 93, pp. 80-85.

knew how to use them. He requested that experienced artillerymen be sent to man the guns and to train the rest of the garrison in this science. During his recent visit to Nacogdoches he had observed that the cannons at that post were lying on the ground and that there were no gun carriages or emplàcements. Near the crossing of the Trinity, he had seen, minus their carriages, two brass cannons which had been abandoned by Gil Ibarbo. These had been taken to La Bahía as ordered by the governor. In May he reported that *Alférez* Cadena had brought back three more brass cannons from the Trinity. These had also belonged to the settlement of Pilar before it was moved to Nacogdoches.[24]

Cortés made a strange request. Pointing out that the church at La Bahía needed a bell, he asked permission to melt the brass cannons to cast bells. The permission was not granted.

A glimpse at conditions in La Bahía is given in a letter of 1797. The commander declared that the settlement was perhaps the poorest in the whole province. The settlers were still totally dependent on the weather for their crops. The chief crop was corn. The daily wages were three *reales* (about 36 cents). The church needed a new roof. At great sacrifice the settlers had patiently gathered the necessary materials, and work had been started. But the citizens desired the governor to give them two new bells. He suggested that two be taken from the abandoned Mission of Nuestra Señora de la Concepción. The two bells at La Bahía were not only too small, but also cracked. He pleaded in the name of charity and out of regard for the sacredness of religion that the request be granted.[25] The petition, which was sent to Nava, was transmitted by the commandant general to Muñoz with recommendations to try to get the bells from the president of the missions in San Antonio.

Commanders at La Bahía. Early in 1797, Juan Bautista Elguezábal was sent to Texas by Nava to investigate conditions at La Bahía. In checking the accounts of the presidial troops, he found that the former commander, Manuel Espadas, had left unpaid an account of four hundred *pesos* due Mission Espíritu Santo. Captain Cortés was asked to retire to San Antonio while the investigation of his administration was being conducted. Cortés retired to Mission San Juan on May 18, 1797, and was replaced in command by Bernardo Fernández, who was appointed by Nava on April 9, but did not arrive at La Bahía until May 27.

[24]Juan Cortés to Manuel Muñoz, January 16, 1795; same to same, May 8, 1795. *Béxar Archives.*

[25]Juan Cortés to Pedro Nava, March 11, 1797. *Béxar Archives.*

Fernández remained in command until April, 1798, when he was replaced by José Miguel del Moral, former lieutenant in San Antonio. Elguezábal, who had carried on an extensive investigation, remained in La Bahía until he was ordered to conduct an inspection of the garrison at San Antonio.[26]

Nava had intended to appoint José Francisco Sosaya, of Coahuila, to the command of La Bahía, and did so in January, 1798, but the lack of experienced officers in Coahuila made him rescind the order in March and select Del Moral to take charge. Immediately after assuming command, Del Moral wrote Governor Muñoz that the wall of the presidio had been so torn apart by the soldiers that it needed to be rebuilt. He explained that work had already been started, and that in order to keep down the labor costs, he had promulgated an ordinance to the effect that all those found guilty of gambling would have to work out their fines by rebuilding the new wall.[27]

False alarm and the exploration of the coast. Shortly after his arrival, Del Moral was unduly alarmed when one day, at about eight in the evening, a messenger from Refugio brought news that foreigners had been observed on the coast. The deduction was that they were either shipwrecks or the advance guard of an invading force. As the repairs on the wall had not been completed, the presidio was in no condition to withstand attack. Del Moral reported the matter to the governor and frantically called for reënforcements. An investigation disclosed that either the rumor was false, or that, if foreigners had been seen, they had reëmbarked shortly afterwards.[28]

Still fearful of prowlers along the coast, Del Moral dispatched Sergeant Francisco Vázquez with eleven men to make a careful exploration of the bay and the surrounding islands. This expedition went down the San Antonio to its mouth, expecting to ask the natives if any foreigners had been seen recently in the bay. They probably reached the vicinity of present Tivoli. Here they found traces of an Indian camp recently abandoned. Vázquez and his companions concluded that the natives had

---

[26]Pedro Nava to Juan Bautista Elguezábal, April 21, 1797; Elguezábal to Nava, May 27, 1797; Elguezábal to Manuel Muñoz, May 28, 1797; Muñoz to Elguezábal, May 29, 1797; Nava to Muñoz, June 13, 1797. *Béxar Archives.*

[27]Pedro Nava to Manuel Muñoz, January 19, 1798; Nava to Muñoz, March 8, 1798; Juan Bautista Elguezábal to Muñoz, April 22, 1798; José Miguel del Moral to Muñoz, May 13, 1798. *Béxar Archives.*

[28]Del Moral to Muñoz, May 28, 1798. *Béxar Archives.*

gone over to the neighboring islands. They decided to give a smoke signal and wait, but no one came. The next day the party went to Paso del Vergantín, probably below Seadrift, where they observed tracks leading to the islands opposite the coast. Unable to cross without canoes, Vázquez and his companions returned to Mosquito Ranch, probably at or near Mission Bay, since they noted that it belonged to Mission Refugio. The following day they went to a point above the confluence of the Guadalupe and the San Antonio to investigate a smoke signal seen the previous day, and discovered that a group of Jaraname Indians from Mission Espíritu Santo were out on a hunt. Not even a trace of the foreigners was discovered, but the exploring party obtained evidence proving a party of Karankawas guilty of stealing fourteen horses and killing fifteen cows at the presidio on June 3, 1798.[29] Although the bay explored is referred to as San Bernardo, it is evident that it was San Antonio Bay.

The fears of Del Moral were again aroused in September, according to information received from Nava, when Muñoz warned him against the danger of foreign attack. He called upon the friendly Indians in the vicinity and offered them a liberal reward for information concerning any strangers along the entire coast from San Bernardo Bay (San Antonio Bay) to the mouth of the Trinity. At the same time he sent, as instructed, a detachment of seven men to reënforce the garrison at Nacogdoches. The walls of the presidio had been repaired and were in good condition, he declared, and he had an abundant supply of powder, besides five thousand cartridges.[30]

On September 15, Del Moral sent a sergeant and nine men to explore Matagorda Bay. Four Indians from Mission Rosario accompanied them as guides. The party was instructed to contact the friendly chiefs and offer them gifts for any information concerning strangers seen in the *rancherías,* or ships along the coast. Four days previously he had dispatched Chief Zertuche, a Coco from Mission Rosario, to reconnoiter the Colorado River. But this Indian was moody and not entirely dependable. The chief returned on September 27, but did not bother to make a report until he was summoned by the impatient commander. Father Garavito, it

---

[29]José Miguel del Moral to Manuel Muñoz, June 5, 1798; Diario de Francisco Vázquez, June 3-5, 1798. *Béxar Archives.*

[30]Del Moral to Muñoz, September 14, 1798.

will be recalled, held in low estimation the loyalty and character of this Indian, whom he referred to as the meanest Indian living.[31]

Captain Cortés had been alarmed three years before by similar fears of foreign prowlers along the coast. On August 27, 1795, he distinctly heard a cannon fired in the vicinity of Mission Rosario. He immediately dispatched Juan Chirino with twelve men to investigate the incident. They proceeded to San Antonio Bay, but could find no trace of intruders. Governor Muñoz, however, was as alarmed as Cortés, and on September 15, 1795, ordered Corporal José Manuel Granados to make a new reconnaissance of San Bernardo and Matagorda bays. Taking six men, Granados left immediately and marched as far as Salado Creek. The following day he reached La Tortuga, a ranch located in the vicinity of modern Nixon. Granados crossed the Guadalupe in the vicinity of Victoria on September 17, and the next day reached the coast at a place which he called Los Laureles (Oleanders), possibly near Port Lavaca. On September 18 he continued along the shore to what he called the Port of Matagorda, which may have been modern Port O'Connor or Magnolia Beach. Since the direction and distance travelled are not given, it is difficult to ascertain just where Granados was at this time.

In the vicinity of what he called the Port of Matagorda, which could also have been near present Seadrift, he met two Karankawa Indians and their families from the *ranchería* of Chief Frazada Pinta. When asked if they had heard cannon fire or seen any strange ships, they replied in the negative, and assured the visitors they had not seen strangers in their lands. Granados explored the coast to the north on September 20, but found no trace of foreign prowlers. He next explored the country to the west as far as what he called Laguna Verde (Green Lake), which may be the lake north of modern Mission Bay. There is a strong probability that it was, as in its vicinity the party met Chief Frazada Pinta and six of his warriors. They declared they had neither seen nor heard anything about strangers.

The fact that Granados and his companions marched back to the Guadalupe the next day confirms the opinion that they had been north of Mission Bay the day before. They probably reached the Guadalupe just below Victoria. The river was high and the party had to construct a barge to cross. This delayed them a day. On September 23 they resumed

---

[31]Manuel Muñoz to Del Moral, September 23, 1798; Del Moral to Muñoz, October 27, 1798. *Béxar Archives.*

their journey to San Antonio where they arrived on September 25, having sustained the loss of only one man.[32]

Indian hostilities at La Bahía. In the fall of 1795, a band of Comanches made a raid upon Espíritu Santo Mission. An investigation into the cause disclosed that the Comanches resented the aid given by the mission Indians to the Mescalero-Lipans. Governor Muñoz instructed Captain Cortés at La Bahía to warn Chiefs Canoso, Chiquito, and Moreno of the Karankawas, Cocos, and Orcoquisacs, that they must not harbor or give assistance to the Mescaleros in their *rancherías*. Should they persist in this practice, they would be deprived of gifts and the friendship of the Spaniards. Cortés transmitted the message through Antonio Cadena, Indian interpreter, who advised the chiefs to prove their loyalty to the Spaniards by arresting all Mescalero-Lipans who came to them for help or refuge. The chiefs solemnly agreed to follow the counsel.[33]

The visit of rival nations often caused difficulties. On July 12, 1797, a Comanche, Chief Soxas, and a Tawakoni, Chief Quiscat, son of the elder chief of this name, arrived in La Bahía, accompanied by one hundred eighteen warriors and six squaws. The next day Chief Zertuche and ten Indians from Missions Rosario and Refugio were on their way to the presidio when the Comanches and Tawakonis, mistaking them for Lipans dashed out to kill them. The presidio guards rushed to their rescue. After a brief scuffle they succeeded in restoring order and establishing the identity of the newcomers. The party then continued in peace to Mission Espíritu Santo.

But the following day a Lipan chief named Bautista, who was at the presidio with a group of followers, started for Espíritu Santo Mission and met four Tawakonis. Forgetful of the fact that both groups were guests of the Spaniards, the Lipans gave a blood-curdling yell and dashed upon their enemies; the Tawakonis fired upon the charging band, and Bautista's horse was killed.

The Jaranames in Mission Espíritu Santo, having heard the yell, rushed out and joined the fray. Shots flew thick and fast, but before any one was seriously wounded, the garrison had stopped the fight. The Tawakonis, Comanches, Lipans, and mission Indian chiefs were all invited to the presidio, a parley was held, the pipe was smoked, and the

---

[32]Diary of José Manuel Granados, September 15-25, 1795; Cortés to Muñoz, August 28, 1795. *Béxar Archives.*

[33]Governor Muñoz to Pedro Nava, November 8, 1795. *Béxar Archives.*

Comanches and Tawakonis swore to observe the peace with the mission Indians of Rosario and Espíritu Santo.

On July 15 Chiefs Soxas and Quiscat departed. The commander of the presidio furnished them an escort of a sergeant and five soldiers to accompany them as far as the Guadalupe. Before their destination was reached, all the Comanches and Tawakonis, with the exception of four, went on the warpath to hunt Apaches and Lipans. They assured the soldiers that they would not harm either the Spaniards or the mission Indians.[34]

Chief Quiscat aspired to be honored, as his father had been, by being appointed governor of his tribe. The Tawakonis of Chief Quiscat were influential allies of the Spaniards. When Nava heard of the visit to La Bahía and of the difficulties that had arisen, he recommended that Chief Quiscat, the younger, be treated with all consideration and his pride flattered in order to win his support. He suggested that Chief Quiscat, on his next visit, be presented with the baton (a silver cane) of an Indian governor, and that he be given four braided coats.[35]

But it was almost impossible to maintain peace among lifelong enemies who hated each other as much as the Lipan-Apaches hated the Comanches. A little more than a year later, three Tawakonis informed the commander of La Bahía that a party of Comanches was again on the warpath searching for Lipans. The Karankawas at Refugio and Rosario hated the Comanches as much as they hated the Lipans. They decided to go out to ambush the Comanches. The garrison immediately took steps to prevent the clash. To avoid a possible incident, the commander placed the Comanches in a house for safe-keeping during their visit to the presidio. On the night of September 12, 1798, a Karankawa Indian bored a hole through the wall of the house, and fired point-blank at the inmates, wounding two Comanches, one in the leg and another in the knee. The Comanches rushed out of the house to avenge the insult. A serious break was prevented when Chief Andrés agreed to turn over the guilty party. Next morning it was learned that the Indian who had attacked the unwelcome visitors was a Karankawa, whose brother had been killed in a raid by the Comanches. The barber dressed the wounds, the injured parties shook hands, smoked the peace pipe, and tranquillity was restored.[36]

---

[34]Juan Bautista Elguezábal to Manuel Muñoz, July 20, 1797. *Béxar Archives.*
[35]Nava to Muñoz, September 25, 1797. *Béxar Archives.*
[36]José Miguel del Moral to Manuel Muñoz, September 14, 1798. *Béxar Archives.*

On September 29 of the same year three soldiers were driving twenty-one head of cattle to Mission Espíritu Santo. As they approached the presidio in the dark, they were suddenly attacked by a group of Indians. One soldier was shot in the arm, but they succeeded in reaching the fort. The attackers were quickly dispersed by the garrison who rescued the cattle. An investigation disclosed that the Indians, estimated to number from forty to fifty men, were Karankawas from Mission Refugio. They had been granted permission on September 17 to go to the seashore. They explained that they had mistaken the soldiers for Comanches who, they thought, were driving their cattle away—a lame explanation at best. Nava, however, suspected the Comanches of having some connection with the attack and instructed Muñoz to impress upon the missionaries the need of preventing the Indians from leaving their missions. At the same time he gave orders for greater vigilance to be observed by the garrison at La Bahía.[37]

Chief Frazada Pinta was a constant source of irritation and trouble to the missionaries of Refugio and the commanders of the presidio at La Bahía.[38] In July, 1796, Captain Cortés reported that late one evening Chief Frazada Pinta had surprised a group of settlers, who had gone to the Guadalupe to cut wood, killed one, and carried off their horses. The party sent in pursuit followed his tracks to the coast and noted where he had crossed to the neighboring island of El Sombrero.[39]

José Miguel del Moral was seriously worried late in 1798 by rumors that the troublesome chief had entered into an alliance with the Orcoquisacs (Arkokisas) and that he was planning a series of extensive raids on the settlements. Aware of the fact that the wily chief maintained spies in the mission to keep informed, Captain Cortés publicly declared he would make ready for the attack. The stockade was repaired, the cannons were remounted, and the old fort bustled with preparations for defence.[40] The threat did not materialize.

In June, 1801, the new commander at La Bahía enthusiastically reported that at last Chief Frazada Pinta was willing to make peace. The governor went to the coast in hope of concluding a permanent agreement, but only a temporary truce resulted.[41]

---

[37]José Miguel del Moral to Muñoz, October 1, 1798; Muñoz to Del Moral, October 8, 1798; same to same, November 6, 1798. *Béxar Archives*.

[38]See pp. 82, 90, 106, 123.

[39]Juan Cortés to Manuel Muñoz, July 21, 1798. *Béxar Archives*.

[40]José del Moral to Muñoz, November 13, 1798. *Béxar Archives*.

[41]Nava to Governor of Texas, June 26, 1801. *Béxar Archives*.

That fall all the settlements in Texas were thrown into consternation by persistent rumors that the Comanches, the Tawakonis, and the Taovayas, urged by foreign agents, were holding meetings to plan the destruction of the Spaniards. The governor warned the commander of La Bahía and ordered him to double the vigilance against surprise, to move the garrison horses as near to the presidio as possible, and distribute ammunition and arms to the settlers and to the friendly Indians who could be counted upon to aid in repelling an attack. He was to report by special messenger any news.[42] There were good grounds for the alarm as will be seen in the subsequent chapters.

Mission Espíritu Santo and the Jaranames. The Mission of Espíritu Santo had been practically abandoned before 1790. Father Reyes had attempted to revive it in 1789. It was during the following year that Father Garza and Father Silva came. The former reported to Governor Muñoz in June, 1791, that a group of thirty-two Jaranames, former inmates of Mission Espíritu Santo, had told him that if he would go with them to the San Xavier River, ninety-seven more would return with him to join their former mission. Governor Muñoz immediately authorized Father Garza to go to the San Xavier River and furnished him an escort on June 29.

After a sojourn of almost a month, Father Garza left for La Bahía with fifty-eight apostate Jaranames who agreed to return to Mission Espíritu Santo. Fray Luis Mariano de Cárdenas, who was then in charge, welcomed the wayward neophytes with open arms and the mission obtained a new lease on life.[43] On March 1, 1794, Father Fray Juan José Aguilar was appointed to take charge of Espíritu Santo, but he was unable to leave Zacatecas until the 17th. It was not until early in April that he arrived at La Bahía. He was still caring for the mission at the end of 1797.[44]

Exemption granted Mission Espíritu Santo. It was Fray Aguilar who requested Governor Muñoz to dispense Mission Espíritu Santo from the payment of the *mesteña* tax (tax paid on wild or unbranded cattle killed). He explained that the mission was too poor to pay this impost

---

[42]Governor to Uranga, October 5, 1801. *Béxar Archives.*

[43]Manuel Muñoz to Revillagigedo, July 14, and August 29, 1791. *Béxar Archives.*

[44]Juan José Aguilar to Manuel Muñoz, February 23, and July 30, 1795; Aguilar to Elguezábal, May 11, 1797. *Béxar Archives.*

and that it was so short of hands that it was unable to brand its own cattle. Governor Muñoz granted the request on August 8, 1795.[45]

In January, 1797, Fray Aguilar wrote Nava that the Presidio of La Bahía owed the mission four hundred *pesos* for the transportation of supplies from San Antonio. He explained that all efforts to collect this amount from the commander of the presidio had proved futile. Captain Juan Bautista Elguezábal had been commissioned at this time to investigate the state of affairs at La Bahía. Nava had suspected for some time that Lieutenant Manuel Espadas, burser of the company at La Bahía, was not discharging his duties with honesty and dispatch. He instructed Elguezábal, therefore, to ascertain the circumstances of the claim advanced by Father Aguilar, which, if found to be correct, would have to be paid to the mission by Espadas. When Elguezábal asked Father Aguilar for particulars, the missionary explained that the mission had paid four hundred *pesos* to the conductor of a train of supplies brought to the presidio in 1795, that subsequent efforts to collect this amount from Captain Cortés and Lieutenant Espadas had proved useless, and that the mission was now in sore need of that sum to secure supplies for the maintenance of the Indians.[46] Satisfied with the explanation, Elguezábal shortly thereafter ordered the payment of the amount.

When Rosario was temporarily abandoned, part of the mission property was sold. Out of the proceeds, two hundred six *pesos* were given to Father Reyes for the projected new mission of the Orcoquisacs, and two hundred, to Fray José Rafael Oliva of Mission San Juan Capistrano. The governor now suggested that these sums be repaid in horses and tools, both of which were needed to round up the herds and to cultivate the farm of the old mission.[47]

Such were the conditions found by Father Silva in 1791, when he informed Governor Muñoz that Father Reyes had been granted permission to retire to Zacatecas and Father José Francisco Jaudenes had been appointed his successor on February 26. The governor shortly afterwards requested authorization from the viceroy to pay Father Reyes his salary for fifteen months and twenty-two days, the time, according to Father Silva, that he had served at Rosario since its restoration. This helps to

---

[45]Fray Juan José Aguilar to Manuel Muñoz. *Béxar Archives.*

[46]Pedro Nava to Manuel Muñoz, March 10, 1797; Nava to Juan Bautista Elguezábal, March 21, 1797; Juan José Aguilar to Elguezábal, May 11, 1797. *Béxar Archives.*

[47]Manuel Muñoz to Revillagigedo, January 14, and 30, 1791. *Nacogdoches Archives*, Vol. 7, pp. 2-3; 5-7.

fix the date of the formal reoccupation of Mission Rosario as December 4, 1789.[48] The request was granted and Father José Francisco López, president of the missions in San Antonio, received five hundred *pesos* which were paid out of the Mesteña Fund.

Conditions at Mission Rosario.   In his letter of March 26, the governor explained that since Jaudenes had taken charge, the mission walls had been rebuilt and sufficient lumber had been cut to reroof the church, all with the help of the Indians, who seemed to be enthusiastic and well pleased with the restoration of the mission. He had sent twelve bundles of tobacco, six axes, six hoes, and various other tools. He assured Nava that he would make every effort to supply the most urgent needs.

By August there were eighty-five Indians living at the mission. Father Jaudenes had almost completed repairing the church and the quarters of the *Padres*. One hundred *pesos* out of the Mesteña Fund, and five large copper cooking kettles were turned over to Father López in San Antonio to be sent to Father Jaudenes. On October 9, 1791, the new church was blessed and dedicated. The governor reported that he was doing everything in his power to contribute to the success of the enterprise, and that he would soon send a brick mason and a carpenter to make an estimate of the cost of other improvements desired by Father Jaudenes.[49]

The problem of feeding the neophytes became acute during the fall. The crop planted by the Indians had been lost for lack of rain. The mission had no cattle, for its herd had been scattered during the period of its abandonment. Father Cárdenas, of Mission Espíritu Santo, had been obliged to furnish meat to Father Reyes the previous year. Governor Muñoz now asked Father López, president, if the San Antonio missions could help feed the natives of Rosario. At the same time he inquired from the captain at La Bahía if it would be possible to round up wild cattle to supply the needs of the mission. He suggested that the settlers be asked to help the soldiers and neophytes, and be promised a share in the cattle rounded up or killed. Carlos Martínez, one of the settlers, succeeded in rounding up some of the former mission cattle, and the missions in San Antonio agreed to help in proportion to their now very

---

[48]Manuel Muñoz to Revillagigedo, March 26, 1791. *Nacogdoches Archives*, Vol. 7, pp. 45-49.

[49]Muñoz to Revillagigedo, March 26, August 15, and October 10, 1791. *Nacogdoches Archives*, Vol. 7, pp. 45-49; 100-101; 117-119.

slender means. In this way Father Jaudenes was enabled to keep his little flock together through the winter.[50]

Early in the spring of 1792, Governor Muñoz sent Jaudenes clothes for the Indians, forty-eight blankets, other miscellaneous supplies, and two hundred *pesos* in cash. In his report the governor estimated the cost of the supplies sent at this time as six hundred twenty-four *pesos*.[51]

Little wonder that Governor Muñoz was much displeased to learn late that fall that Father Jaudenes had complained of lack of coöperation and had requested two thousand *pesos* as reimbursement for the expenses incurred in restoring the mission. Father Jaudenes had appealed to Nava in a memorial in which he explained the conditions he had found on his arrival, and that he had been obliged to rebuild practically the whole mission at the request of the governor. He had taken it for granted that the king would defray the expenses. To do the work he had had to borrow two thousand *pesos,* he declared. It was this sum which he now requested the commandant general to repay him.

It seems that Father Jaudenes decided to take this step after he had written to Muñoz on October 19 to ask him for a fixed annual allowance to assist in the maintenance of Rosario. This was an unusual request, and the governor naturally replied that he had already given the customary assistance allowed a mission during its first year; that to continue it, would require the approval of the viceroy.[52] The controversy grew warm and as late as the summer of 1794 had not been settled. Father Jaudenes maintained that the sum he requested had been spent in the construction of the church, the lodgings, and the new wall.[53]

Progress during the first few years was slow and halting. Lack of adequate supplies prevented the missionaries from keeping the Indians constantly under instruction. Every three months the neophytes had to be permitted to hunt food. When Father Cárdenas in San Antonio appealed to Muñoz, the governor replied that there was little he could do to relieve the gravity of the situation. The custom of permitting the Indians to absent themselves had been started by Father Reyes and soon was regarded an unavoidable evil. When in August, 1794, the

---

[50]Muñoz to Revillagigedo, October 1, October 10, and November 7, 1791. *Nacogdoches Archives,* Vol. 7, pp. 120-125.

[51]Muñoz to Revillagigedo, March 12, 1792. *Nacogdoches Archives,* Vol. 7, pp. 189-190.

[52]Jaudenes to Nava, November 17, 1793. *Béxar Archives.* Muñoz to Revillagigedo, October 21, 1792. *Nacogdoches Archives,* Vol. 7, pp. 248-249.

[53]Nava to Muñoz, May 7, 1794. *Béxar Archives.*

captain of La Bahía notified Father Jaudenes that the five soldiers assigned to the mission were to be withdrawn, the friar replied that such action would force him to abandon the mission. To remain at his post under the circumstances would endanger his life. The unhealthful climate, constant labor, and endless privations had undermined the strong constitution of the missionary, and in September of that year he had to go to San José for treatment and rest. Father Cárdenas sent Father Pedrajo to care for Rosario during the *interim*.[54]

It will be recalled that Governor Muñoz had made a personal visit to La Bahía that fall in connection with the secularization order of April 10, 1794. He found the conditions such that he urgently requested the postponement of secularization, a plea that was granted by Nava. But conditions grew worse. In 1796 some of the Indians of Rosario went to live in Refugio, and others returned to the woods. Father Jaudenes went to Boca de Leones in Nuevo León for supplies and aid in order to be able to continue his labors. By September of that year he was back in Rosario and informed Muñoz that the natives had returned to the mission on September 9. In spite of previous hardships and disappointments, he was as enthusiastic as ever. He told the governor that many more Indians had sent word that they would come soon. The neophytes had elected Manuel Zertuche governor of the mission pueblo, and Captain Cortés had invested him with the insignia of his office. In a supplementary report made on October 23, he explained that of the one hundred seven Indians actually living at the mission, only thirteen were not receiving instruction in catechism.[55]

Request of Cocos to be taken into Rosario. The high hopes of Father Jaudenes were probably the result of a request made at this time by ninety-seven Cocos and Karankawas to enter Mission Rosario. He wrote Muñoz that, shortly after his return, these Indians had solicited permission to join the mission. They were not members of Chief Frazada Pinta's tribe, nor had they ever been in a mission. They came from beyond the mouth of the Colorado River. He had told them to return in two weeks, and although he had not expected to see them again, they came back on April 5.[56]

---

[54]Manuel Muñoz to Cárdenas, May 15; Francisco Vázquez to Fray Jaudenes, August 11; Cárdenas to Muñoz, October 2, 1794. *Béxar Archives.*

[55]Cortés to Muñoz, January 15; Jaudenes to Muñoz, September 9, and October 23, 1796. *Béxar Archives.*

[56]Juan Cortés to Muñoz, March 24; Jaudenes to Cortés, April 5, 1797. *Béxar Archives.*

In reporting the incident, Captain Cortés pointed out that the mission was without sufficient supplies to care for the newcomers. Muñoz sent fifty *fanegas* (one hundred bushels) of corn. The governor instructed him to ascertain the sincerity of the petitioners, whether they had come impelled by hunger, or fear, or by a desire for leisure and security. If they wanted to live in a mission, Cortés was instructed to try to convince them of the greater advantages which San Antonio offered them, for Muñoz believed that they could be cared for in one of the abandoned missions at considerably less expense to the royal treasury.[57]

While waiting for the Indians to come to see him, Cortés sent the governor a list of the supplies which he estimated were needed to care properly for the newcomers. During the first year four bulls were to be slaughtered for the weekly supply of meat, and four bundles of tobacco were to be distributed to keep the Indians contented. Among other things, he requested seventy-five blankets, four suits of clothing for the chiefs, sixty-two knives, seven bolts of cloth for skirts, six bolts of brown domestic, six *metates* (grindstones), six large kettles, six *comales* (flat cooking irons), and thirty or forty pounds of powder.

When on April 22 the Cocos and Karankawas met with the captain, he reminded them that they had come three years before with a similar petition but with no intention of staying. The Indians solemnly replied that they had come in 1794 seeking permission to enter a mission and that they had stayed in Mission Rosario until the missionary had departed, obliged to leave to secure food. They explained that they had continued to baptize their children whenever possible, that they had not committed any depredations against the presidio or the missions, and that they had always helped the mission Indians of La Bahía to get wood, bring water, and cultivate the fields. When Father Jaudenes went away, they had gone back to the woods, but they had promised him they would return when he did. They added that they knew how to plant and cultivate corn, beans, pumpkins, melons, and other things, and that they were good *cíbolo* and deer hunters. Cortés explained to them that they would have to live in the mission, work for the *Padre*, and obey all his commands. The Indians replied that they were willing to do all this if they were given lands and received seed and tools for cultivation. When Cortés suggested that they go to San Antonio, where Father Jaudenes would take them, they replied that they wanted to live in Mission Rosario and nowhere else.

---

[57]Manuel Muñoz to Cortés, April 1, 1797. *Béxar Archives.*

Cortés reported to the governor that he was convinced of their sincerity. He pointed out that these Indians, being sedentary in their habits, had permanent pueblos similar to those of the Bidais, the Tejas, and the Orcoquisacs. In recent years they had maintained peace with the Spaniards. The women were excellent workers and knew how to grind corn and make very good tortillas (hand-patted corn cakes). Cortés believed that they would soon learn to make their own clothes. He was particularly impressed with their industry. While waiting for an answer to their request, they had busied themselves in clearing a field, plowing it, and planting a bushel of corn.[58]

Nava, when informed of the incident, agreed with Muñoz in that the Indians should be induced to come to San Antonio, if possible. Only as a last resort were they to be permitted to stay at La Bahía, in which case, the Cocos should be placed in Rosario and the Karankawas sent to Refugio. In either event the approval of Father Cárdenas, president of the missions, should be obtained. The expenses incurred in their reduction to mission life were to be met out of the funds assigned to the mission and not the Mesteña Fund which had been drawn upon to pay for the fifty *fanegas* of corn sent by the governor. Muñoz was instructed to furnish only the most essential supplies for the new arrivals.

Not having heard the ultimate disposition made in the case, Nava again urged in July that both the Cocos and the Karankawas should be induced to come to San Antonio where they would enjoy the advantages of irrigation for cultivating the fields and much better protection against their enemies. If they preferred to remain in La Bahía, they were to be made to understand that they would have to work in the fields and help raise crops for their maintenance in order that they would not become an added burden to the royal treasury.[59]

Mission guards at Rosario and Refugio. The arrival of the party of Karankawas and Cocos had made Father Jaudenes appeal to Captain Cortés for three or four additional guards. Three more soldiers were accordingly assigned to Rosario with the approval of Elguezábal. But since these had to be taken from Mission Refugio, Father Puelles, who was temporarily in charge, ardently protested the action to Governor Muñoz. In his deprecation Puelles maintained that the life of a missionary—one of hunger, suffering, and endless privations—was difficult

---

[58]Cortés to Muñoz, April 7; list of supplies needed, same date; Cortés to Muñoz, April 22, 1797. *Béxar Archives.*

[59]Pedro Nava to Muñoz, May 2, June 13, and July 1, 1797. *Béxar Archives.*

enough. He was sincerely apprehensive of the effect on Refugio of leaving only one guard.[60]

Finances of Mission Rosario. In the investigation conducted by Captain Elguezábal, it was disclosed that the mission owed the presidio twelve hundred fifty-three *pesos.* Father Jaudenes admitted the records were correct, but declared that it was impossible for the mission to pay one cent. He reminded the officials of the destitute condition of Rosario and of his chronic inability to provide food for the Indians. He recounted how the expense of rebuilding the church, the *Padre's* quarters, and the mission wall had never been paid by the royal treasury, and he again asked to be reimbursed for this debt. Elguezábal seems to have been impressed with the justness of the complaint and joined the missionary in his request.

When the matter was presented to Nava, he referred the case to his *auditor,* Galindo Navarro, who made a detailed report on the subject on August 1, 1797. He explained that the royal treasury had paid six thousand *pesos* in 1758 for the original establishment, that one thousand more were paid the first year for the upkeep of the Indians congregated, and four thousand one hundred one for the construction of mission buildings, a total of eleven thousand one hundred one *pesos.* When, at the insistence of Father Reyes, it was reëstablished in 1789-1790, the royal treasury had paid various sums of money advanced by different officials for the maintenance of the Indians during the first year and for tools, utensils, and other things requested. In spite of this, Father Jaudenes had asked for additional aid on October 19, 1792, part of which was granted by the commandant general after the refusal of the governor. The missionary had been specifically warned at that time to impress upon the Indians congregated that they must become self-sustaining.

Not until November 19, 1793, had Father Jaudenes presented a formal claim for the two thousand *pesos* spent in the reëstablishment of the mission. The request had been repeated on April 25, 1794, at which time Father Ignacio María Laba, guardian of the College at Zacatecas, supported the claim in his letter of June 10, in which he intimated that if the amount were not paid, the mission might have to be abandoned for lack of means to keep the Indians under instruction. Governor Muñoz, when consulted on June 29, gave a favorable opinion. But when the

---

[60]José Francisco Jaudenes to Cortés, April 5; Juan Bautista Elguezábal to Muñoz, June 8; José Mariano Puelles to Manuel Muñoz, November 6, 1797. *Béxar Archives.*

matter was submitted to the *Junta Real de Hacienda,* on September 19, 1794, the claim was denied.

Under the circumstances, the revival of the old claim should be disregarded, declared Navarro. Elguezábal should be informed of the antecedents and instructed to proceed to investigate whether or not the mission was able to pay. Whatever property, seed, cattle, or other goods, that was not actually needed for the support of the Indians, was to be attached. If the mission was as destitute as Father Jaudenes claimed, the governor should be notified in order that he might determine the cause for its failure. A report on the number of Indians at the mission, their daily occupation, and the resources of the establishment would enable officials to decide whether the mission should be continued or abandoned. Elguezábal evidently must have concluded that the mission was able to pay the amount, for on January 19, 1798, Nava authorized him to collect the debt.[61]

Population of La Bahía. The census report of 1797 showed there were twelve hundred twelve persons living at La Bahía. Of this number, four hundred sixteen were Spaniards; the others were Indians in the two missions. In January, 1798, Elguezábal reported the population as thirteen hundred seventy, showing an increase of one hundred fifty-eight persons. The chief occupations were agriculture and cattle raising, but he added that without irrigation the crops were uncertain.[62]

Conditions in San Antonio. When Ugalde recommended in 1789 the improvement of the fortifications in Nacogdoches and La Bahía, he also called attention to the deplorable conditions that existed in San Antonio, pointing out that since this was the seat of government and the only settlement worthy of the name, it deserved more consideration in the plans for defence. It is to be remembered that it was Ugalde who argued so strenuously at that time for the preservation of the office of governor.[63]

Not until Viceroy Revillagigedo took charge the following year were the recommendations of Ugalde respecting Texas acted upon. Muñoz declared in the meantime that the most urgent need was the construction of a guard-house. The property necessary for the purpose had been ceded

---

[61]Elguezábal to Nava, June 25, 1797; Dictamen del Auditor Galindo Navarro, August 1, 1797; Nava to Elguezábal, January 19, 1798. *Béxar Archives.*

[62] Census reports in the *Béxar Archives.*

[63]See pages 111-113.

by Luis Antonio Menchaca, and part of the materials had been gathered. The work was to be done by the soldiers when not on duty, but since funds were necessary for the purchase of materials, the governor asked permission to use two hundred *pesos* which had been appropriated for the construction of a fort on the Cibolo and were still held on deposit. If this money could be used, the soldiers could build not only the guardhouse indicated but a powder magazine and a much needed warehouse in which to store the supplies of the garrison.[64]

Agreeable to an order of December 10, 1790, Muñoz commissioned Pedro Huizar to make a survey and draw plans for the reconstruction of the presidio and the improvement of its defences. Huizar in his report pointed out that the crooked streets, the irregularity of the terrain, and the haphazard development of the city presented a serious problem in the improvement of the presidio. The new wall would necessitate cutting across some of the occupied lots, and moving several of the houses. He recommended that the *jacales* (mud and straw huts) outside the new wall be demolished. The actual damage to property would, in reality, be slight, the governor explained, because only a few stone houses were not within the proposed new wall and most of these were already in ruins. The reconstruction would be a blessing, as it would afford much more effective protection and correct the irregular plan of the city. According to the estimates and drawings prepared by Huizar the cost of reconstructing the presidio and of building a new wall amounted to six thousand three hundred eighty-five *pesos*.[65]

Posada, the *fiscal,* who appears to have been a narrow-minded official, took exception to the recommendations. He protested that while the cost of construction was indicated, no details were given as to the length, the height, or the thickness of the new wall. He wanted to know, furthermore, the depth of the San Antonio River along the east side of the proposed enclosure. He feared that if the stream could be forded, the city would be exposed to attack by the Indians or other enemies. In view of this statement, his last argument against the reënforcement of the defences of San Antonio was indeed curiously illogical, for he maintained that if San Antonio was made absolutely

---

[64]Manuel Muñoz to Revillagigedo, February 9, 1791. *Béxar Archives.*

[65]Muñoz to Revillagigedo, March 26, 1790. *Nacogdoches Archives,* Vol. 7, pp. 42-45.

safe, its citizenry would relax all vigilance and become more indolent and indifferent than ever.[66]

When Ramón Castro assumed command in 1792, he wrote Viceroy Revillagigedo protesting the abandonment of the project to strengthen the fortification of San Antonio. He argued that Ugalde and Muñoz were correct in maintaining that this frontier outpost should be adequately fortified. He explained that there were eight and one-half lots along the west, the San Pedro Creek side; five lots on the north, and six on the south; that since each lot was sixty *varas,* the wall on these three sides would be eleven hundred seventy *varas.* The height of the proposed wall, including the foundation, was to be four and a quarter *varas,* and its thickness three-quarters of a *vara.* Each lineal *vara* of the proposed wall, if built according to specifications, would take four and one-half cart loads of rock. Castro assured the viceroy that the estimate of the cost made by Huizar was reasonable.

With regard to the few *jacales* recently built near San Pedro Creek, these occupied ground protected by a bulwark erected by Castro when in San Antonio the previous year, at which time also the new powder magazine was constructed near the creek. Castro sent a map with his report, concluding it with a criticism of the objections raised by Posada to the proposed improvements.[67]

But Posada was unconvinced. He was personally hurt by Castro's insinuation that it was not his business to inquire about river soundings. He warmly replied that Law 72, Title 2, Book 2 of the *Laws of the Indies* authorized him to ask for such information; that it also empowered him to pass on military matters. To prove that he was correct in his opinion, he recommended that the whole matter be referred to the capable and well-known engineer, Miguel de Constansó, and to Jacobo Ugarte.[68]

Difficulties with the curate of San Antonio. When *Bachiller* Francisco Gómez Moreno, curate of San Antonio, took an active part in siding with Governor Martínez Pacheco against Manuel Muñoz in 1790, it was not the first time that the parish priest found himself in difficulties. Like

---

[66]Dictamen del Fiscal Posada, May 31, 1791. *A. G. M., Historia,* Vol. 93, pp. 67-69.

[67]Ramón Castro to Revillagigedo, May 15, 1792. *A. G. M., Historia,* Vol. 93, pp. 71-79.

[68]Dictamen del Fiscal Posada, June 26, 1792. *A. G. M., Historia,* Vol. 93, pp. 180-182. The report of Constansó and the map of Castro may some day be found in the archives in Mexico.

some of his predecessors, he was a high-spirited man, who had taken a strong dislike to Muñoz and to the missionaries in San Antonio. In the investigation conducted by Martínez Pacheco, he stretched his testimony against Muñoz, and when early in 1791 Fray José Manuel Pedrajo, an experienced missionary, attempted to reconciliate him with the other missionaries at the request of Gaspar González de Candamo, administrator *ad interim* of the diocese of Nuevo León, Moreno publicly insulted him and refused to return the courtesy call.

Governor Muñoz, who had returned after the fruitless investigation against him, abstained from interfering with the irate priest. There was good reason. One of the servants of the household of the governor named Gabriel Gutiérrez had been falsely accused of illicit relations with the wife of Francisco Galán, who, as a result of the charges, had separated from his wife. Circumstances pointed to Moreno as the chief instigator of the false rumors in an attempt to implicate the governor for his tacit approval of the alleged scandalous conduct of his servant. But when on November 13 a severe beating was administered to Ignacio Santos Coy, former sacristan, under circumstances that pointed clearly to Curate Moreno, Governor Muñoz was forced to undertake an investigation which revealed the complicity of Moreno and his new sacristan, Francisco Mata.

In a letter to the administrator of the diocese, Muñoz deplored the situation but felt duty bound to report that Moreno was lax in his duties, that he rarely if ever preached a sermon, and that the people lacked spiritual guidance and instruction. He politely expressed the hope that González de Candamo would take steps to remedy the situation. As early as May 9, 1791, Muñoz had remonstrated with the viceroy against the conduct of the curate. Repeating his complaint in August, he pointed out the disagreement between the curate and the missionaries. The matter was eventually brought before the advisors of the viceroy, who, in a formal opinion, declared that for the welfare of the community of San Antonio it would be well to ask the Most Reverend Andrés Ambrosio de Llanos y Valdez, the bishop-elect of Nuevo León, then in Mexico, to appoint a new parish priest. A formal investigation was instituted concerning the accusation against the character of Herlinda Bustillos, wife of Francisco Galán. She was completely exonerated, and Galán was ordered to live with her as man and wife. This affair, while of no great importance, was, nevertheless, reported to the secretary of the king by Viceroy Revillagigedo as a matter of record.[69]

Curate Francisco Gómez Moreno appears to have been replaced soon thereafter by *Bachiller* José Clemente Arocha, who on April 11, 1793, signed a receipt for an altar, a copper baptismal font, a silver baptismal shell, a silver ciborium, and a host mold. These had been obtained from the secularized Mission of San Antonio de Valero for the chapel that had been set up in the old mission headquarters for the company of troops from El Alamo.[70] Early in 1793, Bishop de Llanos y Valdez took charge of the diocese of Nuevo León, the seat of which was in Monterrey, and in which Texas was included. He died in December, 1799, and was succeeded temporarily by Miguel Ignacio de Zárate who was appointed vicar.[71]

Recognition bestowed on curate of San Antonio. Towards the close of the century Father Gabino Valdez was the curate of San Antonio. A native of Saltillo, he had attained fame on the frontier outposts of New Spain for his eloquence. In July, 1800, he asked permission to absent himself for a week in September so as to attend a commemorative feast being celebrated in Saltillo, where he was to deliver the principal sermon. Governor Elguezábal readily granted the request and Nava, when informed, heartily approved the action.[72]

Fixing the time for Mass. It seems that complaints were made to Commandant General Nava concerning the irregularity of the time at which Mass was said for the soldiers and the settlers in San Antonio on Sundays and feast days. At this time the curate was also the chaplain of the garrison stationed at San Antonio de Béxar. Nava wrote Governor Elguezábal that Mass should be said at the same hour on Sundays and feast days. He suggested that nine o'clock in winter and eight o'clock

---

[69]Muñoz to Revillagigedo, May 9, and August 29, 1791; Muñoz to Gaspar González de Candamo, November 21, 1791. *Nacogdoches Archives*, Vol. 7, pp. 77-79; 105-106; 143-144. Dictamen del Auditor, 1793, Conde de Revillagigedo to Conde del Campo de Alanza, January 31, 1793. *A. G. I., Audiencia de México*, 89-6-21 (Dunn Transcripts, 1792-1799, pp. 59-67).

[70]Receipt certified by Bachiller José Clemente Arocha, April 11, 1793. *Nacogdoches Archives*, Vol. 8, p. 44. The stationing of this military company formerly at a post called El Alamo in Coahuila, is responsible for the name that today attaches to the old Mission of Valero.

[71]Ecclesiastical Cabildo to Elguezábal, December 30, 1799. *Béxar Archives*.

[72]Gabino Valdez to Elguezábal, July 9, 1800; Nava to Elguezábal, August 5, 1800. *Béxar Archives*.

in summer as the hour most convenient for both the soldiers and the settlers. The chaplain of the garrison should be instructed to follow this suggestion with all regularity. Furthermore it was customary to ring the bells three times at intervals before the hour at which the Mass was to begin. He advised that this be done, beginning fifteen minutes before the hour and twice thereafter at five-minute intervals. He reminded Elguezábal that local commanders had no authority to change the time of Mass, except on the eve of setting out on a campaign.[73]

Religious political refugee. A Capuchin friar by the name of Buenaventura de Castro appears to have fled from New Orleans and taken refuge in Texas early in 1800, probably because of his sympathies for the French Revolution. Captain José Miguel del Moral, commander at Nacogdoches, informed Elguezábal that it had come to his notice that the fugitive friar had been harbored in Nacogdoches by Father Vallejo. Castro evidently did not stay long, because he is next heard of from Monterrey, where Miguel Ignacio de Zárate, the vicar of the vacant diocese, was requested by the bishop of Louisiana to make a diligent search for the fugitive. Zárate wrote Elguezábal that, according to the information he had received, Fray Castro was a fugitive from justice, that he had gone first to Nacogdoches, thence to San Antonio, and was now probably in that city living incognito. Del Moral had stated that Castro claimed to have been the curate of Galveston. Governor Elguezábal was asked to arrest him and send him back to New Orleans. There seems to be no indication that he was ever apprehended.[74]

Aid for canonization of San Felipe de Jesús. Commandant General Nava informed Governor Muñoz in January, 1798, that he had granted permission for a collection to be taken up by the parish priests in all the towns and settlements of the Interior Provinces for the canonization of San Felipe de Jesús.[75] The archbishop of Mexico had undertaken to promote the canonization of this saintly missionary, the first native-born Mexican to suffer marytrdom. He was crucified on February 5, 1597, with twenty-six Franciscan and Jesuit missionaries in Nangazaque, Japan.[76]

---

[73]Pedro Nava to Juan Bautista Elguezábal, July 10, 1800. *Béxar Archives.*

[74]José Miguel del Moral to Elguezábal, April 26, 1800; Miguel Ignacio de Zárate to Elguezábal, October 12, 1801. *Béxar Archives.*

[75]Nava to Muñoz, January 31, 1798. *Béxar Archives.*

[76]Pichardo, *Vida de San Felipe de Jesús,* 454-471.

Improvement of the military. The antiquated arms of frontier troops were replaced in the fall of 1800 by an improved rifle with bayonet. Nava urged the governor to use all the time necessary to acquaint the soldiers in San Antonio with the use of the new guns. He recommended that the men be drilled with more regularity. Mindful of the inadequate number of troops in the Interior Provinces, he authorized the governor to organize a militia of volunteers from among the able-bodied men. Pursuant to these instructions, Muñoz enlisted forty men in a company of San Antonio militia, who elected Pedro Zambrano as captain.

When the governor reported the organization of the volunteer corps and indicated that he had assigned them a monthly allowance, Nava pointed out it was not customary to pay volunteers. In view of the conditions that prevailed in Texas, however, he authorized the governor to pay the men enlisted at the rate of ten *pesos* a month for such time as they were occupied in active service. This rate had been approved by the king in the organization of a similar militia company in Mazatlán. If the men needed horses for the performance of their duties when called, these could be furnished at the king's expense, but such horses were not to be used by the volunteer troops except when on active duty. Nava explained that only one-third of the total number of men participating in a campaign could be taken from the militia, who were intended primarily as a home guard.[77]

Building a new guard-house. The need for an ample and safe place of detention had long been felt. Governor Muñoz appealed to Nava for aid. He informed the commandant general that the citizens had agreed to contribute two hundred ninety-eight *pesos* by voluntary subscription. The construction of the new jail, however, would cost eleven hundred ninety-five *pesos*. Muñoz asked that in order not to burden the royal treasury, he be permitted to collect a special assessment of one *peso* on each barrel of *aguardiente* (fire water), and fifty cents on each barrel of wine sold, until the desired amount was raised. To this proposal, Nava replied that the assessment was illegal. He suggested that the governor take three hundred *pesos* from the military fund, urge the citizens to contribute more generously, and save on the cost of labor by requiring persons convicted by the courts to work on the new building.[78]

---

[77]Nava to Muñoz, December 28, 1800, and May 12, 1801. *Béxar Archives.*

[78]Nava to Muñoz, May 12, 1801. *Béxar Archives.*

Archives and bullets. The muzzle-loaders of frontier days required paper wads to press the charge close to the shot. Paper wads were essential to the defence of the frontiers of New Spain. But paper was a scarce commodity in those days. The supply of the enlarged garrison of San Antonio at the close of the century became depleted. It occurred to some sergeant that the musty archives cluttering the commander's crowded quarters could be put to a more useful purpose. Fortunately not even waste paper could be disposed of without the consent of the commandant general. Imagine the shock of Nava upon the receipt of a formal request for authorization to use the old books and records of the presidial company of San Antonio as paper wads. Posthaste he dispatched strict orders not to use one single sheet of the old records for that purpose. He gave ample authority to the commandant of the post to purchase all the scrap paper he needed in Saltillo or any other place. The archives were saved.[79]

Governors of Texas at the close of the century. Manuel Muñoz had served his king loyally in Texas since 1790. He was not a young man when he took office. His long career on the frontiers of the Interior Provinces had undermined his powerful constitution, and the strenuous duties that devolved upon him in the eventful years of his residence in Texas completed the ruin of his health. Early in 1796 he had asked Nava for permission to retire in order to seek treatment for his increasing ailments. Nava thanked the old commander and assured him his request would be forwarded to the king with a full record of his services. In the meantime Juan Bautista Elguezábal would be appointed to assist him in the administration of the province.[80] In January, 1797, Muñoz was informed that the king had granted his request and promoted him to the rank of colonel in his royal armies. Governor Antonio Cordero, of Coahuila, had been designated as his successor, but this officer was engaged in a campaign against the Apaches, to terminate which was very important. Muñoz was asked to remain in office until further notice, and to indicate where he wished to retire, in order that the king's approval might be secured.

Two months later, Cordero informed Muñoz that, due to the death of Governor Gutiérrez on March 17, 1797, he had become lieutenant-governor of Nuevo Santander; this would delay his coming to Texas.

---

[79]Nava to the governor, October 12, 1801. *Béxar Archives.*
[80]Nava to Muñoz, October 16, 1796. *Béxar Archives.*

In August of that year, Nava wrote that Colonel José Irigoyen had arrived in Mexico with a blank royal appointment to the first vacancy in any of the provinces. The viceroy had, consequently, appointed him to succeed Muñoz. But Irigoyen had fallen sick after his arrival and was unable to relieve him immediately. Nava begged him to stay in San Antonio a little longer and named Elguezábal, his able and energetic assistant, governor *ad interim*. But months lengthened into years. Muñoz became an invalid confined to his bed, and although he had received royal permission to retire to the military hospital at Durango on one-third pay, he had to remain until his successor arrived. On July 27, 1799, the old governor died in San Antonio, and Juan Bautista Elguezábal took over the administration of the province.[81] He continued in office until October 5, 1805, when, like his predecessor, after many hardships that undermined his health, he died in SanAntonio.[82]

Pedro Nava, the commandant general at Chihuahua, on whom rested the responsibility for the defence of the Interior Provinces and the solution of the numerous problems which the rapidly changing conditions brought up, did not long survive Muñoz, his old friend and companion. Elguezábal received a royal communication in 1800, informing him that the king had appointed Nemesio Salcedo to succeed Pedro Nava, who had asked for permission to retire on account of illness. On July 14, 1801, Salcedo, the new commandant general of the Interior Provinces, notified Elguezábal that he had taken possession of his office. The new commandant was an experienced officer of the king, having seen extensive service in various countries of Europe. He came to his new post by way of New Orleans where he wrote Elguezábal to inform him of his arrival.[83]

Medical practitioners and epidemics in San Antonio. At the close of the century, Spanish settlers as well as mission Indians in Texas were still chiefly dependent on the barber for surgical service, particularly bleedings. A barber by the name of Rafael Navarrete attained considerable renown as a bleeder and general healer. Stationed oiginally in La Bahía, he was called to San Antonio to treat Francisco Arocha, a

---

[81]Nava to Muñoz, October 16, 1796, January 1, and March 7, 1797; Antonio Cordero to Muñoz, March 28, 1797; Nava to Muñoz, May 16, 1797, and August 17, 1798; Nava to Ayuntamiento, August 17, 1799. *Béxar Archives.*

[82]Nemesio Salcedo to Antonio Cordero, November 4, 1805. *Béxar Archives.*

[83]*Real Cédula*, August 26, 1800; Nemesio Salcedo to Elguezábal, July 14, 1801. *Béxar Archives.*

prominent citizen. His patient recovered rapidly and Navarrete stayed because his services were much in demand.[84]

In 1795 and 1796, a strange malady made its appearance in Texas. This was promptly named *mosezuela,* which, freely translated, means "infant's disease." The ailment appears to have been common also in Havana, where it was called *mal de siete días* (seven-day ailment). It was a sort of epilepsy which affected infants on the seventh day after birth and which proved fatal in almost every case, for which reason it was declared incurable. Those few who survived seem to have been subject to a recurrence of the ailment on the seventh or twenty-first year. But just as the epidemic broke out in San Antonio in 1795, an effective remedy was being discovered in Cuba. This consisted of *aceite de palo,* known also as *aceite canimar,* or *bálsamo de copaiba.* This was applied to the umbilical cord when cut. It proved a successful preventive in every case in Cuba. The officials of San Luis Potosí, upon being consulted, advised its use in Texas.[85]

Smallpox still continued to be the most feared scourge on the frontier. La Bahía was frequently visited by the malady. In November, 1798, during an epidemic, Captain José Miguel del Moral informed Governor Muñoz that he was sending two soldiers to San Antonio to purchase thirty *pesos* of *piloncillo* (brown sugar) needed for the treatment of the disease. He did not explain how the ingredient was to be used in the cure of smallpox. The disease was endemic, it seems, in the coast region. When in January, 1799, the governor ordered Captain del Moral to send some Indian allies to Laredo, he replied that the natives were unable to go because of the prevalence of smallpox in their villages.[86]

Cattle industry. It is of interest to note how the importance of the cattle industry occupied the attention of the king himself. A long and interesting royal decree was issued May 8, 1800, detailing measures for the improvement of the stock. Instructions were given for the separation of the bulls from the cows each year and the selection of one third of the best bulls for breeding purposes in order to improve the quality of the herds. The other two thirds were to fatten in separate pastures to be used as oxen, or sent to the market. The recognition of the importance

---

[84]Cortés to Muñoz, June 20, and July 7, 1795; Muñoz to Cortés, June 26, 1795. *Béxar Archives.*

[85]Circulars dated September 23, 1795, and December 17, 1796. *Béxar Archives.*

[86]José Miguel del Moral to Governor Muñoz, November 21, 1798; Muñoz to Del Moral, January 14, 1799; Del Moral to Muñoz, January 18, 1799. *Béxar Archives.*

of the adoption of scientific methods for the improvement of the numerous herds is significant and unexpected at this early date in the Spanish dominions.[87]

Nacogdoches, the gateway to Texas. This post was the eastern spearhead of Spain's dominion in North America. More than one hundred miles of open country lay between it and Natchitoches, the nearest settlement in Louisiana. The treaty of 1783 had brought the enterprising pioneers of the West to the very banks of the Mississippi. The boundary between the possessions of His Catholic Majesty and the infant republic was not defined until 1795. Is it strange that in the closing years of the century the importance of this distant outpost should have attracted more and more the attention of Spanish officials and should have become the major consideration in determining new policies directed to protect and defend the frontier? It is remarkable that this obvious fact should not have been realized sooner. The hesitant attitude is traceable to the importance attached to Louisiana in the general plan to check the American advance.

Difficulties in closing the door. Again and again the commandant general of the Interior Provinces and the governor of Texas issued strict orders against illicit trade with Louisiana, the introduction of foreign traders, and the admission of foreigners. The coöperation of the officials in Louisiana was earnestly sought, but they were equally powerless in stemming the impetuous flow of the American frontiersmen. The commander at Natchitoches wrote Governor Muñoz in 1793 that he was as helpless as the captain of Nacogdoches in keeping Americans without passports from penetrating into the interior of Texas. He admitted that he knew they entered clandestinely, killed wild cattle, stole horses, traded with the Indians, and committed numerous outrages, but the vast expanse of the unguarded frontier prevented the effective enforcement of restrictions.[88]

Elguezábal issued a proclamation as late as 1799, prohibiting the introduction of merchandise from Louisiana on whatever pretext. Violation of the new order would result in the confiscation and sale at auction of all the property of the violator. The goods brought into the province prior to the promulgation of the decree were to be reported

---

[87]*Real Cédula*, May 28, 1800. *Béxar Archives.*
[88]Louis Blanc to Manuel Muñoz, April 26, 1793. *Béxar Archives.*

and their sale suspended. Equally stringent regulations were made concerning the admission of foreigners into the king's dominions.[89]

José María Guadiana, commander of Nacogdoches, reported he was doing everything possible to carry out his instructions in regard to foreigners. He had refused permission to Harold (?) Wiggins and Harry (?) Crow from Rapide, Louisiana, to hunt in the vicinity of Nacogdoches; he had ordered John Farrel, an American who had come with a passport from the commander at Natchitoches, to leave the province; and he was keeping an eye on Samuel Davenport, another American business partner of Eduardo Morfil of Natchitoches, and of William Barr of Nacogdoches. Barr had been licensed by Spanish officials to trade with the Indians, and Davenport enjoyed the same privilege as his partner. The latter was a native Philadelphian, whose family took him to Cumberland while a young boy and later to Natchez; from there he had migrated to Nacogdoches in 1794, as a loyal subject of Spain and a Roman Catholic.[90]

Casa Calvo, of Louisiana, informed Elguezábal in March, 1800, that he had issued stringent orders to prevent the introduction of foreigners from the United States or Louisiana into Texas and to arrest immediately all unlicensed traders found among the Arkansas. He deplored the difficulties encountered in the enforcement of these regulations. The treaty of limits of 1795 had left the frontier along the Mississippi entirely unprotected for a distance of almost three hundred leagues.[91]

It was evident that, if the restrictions against foreigners were to become effective, a larger force had to be stationed in Nacogdoches to patrol the frontier. Nava ordered Elguezábal in August, 1800, to reënforce the garrison with forty men from San Antonio, who would be replaced by an equal number sent from the Presidio de Río Grande. But this increase proved far from adequate to accomplish the end desired. In an illuminating report made by Elguezábal in 1803, he wisely pointed out the futility of attempting to enforce a policy which circumstances made inadvisable. Nacogdoches, he explained, was "situated about one hundred and fifty leagues to the northeast upon the frontier of Louisiana, whence all the settlers obtain such articles as are necessary for the maintenance of life. Because of its proximity to Louisiana and because of the insuper-

---

[89]Decree issued by Juan Bautista Elguezábal, May 20, 1799. *Béxar Archives.*

[90]Guadiana to Muñoz, January 3, 1799; affidavit of S. Davenport, June 16, 1809. *Béxar Archives.*

[91]Casa Calvo to Elguezábal, March 1, 1800. *Béxar Archives.*

able difficulties presented by the extensive, unsettled region [between Nacogdoches and this place] which is full of rivers and liable to terrible floods, the settlers are deprived of the hope of securing anything . . . from these regions." Any attempt to deprive them effectively of trade with Louisiana would result in starvation and the abandonment of this advanced post.[92]

Extent of leakage. Fortunately, a list of the foreigners in Nacogdoches and its vicinity was prepared in 1804, which reveals how many had succeeded in squeezing through the half-closed door and in establishing themselves in Texas. Of the sixty-eight on the list, fifty had been in the province three or more years. In this group were included Americans, Irishmen, Frenchmen, and Englishmen. The earliest foreigners to settle in Nacogdoches seem to have been French who entered in 1778; the first English arrived in 1783, and three years later the Irish appeared upon the scene. By 1789 Americans had begun to trickle into Texas. Those listed are far from the actual number who slipped unobserved across the frontier and penetrated far into the interior to trade with the natives and to steal horses.[93]

Typical of the latter is the case of Juan Calbert, whose name does not appear in the list cited. He was caught in the villages of the Tawakoni and Taovaya Indians in the summer of 1795, and taken first to Nacogdoches, and then sent to San Antonio. Upon being questioned by the governor, he answered that he was a native of Philadelphia, a Presbyterian, gunsmith by trade, and that about six years before he had gone to Fort Pitt on the Ohio, then drifted down that river to the Mississippi. He had lived for a while in Natchez and New Orleans, later moved to Natchitoches, and finally had gone directly to the country of the Tawakonis and Taovayas. He had lived among them for fourteen months, during which time he had gone hunting buffalo with them. He had kept their guns in repair. Asked how far it was to his home in Pennsylvania, he estimated the distance to San Antonio to be seven hundred leagues. Calbert requested permission to settle in Spanish territory and to practice his trade. The commandant general acceded to the request and instructed Muñoz to permit him to settle in Coahuila. The following year he was arrested in Candela, but was released upon presenta-

---

[92]Nava to Elguezábal, August 4, 1801. *Béxar Archives;* Hatcher, M. A., *The Opening of Texas to Foreign Settlement, 1801-1821,* 304.

[93]List of the foreigners in the pueblo . . . Nacogdoches, January 1, 1804. Cited in Hatcher, *The Opening of Texas,* 297-300.

tion of his permit. He claimed at that time that he had been baptized a Catholic. The king on April 5 ordered his arrest and deportation to Havana. Calbert evidently learned of his impending doom and started for Nacogdoches shortly after his release, because on September 3, 1796, Nava asked Muñoz to send a detachment to take him into custody before he reached the frontier.[94]

In the meantime Nacogdoches had been placed in as good a state of defence as possible. Captain José del Moral informed Governor Elguezábal in January, 1800, that the stockade had been rebuilt and the artillery in the post had been mounted and reconditioned for any emergency.[95]

Commanders at Nacogdoches, 1795-1800. In January, 1795, Nava inquired from Muñoz if sickness or some other cause had prevented Bernardo Fernández from assuming command at Nacogdoches. If he was still unable to take over, Manuel Espadas of La Bahía was to be sent to take charge temporarily. The urgency of filling this position brooked no delay. Muñoz replied that Fernández was already in Nacogdoches with a detachment of twenty men, as ordered on November 21, 1794. Fernández remained in Nacogdoches until September, 1795, when he was replaced by José María Guadiana. Nava had promoted Fernández to a captaincy in the light cavalry. Muñoz had been asked to send Francisco Amangual to replace Fernández, but his illness prevented the execution of the order.[96]

Guadiana informed Nava in October, 1796, that he had taken charge of the garrison. He remained in command until May, 1799, when he was replaced by José del Moral from La Bahía, who had been ordered to Nacogdoches in March, but had been unable to leave until Captain Francisco Xavier de Uranga arrived. Guadiana had been accused of laxness in enforcing the laws on contraband trade and the introduction of foreigners. He was reprimanded in the fall of 1798, and although he had promised in January, 1799, to observe his instructions more carefully, Nava decided that a change was advisable. Shortly after the

---

[94]Nava to Muñoz, July 29, 1795; Miguel José de Amparán to Muñoz, August 10, 1796; Nava to Muñoz, September 3, 1796. *Béxar Archives.* Nava to Duque de Alcudia, November 3, 1795. *A. G. I., México, Leg. 18, Núm. 51.* (Dunn Transcripts, 1792-1799.)

[95]Del Moral to Muñoz, January 28, 1800. *Béxar Archives.*

[96]Nava to Muñoz, January 27, and February 10, 1795; Muñoz to Fernández, September 27, 1796; Nava to Muñoz, October 1, 1796. *Béxar Archives.*

appointment of his successor, Nava informed Elguezábal, the new governor, that in the future the commander at Nacogdoches was to be changed every four or five months to prevent him from becoming too intimate with smugglers and foreign intruders.[97]

How jealously Nava watched contraband trade in Nacogdoches is revealed by his action upon the request of Captain Cortez, former commander of La Bahía, to be permitted to reside in Nacogdoches after his retirement. Nava wrote Muñoz that Elguezábal, who had conducted the investigation of Cortez's administration at La Bahía, suspected Cortez of having engaged in contraband trade. Consequently he was not to be allowed to settle in Nacogdoches or even to remain in Texas. He was to be ordered to retire to some post in Coahuila as far removed from the frontier as possible. His pension was to be paid by the treasurer at Saltillo.[98]

A new church. Neither the unsettled condition of the frontier, nor the approaching hurricane that threatened to sweep away Spain's dominion in America, nor the military worries of the officials discouraged the earnest missionaries in Nacogdoches from making plans for the erection of a new church. Fray José Francisco Moreno (not the former curate of San Antonio) secured the necessary permission from the governing *Cabildo* of the Cathedral of Monterrey to embark upon the enterprise. He then wrote Governor Elguezábal for his approval. He explained that the church being used by his parishioners was about to crash upon their heads. Its roof afforded little protection against the rain and its walls did not keep out the cold. It was located too far from the settlement and many were kept from attending services in bad weather. The people wanted a new church. They had already gathered a large part of the materials for the building, and he had secured the consent of the ecclesiastical authorities of the diocese. He now needed only the approval of the governor. The permission was granted and work started immediately.[99] Thus in the encircling gloom of the approaching storm, the missionaries on Spain's farthest and most exposed frontier continued to raise the cross, a symbol of faith, a promise of hope in the future.

---

[97]Guadiana to Muñoz, October 25, 1796, March 20, 1798, March 19, 1799, and May 14, 1799. *Béxar Archives.*

[98]Nava to Muñoz, July 20, 1798. *Béxar Archives.*

[99]José Francisco Moreno to Elguezábal, August 26, 1800. *Béxar Archives.*

CHAPTER VII

FROM SAN LORENZO TO THE RETROCESSION OF LOUISIANA, 1795-1801

Treaty of San Lorenzo, 1795. After prolonged negotiations and considerable wrangling over the limits between the United States and the dominions of His Catholic Majesty in America, a treaty was signed on October 20, 1795. Article II stipulated that the southern boundary was to be the thirty-first parallel of north latitude from the Mississippi River eastward to the Chattahoochee River, thence along a line running due east from the mouth of the Flint River to the head of the St. Mary's River, and thence down the middle of that river to the Atlantic Ocean. Article IV defined the western boundary as running along the middle of the Mississippi River from its source to the intersection of the thirty-first parallel of north latitude on the said river. But the people of the United States were granted the right of navigation from the source of the Mississippi to the sea, and permitted the use of New Orleans as a place of deposit free of all duty for a period of three years. The treaty further provided for the immediate appointment of commissioners to survey the line agreed upon, and for the evacuation of the troops and garrisons of the signatory powers to their respective jurisdictions within six months from the date of ratification. The subjects of the two powers were likewise to be at liberty to move if they so desired.[1]

Such were the stipulations concerning the limits between the two countries embodied in the treaty of amity and commerce of 1795. The completion of the negotiations put an end to the intrigues of the governor of Louisiana with the agents of the disgruntled West, but it gave rise to new difficulties and misunderstandings which deeply affected conditions in Texas. The American frontier had moved to the Mississippi River; the aggressive pioneer had been brought one step closer to the thinly populated and weakly held outposts of northern New Spain. Before the new boundary was definitely established, Louisiana was to be returned to France and Napoleon was to sell it to the United States, bringing the frontier beyond the Mississippi to the eastern border of Texas.

Complications resulting from the war with Great Britain. Even as the terms of the treaty of 1795 were being discussed, relations between

---

[1]*Treaties, Conventions, and International Acts, Protocols, and Agreements between the United States and Other Powers, 1776-1909,* II. (Washington, 1910.)

Spain and Great Britain became strained and eventually led to a declaration of war on October 7, 1796. As early as March, 1795, the Duke of Alcudia had informed Viceroy Branciforte that a break with the British was imminent and warned him against attack from Canada on New Spain. Branciforte replied in July that he was making every effort to strengthen the defences of his jurisdiction. He pointed out that on the west coast, San Francisco had only a small garrison with eight cannons, that San Diego and San Blas were unprotected, and that Acapulco lacked the means to repel a serious attack. The immense distance from the last mentioned port to San Francisco precluded the possibility of effective coöperation between it and the outposts along the west coast.

The eastern frontier was in no better position. The provinces of New Mexico, Coahuila, Texas, and Louisiana now bordered upon the independent American colonies. The common interest of the British and the Americans in the navigation of the Mississippi made their coöperation, in the event of hostilities, a serious menace. He expressed concern, furthermore, about the loyalty of the settlers of Louisiana, almost all of whom were French. He pointed out that this province had been a heavy drain on the resources of New Spain, as its revenue was inadequate to defray the expenses of administration and defence. He had just sent 298,000 *pesos* requested by Carondelet. The urgent need of reënforcing the defences of Texas and New Mexico would render further help to Louisiana impossible.[2]

To the serious danger of the impending English attack was added the fear of American aggression. The negroes in Louisiana and the Indians in Texas were showing signs of increasing unrest. It was suspected on good grounds that American emissaries were encouraging the former to revolt and the latter to prey upon the Spanish outposts. A group of Iowas, Wichitas, and Taovayas had come to Nacogdoches with Chief Irissac to complain of damages suffered at the hands of American settlers and their Indian allies. Commandant Nava asked Muñoz to make an investigation and to report how far the lands of these natives were from the American settlements, what the extent of the depredations was, and what the relations were between the Iowas and other northern tribes.[3] Warnings were issued to the Count of Sierra Gorda in Nuevo

---

[2]Marqués de Branciforte to the Duque de Alcudia, July 3, 1795. *A. G. I., Papeles de Estado, México, Legajo 4, Núm. 7.* (Dunn Transcripts, 1795-1817, pp. 1-13.)

[3]Nava to Muñoz, March 13, 1795. *Béxar Archives.*

Santander and to Simón de Herrera in Monterrey (Nuevo León) to keep the closest vigilance and to maintain constant communication with the commandant general. A royal order was transmitted to all frontier commanders in New Spain, instructing them to be on the alert against surprise. The commander at Nacogdoches was ordered to arrest all foreigners found among the Indians, and to offer to the friendly natives liberal rewards in the form of gifts for news of the presence of strangers within the Spanish dominions.[4]

As the summer wore on, rumors were rife of a combination of English and American forces, who would assemble on the shores of Lakes Superior, Michigan, and Erie to descend the Mississippi to New Orleans and attack Texas and New Mexico. Nava repeated his orders to maintain the strictest vigilance and suggested that the Gulf coast be watched from the bay of San Bernardo to the Mississippi. At the same time he informed the Duke of Alcudia that upon receiving the first news of the appearance of the enemy in the northern provinces, he would move to the frontier to take personal charge of operations. The friendly Indians of New Mexico and Texas had been asked to report the presence of foreigners or their approach. Just recently they had captured and brought to Nacogdoches an American trader. But two Frenchmen, Dupont and Gachard, who were in his company, had succeeded in escaping. To prevent a possible surprise on the unprotected coast line of Texas, he had ordered a reconnaissance to be conducted by Governor Muñoz.[5]

Fear of French invasion. The strain felt by frontier officials was perceptibly increased in September when Bernardo Dortolán, captain of Natchitoches, reported to Governor Muñoz that he had learned from the Iowas that a Mr. Genêt, former captain of the guards of Louis XVI, had planned to invade Louisiana. Genêt had maintained correspondence with a certain Burgos, resident of Havana, to whom he was going to send arms and munitions from Philadelphia. It seems that the conspirators had counted upon American support, but President Washington had resolutely opposed the scheme. Burgos had been arrested in Havana and the plot had failed. The news given Dortolán was confirmed by a full report of the whole affair received by Governor Carondelet of Louisiana.[6]

---

[4]Marqués de Branciforte to the Count of Sierra Gorda, July 10, 1795; Nava to Muñoz, July 30, 1795. *Béxar Archives.*

[5]Pedro Nava to the Duque de Alcudia, August 6, 1795. *A. G. I., Papeles de Estado, México, Legajo 13, Núm. 2.* (Dunn Transcripts, 1792-1799, pp. 95-102.)

[6]Bernardo Dortolán to Muñoz, September 6, 1795. *Béxar Archives.*

Negro insurrection in Louisiana. Late in the summer the fear of a negro revolt became a reality and only the determined and quick action of Carondelet prevented its spread. A slave named Sarasai headed the rebellion which broke out on the plantation of Julian Poydras in Pointe Coupee Parish. It was the plan of the slaves to surprise and murder their masters simultaneously in all the plantations. Several hundred were involved in the plot but the brains of the conspiracy were a Frenchman named Bullabal and a German named Rotenburg. The prompt action of the authorities overpowered the slaves. After a summary trial of the leaders, Sarasai and twenty-one others were publicly hanged and forty were condemned to the galleys. The masters of the slaves were compensated at the rate of two hundred *pesos* for each slave.

Still fearful of a repetition of the incident, the *Cabildo* of New Orleans on February 29, 1796, requested Governor Carondelet to prohibit the future importation of slaves into the province. Carondelet acceded to the request and issued a provisional proclamation.[7]

Guarding the coast line. Early in January the viceroy agreed to send the *Flor de Mayo* to reconnoiter the coast from the mouth of the Río Bravo or Del Norte (Río Grande) to the Mississippi. Nava instructed Muñoz to order a detachment from La Bahía to be stationed on the bay of San Bernardo to await the vessel and to render it such aid as it might need. He suggested that the soldiers keep a bright fire burning at night to guide the exploring crew. On April 15, formal orders were issued to Don Joaquín de la Moneda, commander of the coast guards at Vera Cruz, to carry out the reconnaissance with two ships, the *Flor de Mayo* and the *Zaeta*, which were to contact the detachment sent to San Bernardo Bay. But shortly afterwards the order was countermanded and the projected exploration was abandoned.[8]

The strained relations with England and the fear of American aggression made the viceroy realize the importance of building a second line of defence in Texas. In a letter to Godoy, the viceroy boldly stated that, should Louisiana be lost by a surprise attack, Texas would become the only barrier to stem the tide of American colonists who would sweep

---

[7]Dortolán to Muñoz, September 6, 1795. *Béxar Archives.* Fortier, *A History of Louisiana*, II, 164.

[8]Nava to Muñoz, January 9, May 10, and July 2, 1795. *Béxar Archives.*

across the vast expanse of the Interior Provinces to the very outskirts of Mexico City. There was no time to lose in fortifying this province.[9]

Difficulties of the Boundary Commission. In the midst of the uncertainty and the fears of puzzled Spanish officials, the United States appointed Colonel Andrew Ellicott to proceed to the survey of the boundary established by the treaty of 1795, and Spain named Brigadier-General Manuel Gayoso de Lemos as her representative. Late in 1796, Ellicott and his military escort reached the Mississippi by descending the Ohio. On January 16, 1797, his party met Philip Nolan on his way from New Madrid to Massac. Ellicott remarked of the newcomer that he was well known "for his athletic exertions and dexterity in taking wild horses." The young adventurer, who was to meet an inglorious death in Texas,[10] gave Ellicott much useful information "which eventually I found extremely useful," declared the commissioner. It was a fortunate chance meeting, for few men knew more about frontier conditions than the young protégé of the wily General Wilkinson.[11]

Ellicott and his party arrived on February 2 in New Madrid where the Spanish garrison fired a salute and welcomed the American party with characteristic Spanish hospitality. Here Ellicott met Father Maxwell, an Irish priest, "a well informed liberal gentleman, who acted as an interpreter." A letter of Governor Carondelet of November was shown to the commissioner in which the commandant was instructed not to allow the commissioner to proceed down the river until the Spanish forts had been evacuated. This surprised Ellicott, who protested, and was permitted to continue the next day.

By February 3 he was in Chickasaw Bluffs where the Spaniards were evidently surprised to see him and received the visitors with cold but impeccable hospitality. Ellicott was perplexed and his suspicions of the action of Spanish officials were rapidly aroused. Nolan warned him, "keep your suspicions to yourself . . . the utmost caution will be necessary both for your success and my own safety." After a few days' delay, the party continued down the river to Walnut Hills (Nogales). Here the Spaniards had erected a strong fortification which Ellicott observed could be converted into an almost impregnable post.

---

[9]Marqués de Branciforte to the Prinicipe de la Paz, May 27, 1796. *A. G. I., Papeles de Estado, México, Legajo 5, Núm. 64.* (Dunn Transcripts, 1792-1799, pp. 169-172.)

[10]A full account of his activities and death is given in Chapter VIII.

[11]Ellicott, Andrew, *Journal of . . . during part of 1796, the years 1797, 1798, 1799, and part of 1800,* 20-30.

The Spanish commander was coldly polite, asked the occasion of the visit, and feigned absolute ignorance of the treaty of 1795. Ellicott was by now convinced that the Spanish officials desired to postpone the survey of the boundary and the evacuation of the territory now occupied. Here he received a letter on February 21 from Gayoso de Lemos who explained that lack of adequate facilities to withdraw the troops would delay the survey. He politely asked Ellicott to leave his military escort at Bayou Pierre before continuing his journey to Natchez. Agreeable to the request, the American commissioner proceeded next day without the escort to the post just above Natchez where he met Gayoso de Lemos on February 24 and, after a brief interview, set March 19 as the date for beginning the survey.[12] While in Natchez, Ellicott learned the cause for the hesitation of Spanish officials and their desire to postpone the execution of the terms of the treaty of 1795.[13]

The Natchez affair. Ellicott discovered that rumors of a possible French seizure were rife and that French relations with the United States had become strained as a result of Citizen Genêt's affair. Exceeding his powers, he sounded out the opinion of the settlers in and around Natchez and found out that the majority favored becoming citizens of the United States. He injudiciously hoisted the American flag in his camp, and began to organize American sympathizers for resistance by force of arms. The Indians in the vicinity now became openly hostile and threatened the American camp with destruction. Ellicott protested. Gayoso hastened to explain that the hostility of the natives was due to the hoisting of the American flag. This had aroused their fears and hatred. On March 16 Ellicott used the incident to move the escort from Bayou Pierre to the American camp.[14]

The Spanish fort at Natchez was dismantled on March 17, but suddenly the guns were remounted and the garrison reënforced. Ellicott protested, and Gayoso replied that the evacuation would have to be delayed because of Indian unrest. The natives had complained against American friendship with the Choctaws. Irritation continued to increase, and on March 29 Gayoso issued a proclamation to calm the inhabitants of Natchez and to assure them that Spanish law would continue in force until the country was officially turned over to the United States.[15]

---

[12]Ellicott, *Journal*, 32-40.

[13]*Ibid.*, 44.

[14]*Ibid.*, 44-55.

[15]*Ibid.*, 57-67.

Conditions grew worse as time passed. A Mr. Green from Tennessee made an offer to Ellicott to raise one hundred men to take Fort Natchez by force, and a Mr. Anthony Hutchins, a British agent, offered to capture Gayoso and deliver him to the Chickasaws to avoid responsibility for his fate. Ellicott refused both proposals, but he condoned the enlistment of men for service in the United States Army.[16]

On May 30 Governor Carondelet issued a proclamation in French, in which he declared that the Spanish minister to the United States had learned on good authority that an English expedition was being organized on the Great Lakes to attack the country of the Illinois and to invade Louisiana. In view of these circumstances, the evacuation of Natchez and Nogales, already begun, would be suspended as a means of defence. The measure was made all the more imperative by the information received from Natchez itself that a division of the American Army on the Ohio had been ordered to this post, and that the militia of Cumberland had been instructed to be in readiness. Gayoso had communicated this information to Ellicott thirty days before with a request that he ask the American Government to deny permission to the English to march through American territory, and to explain the postponement of the execution of the terms of the treaty of 1795 was necessary in view of the turn of affairs.[17]

By his own admission, Ellicott's conduct after May 1 was not above reproach nor in keeping with international law. On May 16 he set down in his diary that he had undertaken to win over the Choctaws and planned to fortify Baton Rouge. He kept these activities secret, he said, because "its being known would injure, if not ruin, Mr. Nolan." But he explained in his entry for June 5 that his relations with the Choctaws were dictated by his desire "to render the Indians harmless in case of a rupture."[18] That a rupture was not a remote possibility was pointed out by Carondelet in his proclamation of May 30, when he referred to the strained relations between the United States and France as a result of Citizen Genêt's activities and the fact that France was the "intimate ally" of Spain.[19]

---

[16]*Ibid.*, 74-79.

[17]Proclamation of Governor Carondelet, New Orleans, May 30, 1797. Spanish translation by José Piernas in *Béxar Archives*. Ellicott, *Journal*, 80-82; Fortier, *History of Louisiana*, II, 168-169. Ellicott in his diary referred to the proclamation in his entry for May 24, indicating its probable publication before May 30. Fortier gives the date as May 31.

[18]Ellicott, *Journal*, 80-99.

[19]Fortier, *op. cit.*, II, 168.

The matter was brought to a head at Natchez through the activity of a Baptist minister by the name of Hanna, an itinerant pioneer preacher. Permission was obtained on June 4 for him to hold a quiet meeting in Ellicott's camp. The news spread rapidly, and a large crowd gathered to witness the unusual sight. The enthusiastic minister in his fervor denounced Catholicism. He was reprimanded by Gayoso a few days later. His impudent reply resulted in his prompt arrest and an order on June 9 that he be put in the stocks. In vain did he appeal to Ellicott, who wrote in his *Journal* that he "spent a great part of the night devising plans to direct the commotion that was now inevitable to the advantage of the United States, without committing either the government or its officers." The next day a mob forced Gayoso to take refuge in the fort, and for twelve days the boundary commissioner and governor of Natchez was a virtual prisoner until terms were dictated by the rebellious citizens who were encouraged in their actions, guided in fact, by Ellicott.[20]

Although the incident just narrated may seem unrelated to Texas, it had a very direct bearing on the policy ultimately adopted by the Spanish officials for the defence of the province, and should be considered in relation to other contemporary incidents to fully understand the events that followed in Texas.

James Wilkinson and his schemes.   A singular character, as unscrupulous as he was shrewd, a double-crossing villain, a good-natured rogue, this man played a sinister roll upon the Spanish frontier. At the close of the war for American independence, he retired from the army with the rank of colonel and brigadier-general by brevet. In 1787 he was engaged in business in Kentucky. In June of that year he arrived in New Orleans with a cargo of tobacco, flour, butter, and bacon, which were promptly seized by Spanish officials. He appears to have won the confidence of Governor Miró shortly afterwards, however, and to have ingratiated himself with Miró by a memorial which he presented at this time. The goods were released, and before the close of the year Wilkinson had sold them at a handsome profit without paying a cent of duty.

The secret of his success is found in the proposals made to Governor Miró in his memorial. He argued that the settlers of the West had an inalienable right to follow the rivers flowing from their country to the sea. Spain was pursuing a short-sighted policy in attempting to close the Mississippi to them. They were greatly aroused by the rumors that

---

[20]Ellicott, *Journal,* 98-102.

the United States was about to sacrifice their dearest interest by ceding to Spain, for twenty years, all rights to the Mississippi. They were so completely dissatisfied with their government that they were on the point of seceding from the Union. Spain should try to win their friendship by permitting them to navigate the Mississippi, rather than to provoke them into an invasion of Louisiana. He concluded by offering his services in the promotion of the policy outlined. How far these treasonable designs had advanced, is revealed by Miró's letter of January 8, 1788, in which he wrote: "The delivery of Kentucky to His Majesty, the principal object to which Wilkinson has promised to devote himself entirely, would assure forever this province as a rampart to New Spain."[21]

On May 15 Wilkinson wrote the Spanish governor an incriminating letter in cipher, which was brought to New Orleans in a pirogue by Colonel Dunn. He assured Miró that Kentucky would soon separate from Virginia. The separation would be followed by open negotiations through an agent "with power to treat of the union in which we are engaged. . . . I anticipate no obstacle on the part of Congress," he added, "because of the weakness of this body under the Confederation and the uncertainty of the establishment of a new congress."[22]

Miró was not completely fooled. His suspicions, aroused by the ambitious commercial transactions of the would-be conspirator, are expressed in a letter of June 15. "Although his candor and whatever information I have obtained from many who have known him," he says, "seem to assure us that he is working in all cordiality, I am aware it is possible that his intention may be to enrich himself by means of inflating us with hopes and advantages, knowing that they will be in vain." There were good grounds for the suspicions. The message of May had been followed by the arrival of five boatloads of tobacco which were sold for seven thousand *pesos*. This money was reinvested in merchandise valued at more than eighteen thousand. In 1789 Wilkinson visited New Orleans again. It was at this time that he wrote the incriminating letter of February 14, 1789, signed *"Un buen Español"* (A good Spaniard). The open hints for remuneration were answered by Miró with the statement, "according to the answer of the court [of Spain], you are our agent, and I am ordered to give you hopes that the king will recom-

---

[21]Whitaker, A. P., *The Spanish-American Frontier*, 97-99; Fortier, *op. cit.*, II, 131-132.

[22]James Wilkinson to Miró, May 15, 1788. Cited by Fortier in *A History of Louisiana*, II, 133-135.

pense you as I have already intimated."[23] He was advanced a loan of seven thousand *pesos* at this time by the Spanish governor who on May 22 recommended that he be retained in the service of Spain with a pension of two thousand *pesos*. This pension was formally granted by the king in 1792.[24] Such hopes as Wilkinson and his friends may have seriously entertained had, in fact, been blasted by the rejection of a proposal for the secession from the Union by the Convention of Kentucky held in July, 1788.

Interest in the schemes of Wilkinson waned between 1789 and 1794. In January and February of this year, however, he again wrote enthusiastically that the time for decisive action had arrived. Kentucky was tired of the inefficiency of the Federal Government, and its people were determined to gain accession to the Mississippi either by secession from the Union or by conquest of Louisiana. The visit in the winter of 1793 of Michel Lacassagne, a French merchant from Kentucky, who came to New Orleans to collect six thousand *pesos* on Wilkinson's pension account, had prepared Carondelet for the news. From April to July, the Spanish governor urged Godoy to make a decision between strengthening the outposts of Louisiana and Texas and stirring up the Indians against the Americans on the one hand—and on the other, scheming for the withdrawal of Kentucky from the Union to constitute a buffer province. The latter policy involved, among other expenses, the increase of the pension of General Wilkinson. In fact, Carondelet, on his own initiative, early in 1794 sent Wilkinson sixteen thousand dollars, of which he received only fifty-one hundred; Lacassagne received four thousand more, of which he kept fourteen hundred; and of the twelve thousand sent by Henry Owens and Henry Collins, only twenty-five hundred reached Wilkinson, because Owens had been murdered and robbed by his Spanish escort, and Collins had incurred heavy expenses in conducting the money.[25] Wilkinson justified his demands for additional money by alleging he had sustained considerable expense in buying off George Rogers Clark. But he failed to come to New Orleans as he had promised, or to send delegates for a final agreement. Suspicion of the sincerity of the American conspirator, the inherent danger of war with the United States, the strained relations with Great Britain, and the fear of a general uprising of Indians finally resulted in the Council of the Indies' abandoning,

---

[23]Fortier, *op. cit.*, II, 135-142.
[24]Whitaker, *op. cit.*, 117; Fortier, *ibid.*, II, 143.
[25]Whitaker, *The Spanish-American Frontier*, 190-196.

on July 25, 1794, the treasonable schemes which led eventually to the treaty of San Lorenzo of 1795.[26]

French, British, and American complications. The treaty of San Lorenzo was the immediate outcome of the peace concluded between Spain and France at Bale in July, 1795. Spain was fully aware that the resentment of Great Britain would result in an open break; hence her decision to settle the long standing dispute with the Americans to obviate an alliance with the British. Godoy admitted the facts in a conversation with Earle Bute, the British ambassador, when he told him in May, 1796, that Britain's hostile preparations against Mexico in the previous year had forced him to make extensive concessions to the United States.[27] But the sacrifices proved futile. The French and the American treaties served only to exasperate the English and did not win for Spain either the friendship of the United States or the support of France.

In July, 1797, Nava wrote Muñoz in Texas that the English were still planning an invasion from Canada; that an expeditionary force of nine or ten thousand men was being assembled at Halifax; and that the attack would be made either on the Mississippi or on the coast of Texas. He urged the governor to maintain the strictest vigilance, to court the friendship of the natives, to reënforce all outposts, and to send detachments frequently to patrol the Gulf coast. Soldiers from La Bahía should explore San Bernardo Bay two or three times a week, and the natives should be asked to report the presence of foreigners along the coast. Nava warned Muñoz that an agent was being sent to arouse the Indians and promote a rebellion. This agent was no other than Francisco de Miranda whose description read thus: "two *varas* in height, brunette, heavy black beard, black hair, oblong face, wide forehead, sunken cheeks, brown eyes, slim, bony, dress and manner English, age about fifty." If found, he was to be arrested and his papers and belongings seized.[28]

Nava was not convinced, however, that the contemplated attack would be through Texas and Coahuila. In a letter to Godoy, he declared that these provinces were too vast, too poor, and too desolate for a successful invasion. There was greater likelihood that the expedition would be directed against lower Louisiana. Elguezábal reported in August that a sharp lookout was being kept both at Nacogdoches and all along the coast

---

[26]*Ibid.*, 197-200.
[27]Whitaker, *op. cit.*, 207.
[28]Nava to Muñoz, July 17, 1797. *Béxar Archives.*

against any surprise. The friendly Indians had been propitiated by gifts, and a detachment had been sent to San Bernardo Bay.[29]

It was at this time that Ellicott, exasperated by the hesitating policy of Gayoso in putting into effect the terms of the treaty of 1795, was stirring up trouble in Natchez. His activities among the Choctaws have been noted. Nava explained to Godoy in September that these Indians, urged by American agents, were molesting the friendly tribes in order to convince them of the Spaniards' impotence to protect them.[30]

In 1798 Franco-American relations became seriously strained. Nava warned Muñoz in August of this year that Congress had authorized American ships to attack French vessels found in coast waters. He expressed fear that the close relations binding France and Spain might cause American hostility to extend to the dominions of His Catholic Majesty. Vigilance along the frontier and the Gulf coast should be redoubled. He suggested that Nacogdoches be reënforced by fifteen or twenty men from Béxar or La Bahía, and an advanced post be established beyond Nacogdoches to keep a closer watch on developments in Louisiana. All foreigners without passports were to be arrested; only licensed traders were to traffic with the natives; and constant communication with Natchitoches and the governor of Louisiana was to be maintained. The instructions were repeated in October, but there was added a strong recommendation to watch the natives in particular.[31]

Activities of William Augustus Bowles.   This interesting adventurer was a native of Maryland, who fought on the side of the British during the American Revolution. While in Florida in 1777, he was dismissed for insubordination. He took refuge among the Indians and married the daughter of one of the Creek chiefs. He now became an irreconcilable enemy of Spain. For some years he preyed upon Spanish commerce as a pirate, and later became the agent of English trading houses in the Bahamas. Bowles was among the Creeks in Florida early in 1792. Governor Carondelet sent an expedition which succeeded in capturing him. After he was brought to New Orleans in March, his attractive personality and his plausible manner made the governor put more faith

---

[29]Nava to Principe de la Paz, August 1, 1797. *A. G. I., Papeles de Estado, México, Legajo 18, Núm. 21.* (Dunn Transcripts, 1792-1799, pp. 181-183); Elguezábal to Muñoz, August 3, and 7, 1797. *Béxar Archives.*

[30]Nava to Principe de la Paz, September 5, 1797. *A. G. I., Papeles de Estado, México, Legajo 12, Núm. 22.* (Dunn Transcripts, 1792-1797, pp. 222-226.)

[31]Nava to Muñoz, August 28, and October 30, 1798. *Béxar Archives.*

in the account of conditions among the Indians than the character of
the informer warranted. Carondelet, having obtained the desired information, sent him to Havana, whence he was taken to Cádiz for trial,
and eventually to Manila to serve out his sentence. Several years later,
however, he succeeded in escaping.[32]

In 1797 he was back in England where he appears to have enjoyed
the friendship of the Duke of Portland. He shortly afterwards returned
to the Bahamas and then to his old haunts in Florida and Louisiana.
Alarming news about his activities aroused grave apprehensions in the
mind of the commandant general. Nava wrote to the governor of Texas in
November, 1799, that he had just learned of the recent arrival in Nassau,
of a certain Mr. Bowles, said to be a Virginian, who was chief of the
Indians of Florida, Pensacola, and Louisiana. According to the reports
received, he had an English secretary who spoke Spanish and French
fluently. The English had conferred upon him the rank of lieutenant-colonel
and given him a French aide-de-camp. The ship that took him to his
destination carried three thousand guns and the corresponding ammunition. This information had been given by a Spaniard recently taken
prisoner while on his way from Philadelphia to Cuba. He added that
Bowles was to go to Savannah where he was to promote rebellion among
the natives nearest the Spanish frontier. The rebellion could easily extend
from Louisiana to Texas, Nava warned. A close vigilance of the natives
was more necessary than ever. José Miguel del Moral dispelled the fear
entertained by officials in Texas in April, 1800, by informing Elguezábal
that the commandant at Natchitoches had learned that the Indians did
not accept Bowles as leader. There was, consequently, no immediate
danger.[33]

Bishop of New Orleans warns against Americans.   The pioneers who
had by now filtered into Louisiana were openly expressing their designs
on Mexico. Bishop Peñalver wrote in November, 1799, that the province
was "infested" with adventurers from the West, who had settled in the
districts of Ouachita, Attakapas, Opelousas, and particularly Natchitoches. All these areas bordered the Texas frontier. He had noticed

---

[32]For an interesting account of this singular character, see *The American Historical
Review*, VI, 708-709; also Cox, I. J., *The West Florida Controversy, 1798-1818*,
140-141; Fortier, *A History of Louisiana*, II, 151; Lac, Perrin du, *Voyage dans les
deux Louisianes;* Whitaker, *Spanish-American Frontier*, 163-164, 166-167.

[33]Nava to governor of Texas, November 20, 1799. *Béxar Archives*. Hatcher,
M. A., *The Opening of Texas to Foreign Settlement*, 42.

that the westerners were in the habit of striking their sons on the shoulder if they were unusually robust, and of saying to them, "You will go to Mexico by and by."[34]

A brief quotation from the illuminating *Memoir* of Colonel Joseph Xavier Delfau de Pontalva serves to emphasize the repeated warnings which Spanish officials received concerning the ulterior designs of the American pioneers and the danger they represented. "The Mississippi is the natural barrier," he declared. "It should be rendered impenetrable as . . . the surest way to destroy forever the bold projects with which several persons in the United States fill their newspapers, designating through Louisiana the road to the conquest of Mexico; especially since the disputes that have arisen about the frontier. . . .

"Since the Americans have been in possession of the new limits, it becomes more important than ever to assure a rampart for the protection of Mexico."[35]

Keeping watch against foreign surprise. Under the circumstances it was only natural that in the closing years of the century strenuous efforts should have been made to prevent encroachments. A hunter of wild horses reported to the commander of La Bahía that he had heard cannon fired on the coast. On January 5, 1799, Captain Del Moral dispatched a group of mission Indians from Refugio to investigate. Having made a careful exploration of Aransas and Matagorda bays, they returned thirteen days later to report no trace of foreigners.[36]

Not long afterwards rumors reached Captain Guadiana at Nacogdoches through the Arkokisas that a trading post had been established by foreigners in the vicinity of the mouth of the Sabine River. He immediately sent Bernabé del Río, trusted Indian interpreter, to investigate the report. A vacant log house was found at the place indicated, which, according to the natives, had been occupied two years before by an Englishman named Juan Barney, and his companion, who were now living in Natchitoches. Guadiana inquired from the commander at Opelousas if any settlers from Louisiana had moved recently into Texas. The reply was that he knew of none.

Before the end of January, Del Moral, still suspicious, sent four soldiers to make a careful exploration of the mouth of the Colorado and the coast

---

[34]Cited by Fortier, *op. cit.*, II, 175.

[35]Pontalva, Joseph Xavier Delfau de, *Memoir*, September 15, 1801. Quoted in full in Fortier, *op. cit.*, II, 192-193.

[36]José Miguel del Moral to Muñoz, January 5, and 13, 1799. *Béxar Archives*.

in its vicinity, the eastern end of Matagorda Bay. He wanted to learn if the river was navigable. The party reported that the mouth of the river was lost in a group of shallow inlets five or six leagues from the coast. There was no danger of the enemy penetrating by this route into the interior. Del Moral observed that the Trinity River was a much better entry.[37]

A few straggling settlers, mostly French, had established themselves on Arroyo de las Piedras, east of the Sabine, but within the jurisdiction of the commander of Nacogdoches. Pablo Bevel Lafitte was the *Justicia* (judge) of the district and even had an old cannon as defence against the Indians. Shortly after the death of Nolan, all settlers east of the Sabine were ordered taken to Nacogdoches, together with their cannon.[38]

Relations with Choctaws and other nations. The Choctaws, it will be remembered, had been befriended by Ellicott at Natchez. They had been committing depredations ever since then, protesting all the while their friendship for the Spaniards. On January 20, 1800, they attacked a group of Caddos near Natchitoches without provocation. In reporting the incident, Del Moral pointed out that these Indians were the inveterate enemies of all the northern nations. In June a band of Choctaws raided the ranch of José Ignacio Ibarbo, near Nacogdoches, killed two friendly Ais Indians, cut off their heads, and bound a Spaniard hand and foot before driving away the cattle. Again Del Moral warned Elguezábal against befriending these Indians who were a real menace to Texas. He explained that the enraged friendly tribes had solicited his aid for a campaign of extermination. There were thirty-three men in the garrison at Nacogdoches, but if the governor approved the idea, one hundred sixty volunteers could be enlisted.[39]

The exasperation of Del Moral at the proposal of Valentín Layssard, commander at Rapide, Louisiana, that the Choctaws be granted lands to settle in Texas may be imagined. He wrote to Elguezábal in July vigorously opposing the plan. He declared that the Choctaws were hostile to the tribes now in Texas, that they were under the influence of the English and the Americans, and that they were widely connected with other hostile tribes in Louisiana. Their admission would bring no benefits

---

[37]José María Guadiana to the Governor, April 2, 1799; José Miguel del Moral to Elguezábal, January 28, and March 5, 1800. *Béxar Archives.*

[38]Músquiz to Elguezábal, May 1, 1801. *Béxar Archives.*

[39]José Miguel del Moral to Elguezábal, January 28, and June 26, 1800. *Béxar Archives.*

whatsoever, because they would continue to trade in Rapide, and there was danger of terminating the peace. Elguezábal, who knew the allegations were well founded, appealed to the governor of Louisiana to prevent the emigration of the Choctaws. At the same time Del Moral wrote Layssard to delay their departure until a decision was made by the higher officials, to whom the matter had been referred.[40]

Commandant Nava promptly adopted the recommendation of Elguezábal, and the governor issued orders to prevent their admission. But Layssard was not discouraged in his plan. He realized that the only valid objection to his protégés was the existing enmity between them and the Texas tribes. If this was removed, the Choctaws would have to be admitted. Immediately, he prepared a speech praising the virtues of peace which he forwarded to José Vidal, Spanish consul at Natchez, with instructions for its prompt delivery to the grand chief of the Choctaws. Following the instructions of their patron, they applied again for admission, and after a short time succeeded in obtaining their end.[41]

Trade in horses and cattle. The scarcity of horses and cattle in Louisiana had long been recognized, and officials in Texas had repeatedly been authorized to give temporary relief. On May 1, 1780, the king, in approving the action of the viceroy in this respect, gave blanket authorization for the future, conditioned on the request of the governor of Louisiana. "The king," wrote the secretary, "has approved your action in ordering the governor of Texas to send fifteen hundred head of cattle to Louisiana immediately to replenish the notable want in that territory. His Majesty has likewise approved your instructions to the governor of Texas, requesting him to give any help or assistance within his power to the governor of Louisiana without awaiting his royal authorization. It is his will that your lordship order that stock continue to be sent to Louisiana whenever its governor requests it."[42] This provision let down the floodgate and permitted numerous foreign traders to penetrate even beyond Texas to distant Coahuila and Nuevo Santander in search of wild horses and cattle.

An idea of the extent of traffic in horses may be judged by the reports made on this subject in 1801 alone. On April 20, Miguel Músquiz wrote

---

[40]Del Moral to Elguezábal, July 11, and 27, 1800. *Béxar Archives.*

[41]Nava to Elguezábal, August 4, and September 30, 1800; Layssard to the Great Chief of the Choctaws and Other Nations, September 15, 1800; Layssard to Vidal, same date. *Béxar Archives.*

[42]*Real Orden*, May 1, 1780. *A. G. M., Historia*, Vol. 413, pt. 1.

Governor Elguezábal from Nacogdoches that Juan Bautista Fortiere had arrived there with sixteen horses which he claimed he had caught near La Bahía. Upon being asked to present his passport and permit, he was unable to produce them; whereupon Músquiz confiscated the horses and sold them at auction on April 18. Fortiere was sentenced to two weeks' work on the new church being built in Nacogdoches.[43]

Vicente Fernández Tejeiro requested permission on May 23 to take three hundred horses, three hundred mares, and twenty-five asses each year for two or three years, to the new settlement of Baron de Bastrop in Louisiana. These animals were needed for developing the new colony and cultivating the wheat fields.[44] The request was rejected because of the excitement created at this time by the Nolan affair.

In July, Nicolás Lanee, from San Fernando, in Nuevo Santander, sent notice posthaste to Elguezábal that Tomás Luna and two servants, Emeregildo Garza and Gregorio Patiño, had just left for Natchitoches with a drove of stolen horses. According to the information obtained, they were not planning to go by way of San Antonio but would follow along the coast to avoid La Bahía and Nacogdoches, and passing through the country of the Arkokisas, would cross the Sabine at the Juan Mora crossing. Lanee suggested that the horse thieves be intercepted at once before they reached the Sabine. Elguezábal wrote Guadiana on August 12 to send a party out from Nacogdoches to apprehend the horse thief smugglers, but it seems they arrived at the Sabine crossing too late.[45]

On October 13 Juan Lastrope wrote Elguezábal that he had contracted the year before with a certain Manuel Barrera for one hundred eighty or one hundred ninety head of cattle and a drove of horses. But since the death of Nolan and the arrest of his companions, all exportation of both cattle and horses had been strictly prohibited. Lastrope asked that an exception be made in this instance, but Nava was not in a favorable mood and the request was refused.[46]

Horse and cattle smugglers had to risk not only official retribution but the danger of Indian attacks as well. On September 16, Elguezábal reported to Nava a typical example. A group of herders, who had been secretly rounding up wild cattle north of San Antonio, started for

[43]Miguel Músquiz to Elguezábal, April 20, 1801. *Béxar Archives.*

[44]Vicente Fernández Tejeiro to Elguezábal, May 23, 1801. *Béxar Archives.*

[45]Nicolás Lanee to Elguezábal, July 31, 1801; Elguezábal to Guadiana, August 12, 1801. *Béxar Archives.*

[46]Juan Lastrope to Elguezábal, October 13, 1801. *Béxar Archives.*

Louisiana with their catch but were soon afterward attacked by a large party of Comanches who succeeded in taking the herd. Lieutenant Amangual was sent in pursuit, but the herders had delayed reporting the outrage for obvious reasons and so made the venture futile.[47]

Texas mustangs. The horses, strays from the missions, had multiplied with incredible rapidity and sired the numberless droves that attracted so many adventurers to Texas in the closing years of the century. When in 1806, Captain Zebulon Montgomery Pike undertook to explore Red River and the Arkansas by order of General Wilkinson, he was amazed by the number of the wild creatures thundering proudly across the plains, their defiant neighing causing the horses and the mules of the pack train to stampede and follow the herd. "The wild horses," he wrote in his account, "are in such numbers as to afford supplies for all the savages who border on the province, [as well as] the Spaniards, and the vast droves for other provinces of the United States. . . . They go in such large numbers that it is requisite to keep an advance guard of horsemen, in order to frighten them away; for should they be suffered to come near your horses and mules which you drive with you, by their snorting and neighing, they alarm them, and are frequently joined by them and taken off, notwithstanding all the exertions of the dragoons to prevent them.

"A gentleman told me," he continued, "he saw seven hundred beasts carried off at one time, not one of which was ever recovered. In the night they frequently carry off the droves of travellers' horses and even come within a few miles of San Antonio and entice away the horses in the vicinity."[48]

A description of the manner in which the Spaniards were wont to catch them may not be amiss. "They take a few fleet horses," continued Pike, "and proceed into the country where the animals are numerous; they build a large inclosure, with a door which enters into a smaller inclosure. From the entrance of the large pen they project wings out into the prairie to a great distance, and then set up bushes, etc., to induce the horses when pursued to enter within these wings. After these preparations are made, they keep a lookout for such a drove; for if they unfortunately should start too large a one, they either burst open the

---

[47]Nava to Elguezábal, October 13, 1801. *Béxar Archives.*

[48]Pike, Zebulon M., *Exploratory travels through the western territories of North America*, 331-332. (London, 1811.)

pen or fill it up with the dead bodies, and the remainder run over them and escape, in which case the party is obliged to leave the place, as the stench arising from the putrid carcasses would be insupportable, and in addition to this, the pen would not receive others. But should they succeed in driving in a few, say two or three hundred, they select the handsomest and youngest, noose them, and take them into a small inclosure, then turn out the others. . . . They subdue them by degrees, and finally break them to submit to the saddle and bridle. For this business I presume there is no nation in the world superior to the Spaniards of Texas."[49]

Celestino Sant-Maxent appealed in 1801 to Governor Elguezábal in San Antonio for permission to take to Louisiana a large number of horses which he had employed in the transportation of baggage from Puebla to Rancho del Palo Blanco, near Mier. In the petition he explained that he was a captain in the Louisiana regiment stationed in New Orleans, that he had taken his mother to the city of Puebla by way of Vera Cruz, but that he had been granted permission by the viceroy to return by land. He wished to continue his journey from Palo Blanco to New Orleans by way of Espíritu Santo and he desired permission to proceed to his destination with his horses. Nava readily agreed to the request in view of the circumstances.[50]

Father Juan Brady requests permission to move to Texas. On October 29, 1800, Father Juan Brady, a Carmelite, requested permission to move to Texas from Baton Rouge. In his petition he included a certificate from the bishop of New Orleans in which it was set forth that he had studied in Spain and had come to New Orleans in 1795 with a royal patent to serve in the missions. After his arrival in Louisiana he had been sent as curate to Natchez. He had also served as curate of the parish of El Sagrario. Prior to his coming he had been chaplain on one of His Majesty's ships. The bishop testified that he was capable and responsible, that he had good training in theology, knew Spanish, French, and English, and was a zealous priest. The permission was granted.[51]

The retrocession of Louisiana. The success of Napoleon at Marengo on June 14, 1800, had forced Austria to make peace with France, and

---

[49] *Ibid.*, 332.

[50] Celestino Sant-Maxent to Elguezábal, October 14, 1801; Nava to Elguezábal, November 11, 1801. *Béxar Archives.*

[51] Testimony of the Bishop of New Orleans, October 1, 1801; Juan Brady to the Bishop of New Orleans, October 29, 1800. *Béxar Archives.*

made the prospects of peace with England almost a certainty. The First Consul had begun to think of an oversea empire. The former province of Louisiana loomed large in his dreams. He now proceeded to persuade Spain to return it to France. Godoy, Prince of the Peace, was the real ruler of Spain at this time through the absolute power he had come to exercise over the infatuated queen, who, in turn, completely dominated the spineless Charles IV, sitting stupidly upon the throne of his distinguished ancestors. Holding out a tempting territorial compensation at the expense of Italy, and arguing that Louisiana in the possession of France would become an impenetrable buffer to protect the Kingdom of New Spain, Napoleon had little difficulty in securing his wish.

General Alexander Berthier had succeeded as early as October 1, 1800, in negotiating the secret treaty desired by the First Consul. According to the agreement signed at San Ildefonso by Mariano Luis Urquijo for Spain, His Catholic Majesty bound himself to return to France the Province of Louisiana "with the same extent which it has at present in the hands of Spain, and which it had when France possessed it, and such as it should be since the treaties negotiated subsequently between Spain and other States." The retrocession, however, was not to be carried into effect until "six months after the full execution of the conditions and stipulations" concerning the Duke of Parma. These conditions and stipulations dealt with the aid which France bound itself to give Spain in enlarging the dominions of the Duke of Parma in Etruria, and in raising him to the dignity of king. The reason for secrecy was the effect which the French feared the retrocession of this valuable province would have upon the English negotiations then in progress.

On March 21, 1801, Lucien Bonaparte, brother of the First Consul, signed a new treaty at Madrid, confirming the agreement made at San Ildefonso, by which France again bound itself to bestow the Duchy of Tuscany on the Duke of Parma. But it was not until October 15, 1802, that Charles IV finally approved the treaty of San Ildefonso, after adding a very significant amendment which was to be shamelessly ignored by Napoleon within six months. He stipulated that: "France must pledge herself not to alienate Louisiana, and to restore it to Spain in case the king of Etruria should lose his power."[52]

The peace between France and England was at last concluded at Amiens on March 25, 1802. Napoleon immediately prepared to take

---

[52]Fortier, *History of Louisiana*, II, 178, 320-332. In the Appendix to this volume the full French text of the Treaty of San Ildefonso is reproduced.

possession of Louisiana. He appointed General Bernadotte captain-general of the new province, but the demands for troops and colonists made by the future king of Sweden were so exaggerated that the First Consul had to appoint General Victor in his place. The new captain-general was in Holland at the time of his appointment. Bad weather delayed his departure until May, 1803, by which time the peace of Amiens had been broken. The future Marshal of France never set foot on Louisiana. Nevertheless it fell to Governor Manuel de Salcedo and the Marqués de Casa Calvo to turn over the Province of Louisiana to Mr. Laussat, the French commissioner. He arrived in New Orleans in March, 1803, but the formal transfer was delayed until November 30, at first pending the arrival of General Victor, and then of further instructions.

The lack of rapid communication caused the news of Napoleon's sale of Louisiana to the United States to be delayed considerably. Seven months had elapsed since the sale to the United States before the solemn ceremony of the transfer to France took place. Thus, Napoleon sold the province before he had actually taken formal possession of it.

On the appointed day, at high noon, the Spanish troops and militia were drawn up in battle array in the square before the Cabildo. Thousands crowded in the neighboring streets, in the doorways, the windows, and even on the roofs to witness the spectacle. Within the Cabildo, Governor Manuel Salcedo sat in the middle of the council chamber with the Marqués de Casa Calvo at his left and Mr. Laussat at his right. The French commissioner presented his credentials from the First Consul and the order of the king of Spain of October 15, 1802, for the delivery of the province to France. The documents were publicly read by the secretary. Salcedo rose, bowed, and handed the keys of New Orleans to Laussat. The Marqués de Casa Calvo now rose and announced that all Spanish subjects who wished to follow the flag would be at liberty to move with their belongings to the dominions of the king, and that those who chose to remain in Louisiana would be automatically absolved from their oath of allegiance to His Catholic Majesty. The three commissioners went together to the large balcony facing the square, and at a given signal the flag of Spain was slowly lowered and the French flag hoisted in its place amidst the booming of a twenty-one gun salute. The crowd was ominously silent. The people of Louisiana felt no elation. Somehow their beloved France had betrayed them. The news of the sale to the United States had been public knowledge ever since early summer, and the arrival of the American commissioner was expected momentarily. In fact, the instructions to Mr. Laussat were that he transfer the province to the representative of the United States the same day he received it officially from Spain, but Laussat chose to exercise sovereignty for twenty days. Not until December 20, 1803, was the transfer to the United States to take place. At that time, one of the American commissioners was the sinister General James Wilkinson, who was to be so closely and luridly associated with events on the Spanish-American frontier during the next few years.

CHAPTER VIII

FIRST CLASHES WITH THE UNITED STATES

It has been shown that Spanish officials in Texas and New Spain had become fully aware of the importance of conciliating the Indians. Their policy of appeasement as the most likely solution of this vexing problem has already been noted. But more significant was the effect of the full realization of the import of foreign designs on Texas. The Spaniards were now compelled to be on guard against the Spanish vassals in Louisiana whom they distrusted; against the French, whom they could not classify either as friend or foe; against the English, who were openly antagonistic because of their commercial interest in the Spanish colonies; and against the Americans, whom, because of their aggressiveness and daring, they feared most of all. When in the opening years of the nineteenth century the retrocession of Louisiana to France made Texas again the bulwark of Spain's dominions in North America, these considerations naturally determined the new policies adopted for the safeguard of the distant province.

Philip Nolan's activities. No incident prior to 1801 had so profound an influence in confirming the long-felt fears of Spanish officials respecting the ulterior designs of American adventurers than the Nolan affair. It aroused the entire frontier into frantic action; it sowed suspicion so deep that it was never again fully dispelled. The mystery surrounding the activities of the intrepid "dealer in horses," his connection with high American and Spanish officials, the participation of American, French, English, and Spanish subjects in his expeditions, and the dramatic qualities of the adventurer could not help creating a deep and lasting impression.

Nolan first came to New Orleans in 1789 as the trusted business agent of Wilkinson, whom he served as bookkeeper and shipping clerk until 1791.[1] When the general, disappointed by the failure of his tobacco monopoly, decided to reënter the Army this year, Nolan was obliged to

---

[1]Clark, Daniel, *Proofs of the Corruption of General James Wilkinson*, 57-66; Wilkinson, James, *Memoirs of My Own Times*, II, 84. Much conjecture exists about his early years and parentage, but there is no ground for any longer maintaining that he was either the natural son of Wilkinson or that the general reared him from infancy.

seek some other employment. It was in the spring of 1791 that he announced to Wilkinson his intention of going to Texas for the first time, and it is seriously doubted that he had entered the province prior to this year.[2] In spite of the reluctance of Louisiana officials, he secured a letter and passport from Governor Miró and set out for San Antonio. He apparently did not reach his destination, but there is no doubt that he arrived in Nacogdoches and had spent some time there before his goods were confiscated. Disappointed, he took refuge among the Indians between the Illinois and San Antonio, where he claimed he became a favorite of the Comanches in particular.[3] After two years he admitted that he was bored with the wild life of the Indians, and he returned to the Spanish settlements "to repair his fortune." It was his return to Nacogdoches, probably in 1793, which he generally referred to as his second expedition to Texas.[4] He turned hunter, sold pelts, and succeeded in catching fifty wild horses which he drove back to Louisiana. Governor Carondelet received him "as a person risen from the dead."[5]

The third expedition to Texas, 1794-1796. Undaunted by the misfortunes and hardships of the first trip which perhaps was not so completely a financial failure as he would like to make us believe, Nolan immediately made arrangements to return to Texas. By June, 1794, he was back in Nacogdoches with five other citizens of Louisiana and a negro slave, armed with a letter from Carondelet and a passport. Córdoba, commandant at Nacogdoches, gave him permission to catch horses in accord with the request of the governor of Louisiana.[6] When, months later, Nava learned accidentally of the presence of Nolan in Texas, he asked immediately about his identity, and Muñoz reported that he was an Irishman, a relative of the renowned frontier inspector, Hugo Oconor. It seems that Nolan gave the governor this information, but it is seriously to be doubted that he was related to Oconor. While in Nacogdoches he became a good friend of the experienced missionary

---

[2]Nolan to Wilkinson, April 6, 1797. Wilkinson, *Memoirs,* II, Appendix No. 2. Yoakum has asserted he was in Texas in 1785, but gave no authority for his statement. Bancroft and many others have followed him.

[3]Nolan to Wilkinson, June 10, 1796. Wilkinson, *Memoirs,* II, Appendix No. 2.

[4]Wilson, Maurine T., *Philip Nolan and His Activities in Texas.* M. A. Thesis, University of Texas, 1932. (Unpublished.) An excellent study, the best and most thorough available.

[5]Wilkinson, *Memoirs,* II, 117.

[6]Muñoz to Nava, June 6, 1794; Carondelet to Muñoz, September 9, 1794. *Béxar Archives.*

Fray Bernardino Vallejo, in whose company he went to San Antonio where he arrived on December 21, 1794. He now presented his credentials and asked to be permitted to introduce some merchandise from New Orleans to defray the expense of the expedition. Muñoz pointed out the procedure suggested was contrary to law and that he would have to consult Nava at once, but the commandant made a noncommittal reply. Before long, it seems Muñoz winked at the violation of the trade regulations and Nolan appears to have introduced a considerable amount of goods from Louisiana.[7]

By January, 1796, he had returned to New Orleans. The third expedition, as he called it, proved much more profitable than his former ventures. He brought back two hundred fifty horses. After selling the best in Natchez, he drove the remainder to Frankfort, Kentucky. The mystery surrounding his activities between 1791 and the close of 1795, except for the glimpses just related, is explicable in part by the relations between him and Governor Muñoz, and the fact, which he admits himself, that "a letter from a trader in horses to a General of the Federal armies" would naturally arouse suspicions.[8]

Reference to the intrigue of the governor of Louisiana with the agents of the rebellious West and with Wilkinson during these years has been made in the previous chapter. The "accidental" meeting in January, 1797, of Nolan and Ellicott, the American boundary commissioner, has been likewise noted.[9] Leaving Ellicott and Gayoso to iron out their difficulties at Natchez, Nolan seems to have hurried back to New Orleans, where he regaled Governor Carondelet with entertaining, confidential, but not entirely reliable stories, all of which the governor believed, "always more impressed with inconsequential matters than with weighty problems of state."[10] While courting favor with Carondelet to secure permission to embark on a fourth expedition into Texas, he was writing Wilkinson, who now was general-in-chief of the United States Army, that in the event of war he could "cut" his way back and he could be counted upon to aid.[11] The dual game he was playing is revealed in his letter to

---

[7]Nava to Muñoz, January 15, 1795; Muñoz to Carondelet, January 18, 1795; Nava to Muñoz, January 27, 1795; Muñoz to Commandant at Nacogdoches, March 12, 1795. *Béxar Archives.*

[8]Nolan to Wilkinson, January 6, and 10, 1796. Wilkinson, *Memoirs*, II, Appendix 2.

[9]See page 214 of the preceding chapter.

[10]Whitaker, *The Spanish-American Frontier, 1783-1795*, 153.

[11]Nolan to Wilkinson, July 21, 1797. Wilkinson, *op. cit.*, II, Appendix 2.

Samuel Moore, whom he tried to get interested in the venture. After declaring he had finally obtained permission to trade in horses through the recommendation of Wilkinson and the expectation of Governor Carondelet of being furnished plans and information concerning the country visited, he said, "But I shall take good care to give him [Carondelet] no information, unless such as may be calculated to mislead him. Whatever discoveries I can make," he concluded, "shall be carefully preserved for General Wilkinson, for the benefit of our government. . . . I look forward to the conquest of Mexico by the United States; and I expect my patron and friend, the General, will in such an event, give me a conspicuous command."[12]

Suspicion aroused. Governor Carondelet proved an easy mark for Nolan's wiles, but the Spanish boundary commissioner, Gayoso de Lemos, suddenly became distrustful of the enterprising young protégé of General Wilkinson. The rebellious attitude of the inhabitants in Natchez in June and July, who practically drove Gayoso out of the city; the humiliation inflicted upon him by Ellicott and his friends; and the unexpected display of American loyalty, which the double-dealing Wilkinson felt compelled to make at this time, caused Gayoso to realize the betrayal of the trust placed in the new commander-in-chief by Spain. There was little he could do against him, but his agent was perhaps still within his power. He immediately warned Baron Carondelet against Nolan, who, he declared, "will take an active part against us; he is popular and enterprising, secure him." The dislike was mutual. The young adventurer knew Gayoso had seen through his plans, and wrote Wilkinson that Carondelet was trying to shield him (Nolan) from Gayoso's vengeance, of whom he said, "I might be compelled to shoot the monster with a poisoned arrow."[13]

Nolan in Texas and Nuevo Santander. Late in July, 1797, Nolan set out for Texas again, accompanied by John Murdock, William Escot (Scott), four Spaniards, and two Negroes. The party carried twelve good rifles and seven thousand dollars' worth of well-assorted merchandise. Murdock was a Natchez merchant with whom Nolan had entered into partnership.[14] After a short stay in Nacogdoches, he arrived in San

---

[12]Philip Nolan to Samuel P. Moore. Wilkinson, *Memoirs*, II, Appendix IX.

[13]*Ibid.*, II, Appendix 2.

[14]King, Grace, "The Real Philip Nolan," Louisiana Historical Society, *Publications*, X, 100.

Antonio in October, and presented his credentials, adding that he had a special commission from the Louisiana regiment for whom he was to secure horses in Nuevo Santander. This pretension was to arouse much suspicion and to cause even the viceroy to become curious. Nava observed that Nuevo Santander was not under his jurisdiction and suggested he write either or both the governor of that province and the viceroy. Before following the suggestion, Nolan asked Nava in November for permission to introduce two thousand *pesos* of merchandise to enable him to defray his expenses. In January, 1798, Nava acceded to the request on condition that the merchandise be suitable for gifts to the Indians, and that this merchandise be bought by the governor to prevent Nolan from trading directly with the citizens.[15]

When Nolan next tried to secure permission to go to Nuevo Santander, his real troubles began. He applied to an old acquaintance, Francisco Rendón, former intendant of Louisiana and now intendant of Zacatecas, to help him secure the viceroy's consent. Rendón immediately became suspicious and made inquiry from Baron Carondelet who was now president of the royal *Audiencia* of the Province of Quito. The former governor of Louisiana replied that the claim of a commission to buy horses for the regiment "was as false as the letter of recommendation" which Nolan said he had lost.[16]

Gayoso, who had now become governor of Louisiana, at about the same time wrote Viceroy Branciforte that all foreigners in Texas should be arrested, and warned him particularly against Nolan. The viceroy immediately upbraided Nava for permitting his entrance, whereupon the commandant general made a long explanation of the circumstances and the passport and letters of recommendation brought by Nolan. At the same time he wrote Muñoz ordering him to expel all foreigners and arrest those who came without a passport and he revoked the authorization for the purchase of merchandise for Indian gifts from Nolan.[17]

The matter may have ended here, had it not been for the new viceroy. Hardly had Miguel José de Azanza succeeded Branciforte early in the summer, before he began to make inquiries about the elusive "trader in

---

[15]Nava to Nolan, October 31, 1797; Nolan to Nava, November 25, 1797. *A. G. M.*, *Historia*, Vol. 413, pt. I, pp. 194-195, and 292. Nava to Muñoz, January 9, 1799. *Béxar Archives.*

[16]Nolan to Rendón, November 25, 1797; Carondelet to Rendón, January 13, 1798. *A. G. M., Historia*, Vol. 413, pt. I, pp. 196-197, and 200-201.

[17]Nava to Branciforte, March 20, 1789; Nava to Muñoz, same date. *Ibid.*, Vol. 413, pt. I, p. 187.

horses," his character, his activities, and his whereabouts. He instructed Nava not to permit Nolan to go to Nuevo Santander under any circumstances. The commandant general replied that according to his records the adventurer had left Texas at the end of July, 1798. Imagine his surprise to learn incidentally that Nolan was still in Texas in April, 1799![18] Nava wrote Muñoz at once to order Nolan to leave immediately and to warn him not to return. Muñoz, in his reply, tried to dissipate the suspicions of his superior, explaining that Nolan's failure to depart was unintentional, that he was still in Texas because of the difficulties he had encountered in catching and conducting the horses to his pasture on the Trinity, and because of his trip to Nuevo Santander, which had been undertaken with the permission of the governor of that province.[19]

Had Muñoz dispatched a messenger at the time he received his orders from Nava, he could have overtaken Nolan before he left his pasture on the Trinity, where he had one thousand two hundred six horses. But the old governor was very sick, and died on July 27 without informing the unsuspecting Nolan of the strict orders against his return. It is not known just when Nolan finally left the Trinity River, but by November 12 he was already in the United States. On November 20, 1799, he wrote to Cook, his agent in Nacogdoches, that after his return he had learned that Gayoso de Lemos had warned the governor of Texas that he, Nolan, was a heretic, a dangerous man, who should be arrested and kept in close confinement.[20] It was not until August 8, 1800, however, that Nava issued orders to Elguezábal for Nolan's immediate arrest should he ever return to Texas, in order to question him concerning his activities during the last few years and his relations with General Wilkinson.[21]

Nolan's last expedition. Under the circumstances, it is difficult to understand why Nolan undertook a fourth expedition, particularly in view of the opposition of José Vidal, commandant at Concordia, who had him arraigned before the Federal Court of the Territory of Mississippi

---

[18]Nava to Muñoz, April 30, 1799. *Béxar Archives.*

[19]Muñoz to Nava, June 12, 1799. *Quaderno Borrador,* 1799-1801. *Béxar Archives.*

[20]Daniel Clark to Thomas Jefferson, November 12, 1799. Texas Historical Association, *The Quarterly,* April, 1904, VII, 317-321. Nolan to Cook, November 20, 1799. *Nacogdoches Archives.* Nolan was in error as to the letter of Gayoso de Lemos, who, in reality, wrote to Nava on June 1, 1799, a letter that was stronger than Nolan suspected and which, if it had been delivered promptly, would have been fatal to him. Nava to Berenguer, November 27, 1801. *Historia,* Vol. 413, pt. 1, pp. 216-219.

[21]Nava to Elguezábal, August 8, 1800. *Nacogdoches Archives.*

for intended violation of the neutrality laws of the United States. In defiance of Spanish opposition and the odds against him, the bold adventurer was to set forth on his fatal undertaking.

He first attempted to propitiate the commandant of Nacogdoches and to win the friendship of Father José Manuel Gaetán by sending to the former a piece of linen and other gifts, and to the latter a double-barreled gun—strange gift for a priest.[22] To what extent he was influenced by Thomas Jefferson, vice-president-elect at the time, and other officials cannot be determined. That both Daniel Clark and Wilkinson wrote to Jefferson concerning the young adventurer "whom nature seems to have formed for Enterprises of which the rest of Mankind are incapable" and that an interview was arranged with the high dignitary in the summer of 1800, there is no doubt.[23] It is likewise true that immediately upon his return from the East, Nolan made formal application to Governor Casa Calvo, who had succeeded Gayoso de Lemos, for permission "to run the pasture lands to the north." But the new governor, more distrustful of Americans than his predecessor, promptly refused the request.[24]

Undaunted by the refusal, Nolan proceeded to enlist men for the most formidable expedition he had ever undertaken. His boldness smacks strongly of official approval of the American authorities. By October, 1800, he had contracted with eighteen Americans, seven Spaniards, and two Negroes. The Americans were Simon McKoy, Jonah Walters, Solomon Cooley, Ellis Bean, Joseph Reed, William Danlin, Charles King, Stephen Richards, Joseph Pierce, Thomas House, Ephraim Blackburn, David Fero, Robert Ashley, John House, Michael Moore, Mordicai Richards, John King, and Augustus or John Adams; the Spaniards were Luciano García, Vicente Lara, Refugio de la Garza, Juan Joseph Martínez, Lorenzo Hinojosa, Joseph Berbán, and Joseph de Jesús de los Santos; and the two Negroes were Juan Bautista (called Caesar by the Americans) and Robert.[25]

---

[22]Hale, E., "The Real Philip Nolan." Mississippi Historical Society, *Publications,* IV, 310, and 315. See also Elguezábal, June 29, 1801. *Béxar Archives.*

[23]Daniel Clark to Thomas Jefferson, February 12, 1799; Wilkinson to Jefferson, May 22, 1800; Cox, "The Louisiana-Texas Frontier." Texas Historical Association, *The Quarterly,* VII, 310, and 314; X, 58.

[24]Hale, "The Real Philip Nolan." Mississippi Historical Society, *Publications,* IV, 292.

[25]The list was compiled by Miss Maurine Wilson. The last three of the Americans deserted before the expedition entered Texas. Wilson, *Philip Nolan and His Activities in Texas.*

The ostensible purpose of the expedition, according to the declarations of the men after they had been captured and the statements of Nolan before his departure, was to catch mustangs and to bring back the horses which had been left behind on the previous expedition.[26] The men enlisted had been told that they would be employed for a period of three months. Each one had been requested to furnish his own horses and arms. They were to help build corrals and to catch horses. Food and ammunition were to be furnished by Nolan, who was to reward them for their labors with a varying number of horses. If the time of the expedition exceeded three months, the men were to be paid an additional *peso* a day.

José Vidal, commandant at Concordia, kept a close watch on Nolan and reported all his moves to Governor Casa Calvo. He pointed out to his superior the negligence of American officials in permitting such expeditions to be organized and the feeble efforts made to enforce the neutrality laws. Determined to prevent Nolan from setting out, he made formal complaint to Governor Sargent early in October and Sargent was compelled to summon Nolan to appear before the Supreme Court of the Territory of Mississippi. Nolan admitted he was preparing to enter Spanish territory with some companions in search of wild horses, but alleged he had a permit for that purpose from the commandant general of the Interior Provinces and he presented as evidence a letter from that official dated in 1798. Vidal, who appeared in person to press the charges against him, explained that the permit had no longer any value, since Nolan had been forced to leave the Spanish dominions as a fugitive from justice during his last expedition. Nolan reasserted his peaceful purpose and argued that the arms being carried by his men were for defence against thieves and for securing food. The court ruled there was not sufficient evidence to restrain Nolan and his men, declaring: "It is beyond our power and contrary to the constitution of the United States to prevent one or more citizens from leaving their country when it cannot be proved with evidence that their intentions are hostile."[27]

In vain did the enraged Spanish official protest against the decision. Nolan won a victory which made it much easier for him to secure men to join his expedition. However, Vidal kept informed through his spies of the plans of Nolan, who, on the eve of his departure, had to change his proposed route twice. At first he had intended to go west as far as the

---

[26]Testimony given in answer to questionnaire presented to Nolan's men. *Nolan Documents*, Vol. I. (Photostat copies in University of Texas Library.)

[27]Vidal to Casa Calvo, October 11, 1800. *Nolan Documents*, Vol. I, p. 157.

Río Grande by the lower road, leaving Nacogdoches slightly to the north. He then wrote Cook that he would follow the coast "along the sea to avoid troops at Nacogdoches," adding, "I am so well acquainted with the coast from Opelousas to the Río Grande, that they would never be able to overtake and attack us. I have everything so well arranged at Revilla that I shall not be detained two days in that place."[28] But before he finally left Natchez, late in October or early in November, 1800, he again changed his plans and went up the Mississippi to Nogales (modern Vicksburg) where he crossed the river and proceeded to the Ouachita (Wichita). That he expected trouble is evident from the arms which he carried. He personally had a double-barreled shotgun, a brace of pistols, and a carbine. Almost all his men were equally well-armed.[29]

First encounter with Spanish troops. When the party reached the vicinity of the post on the Wichita, on or about November 6, they encountered a group of nineteen men sent by Vicente Fernández Tejeiro of that post to stop them. The Spanish troops had not anticipated meeting so formidable a group and contented themselves with explaining they were out in search of Indian marauders. Nolan, who was allowed to proceed with his companions, nevertheless, made an explanation to Fernández Tejeiro, to whom he wrote a note saying that he was on his way to the Province of Texas, that he did not have a passport, and that he would consequently avoid him embarrassment by not passing through his post.[30] The following day, Fernández Tejeiro sent a force of fifty men to halt the intruders, but to no avail, as Nolan and his men had moved on rapidly to avoid trouble.[31]

The meeting with Spanish troops caused Nolan's men to question him concerning the nature and purpose of the expedition and sowed deep distrust among them. A few days later Richards induced Adams and King to run away. When Richards arrived in Concodia, he immediately went to Vidal and made a full confession.[32]

---

[28]Nolan to Cook, October 23, 1800. *Miscellaneous correspondence concerning Philip Nolan,* pp. 42-43.

[29]Testimony of Charles King and Stephen Richards. *Nolan Documents,* I, pp. 39, and 47.

[30]Nolan to Fernández Tejeiro, November 6, 1800. *Nolan Documents,* I, pp. 135-136.

[31]Fernández Tejeiro to Trudeau, November 7, 1800. *A. G. M., Historia,* Vol. 413, pt. 1, p. 259.

[32]Declaration of Mordicai Richards, December 13, 1800. *A. G. M., Historia,* Vol. 413, pt. 1, pp. 353-358.

Alarm spreads among Spanish officials. Before the news of the encounter in the vicinity of Wichita reached Governor Elguezábal, Vidal had reported, through Commandant Músquiz of Nacogdoches, that Nolan and his party, variously estimated to consist of thirty or forty men, were on their way to the mouth of the Brazos to proceed along the coast to the Río Grande.[33] At this time he also warned Músquiz of the relations of John Cook of Nacogdoches with Nolan. Elguezábal ordered the immediate arrest of Cook and the seizure of his papers and property, but before the order arrived, Cook had left Nacogdoches with Pedro Longueville, Antonio Leal and his wife, Gertrudes de los Santos. The party sent in pursuit overtook the last three and brought them back. Cook was later captured at Rapide and returned to Nacogdoches.[34] Elguezábal issued orders at the same time to Lieutenant Amangual at La Bahía to send out a reconnoitering party every day to keep a constant watch on the coast, and warned Governor José Blanco of Nuevo Santander of the intended violation of his jurisdiction by the bold adventurer.

But by this time a report of the incident at Wichita had reached the alarmed Elguezábal which left no doubt that Nolan had decided at the last minute on a northern route and was well on his way to Texas by now. Bewildered by the elusive adventurer, he instructed Músquiz to send his most trusted Indian agents to the northern Indians to get whatever information was available concerning the appearance and movements of the invaders.[35]

Thoroughly aroused, Governor Blanco of Nuevo Santander, without consulting Felix Calleja, sub-inspector at San Luis Potosí, ordered the captains at Refugio, Reynosa, Camargo, Mier, Revilla, and Laredo to arrest any and all foreigners who entered their settlements without a passport and to place and keep under arms two-thirds of the militia in their respective jurisdictions. When Calleja learned of the danger that threatened the northern provinces and the measures taken for their defence, he instructed Blanco to assemble at Reynosa detachments from

[33]Vidal to Músquiz, October 6, 1800. *Miscellaneous correspondence concerning Philip Nolan,* 1800-1803, pp. 78-80.
[34]Elguezábal to Nava, November 12, and 30, 1800. *Quaderno Borrador de los oficios . . .,* II, pp. 90, and 95-96.
[35]Elguezábal to Nava, November 30, 1800. *Quaderno Borrador,* I, pp. 94-96.

the five villas and repair to that post in person to guard against the appearance of Nolan and his men.[36]

Warned by Blanco, the commandant at Laredo moved the horses of the presidio to the west side of the Río Grande to avoid their capture by surprise. He sent out three detachments to keep a sharp lookout for the invaders: the first was to watch as far as Cerrito de los Apaches, some eighteen leagues upstream; the second, as far as Charco de la Becerra, near the intersection of the San Antonio road with that of the Nueces River; and the third, as far as the intersection of the road from Camargo to La Bahía with the Nueces River. Scouting parties of ten men each were likewise to be sent daily from Revilla, Mier, Camargo, and Reynosa, to explore the surrounding country.[37] At the same time Bustamante, at Laredo, was to report all occurrences to Governor Simón Herrera, of Nuevo León, who was ordered by Calleja to move to Laredo with all available troops and militia from Punta de Lampazos.[38] Calleja warned the viceroy on December 11 of the serious menace of the projected invasion, and on December 22 explained to him that he would have to rely on the forces available in Nuevo Santander and Nuevo León since "Nolan's enterprise was a bold and daring undertaking . . . that did not permit waiting for help from distant parts." He called the attention of the viceroy to the ill assorted calibre of the guns of the provincial troops, their lack of equipment, the urgent need for military aides, and the total absence of sergeants and adjutants in the dragoons under his command.[39]

The viceroy was thoroughly impressed with the danger that confronted the Interior Provinces and fully sympathized with the sub-inspector, but was unable to give aid either in providing equipment or supplying the needed officers. To a third appeal for aid made on December 30, he replied that in case of "absolute necessity" Calleja might put some of the militia on a salary.

In January, the fears of the alarmed commanders along the Río Grande were greatly augmented by rumors of an impending Comanche attack

---

[36]Blanco to the commanders of Refugio, Reynosa, Camargo, Mier, Revilla, and Laredo, November 20, 1800. *A. G. M., Historia,* Vol. 413, pt. 1, pp. 221-222.

[37]Bustamante to Blanco, December 29, 1800. *A. G. M., Historia,* Vol. 413, pt. 1, pp. 274-276.

[38]Calleja to Bustamante, December 21, 1800; Calleja to Herrera, same date. *Ibid.,* pp. 235-239.

[39]Calleja to Viceroy Berenguer de Marquina, December 22, 1800. *Ibid.,* pp. 240-241.

on Presidio de Rio Grande and Laredo, led by foreigners. The stories told by the Lipan-Apaches convinced Spanish officials of the presence of Nolan and his companions among the Comanches.[40]

Governor Blanco late in January set out from San Carlos to the mouth of the Río Grande, making a careful survey of the coast before ascending the river to Laredo. Governor Herrera of Nuevo León had in the meantime taken a position near Revilla with a hundred men, and Governor Cordero of Coahuila had established a line from Laredo to Sierra del Pino with one hundred sixty men, evenly divided among the posts at Aguaverde, Monclova, Pacuache, and Iglesias.[41]

Time moved on while the aroused frontier commanders watched, tensely poised to pounce upon the daring adventurers. Three months had elapsed since the first news. The bewildered governors began to wonder if the enemy would ever arrive. Calleja believed that Nolan and his companions were lying low, because they had been warned of the preparations made and that they were waiting for the vigilance to be relaxed.[42] It was not possible, however, to maintain the vigilance indefinitely. The governors could not remain away from their capitals; the militiamen had to return to their round of daily duties; the treasury could not endure the expense much longer. Fortunately, the strain of the impending danger was suddenly removed by the unexpected news of the death of Nolan and the capture of his companions.

Death of Nolan and capture of his companions. In the meantime Nolan and his men, reduced to twenty-five by desertions, had entered Texas north of Nacogdoches and established a permanent camp in the country of the Tawakoni, near the mouth of a creek which today bears his name.[43] The camp consisted of three irregularly spaced "forts," small enclosures of logs piled five feet high, as protection against Indians. Contrary to the suspicions of Spanish officials, Nolan made no attempt to win the friendship of the natives nor to incite them against the Spaniards. Both the Tawakoni and the Tahuayaces visited the camp

---

[40]Blanco to Calleja, January 15, 1801. *A. G. M., Historia*, Vol. 413, pt. 1, p. 278.

[41]Cordero to Herrera, January 17, 1801. *Ibid.*, pp. 287-288.

[42]Calleja to the Viceroy, February 27, 1801. *A. G. M., Historia*, Vol. 413, pt. 1, p. 307.

[43]Mr. David Donoghue, of Fort Worth, placed the site of the camp near Blum, Hill County, on Nolan River, called by Músquiz "Blanco." Mr. Donoghue arrived at this conclusion from a careful study of Músquiz's "Diary," translated by J. A. Quintero in *Texas Almanac*, September, 1868. The investigation was undertaken at the request of Miss M. T. Wilson.

and showed little friendliness to the newcomers, having been warned by Spanish agents that Nolan was a "bad man." Chief Erías Cooquis, of the Tahuayaces, actually revealed the confidence to Nolan, who could not resist writing a note to Samuel Davenport and William Barr of what he thought of them.[44]

Commandant Músquiz, at Nacogdoches, after a careful study of Mordicai Richards' confession, confirmed by statements of his Indian agents, informed Governor Elguezábal in January that he was ready to go in search of Nolan. In reply to his request for reënforcements, the governor sent thirty men—all he could spare—and authorized Músquiz to enlist thirty citizens of Nacogdoches to complete the number requested. If this force was inadequate, Músquiz was to request aid from Natchitoches and Wichita.[45]

But for various reasons, Músquiz did not set out until March 4. With a force of seventy regulars and fifty militia, led by Indian scouts from the Tawakoni villages, who had visited Nolan's camp, Músquiz made his way to Blanco Creek (Nolan River). The party was well armed and carried a small fieldpiece. On March 21, early in the morning, he came in sight of the camp. Nolan and his men had been there for almost five months. They made a sorry sight, with their long beards, tattered garments, and crude equipment. For several months they had been reduced to eating horse meat, as their two months' provisions had long since been exhausted, and powder could not be spared for game.

Although Músquiz divided his men into three parties for the attack, one under Saucedo, another under Granado, and the third under himself, and advanced with great stealth, their presence had been revealed to Nolan during the night by the restlessness of the horses. As the early morning light became brighter, the three parties advanced to within thirty paces of the camp, and Barr, who accompanied Músquiz, told the adventurers to surrender in the name of the king. Nolan and his men withdrew to the interior of the inclosure and prepared to resist.

Before the fight began, Vicente Lara and Juan José Martínez deserted to the Spaniards; and Refugio de la Garza, Francisco Berbán, Thomas House, and Stephen Richards were captured. Soon the crack of firearms broke the stillness of the morning and a lively fusillade was kept up

---

[44]Nolan to Barr and Davenport, *Nolan Documents,* I, p. 142.

[45]Músquiz to Elguezábal, January 2, 1801. *Miscellaneous correspondence . . .,* 1800-1803, p. 70; Elguezábal to Nava, January 8, 1801. *Quaderno Borrador,* I, p. 104. (Photostat)

until about nine, when a lucky or unlucky ball from the fieldpiece killed the daring leader. Dismayed, his companions attempted to reach the nearby woods and took refuge in a small cave. During the hot pursuit, the Negro César and two of the Spaniards lagged behind and were taken prisoners. Again Barr called upon the little band to surrender. The offer having been refused, the cannon opened fire, and after the third shot William House came out unarmed and asked for water. Músquiz granted the request and urged House to plead with his companions to surrender as he did not want to have to kill them. David Fero, who had assumed command after Nolan's death, asked for terms. Músquiz replied they would have to surrender unconditionally and give up their arms, but he assured them they would be treated humanely. One by one the men came out and surrendered their arms.

Músquiz remained in Nolan's camp until March 23. Fifteen Americans, two Negroes, and seven Spaniards were taken prisoners. Nolan's body was buried by his two negro slaves, after his ears had been cut off. These were sent to San Antonio with a detailed report of the fight, both of which Governor Elguezábal promptly dispatched to Nava together with all the personal papers of the deceased leader. It was William Barr, Indian agent for the Spaniards in Nacogdoches, who, "moved by his well known love for the king," volunteered to carry to San Antonio the ghastly trophy of the dead chieftain's ears, his private papers, and the report of Músquiz.[46]

It is not our purpose nor does space permit us to follow the fate of the companions of Nolan.[47] The effect of this last venture of the daring young "trader in horses" cannot be overestimated. The governors of Louisiana, Texas, Coahuila, Nuevo León, and Nuevo Santander had mobilized all the resources of their respective provinces to check the invader. Every commander on the northern frontier had been held in suspense for almost five months, and more than four hundred men had been employed to guard against a possible surprise. The commandant general at Chihuahua, the sub-inspector at San Luis Potosí, and the viceroy himself had strained every nerve to avert the impending threat. The incident aroused the entire frontier as well as the viceregal officials. It brought to them forcefully the realization of the danger of aggression

---

[46]The summary of the fight and capture of Nolan's men is based on the account in Wilson, *Philip Nolan and His Activities*, pp. 128-141.

[47]The writer is preparing and will soon publish a full account, *Philip Nolan, Filibuster*, in which the subject will be treated in detail.

from the United States. If there had been some indifference in the past, and if there had been some who doubted the serious menace which the enterprising Anglo-American pioneer represented, they were all convinced now that no trust was to be placed in their friendship. When claims were advanced to all of Texas as part of the Province of Louisiana, Spanish officials were not surprised, and the viceroy ordered Simón Herrera of Nuevo León and Antonio Cordero, then governor of Texas, to prevent the advance of General Wilkinson beyond the Sabine. Almost twelve hundred men were mobilized to face the new crisis. Little wonder that three years later Zebulon M. Pike's intrusion was eyed with such suspicion and misgivings, and that the activities of Aaron Burr were viewed with deep concern.

American reaction to the retrocession of Louisiana to France. The retrocession of Louisiana to France created a widespread feeling of genuine alarm among both the officials and the people of the United States, particularly in Ohio, Kentucky, and Tennessee. As long as this important province was held by Spain, the Americans felt that no serious difficulty over the navigation of the Mississippi would arise. But in the hands of the powerful and ambitious emperor of the French, Louisiana represented a serious menace to the future welfare and development of the West. The leaders in the Western states immediately denounced the transfer in loud terms. By the spring of 1802, when the retrocession became generally known, public opinion openly advocated forceful opposition to the military occupation of Louisiana by Napoleon.[48]

As early as November 21, 1801, Rufus King, American minister in London, had written to Secretary Madison to confirm the rumor of the acquisition of Louisiana by France. He had explained at that time the plans of Napoleon for the military occupation of the province and his intention of using Santo Domingo as a base.[49] In the face of the mounting indignation of public opinion, Jefferson at first favored prudence and an amicable settlement through diplomacy rather than a declaration of war against France as advocated by the Federalists. But in a letter to Livingston, minister in Paris, he outlined the policy contemplated by the American Government in view of the circumstances. This letter is

---

[48]Geer, Curtis M., *The Louisiana Purchase and the Westward Movement.* (History of North America, S. C. Lee, editor, VIII, 185-189.)

[49]*Ibid.*, 190-191.

worthy of being quoted. "The cession of Louisiana and the Floridas by Spain to France works most sorely on the United States," declared Jefferson. "It completely reverses all the political relations of the United States and will form a new epoch in our political course. . . . It is impossible that France and the United States can continue long friends. . . . We must turn all our attention to a maritime force, for which our resources place us in a very high ground, and having formed and connected together a power which may render reinforcements of the settlements here impossible to France, make the first cannon which shall be fired in Europe the signal for the tearing up of any settlement she may have made and for holding the two continents of America in sequestration for the common purpose of the United British and American nations."[50]

The mounting resentment against France increased the fears of the already worried Spanish officials of Louisiana, Cuba, and Texas, who, cut off from Spain, heard only distorted and inaccurate accounts of what was happening. On June 15, 1801, Governor Marqués de Casa Calvo wrote to the captain general of Cuba, the Marqués de Someruelos, that he was in a quandary as to his course of action should either France or the United States demand that he turn over the province of Louisiana to them. English papers from Jamaica and American papers from Baltimore repeatedly referred to the recent transfer of Louisiana to France, but the Americans loudly voiced their determination not to allow its consummation. The governor had received no official communication from Spain since August, 1800. What particularly alarmed him was that the United States had recently erected a new fort named General Wilkinson near the Illinois River and garrisoned it with seven hundred men under Colonel Strong. Furthermore General Wilkinson himself had been again ordered to Natchez, only seventy leagues from New Orleans. Under the trying circumstances it had been a relief, he added, to learn that the desperado Philip Nolan had been killed near the Brazos River, and his companions arrested.[51]

The resentment against France was extended to Spain and the situation was aggravated by the ill-advised action of Juan Ventura Morales, intendant at New Orleans, who, on October 16, 1802, published a proclamation abrogating the right of deposit in New Orleans. He declared that the three-year period stipulated by the treaty of 1795 had long

[50]Geer, *op. cit.*, 191-192.

[51]Marqués de Casa Calvo to Marqués de Someruelos, June 15, 1801. *A. G. I., Audiencia de Santo Domingo*, 86-7-27. (Dunn Transcripts, 1763-1818, pp. 271-275.)

since expired. The action was interpreted by the Americans as confirmation of all their fears concerning the effect of the retrocession on the free navigation of the Mississippi. The governor of the Territory of Mississippi, the governor of Kentucky, and William E. Huling, American consul at New Orleans, protested to the State Department. A wave of apprehension swept the West. Congress gave Jefferson full discretion to act and voted two million dollars to purchase the area that controlled the mouth of the Mississippi.[52]

The purchase of Louisiana. Jefferson now appointed James Monroe to go to Paris at once as minister plenipotentiary to negotiate the purchase of New Orleans and a portion of Florida to insure to the West the navigation of the Mississippi. The proposal originally presented by Reuben R. Livingston had been coldly received by Napoleon. Great was the surprise of the American minister when on April 11, 1803, Talleyrand informed him that the emperor had changed his mind and was now willing to sell the whole of Louisiana. Outbreak of hostilities with England was imminent. In view of the circumstances and the need of ready cash, Napoleon had decided that Louisiana should not fall into the hands of the English. In characteristic Napoleonic fashion the deal was swiftly consummated with the astonished American envoys within a month. In signing the treaty, the first week in May, 1803, they far exceeded their powers and instructions. Livingston, however, comprehended the significance of the deal just effected. "From this day," he said, "the United States take their place among the powers of the first rank; the English lose all exclusive influence in the affairs of America."[53]

Attitude of Spain. The Treaty of San Ildefonso had expressly provided that France was not to alienate Louisiana. Spain immediately protested to France against the sale of the province and questioned the validity of the transaction. "Spain had reason to fear the United States more than any other nation, because American aggression would naturally be directed against her other territories, the Floridas, the neighboring islands and Mexico."[54] Jefferson fully realized the feeling of Spain

---

[52]The text of Morales' proclamation and the protests are reproduced in *State Papers and Publick Documents of the United States from the accession of Thomas Jefferson to the Presidency, exhibiting a complete view of our foreign relations since that time, 1801-1806,* II, 185-193. (Boston, 1814.) See also Geer, *Louisiana Purchase,* 191-196.

[53]Geer, *The Louisiana Purchase,* 198.

[54]*Ibid.,* 199.

about the sale of Louisiana, and stated in a message to Congress that the transfer of the province to the United States was "an event as unexpected as disagreeable to Spain."[55] But Spain, realizing her weakness, and out of regard for the good will of the United States, soon withdrew her protest, resigned herself to the inevitable and turned her attention to the prevention of the encroachments which she so greatly feared would immediately follow along the Texas frontier.[56]

The transfer of Louisiana to the United States. In spite of the known protest of Spain, Jefferson appointed General James A. Wilkinson and William C. C. Claiborne commissioners to receive Louisiana from Laussat. Claiborne was, furthermore, appointed governor of the new territory. Because of possible opposition to the transfer by Spain, orders were issued for the mobilization of the militia of Ohio, Kentucky, and Tennessee, which was to hold itself in readiness. The garrison stationed at Fort Adams on the Ohio, accompanied by five hundred Tennessee militia, was ordered to march to Natchez; and a company of volunteer cavalry from the Territory of Mississippi was to accompany Governor Claiborne. Both Wilkinson and Claiborne arrived in the vicinity of New Orleans on December 17, and encamped with their troops outside the city. Word was sent to Laussat, the French commissioner, who had officially received the province from the Spaniards on November 30.[57] After the exchange of the usual courtesies, it was agreed that the formal transfer would take place on December 20. On the appointed day the American commissioners and their military retinue entered the city and were welcomed by Laussat, who delivered to them the keys of New Orleans. In the presence of a solemn but not overjoyous crowd, the French colors were lowered and received by a guard of honor made up of old French settlers and officers. The Stars and Stripes were then raised and a second salute was fired by the artillery. A few cheers greeted the new flag. A heavy air of apprehension and expectancy subdued the volatile spirit of the settlers of Louisiana.[58]

---

[55] Message of the President, December 6, 1805. *State Papers and Publick Documents*, II, 4-6.

[56] Filisola, Vicente, *Memorias para la historia de la guerra de Tejas*, I, 42-43; Message of the President, November 8, 1804. *State Papers and Publick Documents*, II, 228-235.

[57] For description of the ceremony see p. 231.

[58] Fortier, *History of Louisiana*, II, 276-277; Geer, *Louisiana Purchase*, 220-221.

In his message to Congress, January 16, 1804, Jefferson congratulated the country on the significant event. "On this important acquisition, so favorable to the immediate interests of our Western citizens, so auspicious to the peace and security of the nation in general, which adds to our country territories so extensive and fertile . . . I offer to Congress and our country my sincere congratulations."[59] When within less than a month the President again addressed Congress on the same subject, he declared that Spain's objections to "the validity of title to the country of Louisiana" had been withdrawn, but its exact limits "still remained to be settled."[60] What affected Texas was the vagueness with which the boundaries of the vast territory just acquired were defined. France had sold to the United States "the colony or province of Louisiana, with the same extent that it now has in the hands of Spain, and that it had when France possessed it. . ." On the basis of this clause the western boundary was claimed to be the Río Grande in absolute disregard of the well-established title of Spain to the territory between Los Adaes and the Río Grande by continuous and uncontested possession of this territory.

Mutual suspicions. When the transfer took place on December 20, there was a large number of Spanish troops in New Orleans. Seven days later Wilkinson wrote the Secretary of War that his men were in redoubts outside the city limits in tents, for the Spanish troops were still in New Orleans. Before long, Governor Claiborne complained to the State Department that the continued presence of Spanish officers and troops in Louisiana was becoming a nuisance. By April some three hundred Spanish soldiers and officers had embarked for Pensacola and Wilkinson's men had been given possession of the principal barracks, but there were still about one hundred Spanish soldiers and twelve or fifteen officers occupying the hospital and several other buildings.[61]

The irritation aroused by the reluctant withdrawal of Spanish troops gave rise to suspicions concerning the intentions of Spain. Captain Edward Turner, stationed at Natchitoches, wrote Wilkinson that he was convinced the Spaniards in Texas were planning some mischief. Their agents were busy among the Indians and the Negroes. Recently nine

---

[59]Message of the President, January 16, 1804. *State Papers and Publick Documents, II,* 220-221.

[60]Message of the President, February 16, 1804. *Ibid.,* 228-235.

[61]Wilkinson to Secretary of War, December 27, 1803; same to same, April 15, 1804. *State Papers and Publick Documents, I,* 350.

slaves, induced by Spanish agents who assured them they would regain their freedom by taking refuge in Texas, had run away to Nacogdoches. Likewise, it was rumored that the Indians east of Red River had been invited to a great council by the Spaniards to discuss plans for a war against the Americans in Louisiana.[62]

The suspicions of the Americans were further aroused by the deposition of a Choctaw chief who declared to Judge John Sibley at Natchitoches that a party of his warriors, recently returned from a hunting expedition to the bay of St. Bernard, had met two parties of Spanish troops. The Spaniards seemed to have just arrived in Texas by water and were now busily engaged in building a fort near the mouth of the Trinity and another on the Colorado in the country of the Karankawas. The warriors had reported that the work on the new forts was well advanced and that the Spanish officer in charge at the old site of the Orcoquisac (Arkokisas) had commissioned one of the braves as chief, telling him that there was soon to be a big war against the Americans. He told the Indians that the Spaniards were going to build still another fort in the country of the Attakapas and one near Natchitoches. The Spaniards needed spades and offered the Indians a horse for each spade they brought.[63]

The story of the additional troops in Texas was shortly afterward verified by Captain Turner, who reported on May 3, 1805, that the recently arrived Spanish troops had taken possession of Matagorda Bay and the old site of Orcoquisac. Furthermore, a Mr. St. Prie, who had come from Texas to Natchitoches in July, told Judge Sibley that five hundred families had just come to San Antonio for the purpose of establishing settlements in the vicinity of the new forts, and that a considerable number of troops had accompanied them. Shortly one hundred of these were to be stationed at Nacogdoches where fifty were to arrive by July 15.[64]

A singular character, the famous Baron de Bastrop, of whom we will hear more, passed through Natchitoches in August on his way to Texas. He spoke Spanish, English, and French and, being a sociable individual,

---

[62]Turner to General Wilkinson, October 15, 1804. *State Papers and Publick Documents*, I, 352.

[63]John Sibley to Secretary of War, May 1, 1805. *State Papers and Publick Documents*, I, 352-353.

[64]Turner to Wilkinson, May 3, 1805; Sibley to Secretary of War, July 2, 1805. *State Papers and Publick Documents*, I, 353-355.

chatted freely with various persons. He assured everybody that Louisiana would, ere long, be under Spain again. Before the end of the month the rumor had spread to New Orleans, and Governor Claiborne wrote to James Madison, Secretary of State, that he had called upon the Marqués de Casa Calvo to inquire from this ranking Spanish official the source of the report. The Marqués assured him he knew nothing about it and denied any such intention on the part of Spain.[65]

The presence of more troops and of a prominent commander for the Spanish frontier was confirmed by a letter of Barr to Davenport late in September, 1805. Writing to his partner in Nacogdoches from San Antonio, Barr told him he was waiting for the new governor, Colonel Manuel Antonio Cordero, to set out for Nacogdoches. Cordero, who had attained distinction in Coahuila and had seen service abroad, was to take two full companies to the eastern frontier, one of which was to be stationed at Orcoquisac and the other to be divided between Nacogdoches and the abandoned post of Los Adaes.[66]

The rumors of Spanish designs on Louisiana and the mobilization of troops in Texas soon gave way to complaints of actual violation of American territory. In November the brothers Gaspard and Lewis Bodín and Andrew Chamar, residents of Natchitoches, made deposition before Judge Sibley that they, while travelling from Natchitoches to Opelousas, had been accosted on September 8 by a group of five Spanish soldiers about fourteen or fifteen miles from their destination. The leader of the party took their best horse. Saying that it was needed for the king's service, he drove away in the direction of Nacogdoches. The next day Francis Roban, agent for Oliver and Case of Natchitoches, made a similar declaration to Judge Sibley. He stated that he and Joseph Lucas, en route from the Caddo nation to Natchitoches with a train of eighteen horses loaded with some eleven hundred deer skins, stopped at Bayou Pierre (San Pedro Creek) to call on a friend named De Soto. A Spanish guard stationed there arrested Roban and took his train under custody. The following day the declarant succeeded in escaping, but his horses and pelts were carried on to Nacogdoches.[67]

---

[65]Sibley to Secretary of War, August 8, 1805; Claiborne to James Madison, August 26. *State Papers and Publick Documents*, I, 355; II, 306-307.

[66]Turner to Wilkinson, September 30, 1805. *State Papers and Publick Documents*, I, 356.

[67]Depositions made before John Sibley, Natchitoches, November 2 and 3, 1805. *State Papers and Publick Documents*, I, 335-336, and 338-341.

In his message to Congress, December 3, 1805, the President devoted a long paragraph to Spain. He explained that relations continued to be strained, that Spain had refused to ratify a previous claims convention and that "preparations for adjusting amicably the boundaries of Louisiana have not been acceded to." He did not point out how the ambitious claim to all of Texas was the chief stumbling block. He went on to recite that Spaniards had trespassed on the territories of Orleans and Mississippi, had seized American citizens and had plundered property in American territory. He had, consequently, ordered the United States troops to protect "our citizens" and to repel future aggressions by force. Three days later Jefferson sent a special message to Congress "relative to the hostile spirit manifested by the court of Spain toward the United States," in which he practically asked for discretionary power to use the armed forces of the country to carry out his policy. He stated, after reviewing the relations since 1803, that the actions of Spain in the Floridas and Texas "authorized the inference of her intention to advance on our possessions until stopped by force." He concluded with these significant words: "Formal war is not necessary; it is not probable it will follow; but . . . force should be interposed to a certain degree."[68] There is little room to doubt that the United States had determined, if necessary, to compel Spain to settle the pending question of the Louisiana boundary.

What were the true facts concerning the actions of Spain on the Texas frontier? Documents available seem to indicate that her reaction was purely defensive and that she was extremely anxious to avoid a break with the United States. In April, 1805, Commandant General Nemesio Salcedo wrote Cordero, the new assistant governor of Texas, that he was to be guided in his conduct by three principal aims. The danger of being involved in a war with England made it imperative for him to do everything possible: first, to maintain friendly relations with the Indians; second, to avoid altering the *status quo* on the Spanish-American frontier; and third, to keep a close vigilance against any surprise along the coast. To enable him to accomplish these aims, the light-mounted company of Parras and other troops from Coahuila had been ordered to San Antonio. Cordero was, furthermore, authorized to call on volunteers from the settlements in Texas if an emergency arose.[69]

---

[68]Message of the President, December 6, 1805. *State Papers and Publick Documents*, II, 4-6.

[69]Nemesio Salcedo to the Governor of Texas, April 8, 1805. *Nacogdoches Archives*, X, pp. 19-20.

But Spanish officials, too, had become suspicious of the activity of the Americans in Louisiana among the various Texas tribes. In June, 1805, Salcedo informed Cordero that he had learned on good authority that the United States had sent a formal invitation to the Taovayas on Red River to attend a meeting. The commandant general suggested to Cordero that he write to the Marqués de Casa Calvo to ask him to file a protest. He also advised that more details about the incident and the proposed meeting be secured from the natives. He reminded the governor it would be well to attempt to impress upon the Indians the importance of being friends of the Spaniards. Suspicions grew apace and by August, the commandant general wrote Cordero that the United States was contemplating hostilities along the eastern frontier of Texas. To reënforce the Nacogdoches garrison against any contingency, he recommended that Cordero take there such troops as he could muster. As governor of Coahuila and Texas, Cordero was authorized to transfer as many troops from the former to the latter as he deemed advisable. He was warned to be constantly alert to prevent a surprise.[70]

Salcedo, because of the growing tensity on the frontier, felt that it would be best to stop all trade and communication between the settlers of Louisiana and Texas. The commandant general issued detailed instructions designed to stop all trade, but more particularly the sale of horses and mules to Americans in Louisiana. He went so far as to authorize the governor to publish a proclamation imposing the death penalty for the sale of horses and mules to the enemy. He assured Cordero that, on the first certain indication of hostilities on the part of the United States, he would come to his aid in person, bringing arms, munitions, saddles, horses, and all available men. At this time he suggested as a war measure that, should hostilities break out, Cordero might issue a proclamation declaring free all negro slaves who entered the dominions of Spain. It was against this measure that the Americans in Natchitoches so loudly protested.[71]

The dependency of East Texas on supplies from Natchitoches and from other neighboring French settlements is revealed by the request of Governor Cordero that the trade restrictions recommended by Salcedo be relaxed. In November, 1805, the governor wrote the commandant

---

[70]Nemesio Salcedo to Antonio Cordero, June 17, and August 6, 1805. *Nacogdoches Archives*, X, pp. 25, and 28-29.

[71]Salcedo to Cordero, August 20, 1805. *Nacogdoches Archives*, X, pp. 30-31. See page 250 for protest against harboring of negro slaves at Nacogdoches.

general that he was experiencing considerable difficulty in securing the necessary provisions from San Antonio for the new troops stationed at Nacogdoches and on the Trinity. He had come to the conclusion that stores had to be acquired in Natchitoches and Louisiana or the garrisons in East Texas would be forced to retire to San Antonio. He ingeniously pointed out that as long as hostilities did not exist, there was no harm in the trade proposed and that if war broke out, the troops could then secure the needed goods through conquest.[72]

Reënforcement of the Spanish frontier. In conformity with recent instructions the energetic and capable governor of Coahuila and Texas made a personal inspection of the outposts of Texas in the summer of 1805.[73] Cordero, an experienced officer, was deeply impressed by the defenceless condition of the province. He pointed out to his superior that in the event of hostilities the first point of attack by the Americans would be Nacogdoches. The advanced post of observation placed on Arroyo Hondo would fall back on Nacogdoches the moment the enemy appeared in force. The invaders, well provided with artillery, would need to fire only a few shots to capture Nacogdoches in its present condition. If this post fell, the road to San Antonio was wide open. Because of the circumstances he believed it necessary to make use of the discretionary powers granted to him, and began the construction of a fort which would enable the troops stationed there to withstand attack and allow time for reënforcements to be rushed from the Trinity to check the advance of the invading force. He, furthermore, urged that civil settlements be established on the Trinity and the Brazos, as well as on the Guadalupe and the San Marcos, as a part of the defence program. The absence of settlements between Nacogdoches and San Antonio would allow the enemy to advance to the very heart of the province without opposition.[74]

Upon his return to San Antonio he directed his attention to its fortification and defence. The town had originally been built around the two

---

[72]Cordero to Salcedo, November 19, 1805. *Nacogdoches Archives*, X, pp. 46-47.

[73]Early in the summer of 1805, Antonio Cordero, governor of Coahuila, was appointed assistant governor of Texas. Governor Juan Bautista Elguezábal was confined to bed. Although he was given permission to retire, his serious illness prevented him from leaving Texas. He died in San Antonio on October 5, 1805, and was succeeded in office by his able assistant. Cordero thus became governor of Coahuila and Texas. Salcedo to Cordero, July 29, 1805; same to same, November 4, 1805. *Nacogdoches Archives*, X, pp. 26-27, and 45.

[74]Cordero to Salcedo, September 24, 1805. *Nacogdoches Archives*, X, pp. 32-35.

plazas. In the past it had depended for its defence on two cannon placed at each of the four corners of the plaza. But as the city had now grown to the north and west and extended out for several blocks, the defences had become inadequate. Cordero made a careful study of the city and the surrounding country with a view to its protection against the Indians and against a possible invasion. He found that the San Antonio River, the San Pedro Creek, and the San Antonio Springs afforded natural protection along the east, southeast, and southwest. He decided, therefore, to build an extensive stockade along the north and northeast limits of the city. The northwest quadrant was well protected by the small fort and powder magazine erected on the highest hill in that section. He ordered a new redoubt built one and a quarter leagues north of the city, on which he placed two batteries, to be manned by nine soldiers. This outpost would prevent any attack or surprise by the northern Indians who entered the city from this direction. It also covered the thick woods above the San Antonio Springs which had been till then the favorite hiding place for smugglers, thieves, and cattle runners. Construction was begun on September 12 and by the end of the month considerable progress had been made.

Cordero explained that he was using the soldiers in the erection of the new fortifications and expected to have no other expenses than for hiring carts to haul the materials. There would also be some expense in connection with the repair of the gun carriages and the emplacement of the batteries, and before the work was entirely completed he might have to employ a few skilled craftsmen to put on the finishing touches. He was planning, after the outer defences were completed, to rebuild the stockade around the presidio. He promised Salcedo a map of the city and the fortifications.[75]

The reënforcement of the outposts in Texas was an inevitable consequence of the insistent claims of the United States to territory that had never been a part of Louisiana. The fears of the Spaniards were perhaps more real than those of the Americans. In October, 1805, Cordero sent the commandant general copies of a heated correspondence between Lieutenant Dionisio Valle, of Nacogdoches, and Captain Edward Turner, of Natchitoches, in regard to the surrender of American deserters. Turner alleged that General Wilkinson and Governor Gayoso de Lemos had in the past made an agreement concerning the matter. A few days later an

---

[75]Cordero to Salcedo, October 5, 1805. *Nacogdoches Archives*, X, pp. 38-40.

officer from Natchitoches pursued a party of deserters beyond the Arroyo Hondo and arrested them in Spanish territory. To the protest made by Spanish officials, Turner replied that the limits of Louisiana were as yet undetermined; whereupon he was told that until the boundary was settled the old line between the two provinces would have to be observed. Salcedo, when he learned of the incident, gave orders to Governor Cordero that in the future any party or individual who trespassed beyond the established line was to be arrested and held until further instructions.[76]

Growing distrust. The suspense and indignation of Spanish officials heightened as the year drew to a close. In November, Louis Foutier, formerly of Natchitoches but now residing in Nacogdoches, reported to the governor that American officers had questioned citizens of Natchitoches to learn whether or not they would take up arms against Spain in the event of war. In October a new road from Natchitoches to the Illinois was ordered built and more than a thousand men were hired at three dollars a day. Foutier also stated that he had been in Natchitoches on October 22, when Felix Trudeaux returned from New Orleans and said that the Marqués de Casa Calvo had left on October 20 with thirty dragoons and ninety grenadiers aboard three ships for Orcoquisac. But more alarming still was the fact that the American troops in Natchitoches publicly boasted that they would soon help to mark the boundaries of Louisiana, which they maintained extended to the Río Grande. Recently a certain James and a Folston, both Americans, had gone hunting with Indian friends to the country of the Orcoquisacs.[77]

When the commandant general received the report containing the statements made by Foutier, he was seriously alarmed. He immediately informed Cordero that he had dispatched sixty men under Captain Gregorio Fernández from Chihuahua to Coahuila so that Cordero might make use of them as he saw fit. At the same time he had sent an urgent request to the viceroy for six hundred mounted troops, one or two good engineers, and fifteen or twenty artillerymen for service in Texas.[78]

Clashes in the Sabine-Arroyo Hondo area. By the end of the year Spanish forces had reoccupied the abandoned post of Los Adaes; Bayou Pierre, located a short distance from the former; and La Nana, likewise

---

[76]Cordero to Salcedo, October 14, 1805; Salcedo to Cordero, November 2, 1805. *Nacogdoches Archives*, X, pp. 41-44.

[77]Cordero to Salcedo, November 22, 1805. *Nacogdoches Archives*, X, pp. 48-50.

[78]Salcedo to Cordero, December 6, 1805. *Nacogdoches Archives*, X, pp. 55-56.

east of the Sabine. The garrison at Nacogdoches had been reënforced, the old site of Orcoquisac occupied, and a new post on the Trinity established. Spain had taken such measures as she could in order to maintain her claims as far as the Arroyo Hondo. But American suspicions of ulterior designs had again been aroused, and feeling along the Texas-Louisiana frontier ran high.[79]

It was at this time that Captain Sebastián Rodríguez, of Nacogdoches, undertook to reconnoiter the advanced line, and chose to accompany Marqués de Casa Calvo to Natchitoches itself. Major Porter promptly became suspicious of the escort of Casa Calvo and ordered Rodríguez to return with his men to Nacogdoches. The four months' visit of Casa Calvo in Texas had aroused much speculation and was most indiscreet, to say the least.[80]

To a subsequent request of Major Porter that Spanish troops retire west of the Sabine River, which the United States considered the western boundary of Louisiana, Rodríguez replied with arrogance that Arroyo Hondo had always been the eastern boundary of Texas and that he would continue to occupy the territory between the two streams. When on January 4, 1806, Cordero was advised of the incident, he ordered 50 men from the Trinity to reënforce Nacogdoches, called for the volunteer militia, issued a ringing proclamation, and requested 100 men from Coahuila to march to East Texas at once.[81]

"Now indeed the fear of invasion seized both sides. The Americans trembled for Louisiana; the air was rife with tales of Spanish intrigues, and there were evidences of deceit and treachery." But whereas Cordero had become unduly alarmed, Salcedo kept his head, and on January 17 wrote the governor that he had been hasty in his proclamation and the call for volunteers, that there were no grounds for such alarm, that his action might justly create the wrong impression in Louisiana. He condemned in particular the conduct of Captain Rodríguez. As a subordinate, he should not have so answered Major Porter; he should have been content to explain that he was acting under orders, that he had no authority to withdraw forces from the Arroyo Hondo, and that he would have to refer the whole matter to his superiors. Captain Rodríguez was,

---

[79]McCaleb, W. F., *The Aaron Burr Conspiracy*, 105-107; Filisola, *Memorias para la historia de la guerra de Tejas*, I, 43-45.

[80]Rodríguez to Cordero, March 4, 1806; Casa Calvo to Cordero, December 8, 1805; Salcedo to Cordero, January 1, and 28, 1806. *Béxar Archives.*

[81]Salcedo to Cordero, January 17, 1806. *Nacogdoches Archives*, X, pp. 58-63.

consequently, ordered removed from his command and put under arrest for fifteen days. Lieutenant Dionisio Valle was to replace him. The new commander was to exercise the utmost discretion and to avoid scrupulously precipitate action. The fifty men ordered to Nacogdoches were to be recalled and left on the Trinity. He concluded by emphatically declaring that a break with the United States was to be averted at all costs.[82]

But before the letter of Salcedo reached Cordero, Major Porter had received from the Secretary of War an order to request explicit assurances from the commander of Nacogdoches that no further inroads be made east of the Sabine, and to inform him that the American patrols were to be extended to this river. Porter sent Lieutenant Piatt with this formal request to Rodríguez, who again refused to accede to it. On February 1 Captain Turner was ordered to proceed with about sixty men to Los Adaes to command the Spanish troops stationed there to withdraw beyond the Sabine. "They might go in peace if they would, but evacuate they must, even at the cost of blood."[83]

Turner arrived on February 5 at the outpost on Bayou Pierre and delivered his message. González, the officer in charge, protested the violation of Spanish territory but signed a written agreement to withdraw west of the Sabine as soon as his horses were in condition to travel.[84]

Such is the account of events recorded by the Americans. Not until February 19 did Rodríguez report the American incursion to Cordero. Spanish outposts at Comichi and La Nana had been forced west of the Sabine by American forces, who, after setting fire to the temporary barracks built by the Spanish troops, had returned to Natchitoches. The post at Bayou Pierre had not been molested. As a precaution Rodríguez had ordered 100 men to guard the two main crossings on the Sabine, the one leading to Bayou Pierre and the other, to Natchitoches. He had issued strict orders prohibiting all communication with Louisiana, and he had taken every step possible to prevent information about his movements from reaching the Americans. The roads were impassable at this time of the year and Rodríguez had been unable to contact Captain Gerónimo de Herrera, who had gone to make a careful inspection along the coast.[85]

---

[82]Salcedo to Cordero, January 17, 1806. *Nacogdoches Archives*, X, pp. 58-63.
[83]McCaleb, *The Aaron Burr Conspiracy*, 106-107.
[84]*Messages and Reports of the United States Government*, 1806.
[85]Rodríguez to Cordero, February 19, 1806. *Nacogdoches Archives*, X, pp. 71-73.

When the matter was reported to Salcedo, whom Pike described as "a middle-sized man, apparently about fifty-five years of age, with a stern countenance," the cautious and worried commandant of the Interior Provinces again advised the utmost tact to prevent an open break. As he was sick, he did not feel like writing at length. He recommended that Cordero read carefully his letter of January 17. He suggested that the Americans be told that "until the boundary is defined, setting the limits of the provinces of Louisiana and Texas, no point may be abandoned that has until now been known to be within the territorial limits of Spain." He reiterated his disapproval of the plan to call out provincial troops and declared that whatever men should be needed were to be drawn from Nuevo León and Nuevo Santander. The viceroy had already issued instructions to this effect.[86]

Suggestions for establishment of a neutral zone. Salcedo was the first to propose that the area between the Arroyo Hondo and the Sabine be declared neutral ground as a means to prevent a rupture. In a letter to Cordero on February 24, 1806, after repeating that the action of Rodríguez in establishing new posts at Comichi and La Nana had been ill-advised, he declared that a return to the *status quo* was highly desirable. He instructed Governor Cordero, therefore, to send an officer to Natchitoches to explain to the commander that the territory between the Arroyo Hondo and the Sabine was to be considered neutral and until the boundary was defined, neither party was to advance within the area designated. Here, then, are the essentials of the agreement eventually entered into with Wilkinson nine months later.

On March 23 Cordero informed the commandant general that he had followed his instructions in regard to the neutral ground proposal and had ordered the additional troops concentrated at Nacogdoches to return to their former stations. He assured Salcedo that all efforts would be made to prevent an outbreak of hostilities. Intent on avoiding a breach, Salcedo once more advised moderation on the frontier when he informed the governor on April 4 that Francisco Viana, an experienced officer and inspector of military outposts, was to take charge of the garrison at Nacogdoches. Cordero was to instruct Viana to use the utmost discretion in dealing with any situation that might arise.[87]

---

[86]Salcedo to Cordero, February 23, 1806. *Nacogdoches Archives*, X, pp. 74-76; Pike, *Exploratory Travels*, 265.

[87]Salcedo to Cordero, February 24 and April 4, 1806. *Nacogdoches Archives*, X, pp. 77-81, and 89-94. Pike remarks in his diary that Viana was a capable officer but had failed to be promoted because he was too outspoken. Pike, *op. cit.*, 293.

Mounting war fever and complications. But while Salcedo was attempting to maintain peace, American public opinion and the Government itself believed that a Spanish attack was imminent. When the Turner incident was reported to Washington, the President sent a special message to Congress on March 19 "relative to Spanish innovations on the Sabine River," declaring that he had just learned that the Spaniards were advancing "to occupy new posts and make new settlements." He then informed Congress that the officers of the United States Army were ordered "to confine themselves within the country on this side of the Sabine River, which by delivery of its principal post, Natchitoches, was understood to have been delivered up by Spain."[88] The President's message was interpreted by the newspapers as a veiled warning of serious peril. The excitable Westerners violently protested and strongly urged immediate attack on Spain and the liberation of Mexico. By the fourth of July (1806) "there was not a thousand persons in the United States who did not think war with Spain inevitable, impending, begun!" says a well-known historian.[89]

Naturally the general denunciation of Spain reached Spanish officials. Salcedo wrote Cordero as early as April 9 that, ever since France sold Louisiana to the United States, nothing had been left undone "to extend the limits into the Spanish possessions . . . and to secure the twenty-two leagues of land lying between the Arroyo Hondo and the Sabine, the former of which marks the boundary of Louisiana, as the Americans well know."[90] Agents in Louisiana early in the year had warned Spanish officials of an expedition being organized in Kentucky to free Mexico. When Salcedo heard of it, he wrote to Cordero: "It is a very grave matter . . . that some 10,000 men, subjects of the United States, are being prepared in Kentucky with the object of overpowering the uninhabited provinces of this kingdom and our Indian allies, with no respect for the boundaries of Louisiana. You will, therefore, take extraordinary precautions toward putting the country in a good state of defence by bringing up all the auxiliaries." Cordero immediately relayed the news to Viana at Nacogdoches, adding that the real purpose of the expedition was to take possession of Texas. He recommended that every effort be

[88]Message . . . . relative to Spanish innovations on the Sabine River . . . , March 19, 1806. *State Papers and Publick Documents,* II, 152.

[89]McCaleb, *The Aaron Burr Conspiracy,* 110.

[90]Salcedo to Cordero, April 9, 1806. *Béxar Archives.*

made to maintain friendship with the Indians. Friendly chiefs should be asked to report the presence or the approach of foreigners.[91]

It was at this time that Major Freeman and Captain Sparks attempted to make an exploration up the Red River. Viana immediately protested to the commander at Natchitoches, pointing out that the advance of the armed party up the Red River was a palpable violation of neutrality and constituted an unwarranted intrusion into Spanish territory. He recalled the dismissal early in the year of the small military escort of Marqués de Casa Calvo and of the bishop of Nuevo León upon their visit to Natchitoches, and concluded by requesting the immediate withdrawal of the expedition. At the same time he reported to the commandant general the incident and the measures taken, and sent him copies of the correspondence. Salcedo wrote the governor approving the protest of Viana and declared that, judging from the correspondence submitted, the sincerity of the Americans in their professions of peace left much to be desired. Two weeks later, on June 29, he issued specific instructions to Lieutenant Colonel Simón de Herrera to prevent by force, if necessary, the advance of the American exploratory expedition up the Red River.

Viana, accordingly, was authorized to send 230 men under Lieutenant Juan Ignacio Ramón to prevent the Americans from ascending the Red River. The expedition, which had traversed almost 600 miles, was halted on its march into what, there is no doubt, was Spanish territory.[92]

Second crisis on the Louisiana-Texas frontier. The American war fever of the early summer of 1806 aroused the fear of the Spaniards; and Salcedo himself, a staunch supporter of the *status quo,* came to think that it was best to occupy the territory between the Sabine and the Arroyo Hondo so as to repel any invasion of the dominions of His Majesty. By the end of June, 1806, there were in Texas 1,007 soldiers. Cordero informed Salcedo on June 12 that Herrera, governor of Nuevo León, assigned to the frontier in this moment of peril, had left San Antonio that day with the last detachment of troops ordered from Mexico to the Louisiana frontier. He intended to march double-quick in order to assume command on the Trinity as soon as possible. The soldiers

---

[91]Salcedo to Cordero, April 9, 1806. *Béxar Archives;* Cordero to Viana, April 21, 1806. *Nacogdoches Archives,* X, pp. 95-96.

[92]Salcedo to Cordero, June 16, 1806; Viana to Commander of American Expedition, May 10, 1806; Cordero to Salcedo, June 29, 1806. *Nacogdoches Archives,* X, pp. 102-104, 111-114, and 115-120; Message of the President . . . to the Ninth Congress, December 2, 1806. *State Papers and Publick Documents,* II, 158-159.

included veterans and militia and comprised the garrisons stationed on the Trinity, at Nacogdoches, and Orcoquisac. All were fully equipped and well supplied with food to last until August 30. Four kegs of powder had been sent by Cordero to Nacogdoches from San Antonio, as also four cases of cartridges (8,000) for the militia and from the Trinity four more cases for the Coahuila contingent. Father Cipriano de la Garza, of Punta de Lampasos, had been appointed chaplain for the troops in East Texas and a portable chapel for field services had been secured from Parras for his use.[93]

On June 25 Herrera reported that he had arrived safely and had placed his troops advantageously so as to enable him to observe with ease the movements of the Americans from the Trinity to the Arroyo Hondo. Viana was now sent to reoccupy Bayou Pierre which had been abandoned voluntarily in February in accord with the proposal for the establishment of a neutral zone. The Spanish flag was raised at the old post early in July on the site of the abandoned mission, San Francisco de los Tejas. But conditions on the eastern frontier were far from satisfactory. The arrival of fresh troops in Nacogdoches served only to multiply the difficulties of the commissary. On August 4 Viana made an urgent appeal to Nacogdoches for provisions, explaining that his detachment at Bayou Pierre had been four days without rations. Sickness spread rapidly through the crowded camp of underfed men and soon converted it into a wretched hospital.[94]

Exaggerated rumors of the number of Spanish troops on the frontier and of their designs now spread alarm among the Americans. Colonel T. H. Cushing, commander of Natchitoches, sent Major Moses Porter with a letter to Lieutenant Colonel Herrera, in which he stated he had just learned of the recrossing of the Sabine by the Spanish forces recently assembled west of the river. He peremptorily demanded their immediate withdrawal and an explanation of their actions. He declared that Herrera would be responsible for the consequences of a refusal. The question of the true boundary was still the subject of diplomatic discussion. The reënforcement of the American outposts was intended for the protection and safety of the territory of the United States. There was no intention

---

[93]Cordero to Salcedo, June 12, 1806. *Nacogdoches Archives*, X, pp. 109-110; McCaleb, *The Aaron Burr Conspiracy*, 116-117.

[94]Cordero to Salcedo, June 29, 1806. *Nacogdoches Archives*, X, pp. 115-120; McCaleb, *op. cit.*, 111-117.

of invading Spanish territory, but failure of the Spaniards to withdraw west of the Sabine would be considered a violation of American territory.[95]

Herrera replied the next day, in a firm and dignified note, that the troops under his command had advanced east of the Sabine, and had taken positions according to instructions received from the commandant general. His orders were to hold the occupied ground against any invasion of the king's domain. This territory belonged to Spain from time immemorial and was an integral part of Texas. He took occasion to protest against the unjustified attack made recently upon a small Spanish detachment by American troops and warned that he could not permit the usurpation of Spanish territory.[96]

The two commanders now stood poised while the war clouds gathered rapidly. Governor Claiborne, who had been granted a leave of absence to visit his family in Tennessee, was at the time in Concordia near Natchez. He immediately rushed to Natchez for a conference with Cowles Meade, acting governor of the Mississippi Territory. They issued a joint proclamation on August 17, calling upon the people to aid the regular troops in expelling the Spaniards from Bayou Pierre. The *Orleans Gazette* published a sensational account, declaring that 900 men under the governor of Texas had advanced to within twelve miles of Natchitoches.[97]

Claiborne formally took up American grievances with Herrera on August 26. He stated that the territory under dispute should be left unoccupied. The advance of troops east of the Sabine River could be considered in no other light than that of an unfriendly act to the United States. But this was not the only unfriendly act committed recently. Major Freeman and his party had been arbitrarily stopped on the Red River and forced to give up a purely scientific expedition; a group of Spanish troops had entered a Caddo village and had cut down the staff from which an American flag flew; and a party of Spanish soldiers had seized Shaw, Irwin, and Brewster, three American citizens, within twelve miles of Natchitoches and had sent them as prisoners to Nacogdoches. Last but not least, slaves in Louisiana had been encouraged

---

[95]T. H. Cushing to Lieutenant Colonel Herrera, August 5, 1806. *State Papers and Publick Documents*, II, 163-164.

[96]Herrera to Cushing, August 6, 1806. *Nacogdoches Archives*, X, pp. 164-165.

[97]McCaleb, *The Aaron Burr Conspiracy*, 117-118.

to run away and had been given protection in Nacogdoches. The governor of Louisiana demanded an explanation; the release of Shaw, Irwin, and Brewster; and the return of the runaway slaves.[98]

Two days later he reported to the War Department that the Spaniards had advanced their main body to within seventeen miles of Natchitoches and their patrols as far as Bayou Funda (Arroyo Hondo), claimed by them as the eastern boundary of Texas; that their number was said to be 1,000; and that reënforcements were expected daily. Within a week he raised the estimate to 1,200 Spanish troops, composed of 300 regulars brought up by Governor Codero, and two regiments from Vera Cruz expected to land at the mouth of the Trinity.[99]

Attempts to dispel the war clouds. Cordero reported the occupation of the territory as far as Arroyo Hondo to the commandant general on August 23. At the same time he recounted the arrest of three suspicious characters, Shaw, Irwin, and Brewster, who had been sent for examination to Nacogdoches and hence to Monclova. They seemed to be either spies or smugglers. Cordero related he had just arrived in the camp on the Trinity by dint of forced marches and there received Herrera's dispatches of August 17. From all information available, the situation on the frontier appeared serious. The Americans at Natchitoches were on the verge of attacking his troops. He, however, assured the commandant general that, in case of hostilities, he would delay the advance of the enemy until reënforcements could be rushed to his aid. He was expecting on the morrow the arrival of 100 men who were bringing 120 horses from Béjar and the Alamo (post in Coahuila) and others borrowed from La Bahía. These would be replaced by others from Coahuila.

The condition of the forces on the frontier was truly deplorable, he pointed out. The climate, the lack of adequate pastures, and the campaign were hard on the men and horses. Sickness was prevalent in Nacogdoches and the vicinity. More than 200 men had either died or were too sick for active service. All those who were able to travel he had sent to San Antonio to be cared for in the hospital recently established there. He estimated the effective force of the outposts on the

---

[98]William C. C. Claiborne to Herrera, August 26, 1806. *State Papers and Publick Documents*, II, 165-168.
[99]McCaleb, *op. cit.*, 118-119.

Trinity and Sabine rivers, and at Orcoquisac and Nacogdoches as 900 men, but a large number of them was employed in the transportation and distribution of food and supplies from Nacogdoches to the various outposts.

Fearful of a sudden attack and the need of a hasty retreat west of the Sabine, Herrera had requested that a number of flatboats be built on the Sabine. Cordero assured Salcedo that he had given orders for their construction.[100]

To Claiborne's communication of August 26 Herrera replied that the purpose of the Spanish troops on the frontier was to prevent a violation of the king's territory; that Major Freeman had been turned back from the Red River at a point which was far beyond the acknowledged limits of Louisiana; that the incident involving the Caddo Indians had taken place in a village of this nation located within the jurisdiction of Spain and that the Indians had merely been told that if they wanted to fly the American flag they would have to move to American territory. He explained the arrest of the three Americans on the grounds that they had been found spying upon the movements of Spanish troops. He concluded by giving Claiborne positive assurance that his intentions were not hostile, but that he was determined to repel force with force, should the established and acknowledged frontier be violated. Claiborne promptly replied that the explanations offered were unsatisfactory and again demanded immediate withdrawal west of the Sabine.[101]

When Salcedo finally received full details of the occurrences on the frontier, he was somewhat relieved to learn that, in spite of the angry recriminations, no hostilities had resulted. He again advised caution and tact, and instructed Herrera to restrict his activities to periodic inspections or simple patrol duty in the area between the Sabine and the Arroyo Hondo.

In the meantime, as early as May 6, 1806, the War Department, in view of the exaggerated reports rife at the time, had explicitly ordered General Wilkinson: "You will, therefore, with as little delay as practicable, repair to the Territory of Orleans or its vicinity, and take upon yourself the command of the troops in that quarter . . . and you will,

---

[100]Cordero to Salcedo, August 23, 1806. *Nacogdoches Archives*, X, pp. 136-140.

[101]Claiborne to Herrera, August 31, 1806; Herrera to Claiborne, August 28, 1806. *State Papers and Publick Documents*, II, 168-171.

by all the means in your power, repel any invasion of the territory of the United States east of the River Sabine, or north or west of the bounds of what has been called West Florida."[102]

But fortunately for all concerned, Wilkinson was delayed three months in St. Louis by "various and unavoidable obstacles." Subsequent events point strongly to the shady and not satisfactorily explained relations of the general with the colorful conspirator, ex-Vice-President Aaron Burr. These unfortunate relations and the excited state of public opinion both in the United States and the Interior Provinces have sadly confused the true state of affairs. "Burr's designs were complicated with the attitude of the United States Government . . . and the complication confounded contemporaries, most of all the Spaniards. They saw the conspiracy only as an aggressive movement against their territories, organized as it were under the wing of the Government."[103]

Let us return to Wilkinson and the third crisis on the frontier. Although his movements were incredibly slow, the general was loud in his denunciation of Spanish perfidy and his determination to drive the Spaniards beyond the Sabine. "I will soon plant our standards on the left bank of the Grand River [Río Grande]," he said shortly after his orders reached him. The *Orleans Gazette* announced on October 3 that from Fort Adams all the regular troops had marched under Captain Sparks for Natchitoches, and that at any moment Major Ferdinand L. Claiborne was expected to take the Mississippi militia and Captain Farrar's dragoons to the frontier. To General John Adair, Senator, Wilkinson wrote in reply as to the distance from St. Louis to Santa Fe: "Do you know that I have reserved these places for my own triumphal entry, that I have been reconnoitering and exploring the route for sixteen years; that I not only know the way but all the difficulties and how to surmount them?" Shortly after his arrival at Natchitoches in September, he again wrote Adair: "The time long looked for by many and wished for by more has now arrived. More will be done by marching than fighting; 5,000 men will give us to Rio ....; 10,000 to ....; we must here divide our army into three parts and will then require

---

[102]Wilkinson, James, *Memoirs of My Own Time*, Appendix xc. Salcedo to Cordero, August 25, and September 18, 1806. *Nacogdoches Archives*, X, pp. 141-145.

[103]McCaleb, *The Aaron Burr Conspiracy*, 109.

30,000 men to conquer the whole of the province of Mexico."[104] Wilkinson seemed bent on war at all costs from the moment he arrived in Natchez on September 7 until September 27, when Herrera avoided the conflict by ordering a retreat of the Spanish forces west of the Sabine.[105]

But the matter was not definitely settled until November 5, when the celebrated Neutral Ground Agreement was finally concluded. It is necessary to trace the Spanish reaction to the attitude and actions of Wilkinson just described in order to understand the ultimate settlement of the vexing question. It is well to keep in mind also that it was Governor Cordero who was inclined to be bellicose, and that it was Salcedo who had steadfastly advocated avoidance of hostilities. Herrera, the governor of Nuevo León, had been ordered to the frontier to assist Cordero because of his knowledge of English, his acquaintance with the United States where he had spent some time, and his known moderation and tact.[106] Governor Claiborne's letter of August 26 and a copy of Herrera's reply had been forwarded to Salcedo.

On September 18, the commandant general, still unaware of the arrival of Wilkinson on the scene, wrote a long letter to Governor Claiborne. Had this letter reached Claiborne sooner, the subsequent disagreeable events might never have occurred. He took up the various complaints and answered them in detail. To the protest against the occupation of the territory east of the Sabine River by Spanish troops he replied that Spain had always had an indisputable claim to the land as far as the Arroyo Hondo, as shown by the permanent maintenance of Los Adaes until 1772, when it was abandoned after the cession of Louisiana to Spain. He further cited in support of this contention that in 1745 France had tacitly admitted that, on the occasion of a controversy over deserters from Natchitoches, Arroyo Hondo was the boundary. When Governor Miró had proposed in 1790-1791 the extension of the limits of Louisiana to the Sabine River, the request was denied. Salcedo assured

---

[104]McCaleb, *The Aaron Burr Conspiracy*, 122-131; *Orleans Gazette*, October 3, 1806; Wilkinson, *Memoirs*, Appendix lxxvii. Blanks in the quotation are in the original manuscript.

[105]Wilkinson, *op. cit.*, Appendix xcii; McCaleb, *op. cit.*, 184.

[106]Herrera's wife was an Englishwoman. Pike says of her: "Herrera married an English lady in early youth at Cadiz, who, by her suavity of manners, makes herself as much beloved and esteemed by the ladies as her noble husband is by the men. By her he has several children, one now an officer in the service of his royal master." Pike, *Explorations*, 289.

the American commander that the Spanish troops on the frontier were animated by no hostile intention, and that they were operating within territory recognized as Spanish from time immemorial.

Respecting Major Freeman and his party who had been ordered back by Spanish troops on the Red River, the commandant general explained that French jurisdiction had never extended up the Red River beyond Natchitoches. The Government of the United States was fully aware of this, he declared, as shown by the fact that application had been made for a Spanish passport for a Mr. Dunbar, who was originally intended to lead the expedition. Major Freeman was appointed only after Dunbar was refused the passport. For a country to permit an armed group of foreigners to go freely through its territory was contrary to the practice of nations.

The flag incident in the Caddo village had been misrepresented. The national emblem had not been taken down from a flagpole. It had been found in a deserted Indian hut in an Indian village, together with a Spanish flag bearing the Burgundian cross. The two flags had been confiscated and the Indians warned not to fly the American flag within Spanish jurisdiction.

The three Americans, said to have been arrested, in fact had been detained merely for questioning and sent with an escort to San Antonio. They had been found under suspicious and compromising circumstances. But in spite of their unsatisfactory explanations, the order for their immediate release had been issued and they should have already reached the frontier.

The question of the runaway slaves had been carefully investigated. It turned out that on May 23, there came to Nacogdoches three negro brothers, and a negress with three children. They had presented a safe-conduct signed by the justice of the peace. An examination of the document proved it was false. On July 12 a Mr. Jacob Bean, resident of Opelousas, had come to Nacogdoches and claimed the slaves as runaways. He explained that the Negroes had robbed him and made their escape. Under the circumstances the request for their return was refused. But instructions had since been issued to all officials along the frontier that in the future runaway slaves were to be returned promptly on demand of the legal owner presenting adequate proof. These instructions were, of course, subject to the approval of the king.

With regard to the troops east of the Sabine, he assured Governor Claiborne that they would not establish permanent quarters within the territory under dispute, nor would they make any innovations. They were present merely to prevent the invasion of Spanish territory before the permanent boundary was settled by diplomatic negotiation.[107]

Wilkinson's ultimatum. Determined to provoke an incident, General Wilkinson, upon his arrival in Natchitoches—three and a half months after he had been ordered to proceed to the frontier with all possible haste—addressed a harsh remonstrance, not to Lieutenant Colonel Herrera, but to the bellicose Governor Cordero. He dramatically began by declaring that "peace or war hangs in the balance." He then stated that the territory under dispute must not be occupied until the question was settled by the representatives of the respective Governments. In a grandiose manner he continued, "pending negotiations . . . nothing shall be attempted against his Catholic Majesty's subjects, or territories, by the troops under my command; unless his officers should attempt, as they have already done, to innovate the *status quo* . . . by occupying new ground, or erecting new posts." He then launched into a discussion of the history of the boundary between the two provinces and concluded by saying that Mr. Laussat, the French commissioner who had turned Louisiana over to the United States, had asserted that its western limits extended to the Río del Norte (the Río Grande). But the United States had modestly claimed only as far as the Sabine River. He, therefore, demanded the immediate withdrawal of all Spanish forces to the west bank of said river. He explained that he had been commanded by the President of the United States to extend jurisdiction to the Sabine River, for the territory east of this river was "fully within the limits of the country surrendered by France to the United States." Any attempt to disturb the present state of affairs would be considered an actual invasion of American territorial rights. He closed his long epistle with an impassioned plea, "Retire, then, Sir, I conjure you, the troops of your command . . . and spare the effusion of human blood."[108]

Cordero replied promptly, regretting his inability to decide the question. The decision could be reached only by the commandant general, to whom he had forwarded the general's communication by special mes-

---

[107]Salcedo to Governor Claiborne, September 18, 1806. *Nacogdoches Archives*, X, pp. 146-156.

[108]Wilkinson to Cordero, September 24, 1806. *State Papers and Publick Documents*, II, 172-175. The copy in the Béxar Archives is dated September 23.

senger. Until he had received instructions to the contrary, the Spanish forces east of the Sabine would remain in their present positions.[109]

But two days previously, on September 27, "While Burr sat at a banquet in Nashville and the crowd lustily cheered the toast of Jackson, 'millions for defence; not one cent for tribute'; while the American army burned with eagerness to try their metal on the foe, and Jefferson listened tremulously for the announcement of the rupture, Herrera, exercising his own discretion, ordered a retreat—and the Spanish flag had waved for the last time over Bayou Pierre! The crisis was past."[110]

The Neutral Ground Agreement. Wilkinson's orders were to assert the authority of the United States unequivocally as far as the Sabine River and, although the decision of Herrera to withdraw voluntarily made Wilkinson's march unnecessary, he informed the Government on October 4 of his determination to carry out his orders. At the same time he answered Cordero in a conciliatory tone that he would dispatch his troops to the Sabine as ordered, but that he hoped the governor would interpret the move as "signifying the pretensions of the United States to the east bank of the river, and not as an act of hostility against the Spanish troops." He explained that the honor of the United States demanded the move. In the meantime, Herrera had, true to his word, removed immediately all Spanish outposts east of the river, and on September 30 crossed to the west side. But in all justice, be it said that Cordero did not approve of Herrera's action and that the momentous decision separated the two old friends for a while. It was, therefore, not entirely idle talk when the governor replied to Wilkinson that, much to his regret, he would have to oppose with force the advance of American troops beyond the Arroyo Hondo, because he was committed by the orders of his superior "to oppose myself to the aggressions of the United States and to preserve entire . . . the dominions of my sovereign." Cordero was at this time still in Nacogdoches.[111]

Wilkinson strangely remained in Natchitoches for almost a month before he proceeded to put into execution his loudly proclaimed march to the Sabine. But he was not exactly idle during this month, for he kept more than busy preparing the ultimate betrayal of his friend and fellow conspirator, Aaron Burr. That the Spaniards saw through his

---

[109]Cordero to Wilkinson, September 29, 1806. *Ibid.*, II, 175.
[110]McCaleb, *The Aaron Burr Conspiracy*, 134.
[111]McCaleb, *op. cit.*, 137-138.

plan to cause an outbreak is evident. Cordero had written Herrera on October 19 that the determination of the pretensions of the United States rested with the king. However, it would be best in the meantime to avoid giving the Americans a pretext for an open break by opposing their advance to the Sabine by force. The orders of the commandant general in this respect were with reference to scouting parties and patrols, "not against the advance guard of a regular army, looking for an excuse to attack." He, therefore, suggested allowing the Americans to advance unopposed as far as the Sabine.[112] A few days later came Salcedo's confirmation of the policy adopted by Herrera. From the Hacienda de los Hornos he wrote to Cordero that under no circumstances was an attack to be made upon the Americans. Better that the disputed territory be occupied by them than to jeopardize the claim of Spain to it by hasty action.[113]

Not until October 22 did Wilkinson finally set out on his triumphal march to the Sabine. "It was an idle march," says McCaleb, "selfishly begun and disgracefully ended."[114] They proceeded unopposed to the east bank of the Sabine where they halted on October 29. On the previous day Wilkinson had sent his trusted aide-de-camp, Walter Burling, of whom we will hear more, to Cordero in Nacogdoches with the proposal that without yielding a pretension or ceding a right, the two powers should retire to Nacogdoches and Natchitoches respectively; and that until the boundary question was settled, the Spaniards were not to recross the Sabine, and the Americans, the Arroyo Hondo.

Burling left with Herrera a copy of the proposals which were substantially those made in February by Salcedo,[115] and hurried on to Cordero. He appears to have delivered his dispatch to the governor in Nacogdoches at noon on November 1. Here he remained until the third, when Cordero, with characteristic stubbornness, replied that the decision rested with the commandant general. He regretted he could do nothing about the matter, but assured Wilkinson's emissary that he was sending the proposals with all haste to Salcedo. Herrera, more practical than diplomatic, realized there was no time to lose. When Burling returned to the Sabine on November 4 with the noncommittal reply of Cordero, he again seized

---

[112]Cordero to Herrera, October 19, 1806. *Nacogdoches Archives*, XI, pp. 2-3.

[113]Salcedo to Cordero, October 24, 1806. *Béxar Archives*.

[114]McCaleb, *op. cit.*, 149; Wilkinson to Secretary of War, October 21, 1806. *State Papers and Publick Documents*, II, 176-177.

[115]See page 260.

MAYOR GENERAL
JAMES WILKINSON

A. BURR

LIEUT.
Z.M. PIKE

PROTAGONISTS IN THE ANGLO-AMERICAN MARCH TO THE WEST: JAMES WILKINSON,
AARON BURR, ZEBULON M. PIKE
Ink drawings by H. Medina-Neri.

the opportunity to prevent a rupture and, assuming full responsibility, announced his acceptance of the articles proposed. The next day, November 5, Inspector Francisco Viana arrived in the American camp on the Sabine and signed the agreement with Wilkinson which has been known ever since as the Neutral Ground Agreement.[116]

Thus was concluded an unofficial treaty that was indubitably a victory for Spain. "Without warrant of Congress, without the consent or advice of the Executive," declares McCaleb, "Wilkinson compromised the claim of the United States to what was known as the Neutral Ground; and without the shadow of authority rendered ridiculous our pretensions to the Rio Grande as the western limit of Louisiana!"[117]

Filibusters and the Aaron Burr conspiracy. The activity of filibusters and the frustrated conspiracy of the ex-Vice-President of the United States are closely related to the incidents just recounted. The connection of Wilkinson with the latter has been the subject of numerous discourses. Daniel Clark, accused by the general as one of the conspirators, declared that the entire plan probably originated with Wilkinson himself, and that "it was the impracticability, not the wickedness of the scheme" that induced him to abandon it. A brief statement of the principal events will explain, in part, the conduct of Wilkinson in the negotiations of the Neutral Ground Agreement. It is necessary to go back in the narrative to understand the bearing of the treaty on Texas.

As early as August, 1803, Miguel Músquiz, the commander of Nacogdoches who had succeeded in killing Nolan and in taking his companions prisoners, warned the governor of Texas that others were following in the footsteps of the scheming trader in horses. José Vidal, at Concordia, had informed Músquiz that a party of ten men had left Natchez for Texas, and that this group was headed by a Mr. Ashley, a member of Nolan's party who had escaped from Nacogdoches. They had crossed the Mississippi at Nogales (Walnut Hill) to follow the route taken by Nolan. Músquiz said he had asked Santiago Gil and Manuel Menchaca, who had gone to hunt on the upper Brazos, to keep a watch for the intruders and he suggested that the friendly Indians be questioned for information.[118]

---

[116]Wilkinson, *Memoirs,* II, Appendix xcvii.

[117]McCaleb, *op. cit.,* 156.

[118]Miguel Músquiz to Governor of Texas, August 20, 1803. *Nacogdoches Archives,* X, pp. 9-10.

The disgruntled Vidal, who had never forgotten the mock trial of Nolan in the Territorial Court of Mississippi, warned Elguezábal in October. After fourteen years of faithful service in Louisiana, he was on the point of setting out on a year's vacation. "Woe to our possessions in Mexico with such an order of things!" he wailed. The Americans, in his opinion, were ambitious, restless, treacherous, and their Government was the "most meddlesome on earth." Inflexibility seemed to be the only way of restraining them. Hypocritical Protestants thought nothing of posing as zealous Catholics in order to obtain land grants and establish new homes within the Spanish dominions.[119]

The bishop of Nuevo León in 1804 reported directly to José Caballero, Secretary of State of Spain, that his frequent visitations to Texas had convinced him that its fertility, wild horses and cattle, and fine rivers were an irresistible magnet drawing to Texas the greedy Anglo-Americans, particularly those in Louisiana. The few settlers in the vast province were scattered on ranches and *haciendas* many miles apart. Two years later he reported to Viceroy José de Iturrigaray that more than 2,000 French and American settlers had established themselves on the eastern frontier where they lived *"muy olvidados de la Religion"* (oblivious of religion).[120]

When in June, 1805, Aaron Burr visited New Orleans and was entertained by Daniel Clark, the officials of the city, and Governor Claiborne, he found a host of friends who were in complete accord with his long-meditated plan of leading a filibustering expedition into Mexico. The Mexican Association, headed by no less personages than Mayor John Watkins and James Workman, Judge of the County Court, had been formed for the avowed purpose of collecting Mexican data which would be useful for the United States in the event of war with Spain. The members naturally entered into Burr's scheme with unfeigned enthusiasm. It is worthy of note, too, that Burr brought to New Orleans letters of the strongest recommendation from no other than General Wilkinson himself. Whatever Burr's plans may have been in regard to the disruption of the Union by the withdrawal of the western states,

---

[119]José Vidal to Governor of Texas, October 4, 1803.

[120]Primo, Obispo de Nuevo León to José Caballero, Secretario de Estado, March 7, 1804. *A. G. I., Audiencia de Guadalajara*, 104-2-19; Primo, Obispo de Nuevo León to José de Iturrigaray, June 20, 1806. *A. G. I., Audiencia de Guadalajara*, 103-3-19. (Dunn Transcripts, 1800-1819, pp. 66-70, and 152-157.)

there is no doubt that his primary aim was directed to what he and his companions referred to as the "liberation of Mexico."[121]

We are here concerned only with the Mexican aspect of the conspiracy and its effect on Texas and Spain. It seems that during his visit to New Orleans, Burr enlisted the coöperation not only of the high officials, as already indicated, but also of the clergy. The bishop of New Orleans himself was interested and seems to have actually appointed three Jesuits to act as agents for the revolutionists in Mexico. In his *Memoirs,* Burr writes, "The bishop was an intelligent and social man. He had been in Mexico, and spoke with great freedom of the dissatisfaction of the clergy in South America." It was agreed that the religious establishments of the country were not to be molested. The Superior of the Ursuline Convent, Madame Xavier Tarjson, was in the secret also, and some of the Sisters were to be employed in Mexico.[122]

Francisco Morales, the former intendant of New Orleans who abrogated the right of deposit on the eve of the Louisiana Purchase, daily became more distrustful of the Americans and from Pensacola warned Viceroy Iturrigaray in May, 1806, that there was a strong and active party in New Orleans whose object was to revolutionize Mexico. He wisely added that conditions on the frontier were entirely favorable for such a design. In June, Inspector Viana wrote Cordero from Nacogdoches that persistent rumors indicated that a large force was gathering in Kentucky to invade Texas. "I have neither munitions, arms, provisions, nor soldiers wherewith to uphold our authority." A more concrete, if exaggerated, report of the danger that threatened New Spain in general and Texas in particular is found in the letter of Vicente Folch, governor of West Florida. In October, 1806, he advised Iturrigaray that the movement to revolutionize Mexico was stronger than ever. According to the plans of the conspirators, the weather permitting, the expedition was to set out in February or March. It was to consist of 10,000 Kentuckians, 3,000 regular troops, and 8,000 or 10,000 militia from Louisiana. A corps of 5,000 Negroes were expected to be recruited on the plantations by offering

---

[121]The bibliography of Burr's conspiracy is so voluminous as to be appalling. Few subjects have elicited more profuse and contradictory treatises and discussions. One of the best, in the opinion of the writer, is McCaleb, W. F., *The Aaron Burr Conspiracy.* Useful printed sources are: Clark, Daniel, *Proofs of the Corruption of Gen. James Wilkinson, and of his connexion with Aaron Burr* (Philadelphia, 1809); Wilkinson, James, *Memoirs of My Own Time;* and Davis, Mathew L., *Memoirs of Aaron Burr.*

[122]Davis, *Memoirs of Aaron Burr,* II, 382.

the slaves their liberty. Natchitoches was to be the meeting point for most of the forces. Once gathered, part of the army was to embark for the Río Grande. The presence of Spanish troops at Los Adaes was to be the pretext for the attack.[123]

Just what were Burr's plans in regard to Mexico? One of his associates said: "Colonel Burr would be king of Mexico, and Mrs. Alston, daughter of Colonel Burr, was to be queen of Mexico whenever Colonel Burr died." He had in the past made fortunes for others but now he was going to make something for himself. The witness added: "He had a great many friends in the Spanish territory; no less than 2,000 Roman Catholic priests were engaged, and all their friends too would join, if once he could get to them."[124]

But the whole scheme hinged on Wilkinson and on the outbreak of hostilities with the Spaniards on the Texas frontier. The dilatory movements of the American commander, viewed in this light, take on an added significance. Burr's plans miscarried in upper Mississippi—the Spaniards refused the challenge of an open appeal to arms made by Wilkinson. Herrera saved the day, and the bosom friend and chief collaborator of Burr, General Wilkinson, seeing the possibilities of success grow dim, turned informer and played the heroic role of "savior of his country" against the foreign aggressor and the domestic conspirator who threatened to disrupt the Union.

With an eye to business as well as to glory, the veteran schemer of the frontier, who had once been a pensioner of Spain, now tried to capitalize on the situation and pose as the savior of the dominions of the king of Spain in America. At almost the same time that he denounced Burr to the American Government, he sent a personal emissary to Viceroy Iturrigaray to request more than $100,000 for his invaluable service in frustrating the invasion of Mexico by an American filibustering expedition. The duplicity of the commander-in-chief is vividly portrayed by McCaleb: "At the moment Wilkinson wrote to Freeman in New Orleans to rush the works of defence; to Cushing to 'hurry, hurry'; to Claiborne that he was surrounded by dangers of which he did not dream; and to the President that a 'deep, dark, and wicked conspiracy' was about to

---

[123]Francisco Morales to José de Iturrigaray, May 12, 1806; Viana to Cordero, June 3, 1806. *Bexar Archives;* Folch to Iturrigaray, October 1, 1806, cited by Mc-Caleb, *op. cit.,* 98.

[124]McCaleb, *The Aaron Burr Conspiracy,* 89-90.

shake the nation to its foundation—at that very moment he was making final arrangements to send Walter Burling to Mexico on as shameful an undertaking as our history chronicles."[125]

The Walter Burling mission. Ostensibly to warn Mexico of the danger to its integrity, but really to secure at the same time information of the practicability of the land and water routes to Mexico, "and the means of defence the Spaniards possess," Walter Burling was provided with a passport on November 17 to proceed to Mexico via Texas and the Interior Provinces. But his mission included much more than spying upon the Spaniards. He was given a letter from Wilkinson addressed to Viceroy Iturrigaray, the import of which will soon be seen. By the end of November he had crossed the Sabine. In an interview with Herrera, Burling skillfully half disclosed the nature of the letter addressed to the viceroy in order to win his confidence, and to obtain permission to go by the lower road so as to avoid impertinent questions in Nacogdoches. He continued to San Antonio by way of La Bahía. To hasten the messenger on his way to Mexico, Herrera sent Captain José María Sada and his own son, a cadet in the infantry, to accompany him as far as Monterrey.[126]

News of the mission of the strange emissary preceded Burling to Mexico, where he arrived on January 21 and delivered his letter to Viceroy Iturrigaray. The day before, the viceroy had written to the Secretary of State of Spain that General Wilkinson was sending him his aide-de-camp. "He brings me messages," he said, "the designs of which, I suppose, must be concerning the ex-Vice-President Burr." Evidently news of the conspiracy had long since been reported to Spanish officials.

An American merchant in Mexico City by the name of John Kelly translated the letter of Wilkinson, written at Natchez and dated November 17, 1806. Assuming that the viceroy knew nothing about the conspiracy, Wilkinson, true to form, began by declaring that in the fulfillment of his sacred duty, he felt compelled to reveal the villainous design of American citizens, who, in violation of the good faith of their country, were plotting to overthrow the Mexican Government. This fact explained his hasty withdrawal of troops from the Sabine and their concentration in New Orleans without awaiting orders from Washington.

---

[125]McCaleb, *The Aaron Burr Conspiracy*, 164.
[126]Herrera to Cordero, December 1, 1806. *Béxar Archives.*

Referring to the plot as the "infernal conspiracy," he went on to say that it was made up mainly of Kentucky frontiersmen and settlers of the Ohio Valley, who, led by able and ambitious veterans of the Revolutionary War, and aided by the British Navy, planned first to gain possession of New Orleans, then to descend upon Vera Cruz and march on Mexico City. He assured the viceroy, however, that he would obstruct their designs and emulate the example of the great Spartan Leonidas. He suggested that Vera Cruz be reënforced by 10,000 men and that vigilance along the entire coast be redoubled.

He also warned Iturrigaray against a possible understanding between the leaders of the conspiracy and the daring spirits of the Interior Provinces. Burling, the bearer, could give him any additional information he might desire.

In an effort to shroud the whole affair in mystery, yet to put himself in a heroic light, he concluded by stating that he had risked his life, his fame, and his fortune to ascertain the facts just recounted in order to safeguard the king's possessions in America. He begged the viceroy, therefore, to destroy the letter and when making the information public, not to reveal his identity, particularly to England, France, and the United States.

He finally came to the real point of the whole farce. In securing this vital information for the safety of Mexico and in foiling the purpose of the conspirators, he declared he had spent $85,000, besides $36,000 paid to spies and special agents. He did not doubt that the generosity of the king would reimburse him for these expenses and liberally reward him for his services.[127]

Even a child could have seen through such a rustic ruse. Iturrigaray replied politely, however, to Wilkinson the very day he received the letter and thanked him for his great diligence and extreme concern. But one can see the viceroy's contempt in his statement that the newspaper accounts of the conspiracy had for some time made him aware of the plot. The general need not worry himself about the danger to New Spain. The forces of the viceroyalty were fully capable of coping with any emergency that might arise. Iturrigaray deeply regretted his inability, without an order from the court, to reimburse the general for the expenses incurred in the performance of his duty. He assured

---

[127]Wilkinson to Iturrigaray, November 17, 1806. *A. G. I., Audiencia de México,* 90-1-8. (Dunn Transcripts, 1800-1819, pp. 25-28.)

Wilkinson that he would report the whole matter to the king, and extend every facility to Mr. Burling for his prompt return.[128] Burling left Mexico shortly afterwards for Vera Cruz, where he embarked February 10, 1807, on the American schooner *Liberty* for New Orleans.

True to his promise, Iturrigaray reported the disgraceful proposal to Godoy on March 12, sending him a copy of the translation of Wilkinson's letter, and stating that, agreeable to the request of the general, the original draft had been destroyed in the presence of Mr. Burling. The report is most revealing. Iturrigaray pointed out the great stress placed upon the measures alleged to have been taken by the general "at the risk of his life, his fame, and his fortune in order to save, or at least protect the Kingdom," but in reality to come finally to "what I had anticipated, the question of payment for his services." He explained that he had refused to pay one cent and added, "I gave him to understand [in my reply] that the revolutionists had not caused me any alarm; for I had been long prepared to repel them by force, even though their number had been much greater."[129]

By a curious coincidence, the same day that Iturrigaray reported the Burling mission to Godoy, "the General forwarded to Jefferson a report of the condition of Mexico, purporting to have come from Burling. This was accompanied by the request for one thousand five hundred dollars, the amount alleged to have been expended on Burling's praiseworthy undertaking. And Jefferson had not the heart to deny one whom he regarded a faithful servant."[130]

Pike's expedition. Closely associated with Burr's conspiracy and Wilkinson's shady activities was the expedition undertaken by Zebulon M. Pike in 1805. The purpose of the enterprise has never been absolutely clear. He received his instructions from General Wilkinson on June 24, 1805, just as the frontier situation was becoming acute, and as Burr was planning to make his tour of Louisiana. Contrary to general belief, the expedition was ordered, not by the Secretary of War, but by the new commander-in-chief of the Army. It is not strange that under the circumstances the Spaniards should have regarded Pike's expedition with

---

[128]José de Iturrigaray to Diego (James) Wilkinson, January 21, 1807. *A. G. I., Audiencia de México*, 90-1-8. (Dunn Transcripts, 1800-1819, pp. 29-30.)

[129]Iturrigaray al Principe de la Paz, March 12, 1807. *A. G. I., Audiencia de México*, 90-1-8. (Dunn Transcripts, 1800-1819, pp. 31-33.)

[130]McCaleb, *The Aaron Burr Conspiracy*, 171.

suspicion. Relations with Spain had been strained almost to the breaking point, because fantastic claims were still being advanced and pressed in regard to the western limits of Louisiana.

Although the instructions were issued in the summer of 1805, it was not until September 1, 1806, that Pike and his party, consisting of two Indian interpreters, a doctor—the notorious Doctor Robinson—two sergeants, one corporal, fifteen privates, three Pawnees, four chiefs of the Grand Osage, and twenty-six warriors, set out from the country of the latter, ostensibly for the headwaters of the Arkansas and Red rivers. All through the summer Pike, who was essentially a soldier and a natural-born leader and explorer, had made careful preparations for the undertaking.

But news of the proposed expedition did not escape the watchful Spanish agents, for they had already reported the plans to the Spanish commander at St. Louis. He immediately relayed the information to Sebastián Rodríguez at Nacogdoches. He, in turn, advised Governor Cordero, and this official notified Commandant General Salcedo at Chihuahua. Thus, Pike and his men had hardly started preparing for the expedition before the Spaniards sent a scouting party to intercept and arrest them.

By September 25, 1806, Pike and his men had reached the village of the Pawnees on the La Platte River. Here he learned from the Indians that an expedition had been sent against him. The chief was inclined to prevent Pike and his men from continuing, and the party, delayed by the reluctance of the Indians to sell them horses, was obliged to stay in the village until October 6. After resuming their march, they reached the Arkansas on November 1, and saw a herd of wild horses for the first time. When these animals noticed the strangers, they thundered across the plains "like a charge of cavalry," making the earth tremble, says Pike. By February 5 the party had established a camp and built a stockade on the north bank of the western branch of the Río Grande, about five miles above the point where it flows into the Río Grande, just below Culebra River, and not more than fifty miles north of Taos.[131]

It is difficult to believe that Pike did not know that he was on the Río Grande at this time. When discovered by the Spaniards shortly afterwards, he feigned complete ignorance of the fact. Confirmation of his

---

[131]The summary thus far presented is taken from Pike, Zebulon M., *Exploratory travels through the western territories of North America*, 1-231.

knowledge of the country is found, however, in the departure of Dr. Robinson on February 6 from Pike's camp to go to Santa Fe. His arrival in the capital of New Mexico brought the Spaniards immediately to the camp.

But let us follow the Spanish expedition sent by the harrassed commandant general, Salcedo, to pursue the intruders. At almost the very time that Pike was making preparations for his daring exploration, Captain Facundo Melgares, an experienced and able officer who had seen service in Europe and fought Apaches in America, started from Chihuahua with a company of 100 dragoons. His instructions were to proceed to Santa Fe, where he was to be reënforced by 500 militia, and then to continue his march to the headwaters of Red River. He was to follow this stream until he met Pike and his men. If they refused to obey the order to return to the United States, they were to be taken into custody and brought to Chihuahua for examination.

The expedition that left Santa Fe under Captain Melgares was an imposing array. The 600 men carried full equipment. There were two extra mounts and a mule for each soldier. They were supplied with provisions and ammunition for a six months' campaign. As they made their way to the headwaters of Red River, there were 2,075 beasts of burden in the long supply train following the soldiers. They first went down Red River approximately 230 leagues (about 500 miles) but, finding no trace of the intruders, turned northeast to the Arkansas, where they left 240 men with their tired and lame horses, and proceeded to the country of the Pawnees, where they arrived more than two months before Pike. This explains the attitude of the chief toward Pike when he put in his appearance. On their long march they had driven out or taken prisoner all American traders found among the various Indian nations they visited. Both the men and the horses were tired and worn out, for they had made more than 1,200 miles through difficult and almost unknown territory. Captain Melgares decided to return from the Pawnee village, and by October was back in Santa Fe again. Here he disbanded the militia, and decided to wait for news of the trespassers.[132]

Let us return to Pike and his men on the upper Río Grande. On February 16, 1807, ten days after Dr. Robinson had left Pike's camp, a dragoon and an Indian guide visited the Americans. Ten more days passed before fifty dragoons and fifty militia, commanded by Ignacio

---

[132]Pike, *Exploratory Travels*, 181-183.

Salcedo and Bartolomé Fernández appeared, politely informed Pike that he was on the Río Grande, and offered to escort him and his party to Santa Fe. Treated with every courtesy possible, Pike and his men arrived at Santa Fe on March 3, and after a stay of a few days, continued to Chihuahua. On March 7 the party stopped in Albuquerque. The next day they met Captain Melgares and his men, who took charge of Pike and conducted him to Chihuahua, where he arrived on April 2. After a delay of twenty-one days, Pike was informed that all his papers would be confiscated, but that he was at liberty to return by way of Natchitoches and was to be furnished an escort. Not until April 28 did he set out with an escort for Monclova, where he arrived on May 25, having passed by the Bolsón de Mapimí and through a good portion of Coahuila and the vast estate of the Marqués de Aguayo. By June 1 he was in San Juan Bautista (near present Eagle Pass). Six days later he arrived at San Antonio, where he stayed until June 14. Seven days' march brought him to the Sabine, and on July 1, 1807, he crossed Arroyo Hondo and arrived at Natchitoches.[133]

"For hospitality, generosity, docility, and sobriety, the people of New Spain exceed any nation perhaps on the globe," he wrote in his diary, and well he might, for he had met with courteous treatment and consideration everywhere. In describing the eastern frontier dragoons, he has perhaps given us the origin of the cowboy boot. "The dragoons wear . . . a sort of Jack-boot, made of seal leather, to which are fastened the spurs by a rivet, the gaffs of which are sometimes near an inch in length. But the spurs of the gentlemen," he added, "although clumsy to our ideas, are frequently ornamented with raised silver work on the shoulders and the strap embroidered with silver and gold thread. They are always ready to mount their horses, on which the inhabitants of the Interior Provinces spend nearly half their lives." Of their horsemanship he wrote: "Mounted, it is impossible for the most vicious animal to dismount them. They will catch another horse when both are running at full speed, with a noose and hair rope, with which they will soon choak [sic] down the beast they are pursuing. In short, they are probably the most expert horsemen in the world."[134]

The news of the arrest of Pike and his men was first transmitted to Spain in the fall of 1807 by the Marqués de Casa Yrujo, Spanish minister

---

[133]Pike, *Exploratory Travels*, 272-295.
[134]*Ibid.*, 336-342.

to the United States, who learned of it after Pike's return to Natchitoches. When the commandant general made his official report, stating that he had released the prisoners after taking their papers among which were many suspicious letters and instructions—Secretary Ceballos replied that the king approved of the diligence displayed in their capture and the prudence shown in the handling of the matter, but he disapproved of their release. The commandant general was informed that he should have detained them until formal request for their release had been made by the American Government. This course would have permitted Spain to protest formally the unwarranted violation of Spanish territory. The chargé d'affaires to the United States was instructed to inform the American Government that the most rigorous measures would be taken in the future against such transgressors.

Salcedo realized too late that he had been hasty in the release of the prisoners and hurried to report on November 24, 1808, that seven men were still in custody and could be held until further instructions. In a personal brawl one of them, Julian Mike, had killed his companion, Millian Doliet. The king replied that, since the leader had been released, it would be unjust to hold the soldiers who were still in Chihuahua. He ordered that all, except Julian Mike, be set at liberty.[135]

Antonio Glass's expedition to the Red River, 1808. But neither the difficulties of Pike, the negotiation of the Neutral Ground Agreement, nor the arrest and trial of Burr dissuaded ambitious adventurers from attempting to penetrate Texas and New Mexico. Late in the summer of 1808, Juan Cortés, Spanish agent in Natchitoches, warned the commander of Nacogdoches that a certain Antonio Glass, with about one hundred men, had probably set out for the country of the Taovayas on the Red River. He intended to prospect for mines, establish trade with the Taovayas and the Comanches, and penetrate perhaps as far as Santa Fe. Another party was to join his band in New Mexico. The men were desperate characters and were well armed.

Further details of this expedition were learned a few days later by Herrera in Nacogdoches. It seemed that the primary object of Glass and his companions was the discovery of silver mines in the country of

---

[135]Pedro Ceballos to Comandante General de las Provincias Internas, November 21, 1807; Ceballos to the Gobernador del Consejo de las Indias, November 24, 1808; Salcedo to Martin de Garay, August 8, 1809. *A. G. I., Audiencia de Guadalajara,* 104-3-15. (Dunn Transcripts, 1800-1819, pp. 189-191.)

the Taovayas and the Pawnees. Their number was now thought to be sixty. Carrying tools and implements, they had set out from Natchez and had passed north of Nacogdoches. But another party of twenty-eight was to join them, and a group of about one hundred men from New Madrid (on the Illinois above the Caddo country) was to follow. Although they were principally interested in the discovery of mines, they were also anxious to catch horses, and might even raid some of the Spanish settlements. Herrera expressed the hope that the governor of Texas might succeed in catching and hanging the intruders.

When the matter was reported to Salcedo, he replied that it would be best to be cautious, and not to send troops against Glass until more definite information concerning his whereabouts, the number of his men, and their real intention could be ascertained. He suggested that much could be learned by questioning the friendly Indians.[136] Nothing more was heard of the expedition, but it helped to continue the high tension prevailing thereafter on the eastern frontier. The fears of the Spaniards had become a horrible reality. The aggressive and enterprising Americans could not be restrained. Determined to penetrate the king's dominions, they filtered through like sand. Soldiers alone could not keep them out of Spanish territory. Only one other recourse remained, the establishment of settlements.

---

[136]Cordero to Salcedo, August 11, 1808; Herrera to the Governor, August 14, 1808; and Salcedo to the Governor, August 31, 1808. *Nacogdoches Archives,* X, pp. 12-14; XI, pp. 94-95.

CHAPTER IX

The Beginning of Formal Colonization, 1803-1810

The mission as an agency for the control of the Indians and the maintenance of Spanish sovereignty had definitely proved ineffective against the resistless tide of foreign aggressors. The pressing need of defending the territorial limits of Texas against the ambitious claims of the United States and to guard against American filibusters, foreign adventurers, and enterprising traders had been met by the mobilization of a fairly large body of troops, as shown in the previous chapter. This was a temporary measure to meet an emergency. Slowly the Spaniards were becoming convinced that the permanent salvation of Texas depended now more than ever on colonization rather than on new missions and military outposts. Spanish officials had realized this for some time before the crisis of the Neutral Ground developed. But many difficulties cropped up. Where obtain settlers? What inducements should be offered them? How was Spain to make certain that the new settlers would defend her interests and remain loyal? Was it wise to permit Americans to settle near the border? These and many other similar questions presented themselves to the worried and harrassed officials.

With a realistic sense that does him honor, Governor Cordero wrote in September, 1805—immediately after he had made a survey of the province — that, after the strengthening of the military defences of San Antonio, La Bahía, and Nacogdoches, next in importance was the founding of civil settlements to help maintain the new military establishments, to give permanence to the occupation, and to offer effective resistance to the invader. Settlements on the Trinity and the Brazos, he continued, were indispensable for more effective and secure communication between San Antonio and East Texas. Primarily a man of action, Cordero did not wait for approval; but, using the discretionary power with which he was fortunately vested, he immediately dispatched four families to begin a civil settlement on the Trinity near the new outpost. He explained to Salcedo that these families would supply the military outpost with the much-needed milk, eggs, meat, and other fresh provisions. When asking for approval of the projected settlement, he requested that the four families, who had gone to start it at his bidding, be accorded all the exemptions, privileges and distinctions of first or pioneer settlers as provided by the *Laws of the Indies*.

He sent a party at the same time to scout for the most suitable location for a permanent settlement on the Brazos, where he intended to establish also a post of twenty-five soldiers to guard and manage a ferry. He pointed out that a ferry on this river was of the utmost military importance to maintain communications, as well as to facilitate the movement of troops and supplies. The military outpost and the civil settlement here, as on the Trinity, would be of mutual benefit and support. Furthermore, the projected settlements would be invaluable in preserving good relations with the important Indian nations of the Tawakoni, the Tonkawas, and the Comanches. In fact, these Indians had already signified their willingness to coöperate, for they had agreed to trade with the new settlements and help stop petty thieving. The good will and friendship of the natives would assure to the settlers a profitable trade in pelts and hides.[1]

First regulations concerning settlers. But it was the cession of Louisiana to France and its subsequent sale to the United States that started the flood of immigrants into Texas. Immigration, at first a mere trickle—which the officials sedulously tried to control and prevent from becoming a tidal wave—soon grew into a steady stream that wore down resistance, and at last burst the dam to rush with a mighty sweep into the vast unpopulated province. Let us trace its origin and development.

As the news of the sale of Louisiana spread, the governor of Texas, Juan Bautista Elguezábal, began to be importuned with requests for permission to move into Texas. The petitioners generally alleged that, as faithful subjects of His Catholic Majesty, they desired to continue to live under his benign protection and declared that they could not entertain the idea of living under a foreign power. In April, 1803, the governor decided to consult the commandant general on the course he should follow. Salcedo was anxious to develop the remote province of Texas, which had again become a frontier province and the main bulwark against the westward march of the Anglo-Americans. The appeal of the former subjects of His Catholic Majesty for permission to continue to live under his jurisdiction by removing to Texas found a strong and

---

[1]Cordero to Salcedo, September 24, 1805. *Nacogdoches Archives*, X, pp. 32-35.

sympathetic response in the stern commander, who felt compelled to furnish a refuge for the Spanish vassals of Louisiana, now "abandoned to a foreign country."

Cautious as usual, Salcedo instructed Elguezábal on May 23 to admit all petitioners, but to require each applicant, before accepting him as a settler, to prove that he had been a vassal in Louisiana by submitting, when possible, certificates of good character and a passport. Every applicant was also to state the number in his family and the amount and kind of personal property he intended to introduce. Salcedo wanted to be certain that the would-be settlers did not take advantage of their admission so as to bring in large quantities of goods for trade. He further advised that former vassals whose loyalty was not entirely above reproach would be permitted to settle within the dominions of the king, but not in the Province of Texas. Lands would be assigned them in Coahuila or Nueva Vizcaya. In order to keep a close supervision over the newcomers, all petitions, together with the governor's recommendations for final approval, were to be referred to the commandant general.[2] Such were the first provisional regulations for the admission of settlers. It is important to note the reluctance of Salcedo. The provisions reflect his inherent distrust of Louisianians and his misgivings of the plan for colonizing Texas. His hesitant policy and his opposition to the indiscriminate admittance of settlers from Louisiana brought him into open conflict with officials in Texas, and the resulting bitterness put an abrupt end to the colonization movement within a few years. The attempt to shut off immigration, however, proved futile. The stemmed flow gathered pressure and soon swept away all obstacles.

Before the regulations of Salcedo reached the throne, the appeals of the Spanish vassals had softened the heart of the king. A royal decree issued on September 24, 1803, permitted Spanish vassals in Louisiana immigrating to Spanish dominions to bring in their personal property and effects free of duty. Two months later, royal approval was given to the regulations of the commandant general, and the gates of the dam were partially opened to immigration.[3]

Proposal for new settlements between Béxar and Nacogdoches. On the eve of the formal transfer of Louisiana to France, Captain Juan de

---

[2]Salcedo to the Governor of Texas, May 23, 1803. *Béxar Archives*. Salcedo to Ceballos, June 7, 1803. *A. G. I., Audiencia de México, Leg. 18, Núm. 27.*

[3]*Cédula* of September 24, 1803; Salcedo to Elguezábal, March 27, 1804. *Béxar Archives.*

Ugarte, commander of Nacogdoches, pointed out the advisability of establishing one or two settlements in the vast region lying between this distant outpost and San Antonio. Ugarte had reached this conclusion after the prohibition of all trade with Louisiana was strictly enforced. The proposed settlements would make it easier for the garrison at Nacogdoches to secure necessary supplies. When the governor was consulted, he admitted that San Antonio was a long way from Nacogdoches, and that in the intervening country there were numerous streams to supply the fertile valleys with an abundance of water. He admitted, too, that these valleys were well suited for such settlements, and that they might prove very useful. But he pointed out that these sites were no better than those in the vicinity of San Antonio, where much of the land could be irrigated, and where settlers could help considerably to strengthen this old post. The idea of founding new centers of population was good, but the difficulty was in securing settlers. He gave a discouraging summary of the poor results of previous efforts, pointing out that from 1718 to the time he was writing, only three permanent settlements had been established: San Antonio, La Bahía, and Nacogdoches. Civil establishments had failed because the Spaniards in Texas were not agriculturists. He concluded by declaring that the proposal of Ugarte would be impractical unless settlers could be brought from other provinces and given adequate protection against the Indians.[4] The governor had analyzed the situation with remarkable clarity and frankness. Ugarte's proposal was a bit premature, for conditions in the frontier province had not as yet become desperate, nor had officials decided to give the French and the Americans of Louisiana a trial as settlers in Texas.[5]

Governor Elguezábal, in fact, had already pointed out the deplorable condition of Texas and indirectly advocated a more liberal policy for its development. In a general report made to Salcedo in June, 1803, he estimated the population of Béxar as 2,500, that of La Bahía as 618, and that of Nacogdoches as 770. The total population of the province, including the settlers in the various missions, was about 4,000. He deplored the absence of all industry and the backward condition of agriculture. In a country filled with fine pastures and large rivers,

---

[4]Governor of Texas to the Commandant General, January 18, 1804. *Quaderno Borrador*, January 4, 1804, to December 19, 1804. *Béxar Archives.*

[5]The best and most detailed study of the opening of Texas to colonization is to be found in M. A. Hatcher's *The Opening of Texas to Foreign Settlement*, 1801-1821. (University of Texas Bulletin, No. 2714, April 8, 1927.) The work is indispensable for the study of Texas colonization, but it is unfortunately out of print.

ROYAL ORDER OF SEPTEMBER 24, 1803, OPENING DOOR TO IMMIGRATION INTO TEXAS AFTER THE SALE OF LOUISIANA
TO THE UNITED STATES

the people often had to depend on the chase for food. He went as far as to aver that horseflesh (wild) had saved the population from starvation on more than one occasion. The fertile lands and the abundant resources of wild cattle and horses in Texas could not help attracting the French, the Americans, and the Indians from the United States. The retrocession of Louisiana to France (its sale to the United States was yet unknown) would bring a host of scheming foreigners into the province.[6]

The following year, in March, 1804, the bishop of Nuevo León wrote José Ceballos, Secretary of State in Madrid, to warn him against the dangers which beset the remote province and openly to recommend the establishment of settlements. His frequent visitations through the diocese had often taken him to the distant confines of Texas. He had been amazed by its marvelous fertility, its numerous large rivers, and its vast herds of wild cattle and horses, and for that reason he had been the more vexed that it was so sparsely populated. These things were powerful attractions for the Anglo-Americans of Louisiana. There were not sufficient troops or settlers in this important and rich province to check effectively the advance of the ambitious and enterprising frontiersmen. He suggested the founding of new centers of population, the establishment of towns and parishes, and even offered to help defray the expenses of Christian settlers from his diocese of Nuevo León.[7]

The crown takes a personal interest. But the frontier commanders, the governor of Texas, and the commandant general were not the only ones who recognized the importance of developing the province in order to make it an effective buffer or bulwark against American aggression. Fully aware of this menace, the Prince of the Peace, Manuel de Godoy, had the king issue an order dividing the Interior Provinces into the eastern and western commandancies-general. The purpose of the change was declared to have been the need of bringing the frontier provinces into closer control so as to offer more effective resistance to the Americans. It seems that the spineless Charles IV actually granted the Province of Texas to Godoy as an appanage.[8] According to the royal

---

[6]Elguezábal to Salcedo, June 20, 1803. *Béxar Archives.*

[7]Primo, Obispo de Nuevo León, to José Caballero, Secretario de Estado, March 7, 1804. *A. G. I., Audiencia de Guadalajara,* 104-2-19. (Dunn Transcripts, 1800-1819, pp. 68-70.)

[8]Smith, Ashbel, *Reminiscences,* 27; "British Correspondence Concerning Texas," *Southwestern Historical Quarterly,* XIX, 293.

order, issued on May 8, 1804,[9] the Eastern Interior Provinces were to include Texas, Coahuila as far as Bolsón de Mapimí, a part of Nuevo León, and Nuevo Santander from the Río Bravo (Río Grande) west to Río del Pilón and north to Saltillo and Parras. The Western Interior Provinces were to comprise Sonora, Sinaloa, Nueva Vizcaya, and Nuevo México. Salcedo was to become the commandant general of the western division and a new commander with the same authority and privileges was to be appointed for the eastern division.

The decree authorized the organization in New Spain of a regiment of infantry for the eastern commandancy, in addition to a body of troops of 200 men, who were to be recruited in Spain from among married men under 50 years of age and who had served 15 years or more. A company of artillerymen was likewise to be organized in Spain under the same conditions and for the same purpose. The decree further stated that it was the desire of the crown to encourage deserving veterans to go to Texas in order to establish military colonies which would form an effective barrier against the Americans. The necessary supplies for the projected military colonies were to be collected in Coahuila, where the settlers and troops were to assemble preparatory to the assignment and distribution of lands.

The settlements were to be founded along the coast, starting at the mouth of the Río Grande and extending northward to Galveston Bay. A special survey was to be made of the bays of Espíritu Santo and San Bernardo for suitable sites. The captain general of Cuba and the viceroy of Mexico were requested to coöperate, and two ships were ordered to be placed at the disposal of the settlers to transport them, their families, and all their belongings. The decree authorized the organization of an additional regiment of cavalry and one of infantry when the new project reached the stage of development as to warrant it. These were to be recruited in New Spain, with the exception of one-third of the officers, who were to be sent from Spain.[10]

Appointment of Grimarest and preparations for the military colonization of Texas. Agreeable to the decree, and at the suggestion of

---

[9] Such is the date given in the letter of transmittal of José Antònio Caballero, cited by Salcedo in his letter of May 20, 1805, to Governor Elguezábal. Mrs. M. A. Hatcher, in her study, *The Opening of Texas to Foreign Settlement*, cites it as "Real Cedula de 30 de mayo de 1804," p. 84, n. 35.

[10] Salcedo to the Governor of Texas, May 20, 1805. *Nacogdoches Archives*, X, pp. 22-24.

Godoy, the king appointed on May 22, 1804, Colonel Pedro Grimarest commandant general of the Eastern Interior Provinces of New Spain with a salary of 10,000 *pesos*. Grimarest had been commander of the third battalion of the Regiment of Infantry of Extremadura. At the same time Lieutenant Colonel Luis Baccigalupi, sergeant major of the Royal Corps of Engineers, was named his assistant and second in command.[11] Orders were immediately issued for the soldiers and settlers intended for Texas to assemble without delay in Cádiz, where they were soon to embark for America. On July 31 Godoy gave instructions for two sergeants, one corporal, and sixteen men from the fourth regiment of artillery stationed at La Coruña to proceed at once to Cádiz. They were to be joined there by one sergeant, three corporals, and twenty-nine artillerymen from Segovia, and by one sergeant, four corporals, and twenty-seven men from Sevilla, to complete the company of mounted light artillery for the Texas expedition. They were to be ready to embark on September 1. Lieutenant Antonio Vásquez was to be in command.[12]

A careful selection was made for the eighty-six ranking officers and officials, who were formally appointed by the king on August 6. It is interesting to note that among them, the Presbyter, José González Olivares, theologian, preacher, confessor, and consultant of the bishop of Astorga, was appointed chaplain for the Texas regiment of infantry, and Bachiller José Flores y García, former chaplain in the Royal Factory of China, chaplain for the regiment of cavalry. A distinguished surgeon, Don Bernardo Herrera, attached to the Prince's Regiment, was named surgeon general of the *Tercios de Texas,* and Don Antonio Bastus y Faya, chemist and botanist with a licentiate in pharmacy, had charge of the military medical supplies.[13]

On August 12 the *Generalísimo* Prince of the Peace ordered "all officers, troops, families, and supplies destined for the Province of Texas in North America to assemble in Cádiz by the end of the month," and he authorized the chartering of the necessary vessels for their transportation to Cuba. The expedition was to be convoyed by the royal frigates of His Majesty.[14]

---

[11]José Caballero to Miguel Cayetano Soler, Minister of War, May 22, 1804. *A. G. I., Audiencia de Guadalajara,* 103-6-17. (Dunn Transcripts, 1800-1819, pp. 74-75.)

[12]Royal orders of July 31, and August 13, 1804. *Ibid.,* pp. 77-78.

[13]*Real Cédula,* August 6, 1804. *Ibid.,* pp. 78-83.

[14]Antonio Samper and José Navarro to Miguel Cayetano Soler. *Ibid.,* p. 84.

Arms, munitions, equipment, tools, supplies, and vast stores of provisions and goods of various kinds were collected. Numerous families brought all their worldly possessions to embark with this formidable expedition to found new homes in Texas. Their number has been estimated as high as three to five thousand persons.[15] But fate decreed otherwise. It is idle to speculate on what the effect of this pretentious and formidable colonization movement would have had on the history of Texas. September came and went, but the expedition did not sail. An English fleet was hovering outside the Bay of Cádiz and the relations with Britain became more strained each day. Finally four Spanish frigates, part of the convoy, were captured by the British, a rupture followed, and the Texas expedition of Grimarest never left the port of Cádiz.[16]

Nevertheless, as late as September, 1805, the arrival of Grimarest and his military colonists was still expected in Texas. Captain Turner reported to Wilkinson that a Mr. Shabus (Chávez), of Natchitoches, had just received a letter from Father Puellet (Puelles), of San Antonio, stating that General Grimaré (Grimarest), who was coming directly from the court of Spain, was expected to arrive at the mouth of the Río Grande any day, and that a large number of persons from San Antonio had gone to welcome him. According to the information available, he was bringing seven full companies with which he was to establish military colonies in Texas, and was to make San Antonio his headquarters.[17] Salcedo himself fully expected Grimarest to come. Early in January, 1805, he wrote Ceballos, the king's secretary, that he was leaving to his successor the decision of admitting a large group of settlers from Louisiana, because he felt that such matters as involved policies should be left to him.[18] The officers and troops appear to have remained in Cádiz until June, 1805, at which time they were instructed by order of the king to return to their respective regiments where they

---

[15]Filisola, *Memorias para la historia de Tejas*, I, 46-48; Arthur Wavel, "Account of the Province of Texas," in Ward, H. I., *Mexico in 1827*, II, Appendix B, 556.

[16]Filisola, *op. cit.*, 46-48; Ward, *ibid.*, 556.

[17]Turner to Wilkinson, September 3, 1805. *State Papers and Publick Documents*, I, 355-56.

[18]Salcedo to Pedro Ceballos, January 8, 1805. *A. G. I., Audiencia de México, Leg. 18, Núm. 27.* (Dunn Transcripts, 1795-1817, pp. 143-144.)

were to be restored to their former rank. They were, however, to be promoted at the first opportunity to the rank assigned them in the regiment which had been destined to go to Texas.[19]

Attempts to control immigration from Louisiana. The formal transfer of Louisiana to the United States in December, 1803, started a host of immigrants to Texas similar to that following the cession of French territory east of the Mississippi to the English in 1763. Spaniards, Irishmen, Frenchmen, Englishmen, and disguised Americans began to pour across the border and to present themselves to the commander of Nacogdoches, or to the governor in San Antonio, seeking permission to settle preferably in Nacogdoches or its vicinity. On the one hand, the rather broad regulations concerning the admission of former Spanish vassals, issued on May 23, 1803, made it impossible to prevent the entrance of scheming and unscrupulous Americans, or to weed out undesirables. On the other hand, the situation had become acute, and the necessity of immediately building an effective barrier against an aggressive and enterprising neighbor was now so urgent that it could not be put off or ignored. Impelled thus by circumstances but anxious to supervise as carefully as possible the immigrants so insistently knocking at the door and so much needed to populate the vast expanse of the province of Texas, Salcedo gave more detailed instructions to Governor Elguezábal on March 27, 1804.

As before, the governor was to continue to receive all applications of Spanish vassals in Louisiana who wished to settle in Texas; he was likewise to admit those eligible under previous orders, and to assign them lands, subject to the ultimate approval of the commandant general. But though such immigrants might settle either in Texas, Coahuila, or Nueva Vizcaya, no one was to be permitted to remain permanently in Nacogdoches or its vicinity. Strongly suspicious of contraband trade, he preferred that the area bordering on the American frontier remain thinly populated. Most of the applicants came generally as far as Nacogdoches and waited there for a decision. Every effort was to be made to shorten as much as possible the time required to decide each case safely. The officials were to try to induce immigrants to settle in, or near San Antonio, or in the adjacent provinces of Coahuila and Nueva Vizcaya. Applicants who wished to follow a trade or profession,

---

[19]*Real Orden*, June 24, 1805. *A. G. I., Audiencia de Guadalajara*, 103-6-17. (Dunn Transcripts, 1800-1819, pp. 89-90.)

and others who were not principally interested in agriculture, were to be urged to settle in Coahuila or farther in the interior rather than in Texas. With regard to American deserters — there were a number of them now — they were to be given asylum but were not to remain in Nacogdoches or on the eastern frontier any longer than was absolutely necessary to ascertain their identity. They were to be sent to San Antonio, where every assistance was to be given them in selecting lands for their permanent settlement.[20]

Until this time those Spanish vassals from Louisiana who had been admitted, had been restricted in their choice of lands for settlement to the Interior Provinces under the jurisdiction of the commandant general who had reluctantly acceded to their insistent demands. Viceroy Iturrigaray had been even more hesitant in permitting them to enter his dominions. Thus, Nuevo León and Nuevo Santander continued to be forbidden territory until May, 1804, when, in view of the favorable attitude of the crown towards immigration and settlement evinced in the royal decree of September 24, 1803, and the approval of the regulations of Salcedo in November of the same year, Iturrigaray relaxed his vigilance. Salcedo, however, imposed an added restriction on those entering New Spain. He ordered that all settlers be warned to terminate their business in Louisiana before setting out, because they would not be permitted under any condition to revisit their former homes.[21]

American Indians join the immigrants. Closely related to the problem of the defence of the frontier was the Indian question. The friendship of Louisiana Indians, with whom trade had been established during the period Spain held that province, was naturally considered of importance. The governor was instructed to tell all the Indian chiefs of the nations of the north visiting San Antonio that the Americans were cruel and treacherous in their dealings with the natives, and to point out, as an example, that they had forced the Alabamas, Choctaws, and Apalaches to seek refuge among their friends, the Spaniards.[22]

As early as 1804, a group of Tinzas and Apalaches made application for settlement in Texas through their agent, Valentín Layssard. Governor Elguezábal was suspicious of Layssard. Commandant General Salcedo, following his recommendations, refused to grant the permission

---

[20]Salcedo to the Governor of Texas, March 27, 1804. *Béxar Archives.*
[21]Salcedo to the Governor of Texas, May 22, 1804. *Béxar Archives.*
[22]Salcedo to the Governor of Texas, May 22, 1804. *Béxar Archives.*

until more proof of the good conduct and loyalty of the Indians in question was presented. That the governor was not entirely wrong in his suspicions of Layssard is shown by the latter's petition, presented shortly afterwards, that he be made agent for the Indians in Texas. When it was referred to Salcedo, he replied that William Barr was already in charge of the Spanish trade among the Indians in the province.[23]

Undismayed, the Indians again appealed to the governor, stating that they desired to move to Texas because they preferred the rule of Spain, that they were Catholics, and that they were anxious to receive religious instruction. Their chief was Luis Tinza. They were living at the time in Opelousas and Rapide. Their second petition was endorsed by the commander of Nacogdoches. Juan Manuel Salcedo, governor of Louisiana and brother of Nemesio, joined him in pleading for the admission of the Tinzas and Apalaches. Juan Manuel testified that the applicants were good Catholics; that they loved the Spaniards and hated the Americans. Shortly afterward the governor of Texas himself declared that an investigation had disclosed that the Tinzas and Apalaches were good Catholics, good farmers, and peace-loving friends of the Spaniards. Their extensive connections with the various tribes of Louisiana would prove of great value in extending Spanish influence over other tribes. Faced with this evidence of Governor Elguezábal, Commandant General Nemesio Salcedo granted their request and instructed the governor to assign them lands along the coast in the area between the Sabine and the Trinity. They were to be told that they were not to extend their settlements beyond these two rivers, and that they were expected to be self-supporting. The commander of Nacogdoches was to have general supervision over their establishment in Texas. They would be expected to keep him informed of the movements of the other tribes.[24]

Again the Spaniards, in their anxiety to create a buffer against the Americans, had made a fundamental mistake. The applicants were not different from any other natives. In spite of the Indians' protestations of loyalty, little trust could be placed in their word. Their long asso-

---

[23]Elguezábal to Salcedo, February 29, 1804; Salcedo to the Governor of Texas, March 13, and 25, 1804. *Béxar Archives*.

[24]Ugarte to Elguezábal, April 3, 1804; Juan Manuel Salcedo to Nemesio Salcedo, November 11, 1803; Elguezábal to Manuel Salcedo, April 11, 1804; M. Salcedo to the Governor of Texas, May 8, 1804. *Béxar Archives*.

ciation with French and American traders had predisposed them against the milder and more paternalistic policy in Indian relations generally followed by the Spaniards. The location assigned them between the Sabine and the Trinity was as advantageous for continuing illegal trade relations with the French and the Americans as it was excellent for preventing clashes between the Texas tribes and the newcomers. The admission of the Tinzas and Apalaches, as could be expected, proved to be the spearhead or entering wedge for other equally undependable Louisiana tribes, such as the Choctaws, the Coshates, and the Alabamas, who, making a precedent of the decision favoring the Tinzas and Apalaches, followed in their wake.

Unfortunately, too, the mouth of the Trinity, an important port, soon became a coveted area; and the Spanish officials were, consequently, compelled to move the Indians in order to make room for more ambitious settlers. This action did not increase the love of the new friends, who soon lost faith in their protectors, the Spaniards.

Proposal for formal colonization. Heretofore, only individuals had asked for permission to settle in Texas. On April 10, 1804, Father Brady, of whom we have already spoken, and Bernardo Martín Despallier made a formal proposal for the establishment of a colony of Louisiana families. They requested permission to introduce a large number of families from Baton Rouge and Rapide. This may be called the first application for an *empresario* grant. The petitioners stated that the plan had originally been conceived by Casa Calvo. They explained that most of the families whom they intended to bring were French. They estimated that more than a thousand were ready to abandon their homes in Louisiana in disgust because of American rule. Of these, about two hundred were Spaniards. Most of them were of noble descent, were influential and prosperous citizens who had come to Louisiana while the province was under the jurisdiction of Spain. Some of them had immigrated to the province at royal expense and felt a deep affection for the king. If permission was granted, they would move into Texas just as soon as they were able to dispose of their property.

Among the various reasons given for the desire to immigrate, those stressed were the dissatisfaction felt by Catholics with a country in which religious faith and observance had now become a matter of indifference, and the love and affection felt for the benevolent government of Spain. They made an appeal to national pride by declaring that the immigrants wished to follow the flag of Spain and, impelled by a sense of gratitude for all that the king had done for them, they were ready to shed their blood for it, if need be. It was pointed out that, should war break out between Spain and the United States, the petitioners would find themselves in the deplorable predicament of being forced to take up arms against Spain. Such a situation should not be permitted to arise.

Skillfully, the petitioners then recited the benefits that would accrue to the crown from the admission of this substantial group of settlers. Their immigration would weaken a strong and aggressive neighbor and greatly strengthen the frontier defences of Spain by contributing to the development of the vast, unpopulated, and undeveloped province of Texas. The new colonists would devote themselves primarily to the cultivation of tobacco, hemp, cotton, and other staples. Their labor, enterprise, and initiative would soon convert into productive fields the fertile lands that now lay unused. Spain would then possess in Texas the products essential for developing a powerful navy without having to depend for them upon foreign countries. The increased population would tend to check Indian hostilities and eventually put a stop to the heavy expense of maintaining peace with the natives through the wasteful distribution of gifts. Time and circumstances had conspired to help Spain. This was a golden opportunity to build an effective barrier to the economic as well as to the political penetration of the scheming Americans.

The widespread dissatisfaction of the inhabitants of Louisiana with the Government of the United States would surely drive large numbers from that province. If Spain did not permit them to move into Texas, as they ardently desired, they would have to go somewhere else. The plan proposed would bring to the province many men of varied and useful trades and put new life into industry. With the increase of industrious settlers, the troops stationed on this remote frontier would no longer experience difficulty in obtaining supplies.

Having outlined the advantages of the proposed colony, Brady and Despallier then made a bold request which seems to indicate, incidentally, the true purposes of the enterprising petitioners. A port, they declared, was essential to the success of the new colony; as a matter of fact, without it the families could not immigrate, and the whole plan would be doomed to failure. They went on to explain that a port, through which the colonists could export their products, would develop commerce rapidly, and the duties collected on exports and imports would be sufficient to defray the cost of governing all the Interior Provinces.

Legitimate commerce would put an end to contraband trade, furnish means for more effective protection of the coast, encourage agriculture and industry, and stimulate settlers to such an extent that even the laziest would be induced to work. Should the *Consulado de Mexico* (an association of merchants of Mexico City) oppose the opening of a port as an encroachment on their monopoly, the petitioners suggested that arrangements be made with the *Consulado* itself, or with a similar agency in Vera Cruz, Havana, or some other port to handle the trade of the new colony.[25]

This bold plan for the establishment of a settlement in Texas included many innovations that were diametrically opposed to Spain's time-honored policy for colonial trade and industry. Governor Elguezábal transmitted the petition to Salcedo, and called his attention to the principal suggestions of the plan. It would be well, he said, to keep in mind that several nationalities of different religious sects comprised the population of Louisiana, whence most of the colonists were to be drawn. A measure of religious freedom had been granted by the Spanish officials of Louisiana to the settlers admitted west of the Mississippi after the cession of this province to Spain.[26] In an analogous situation, Elguezábal inquired what the religious policy was to be. He asked, too, if any particular nationality was to be barred from the new colony, and if the new settlers were to be permitted to cultivate tobacco. As the Government had long maintained a tobacco monopoly, he desired to be informed whether or not an exception was to be made in this instance. If none was intended, he believed it would be well to inform the newcomers explicitly, in order to avoid any misunderstanding. Last, he called attention to the need of very specific instructions regarding the kind and amount of property that the settlers were to be permitted to bring, so as to prevent the introduction of contraband goods.[27]

It is to be noted that Brady and Despallier had not even hinted at the location of the proposed colony. They prudently left the whole matter for the officials to decide. Governor Elguezábal was the first to offer a suggestion on the subject. In a letter to Salcedo he mentioned

---

[25]Juan Brady and Bernardo Martín Despallier to the commandant general, April 10, 1804. *Béxar Archives.* The full text of this interesting petition is printed in Hatcher, *The Opening of Texas to Foreign Settlement,* Appendix 8, 307-311.

[26]Petition of Baron de Bastrop, June 20, 1796. *A. G. I., Sto. Domingo, Louisiana, and Florida,* 86-7-17.

[27]Elguezábal to Salcedo, April 25, 1804. *Béxar Archives.*

that along the Guadalupe River there were many places suitable for settling Louisiana families. This area had water in abundance, extensive and fertile fields of gentle slope, and navigable lakes and lagoons that connected the region with Matagorda Bay. Elguezábal, in full accord with the plans of Brady and Despallier, studiously avoided committing himself on the matter of the port, but pointed out that the prospective immigrants would be saved considerable trouble and hardships in reaching their new homes, if the Guadalupe River was designated as the location for the proposed settlement.[28]

Prompt was the decision made by the commandant general. It seems that, as reluctant as he was to consent to the admission of foreigners, he could not escape the fact that a barrier was an absolute necessity, and to that end the settlement of Texas was indispensable. He, accordingly, on May 23 gave his formal approval to the petition and assented to all but a few of the proposals made. Following Elguezábal's suggestion, he drew up a set of instructions for the new settlers. Immigrants from Louisiana were not to bring Negroes, mulattoes, or any other servants, unless they, like their masters, were practical Catholics. Lands were to be assigned in proportion to the size of the family and the means of the applicant. Justifiable requests for other land for cultivation, cattle raising, and mining were to be granted. Settlers were to be permitted to plant any crop except tobacco. Commerce through Matagorda Bay or any of the neighboring harbors was to be strictly prohibited, and colonists were not to venture forth into the Gulf without the consent of the Government. Immigrants were not, however, restricted to settle on the Guadalupe. They could choose a location in or near San Antonio, La Bahía, in any part of Coahuila or Nueva Vizcaya, or in any other province under the immediate jurisdiction of the viceroy. No one could settle in or near Nacogdoches, as this locality was unsafe and unsuitable for colonization. The real reason for this restriction was the distrust which Salcedo and all other Spanish officials had always felt for those, who, while loudly protesting against American misrule, yet sought permission to settle in Texas as close as possible to the frontier.

The governor was ordered to instruct the prospective settlers to terminate their business in Louisiana before setting out, and to make the necessary preparations to bring all their effects in one trip, because they would not be permitted to return under any conditions. Upon notification, the Spanish officials would extend the help and protection

---

[28]*Ibid.*

needed to reach their destination. Implements, tools, machinery, and household goods could be brought in free of duty; but all articles on the prohibited list found among the effects of the immigrants would be confiscated. To prove their good faith, they were to be asked to submit with good grace to a thorough examination of their baggage and equipment.[29]

A letter of Father Antonio de Sedella, of New Orleans, throws an interesting light on the character of the whole scheme and on the kind of immigrant that was likely to come in under the permission just granted. In a communication to Governor Elguezábal Father Sedella declared that he had received a letter from a discalced Carmelite, Father John Brady, Irish curate of Baton Rouge. Father Sedella, after the sale of Louisiana to the United States, had been requested by the former subjects of His Catholic Majesty to seek permission to remain in New Orleans and the king had granted his petition. Father Brady had just apprised him of his recently acquired contract permitting him to introduce 1,500 Catholic families into Texas. The news aroused the suspicions of Father Sedella, who had come to know Americans rather well in his twenty-seven years in New Orleans. "Catholics, God knows!" he exclaimed. Pointing out that American settlers had no scruples in claiming that they were Catholics in order to deceive the Spaniards, he added angrily, "Better to leave Texas to the natural protection of its untrodden forests than to clear the fields on which to permit disguised enemies to live under the honorable title of Catholics." His opinion of Father Brady was no more flattering. "If such is the leader," he commented, "the governor may judge the character of the settlers."[30]

Governor Elguezábal was spared the embarrassment of refusing admission to Father Brady, for he seems to have withdrawn from the enterprise at about this time. When the regulations of the commandant general arrived, Elguezábal wrote Salcedo that he was requesting Despallier to come to San Antonio to discuss the details of the settlement of Louisiana families in Texas. Salcedo, still uneasy about the true designs of the settlers, hastened to inform Elguezábal that the colonists, if they preferred, could come by water through any port on the coast, but that

---

[29]Salcedo to Elguezábal, May 23, 1804; Copia de los once capitulos de Orn del Sor Comdte gral de 22 de Mayo de 1804. *Nacogdoches Archives*, XI, pp. 30-32.

[30]Antonio de Sedella to Elguezábal, July 6, 1806. *Nacogdoches Archives*, X, pp. 121-123.

they could not communicate regularly with foreigners through any harbor or port, or sail out on the Gulf without the express consent of the Government.[31]

Despallier's request for a port. But Despallier and his colonists appear to have been more interested in trade than in simple agriculture, and more desirous of maintaining close communications with their former associates and the world at large than of becoming good Spanish isolationists. When informed of the restrictions imposed on overseas communications, Despallier appealed to the viceroy, stating definitely that his settlers preferred the Trinity to the Guadalupe. He wrote that the majority of the colonists who planned to emigrate from Louisiana were families of substantial means, their immigration would be an expensive enterprise, and preparation of the fields for cultivation and construction of new homes would consume a considerable amount of time during which they would be unable to carry on productive activities. He continued that, in view of these circumstances, he wished to be allowed to settle on the banks of the Trinity River—a location which offered greater opportunities for export trade. He believed that a port on San Bernardo Bay at the mouth of the Trinity should be opened in connection with the new settlement. He ignored the fact that this was the very thing Spanish officials desired to prevent. He went on to argue that the development of the colony would be not merely retarded but made impossible if trade with Vera Cruz, Havana, and other Gulf ports should be disallowed, because restrictions on the exportation of stock to Louisiana deprived the prospective settlers of the means of making the trip overland. A port, he was convinced, was indispensable not only to the success of the proposed colony but also to the welfare of the entire province. Despallier terminated his petition by strongly protesting that the settlers of his colony were loyal and enthusiastic supporters of Spain, and were ready to defend her interests and their new homes against all enemies. In a second petition transmitted through the governor, Despallier added that rich immigrants could bring their stock, slaves, furniture, tools, and resources only by sea, and would come on the condition that a port be opened for their benefit.[32] These two memorials left no room for doubt about Despallier's designs, if there had been any before.

---

[31]Elguezábal to Salcedo, June 20, 1804; Salcedo to Elguezábal, July 17, 1804. *Béxar Archives.*

[32]Despallier to Salcedo, and Elguezábal to Salcedo, December 5, 1804. *A. G. I., Audiencia de México, Leg. 18, Núm. 28.*

The petitions were sent to Commandant General Salcedo, who replied immediately that he was referring the whole matter to the king. He suggested that Despallier appeal to the new commandant of the Eastern Interior Provinces, General Grimarest, who was expected to arrive soon. But Grimarest never came, and it was almost a year before the king finally took action. He instructed the new governor, Antonio de Cordero, to permit Despallier and his colonists to settle on the most suitable location on the Trinity. The governor was careful, however, to warn the officials not to allow anyone to enter the province as a settler whose loyalty or integrity was questionable. Useless precaution. In abandoning Salcedo's policy of refusing foreigners permission to settle on the frontier so far from Spanish officials, the king had unwittingly thrown open the floodgates. A few months later he opened the gates still wider when he authorized the Port of San Bernardo. Salcedo issued a proclamation in consequence of this royal order. In it he stated that His Majesty was mindful of the hardships experienced by the inhabitants of Texas in securing necessary supplies and in exporting their products because of the great distance to Vera Cruz, the nearest Gulf port, and, therefore, had decided to open San Bernardo Bay as a means of communication and trade for the Province of Texas.[33] The king, in spite of the opposition of his experienced commandant general, had been induced by Despallier to grant both the settlement and the port.

Barr's Orcoquisac settlement contract. At almost the same time that Brady and Despallier were promoting their colonization plans, William Barr, Indian agent for Spanish officials in Nacogdoches, conceived the idea of establishing a settlement on the site of abandoned Presidio Orcoquisac (near present Liberty). He wrote Don Nemesio Salcedo that it would be well to reoccupy the presidio with settlers in order to prevent unlicensed traders from clandestinely visiting and establishing trade with the Indians in the vicinity of the mouth of the Trinity. He offered to start the settlement immediately with 40 of his own Negroes who could begin clearing the ground, and to bring 200 families from Louisiana within two years. He took occasion to ask permission to sell in Florida the horses obtained from the Indians. He desired to continue purchasing in New Orleans gifts for the Indians, and requested permission to bring the goods in his own vessels to Orcoquisac, should his proposed settlement be approved.

---

[33]Salcedo to Cordero, January 1, 1805; Cordero to Salcedo, May 20, 1806, transmitting the text of the royal order of September 8, 1805, concerning the settlement on the Trinity; Proclamation of Nemesio Salcedo, February 11, 1806. *Béxar Archives.*

It is interesting to note how differently Salcedo reacted to this proposed settlement on the Trinity. He wrote Barr that he could proceed at once with the reoccupation of Orcoquisac with his Negroes, but that he was to make a report on each prospective settler from Louisiana. Salcedo stipulated that only Catholics were to be admitted to Texas as settlers. Almost two years later Salcedo instructed Cordero to notify Barr that his failure to fulfill the contract within the specified time rendered the original grant null and void. He added significantly that neither Barr nor anyone else would ever again be given permission to establish a settlement at this post, because it was advisable to keep foreigners from establishing themselves too near the American frontier.[34]

Father Delgadillo and the Orcoquisac Mission. It was during this time, too, that Father José María Delgadillo requested the commandant general's permission to reëstablish the abandoned mission of the Orcoquisacs (Arkokisas). Elguezábal, in reply to an inquiry of Salcedo, made a detailed report on August 15. He recounted the origin of the old post among the Orcoquisacs, the Blancpain episode and the measures adopted by viceregal officials to prevent a recurrence of the incident. The site had been chosen for the presidio and mission, he said, because it was a strategic point from which to keep close watch along the coast for enemies and contraband traders. To that end, he had already given instructions to the commander of Nacogdoches for sending at regular intervals a picket of soldiers to visit the old site and report anything unusual.

The Orcoquisac nation, once a powerful tribe, now numbered about two hundred and fifty men, women, and children. They were, he explained, kin to the Bidais, another tribe that ranged north and east from the coast and numbered some three hundred in all. If a mission was to be founded for the Orcoquisacs, it should be so planned that it could care for as many of the Bidais as would choose to join their kinsmen. The governor frankly expressed his lack of confidence in Father Delgadillo and his plan. He was too young and inexperienced. As far as Elguezábal knew, Father Delgadillo had never been among either the Orcoquisacs or the Bidais. Everything he had stated about them in his petition was based on second-hand information.

The governor believed that, although these Indians had always been on friendly terms with the Spaniards and very fond of the missionaries,

---

[34]Salcedo to Barr, August 29, 1804; Salcedo to Cordero, August 24, 1806. *Béxar Archives.*

all natives were fickle. It would be best to ascertain their real attitude towards the contemplated mission by sending Father Vallejo with an escort to visit them. He could at the same time investigate the claims advanced for a new mission location on a spring about five leagues west of the old site. It was claimed that the spring, near the Trinity, would provide sufficient water for irrigation, and that the forests in the vicinity would afford the timber necessary for the construction of the church and other mission buildings.

Taking up the question of equipping the proposed mission, Elguezábal recollected that a similar plan had been proposed before, and that the sacred vessels and furnishings provided at that time were at Refugio. These articles could now be used for the reëstablishment of Orcoquisac Mission. At any rate, the property of Mission Valero, with the exception of a few pieces lent to the parish church of San Fernando, was still stored in a government warehouse. What perplexed the governor was the offer made by Father Delgadillo to furnish the mission with all the necessary equipment, besides 2,000 sheep, and 400 cows. The young friar was not known to possess the independent means to make good so liberal an offer. The governor warned that, while alms and donations for the conversion of the natives might be counted upon, they should not be relied on too much. He let it be known that he realized that the royal treasury would have to defray most of the expense in reëstablishing the mission and maintaining it during the first year or two, or until the congregated Indians could become self-supporting.

The governor recommended that an adequate military guard be provided to protect the mission as well as to keep an effective watch on the coast. The missionary who was to take charge of the enterprise should be an experienced, patient, and virtuous man. He hinted broadly that Father Delgadillo, because of his youth, inexperience, and lack of judgment, did not meet these requirements.[35]

In September Salcedo wrote that he agreed with the governor and the missionary that the abandoned site of the presidio should be reoccupied, and perhaps a mission and military post reëstablished; but in view of the contemplated change in the organization and administration of the Eastern Interior Provinces outlined in a recent order of the king, he deemed it advisable to suspend action and to refer the matter to his successor. He approved the orders issued to the commander of Nacog-

---

[35]Elguezábal to Salcedo, August 15, 1804, draft No. 276, *Quaderno Borrador,* January 4-December 19, 1804. *Béxar Archives.*

doches for keeping a close watch on the mouth of the Trinity, and thanked Elguezábal for his detailed report.[36] Father Delgadillo's plans collapsed with the failure of Grimarest to come as scheduled.

Minor's proposed Trinity settlement. Interest in the area between the mouth of the Trinity and that of the Sabine appears to have become widespread. We have already seen how Despallier eventually came out frankly with the statement that he desired to establish a colony in this region. We have seen, too, how both Barr and Father Delgadillo presented plans which would have resulted in the occupation of the mouth of the Trinity. Before the end of 1804, another such plan was placed before Salcedo by John Minor. He was a prominent citizen of Natchez, a man of culture, wealth and political ambitions. He was related to Nolan by marriage, and had been connected with the Aaron Burr conspiracy. He asked Commandant General Salcedo on October 16 for permission to enter the Interior Provinces as a settler and explore the country from the mouth of the Trinity to the Sabine in search of a location suitable for a settlement of Louisiana families.[37] He alleged that he was a Catholic, and a native of Pennsylvania; that he had lived in Natchez under the Spanish flag for sixteen years, and desired to be again under the benevolent rule of the king of Spain. He claimed to have served for five years in a Louisiana company of militia organized by Governor Gayoso. Commissioned by the Marqués de Casa Calvo to inspect the coast from the Trinity to the Sabine—preliminary to determining the boundary between the possessions of the United States and Spain in America—he had come to Texas in a semi-official capacity. He had brought no papers, because the order requiring such papers had not been published at the time of his departure for Texas. Both his brother Stephen and Casa Calvo were interested in learning whether or not the country between the two rivers would afford a good site for the settlement of a large group of Louisiana families who were likely to immigrate to Texas, if this area remained in possession of Spain.[38]

Minor, like many others who were seeking admission at this time, came to Nacogdoches in person. Here he remained to await the reply to his petition, because he was not permitted to proceed to

---

[36]Salcedo to Elguezábal, September 11, 1804. *Béxar Archives.*

[37]Petition of John Minor, October 16, 1804. *Béxar Archives.* John's brother, Stephen, was the brother-in-law of Philip Nolan. *Louisiana Historical Quarterly,* IX, 100.

[38]John Minor to Salcedo, October 16, 1804. *Béxar Archives.*

San Antonio to see the governor. Captain Ugarte was so favorably impressed by the applicant that he endorsed his petition. But Elguezábal and Salcedo, who were much more experienced than Ugarte and were with reason suspicious of Americans, had misgivings about permitting the exploration of the coastal region, particularly at that time. Since the Louisiana Purchase, relations between Spain and the United States had become strained over the boundary dispute. Minor was immediately informed, therefore, that he could not carry out the commission of Casa Calvo, and that the decision on his request to enter Texas as a settler was still pending. A few months later, on August 4, 1805, Governor Elguezábal, after making a thorough investigation, recommended to Salcedo that Minor be refused permission to settle in Spanish territory. He also made the observation that Ugarte had been hasty in judging Minor's character. Shortly thereafter he was informed of this decision, and asked to leave the province.[39]

Casa Calvo's interest in the settlement of Texas. The Marqués de Casa Calvo evinced an unusual interest in the settlement of the lower Trinity and the area between this river and the Sabine. A possible explanation for this interest may be found in his friendship with C. C. Robin, a French traveler, with whom he had become familiar in New Orleans. Robin made an interesting and detailed report to the French Government, in which he outlined the policy that France should adopt for North America. Some of the measures he advocated seem to be reflected in the actions of Casa Calvo. It was Robin's opinion that the country lying between Texas and the interior of Mexico was most valuable and enticing. He pointed out that, if Spain made no effort to occupy this territory by establishing settlements with immigrants from Europe and America, as had been done on the Wichita, the American frontiersmen would take it. He then suggested the settlement of this area with French immigrants, who, he declared, would prove more than a match for the unscrupulous Americans.[40] May not this explain in part the interest of Casa Calvo in the colonization of the lower Trinity?

---

[39]José Joaquín Ugarte to Elguezábal, October 1, 1804; Salcedo to Elguezábal, October 22, 1804; Elguezábal to Salcedo, November 21, 1804, *Quaderno Borrador,* January 4-December 19, 1804; Dionisio Valle to Elguezábal, April 5, 1805. *Béxar Archives.*

[40]Memoire par C. C. Robin, Auteur du Voyage a la Louisiane et les Colonies et Conduite que doit tenir la France Relativement au continent de L'Amerique Septentrionale par C. C. Robin. *Affaires Etrangeres, Etats Unis, Paris Archives,* LX, pp. 337-341.

Clouet's proposed settlement. Brady and Despallier, like Minor, claimed that their plans had originated with Casa Calvo. The petitioners listed thus far were not the only ones who were inspired by the Marqués. On June 12, 1804, the new commander of Nacogdoches reported that Juan Garnier and Pedro Arsenaux, residents of Attakapas, Louisiana, had just arrived in the vicinity of Orcoquisac. Upon being questioned, they said that they had come to find a location suitable for the settlement of 300 Louisiana families who had promised the Spanish Boundary Commissioner to move to this area.[41] Garnier claimed to be a Spanish subject and a Catholic. He had been born in France, but had been taken at the age of four to Attakapas, where he had lived ever since. In spite of his long residence in Louisiana under the Spanish flag, he could not even understand much less speak Spanish.[42]

No immediate action appears to have been taken. Salcedo several months later sent the governor written instructions that the settlers who, in fulfillment of Casa Calvo's plans, came to establish themselves on the lower Trinity were to be made to comply with the general regulations before they could be admitted. He pointed out that since the petition of Barr to reoccupy the abandoned presidio of Orcoquisac had been granted, Garnier and Arsenaux should be requested to come to San Antonio to discuss their contemplated settlement and to report on the families they intended to introduce. If the petitioners gave unmistakable proof of their loyalty to Spain, they were to be permitted to immigrate and to introduce approved settlers. Salcedo seemingly was dubious of them, for he instructed the governor to inform Garnier and Arsenaux that such families as were brought could settle either on the Guadalupe or in some other location designated by the governor. They could come by water if they desired, but their arrival was to be reported immediately to the Spanish officials in order that an agent might be commissioned to assign them lands.[43]

It turned out that Garnier and Arsenaux were the agents of Lieutenant Brogné de Clouet, of Attakapas. On October 18, 1805, Acting Governor Antonio de Cordero informed Clouet that he could introduce 300 families and establish them anywhere between the Trinity River and San Antonio

---

[41]Valle to Elguezábal, June 12, 1804. *Béxar Archives*.

[42]Affidavit of Garnier, October 10, 1805. *Béxar Archives*.

[43]Salcedo to Elguezábal, July 9, 1805. *Béxar Archives*.

de Béxar. He was to see to it that the colonists fulfilled the requirements for all prospective settlers set forth in the general instructions
of the commandant general.[44]

An effort to make immediate use of the permit appears to have been
made by Clouet. In November the commander of the small detachment
stationed at Atascosito reported that he had been informed by two Indians
that a group of French and Spanish settlers from Attakapas had sailed
for the abandoned Presidio of Orcoquisac. Orders were issued for their
reception, as well as for the Tinza Indians, who had previously been
promised land in the same area.[45] But there is no indication that the
300 families supposedly sent by Clouet ever arrived.

Evasion of regulations. Although not one of the various proposed
settlements by these pioneer *empresarios* became a reality, many adventurous individuals—never intended to be allowed to immigrate—succeeded
in gaining admission. Salcedo himself was responsible for the loophole
enabling them to enter Texas. In a moment of generosity, he ruled that
since conditions in Louisiana after its acquisition by the United States
made it very difficult for prospective immigrants to obtain proof of their
good character, their former allegiance, and their loyalty to Spain, a
simple affidavit would suffice.[46] The authorities in Nacogdoches and the
people themselves had generally favored contraband trade and illegal
admission of foreigners. The new regulation afforded them the opportunity lawfully to relax the enforcement of the former instructions and
to admit into Texas many who were neither Catholics nor loyal citizens
of Spain. Won over slowly to the plan of colonization as a means of
defence, Salcedo did not intend to allow Americans to gain entrance
to Spanish territory. His idea was to reënforce the frontier by settling
the vast unoccupied areas of the Interior Provinces with former Spanish
subjects. Salcedo's efforts to correct his mistake of July 1, 1805, proved
futile. He repeatedly issued stringent orders designed to keep Americans
out of Texas, to stop unauthorized traders from dealing with the native
tribes, and to prevent groups from exploring large sections of Spanish
territory. Making Catholicism the *sine qua non* for admission, he believed,

---

[44]Cordero to Salcedo, October 18, 1805, transmitting a copy of the permission
issued to Clouet on the same date. *Béxar Archives.*

[45]Salcedo to Cordero, November 2, 1805; Cordero to the commandant of La Bahía,
November 25, 1805. *Béxar Archives.*

[46]Salcedo to Elguezábal, July 1, 1805. *Béxar Archives.*

would prevent Americans from gaining admittance to Texas; but they filtered through the loosened net of entangling regulations in constantly increasing numbers.[47]

Cordero's views on immigration and plans for settlements. Distrust of Americans by both Governor Elguezábal and Commandant General Salcedo has been noted. But in July, 1805, the advocates of unrestricted immigration gained a powerful ally in Antonio de Cordero, who, because of Elguezábal's illness, was appointed acting governor of Texas. He not only had served under all the commanders of the Interior Provinces— the Cabellero de Croix, Neve, Rengel, Ugarte, and Nava—but also had been instrumental in establishing two new settlements in Coahuila: Cuatro Cienegas and San Andrés de Nava. The latter was partly named to honor his superior. He realized the importance and strongly advocated the policy of settling the vast unoccupied territory that lay between New Spain's far-flung frontiers and its distant centers of population.[48]

Cordero's determined action in behalf of colonization has been noted in the beginning of this chapter. No sooner had he received a favorable answer from the commandant general than he issued a formal proclamation calling for volunteer settlers for two colonies. The one, called San Telésforo, was to be located at the crossing of the Brazos on the San Antonio Road; the second, named Santísima Trinidad de Salcedo in honor of the commandant general, was to be at the intersection of the upper and lower roads on the Trinity River. He promised prospective colonists free lands, the customary exemptions from taxation and dues, and the privileges extended to first settlers by the *Laws of the Indies*.[49]

The increasing gravity of the frontier disputes with the new, aggressive neighbors did not deter Cordero from his colonization plans. He seems, on the contrary, to have been spurred to even greater colonizing efforts by the very gravity of the situation. Thus, on November 11, 1805, before the colonists set out for the two authorized settlements, he presented a new plan to Salcedo. He now proposed that similar villas be founded on the Colorado, the San Marcos, and the Guadalupe, at or near the point where these rivers intersected the road to Nacogdoches.

---

[47]The attempts to stop illegal trade and exploratory expeditions have been described in detail in the previous chapter.

[48]Cordero to Bonavía, July 21, 1809. *Béxar Archives.* Portillo, Esteban L., *Apuntes para la Historia Antingua de Coahuila y Texas*, 466-476.

[49]Proclamation of Governor Cordero, October 18, 1805. *Béxar Archives.*

His idea was to establish settlements along the road between San Antonio and Nacogdoches as the best means of defence against a possible invasion by the Americans.

The commandant general gave his consent to the new plan on December 16, but stipulated that the newly proposed villas were not to be started until the two previously authorized settlements had been established. Cordero, in enlarging upon his original plans, suggested the possibility of utilizing the numerous Louisiana families who were seeking admission into Texas. Although Salcedo approved the plans, he warned that the employment of immigrants in establishing new settlements might prove an unsound policy. He went as far as to say that he thought it unwise to attempt founding that many settlements at one time. He pointed out that the dispersion of the old Spanish settlers and the intermixture of immigrants in the new villas would require many more soldiers to police and protect them. He suggested, therefore, that these Louisiana families be settled preferably in Béxar and La Bahía to replace the inhabitants of these older settlements who, in turn, might move to the new establishments. He recommended, in conclusion, that Cordero start only those villas for which a sufficient number of colonists could be obtained.[50]

But Cordero had made up his mind. He was to find, however, that the inhabitants of San Antonio and La Bahía were not to be lured into abandoning their homes by the inducements of the proclamation. From them came little or no response to the call for volunteers to pioneer in East Texas. San Antonio, it must be remembered, had no surplus population, and had struggled too long and too hard against the elements, the Indians, and the incompetent officials to be easily drawn from their homes to start life anew on the frontier. But the news of the projected settlement on the Trinity did arouse considerable interest in Louisiana. A citizen of Opelousas, for example, wrote to Simon McKoy, one of Nolan's associates, stating that the people of Opelousas, who were quite dissatisfied with American rule, had heard that the Spaniards were planning to establish a new town on the Trinity and were offering many inducements to settlers. Because the rumor had become widespread, many inhabitants of Opelousas were selling their lands and preparing to immigrate in the hope of finding new homes.[51]

---

[50]Salcedo to Cordero, December 16, 1805. *Béxar Archives.*

[51]Hatcher, *The Opening of Texas to Foreign Settlement,* 101.

Santísima Trinidad de Salcedo. As soon as Cordero received formal approval of the project, dated October 8, 1805, he began preparations in earnest for the realization of his cherished dream, the founding of Santísima Trinidad de Salcedo. He called for volunteer settlers, and interviewed Father Vallejo, president of the missions, to obtain a missionary to minister to the spiritual needs of the settlers. Shortly afterwards, he sent instructions to Pedro Nolasco Carrasco for selecting the site and formally establishing the villa.[52]

Father Vallejo, who had spent many years in Nacogdoches and who loved East Texas, readily acceded to the request and on November 5 instructed Father Mariano de Jesús Sosa to proceed without delay to the new post on the Trinity. Father Sosa wrote Governor Cordero on December 4 that he would set out the following day.[53] In the meantime, Salcedo had learned and heartily approved of this arrangement, and authorized Cordero to take from secularized Mission Valero whatever Father Sosa needed for divine services.[54] In company with Sebastián Rodríguez, who was soon to take command of the new villa, Father Sosa journeyed from Nacogdoches to the site of the new town. It was at the crossing of the river, where the upper and the lower roads from San Antonio and La Bahía to East Texas came together, probably just beyond the northern boundary of Madison County, in the vicinity of modern Midway. The location was almost the same as that of Nuestra Señora del Pilar de Bucareli (founded by Ibarbo, and later abandoned in favor of Nacogdoches), except that Bucareli had been on the west bank, whereas Trinidad de Salcedo was just east of the river.[55]

Pedro Nolasco Carrasco on January 4 wrote Cordero acknowledging his detailed instructions of December 19 for the founding of the new villa.[56] They were in accord with the prevailing regulations for the establishment of new settlements in the Interior Provinces, and were modeled upon the instructions which had been drawn up for the founding of Villa de Pitic, Sonora, and which had been approved on August 23, 1783, by the king.

---

[52]Salcedo to Cordero, October 8, 1805; Puelles to Cordero, December 4, 1805; Mariano de Jesús Sosa to Cordero, December 4, 1805. *Béxar Archives.*

[53]Mariano de Jesús Sosa to Cordero, December 4, 1805. *Béxar Archives.*

[54]Salcedo to Cordero, December 2, 1805. *Béxar Archives.*

[55]For the founding and location of Bucareli, see *Our Catholic Heritage in Texas,* IV, 312-314; Puelles to Cordero, December 5, 1805. *Béxar Archives.* Puelles wistfully commented in his letter that he had hoped to get the new assignment.

[56]Carrasco to Cordero, January 4, 1806. *Béxar Archives.*

A villa, according to the *Laws of the Indies,* could be founded either by agreement or contract with one person, or with individual settlers who moved of their own initiative to the desired location at their own expense. In either case, the four square leagues granted for the town could be in the form of a square or rectangle—whichever would prove to be more convenient for the subsequent subdivision of the land.

The site having been selected, the town was to be surveyed and its subdivisions properly marked by the commissioner appointed to take charge of the settlement. This officer had control over the distribution of the building lots and farm lands, the assignment of water rights, and all matters pertaining to the administration and development of the settlement.

But whenever the town had thirty heads of families and adult citizens, a public meeting could be held to elect a *cabildo* or *ayuntamiento* (city council), which was to consist of two *alcaldes* (mayors), six *regidores* (city magistrates), one *procurador* (solicitor), and one *mayordomo de propios* (city steward). These officials, under the supervision of the commissioner, were to take over all matters of local administration, police, and public welfare. The results of the election were to be reported to the governor for his formal approval.

Within the four square leagues granted to the villa, sections of pasture and woodland were to be set aside for the common use of the settlers. All were to share in the *tierras de propios* (lands cultivated in common within the city limits), the proceeds of which were to meet the expenses of administration and public improvements. As a special privilege, settlers of new villas were to be allowed to pasture their cattle, gather wood, fish, and hunt on vacant royal lands beyond the town limits.

In order to give symmetry to the town, the church and public buildings were to be erected around a central square or plaza; and to the rear, the the house lots were to be arranged in rows to form streets. After the blocks had been laid out, the commissioner could grant to a settler— according to his needs—a whole, a half, a quarter, or an eighth block. To avoid complaints of favoritism in granting building sites, the first settlers were to draw lots to determine the location of their property. Beyond the town limits, lands were to be set aside in all four directions for the common benefit of all for amusement, pasture, and cultivation. It was from this outlying land that grants were to be made to new settlers. The land adjoining the villa could be assigned to individuals for farming. These grants, called *suertes,* averaged 200 by 400 *varas.*

A settler could be given as much land as he needed for his family and was able to cultivate. To prevent confusion and to afford tenure in security, the commissioner was charged with keeping a *cuaderno* (memorandum) in which each grant with its exact bounds was to be recorded. A duplicate *(hijuela certificada)* was to be given as a title to the grantee. In the event that he lost this document, he could apply to the commissioner or the city council for another.

The grants were to be made out in the name of the king for the enjoyment of the individual grantee, his heirs, and assignees. The recipient, on his part, was to agree to keep supplied with arms and mounts, be in readiness to defend the villa against all attack, and to pursue the enemy when ordered. He was, likewise, to bind himself to have his farm lands under cultivation and start building his home within two years. He was to reside with his family in the villa for at least four years, during which time he was not to alienate, transfer, mortgage, sell, or in any way encumber the lot or the lands received. Failure to keep any of these promises constituted sufficient reason for the revocation of the grant and for the assignment of the lands to more industrious settlers. Those grantees who complied with the terms were, after the four years, to obtain absolute title to the property with the consequent right to dispose of it. The one restriction on disposal forbade settlers to sell or alienate any of their property in the villa to a church, monastery, priest, ecclesiastical community, or any other organization which could hold it in mortmain.

In order to prevent damage to crops from stray stock, it was provided that the city council appoint two *alcaldes de campo* (field watchmen)—one for day duty and the other for night duty—to drive into the city corral (pound) all livestock found in fields under cultivation. Before the owners could recover their animals, they would have to pay the damage caused by the strays.[57]

These detailed ordinances reveal the foresight of the Spanish authorities and their wisdom in formulating regulations designed to take care of many problems connected with the founding of new communities.

---

[57]Instructions for the Establishment of the New Villa of Pitic in the Province of Sonora, Approved by His Majesty and Ordered Adopted for Other Projected New Villas to be Established in this General Commandancy. The copy in Spanish is in the *Béxar Archives.* The English text is reproduced in full by Hatcher, *The Opening of Texas to Foreign Settlement,* Appendix 12.

Many of the basic principles were incorporated into the colonization law
of Mexico, under which American immigrants were to pour into Texas
after 1821.

Pedro Nolasco Carrasco, who had aided Cordero a few years before
in founding Villa de San Andrés de Nava, Coahuila, was given orders
on September 17 to proceed with a detachment of 120 men to the site
proposed for the new settlement of Santísima Trinidad de Salcedo. These
troops proved to be, in reality, the first settlers, although they were sent
to establish a military post and to guard the settlers en route to, and
after their arrival on the Trinity. Carrasco's orders stated that several
families—intended as a nucleus for a villa near the military post—were
to accompany the troops, but their number was not given, nor were their
names. Carrasco was instructed to watch the civilians closely to prevent
them from engaging in contraband trade. He was reminded, in particular, that the importation of goods from Louisiana and the exportation
of horses, mules, and cattle from Texas were strictly prohibited. Violators
of the law were to be arrested and sent to San Antonio for trial, and
their property was to be seized and confiscated.

It is to be noted that a carpenter, who had contracted to build a flat
ferryboat and two canoes, went with the troops. Before leaving San
Antonio, he had been paid 40 *pesos,* and upon completion of the work
according to specifications he was to be paid 100 *pesos* more. Perhaps
another reason for sending a carpenter at this time before the formal
approval of the villa, was that a carpenter would prove invaluable to
settlers in building their homes.[58]

Not until December 20 did the first and only group of official settlers
from San Antonio set out for the Villa de Salcedo, as the new settlement generally came to be designated.[59] Although the details of Villa
de Salcedo's formal founding are meager, we know from Governor Cordero's letter to Commandant General Salcedo that a group of volunteers
set out on that date. The 1809 census indicates that the group included
Pedro Cruz; his wife, Juana María Amador; their sons, José Antonio
Cruz (born in La Bahía 18 years before); and two younger children,
Estanislado and María Cesaría, aged 7 and 9. respectively; José Borrego
and his wife, María Manuela Ramona; José Manuel Casanova and his
wife. María del Carmen; Francisco Travieso and his son, José Antonio;
José Luis Durán and his wife. Guadalupe Travieso, and their two

---

[58]Instructions to Pedro Nolasco Carrasco, September 17, 1805. *Béxar Archives.*
[59]Salcedo to Cordero, January 28, 1806. *Béxar Archives.*

children, Augustín and Manuel, 7 and 8 years old, respectively; and José Alderete. In all, there were 16 persons in the little group.[60] Provision had been made in anticipation of their arrival, for on January 4, 1806, Barr, the Indian agent at Nacogdoches, delivered to Carrasco supplies for the new settlers billed at 167.75 *pesos*.[61]

The little caravan, having spent Christmas en route to their new homes, arrived in Trinidad de Salcedo early in January. They did not find it a desolate waste, because several Louisiana immigrants had arrived in the meantime. Among them was Don Bernardo Martin Despallier. As early as 1804, he had come from New Orleans to Nacogdoches, where he had married María Cándida Grande. After trying to found a settlement at Orcoquisac, he had finally moved to Villa de Salcedo with his wife and two children, José Bernardo and Blas Felipe, 2 years and 1 month, respectively. Miguel Quin, an Irishman from upper Louisiana, had come in October. Also from upper Louisiana was Juan Meguin (McGee), another Irishman, who had brought his American wife, Sarah Burxer, and his four children: José, Juan, María, and Anna, the eldest of whom was 6 years old, and the youngest, 15 months. Pedro Lartigue and his two sons, Francisco and Julián, 15 and 18 years old, respectively, were also found by the newcomers. Another Louisianan, a German, Enrique Seridan (Sheridan?) had made his home here with his wife, Christina Hench, and five children: Jacobo, Juan, Isabel, Anna, and Sarah, who ranged in age from 15 to 22. The wife of Juan Lunn, Rebecca Cheridan (Sheridan), who had come alone from Louisiana, and Hugo Coyle, an Irish surveyor, made a total of 23 persons.[62]

The date of the arrival of the San Antonio settlers is not known, but the group was evidently in Salcedo by January 23, for on that day Lieutenant Juan Ignacio Arrambide, acting commandant of the military and *justicia* of the villa, recorded the first formal grant of a *solar* (lot for a house) to José Luis Durán. According to the terms of the deed, Durán agreed to fence, keep clean, and build a house on his lot, which had a frontage of 30 *varas* (about 83 feet), and promised to perform all other duties expected of citizens.[63]

---

[60]Census report of the Villa de Trinidad de Salcedo, October 6, 1809. *Béxar Archives.*

[61]Carrasco to Cordero, January 4, 1806. *Béxar Archives.*

[62]Census Report of the Villa de Trinidad, October 6, 1809. *Béxar Archives.* The list given in Hatcher, *The Opening of Texas to Foreign Settlement*, 102, includes Gerónimo Hernández and his family who did not come until 1808, but omits Pedro Lartigue and his family.

[63]Merced a José Luis Durán, January 23, 1806. *Béxar Archives.*

Progress and development of Salcedo. Carrasco asked for additional supplies on February 16, wax in particular, evidently for candles. Captain José Ugarte, of Nacogdoches, transmitted the request to Governor Cordero on February 20, and reported that he had sent 6 pounds of wax.[64]

Some of the applicants were not from Louisiana, and some of those who did file application failed to come. José María Mora, a resident of Nacogdoches, asked permission on March 26 to move to the new settlement. He believed that he would not suffer the heavy losses in stock at Salcedo that the wild animals around Nacogdoches were inflicting upon him. He promised to hold himself in readiness to defend the interests of the king and to do anything else that might be required of him.[65] For some unknown reason, he seems not to have moved, although he was given permission.

In March, however, there arrived from Louisiana a large family of Germans. Frederich Ecstozman brought his wife, Catalina Bonete, and six children, ranging in age from 5 to 22: Jorge, Enrique, Juan, Pedro, José Antonio, and Margarita. They were granted a lot 30 by 60 *varas* and a *suerte* for cultivation. That same month brought another Louisianan, an American named Juan Sii. Although a bachelor, he succeeded in obtaining two building lots, each 30 by 60 *varas* and one *suerte* of land. Santiago Fierr (Fear?), also of Louisiana, came in June with his wife, Anna Calaxan (Callahan), and two children, José Ignacio and María Loreto. Fierr, a carpenter, likewise obtained two building lots, each 30 by 60 *varas* and one *suerte*.

A few others came to the settlement in 1807. Early in this year, Carlos Dupon (Dupont?), another Louisiana carpenter, arrived. An Irishman, Juan Malroni, and Cilas (Silas) Luci came from Nacogdoches. Elisha Nelson brought his wife, Yhan (Joan) Harman, and five children: Betsi, Poyi, Ana, Sally, and Patsy, ranging in age from 2 to 12 years. The interior of Mexico gave José Miguel de Sosa, resident of Acambaro, in January. Zedo Charman and his wife, Betsy Clark, moved in March from Nacogdoches to the new villa, and obtained two building lots, but went to live in the country, where they established a good ranch with more than two hundred head of cattle. The end of the year saw the arrival of a Canadian carpenter, Bautista Canaliano, who moved from Atascosito. He, however, did not receive either a *solar* or a *suerte*.

---

[64]Joaquín Ugarte to Cordero, February 20, 1806. *Béxar Archives.*
[65]José María Mora to Cordero, March 26, 1806. *Béxar Archives.*

Slowly the little community continued to grow. Early in 1808, Gerónimo Hernández, originally of Havana, moved from Natchitoches with his wife, Isabel de Racal. José Quiroz, originally of Illinois, arrived in March with Celeste Ruberson (Robertson), and two children, José Angélico and Angélica. Before another year, he had 100 head of cattle and 30 horses. Carlos Trahan came the same month from Opelousas with his wife, Celeste Leesuhene, and four children: Salanxe, Carlos, Celeste, and Celesia. Within a year, they had built a house on their lot, and had 100 head of cattle grazing on public lands. Nacogdoches lost Pedro Patterson, carpenter, and Guillermo Burxer, stone mason, to Trinidad de Salcelo in August. Vicente McLaughlan, of Louisiana, his wife, Martha Thompson, and two daughters, Queta (Katy) and Rebecca, coming in October, seem to have been the last settlers to arrive at Salcedo—soon to be abandoned. The census, taken in October, 1809, revealed nothing about the following except their names: José Leal, Juan Macfale, Jaime Mirlan, José Giru, Luís Grande, Pedro Brase, Jacobo Dast, Joshua Ris (Reese), Genaro Pon, and Francisco Lacomba.[66] The total population at this time was 101.

Pedro Nolasco Carrasco, in charge of both the garrison and the settlers, was, on June 27, made chief supply officer for the 300 men in the advanced posts along the eastern frontier. Of this appointment he immediately notified Valle at Nacogdoches so that he could be replaced at Salcedo by another officer.[67] Almost a month later Cordero reported to Salcedo that Valle, who had been named to take charge of Salcedo, could not obey the order until Simón de Herrera or Francisco Viana had returned to Nacogdoches. In the meantime, Carrasco, like many others at the new settlement, had taken sick, for the climate, floods, and malaria-bearing mosquitoes wrought havoc among the inhabitants of the new villa. Since the relief of Carrasco was urgent, and since the appointment of a capable officer to succeed him was important, the governor ordered Captain Juan Ignacio Arrambide to repair to Salcedo. He had been in charge of the mobile unit assigned to guard river crossings along the road from San Antonio to Nacogdoches. Cordero informed Salcedo in the same communication that *Alférez* Miguel Serrano was assuming Arrambide's duties.[68]

---

[66]Census of Villa of Trinidad de Salcedo, October 6, 1809. *Béxar Archives.*
[67]Carrasco to Valle, June 27, 1806. *Béxar Archives.*
[68]Cordero to Salcedo, July 24, 1806. *Béxar Archives.*

One of the Irish settlers, John McGee, requested that he be granted the lands on which he had built a flour mill and planted an expected yield of 1,200 bushels of corn. His lands were located about five leagues north of Salcedo, on the San Francisco River. He also asked for a town lot on which to build a family residence. In the endorsement of the petition sent to the governor, Arrambide testified that the McGee family was already living in the villa, that McGee was cutting timber for his home, and that his mill, which was small and had iron grinders, was to be enlarged in anticipation of the large wheat crop. The three leagues of nonirrigated land were granted by Cordero.[69]

Upon learning that Cordero, in his enthusiasm for new towns, had burdened Lieutenant Colonel Simón de Herrera, the military commander of the frontier, with the duties of admitting prospective settlers and of attending to the general supervision of the villas, Commandant General Salcedo became quite displeased. He wrote Cordero a curt note on July 13, instructing him to relieve Herrera of these additional duties, and reminding him that the chief purpose of Herrera's mission on the eastern frontier was the military defence of the province and that nothing should be allowed to interfere with this important duty.[70]

José Alderete, one of the San Antonio band first settling in Villa Salcedo, became sick that fall. Early in October, he decided to return to Béxar; but by the time he arrived in Mission San Juan Capistrano, he was so ill that he could go no farther. He died at the mission on October 5, without having made a will.[71]

In founding the new villa, the royal treasury had to bear only the cost of a small chapel and rectory. Cordero reported to Salcedo on December 3, 1806, that he had just ordered 1,152 *pesos* to be paid out of the Mesteña Fund for this purpose. Payment was made on December 7 by José Antonio Saucedo.[72]

In December, 1806, the villa barber, Domingo Delgadillo, ran away with the horse of one of the soldiers, José de Jesús de Lima. Delgadillo appears to have come to the settlement with Carrasco. At any rate, he was there when Arrambide took charge late in May, as Arrambide assigned him a soldier's pay for taking care of the tonsorial needs of the troops.

---

[69]John McGee to Cordero, August 30, 1806. *Béxar Archives.*

[70]Salcedo to Cordero, July 13, 1806. *Béxar Archives.*

[71]Report on death of José Alderete, October 5, 1806. *Béxar Archives.*

[72]Cordero to Salcedo, December 3, 1806. *Béxar Archives.*

Seemingly, he decided to depart without complying with the formalities of obtaining a passport. Nothing more was heard of him.[73] Arrambide himself left the new villa soon afterwards. On December 15 he had been commissioned second lieutenant of the Béxar Company, and departed for San Antonio to assume his new duties.[74]

Proposed settlement of Jaen. To establish quicker and safer communications between San Antonio, the Río Grande, and the Coahuila interior, Governor Cordero was anxious to found settlements west of San Antonio also. Early in March, 1806, he sent Prudencio de León and José Menchaca to explore this western region to find a suitable location for the contemplated settlement of Jaen. León reported on March 15 that a careful examination of the country for a distance of 10 leagues (some 25 miles), had revealed no site on which a successful settlement might be established. The only stream they had found within the area, probably Leona Creek, appeared not capable of providing sufficient water for irrigation.[75]

Just as Cordero was becoming reconciled to abandoning plans for Jaen, José Antonio Ramírez, a resident of Nuevo Santander, made a petition that revived the governor's hopes. He wished to found a settlement with twelve other families on the Nueces, where he desired a grant of land suitable for cattle raising. The motive prompting him and his companions to seek new homes, he said, was the need of large tracts for grazing their stock. Cordero avidly seized this opportunity to found a new settlement, and thereby establish closer relations between Nuevo Santander and Texas. He listed the advantages of the proposal and urged Salcedo to give his approval. The commandant general, however, did not believe in scattering the meager frontier resources and dissipating their energies on too many projects at one time. He replied unenthusiastically. He declared that the proposed settlement on the Nueces would have to wait until the projects already started on the Trinity and the San Marcos rivers had been completed.[76]

New grazing land policy. Cordero, in urging the approval of the request of Ramírez for grazing lands, referred to the king's *cedula* of

---

[73]Arrambide to Viana, December 9, 1806. *Béxar Archives.*

[74]Salcedo to Cordero, December 15, 1806. *Béxar Archives.*

[75]Prudencio de León to Cordero, March 15, 1806. *Béxar Archives.*

[76]Cordero to Salcedo, May 1, 1806; Salcedo to Cordero, June 3, 1806. *Béxar Archives.*

February 14, 1805, relative to grants of *realengas* (royal grazing lands), which had inaugurated a new policy. Until the issuance of this royal decree, the policy had been to give to prospective cattlemen for practically nothing immense tracts of land along the thinly populated northern frontier of New Spain. Against this practice the settlers in this isolated region had complained bitterly, because it hindered normal development. Protests were made to the king, who finally instructed the Council of the Indies to investigate the matter and make recommendations for royal action.

The Council of the Indies had then requested the governors of Nuevo Santander, Nuevo León, Coahuila, and Texas to furnish the desired information, and express their views on the policy which they considered best to adopt.

The first to reply was the governor of Nuevo Santander. He was of the opinion that large tracts of land should not be granted or sold to persons who did not intend to establish homes thereon and would not undertake their immediate development. The tenure of vast stretches obtained for practically nothing by absentee stock raisers was seriously impeding the growth of the country through settlements and consequently was imperilling its very defence. He suggested, as one means of correcting the evils of the wasteful policy in force, the adoption of price scales for the various kinds of land. In his opinion, a fair price would be 25 *pesos* for nonirrigable, 50 *pesos* for irrigable, and 100 *pesos* for fluvial lands per *sitio de ganado mayor* (one square league).

A comparison of the documents reveals that the opinion of the governor of Nuevo León was in agreement with that of the governor of Nuevo Santander that the practice of gratuitously granting immense tracts to absentee stock raisers produced evil effects. He advocated, however, not a graduated price scale, but a uniform rate of 30 *pesos* per *sitio*—a fair price, he thought. This policy would tend to bring about a decrease in the number of large ranches held by absentee stockmen, and at the same time would encourage cattlemen of little means to start ranches on the frontier, especially if they were permitted to make payment in ten installments, each of 3 *pesos* per *sitio*.

The governor of Coahuila was even more liberal. He recommended that the prices range from 10 to 30 *pesos* for the three kinds of land described by the governor of Nuevo Santander.

As a result of these conflicting opinions, a special *Junta* had been called to meet in San Luis Potosí to discuss the whole matter and make recommendations to the Council. The *Junta* concluded that, irrespective of prices, the wealthy should be limited to 30 *sitios*, and cattlemen of lesser means, to 10 *sitios*. Persons obtaining lands should be required to settle and improve them within two years. In disposing of the king's domain, the *Junta* recommended that preference should be given the landless. As for prices, the *Junta* was inclined to be liberal. It recommended the adoption of a price scale from 10 to 60 *pesos* per *sitio*, according to land quality and water availability.

In preparation for his own recommendations to the king, the *fiscal* of the Council of the Indies had reviewed the various recommendations in November, 1804. He concluded that the prices suggested by the San Luis Potosí *Junta* were equitable and should be adopted, but that there was no reason to enact measures pertaining to payment procedure or to settlement and improvement requirements, since these matters had already been provided for and clearly defined in the *Laws of the Indies*.[77]

The king had adopted the recommendations of the Council, and in the final decree of February 14, 1805, made the stipulation—contrary to his *fiscal's* opinion of its necessity—that in the future, all royal lands obtained for cattle raising were to be occupied and improved at once.[78]

Louisiana Indian settlements on the Sabine. Commandant General Salcedo had to cope with problems other than those of defence, land policies and infiltrations of undesirable settlers. Early in July, 1806, four Choctaw chiefs sought permission to move their people to Texas. In transmitting the request to Salcedo, Governor Cordero called his attention to the fact that the lands between the Trinity and Sabine rivers had already been granted to the Tinzas. He suggested, therefore, that the Choctaws be permitted to occupy the lands along the coast between the Colorado and the Trinity.

Salcedo, who had a more comprehensive plan for the development of the province and the distribution of its lands among Indians and white men replied to the governor that there were good reasons for not assigning the coastal plains to the Choctaws. He pointed out that the Tinzas and the Choctaws were good friends, and should be allowed to settle in the same area along the Sabine River, where there were game, good water, and rich soil in abundance. He asked Cordero, therefore, to suggest

---

[77]*Laws of the Indies,* Book VIII, Title XXVI, Law XVI; Book IV, Title XII, Law XI.

[78]Informe del Consejo, November 23-December 15, 1804. *A. G. I., Audiencia de México,* 88-1-4 (Dunn Transcripts, 1800-1819).

to the Choctaws to try to find a suitable location on this river. There were good reasons for their settlement in the area indicated. The Choctaws would help form with the Tinzas a cordon of defence along the Sabine River, and the coastal lands would be saved for white settlers who might later establish villas in that region.[79]

Colonel Simón de Herrera reported to Salcedo at about the same time that a group of Pascagoulas were seeking permission to enter the province. An investigation, he declared, had convinced him of the sincerity and loyalty of these Indians, and he recommended, therefore, that their petition be granted, and requested that he be instructed where to establish them.

Salcedo replied that just as the Tinzas and the Choctaws had been persuaded to settle along the Sabine River, so Chief Gonzalo Conché Blonhin should be induced to settle his Pascagoulas in that area by pointing out to him the natural advantages of the region in which his tribesmen would find themselves located among former Louisiana friends. The commandant general was, indeed, following a policy consistent with the best interests of the Indians and Spain by sending all new tribes to a locale suited to their needs, and at the same time along the frontier where they would constitute a buffer against American aggression.[80]

Immigration restrictions. The establishment of the new villa of Salcedo and the rumors of the authorization of a port on the Gulf had spread like wildfire throughout Louisiana. In constantly increasing numbers, by land and by water, immigrants began pouring in, seeking permission to settle in either Nacogdoches, Orcoquisac, Atascosito, or near the mouth of the Trinity. Commandant General Salcedo's insistence on keeping the frontier free of foreigners seems to have finally made an impression on Cordero, for when Richard Mordicai, one of Nolan's companions(?) and formerly a forester in Louisiana, asked permission in September, 1805, to settle in Nacogdoches, Cordero sent him to Chihuahua for a personal interview with the commandant general.[81] On October 7, 1805, Carlos de Grand Pré, commander of the post at Baton Rouge, issued a passport to Herman Wellet, authorizing him to proceed to San Antonio in quest of permission to establish his residence in that city. The passport stated that Wellet had been a settler of the

---

[79]Salcedo to Cordero, August 16, 1806. *Béxar Archives.*
[80]Salcedo to Cordero, August 16, and December 5, 1806. *Béxar Archives.*
[81]Cordero to Salcedo, September 25, 1805. *Béxar Archives.*

Spanish colony at New Madrid.[82] Bernardo Guizarnat, a resident of Louisiana, sought permission in June to settle in Nacogdoches, but was promptly informed by Salcedo that no foreigner could be permitted to settle in that area. Salcedo took occasion to remind Cordero of this regulation and to recommend its strict observance. He suggested that prospective immigrants be informed of this prohibition to save them unnecessary hardships and disappointments.[83] In July, Louis Dannequien and José Nicolas Landrés, of Lafourche de los Chetimas, Ascension Parish, Louisiana, declared that they were ready to sell all their property in Louisiana, provided they would be granted permission to settle in Texas.[84]

Whether or not Mordicai and the rest were refused is not known, but other petitioners, men of substantial means, were rejected.[85] One of them, Francisco Marceau Desgraviers, sought in October sufficient land on which to settle his household of 15 persons, as well as to graze 300 cattle and an equal number of horses. At the same time his friend, Juan Francisco Warnet, Baron de Lambercy, requested a similar grant for the same number of immigrants.[86] But when they were refused permission to settle at Orcoquisac, apparently the only place in Texas they wanted to remove to, they abandoned their plans.

Armed with a passport from the governor of Florida, Juan Eugenio Marchand, another prominent citizen, came to Nacogdoches on November 22 to seek a home in Texas. An experienced seaman, he had heard of the opening of a port, and had decided to come to the new settlement. He explained that he had left New Orleans for Balize on September 5; that in eleven days he had made his way to the mouth of the Sabine, but because the water was too shallow to enter the stream, he had continued as far as Galveston Bay in search of the Trinity. Having arrived in the bay on September 18, he had spent ten days looking in vain for the mouth of the river. Thereupon, he had returned to Attakapas to unload the tools and provisions which he said he had brought for his

---

[82]Carlos de Grand Pré, Passport to Herman Wellet, October 7, 1805. *Béxar Archives.*

[83]Salcedo to Cordero, July 14, 1806. *Béxar Archives.*

[84]Petition of Louis Dannequien and José Nicolas Landrés, July 16, 1806. *Béxar Archives.*

[85]The loss of the archives of the *Provincias Internas* makes it impossible to ascertain the ultimate disposition of their cases.

[86]Petitions of Desgraviers and Warnet, October 22, 1806. *Béxar Archives.*

workmen, and then had gone back to New Orleans, whence he returned overland to Nacogdoches. In his petition for a land grant, he declared that he had several hands, all the necessary farm implements, and the means to immigrate in accord with the king's decree. He stated that he was familiar with the coast from Vera Cruz to Nuevo Santander and desired to explore Matagorda Bay and the mouth of the Trinity. In return for permission to undertake the reconnaissance, he would be glad to furnish the governor with maps showing the results of his exploration.

But his knowledge of the Nuevo Santander coast, his intention of returning to New Orleans for tools and supplies (he had been caught contradicting himself), and his desire to explore Matagorda Bay and the new port cast him in a doubtful role. Salcedo warned Cordero on December 10 that Marchand was a suspicious character who should be sent to San Antonio for further investigation by Viana, the commander of Nacogdoches. The applicant apparently was able to allay suspicions to the extent that he was permitted to settle in Texas, but not at the new port, Atascosito, Orcoquisac, or Nacogdoches. It was not long, however, before Marchand's permit was revoked, because he had been trading in contraband. The prospect of huge profits from an illegal business doubtless was his real motive for moving.[87]

It will be remembered that the agents of Brogné de Clouet, Garnier and Arsenaux, had been refused permission to settle 300 Louisiana families in the vicinity of Orcoquisac because William Barr had been granted a contract the previous August (1804) to occupy the site of the abandoned presidio with 200 Louisiana families. In the light of these antecedents, Commandant General Salcedo's displeasure at the news that eleven families from Louisiana had settled there is understandable. Captain Gerónimo Herrera, commander of Atascosito (below Orcoquisac), had requested authorization in July, 1805, to remove them to the interior of the province according to instructions. Upon being informed of the regulations which compelled them to remove to the interior, the settlers were disappointed and desired to return to the United States. As he did not have the horses to move them and their effects, Herrera requested the Government to assume the expenses. He went on to report that sixty other families, who had started from Opelousas and Attakapas, turned back when they heard of the new regulations requiring them to settle in the interior.

---

[87]Juan Eugenio Marchand to Viana, November 24, 1806; Salcedo to Cordero, December 10, 1806, February 24, and April 27, 1807. *Béxar Archives.*

Salcedo replied that these families at Atascosito should not have been permitted even to stop there; they should have been ordered to continue to the areas opened to colonists by the officials. He repeated his former orders, and insisted that they be strictly observed. The eleven families were to be informed that they might be permitted to go to the new villa on the Trinity after it was started; but for the present, they must either return to their Louisiana homes or move to the interior. As for the expenses for removal, the Government could supply only the most essential needs.[88] Eventually, these settlers were escorted to the Louisiana border at a cost of 1,350 *pesos* to the royal treasury, and told not to return.[89]

Imagine, then, Salcedo's reaction when he learned in February, 1806, that Bernardo Despallier had been appointed second in command at Atascosito. Governor Cordero's specious explanations for Despallier's appointment and monthly salary of 70 *pesos* out of the Mesteña Fund only exasperated Salcedo all the more. The governor attempted to justify this unprecedented action of taking into the king's employ a Louisiana immigrant — not yet formally admitted — by pointing out that his knowledge of Indian languages, his intimate acquaintance with the Alabamas, the Choctaws, and the Coshates, and his experience as a forester in Louisiana made his services indispensable in winning and maintaining the friendship of these and other tribes. In fact, Cordero had given Despallier, now in San Antonio, a number of blank commissions to issue to the chiefs of the various tribes.

Salcedo acted promptly to order the immediate discharge of the new Indian agent. He informed Cordero that he had been both hasty and injudicious in making the appointment. He instructed the governor to stop Despallier's pay at once, and to consult the commandant general on all such matters in the future.[90]

Despallier, meanwhile, had set out with an armed escort from San Antonio on February 15 to explore the country along the coast and to contact the various Indian tribes. The next day he camped on the San Marcos; two days later he was on the Colorado, and three more days brought him to the Tawakoni villages on the Brazos River. By February 24 he arrived at the place near the Trinity where Philip Nolan had

---

[88]Salcedo to Cordero, July 7, 1805. *Béxar Archives.*

[89]Salcedo to Cordero, December 9, 1806. *Béxar Archives.*

[90]Cordero to Salcedo, February 15, 1806; Salcedo to Cordero, March 11, 1806. *Béxar Archives.*

camped. During the next five days he explored Leona River, Carriso Creek, and Buena Vista Creek, and on March 2 reached Monte Grande, or the timber belt. If it were his intention to explore the coastal area, he was certainly far off his route.

Having reached Monte Grande, he seems to have gone to the headwaters of the San Jacinto. Here he met five Choctaw chiefs, who asked him what he was doing in this region with an armed force. Despallier answered that he was exploring the country to find a place suitable for a new settlement, that the Spaniards were their friends and would take care of them. The Choctaws attested to their friendship for the Spaniards by expressing their willingness to fight for them. Despallier went on to Atascosito, where he arrived on March 4.[91]

The presence on the San Jacinto of the Choctaws who had been expressly restricted to the Sabine area is just another illustration of the difficulties encountered in enforcing the commandant general's instructions. The physical impossibility of effectively patrolling the country and the half-hearted coöperation of Governor Cordero make the failure of Commandant General Salcedo's policy on immigration and colonization more understandable.

Orcoquisac and Atascosito closed to settlers. On May 26, Cordero transmitted to Salcedo the petition of five Louisiana settlers, Juan Bautista Le Conte, José Darbani, Juan Bautista Anti, Remigio Lambré, and Augustine Langlois. They had requested 580 *arpents* (about 870 acres) of land at Orcoquisac to be distributed among them. The governor suggested that it might be better to maintain the established Spanish land measures by making the grants in *sitios* rather than in French *arpents*. He assured his superior that he had investigated the character of the prospective immigrants and found no reason to question their integrity or loyalty.[92]

Salcedo on June 16 repeated his regulations that no immigrants could be permitted to settle in Nacogdoches or Orcoquisac. He added that it would be injudicious to authorize a new settlement before the two villas had been established. He reminded Cordero that he had been explicitly instructed that the amount of land which could be allotted to an individual settler depended on the number of persons in his family and his

---

[91]Diario de Bernardo Martín Despallier, February 15-March 4, 1806. *Béxar Archives.*

[92]Cordero to Salcedo, May 28, 1806. *Béxar Archives.*

means for its cultivation. Moreover, land grants must be according to the Spanish system of land measures. Before admitting the petitioners, however, he was to conduct another investigation and require each to adduce proof of his character and loyalty. Upon presentation of satisfactory evidence, they were to be permitted to settle in the interior of the province, or in one of the villas already authorized.[93] Informed of Salcedo's instructions, the applicants resented what they considered his groundless suspicions as a reflection on their integrity and gave up their plan to emigrate.

Daniel Boone, a nephew of Kentucky's famous Boone, made application on June 11 for permission to settle in Orcoquisac. He declared that he was a native of North Carolina, and that from Opelousas, where he had been living for the last twelve years, he had moved to Atascosito with his family because of dissatisfaction with American rule. Boone now sought the grant of a building lot and lands on which to continue life as a farmer.[94] Although he had entered the province without waiting for permission, his petition was granted to the extent that he was permitted to establish his residence in the interior of Texas. He appears to have moved to San Antonio, where he worked for several years, not as a farmer, but as the garrison's gunsmith.[95] According to tradition, Boone was killed by Indians in 1817.[96]

The summer of 1806 brought numerous applications to settle in different parts of Texas. Daniel Colman Jones, an Irish native of Halifax, his family, together with his friends, John Ronells and Benjamin Thomas, desired to take advantage of the law permitting removal from Louisiana to Texas. They asserted that they were Catholics, and had lived in Louisiana for some years before it was sold to the United States. John Andreton (Anderson?), another Irishman, originally of Brunswick, Virginia, petitioned to immigrate with his family, his sons-in-law, and a friend, David King—all Catholics and residents of the neighboring province during the past eight years. Guillermo Gardner, an Irish Catholic, resident of Opelousas for more than seven years, likewise wished to bring his family, stock, and farm implements to found a new home in Spanish Texas. Three other Opelousas citizens expressed their desire

---

[93]Salcedo to Cordero, June 16, 1806. *Béxar Archives.*
[94]Petition of Daniel Boone, June 11, 1806. *Béxar Archives.*
[95]Bill of March 4, 1809; N. Salcedo to M. de Salcedo, April 8, 1809.
[96]Hatcher, *The Opening of Texas to Settlement,* 109.

to move to Texas with their families and possessions; Francisco Mercantel said that he had been born in Louisiana, and Sebastián and María Magdalena Benoit attested they had lived in Louisiana for nineteen years. Juan Fear, another Irishman, resident of Louisiana for nineteen years, asked permission to settle at Orcoquisac with his sons-in-law, Patricio Gurnet and Juan Nevil. Fear assured the Spanish authorities that all twenty-six persons in the party were Catholics and loyal to Spain.[97]

According to the records, some of the applicants were admitted on condition that they either settle at one of the villas already established or move into the interior of the province. The others—Jones and Gardner among them—were required to adduce further evidence of good character and loyalty to the king. None of them, however, except Sebastián and María Magdalena Benoit, seems to have actually settled in Texas.[98]

In July, 1806, Father Domingo Joaquín de Solana, former pastor of San Bernardo de la Nueva Godoy, Louisiana, arrived at Atascosito. He had made the trip from New Orleans by water. Gerónimo Herrera, the commander of the lonely post, considered his arrival short of miraculous and was only too happy to permit him to remain until his case was decided, "since Divine Providence had sent him for the spiritual comfort of the men and their families in these critical times when the soldiers and the small group of families at this post are suffering from an epidemic of fever." The priest presented his royal appointment of July 27, 1804, as pastor, the order for the cessation of his salary, and a passport signed by Casa Calvo. Father Solana, it appears, came as the agent of Juan Evalvez, a wealthy and highly respected Irishman of New Orleans, who desired to found a settlement at Orcoquisac provided he could secure lands for its establishment.[99]

Salcedo replied in emphatic language that, in view of the advisability of keeping foreigners from settling too near the American frontier, no one would ever again be given permission to establish a settlement at this post. The commandant general took this occasion to instruct Governor Cordero to notify Barr that his failure to fulfill the contract within the specified time of two years rendered his grant null and void. Father

---

[97]Petitions of Jones and others, June 9-August 13, 1806. *Béxar Archives.*

[98]Salcedo to Cordero, July 15, 1806; Simón de Herrera to Cordero, September 20, 1806. *Béxar Archives.*

[99]Cordero to Salcedo, July 30, 1806. *Béxar Archives.*

Solana's mission not only proved futile but also brought him misfortune. In early fall he informed Cordero that he was still in Atascosito, because he was sick of malaria.[100]

Illegal entries. Immigrants persisted, however, in penetrating the province in search of new homes, and some of them failed to report at Nacogdoches to make formal application for admission. A detachment of soldiers sent by Captain Gerónimo Herrera from Atascosito to explore the coast reported on November 21, 1806, that they had found five families who had been shipwrecked at the mouth of the Neches. They had set out from Calcasieu, Louisiana, to join one of the recently authorized settlements, but a storm had destroyed their frail vessel, and they had lost all their baggage and provisions. When found, they were in a destitute condition. They were taken to Atascosito to await the decision of the governor.[101]

The case of Francisco Roquier and his ten companions leads one to suspect that some enterprising citizens of Louisiana saw the possibility of evading the laws on the exportation of horses. Posing as prospective settlers, Roquier and his friends came to Nacogdoches to ask permission to take back a sufficient number of horses to move their families and belongings. Salcedo, suspicious of them, instructed the governor to require the applicants to comply with all the regulations for admission and to furnish affidavits stipulating the exact number of horses needed for removing their effects to Texas before granting them permission either to return with the horses or to enter Texas as settlers. Roquier was not heard from until a year later, when he again sought admission. His conduct had aroused the suspicions of Salcedo who now denied him admission, because he had not availed himself of the previous offer.[102]

A similar instance was that of Juan Carlos Casili (Cashily). After making application to settle in Texas, he was granted admission by the governor in the summer of 1806. Before he reached his destination, however, he was arrested as a contraband trader, and his goods were seized and sold. Although he was expelled and ordered never to return, he made application for readmission in 1811.[103]

---

[100]Salcedo to Cordero, August 24, 1806; Solana to Cordero, September 25, 1806. *Béxar Archives.*

[101]Gerónimo Herrera, Diario de acontecimientos, November 21, 1806. *Béxar Archives.*

[102]Salcedo to Cordero, May 6, 1806, and July 13, 1807. *Béxar Archives.*

[103]Petition of Juan Carlos Casili, May 12, 1806, and accompanying documents; petition of 1811. *Béxar Archives.*

American deserters. As early as September, 1805, Cordero had warned the commander at Nacogdoches against deserters from the United States Army seeking admission as refugees. No such persons, he had been instructed, were to be permitted to enter the province as settlers until a careful investigation of each case had been made. Those who were suspected of being spies were to be sent under guard to San Antonio to be cross-examined by the governor.[104] Spanish distrust of Americans, and particularly of deserters, increased after the Wilkinson and Burr affairs, even though these international incidents culminated in the Neutral Ground Agreement. Instructions were issued to take special precautions to prevent the entry of Americans under any pretext. Late in 1806, the commandant general advised the governor that deserters professing Catholicism were to be granted permission to settle on condition that they choose locations in Coahuila or Nueva Vizcaya, and those who were Protestants were to be kept under surveillance.[105]

The alarm of Spanish officials in this respect, however, seems to have been unfounded. A special list of foreign deserters in San Antonio, made in 1808, shows that only nine had been admitted. An Irish Catholic, Thomas Starr, tailor by profession, ran away. Two carpenters, both Catholic, were James Orr, an Irishman, and Juan Estapelton (Stapleton), an Englishman. Another Englishman, Eduardo Hinks, professed no religion. Two other Englishmen, Anglicans, following no particular trade, were Benjamin Cant (Kant), who had gone to Monclova, and John Hicks. The ninth, a Canadian Catholic, Augustin Bernar (Bernard), likewise, had no trade and had gone to Monclova.[106]

Further immigration restrictions. Before the end of 1806, Salcedo had become alarmed at the rapidly increasing number of those applying for admission and at their irregular methods of gaining entrance into Texas by land and sea. The Burr conspiracy and the Wilkinson incident, in the fall of this year, made him more than ever suspicious of the intent of all American immigrants. He, consequently, issued orders on August 4 to all officials in Texas to be extremely careful whom they admitted as settlers from the United States.[107] These instructions he supplemented

---

[104]Cordero to Viana, September, 1805. *Béxar Archives.*

[105]Salcedo to Cordero, December 9, 1806. *Béxar Archives.*

[106]Estado que manifiesta los Extranjeros Desertores que existen en el [Real Presidio de Béjar] desde el año de 1808. *Béxar Archives.*

[107]Salcedo to Cordero, August 4, 1806. *Béxar Archives.*

with others on December 4, and again on December 10. He issued strict orders that those foreigners who left Texas were not to be readmitted under any condition. This measure was intended to stop the practice of going back and forth between Louisiana and Texas. Each applicant was to be certified by the commander of Orcoquisac, Nacogdoches, or Trinidad de Salcedo, and each was to present satisfactory evidence that he had lived under Spanish rule and was to agree to settle either on the Trinity or the Guadalupe.

In order to teach a lesson to those who had settled without awaiting the formality of securing a permit, the governor was instructed to order all who had entered without first complying with all the laws to leave within eight to fifteen days from the date on which the order was published. Cordero was told emphatically to purge Nacogdoches of all foreigners who had gained admission illegally.[108]

But in spite of all efforts to check the stream of immigrants from the United States, they continued to come. Clouet, undismayed by the relentless opposition of the commandant general to his proposed settlement at Atascosito or Orcoquisac, was still trying in the winter of 1807 to introduce families. Subject to the ultimate approval of the king, Clouet gave a passport to Andrés Veran and Antonio Molinar, sailors, and to José Olivero and Nicolás Bouquet to explore the country in the vicinity of Atascosito in search of a suitable location for his proposed settlement. Upon learning of the incident, Salcedo ordered their immediate arrest and detention as suspicious characters. His suspicions were not unfounded. When they were apprehended, a considerable quantity of furs secured from the Indians in exchange for contraband goods was found in their possession. In consequence, they were soon afterwards officially expelled from the province.[109]

Individuals, however, continued to present themselves in Nacogdoches to make application for admission. Among them was Anthony Glass. In March, 1806, his request to move to Texas was granted, but he failed to take advantage of the permit. Then he asked permission in the fall of 1807 to come by water from Baton Rouge to Orcoquisac. He claimed that the cause of his delay in moving was the disturbed conditions in Louisiana occasioned by the Burr affair. But Viana, the commandant at

---

[108]Salcedo to Cordero, August 4, and December 10, 1806. *Béxar Archives*. Salcedo to Cordero, December 4, 1806. *Nacogdoches Archives*.

[109]Passport issued by Clouet and letter to Gerónimo Herrera, December 17, 1807; Salcedo to Cordero, March 8, May 31, and August 5, 1808. *Béxar Archives*.

Nacogdoches, noted that the applicant had brought neither family nor property. When expressing his suspicions to Cordero, Viana pointed out that the request to come by water might be a ruse to enable him to introduce contraband goods. After an investigation, the applicant was refused the desired permission, because he had been engaged in filibustering activities and closely connected with Dr. John Sibley, the wily American Indian agent at Natchitoches.[110]

Another who found himself expelled was Miguel Solivello. He received permission to settle in one of the new villas on either the Trinity, the Brazos, or the Guadalupe. Not content, the applicant asked and was given permission to remain in Nacogdoches until he could make arrangements for transportation to whichever villa he would choose. Apparently, Solivello had no other intention than that of remaining in Nacogdoches to engage in the profitable contraband trade, which seemed to thrive in spite of all efforts to stop it. Viana protested to the governor against Solivello's prolonged stay at Nacogdoches. Cordero immediately ordered the commander to compel him either to move into the interior or return to Louisiana.[111]

Establishment of the Villa de San Marcos de Neve. Governor Cordero had not forgotten his proposed settlement on the Guadalupe, which Salcedo had authorized when he approved the plans for Trinidad de Salcedo. Villa de San Marcos de Neve was to be located at or near the point where the *Camino Real* (Royal Highway) crossed the Guadalupe River. But the problems of 1806—Burr's conspiracy, Wilkinson's dubious activities, Trinidad de Salcedo's difficulties, and American immigration—prevented Cordero from giving much attention to this second project.

The unpleasant experience with the villa in East Texas had convinced even the enthusiastic Cordero that it might be better to try to secure settlers from the interior of Mexico for Villa de San Marcos de Neve. The struggling and thinly populated outposts of northern New Spain seemed to offer an unpromising source from which to draw recruits for the hazardous undertaking. But after prolonged negotiations with Felipe Roque de la Portilla, of Nuestra Señora del Refugio (a recently founded settlement in Nuevo Santander, located where Matamoros stands today), a group of about sixteen families set out in December, 1807, to found the new villa. In accord with the terms agreed upon, Cordero furnished

---

[110]Petition of Anthony Glass, October 31, 1807; Viana to Cordero, October 22, 1807; Cordero to Viana, July 1, 1808. *Béxar Archives.*

[111]Cordero to Viana, July 1, 1807. *Béxar Archives.*

the settlers with the necessary supplies, and sent a guard to the Nueces to escort the pioneers to their destination.

The caravan proceeded by way of San Antonio along the *Camino Real* to the crossing on the San Marcos River, located a few miles above its confluence with the Guadalupe, probably just below the modern city of San Marcos. Here they began to build the new villa. Governor Cordero proudly reported on January 6, 1808, that Villa de San Marcos de Neve had been established. Lieutenant Juan Ignacio Arrambide, Carrasco's successor in charge of Trinidad de Salcedo, was appointed *justicia* of the new villa.[112]

According to the census taken the following year, most of the settlers came from Refugio, Nuevo Santander, but there were a few from Mier, Béxar, Nacogdoches, Boca de Leones, and Camargo. The founders of the new villa deserve to be remembered, even though their efforts to hold the settlement permanently soon proved unavailing. The leader of the group, as previously stated, was Felipe Roque de la Portilla, a native of Spain, who was accompanied by his wife, María Ignacia de la Garza, a native of Mier, and his seven children: Juan Calixto, Juan, María Dolores, José Francisco, María Tomasa, Luciana, and María Monica. He brought 380 cattle, 388 mares, 200 mules, 20 horses (6 tame), and 25 donkeys. Arrambide granted Portilla a 30 by 60 *vara* lot on the main square and several *sitios* for a ranch, 12 leagues downstream.

Five of his ten herders were married men, but one of them, Manuel Landa, a native of Camargo, left his family at home in Nuevo Santander. Pedro Salazar brought his wife, María Ignacia Salinas; Basilio Gómez was accompanied by his wife, María Guadalupe; Santos Hernández took along his wife, Juliana García, and their two children, José Sabas and Pedro José; and Jesusa Salas came with her husband, José María Castañeda. The bachelors in the group were Máximo and Estanislao Salazar, Pedro and Francisco Gómez, and José Eleuterio. Portilla's party also included two housemaids, María Gregoria, a widow, and her daughter, María Ignacia.

Jesús Solís, a stockman from Refugio, and his herder, Nepomuceno Munguía, left their families in Nuevo Santander, and drove 180 head of cattle, 5 horses, and 3 mules to San Marcos de Neve. Solís' failure to bring his family seems to account for his not having been assigned either a lot for a home or lands for a ranch. He appears, however, to

---

[112]Cordero to Felipe Roque de la Portilla, December 16, 1806; Cordero to Salcedo, January 6, 1808. *Béxar Archives.*

have been permitted to pasture his stock on the common lands until his family could come. But before he could take steps to have them join him, the whole project was abandoned.

Another settler of San Marcos de Neve was Mateo Gómez, who gave his age as 60 and his occupation as farming. He, too, was accompanied by his wife, María Josefa, and also a young Indian servant named María Rafaela. They had 6 cows, 2 yoke of oxen, and 3 horses, and received a 40 by 60 *vara* lot for a home, and land for cultivation.

Pedro Flores brought his wife, Rita de la Garza, and two children, José Felipe and José Bernardino. He drove 30 head of cattle and 2 oxen, 26 mares, 6 horses, and 12 mules. He was assigned a lot facing on the main square, and a grant of land for a ranch.

With his wife, Barbara Músquiz, and his two children, María Telesfora and María Matiana, Victorino Losoya, a carpenter from Béxar, joined the settlers in San Antonio. He had 6 oxen and 2 horses, and received a lot on the main square, on which he immediately built a house—one of the first in the new villa.

Also in San Antonio, the settlers were joined by Salvador Bermúdez, a bachelor, whose occupation as herder possibly explains his sole equipment, 2 saddle horses.

From distant Nacogdoches came Juan Soto, a laborer. At the time the caravan set out, he was living in San Antonio with his wife, Feliciana Rodríguez, a native of Béxar. They had four children: José Tomás, María Encarnación, José Soto, and José Lorenzo. He had Cesario Sánchez help him bring the 2 work horses and 2 yoke of oxen. Soto received a lot on the plaza, where he immediately built a home.

The town of Mier gave to the new settlement Juan Ramírez, his wife, Dolores de la Garza, and their three children: José Macedonia, María Nicolasa, and María Salomé. They brought 160 head of cattle, 22 horses, 16 mules, and 5 donkeys. Alejandro Peña, Manuel Barcenas, and Jesús Valdés, laborers, came with this family. They were granted a *solar* on the main square and land for a ranch. Francisco Farías, another cattle- man from Mier, brought his two motherless children, María Petra and José Ignacio. He, too, was given a *solar* and land for his stock, 105 head of cattle and 7 horses. The third Mier family consisted of Gil Gómez, his wife, Antonia Garza, and one son, Santiago. They possessed 40 head of cattle, 8 mares, and 4 horses.

From San Antonio came José Salinas and his wife, Margil Chirina, with their two daughters, María Josefa and María Francisca. They received a *solar* on which they built a house, and land for their 40 head of cattle, 13 horses, 3 mares, and 97 sheep.

Pedro Gallego and his wife, María Michela, with their daughter, María de los Angeles, and a herder, Luis Villarreal, came from Boca de Leones with 45 cattle, 2 yoke of oxen, and 5 horses.

José María Carrillo had his wife and three children with him. He and his servant, Trinidad Montoya, drove 16 head of cattle, 1 yoke of oxen, and 2 horses from Boca de Leones.

La Bahía, noted for its cattle herds, contributed Juan Almontes; his herder, José María García; and a servant, the widow, María Prudencia. His stock consisted of 2 droves of mares, 28 horses, 5 donkeys, 11 head of cattle, and 3 yoke of oxen.

Manuel Landa, a native of Camargo, who had helped Portilla drive his cattle, lived on the Portilla ranch 12 leagues down the river.

Shortly after the establishment of the new settlement, a bachelor, José Estevan García, left Camargo to join the pioneers. It seems that he did not find much employment for his talents as a teacher in this community of cattle raisers, and left San Marcos before the end of the year to try his luck in Salcedo.[113]

The new villa had a population of 82 persons. Its establishment cost the royal treasury much less than did Salcedo, only 79 *pesos*. But it appears that Governor Cordero personally invested a considerable sum in the enterprise, possibly for some selfish reason. According to the census records, the cattle and horses brought by Portilla belonged to the governor. He had agreed to finance another group of settlers, but was forced to inform Portilla in December, 1807, that he would be unable to fulfill his promise until he had received additional funds from Saltillo.

After the establishment of the Villa de San Marcos de Neve, Portilla contracted for the transportation of six more families from Nuevo Santander. Four of these families could boast servants; the other two, only numerous children. Cordero agreed to send an escort to meet them on the Nueces to accompany them to the new settlement.[114] But it seems that they never came, for no new names were added to the list of settlers.

The details of the subsequent history of the villa are, indeed, meager. We catch only glimpses of hardships and tribulations. Shortly after the establishment, the poorer members of the settlement appealed to the Gov-

---

[113]Padrón General, July 12, 1809; Prieto to M. de Salcedo, December 4, 1809.
[114]Portilla to Cordero, August 29, 1808. *Béxar Archives.*

ernment for help and were given temporary relief in the hope that they would soon become self-supporting.[115] Hardly had the struggling settlers begun to build their homes, however, when on June 5, 1808, a flood practically swept away the villa. The water roaring through the main square gave the inhabitants barely enough time to gain the surrounding hillsides. Serious doubts about the suitability of the location arose. Plans were presented for the removal of the villa to higher ground, but were never put into effect. To the many hardships of the settlers was added the constant fear of Indian attack, for the savages frequently raided the colony until it was finally abandoned in 1812.

---

[115]Noticia de lo subministrado a los Publadores de San Marcos, April 3, 1808. *Béxar Archives.*

CHAPTER X

French Intervention in Spain and Its Reaction in Texas

Spain had been reluctant in 1803 to open the door even halfway to immigration. But the insistent knocking of those who called themselves "loyal" subjects, and the urgent pleading of liberal Spanish officials for populating the vast, uninhabited region along the American frontier as the most effective means of preventing further encroachments had at last forced the commandant general of the Interior Provinces to relent and issue instructions for the admission of settlers. The trickle of immigrants, however, soon threatened to take on the proportions of a flood, in spite of all precautions to check the flow. Conflicting views on immigration were largely responsible for the failure to enforce the restrictions which would have kept it within the bounds desired. Governor Cordero of Texas, as well as his able assistant, Simón de Herrera, commander of Spain's forces in Texas, was convinced that immigration was the solution to the problem of defence on this distant and exposed frontier. Cordero did not perceive the danger in the new policy, nor did he foresee the designs of France's ambitious Emperor, or of the grasping American pioneers. Designedly and unwisely, he ignored the efforts of his superior to stop the introduction of foreigners—until it was too late.

The Bayonne conference. While officials on the northern frontier wrangled over the methods to be used in sincerely trying to safeguard the king's best interests in America, the royal family was making a sorry spectacle of itself before the whole world. The infatuated queen, her ambitious Godoy, the vain and selfish Ferdinand, and the spineless Charlves IV were shamelessly disputing among themselves for power, while Napoleon overran the State supposedly to invade Portugal. In order to enforce his Continental System in Europe, the Emperor felt that he had to have absolute control of Spain. He was on the point of forcibly seizing the Crown—a large army was already in northern Spain—when the family quarrel burst to give him the opportunity he was seeking without compelling him to resort to arms.

Napoleon, at this juncture, precipitated the crisis. He demanded practically the whole of northern Spain as far as the Ebro River. Ferdinand and his sympathizers accused the favorite Godoy of having sold out to Napoleon in order to prevent the Prince of Asturias from becoming king. A mob raided Godoy's palace on March 17, and forced Charles IV to dismiss him. The next day, the favorite was imprisoned after a scuffle in which he was slightly wounded; Charles IV had to appeal to his son, Ferdinand, to protect Godoy. The emotional tension of these three days proved too much for the king. On March 19, 1808, he abdicated in favor of Ferdinand. The news was hailed by the populace with the greatest joy. Their jubilation, however, was short-lived, and Napoleon, who had manipulated the whole incident, was disappointed. He had hoped that the royal family would follow the example of the Portuguese and flee to America. He refused, therefore, to recognize Ferdinand VII until it was proved that Charles IV had abdicated voluntarily.

The excitement over, Charles IV recovered his equanimity and, regretting his hasty action, made the foolish mistake of appealing to Napoleon for help and of placing himself entirely in his hands. The Emperor, supposedly on the way to Madrid, invited the old king and queen and Ferdinand VII to discuss the situation with him at Bayonne, just beyond the border. Both Charles IV and Ferdinand VII proved to be as putty in the hands of the clever Emperor. Two treaties were soon drawn up—one signed on May 5 and the other, on May 10, 1808—which bound Charles and Ferdinand to renounce all claims to the Spanish throne in favor of Napoleon, and authorized him to bestow the crown on whomsoever he pleased.[1] The astonishment of Spain, her colonial empire, and all Europe quickly gave way to protests. The Corsican had loosed forces which were soon to crush him and his empire, and set free the Spanish colonies in America.

On May 11, 1808, Joseph, Napoleon's elder brother, then King of Naples, received a brief note: "The Nation, through the Supreme Council of Castile, asks me for a king. I destine this crown for you."[2] *Juntas* sprang up overnight throughout Spain to denounce the action of Napoleon. Swearing undying fealty to Ferdinand VII, they voiced their determination to rule in Spain and in the colonies until their legitimate king was restored. "Their indignation rumbled hoarsely for

---

[1]The summary here given is based largely on the accounts of Altamira y Creveam, Rafael, *Historia de España*, IV, 98-103 (Barcelona, 1911); Oman, Charles, *A History of the Peninsula War*, I, 1-20; and Rydjord, John, *Foreign Interest in the Independence of New Spain*, 254-258.

[2]*The Confidential Correspondence of Napoleon Bonaparte with His Brother Joseph, Sometime King of Spain.* I, 320. (2 vols., New York, 1856.)

a time," says a modern historian, "like a volcano in labour, and then burst forth in an explosion of fury."[3]

Napoleon's interest in the colonies. How Napoleon, without a fleet, intended to make use of Spain's vast colonial empire is still a matter of conjecture. But even before the fateful overthrow of the Bourbon dynasty in Spain, he had begun preparations to win the friendship and trade of the Spanish colonies. As early as April 15, 1808, he had written to his Minister of the Interior to establish and foster trade with the Spanish colonies by all means possible. He suggested at this time that commercial companies be organized with Government subsidies in leading French ports, and ordered ships to be built especially for this purpose. Aware of the possibility that the French might not be well received, he planned to counteract American antipathy by sending agents to prepare Spain's colonials for the change that was to take place. The agents were to show the colonists the advantages they would derive from the new order of things. On April 25 Napoleon wrote Vice Admiral Decrés to learn whether or not he had dispatched the agents to Mexico and Montevideo as instructed, and to order him to send more.[4]

In support of these emissaries, he issued instructions for sending ships and arms, particularly to La Plata and Mexico. Six light vessels were to be built for fast communication with the colonies. Marshal Junot was ordered to reserve three ships for carrying dispatches to the viceroy; one was to depart for Vera Cruz every eighth day. A public announcement was to be made in Madrid on May 22 to acquaint the people with the fact that six ships had already left French ports with letters, proclamations, and instructions for the Spanish authorities in America. The colonists were to be assured of France's protection against England and told that the French were their best friends.[5]

Napoleon offered Gregorio de la Cuesta the office of viceroy of Mexico on May 25, and urged him to accept the position for the sake of securing Mexico for Spain, the vassal of France. He desired to see Mexico recognize Joseph as king so as to forestall a rupture with the mother country. The following day, the Emperor wrote to the Duc de Berg to inform him of Cuesta's appointment and to suggest that he draw up the commission, and name three or four colonels, brigadiers, or field

---

[3]Rose, John H., *The Life of Napoleon I*, 154.

[4]*Correspondance de Napoléon Ier*, XVII, 1-2; 47. (32 vols., Paris, 1865.)

[5]Napoleon to Junot, May 15, 1808; Napoleon to the Duc de Berg, May 22, 1808. *Ibid.*, XVII, 104; 110-111; 157.

marshals for Mexico. The Duc de Berg was instructed to put the *Flora* in readiness to take the new viceroy to Mexico, and transport 3,000 guns, armaments, and the munitions necessary to assure the desired result. But Cuesta refused the appointment, because he was in ill health; and before anyone could assume the office, Mexico had taken steps to resist all of Napoleon's efforts to take over the Government in Mexico.[6]

The Emperor's strategy seemingly called for general discontent, particularly discord between the Creoles and the Spaniards in the colonies, and a pro-French party to make it possible for him to bring the rebellious colonies directly under the protectorate of France. In this scheme of things it was of the utmost importance to penetrate Mexico either by way of Vera Cruz or through the northern frontiers of New Spain. Hence, the importance of Texas. He, accordingly, sent to the United States as chief of his emissaries a certain Desmoland, who was to dispatch special agents to various points in the Spanish colonies. Their task was to foment discord and win the colonies over to France and Napoleon.[7] The Emperor planned to use for his own ends the division existing between the upper clergy, or Peninsular Spaniards, and the lower clergy, or Creoles. He hoped to gain the support of the Creoles by holding out to them the possibility of establishing with his aid an independent Government which they could control.

The General D'Alvimar incident. The Spanish officials in Mexico were not ignorant of Napoleon's plans or of his agents. Early in May Commandant General Nemesio Salcedo warned Governor Cordero of what was impending. He had received confidential information that a certain General Alvina, an Italian member of the Legion of Honor, had just arrived in the United States with a group of French officers. Their plan was to proceed by way of Philadelphia and New Orleans across the frontier to arouse the peaceful inhabitants of New Spain to revolt. The governor was instructed to maintain patrols at Nacogdoches and all other posts along the frontier and coast. Strangers presenting passports from the Court of Spain with the purpose of gaining admission into Spanish territory were to be permitted to proceed under escort

---

[6]*Correspondance de Napoléon Ier*, XVII, 237; 246-248; 297. General Castaña was offered the position, but the Marquis de St. Simon, it seems, was finally appointed.

[7]Bancroft, *History of Mexico*, IV, 70-81; Hatcher, *The Opening of Texas to Foreign Settlement*, Appendix 15; Fisher, Lillian E., *The Background of the Revolution for Mexican Independence*, 365.

to San Antonio, where they were to remain until further instructions. Failure to present a passport would be sufficient reason to order them out.[8]

Rumors about the character and importance of the expected agent increased the apprehension of Salcedo. It was said that Alvina (later ascertained to be General Octaviano D'Alvimar) was a relative of Napoleon; that, prior to the transfer of Louisiana, he had been sent to Santo Domingo to help put down a rebellion; that he had been commissioned to secure aid from Caracas, Cartagena, and Santa Fe for the French; that he had since returned to Havana, and was now ready for new duties.[9]

These rumors were not entirely unfounded, for D'Alvimar had gained considerable experience both in Europe and America, and was particularly fitted for the mission entrusted to him. He was related, not to Napoleon, but to General Le Clerc, whom he had accompanied on the unsuccessful expedition to Santo Domingo. It was in a futile attempt to secure aid for Le Clerc that he had visited Caracas and other colonial cities. Vidal, the Spanish vice-consul at New Orleans, informed of his presence by Wilkinson and Claiborne, wrote directly to the viceroy of Mexico to warn him of the proposed visit of the dangerous agent. Vidal described him as "a man of talent, high enterprise, with no morality; cruel, and with his apparent and assumed affability, capable of insinuating himself into the hearts of the most imperturbable, and of playing upon the ignorant at will."[10] It is not strange then that Salcedo should have repeated on July 12 his instructions of May 27, and added that, even if General D'Alvimar presented a passport, he was to be arrested upon arrival and held until further instructions. This order was to be applied to the companions of the general, as well as to any other suspicious foreigner who presented himself on the frontier.[11]

Before these last instructions reached Nacogdoches, Captain José María Guadiana found himself face to face with D'Alvimar. A scouting party returned from the Sabine with the general on August 5, 1808. Guadiana was puzzled as to the course he should pursue. The man's name was not Alvina, he found, nor was he an Italian. Guadiana wondered if the orders of May 27 applied in this case. When the puzzled frontier commander asked for his passport, D'Alvimar, feigning

---

[8]N. Salcedo to Cordero, May 27, 1808. *Nacogdoches Archives*, XI, pp. 81-82.
[9]Cavo, *Tres Siglos de México*, 258-259; Alamán, *Historia de México*, I, 297.
[10]Cox, *West Florida Controversy*, 313-314.
[11]N. Salcedo to Cordero, July 12, 1808. *Nacogdoches Archives*, XI, pp. 91-92.

amazement at such effrontery, declared that for years he had been visiting Spanish colonies and had never been subjected to such an insult. He presented documents to prove that he had served on various missions in the Spanish possessions; his passport in French astonished Guadiana, for it had "not a word in Spanish." D'Alvimar had come without servants or officers, not from New Orleans, as expected, but directly from Baton Rouge. The French agent volunteered the information that he had landed in Philadelphia; that he had waited there several months for instructions; and that he had received orders from the Emperor to proceed without delay to Mexico City. He explained that his overland trip to Nacogdoches was to avoid possible delays which might arise out of the American embargo and the tense Franco-American relations that had developed since his departure from Europe. Guadiana was highly impressed by the tone and bearing of Napoleon's emissary. His instructions of May 27, however, compelled him to inform the Frenchman that, since he could not exhibit a passport from the Spanish Court, he would have to return to the United States. D'Alvimar replied that he could not possibly turn back, because his orders were to proceed to Mexico without delay. Sympathizing with Guadiana for being charged with the execution of such unreasonable instructions, he deigned to concede a point and wait in Nacogdoches for permission to proceed on his mission. Guadiana lost no time in reporting D'Alvimar's case to Cordero and asked to be advised immediately.[12]

Impatient by nature, and bored with the monotony of squalid, frontier Nacogdoches, D'Alvimar wrote to Governor Cordero on August 9. He gave him a detailed account of his mission, and expressed in vigorous terms his displeasure at the delay. He informed Cordero that it would be futile to try to stop him. To Cordero he, likewise, manifested surprise at the unfriendly reception accorded him—an experience to which he had never before been subjected. He went on to state that he had left France in December, 1807, for the United States, there to await further orders. He admitted that he had done some travelling in the United States until he received instructions to report to the viceroy of Mexico in all haste. Fearful of a Franco-American rupture which might prevent him from reaching his destination, he had left his entourage behind and proceeded as fast as possible to the Spanish frontier. Because of the close relations existing between Spain and France, he had hoped to find a friendly welcome. He protested that he would never

---

[12]Guadiana to Cordero, August 5, 1808. *Nacogdoches Archives*, XI, pp. 96-98.

have exposed himself to the indignity of detention, had it not been for the American embargo. The reason he gave for writing to Governor Cordero rather than to Commandant General Salcedo was that he was certain that Salcedo would take months to decide his case, and he could not suffer the indignity of having to wait that long.[13]

The French envoy was shrewd. He reasoned that the governor of this remote province would be less well informed on the true state of affairs than the commandant general and, consequently, would be more likely to permit him to continue his journey. D'Alvimar did more than plead. He warned, "You may block my official entrance [by way of Texas], but how can you prevent me from reaching Mexico City by some other route?" He maintained that he preferred to enter legally, but that if he was delayed much longer, he would be obliged to resort to other methods to carry out his orders. Significantly, he added that he was only one agent, and that others were to follow.

He tried to circumvent the law requiring passports of strangers by declaring that it was ridiculous to demand a passport of a military envoy. He had visited almost all the other Spanish colonies, and had never before been asked to show one. As a matter of fact, he had no more returned from Madrid than he was ordered to go to America. He had spent three months in Spain prior to his embarkation from Bordeaux. His passport, dated in that port November 27, 1807, had been issued by order of Napoleon who instructed all officials, military and civil, to allow the general, an officer of the Legion of Honor, native of Paris, to proceed on a special mission to the United States, thence to the Spanish colonies.[14]

D'Alvimar tactfully tried to play upon the pride of the provincial governor. Expressing his conviction that the whole thing was just a mistake, he lamented the difficulty experienced by officers in charge of such remote provinces in keeping themselves informed of what went on in the world at large. He could well understand why they, lacking information, would be suspicious. But he could not postpone his mission to the Marquis de St. Simon, who by now must be the new viceroy of Mexico. He would remember to mention to the Marquis the treatment accorded him in Texas. He felt outraged at having to exhibit his

---

[13]D'Alvimar to Cordero, August 9, 1808. *Nacogdoches Archives*, XI, p. 98.

[14]Passport issued to General Octaviano D'Alvimar, Bordeaux, November 27, 1807; copy sent to Cordero, August 9, 1809. *Nacogdoches Archives*, XI, pp. 98-101.

passport, but to save a subordinate embarrassment, he consented to send it as requested by Guadiana.[15]

Governor Cordero, in the meantime, had gone to La Bahía, and left Simón de Herrera in command at San Antonio with special instructions to notify him at once if anything important developed. Great was his surprise on his return at 11 o'clock the night of August 10, to learn that only two hours before, a messenger had arrived from Nacogdoches with the report of D'Alvimar's arrival at that post, as well as with D'Alvimar's letter and other documents. Cordero hastened to send copies of everything to Commandant General Salcedo the following morning; he explained that the order of July 12 had not been received in San Antonio until July 30, and that he relayed it the same day to Nacogdoches. Guadiana evidently had not received it by August 5, the day of D'Alvimar's arrival. Fortunately, Guadiana had acted in accord with the spirit of the order. Cordero now asked Salcedo to instruct him what course to follow in view of the circumstances. At the same time he informed Guadiana that he had forwarded all the documents to the commandant general, and until he received further instructions, he was to guard D'Alvimar closely and not permit him to leave.[16]

D'Alvimar's assertion that the disposition of his case would take forever if referred to the commandant general, proved prophetic. Instead of immediately ordering his arrest or expulsion, Salcedo submitted the case to his *asesor* and *auditor* of war for an opinion. This official, after a thorough study of all the documents transmitted by the governor, gave his report on August 23, 1808. The appearance of the French officer on the Spanish frontier at this time, he asserted, assumed extraordinary significance in view of the political crisis that had developed in Madrid. He was amazed that D'Alvimar did not have a Spanish passport and the more so, because the visitor could boast that he had visited many other Spanish possessions without one. If his mission were legitimate, there was no reason for his not having a Spanish passport. The scientific mission to the equator, he recalled, had been provided with a passport from the Court of Madrid, as had the distinguished scientist, Baron de Humboldt, during his recent visit.

It seemed more than a mere coincidence, the *auditor* pointed out, that the original orders to D'Alvimar to embark for the United States

---

[15] D'Alvimar to Cordero, August 9, 1808. *Nacogdoches Archives,* XI, pp. 98-101.

[16] Cordero to N. Salcedo, August 11, 1808; Cordero to Guadiana, August 12, 1808. *Nacogdoches Archives,* XI, pp. 101-102.

to await further instructions had been issued at the very time that French troops began to move en masse into Spain, and that the subsequent orders to hasten to Mexico had been given at about the time of the Bayonne incident. It appeared to be a part of the Emperor's general plan to gain control of the Spanish colonies by means similar to those employed in seizing the Crown of Spain. D'Alvimar's reference to the Marquis de St. Simon as viceroy of Mexico by appointment of Napoleon was significant indeed. How had D'Alvimar learned of this fact? Why had he stated that it did not matter whether or not he would be given permission to go to Mexico? What had he meant when he said that others would follow? The evidence at hand proved to the *auditor* that the emissary of Napoleon was a dangerous enemy. Since this agent's departure from Europe, Napoleon had seized the Spanish Crown which he attempted to place upon his brother's head. But the people of Spain and of her colonies had sworn fealty to Ferdinand VII as their only legitimate sovereign. The *auditor,* better informed on recent events in Europe than would be expected of an officer residing on the remote frontiers of New Spain, went on to declare that in the name of Ferdinand VII, the Duque del Infantado had since declared war on Napoleon and the usurper Joseph.

In view of these circumstances, he concluded that General Octaviano D'Alvimar could be considered in no other light than that of an enemy; that he should be immediately conducted as a prisoner under guard to San Antonio; that his papers be seized and examined; and that the viceroy be kept informed and consulted on the ultimate disposition of the prisoner.[17]

While the advisor of the commandant general prepared his report and made his recommendations, which were sent on August 23 to Cordero for his guidance, D'Alvimar's patience was being sorely tried. The whole thing seemed farcical, he wrote on August 29 to Guadiana. He said that he had been waiting for almost a month, and had decided to go on to Mexico with or without permission of the commandant general. "You know well," he warned Guadiana, "that there are a thousand ways which I may choose to attain my end, none of which you can obstruct." Threatening and cajoling by turns, he said that he did not hold the governor responsible for this shameful conduct; it was the

---

[17]N. Salcedo to Cordero, August 23, 1808, transmitting the report of the *asesor* and *auditor* of war and ordering his recommendations to be carried out. *Nacogdoches Archives*, XI, pp. 106-115.

commandant general who was responsible; the day would come when Salcedo would wish he had never issued such orders. He then proposed to surrender himself to Guadiana as a voluntary prisoner on condition that he be sent to San Antonio. He pledged his word of honor not to attempt to escape. If this offer was not accepted, he warned Guadiana that he would be obliged to have recourse to other means to continue his journey.[18]

The astonished commander of Nacogdoches was at his wit's end to know what to do with the impetuous Frenchman. Finally, without awaiting further instructions, he agreed to the proposal, and wrote Cordero that he had decided to send D'Alvimar to San Antonio, because he thought that the governor was in a better position in San Antonio to prevent D'Alvimar's escape. He feared that the continued presence of the French emissary in Nacogdoches might arouse the populace. Again, D'Alvimar, driven to despair, might commit some rash act. Guadiana with a sigh of relief sent him to San Antonio under an escort of a corporal and six soldiers. At the same time he dispatched by special messenger a copy of D'Alvimar's letter for Cordero; and for Salcedo, a communication and a report of all that had transpired prior to the departure of the irate agent.[19]

D'Alvimar's letter to the commandant general was impudent and insulting in tone. The Frenchman assured Salcedo that he had waited this long only out of regard for a subordinate lacking responsibility, and that the whole performance impressed him as a poor farce. He was aware of the severity with which the commandant general ruled the Interior Provinces, and hoped that he would not deal too harshly with the commander of Nacogdoches for accepting his proposal to be sent as a voluntary prisoner to San Antonio under escort. Only his sense of honor had restrained him from accepting the offers of Indians and citizens of Nacogdoches to guide him to Mexico City. He had decided to surrender himself voluntarily in order to continue the journey. He was convinced of the futility of remaining longer, because the evasive reply, which would doubtless be made to his request for permission to proceed, would but delay him the more. He concluded in an arrogant tone that he was willing to forget all the vexations caused him, if he was allowed to fulfill his mission without further inconveniences. It

---

[18]D'Alvimar to Guadiana, August 29, 1808. *Nacogdoches Archives*, XI, pp. 102-103.

[19]Guadiana to Cordero, August 29, 1808. *Nacogdoches Archives*, XI, p. 103.

would be a pity to let insistence on trifles ruin so excellent a record of faithful service as Salcedo had.[20]

When the messenger from Nacogdoches arrived in San Antonio on September 2, Cordero had not yet received the report of the *auditor*, nor the orders for the formal arrest of D'Alvimar issued on August 23. The governor, therefore, found himself sharing Guadiana's predicament when the French general first made his appearance in Nacogdoches. The next evening, while still pondering the course of action he should follow, the orders of the commandant general of August 23 arrived at eleven o'clock. He had no choice in the matter now. He was to place D'Alvimar under arrest as a prisoner of war, seize his papers, and hold him after a preliminary examination until further instructions.

While the French general was leisurely making his way to San Antonio, Cordero called a Council of War for September 5. Lieutenant Colonel Simón de Herrera, governor of Nuevo León and commander of all Spanish forces on the frontier, Mariano Varela, captain of San Juan Bautista, Captain Miguel de Arcos, commander of the Nuevo Santander militia, and Cordero met in the governor's home on the appointed day. Governor Cordero informed them of the arrival of D'Alvimar in Nacogdoches on August 5, his impatience at having to wait for the commandant's decision, his recent departure on August 29 as a voluntary prisoner, and of the orders concerning him issued by Salcedo on August 23. He asked the Council members to examine all the documents in the case and recommend what he should do with D'Alvimar upon his arrival in San Antonio. After due deliberation, the Council agreed that D'Alvimar's conduct in Nacogdoches, his lack of a Spanish passport, and his impudent letter to the commandant general—which he had sent unsealed—proved conclusively the suspicious character of his mission, and deprived him of all rights which voluntary prisoners could claim. In view of these facts, the Council concluded that it would be best to send a guard to conduct him safely to San Antonio, where he was to be informed officially that Ferdinand VII was the only legitimate king of Spain and that in Ferdinand's name the Spanish nation had declared war on France. He was then to be advised that he would be held as a prisoner of war, and was to be ordered to turn all his papers over to the governor. The Council further recommended that the governor examine his papers before forwarding them to the commandant general in order to determine whether or not they contained any information that might

---

[20]D'Alvimar to Salcedo, August 29, 1808. *Nacogdoches Archives*, XI, pp. 104-5.

require immediate action to prevent a surprise attack upon the frontier outposts of the province.[21]

Cordero, as a matter of fact, had already dispatched fifteen men under Lieutenant Santiago Tijerina to meet the Nacogdoches escort and take over the duty of conducting General D'Alvimar to San Antonio as a prisoner of war. They were instructed to observe every courtesy due his rank and mission. Upon his arrival on September 8, he was taken to the governor's residence and immediately notified of the resolutions adopted by the Council of War and of the last orders issued by the commandant general. D'Alvimar protested against the proceedings, but submitted without resistance. He unlocked the four small trunks that constituted his baggage and opened his two large bags and a case in which he kept all his papers. Surrendering all documents and effects, he declared under oath that this was all he had, that the rest of his papers were by now probably in Vera Cruz, as that was the city for which his retinue had embarked from New Orleans.[22] His papers revealed no information of importance, and seemed to indicate that he was a soldier of fortune.

Shortly afterwards, D'Alvimar was sent under guard to Monclova. After attempting to escape, he was conducted to Perote by order of Salcedo. He was later taken to the famous prison of San Juan de Ulloa. Finally, after his jewels and money had been confiscated, he was sent to Spain on board an English vessel.[23] The appearance of General D'Alvimar on the frontier in the fall of 1808 strengthened the conviction of the commandant general that it was most dangerous to admit immigrants carelessly and indiscriminately.

Effects of the D'Alvimar incident. Although D'Alvimar failed to stir up a revolt in Mexico, the incident served to increase the apprehensions of Spanish officials both in Spain and in America. The viceroy of Mexico informed the Supreme Central Council of Spain (at Seville) controlling the Government in the absence of Ferdinand VII, of the perfidious activities of French agents and sympathizers in the colonies. The Supreme Council issued orders on November 12 for the arrest of

---

[21]Council of War, September 5, 1808. *Nacogdoches Archives*, XI, pp. 83-89; 115-119.

[22]Certified statement by Cordero, September 8, 1808. *Nacogdoches Archives*, XI, pp. 120-121.

[23]Rydjord, *Foreign Interest in the Independence of New Spain*, 260-261; Hatcher, *The Opening of Texas to Foreign Settlement*, 130-131.

all French agents, warned colonial authorities against intrigues in Louisiana, and advised them to avoid all cause for misunderstanding with the United States.[24]

With the French struggle going on in Spain, the Supreme Council, however, was unable to give anything more than moral comfort to the colonies in their defence against foreign agents. The viceroy made diligent inquiries to determine the best plan of defence to be adopted; but he, like the Supreme Council, was in no position to do much more than to send warnings and issue precautionary measures. The chief responsibility of safeguarding the vast frontier of New Spain, therefore, devolved upon the conscientious commander of the Interior Provinces. Although he feared the spread of seditious propaganda by French agents, he was more immediately concerned about the designs of the aggressive American pioneers and the machinations of their Government.[25]

Precautions against Americans. Even before the appearance of D'Alvimar, Salcedo had attempted to neutralize the efforts of enterprising American traders by sending special agents to some of the tribes among whom the Americans had been trading.[26] Earlier still, at the very beginning of 1808, Salcedo had instructed Cordero to prohibit all communication between Nacogdoches and the advanced Spanish post on Bayou Pierre to prevent trade with Louisiana. Bayou Pierre was to communicate with Nacogdoches only to secure food or the services of a priest.[27] Upon learning that there were in Nacogdoches twenty-seven slaves who had escaped from Louisiana, he ordered them transferred to Villa de Salcedo on the Trinity so as to prevent the Indians from capturing them before they could be returned to the Americans. His letter to the viceroy, written in November, 1808, assumed him that his most important task was to hold Texas against the Americans.[28]

New Texas governor. Antonio Cordero had been acting governor of Texas since the death of Elguézabal. On April 24, 1807, the Council of the Indies appointed Manuel María de Salcedo, son of the former

---

[24]Copy of decree of the *Junta Suprema Central* transmitted with the letter of N. Salcedo to Cordero, March 13, 1809. *Béxar Archives.*

[25]N. Salcedo to Velasco, August 24, 1808; N. Salcedo to Cordero, August 23, and December 3, 1808. *Béxar Archives.*

[26]N. Salcedo to Soto, March 13, 1808. *Béxar Archives.*

[27]N. Salcedo to Cordero, January 12, 1808. *Béxar Archives.*

[28]N. Salcedo to Cordero, May 31, 1808; N. Salcedo to the viceroy, November 8, 1808. *Béxar Archives.*

governor of Louisiana, and permitted him to take the oath of office before the Judge of Cádiz.[29] Shortly afterwards, the new governor set out for America, and eventually arrived in Texas during the summer of 1808. The commandant of the Interior Provinces ordered Cordero to remain in Texas, however, to acquaint the new appointee with the duties of his office and the grave problems of his province.[30] The new governor proved himself worthy of his distinguished associates on the distant frontier of New Spain. Like Cordero and Herrera, he firmly believed in colonization. It was, consequently, not necessary to convince him of the urgent need of populating his vast province as the best means of safeguarding it against attack and encroachments. He was liberal in his ideas with regard to trade, sincere in his desire to promote the welfare of Texas, and enthusiastic in his support of all measures designed to develop its resources and make it self-supporting. He had not been in Texas three months when he began pleading for the admission of settlers, even those whom anyone observing just casually would have considered undesirable. Governor Manuel de Salcedo argued with Commandant General Nemesio Salcedo that these people should be permitted to settle in the new colonies on the San Marcos and the Guadalupe since they had voluntarily severed connections with Louisiana and had made no effort to return to that province. Many of them might be allowed to settle even in Béxar itself, where, plying their several trades, they would contribute much to the community.[31] It is remarkable, and at the same time indicative of the importance attached to Texas by Spanish authorities, that during these trying years, when the whole viceroyalty was beset with serious dangers, three of the most able officials in the viceregal administration, rich in experience, liberal in attitude, and resourceful in action, were retained on this distant frontier. Within a year, a fourth was to be sent from Durango.

Immigration control. Before the Bayonne meeting and the D'Alvimar incident, the commandant general had begun to try to regulate the flow of immigration and to deport undesirables. But his efforts had repeatedly been nullified by the lack of coöperation on the part of Cordero and Herrera. He was to get no support from the new governor,

---

[29]Appointment of Manuel María de Salcedo, April 24, 1807; Titulo de Gobernador de la Provincia de Texas . . ., May 1, 1807. *A. G. I., Audiencia de Guadalajara,* 103-4-1 (Dunn Transcripts, 1800-1819, pp. 170-174).

[30]N. Salcedo to Cordero, March 24, 1809. *Béxar Archives.*

[31]M. de Salcedo to N. Salcedo, November 30, 1808. *Béxar Archives.*

M. de Salcedo. Infractions of the carefully drawn regulations have already been noted in connection with the development of Villa de Salcedo and the persistent attempts to occupy Orcoquisac and Atascosito. Other violations during this year (1808) should be cited to illustrate the various ways in which many undesirables succeeded in evading the immigration regulations of the commandant general, who had to depend on his subordinates in Texas for their effective observance.

The commandant general became alarmed early in 1808, when he learned through Father Solana, who was ministering to the soldiers and their families at Atascosito and Orcoquisac, that there were in that region numerous English and French settlers, perhaps squatters, who could not speak a word of Spanish. He immediately inquired of Cordero why he had permitted such a situation to arise, since he had repeatedly issued strict orders forbidding the establishment of any settlers in the area. Cordero disregarded the question of the nationality of the immigrants—the real issue—and explained that the families to which Father Solana referred, were not settled in that region, but were there only temporarily, waiting to secure means of transportation to move into the interior.[32] It was this willingness to relax the observance of the regulations that made possible the entrance of many immigrants, who were later to cause Spain much trouble.

Another interesting example illustrating the carelessness of Cordero and the new governor in admitting suspicious characters is that of Miguel de Larrua and his companions. At the beginning of 1808, a party of eight, including one woman and one child, landed at Atascosito. Investigations disclosed that Larrua, who claimed to be a Catholic and a native of Vizcaya, had no papers to prove either contention. He said that he had been educated in France; had come to Louisiana; and, with the consent of the commander of Nacogdoches, had moved (in 1798) to that post, where he had resided for many years. Cordero had signed his passport on February 6, 1807. Larrua brought with him his son, who had been baptized in Nacogdoches, and an Italian manservant named Rumanoli. When asked for his certificate of baptism, Rumanoli told a lengthy story to explain the reason he could not produce one. Juan Eugenio Michamps, a native of Paris, was another member of the party who had to explain his inability to produce his baptismal certificate. He declared that he had been induced to come to Texas by the king's

---

[32]N. Salcedo to Cordero, February 13, 1808; Cordero to N. Salcedo, March 14, 1808. *Béxar Archives.*

proclamation admitting Louisianans. He brought with him his wife, Rosa Francisca Vechan, and two servants, Pedro Esteban and Pedro Flogny. His wife, who was a native of Naples, showed her marriage certificate signed by a priest in New York City to prove that she was a Catholic. Pedro Esteban said he was a German and a Catholic, but he was unable to prove that he had been baptized. The fourth member of the party, Pedro Flogny, stated that he was a Frenchman and a Catholic and maintained that his baptismal certificate had been lost during the Negro insurrection in Santo Domingo. It was evident that of the seven, only the woman and the boy could produce satisfactory evidence to prove that they were Catholics. In spite of the explicit regulation barring non-Catholics, they were, nevertheless, all permitted to settle in Texas. In the report on the investigation, the governor commented on each one of the immigrants. He remarked that Larrua was *"bueno,"* and made the observation that since Rumanoli was young and single, he might make a useful citizen of Béxar. He contended that because the Michamps had been legally married, there were no grounds for refusing them. He approved of Esteban for the strange reason that he had a trade, and tradesmen were needed. As for Flogny, Cordero admitted that he really did not meet requirements, nor did he have anything in particular to recommend him; but he let Flogny remain, for a still stranger reason, to save the expense and inconvenience of sending him back to Louisiana.[33]

The case of Carlos Tessier was an even more flagrant violation of the immigration law—and that with the full connivance of Governor Salcedo. Early in November, the commander of Atascosito reported the arrival of Carlos Tessier from Louisiana, who declared that he was on his way to Béxar with some personal property and certain effects belonging to the new governor's wife. Although he interned the crew of Tessier's vessel until he received further orders, he permitted Tessier to continue his journey to Béxar because he had a passport. Governor Manuel de Salcedo was an old friend of Tessier's, whom he had met in Louisiana, and he wished to employ him as his secretary. But Commandant General N. Salcedo refused to approve the appointment. Determined to keep his protégé in Texas, the governor advised him to make formal application for settlement in Villa de Salcedo, and gave him permission to remain in that settlement until he obtained action on his petition. The governor went further. He was willing to extend

---

[33]Report on Larrua and party, October 11, 1808. *Béxar Archives.*

the same privilege to even Tessier's two servants, if they could prove that they were Spaniards and had lived under Spain's jurisdiction. The ship was ordered to return to Louisiana and the crew were warned against introducing contraband goods. Tessier's request was naturally refused by the commandant general; but in the meantime—thanks to the collusion of the governor—Tessier had been enabled to remain in Texas at least six months. Commandant General Nemesio Salcedo asked ex-Governor Cordero to explain to Governor Manuel de Salcedo the importance of excluding Louisiana settlers from certain frontier areas so as to prevent contraband trade and communication with their former friends and relations.[34]

The De la Rosa incident. An enterprising character, Francisco de la Rosa, appeared late in December, 1808, at Atascosito with two slaves and two servants. De la Rosa was no stranger to Texas or the other northern provinces of New Spain, where for years, it seems, he had successfully engaged in contraband trade.

During an investigation held in 1806, José Plácido de Monzón testified that De la Rosa had brought a load of linen handkerchiefs and muslins to Presidio de San Juan Bautista and had sold a good part of his merchandise to the garrison. The rest of the goods he had sent to Punta de Lampazos, in Coahuila, to be sold there by a certain Arispe. This agent absconded with the proceeds of the sales, convinced, perhaps, that the owner could not prosecute him because he was himself engaged in illegal business. Another witness, José Andrés Cadena, declared that Barr habitually sent to Natchitoches to secure trains of goods from De la Rosa and that, while stationed as a soldier at Villa de Salcedo when Arrambide took charge, he had seen De la Rosa there with a train of mules.[35]

De la Rosa appears also to have coöperated with Barr in illegally exporting horses and mules to Louisiana. From San Marcos, Lieutenant Arrambide, who was at that time in command of the mobile detail guarding the river crossings between San Antonio and Nacogdoches (March 30, 1806), reported to Cordero that José María Salinas and eight muleteers had arrived from San Antonio with eleven loads of

---

[34]Cordero to M. de Salcedo, December 1, 1808; M. de Salcedo to the Commander of Atascosito, December 5, 1808; N. Salcedo to Cordero, December 11, 1808. *Béxar Archives.*

[35]Declarations of José Plácido de Monzón and José Andrés Cadena. *A.G.I., Audiencia de Guadalajara,* 104-2-9 (Dunn Transcripts, 1800-1819, pp. 136-137).

goods for the king's troops at Nacogdoches and a consignment of
nineteen loads for Francisco de la Rosa in New Orleans. The train
master asserted that the loaded beasts and the other twenty-six mules
and twenty-six horses belonged to De la Rosa. Upon being informed
that it was against regulations to permit the exportation of horses
and mules and that he could continue with only the number indispensable
for transporting the freight, Salinas remonstrated that he needed twenty-
four horses and eight mules for relays, besides those in the train.
Arrambide reported on April 2 that, in accordance with the instructions
received on March 31, he had permitted Salinas to resume his journey
with the extra twenty-four horses and eight mules which were to be
turned over to Barr in Nacogdoches, presumably to be driven on to
De la Rosa. He sent back to San Antonio the other sixteen mules
and two horses, because their use could not be justified by the train
master.[36]

When in May, 1806, Francisco Bermúdez brought countercharges
against De la Rosa, who was attempting to collect certain moneys
which Bermúdez had embezzled, Governor Cordero came to the defence
of De la Rosa. He explained that the case had originated in New
Orleans before the Justice of the Peace of that city, and that De la Rosa
had been authorized by the Marqués de Casa Calvo to appear in the
courts of Coahuila to press the collection of the money due him by
Bermúdez. Strangely enough, Governor Cordero asserted that the
accusation now brought by Bermúdez that De la Rosa had sent large
numbers of horses to Louisiana in violation of regulations was utterly
without foundation. He maintained that De la Rosa had rendered
singular service to the king in the past by permitting the use of his
private pack trains to help keep the East Texas troops in supplies.[37]

Such were the antecedents of the applicant for admission. He now
informed the commandant at Atascosito that he had come to settle in
the Spanish dominions, and presented his documents which were in
order and duly signed by José Vidal, vice-consul in New Orleans. He
explained that he had made his way up the Trinity in a small boat,
because the ship which brought all his worldly possessions, his other
servants, and his family, nineteen persons in all, could not negotiate
the Trinity, and he was compelled, therefore, to leave them behind on

---

[36]Arrambide to Cordero, March 30, and April 2, 1806. *Ibid.,* pp. 135-136.

[37]Cordero to N. Salcedo, May 21, 1806. *A. G. I., Audiencia de Guadalajara,*
104-2-9 (Dunn Transcripts, 1800-1819, pp. 134-35).

Culebra Island. It was impossible, of course, to expect him to leave his family and effects there, and he asked permission to continue to Matagorda Bay, where he could effect a landing. As his explanation seemed plausible and his request fair, the commander of Atascosito, without consulting either Salcedo or Cordero gave him permission to proceed to Matagorda. When he did report to the governor, Cordero readily approved of his action and issued instructions for the settlement of De la Rosa either at Villa de Salcedo or San Marcos.[38]

Not so, the commandant general. Salcedo immediately recalled the applicant's previous record; he suspected that his flimsy excuses were a ruse to introduce contraband goods through the unauthorized Port of Matagorda. He wrote to Cordero at once to express his doubts about the true intent of De la Rosa and to make the observation that he could not have come from New Orleans, unless he had evaded the American embargo now in force. In view of the circumstances, Salcedo ordered him arrested, his goods seized, and the case reported to the king for his decision. But by the time the orders reached Atascosito, De la Rosa had long since departed. Two months passed without news of him. Then one day he reappeared at Atascosito with a touching story of misfortune. He recounted to the astounded commander that shortly after sailing from Culebra Island, he had been blown off his course by a terrific storm which swept him all the way to Campeche. After many hardships, he had succeeded in making his way back to Matagorda Bay, where he had left his ship and come in search of food for his "starving people." Unaware that in two months De la Rosa could have been all the way to the coast of Yucatan and back to New Orleans for fresh supplies and contraband goods, the gullible commander, instead of detaining him, sympathized with him and permitted him to depart again for his ship.

Not until April 8 did he finally enter Matagorda Bay and present the papers he had secured from Vidal to justify his large supply of contraband goods. De la Rosa explained that in order to immigrate to Texas he had been obliged to dispose of his extensive property and many slaves. But since it was not possible to secure money, he had been forced to take merchandise and provisions to the value of 3,000 *pesos,* consular invoices for which had been furnished him. He intended to subsist on the sale of the goods while he was waiting for permission to settle. The cargo was checked and rechecked three times, and each

---

[38]Cordero to M. de Salcedo, January 19, 1808. *Béxar Archives.*

time the results of the inventories were different. When the commandant general was again consulted, he referred the matter to his legal advisor, who, in spite of the incriminating evidence and the record of the applicant, rendered a favorable opinion. He declared that De la Rosa, a Spanish vassal desirous of settling in Spanish territory and possessing the means to live anywhere he chose, was entitled to admission under the decree of September 24, 1803. He had amply proved his good faith, argued the *auditor*, by bringing his family with him. If his intentions had been improper, he would have left them in a safe place. Furthermore, great advantages would accrue to the Spanish dominions from the encouragement of immigrants of this kind; industry would be developed; commerce would thrive; and vast, unproductive regions would be cultivated. All this would result in the spread of the Catholic religion, the development of the country, the happiness of the people, and the glory of the nation. As a precaution, however, it might be well to make De la Rosa and each member of his party take an oath that they had come with good intentions, that they would be faithful vassals of the king, and would obey all local authorities. Reluctantly, the commandant general accepted the recommendations, but added that De la Rosa be required to locate in Coahuila or Nueva Vizcaya, and promise to give information to the Government of all persons whom he might suspect of disloyalty. The members of the crew and the others who were not of the applicant's family were to be ordered to return to Louisiana. After taking an accurate inventory, the authorities were to release the property to De la Rosa; but returns on the sales were to be deposited with and held by the treasurer of Saltillo until the king was consulted and a decision rendered.[39]

In the meantime, the new commander of the frontier, Brigadier General Bonavía, had refused admission to only Juan Narrán, a Sardinian member of the crew, who was married to a Spanish woman. Convinced in his own mind of the good intentions of De la Rosa, and induced by his pleas to save his merchandise from the ravages of constant exposure and to provide a livelihood for his family of nineteen, Bonavía had permitted him to sell it on condition that he post a bond of 2,000 *pesos* with Governor M. de Salcedo to cover the duties. It is not known how much he sold, but he did manage to place an order

---

[39]El Comte Gral. de las Provas Ynterns. de N. E. Acompaña constancias . . . *A.G.I., Audiencia de Guadalajara,* 104-2-9 (Dunn Transcripts, 1800-1819, pp. 258-259).

with the paymaster of the troops in Texas in the amount of 19,000 *pesos*. Bonavía approved of the order at the request of the soldiers, who alleged that De la Rosa gave them better prices than they could get at the annual fair in Saltillo. Bonavía officially notified Viceroy Francisco Xavier Lizaña of the transaction and asked him to instruct the officers of the royal treasury in Vera Cruz to honor the draft, which would be covered by the treasury in Saltillo. Bonavía then stressed the importance of making use of De la Rosa's vessel to ship supplies for the troops in Texas directly from Vera Cruz to Matagorda Bay. He informed the viceroy that he had authorized De la Rosa to sail in ballast to Vera Cruz, so that he could bring back a shipload of supplies if the plan was approved.[40]

It seems strange indeed that Bonavía should have been deceived so completely by De la Rosa. When the commandant general learned of Bonavía's action, he immediately denounced him in the strongest terms to Viceroy Lizaña for having exceeded his powers in requesting the payment of 19,000 *pesos* by the Vera Cruz treasury, and in authorizing De la Rosa to proceed to that port in ballast to bring back supplies for the troops in Texas, especially after he had been warned of De la Rosa's character. He also accused Herrera of collusion in this transaction, but held Bonavía responsible for the consequences. He should have consulted the commandant general before granting permission for his departure for Vera Cruz, Bonavía was told, and he should have requested from Saltillo the money he needed to pay for the supplies. N. Salcedo insinuated in his letter to the viceroy that De la Rosa intended to take advantage of his commission in order to introduce contraband and secure other goods to export without paying duty.[41]

Bonavía hastened to explain to Commandant General Salcedo that he thought De la Rosa had been exonerated by the investigation held upon his first arrival. He apologized for having requested the viceroy to honor his draft on Vera Cruz and promised N. Salcedo to write immediately to Viceroy Lizaña to stop payment. He assured the indignant commandant general that he would comply with his previous orders to arrest De la Rosa, and seize all his property and documents; he requested instructions on the disposition he was to make of the ship and the provision he should make for the family until such time as the case

---

[40]*Ibid.*, *pp.* 259-260.

[41]N. Salcedo to Viceroy Francisco Xavier Lizaña, October 31, 1809. *A. G. I.*, *Audiencia de Guadalajara*, 104-2-9 (Dunn Transcripts, 1800-1819, pp. 250-251).

was decided. In a subsequent letter he attempted to demonstrate the importance of utilizing De la Rosa's vessel to bring sorely needed supplies, such as iron, paper, glass, china, and general food supplies, directly from Vera Cruz by way of Matagorda Bay. To this suggestion the commandant replied that Bonavía was to carry out his explicit instructions: that De la Rosa and his family were to be settled in Coahuila or Nueva Vizcaya—as far removed from the coast as possible; that he was to require De la Rosa to make a sworn statement on all the goods he had sold or handled, in addition to the 19,000-*peso* order for the Texas troops; that he could dispose of the ship as he saw fit; that the proposal for trade between Vera Cruz and Matagorda Bay had not been authorized, since conditions had arisen which made the opening of the latter port inadvisable at this time; and that there was no need of Bonavía's worrying about the De la Rosa family, because the case had already been decided.[42]

In the meantime, De la Rosa, who had sailed supposedly in ballast for Vera Cruz, stopped on the way in the Port of Tampico, and was detained by the officials for carrying contraband goods. As usual, he managed to extricate himself from the embarrassing situation and continued to Vera Cruz, where he must have arrived early in October. He presented his draft to the royal treasury and received the 19,000 *pesos*. Before his departure, however, orders were received from Viceroy Lizaña, in accordance with Bonavía's request which Bonavía had promised the commandant general he would make. De la Rosa, thereupon, was asked to return the money to the royal treasury to be held until the case was decided. Thoroughly aroused by the warning of the commandant general, the viceroy refused to engage De la Rosa for transporting the supplies. Whether or not he obtained a cargo of merchandise to take back to Texas or Louisiana, and what his activities were during this trip will never be known. On November 1 the *Elena* sailed out of Vera Cruz with her master Francisco de la Rosa, who, for some reason, insisted on leaving without further delay—in spite of the storm warnings that had been issued by the port officials. The next day the *Elena* was shipwrecked in a severe storm at Boquilla de Piedra, a short distance from Vera Cruz. All on board were drowned except one of the two soldiers who had taken passage for Matagorda Bay. Don

---

[42]Bonavía to N. Salcedo, September 20, and November 29, 1809; N. Salcedo to Bonavía, October 27, 1809. *A. G. I., Audiencia de Guadalajara,* 104-2-9 (Dunn Transcripts, 1800-1819, pp. 242-244; 245-246; 269-273).

Agustín Quiroga, an uncle of Manuel María de Salcedo in Vera Cruz, informed his nephew on November 11 of the fate that had overtaken the adventurous and enterprising trader from New Orleans. He remarked that it was fortunate for the heirs that the treasury officials had repossessed the 19,000 *pesos*.[43]

Luisa Gertrudis de la Rua, De la Rosa's widow, presented a formal petition to the commandant general for the recovery of the 19,000 *pesos* that had been taken from her husband by the officers of the treasury of Vera Cruz. As the case was complicated, it ultimately reached the Council of the Indies, where a decision was rendered in favor of the widow. It was stated in the decision that De la Rosa had flagrantly violated the law by engaging in contraband at a time when all trade with Louisiana had been prohibited, and when no port was open to foreign commerce, in absolute disregard of the express warning by officials in New Orleans against such action. The heirs, therefore, had forfeited all rights to this money. But such merciless enforcement of the law was contrary to the natural clemency of the king, who desired to temper justice with mercy. The authorities in Texas had been derelict in performing their duty and had been guilty of grave indiscretion. Bonavía had exceeded his powers by granting De la Rosa permission to proceed to Vera Cruz, and had acted injudiciously in view of the incriminating evidence available to him. The colonial officials were to be instructed, therefore, to ascertain the value of the goods introduced by De la Rosa, in order to determine the amount of duties due the royal treasury. This sum was to be deducted from the 21,000 *pesos* (19,000 held by the Vera Cruz treasury and 2,000 posted as bond with the governor of Texas), and the balance was to be turned over to the widow and children of De la Rosa.[44]

The commandant general remonstrated with the king's secretary in a letter in which he pointed out that this particular case was illustrative of the deceitful spirit permeating practically every Louisiana petitioner. He called the secretary's attention to the fact that something was obviously wrong: the merchandise which De la Rosa brought was

---

[43]N. Salcedo to Saavedra, November 7, 1809; M. de Salcedo to Bonavía, December 17, 1809; Constancias. . . *A. G. I., Audiencia de Guadalajara*, 104-2-9 (Dunn Transcripts, 1800-1819, pp. 132-133; 260; 276).

[44]Luisa Gertrudis de la Rua to N. Salcedo, December 17, 1809; Dictamen de la Contaduría, June 14, 1811; Informe del Consejo, January 4, 1812. *A. G. I., Audiencia de Guadalajara*, 104-2-9 (Dunn Transcripts, 1800-1819, pp. 252-263; 277-278).

worth 3,000 *pesos*—at least it was so certified by Vidal, vice-consul of New Orleans—yet, De la Rosa disposed of it for 19,000 *pesos*. He wondered whether or not Vidal, as well as Simón de Herrera, and the newly appointed commander, Brigadier General Bernardo Bonavía, was also guilty of collusion, and he desired the secretary to acquaint His Majesty with the circumstances of the case in order that those responsible for this flagrant violation of the trade regulations and the immigration laws might be charged with the blame.[45]

New settlers in East Texas. The case of De la Rosa has been given at length, because it furnishes a vivid insight into the character of the immigrants and the difficulties which commanders were confronted with and had to solve. But this was by no means an isolated instance. During the year 1808, many came, as the commandant general persistently contended, for no other purpose than to engage in contraband trade, and became thoroughly angry when obstacles were placed in their way, even though the laws were not enforced with the rigor recommended. Many of those who had been moved from Atascosito to Villa de Salcedo to prevent communication with friends and relatives in Louisiana repeatedly requested permission to return to their former homes under the pretext of bringing back property left behind. Among them were Santiago Fear and Juan Debis (John Davis?). Davis, in particular, complained bitterly of the privations and discomforts endured at Villa de Salcedo. He declared that his wife had been sick ever since her removal, and that it had been extremely difficult, under the stringent regulations in force, to secure the essentials of life.[46] Some did not even take the trouble to secure permission to leave. Salomé Duxen (Solomon Dixon?) resorted to a ruse. He asked permission to go to Atascosito to bring back some property which he had left there. In possession of a passport, and accompanied by a brother and his family, he left with his wife and child ostensibly for Atascosito, but did not stop until he reached Louisiana. Immediately orders were given to all frontier commanders to issue no more such passports except in very special cases, and never to permit anyone without a permit to leave for Louisiana.[47]

The wisdom of this restriction is revealed by a letter of the tireless Clouet, who wrote to Cordero in June, 1808, that everything that went

---

[45]N. Salcedo to Saavedra, November 7, 1809. *Ibid.*, pp. 242-244.

[46]M. de Salcedo to Cordero, June 14, July 12, 1808, and January 19, 1809. *Béxar Archives.*

[47]M. de Salcedo to the commander of Trinidad, December 5, 1808. *Béxar Archives.*

on in Texas was common knowledge in New Orleans. This news could be attributed to no other source than that of the returned settlers—the very ones who had sought permission to enter Texas as former "loyal subjects" of the king.[48] However, there were some who, although not entirely satisfied with conditions and having no particular love for either the Spaniards or Catholicism, were determined to remain in order to reap the fruits of their honest labor as well as the profits of illegal business. Such a one was Juan Dribread, who wrote his wife in Missouri that he could not afford to return to Cape Girardeau to bring his family for fear of losing out on the rise in value of his lands. John Magee boasted to his brother in Coteilla, Louisiana, that he and another brother had been able to secure two excellent pieces of land along the Trinity, which they stocked well with horses and cattle, and that "with the help of God" they were doing well in their commercial enterprises. He had, as a matter of fact, he explained to his brother, been able to buy several ranches which he expected soon to improve so as to enhance their value. Magee dealt mainly in strong liquors, such as mescal and taffia; occasionally, he did sell a piece of calico, some "pelloncey" (brown sugar bars), or a pair of shoes. Not all his customers were men, according to his book of accounts. Among his best customers were his wife, sister of the worthless William Burxer, and a certain Molly Ann, who seems to have appeared quite regularly to satisfy her craving for alcohol. Magee apparently procured his sugar and flour from Béxar, and his liquor and dry goods from Natchitoches. His was a thriving business in Villa de Salcedo, for most of the new settlers were his customers.[49]

More interesting and significant, were the activities of Miguel Quinn. He wrote to a St. Louis lawyer named Beulitt (Judge Bullett?) in October, 1808, that for several days he had kept practically all his goods loaded on a train of horses ready to set out for that place, but that, fearing detection, he had not left. He informed his friend that he had been more than three hundred leagues farther into the interior and had been successful in carrying on some trade, but that it was not always a safe investment because of the uncertainty of the market. He inquired the price of horses in St. Louis, for he was planning to take a drove there, if the settlement of certain business matters with a Mr. Hoistin (Austin?) at La Mina (Mine à Burton?) required his presence. He also asked if the Americans were really going to press their claims

[48]Clouet to Cordero, June 22, 1808. *Béxar Archives.*
[49]Hatcher, *The Opening of Texas to Foreign Settlement*, 140-142.

to the Río Grande, and if they didn't insist on this boundary, how far they would advance their frontier into Texas. He bluntly told Beulitt that he was anxious to secure this information to enable him to buy good locations in the area to be occupied by the United States.[50]

Could this Mr. Hoistin have been Moses Austin of the lead mines of Mine à Burton? This possibility has been suggested, as has been the fact that in 1816, Austin referred to the arrival of a Judge Bullett, of St. Louis, who may well have been the Beulitt to whom Quinn wrote in 1808. This may all have had an influence on the enterprising Austin in determining him to try to recoup his lost fortune in Texas.[51]

The bishop of Nuevo León had visited the distant frontier in 1806, and stated two years later that most of the immigrants had been drawn to Texas by the hope of enormous profits from contraband trade, that they were not Catholics, and that their living conditions were deplorable from the point of view of Christian morals. The commandant general immediately inquired of Cordero if these charges could be substantiated. The governor replied that the immigrants were neither immoral, nor were they confirmed contraband traders, or disloyal subjects. In self-defence, he argued that immigration regulations had been carefully observed, and that, as far as he knew, there had been no disorders. He took occasion to assert that not all settlers were engaged in contraband trade or were responsible for circulating valuable information in Louisiana. Cordero excused illegal trade on the grounds of necessity, and painted a vivid picture of the privations of the settlers in Salcedo and East Texas, of their insignificant commerce with Béxar, Laredo, and San Juan Bautista, because these miserable outposts themselves lacked the necessary supplies. He dwelt at length upon the difficulties encountered by the new settlers in securing stock to develop their ranches. The number of smuggling cases reported did not necessarily afford incontrovertible proof that the settlers had been bent on engaging in contraband trade merely for the profits to be gained therefrom. The large number might possibly indicate that the settlers had been unable to secure necessary supplies within the province itself. He believed, too, that the frontier officials deserved, not condemnation, but commendation for the efficiency they had displayed in enforcing the law in so many cases. With regard to the presence of a large number of slaves and deserters in Villa de Salcedo, Cordero reminded the com-

[50]*Ibid.*, 142.
[51]Hatcher, *The Opening of Texas to Foreign Settlement*, 142-143.

mandant general that he himself had ordered them there.[52] While it is true that Cordero's arguments to exonerate the settlers justified their actions somewhat, nevertheless, the cases cited show that Cordero and his fellow officials had been lax almost to the point of criminal negligence in admitting suspicious characters whose activities more than bore out the fears of the commandant general.

Nemesio Salcedo now attempted to remedy the situation by ordering the expulsion of the worst offenders with the warning that they would be severely punished if they returned. The orders were transmitted early in January, 1809, to the new governor of Texas, Manuel María de Salcedo, who forwarded them to the commander of Villa de Salcedo. The settlers affected immediately protested that they were unable to leave, because they had lost most of their stock during the winter and needed time to gather their scattered property and to dispose of what they had "accumulated by the sweat of their brow during their residence in Texas." They were not without a staunch defender. Father Sosa, who, it will be remembered, had been sent to care for the new settlers of Villa de Salcedo, entered a strong plea in their behalf. He pointed out that they had always shown an interest in the teachings of the Church. They had, however, been greatly impeded in learning the doctrines of the Church by their inability to understand Spanish and their lack of time for taking instructions after working long hours to make a living. Father Sosa reported that, in spite of these handicaps, they all had been baptized and, consequently, must be considered Catholics. Local authorities joined their pastor in his plea and attested to the fact that some of those coming under the expulsion order had been industrious, useful, and loyal. Their combined efforts, nevertheless, proved unavailing. Tomás Dallete, Juan Eromdreke, his wife, Serafina Esmiete, Remigio Bodro, and María Magdalena Benua (charged with immorality) had to leave Trinidad de Salcedo.[53]

Cordero, irritated by the commandant general's repeated incriminations, informed him in January, 1809, that he was planning a tour of inspection of all the new settlements and outposts. Salcedo, thereupon, instructed him to gather all the evidence possible on undesirables and to have them expelled immediately. To avoid difficulty in the future

---

[52]Cordero to N. Salcedo, December 15, 1808. *Béxar Archives.*

[53]M. de Salcedo to the commander of Trinidad, February 4, and March 21, 1809; commander of Trinidad to M. de Salcedo, including the statement by Father Sosa. *Béxar Archives.*

with persons who would only have to be deported later, the commandant general instructed Cordero at this time to refer all applicants in the future to him and to admit no one under any circumstances without his previous consent.[54] Thus, at long last Salcedo took matters into his own hands to put a definite stop to the infiltration of unscrupulous and disloyal adventurers, who tried to take advantage of the royal decree of September 24, 1803, which had opened the Spanish dominions to the king's former subjects in Louisiana. This was the first step in putting an effectual stop to the flow of immigration.

The spectre of French and American aggression. Salcedo, while not minimizing the danger from Frenchmen to the Spanish colonies, still believed that the interest of the United States in the vast territories of His Majesty might prove a still greater menace. His apprehensions, as well as those of Viceroy Pedro de Garibay, were considerably increased early in 1809, by a dispatch from Valentín de Foronda, chargé d'affaires in Philadelphia. He warned that a large fleet was being assembled at Norfolk to transport 4,000 troops to New Orleans. Foronda reported that he had inquired from the United States Government the purpose of this expedition but had received only an evasive answer. Perhaps they were going down to observe the movements of the English, who, he said, "had signified their intention of visiting their friends, the Spaniards, at Baton Rouge." But rumors were current to the effect that more troops were to descend the Mississippi, and that Congress expected to call out 50,000 volunteers, who were to be placed under the command of the troublesome Wilkinson.[55]

The preparations of the United States, suspiciously warlike, were confirmed by Vicente Folch, governor of West Florida, who suspected Napoleon of instigating, or at least abetting, the American move on the Spanish colonies. Strangely enough, the Marqués de Someruelos, Captain General of Cuba, also warned Viceroy Garibay at about this same time that Napoleon was supporting the plans of the United States to further his own ambitions of conquest. He urged the viceroy, therefore, not to lose one moment in fortifying the defences of Texas, Louisiana, and Florida. It was useless to expect aid from Spain, he observed, because the mother country was already calling upon her colonies to help her defeat France. Vidal, whose loyalty was open to doubt because

---

[54]Salcedo to Cordero, March 13, 1809. *Béxar Archives.*

[55]Foronda to N. Salcedo, January 6, 1809. *Béxar Archives.*

of his shady connections with contraband traders, joined the group of alarmists who were pressing the harassed officials of New Spain to greater efforts against the aggressive plans of the United States and France. He pointed out that the French sympathizers in the United States were enjoying great popularity.[56]

Thoroughly aroused to the danger, both Viceroy Garibay and Commandant General N. Salcedo made frantic efforts to meet the threat impending along the frontier of New Spain. The gravity of the situation took on an even more ominous aspect when the commandant general received instructions from Spain's *Junta Central* to prevent the landing of the king and queen or any of their representatives in any port, and to refuse them admission, should they present themselves at the frontier. This communication declared that Napoleon, in desperation, had decided to send the king and queen to America to create dissension, and thus enable him to gain control of the colonies. The order explained that Napoleon was forcing the sovereigns to take refuge in the colonies. Should they appear, they were to be taken into custody, treated with the respect due them, kept from communicating with anyone, and sent back to Spain with all their entourage. Commandant General N. Salcedo sent this order to the officials in Texas and added his own instructions to keep a close watch on Juan Cortés, of Natchitoches, and Baron de Bastrop, who were suspected of being implicated in the French and American plots. He declared that it was absolutely necessary to cut off all immigration and communication with Louisiana as a precautionary measure against spies. No one was to be admitted, therefore, regardless of documents, affidavits, or passports, until further instructions. Moreover, those returning from Louisiana were to be arrested at the frontier.[57]

New military commander for Texas. It was in this crisis that the *Junta Central* decided to send Brigadier General Bernardo Bonavía, governor of Durango, to take charge of military operations and to act as coördinator of defence in the remote province of Texas. This appointment was not intended as a reflection on Cordero, who had served long on the frontier and, according to his liberal ideas, faithfully. Cordero, still governor of Coahuila, was sorely needed there at the time. He

---

[56]Someruelos to Viceroy Pedro de Garibay, February 2, 6, and 12, 1809; Vidal to Garibay, February 13, 1809. *Nacogdoches Archives.*

[57]Order of the *Suprema Junta Central*, March 1, 1809, transmitted with letter of N. Salcedo to Bonavía, June 22, 1809. *Nacogdoches Archives;* and *A. G. I., Audiencia de Guadalajara*, 104-2-25 (Dunn Transcripts, 1800-1819, p. 212).

was instructed by the commandant general, however, to remain in Texas as long as necessary to acquaint the new commander with the duties of administration and the principal problems confronting him.

Bonavía, after Nemesio Salcedo himself, was the ablest officer on the northern frontier. He had played an important role in putting into effect many of the reforms of Charles III on trade and commerce. As early as 1788, he had been named governor of Texas, but due to the need of his services on other frontiers, he was not then able to serve in that capacity. When the Texas-Louisiana boundary dispute became acute in 1806, he, with the governors of Nuevo León and Coahuila, had been ordered transferred to Texas. Again he was unable to join his comrades-in-arms, because he was urgently needed in Durango.[58] Absolutely convinced that free trade was the greatest incentive to the development of all activities, Bonavía immediately joined Simón de Herrera, Cordero, and M. de Salcedo in their efforts to foster immigration and trade relations between New Spain, Texas, and Louisiana.

On March 24, 1809, before Bonavía arrived in Texas, the commandant general had written a long letter to the new commander of defence to acquaint him with his plans and to request him to study certain documents and consult with the three governors already in the province to learn as much as he could about its population, its Indian tribes, and its boundaries, in order to enable him to formulate an effective plan and offer such suggestions as he might deem best to improve conditions and strengthen the defences.

Nemesio Salcedo's defence plans. Commandant General N. Salcedo explained that his plan of defence, conceived several years before, included the development of Villa de Salcedo as a base for the troops on the farthest frontier; the assignment of an adequate number of troops to the crossings on the San Marcos and the Guadalupe rivers, in order to insure safe and rapid communication between San Antonio, Villa de Salcedo, and the other outposts on the Texas-Louisiana frontier; the fortification of San Antonio as the province's principal stronghold to which, in the event of invasion, the troops could retire so as the better to check the further advance of the enemy until reënforcements could be rushed to their aid; and additions to the garrison at La Bahía, which was to become the base of operations for the detachments as-

---

[58]N. Salcedo to M. de Salcedo, March 24, 1809. *Béxar Archives.* For his services in connection with the commercial reforms of Charles III, see Priestley, H. I., *José de Galvéz,* 32-27; 312-390.

signed to patrol the entire Gulf coast. That part of the plan pertaining to the defence of the coastal area called for winning over the Indians in the region in order to secure their coöperation in preventing landings by the enemy or in securing immediate information on such landings. He also hoped to find a place on the coast where he could establish a good port to which supplies could be shipped directly from Vera Cruz; but it was his intention not to occupy or even start settling and fortifying it until circumstances demanded such a measure.

He confided to Bonavía that he intended to abandon Nacogdoches, where there were no means for its fortification, where sickness was prevalent among the soldiers and the settlers the year round, where the surrounding country was so barren that it barely produced the essentials of life, and where disloyal citizens, smugglers, and spies were harbored. Under the circumstances, he felt that this post would offer more comfort to the enemy than protection to His Majesty's dominions. But he was not yet ready to carry out this phase of his plan. The importance of retaining the friendship of the Indians made it imperative to select one or two other strategic places on the eastern frontier where agents might establish their headquarters to trade among the natives. By way of conclusion he explained the existing regulations on Louisiana emigrants, and warned him not to permit any one—under any circumstances—to settle at Atascosito.[59]

It will be recalled that Governor M. de Salcedo immediately upon his arrival in Texas ardently sponsored immigration. On March 20 Don Manuel wrote Commandant General Nemesio Salcedo to suggest that those who were clamoring to enter the province be settled on the vacant lands of the secularized missions in San Antonio. Innocently or not, he set forth the benefits that would accrue to old Villa de San Fernando from the services of these new and industrious citizens, and emphasized the fact that the applicants would be saved much time and labor in getting rehabilitated and becoming self-supporting.

Commandant General N. Salcedo replied on April 2 that the existent regulations were to be observed strictly, and that all applicants now in San Antonio, as well as those who had settled there, were to be sent to Villa de Salcedo. He declared that these regulations resulted, not from arbitrary whims or fancy, but from the lessons of bitter experience. The commandant general instructed Don Manuel to reserve the lands in the vicinity of San Antonio for more deserving subjects of

[59] N. Salcedo to Bonavía, March 24, 1809. *Béxar Archives.*

the king, and reminded him that the principal purpose of immigration was not to make it easy for the newcomers to reap the fruits of predecessors but rather to develop new lands. For the benefit of the new governor, he cited the case of Doctor Federico Zerbán as illustrative of the kind of person who sought to settle in areas already developed. This interesting character Cordero placed in charge of the first military hospital in Texas, although he had to admit that he was compelled to make use of Zerbán's services because there was no other physician available. Recently this American doctor had induced José Joaquín Ugarte, commander of Nacogdoches, to grant a certain Ramón de Legarreta some land at the Indian mounds, just across the Neches River. Fourteen months later, Zerbán, contrary to law, had Legarreta transfer to himself title to this land (5 leagues square). Commandant General N. Salcedo instructed Governor M. de Salcedo, therefore, to nullify the grant immediately and inform the interested party that this action was to serve as an example to all others. Finally, he requested the governor to acquaint himself with the various land grant records in his office and to nullify all similar transactions.[60]

There were only a few exceptions to the order requiring immigrants in San Antonio to be sent to Villa de Salcedo. Among them were Baron de Bastrop, and Daniel Boone; Lorenzo Reveque, who was too old to be sent back; José Rossi, who had established the first pottery shop in San Antonio; Carlos Marasen, who was employed as an interpreter; and Pedro Longueville, who had resided in San Antonio for many years. These instructions of the commandant general reversed his original decision that immigrants be settled in the interior, or at least near Spanish towns already well-established. He, likewise, changed his policy in regard to deserters. They were no longer to be permitted to enter the province as settlers unless they could produce satisfactory evidence of good moral character.[61] Evocative of sympathy as the commandant general's position may have been, his excessive caution was exasperating. Governor de Salcedo, like his fellow officials in Texas, grew restive under the ever-increasing restrictions designed to check immigration.

New plans for defence. Bonavía had arrived at San Antonio in the meantime, on April 17. The new commander of the frontier was

---

[60]N. Salcedo to M. de Salcedo, April 2, 1809. *Nacogdoches Archives*, XI, pp. 235-238.

[61]N. Salcedo to Bonavía, May 12, 1809. *Béxar Archives*.

anxious to secure the opinion of those who had been in the province for several years trying to solve the problems connected with its defence and development. He lost no time in requesting all ranking officials to prepare for him a written statement of their views on these important questions, for in his communication to them he said he wished to devise a plan based on their experience to bring about not only the security of the frontier but also the development of Texas into a prosperous province. Each of the governors complied with the request and expressed himself with frankness. In the opinions rendered, we find an analysis of the causes retarding the development of Texas, and the state of affairs at the time. Their suggestions for improvements might have proved salutary had not certain events intervened to preclude the possibility of putting them into effect.

Cordero's opinion. The first to reply was Governor Cordero, the veteran supporter of immigration. Convinced that the security of Texas was of paramount importance to the safety of all New Spain, he proposed the organization of a regiment of provincial cavalry. This force aided by an adequate body of mobile troops stationed along the frontier and on the principal river crossings would be sufficient, in the event of a sudden attack, to hold the enemy in check until reënforcements could be rushed from the interior. He apparently was not one of those who believed that an open attack by the United States was imminent, but he did believe that deficiency in the number of settlers in East Texas was largely responsible for the advance of American claims to the Sabine. In his judgment, it was important to the defence of this strategic area not only to hold and fortify Nacogdoches, but also to settle the surrounding country—and that as soon as possible. Withdrawal from this outpost would certainly result in the United States' advancing claims to the Río Grande. Fortunately for Spain, the presence of only a small garrison at Bayou Pierre had so far kept the Americans out of the territory occupied solely by Indians.

Immigration was Cordero's panacea for the ills of Texas. Once started on the topic of immigration, he waxed eloquent. Cognizant of the various arguments advanced by the commandant general on different occasions for evacuating the Nacogdoches outpost, he presented arguments in refutation. The sickness and suffering endured by the troops in that region could be remedied by exercising foresight in arranging for their care. More settlers should be established not only at Nacogdoches and in its vicinity but also on each of the rivers between the frontier and San Antonio, as well as along the coast. He reminded Bonavía that the king had three years previously authorized the opening of the Port of San Bernardo. Opening this port now would contribute greatly to the development of all the Interior Provinces, and would at the same time strengthen the defences of Texas.

The maintenance of friendly relations with all the Indian tribes he considered to be equally important. To that end, he advocated the establishment of a general trading house in San Antonio, with branches at Bayou Pierre, Nacogdoches, and Villa Salcedo. These Spanish trading posts would cut down American-Indian trade, which was quite extensive. He pointed out that through trade the natives' friendship was won or lost.

He made one more recommendation. It seemed to him that, in view of the importance of the province of Texas in the general plan for the defence of the entire northern frontier, its commander should be given military jurisdiction over all the Interior Provinces. He suggested that he be invested with powers similar to those which had been granted General Grimarest.[62]

The efforts of Governor Cordero to secure settlers from the interior of Mexico for establishing the proposed settlement west of San Antonio, as well as for the new Villa de San Marcos de Neve, have already been noted. His work as a colonizer had won him some reputation in the northern provinces of Mexico. One of his greatest admirers and best promoters was Father José María Puelles, former missionary of Nacogdoches. Everywhere he went, he told of Cordero's success in founding colonies, and enumerated the natural advantages which the province offered prospective settlers. In March, 1809, Father Puelles wrote Cordero that 100 families, more than 1,500 persons, had decided to go to Texas but were held back only by lack of transportation. They were ready to enlist for military service in the province, provided they were furnished the means of moving their families and effects. The missionary enthusiastically extolled the character of the colonists, and added that many of them were persons of unusual attainments and considerable wealth. He assured the governor that many were anxious to answer his call, because they had heard of his remarkable success in establishing settlements in Texas. This letter, in spite of its exaggeration and flattery, evidences the results of Cordero's efforts in promoting interest in Texas among the inhabitants of the northern provinces of Mexico.

---

[62]Cordero to Bonavía, April 23, 1809. *Béxar Archives.*

Manuel de Salcedo's suggestions. Unlike Cordero, the new governor, Manuel de Salcedo, who had lived in Louisiana and consequently had the advantage of knowing the Government and people of the United States, was of the opinion that Texas was more seriously threatened at this time than ever before. The ambitious claims of the Americans plus their extensive and growing trade with the Indians represented a real danger. The province in its present condition was helpless before their resolute advance. It could not withstand American encroachments unless it could get more settlers and soldiers. His estimate of the population was more than liberal, however, for he declared that there were approximately 8,000 persons exclusive of the 1,069 soldiers. His figure must have included the Indians in the province.

After paying high tribute to the sturdy and resourceful Spanish settlers in Texas, Governor de Salcedo declared that the Americans were still more resourceful than the Spaniards, and were by nature sturdy, courageous, and enterprising. The Texas setup was inadequate to prevent the Americans from penetrating the Spanish dominions. He cited numerous instances of Americans' entering Texas without a permit and travelling from New Madrid, Natchez, Natchitoches, and other places in Louisiana far into the interior. Don Manuel's purpose in extolling American prowess was to impress upon Bonavía, the new commander, the absolute necessity of obtaining additional troops and settlers for more effectively enforcing a policy of exclusion. To offset the natural abilities of the Americans, the officials of New Spain could depend only on the loyalty of the Spaniards in Texas and the attachment of the people in lower Louisiana to the king of Spain, the superb horsemanship and inexhaustible supply of horses of the Spaniards, their intimate knowledge of the country, and their friendship with the Indians who had for years traded with them. The new governor believed that attainment of parity with the Americans required the reënforcement of the scattered Texas establishments with troops and settlers.

Referring to the proposed retirement from Nacogdoches, Governor de Salcedo resolutely opposed that move and any other plan calling for the abandonment of places now held by the Spaniards. He agreed with ex-Governor Cordero that such a step would but invite new encroachments by the Americans, who would advance as quickly as the Spaniards retired. The governor proposed, therefore, that the entire frontier along the Sabine be reënforced, that new posts be established at such points as might be deemed advisable, and that the coast, likewise, be garrisoned.

To strengthen and supply the new military posts he suggested that new settlements be founded in their vicinity. Don Manuel then asserted that the detachment at Atascosito had been unnecessarily subjected to hardships, because colonists who could have supplied the troops with fresh vegetables, meat, and milk had been excluded from that region. He contended, however, that Villa Salcedo should be strengthened if it remained on its present site. The only justification for its continued location at the crossing on the Trinity was, in his opinion, its necesssity to Nacogdoches for assistance; but to be of effective assistance, the villa would have to be developed into a populous center and strengthened by a larger military detachment. Better still, if a suitable place could be found at a more strategic point, closer to San Antonio, the villa should be moved.

The governor presented some very formidable arguments for removing ineffectual restrictions on immigration. He considered it short of criminal for the officials to allow the rich lands of this vast province to remain uncultivated. If the port authorized by the king was opened and trade permitted with the rest of New Spain and the world at large, the province would become prosperous and thickly populated in a very short time.[63] Governor de Salcedo differed with ex-Governor Cordero only on details; they agreed on the fundamentals for developing the province and its defence.

Herrera's recommendations. Simón de Herrera's experience as military commander of the Spanish forces stationed on the frontier of Texas had convinced the governor of Nuevo León that the adequate defence of Texas required a larger permanent army. He agreed with Cordero that the commander should be granted powers similar to those which had been given General Grimarest as Commandant General of the Eastern Interior Provinces. He would then have the authority to dispose all the available forces in the adjoining provinces as circumstances demanded. Herrera considered the opening of the authorized Port of San Bernardo as of utmost importance in maintaining this larger military force in Texas. This port at Bahía on Matagorda Bay, he said, would facilitate acquisition of material directly from Vera Cruz and Tampico with more regularity and at much less expense.

Having been stationed on the eastern frontier for the last three years, he had been enabled to study the conditions and appraise the strategic value of Nacogdoches in the general plan for the defence of the province.

---

[63]M. de Salcedo to Bonavía, April 24, 1809. *Béxar Archives*. Copy in the *Nacogdoches Archives*, XI, pp. 238-254.

He declared that territory was fertile and could be brought under cultivation. It would be well, however, to adopt measures for improving sanitary conditions. That the people of this frontier outpost were not disloyal to the king was attested to by the fact that many of them had served him long and faithfully. He recommended holding both Nacogdoches and Bayou Pierre. Withdrawal would be interpreted as an indication of military weakness by the Americans, who would probably advance on the heels of the Spaniards to occupy the abandoned territory. He urged the maintenance of a respectable force in Texas to guard the frontier and prevent American explorers and traders from penetrating Spanish territory with impunity.[64]

Bonavía's conclusions. Finding that his able associates shared his own opinions and that his position was strengthened by their support, Bonavía wrote to Commandant General N. Salcedo that the situation was grave and required immediate attention to enact effective measures. Texas, he declared, was the keystone to the king's dominions. As such, its defence was imperative—no matter what the cost—but the forces and means at his disposal were inadequate. Referring to his instructions of March 24, which called for evacuation of the Nacogdoches area, reduction of military forces, further restriction of immigration, and postponement of the opening of the Port of San Bernardo, Bonavía presented arguments in refutation of each of these measures which, he declared, were diametrically opposed to the development of the province and its defence. There was no gainsaying the fact that the Americans had been displaying considerable interest in the vast, uninhabited areas along the frontier, and that they would continue their advance into Spanish territory and increase their claims until they reached the Río Grande and even the country beyond—unless these lands were settled by Spanish subjects, and a force capable of commanding respect was maintained in Texas.

Bonavía pleaded for additional forces and the whole-hearted support of the commandant general and the viceroy. He protested his impotence to place the province in a state of defence unless his recommendations were approved and acted upon immediately. It was of vital importance, he pointed out, to take advantage of American inactivity by adopting effective measures and taking the necessary steps to defend the frontier at once against future advance. Of his recommendations, he considered the opening of a port the most important. He expressed great surprise

---

[64]Herrera to Bonavía, April 25, 1809. *Béxar Archives.*

that the people of this remote province had not even heard of the reforms instituted by Charles III in regard to free trade. Bonavía was most interested in these economic reforms, for he had been influential in developing and putting into effect the new liberal policy. He could not understand how a province blessed with so many navigable rivers had been deprived of a seaport for so long. In his opinion, the lack of a port was the factor contributing most to the wretched condition of the people inhabiting a land which possessed every advantage of nature to convert it into the most prosperous region in North America.

Bonavía's solution called for the appointment of a commander with complete and independent jurisdiction over all the Eastern Interior Provinces, as had been intended in the time of General Grimarest. Investing this authority in one responsible person would obviate the endless delays caused by the differences of opinion between the officers on the frontier and the distant commandant general of the Interior Provinces. The Texas frontier, at once the most vulnerable area and the most vital to the safety of Spanish interests, should have a commander with full power to communicate directly with the highest as well as the lowest Spanish and American officials whenever circumstances demanded. This frank criticism was a direct assault on what Bonavía considered the commandant general's obstructionist policy, which had often been inveighed against by Antonio Cordero, Manuel de Salcedo, and Simón de Herrera.

Immigration restrictions Bonavía attacked with the same fearlessness. The frontier commander denounced as fallacious the wishful thinking of those who trusted that the vast, uninhabited areas in Texas constituted an impassable barrier to American advance. The facts disproved that contention. Bonavía drew a sharp distinction between uninhabitable and uninhabited territory. The lands along the Texas-Louisiana frontier were uninhabited, but their fertility made them anything but uninhabitable. Failure of the Spaniards to occupy this rich region had not been deterring the Americans from it, but had been extending a most welcome invitation to them to settle in it. He argued logically that the abandonment of Nacogdoches or of any other point already occupied would only invite the Americans to push their unchallenged advance into this area also. Consequently, every effort should be made, he contended, to increase the number of settlers all along the frontier and throughout the province, preferably by people from the interior of Mexico.[65]

---

[65]Bonavía to N. Salcedo, April 26, 1809. *Béxar Archives.*

At the same time Bonavía wrote directly to Cornel, Spain's Secretary of War, to present the case of Texas as he saw it, for he was convinced that his request for putting a constructive program into operation with regard to immigration and free trade would be refused by the commandant general. In this interesting communication he declared that he and the others who were actually acquainted with the true conditions were in absolute agreement on the policy that should be adopted to defend the province. They, too, opposed the commandant general's plans of not only abandoning certain strategic frontier areas, but also of restricting still further the immigration of former subjects desirous of forming new settlements in Texas. They wished to go on record as in disfavor of those plans and in favor of admitting all immigrants except individuals proved disloyal. "In my opinion," he declared, "encouraging communications by sea and land and permitting free trade would be the best means of increasing the population." The introduction of families at government expense, he believed, should be left out of consideration. Such a scheme would be tantamount to robbing Peter to pay Paul. In the past, the region whence they came was depopulated, the treasury was burdened not only by unnecessary but also by excessive expenses, and the settlers were generally dissatisfied with the place to which they were moved. The policy had ultimately brought misfortune and unhappiness to all concerned. Wisely he remarked, "Wherever people find prosperity, protection, and security, there they will go without being called."

Bonavía did not consider the United States a serious menace, because he thought the Constitution did not allow of the vigor necessary to make for conquest. He realized, however, that the avaricious, unscrupulous, and aggressive citizens had to be watched constantly and held back by an adequate force. The frontier commander pleaded with the Secretary of War for the establishment of the independent command of the Eastern Interior Provinces as previously planned. This he regarded as essential to the effective protection of the province and all New Spain. To postpone enactment of this measure was to continue wasting time and squandering opportunities. He made it plain that he had no personal interest in the matter and was not advocating the measure in order to be appointed commander. "If I had been commandant general of the Interior Provinces," he wrote, "I would have delegated the command of the Eastern Interior Provinces to Colonel Antonio Cordero, who, in addition to expert knowledge on all pertinent matters, possesses the professional skill of a military commander and the ability of a diplomat in maintaining friendship with the Indians."[66]

Neither the detailed opinions of the three governors in Texas nor the arguments of the new frontier commander convinced the cautious commandant general. As early as May 13, N. Salcedo instructed Bonavía to make no changes whatsoever in the existing regulations in regard to either immigration or trade until the whole matter was considered by the viceroy. To a second proposal for adopting simpler regulations he replied on June 22 that, in view of the warning issued by the *Junta Central* concerning the plans of Napoleon, it was imperative to close the doors completely to all Louisianians irrespective of their reasons for seeking admission. To put a stop to all communication between the two provinces, it was necessary also to arrest every Spanish subject returning to Texas.[67]

The new governor, Manuel de Salcedo, was not easily dissuaded. He seems to have been earnestly concerned about developing the province placed in his care. Early in May, before the commandant general had repeated his stringent orders to stop all immigration, the governor made another review of the situation in Texas, and pleaded that more liberal immigration and trade policies were essential to the development of the province. He sought, likewise, the determination of the Texas-Louisiana boundary and the colonization of Texas. Governor de Salcedo severely condemned the removal of settlers from Atascosito to Villa Salcedo. He requested the immediate authorization of new settlements on the Frio, the Nueces, and the Arroyo San Miguel for easier and safer communications between Texas, Coahuila, and Nuevo Santander. Doubtlessly informed by Cordero of the failure in 1806 to occupy the Nueces with immigrants from Nuevo Santander, he adjudged that policy shortsighted, and advocated new settlements in all directions from San Antonio. He suggested that they be established at Tortuga, one of the villages of the Taovayas on Red River; at Palo Alto, in the vicinity of the Tawakoni; at the village of the Tonkawas on the headwaters of the Colorado; and along the coast. The settlements on the Colorado and the Red would prove useful in maintaining communications with New Mexico, while those on the coast would prevent the invasion of Spanish territory from the sea.

---

[66]Bonavía to Cornel, May 31, 1809. The letter is cited in full by Hatcher, *The Opening of Texas to Foreign Settlement*, 157-158.

[67]N. Salcedo to Bonavía, May 13, and June 22, 1809. *A. G. I., Audiencia de Guadalajara*, 104-2-25 (Dunn Transcripts, 1800-1819, pp. 210-212).

Governor de Salcedo possibly had a sympathetic place in his heart for Louisianans. He again pointed out how much cheaper and more convenient it would be to bring settlers from Louisiana than to attempt to bring them from Spain or the interior of Mexico. By opening a port on the Gulf coast and allowing the former subjects of the king to emigrate to Texas, two ends would be attained: the extension of the king's benevolent protection to former subjects, as the king himself desired, and the increase in the population of the province. A port on the Gulf coast would enable the settlers to import the goods they needed at much more reasonable prices and to export their surplus products for much better prices. This measure would result in the rapid development of the province and the prosperity of its people.[68]

In line with the petition of the governor, Bonavía called a new *Junta* to discuss measures for the development of Texas as a means of defence. On June 19, at nine in the morning, the meeting was opened by Bonavía in his residence. The roll call was answered by Colonel Antonio Cordero, governor of Coahuila; Lieutenant Colonel Simón de Herrera, governor of Nuevo León and commander of the auxiliary troops of the viceroyalty on the frontier; Lieutenant Colonel Manuel de Salcedo, governor of Texas; and Captain Mariano Varela, secretary of the *Junta*. Bonavía explained that the development of the province went hand in hand with its defence. A larger body of troops could not be maintained, he said, without a larger population, one capable of supplying the soldiers with food. Likewise, agriculture, trade, and the arts could not develop without an increase in population and adequate protection. Growth in population would bring the development of agriculture, the increase of trade, and the promotion of the arts; settlers would be attracted in larger numbers; and the prosperity of the province would be assured. But it was necessary to begin with the simpler tasks that would lead to the attainment of the desired end. He, therefore, proceeded to make a number of recommendations for the consideration and approval of the *Junta*.

Bonavía first recommended giving more encouragement to immigrants who were former subjects of the king and gave satisfactory evidence of high moral character. This did not at all mean throwing caution to the winds and admitting undesirables. Such an extreme policy would produce nothing but evil consequences.

Improvement of the settlements already established, he believed, was most important to the future development of the province. There was

---

[68]M. de Salcedo to N. Salcedo, May 7, 1809. *Béxar Archives*.

urgent need for the erection of numerous public offices in San Antonio for proper administration.

Lines of communication from San Antonio to other towns within the province and to neighboring provinces should be improved, kept up, and better guarded. The more difficult crossings should be repaired; canoes and ferryboats built and placed on the larger streams; and new settlements established at suitable locations along the old roads by those who were willing to found them. The establishment of these new settlements would be facilitated by discontinuing the practice of forcing all immigrants to settle in only designated areas.

Turning his attention next to the four missions in San Antonio, Bonavía pointed out that the Indians still living in them were so inconsequential in number that they were insufficient to form even the nucleus of a town. The four churches were in good condition, he reported, and were being taken care of by two missionaries. He proposed that the mission lands be surveyed for four new towns, and be subdivided into lots and farms. Worthy subjects of the king should be permitted to purchase or should be assigned land in the new towns for meritorious services. In either event, the settlers should be required to cultivate and develop their property and to maintain school. The regulations pertaining to new settlements now in force in the Interior Provinces would be followed in establishing the proposed towns. He suggested a slight modification be made in accord with the Ordinance of Sierra Morena— to forbid joining or subdividing the lots and plats assigned. Within a specified time the settlers were to fence their lands under penalty of forfeiture.

Equally important to the defence and development of Texas was the establishment of water communications. Water routes would reduce freight rates, and consequently, lower prices on supplies; water routes would also encourage colonization of the Gulf coast region. Bonavía informed the *Junta* that this last recommendation was already being put into effect. A certain De la Rosa had been authorized to proceed from Matagorda Bay to Vera Cruz to determine the feasibility of establishing direct communications between that port and Texas.[69]

Proposals of the Junta. Although the members of the *Junta* were in accord with Bonavía on all his recommendations, they made several suggestions, some of which were radical and ambitious. For example, they

---

[69]Minutes of the *Junta de Guerra*, June 19, 1809. *A. G. I., Audiencia de Guadalajara*, 104-2-25 (Dunn Transcripts, 1800-1819, pp. 227-230).

proposed that the city of San Fernando de Béxar be moved to the east side of the San Antonio River, where the higher ground, better ventilated and less subject to floods, was more healthful. On its original site between the San Antonio River and San Pedro Creek, the city was inundated by every flood, and the citizens were plagued with sickness, because the terrain was damp and the atmosphere humid. The east side, they argued, was more healthful and suitable to habitation, whereas the area occupied by the villa was better for truck farms and fruit orchards.

Removal to the location suggested would not entail too great a hardship, they pointed out, because most of the homes were worthless straw huts. They recommended that the new capital city be laid out to accommodate a maximum of only 20,000 persons. Apparently large cities with their attendant crowded unsanitary conditions were in disfavor with the *Junta* members. Public buildings such as the church, the governor's palace, the jail, the hospital, the treasury, and the military barracks— most of which the city either lacked or could not be proud of, because they were in a very dilapidated condition—could be erected with a royal loan. This outlay, they said, could later be repaid out of the proceeds from the sale of city lots and farms, or from the fees on building permits. They specifically recommended that the expenditures on public buildings be not met by a sales tax on food.[70] The proposed removal was ignored by the commandant general, and nothing was ever done about it.

The *Junta* suggested certain modifications of the proposal made by Bonavía to convert the four missions into four independent municipalities. The *Junta* proposed that San José and La Espada be surveyed for subdivision into lots and plats for two new towns, and San Juan and Concepción be converted into two haciendas. They suggested that, regardless of the claims of the individual missions, each town and hacienda be allotted four leagues square of land. The thirty families from the villas of northern Nuevo Santander who had requested permission to settle in Texas at their own expense were to be assigned lands in either of the two new towns, San José or La Espada, but only after every Indian living at the missions had been given land equal in amount to that assigned the individual settler. At least one hundred families should be required for each town; the first fifty families to arrive at each town were to be given their lands free of charge to encourage their speedy settlement, and the other fifty were to be charged a nominal price. The land of the other two missions which were to be converted into haciendas

---

[70]*Ibid.*, pp. 230-231.

was to be sold at auction, but the Indians living within the area were to be left in possession of their previously assigned allotments. The parish priests were to be assigned a house, a field, and an orchard. They were to receive moderate fees and an allowance from the royal treasury for their maintenance, because the lands of the new towns and haciendas were to be exempt from tithes.[71]

The *Junta,* in taking up the matter of the regulations affecting Louisiana immigrants, went so far as to recommend (they could only recommend) financial assistance for transporting poor farmers and laborers who desired to move to Texas. They referred specifically to the Canary Islanders in Louisiana, said to be some 1,500 persons, who would long since have emigrated if they could have secured transportation.

The *Junta* could not ignore the pressing boundary question, for it was of grave concern to the Government of both Spain and the United States. They declared that it was common knowledge that Louisiana had never exercised jurisdiction over any post west of Natchitoches; that the occupation of even Natchitoches by the French had been with the consent of the Spanish Government, who had acceded to the request out of regard for the inhabitants who had been frequently flooded out of their homes on the east side of the river; that Louisiana under France had never extended to the banks of the Missouri; and that the United States had not presented and could not produce any documentary proof in support of claims as far as the Missouri. The *Junta* asserted that these claims of the United States were born of unbridled ambition and were being pressed on helpless Spain by those who should be grateful to her for having aided them in obtaining their independence.[72]

Bonavía transmitted these recommendations of the *Junta* to the commandant general on June 28 with a strong plea to approve and support them. He asserted that, although the execution of the plans would involve considerable expense, the royal treasury would be amply repaid for the investment by the resultant prosperity. He advocated setting up a special office of the royal treasury to handle the increased expenditures, and declared that his efforts to place the province in a state of defence by developing its natural resources would prove useless if he were not

---

[71]*Ibid.,* pp. 231-232.

[72]Minutes of the *Junta de Guerra,* June 19, 1809. *A. G. I., Audiencia de Guadalajara,* 104-2-25 (Dunn Transcripts, 1800-1819, pp. 232-233).

furnished means to carry out his plans.[73] Bonavía at the same time wrote directly to Francisco Saavedra, Secretary of the *Junta Suprema* in Spain, deploring his inability to take positive action under the circumstances. He explained that, in order to attain the desired end, it was necessary that no obstacles be placed in his way, and that he be furnished the means necessary to put his program into operation.[74]

Port of San Bernardo and free trade. Determined to institute a new era, Bonavía called another *Junta* on July 20 to consider establishing direct water communications between Texas and Vera Cruz and opening a port for free trade. By way of introduction, he informed the *Junta* that he had recently authorized Francisco de la Rosa to proceed from Matagorda Bay to Vera Cruz to place himself at the disposal of the viceroy, to whom he had written recommending the employment of De la Rosa. He had requested at the same time the appointment of someone competent to take accurate soundings and to make a careful exploration and survey for the Port of San Bernardo, near La Bahía on Matagorda Bay. A survey of the port had been ordered by the commandant general three years before, but for some inexplicable reason it had been dropped. He reminded the assembled officials that the royal orders for opening a port on the Gulf coast were tantamount to authorization of free trade. The question in his mind, he said, was whether the king had intended to extend this privilege to only Texas citizens or to all the inhabitants of the Interior Provinces. The new frontier commander said he was inclined to accept the latter interpretation, as he was convinced that the king's intention was to promote the welfare of the entire commandancy. He pointed out that importation and exportation by only the citizens of Texas would encourage smuggling in all the other Interior Provinces. Once started, smuggling would be practically impossible to stop.

It is to be remembered that Bonavía had been instrumental in formulating and establishing the commercial reforms of Charles III, which had granted the colonies a large measure of free trade. He was thoroughly conversant with the subject. As an illustration of what to avoid, he cited the case of Florida, where by royal decree the resident subjects had been exempted from the payment of all duties on imports and exports. The intention of the king had been to encourage the settlement and development of the province. But this exemption, intended to apply only

---

[73]Bonavía to N. de Salcedo, June 28, 1809. *A. G. I., Audiencia de Guadalajara,* 104-2-25 (Dunn Transcripts, 1800-1819, p. 226).

[74]Bonavía to Francisco Saavedra, June 28, 1809. *Ibid.,* pp. 221-222.

to the resident subjects of the king, was sadly abused by unscrupulous officials and residents who imported and exported goods for personal gain.

A more practical policy, Bonavía believed, should be adopted with regard to trade in Texas in order to attain the desired end. He recommended that the regulations stipulate that all exports be duty free, as also imports from Spain or Spanish colonies, but that the levy on imports from foreign countries be the same for the Texas port as that for other authorized ports in America. Bonavía advocated the exemption of tools, farm implements, and machinery from all duties. The *Junta* unanimously approved Bonavía's suggestions, but recommended that Spanish goods carry a 6 per cent *ad valorem* tax and foreign imports a flat rate of 33 per cent, except on tools, implements, and machinery. The importers should be given a receipt to enable them to introduce their merchandise anywhere in the Interior Provinces without further taxes of any kind. They further suggested that since the royal decree (March 29, 1806) permitted ships from other ports of America and the world at large to bring goods to the Texas coast, it would be advisable to authorize the captain of La Bahía to act temporarily as portmaster to check all imports, collect duties, and issue receipts to the importers.[75] The recommendations of the *Junta* were forwarded on July 26 by Bonavía to the commandant general for his approval. At the same time Bonavía wrote Saavedra and sent him a copy of the minutes of the *Junta* for the information of the *Suprema Junta*. He promised to inform him of the commandant general's action in the matter. Every day he became more convinced, he said, of the need of setting up an independent commandancy in Texas. The position of the commander of the frontier under the existing regulations was embarrassing and incompatible with the best interests of the royal service. It was for this reason that he had adopted the policy of directly informing the *Suprema Junta* of every step he took.[76]

Commandant General N. Salcedo did not take long to inform Bonavía what he thought of the project of a Texas port for free trade. On September 7 he wrote that he considered unwarranted the concern of the *Junta* about the opening of the Port of San Bernardo, its recommendations for customs officials, and its decisions on duty rates. He

---

[75]Minutes of the *Junta de Guerra*, July 20, 1809. *A. G. I., Audiencia de Guadalajara*, 104-2-25 (Dunn Transcripts, 1800-1819, pp. 235-239). The date of the *Junta* is erroneously given as July 30 in Hatcher, *The Opening of Texas to Foreign Settlement*, 171.

[76]Bonavía to N. Salcedo, July 26, 1809; Bonavía to Saavedra, July 26, 1809. *Ibid.*, 234-239.

made the sarcastic remark that there was little likelihood of Spanish, much less foreign, ships appearing at the port in the near future; that since the only vessel likely to put in soon at San Bernardo was that of De la Rosa, a whole maritime office was not essential to his reception. He informed Bonavía that as he considered De la Rosa a confirmed smuggler, he had issued orders for his arrest and detention and for the confiscation of all his goods. He instructed Bonavía to remind the governor of these orders and enjoined him to coöperate in their enforcement.[77] Bonavía attempted to disabuse the commandant general of the idea that contraband was general by attempting to prove that it was insignificant; that, as a matter of fact, it was dictated by direst necessity; and that to attempt to stop it completely would prove to be a short-sighted policy. In a long letter to Nemesio Salcedo on September 20 he wrote that the frequent arrest of smugglers reflected great credit on the officials in Texas for trying to enforce the law. The kind of confiscated merchandise and its petty value bore eloquent testimony, however, to the motive that prompted it—not profit, but necessity. The contraband traders in Texas were not defiantly violating the law; the wretched condition of the inhabitants of the province compelled them to deal in contraband in order to supply the necessities of life. It would be better, he advised, to remove the cause of smuggling than to punish with severity those who were constrained to furnish contraband goods. He explained that the majority of the people in Texas were farmers and cattle raisers in possession of a surplus of agricultural products and stock, but in need of clothes, furniture, and the essential comforts of life. For these goods they had to journey once or twice a year to the fair at Saltillo, where they were cheated and robbed by peddlers, who bought their goods on credit at exorbitant prices. Freightage to Texas increased the price on the merchandise. The same articles, but of much better quality, could be secured in the United States at much lower prices. Were the smugglers or the people of Texas to be blamed, Bonavía challenged, for either illegally introducing or purchasing these necessary goods at reasonable prices? Moreover, the unguarded frontier constituted an irresistible temptation to engage in contraband trade. The solution of the problem was to open the authorized port which would enable the inhabitants of the province to obtain necessities legally by exporting surplus products and importing goods they needed either free of duty or on payment of a

---

[77]N. Salcedo to Bonavía, September 7, 1809. *A. G. I., Audiencia de Guadalajara,* 104-2-25 (Dunn Transcripts, 1800-1819, pp. 264-265).

moderate impost. Bonavía made the significant observation that when need and private interest unite, "there is no army or measure capable of stopping contraband trade." For this reason it would be better to remove the cause of smuggling than to continue futile attempts to repress it.[78]

But the flagrant case of De la Rosa before the commandant general at this very time blinded his reason and convinced him of the perversity of the unscrupulous smugglers seeking admission into Texas under false pretexts. He remained adamant after the December storm brought the De la Rosa case to an end. Bonavía wrote Saavedra a dispirited letter in which he gave the Secretary of State a full report on the case and on all his own efforts to induce the commandant general to put into execution the order of the king authorizing the opening of a free port in Texas. He felt discouraged, he said, by the indifference of higher officials in attending to the more immediate and urgent needs of the province. He deplored the lack of energy that characterized the Government in New Spain and the damnable practice of recurring to "endless *expedientes* which of necessity consume very much time."

His patience exhausted, Bonavía spoke out his mind and fearlessly warned that if conditions were not remedied immediately, the time would come when the colonies would take things into their own hands. This was a daring prophecy to make, but it reveals how thoroughly the new commander had analyzed the critical situation facing Spanish authority in America. "Regardless of the wisdom of the commandant general," he exclaimed, "these provinces will continue to waste their slender resources and ultimately be consumed, if they are not given effective and immediate aid by the viceroy until they are in a position to help themselves. . . . I express what I feel and the way I feel, because I am interested in the welfare of the Monarchy. The United States is watching our every move and will not hesitate to take advantage of our mistakes."[79] But the royal officials in Spain continued to support the policies of the viceroy and the commandant general.

Texas militia. As early as August, 1807, Cordero had urged the mobilization of 4,500 men for Texas and the organization of the inhabitants into a well-trained and disciplined militia that could be depended upon to support the troops stationed in the province. In reply to an inquiry concerning military needs, he had informed Nemesio Salcedo

---

[78]Bonavía to N. Salcedo, September 20, 1809. *Ibid.*, pp. 264-266.

[79]Bonavía to Saavedra, December 27, 1809. *A. G. I., Audiencia de Guadalajara,* 104-2-25 (Dunn Transcripts, 1800-1819, p. 275).

that there were 1,050 troops in Texas, a force he considered totally inadequate for effective defence even when strengthened by armed volunteers. He had declared that valor alone could not defeat the better disciplined and numerically superior Americans, and added that the advantages of the Americans were being further improved by their trading activity among the natives of the province.

In view of the circumstances, Cordero had recommended that 3,000 infantry, 1,500 cavalry, and a field artillery train be sent to Texas. The main body of troops, he believed, should be stationed at San Antonio; an adequate number of well-mounted and well-equipped men should be assigned to keep communications open with the frontier outposts: Nacogdoches, Orcoquisac, Atascosito, Bayou Pierre, and La Bahía; and adequate detachments should be stationed at all these outposts, as well as along the coast to keep an effective lookout for any hostile move on the part of natives or foreigners. Merely the knowledge of such a force in Texas, he thought, would restrain the Americans. He went on to paint a gloomy and apprehensive picture of the danger threatening the province and of the serious inroads being made by American traders among the Indians. To counteract their influence, he urged the immediate establishment of two or three trading posts convenient to the various Indian tribes, where the natives in exchange for pelts and stock could secure from the Spaniards the goods they desired.

At the same time he had suggested the organization of local presidial companies in San Antonio, La Bahía, and Nacogdoches, to form the nucleus for a provincial militia, similar to the home guards of Natchitoches. Both the regular troops and the presidial companies, he had advised, sorely needed military instruction and more rigid discipline.[80]

The commandant general had replied early in September that the request for 4,500 troops was preposterous. The entire viceroyalty of New Spain had hardly that many. But even if the men were available and could be sent to Texas, the condition of the province was such that the men could not be properly quartered or adequately supplied. The lack of good roads, the difficult passage of flood-swollen rivers, and the unhealthful climate of the coast region would nullify the effective use of a force as large as Cordero requested. At that time N. Salcedo was inclined to minimize the danger of attack from the United States.

---

[80]Cordero to N. de Salcedo, August 29, 1807. *Nacogdoches Archives*, XI, pp. 58-66.

With regard to the Indians, Nemesio Salcedo had said that the natives were actuated by only two motives: fear and gain. To attempt the establishment of trading posts at this time was out of the question, the commandant general had pointed out, because the goods could not be secured except in the United States and it would be foolish to purchase Indian supplies from the Americans to resell in competition with them. The only solution he could see for the Indian problem was to distribute gifts more liberally to the chiefs and friendly tribes, and to promise them relief after the war.

N. Salcedo had noted that, according to the report of Cordero, there were in the province only 371 men between 18 and 45. He had authorized Governor Cordero to organize three companies for service in San Antonio and La Bahía. He believed that Nacogdoches did not need and could not support more than the 50 men stationed there, because it did not have either quarters or the necessary food supply. The militia was to form a home guard and to receive military instruction. He had empowered the governor to furnish the militia with the 91 guns and bayonets in the armory, for, as he pointed out, this type of rifle was useless to the cavalry. The militiamen were to receive no pay when not on active duty.[81]

More pressing duties and the reluctance of the inhabitants themselves had prevented the governor from organizing the Texas militia. When Governor Manuel de Salcedo arrived in 1808, he became vitally interested in the project and found the new frontier commander, Bonavía, thoroughly in favor of the movement. On June 26, 1809, the new governor called the attention of Bonavía to the fact that the Americans had neither withdrawn nor disbanded the large number of troops mobilized on the Texas-Louisiana-Florida frontier in spite of the fact that the British Fleet had not put in at Pensacola as the Americans had alleged and against which they had armed. Furthermore, Foronda, the secretary of the Spanish minister in Philadelphia, had recently arrived in Vera Cruz on a secret mission. Governor de Salcedo advised Bonavía, therefore, that it was time to prepare against a surprise attack. Time was precious, particularly in a province so lacking in money, ready resources, and manpower. "Great will be our sorrow," he said, "to find ourselves defeated because of overconfidence."

---

[81]N. de Salcedo to Cordero, September 11, 1807. *Nacogdoches Archives*, XI, pp. 67-72.

The new governor believed that there was urgent need of immediately obtaining sufficient troops to restrain the overambitious neighbors. In order to determine the effective manpower of the province, and to train and discipline them, he suggested the enlistment of all able-bodied men. He made the observation that the troops needed more discipline and the officers further training in their duties. He doubted that there were more than two or three officers in the three companies of presidial troops in Texas fitted for taking command in an emergency, or even for commanding an outpost.[82]

Bonavía had already suggested organizing the militia of Coahuila and Texas into regiments. This proposal had been made by Godoy at the time that the plans for reorganizing the Eastern Interior Provinces under General Grimarest were being considered. But the commandant general was unwilling to make the innovation. N. Salcedo argued that the population was too sparse, and that the troops stationed in the various presidios of Texas were doing their part in promoting the development of the province, for upon expiration of their term of service, they took up the life of settlers in the frontier establishments and protected them against Indians.[83]

Governor Manuel de Salcedo conceded that presidial companies were invaluable in establishing new settlements in Indian territory, but he believed that they were not conducive to developing communities of solid and dependable citizens. The presidial troops in Texas had performed their duty, he acknowledged, but they should be reorganized to cope with the better trained troops of the United States or moved to other Indian outposts. Then the new governor employed contradictory arguments to press his point for reorganizing the presidial troops. He asserted that the sale of Louisiana had changed the status of the Texas frontier and had made its defence more important than the establishment of settlements on the frontier. Furthermore, the presidios in Texas were such only in name, for their commanders were subservient to the civil authorities, and their fortifications were absolutely inadequate. Under the circumstances, he believed that the presidial companies should be reorganized into militia.[84]

Bonavía's views were sustained by Cordero, who pointed out that one of the original intentions in organizing presidial companies had been

---

[82]M. de Salcedo to Bonavía, June 26, 1809. *Nacogdoches Archives*, Vol. XI, pp. 12-15.

[83]N. Salcedo to Bonavía, June 27, 1809. *Béxar Archives*.

[84]M. de Salcedo to Bonavía, July 24, 1809. *Béxar Archives*.

to use the families of the troops to form the nucleus of new civil settlements. The policy of permitting the soldiers to remain in the growing communities as permanent settlers after the expiration of their term of service had accomplished the desired effect, for around each presidio there had developed a settlement, pueblo, or villa. It was time, therefore, Cordero thought, to put into effect in Coahuila and Texas the royal decree of May 30, 1804, which authorized the reorganization of the presidios along the entire frontier of New Spain and the creation of provincial regiments to take over the responsibility of defence.[85] Simón de Herrera, too, concurred in the opinion that the presidial companies should be suppressed, and that militia regiments should be organized in Coahuila and Texas. But he would not admit that the presidial troops had accomplished their primary object, the protection of the settlements against the Indians. He argued that if these troops had been unable to afford adequate protection against disorganized hordes of natives, they could hardly be expected to stand up against the disciplined troops of the United States. He urged the organization of provincial regiments as the solution to the problem of creating an effective force for defence.

Nemesio Salcedo was sufficiently removed from the frontier and the viceroy to see in a truer perspective the problems confronting the Interior Provinces as a whole. He sensed the danger to Spanish authority in the proposed provincial regiments. What, he queried, was to prevent rebellion against Spain by these provincial troops, these local volunteers who were far removed from the interior of Mexico and constantly exposed to insidious propaganda? It would be unwise, he said, to train and arm these men, and thereby give the Interior Provinces a military organization that might be used to attain independence. Even before Bonavía sent the arguments of his collaborators to bolster his contention, Commandant General Salcedo had made up his mind. He had written Bonavía on July 9 that he did not consider the organization of provincial militia forces in Coahuila and Texas essential to their defence. The presidial companies had protected and were still protecting the civilian settlements in their vicinity. These companies, in addition, contributed to the development of the settlements by furnishing ready markets for the agricultural products of the community.[86]

Bonavía registered his disappointment in a lengthy and interesting letter to Antonio Cornel, Spain's Secretary of War. After summarizing

---

[85]Cordero to Bonavía, July 21, 1809. *Béxar Archives.*
[86]N. Salcedo to Bonavía, July 9, 1809. *Béxar Archives.*

all his efforts to place the province in a state of defence against attack by the United States, Bonavía gave a detailed account of his repeated efforts to organize two regiments of volunteers in Coahuila and Texas, and enclosed a copy of Commandant General Salcedo's refusal to consent to the proposed reorganization. He advised Cornel of the great need for reviving the old discipline of Spanish troops which had covered Sixteenth Century Spain with glory. When Spain conquered America, he boasted, Spanish troops were renowned the world over for their discipline. Their easy victory over the large native population resulted from this kind of discipline and superior arms. But conditions had changed during the intervening years. The Indians had learned to excel the Spaniards both in horsemanship and marksmanship. They had the advantage of the troops in night attacks; for their arrows disposed of the guards silently, so as to permit them to murder the troops in their sleep. They were so dextrous with their bows at close range that they could shoot six arrows with deadly accuracy before a soldier could reload and fire his second shot. Discipline was the only salvation of regulars engaged in Indian fights; lacking discipline, regulars were unable to stand up against even Indians. The frontier troops, he declared, were as brave and courageous as any he had ever seen, but poor training and poor discipline were responsible for their serious defeats. It was for this reason that he advocated the organization of two regiments of militia. The danger of attack by the disciplined troops of the United States made this measure all the more imperative, he informed Cornel.[87] The sincerity of Bonavía can hardly be doubted. Unfortunately, the commandant general obstinately persisted in retaining his narrow and shortsighted army policy.

Immigration exclusion. The commandant general was losing his patience with his subalterns for insisting that he adopt a more liberal immigration policy in the face of unmistakable signs of an approaching storm. Irritated by what he considered their blindness to the real issues in the situation along the frontier, he bluntly told Bonavía that the recent proposals were not only officious, but also bordered dangerously upon disloyalty to the king.[88] The commander of the frontier remained undaunted. When he again suggested relaxing the immigration regulations in favor of the Spaniards, Nemesio Salcedo wrote: "The measures I

---

[87]Bonavía to Antonio Cornel, August 9, 1809. *Nacogdoches Archives*, XI, pp. 39-42.

[88]N. Salcedo to Bonavía, August 13, 1809; M. de Salcedo to Bonavía, September 15, 1809. *Béxar Archives*.

have adopted to close the doors to all immigration into that province from Louisiana are to be understood by Your Lordship to apply literally to the entire frontier and Gulf coast and to all individuals in accord with the explicit terms of my orders transmitted on June 22, [which were and are] dictated by the necessity of putting a stop to all communication, direct or indirect, with a foreign country." He added that this order fulfilled the express wishes of His Majesty, and was born of his own six years' experience. Good Spanish subjects desirous of immigrating to New Spain, he informed Bonavía, could enter by way of Vera Cruz on the condition that they secured the viceroy's consent. That official would inform the immigrants what they could or could not bring into the country. The reason these petitioners gave for requesting permission to bring in goods — that they could not dispose of their property in Louisiana for cash — was but a pretext, for they could secure drafts if not specie or currency. The royal order of September 24, 1803, which first permitted such immigration, clearly stated which goods the immigrants could bring.[89]

The commandant general added in a postscript to Bonavía that an examination of the documents in the archives of the commandancy-general, copies of which were in the possession of Bonavía, revealed that all the Spaniards and former Spanish subjects admitted from Louisiana were either libertines, smugglers, fugitives from justice, atheists, or restless rovers who had caused the authorities trouble from the moment they had set foot on Texas soil. He cited the cases of Minor, Vidal, Despallier, Clouet, Lausat, and Bastrop. These men and many others had taken advantage of the generosity of the king and the trusting nature of the Spaniards. The commandant general resented particularly the attitude of those immigrants who considered themselves benefactors of Spain and expected to be rewarded for condescending to live among the Spaniards. They expected every petition and request to be granted and became more of a nuisance every day. Nemesio Salcedo concluded with the remark that the immigrants from Louisiana, regardless of race or nationality, were "crows who some day will peck out our eyes."[90]

So emphatic a denial as this should have convinced Bonavía of the finality of Commandant General Salcedo's determination to put a stop

---

[89]N. Salcedo to Bonavía, August 21, 1809. *A. G. I., Audiencia de Guadalajara,* 104-2-25 (Dunn Transcripts, 1800-1819, pp. 217-219).

[90]*Ibid.,* pp. 217-219.

to all immigration. But Bonavía seemed not to know when to cease importuning. On September 20 he again pleaded for the admission of Spanish subjects from Louisiana as a means of strengthening the defence of the province. He asserted that no one distrusted the French more than he, but the Spaniards in Louisiana aroused all his sympathy. He declared that there were in that province not less than 1,500 Spaniards capable of bearing arms, and some 400 Canary Island families, most of them farmers, who would move to Texas if they were given an opportunity and were furnished transportation. Unlike those who had resided in New Orleans and engaged in commerce for years, these settlers, he said, had not been "contaminated" by their American neighbors.[91] Bonavía wrote at the same time to Saavedra in Spain to acquaint the *Junta Suprema* of the circumstances that had thwarted him in putting into effect a more liberal immigration policy. He maintained that the settlement of Texas was essential to the defence of all New Spain and the development of the Interior Provinces, but the commandant general had remained adamant in his opposition to colonization and had irrevocably closed the doors to foreigners and Spaniards alike. For the information of the Secretary of State and of the *Junta Suprema* he sent a copy of his proposed modifications of the regulations which would have permitted the rapid settlement of Texas and would have barred all undesirables.

He contrasted the immigration policy of the United States with that of Spain. The United States opened her arms in welcome to all Europeans; offered prospective settlers cheap land; admitted everyone who was not incapacitated or a confirmed criminal; and was primarily interested in the number of immigrants rather than in their quality. But Spain refused admission to even her own nationals from Louisiana. The former policy was restrictive enough, for it had placed innumerable obstacles in the way of immigrants: prohibiting the introduction of their property, designating the place of settlement regardless of suitability, and expelling them arbitrarily after they had become established at great sacrifice. Contrary to the assertion of the commandant general, Bonavía said he could not find evidence in support of the allegation that all those who had gained admission were libertines, atheists, smugglers, and restless trouble-makers. Spain's policy of absolute exclusion would forever turn Louisianans away from Texas, and Spain should

---

[91]Bonavía to N. Salcedo, September 20, 1809. *A. G. I., Audiencia de Guadalajara*, 104-2-25 (Dunn Transcripts, 1800-1819, pp. 214-215).

remember that Louisiana was the nearest source of settlers to populate the vast province of Texas. "As for me," he wrote, "I prefer a more diplomatic policy of tact and judgment to one of excessive rigor." Although all the other officials in Texas agreed on this point, he said, it would be impossible to do anything else until the commandant general changed his mind. He felt, however, that the facts should be brought to the attention of the authorities in Spain in order that they might help determine a more intelligent course for the future.[92]

American deserters. Intimately related to the exclusive immigration policy was the official stand on American deserters. It will be remembered that early in May, 1809, the commandant general had issued instructions for sending deserters to San Antonio before admitting them as settlers. Shortly afterwards the *asesor* and *auditor* became apprehensive and advised that it might be better to refuse them admission. Acting on this advice, the commandant general ordered Bonavía on July 9 to admit no more deserters.

The order immediately aroused a wave of protest. Governor de Salcedo declared it too drastic. Admitting the difficulty of apprehending French agents who tried to obtain admittance under the guise of American deserters, he believed that the remedy was to be found, not in refusing admission to all deserters, but in framing regulations which would incorporate distinctive provisions for real deserters and French agents. Governor de Salcedo argued that to refuse admission to an American deserter would be inhuman, because a person in that predicament could not return to the United States without facing severe punishment. If ordered to return to his country, the deserter would, out of despair, do either of two things: join the desperadoes in the Neutral Ground area to swell their ranks in this no man's land, or secretly reënter the province and take refuge among the Indians. In either event, the ultimate effect on New Spain would be worse than admission under well-planned restrictions.

Governor de Salcedo suggested, therefore, that all those who presented themselves to Spanish officials on the frontier as deserters be carefully examined to make certain that they were not impostors. Those found to be impostors were to be arrested; but those who gave satisfactory proof that they had escaped from the American Army were to be sent under guard to Monclova, where they could be kept under strict surveil-

---

[92]Bonavía to Saavedra, September 20, 1809. *Ibid.*, pp. 206-208.

lance while working to pay off the expense of their transportation. As an alternative to this plan, Governor de Salcedo proposed the detention of American deserters to exchange them for Spanish deserters. Either plan would reduce the number of desperate squatters in the Neutral Ground who had been rustling horses and cattle as far as the Trinity. To strengthen his contention, he pointed out the danger of international complications that might arise out of a policy which excluded all deserters. The American Government in attempting to capture the deserters in the Neutral Ground area would probably pursue them into Spanish territory.[93]

Bonavía sent the governor's protest to the commandant general, and stated that he himself favored the governor's objections and suggestions except the one pertaining to the proposed exchange of deserters, because he believed it would not solve the principal problem raised by the execution of the orders. The commandant general replied that he considered their objections as treasonable, their suggestions as officious, and their attitude as unbecoming to loyal officers of the king.[94]

Neutral Ground difficulties. Wilkinson's Neutral Ground Agreement had resulted in the creation of a no man's land east of the Sabine and Arroyo Hondo. Questionable characters soon began to drift into the area, which became the refuge for American and Spanish desperadoes. In November, 1808, Cordero had protested the violation of the Neutral Ground by American forces. It seems that, on orders of Judge Sibley, American soldiers had, on November 5, overtaken a train of merchandise belonging to Samuel Davenport, Nacogdoches Indian agent, two and one-half leagues west of Arroyo Hondo. The Americans had taken the train back to Natchitoches, where it, together with Davenport himself, was held by the authorities. The incident produced considerable excitement. It was alleged that Spanish sovereignty had been violated. The new governor, Manuel de Salcedo, was quite disturbed over the report, and felt slighted that the commander at Nacogdoches had not taken the matter up with him immediately.[95] Governor de Salcedo wrote Cordero that the incident involved three points. Seizure of the train was in effect a denial by American officials of the right of Spanish merchants or agents to purchase Indian goods in Natchitoches; in the next place, it was a violation of the Neutral Ground Agreement; and last, the plan to send

---

[93]M. de Salcedo to Bonavía, July 30, 1809. *Béxar Archives.*

[94]N. Salcedo to Bonavía, August 13, 1809. *Béxar Archives.*

[95]Cordero to M. de Salcedo, November 28, 1808; M. de Salcedo to Cordero, November 27, 1808. *Nacogdoches Archives*, XI, pp. 129-139.

an armed expedition to Nacogdoches to rescue American contraband traders held at that post constituted an absolute disregard of Spanish sovereignty. He advised immediate preparations for war. He warned Cordero that the Nacogdoches garrison could not possibly repel the rumored expedition, and that Guadiana was unfit to be its commanding officer. He urged dispatching two auxiliary companies of at least eighty men to Nacogdoches, fifty to the Sabine crossing, and an observation detail of nine to the Atoyaque.

Governor de Salcedo seems to have been particularly interested in the maintenance and promotion of Indian trade. American refusal to permit Spanish merchants to secure supplies in the United States for their traffic with the Indians would seriously affect relations with the natives, whose friendship might be lost. He suggested, therefore, that steps—subject to the approval of the commandant general—be taken immediately to secure the necessary goods either from Florida or from the British West Indies. An agent could be dispatched at once, he thought, to purchase the supplies from the old Florida firm of Juan Ponton, under the management of Juan Forbes, who imported his merchandise directly from England. Letters also could be sent to Governor Vicente Folch, who would probably coöperate. Should this plan be deemed impractical, an agent could be sent to New Orleans for the purchase of a light sailboat, which the American embargo doubtlessly would facilitate. The vessel could sail out of New Orleans in ballast, he explained, without violating the embargo, and make her way to Jamaica or Santo Tomás to purchase in the English islands everything that was needed for the Indian trade at prices much lower than those prevailing in the United States. The vessel might bring back also a cargo of swords, sabers, pistols, rifles, guns, ammunition, and many other supplies needed by the troops in the province.[96]

Cordero forwarded the governor's letter to the commandant general, and remarked that he did not agree with the new governor on the number and disposition of troops that would be required to safeguard the frontier against any eventuality growing out of the seizure of Davenport's cart train and his arrest. Cordero appears to have been a bit piqued at Manuel de Salcedo's forwardness in proffering him advice on military matters. He did not object to suggestions from the governor, he qualified, but he felt that decisions on military policy rested with

---

[96]M. de Salcedo to Cordero, November 27, 1808. *Nacogdoches Archives*, XI, pp. 129-135.

the military commander. He was guarded in expressing himself on the suggestions for improving Indian trade relations through purchases from either Florida or the Indies. He limited himself to the simple statement that this was a matter for the commandant general to decide.[97]

Commandant General N. Salcedo replied that there was no cause for alarm. He advised Cordero and Governor de Salcedo not to protest to the American Government the arrest of Davenport and his drivers and the seizure of his freight train, because the incident resulted from differences between Davenport and his partner in Natchitoches. He considered it only prudent to instruct Guadiana at Nacogdoches to be more watchful than ever against a surprise attack and to repel with force any attempt to rescue smugglers held at that post. The proposals of Manuel de Salcedo for obtaining the goods necessary for Indian trade, he regarded as impractical and nonessential. He had, in fact, already ordered the needed supplies from Mexico. However, if Davenport was released to continue the journey, his goods were to be received as agreed. He closed, reassuring Cordero that there was no imminent danger of attack from the United States.[98]

Manuel Soto, of Bayou Pierre, and Gerónimo Herrera, of Nacogdoches, reported early in 1810 that an unusually large number of objectionable characters had settled recently in the abandoned Presidio Los Adaes and on Arroyo de Piedra. Governor de Salcedo wished to drive them out forcibly, but he recollected that, according to the terms of the Neutral Ground Agreement, armed forces could not lawfully penetrate the area. He accused American border patrols of collusion in permitting settlers to pass into the neutral zone. Bonavía took up the matter with the commandant general. N. Salcedo advised approaching the American commander with a view of securing a mutual agreement to drive all the intruders out of the area. Acting upon the suggestion, Governor de Salcedo presented a formal remonstrance to the commander at Fort Claiborne, explaining that the settlement of the Neutral Ground by American squatters without Spanish authorization was a violation of the Agreement and was causing considerable damage to the communities along the Spanish frontier.[99]

[97]Cordero to N. Salcedo, November 28, 1808. *Nacogdoches Archives*, XI, pp. 136-139.

[98]N. Salcedo to Cordero, December 11, 1808. *Nacogdoches Archives*, XI, pp. 177-179.

[99]Bonavía to N. Salcedo, March 12, 1810; commander of Fort Claiborne to M. de Salcedo, July 7, 1810. *Nacogdoches Archives*, XV, pp. 61-62; 101-102.

It seems that the Spanish Government had officially protested through diplomatic channels against this violation of the Neutral Ground Agreement, for on May 2, 1810, the American Secretary of War had issued instructions to the commander of Fort Claiborne to coöperate with Spanish authorities in removing all settlers from the zone. Accordingly, the American commander informed Governor de Salcedo of his willingness to coöperate in removing all the settlers between the Arroyo Hondo and the Sabine. In order that the necessary arrangements could be made to carry out the plans jointly, he asked how many troops would be used, at what point he wished the American contingent to join them, when they planned to set out, and who was to be in command.[100]

Ten days later Governor de Salcedo informed the American commander that Lieutenant José María Guadiana had been appointed to proceed with fifteen men to Arroyo de la Piedra (in the vicinity of the abandoned Presidio Los Adaes) to remove all squatters who, contrary to the terms of the Agreement entered into by General Wilkinson and Governor Simón de Herrera, had established themselves in the neutral area. He was expected to arrive on August 1 and would wait for the American contingent so as to carry out the commission jointly. He informed the American that he had instructed Guadiana that the settlers were to be shown every consideration and given a reasonable time to gather their property before departing—everything was to be done "in accord with . . . the inalienable rights of the people." Likewise, he was informed that Guadiana was to burn and destroy all houses, even huts, in order to discourage those who were expelled from returning as soon as the troops had departed, and in order to leave nothing that would attract others to the area.[101]

The efforts to dislodge the intruders permanently proved futile. Bonavía informed the commandant general late in November, 1810, that foreigners were still moving into the zone. In his opinion it would be better to leave them alone than to try to force them to return to the United States. Nothing would be gained, and much ill will might result. Always inclined to be lenient with newcomers, Bonavía added that it would be equally useless to attempt to expel some of those who had entered the province, regardless of the circumstances of their entrance.

---

[100]Commander of Fort Claiborne to M. de Salcedo, July 7, 1810. *Nacogdoches Archives*, XV, pp. 101-102.

[101]M. de Salcedo to the commander of Fort Claiborne, November 17, 1810. *Nacogdoches Archives*, XV, pp. 103-105.

If they had to be moved, he said, it would be preferable to order them to the interior of Mexico than to order them out of the country.[102]

Foreign aggression possibilities. As the year 1809 drew to a close, fear of American and French aggression was on the increase again. In spite of the optimistic view of some local officials and their condemnation of the unswerving stand taken by the commandant general on immigrants and foreign agents, events were soon to prove that his exclusive policy was well founded. Even though both the viceroy and the *Junta Suprema* had supported Nemesio Salcedo, Texas officials disregarded their orders. The laxity of the Texas officials is revealed in the case of Daniel Hughes. On October 6, 1809, the commandant general reprimanded Bonavía for having permitted Hughes to visit Chihuahua. Not only had he been known to be an agent of the United States, but he had also been allowed to succeed in returning with a large number of horses. What was more reprehensible was the fact that he had been given the opportunity to obtain full information on the military strength of the Interior Provinces.[103] At about the same time, Don Luis de Onís, unrecognized minister of Spain to the United States, wrote the viceroy that it was common knowledge that many Louisianians were entering the Spanish dominions, claiming that they were Spanish subjects and consequently had the right to emigrate to Texas under the terms of the treaty of 1803, if they found the change of government in Louisiana unsatisfactory to them. Onís warned the Viceroy, Lizaña, that under this pretext Napoleonic agents and unscrupulous Americans were gaining admission as immigrants. He advised greater vigilance, therefore, along the Texas frontier.[104] A month later he hastened to inform the viceroy that he had just learned that a group of discontented Spaniards had joined a number of French and American insurrectionists in New Orleans, who were planning to start a revolution both in Spain and Mexico.[105]

Francisco Saavedra, Secretary of State, also sent warnings from Spain to Viceroy Lizaña concerning the activities of revolutionary agents in the United States. He reported that a certain Francis Belmont had recently left France for Philadelphia with instructions from Napoleon

---

[102]Bonavía to N. Salcedo, November 23, 1810. *Nacogdoches Archives*, XV, pp. 57-58.

[103]N. Salcedo to Bonavía, October 6, 1809. *Béxar Archives*.

[104]Luis de Onís to Lizaña, October 21, 1809. *A. G. M., Operaciones de Guerra* (Barker Transcripts).

[105]Onís to Lizaña, November 24, 1809. *Ibid.*

to penetrate the Spanish dominions at all costs and incite the leaders to rebel against the mother country. Saavedra passed on his information that a group of prominent citizens of Mexico had made proposals to Great Britain to place New Spain under her protection in the event that France subjugated Spain. He expressed deep concern over the presence of General Wilkinson in Louisiana and the large number of French families residing in that province.[106] Bonavía attempted to allay Saavedra's fears. He wrote that he was of the opinion that Wilkinson's presence in New Orleans in itself constituted no danger to Spanish interests and was not indicative of any plan on the part of the United States to attack. He admitted, however, that the large number of French sympathizers in Louisiana did constitute a danger. As for Wilkinson, his character was such that he had lost his Government's confidence. As a matter of fact, Wilkinson had been removed from command and replaced by General Hampton, because he was pro-English, whereas the American Congress was pro-French.[107]

The dissatisfaction of the Creoles in Mexico was in the meantime crystallizing into open rebellion. The officials in Texas were soon faced with the problem of preventing the spread of discontent from New Spain and the entrance of agents into the province. Within a year, the parish priest of Dolores, Miguel Hidalgo y Costilla, raised the standard of revolt against the tyrannical rule of Spain in America and began the struggle for independence which was soon to spread to Texas, and cause the temporary arrest of both the governor and the commandant general. Don Nemesio Salcedo issued a proclamation on October 24, 1810, to warn the inhabitants of Texas against the machinations of French agents, whom he blamed for the revolt in Mexico. He entreated the citizens of Texas not to be misled by false promises, and pointed out that the rebels were the agents of Napoleon, who aimed to usurp authority in the Spanish colonies and destroy religion. He warned against inactivity which would produce disastrous results, and called upon all the officers in Texas to redouble their vigilance. The viceregal decree against the rebels informed the people that those harboring or giving comfort to French agents would be considered traitors, tried as such, and executed within twenty-four hours after pronouncement of sentence; that those found guilty of spreading seditious propaganda would be condemned to

---

[106]Saavedra to Lizaña, December 12, 1809. *A. G. M., Operaciones de Guerra* (Barker Transcripts).

[107]Bonavía to Saavedra, May 16, 1810. *Nacogdoches Archives*, XV, pp. 65-67.

the gallows; and that those proved guilty of spreading false rumors calculated to create panic would be tried for criminal malice and punished according to their deserts.[108]

The storm had at last broken upon the heads of the frontier officials. The end of the Spanish regime was at hand. But it will be well to take stock of conditions in Texas on the eve of Mexico's War for Independence before treating of that struggle.

---

[108]N. Salcedo to the People of the Interior Provinces, October 24, 1810. *Nacogdoches Archives,* XV, pp. 110-117.

CHAPTER XI

Texas on the Eve of the Mexican Revolution

The hesitant policy of the commandant general in regard to the vital question of immigration had defeated the sanguine hopes of the liberal officials in Texas. As the year 1810 neared its end and the ominous clouds of rebellion darkened the horizon in New Spain, Governor Salcedo reported that the vast province under his care had a population of 3,122, and a military contingent of 1,033 men, a total of only 4,155. The jurisdiction of Béxar had a civilian population of 1,700; La Bahía, 405; Villa de San Marcos, 82; Trinidad de Salcedo, 91; Nacogdoches, 655; and Bayou Pierre, 189. For more than half a century, the governor declared, Spain had neglected to settle this remote but rich province. The presidial system adopted for its occupation, he continued, had afforded inadequate protection to the few, scattered centers, and offered little or no inducement to the development of commerce and industry. The retrocession of Louisiana to France and its subsequent sale to the United States, he asserted, had aroused the fear of foreign aggression. Under the liberal leadership of Cordero, wholesale immigration from Louisiana had been encouraged, a larger number of troops had been brought to the province, and trade restrictions had been slightly modified. In spite of the earnest efforts of Texas officials to improve the general condition of the province and to strengthen its defences, however, little had been accomplished, the disappointed governor commented.

Governor Salcedo reviewed the circumstances that were responsible for the backward condition of Texas. It was impossible for trade and industry to develop because the nearest legal port open to its settlers was Vera Cruz, more than 500 leagues distant. Blessed by nature's abundant resources and rich lands, the colonists had endured untold hardships and privations as a result of the unreasonable trade regulations. A different policy in this respect and in regard to immigration would have to be adopted, he maintained, if Texas and the rest of New Spain was to be saved. Making an about-face, he now admitted that the United States, bordering upon Spain's American possessions, represented a serious danger. He advised that the number of troops in Texas be increased regardless of the sacrifice which such a measure might entail. He insisted, likewise, that the population be augmented either by encouraging settlers from Louisiana or bringing them from Spain and the interior of Mexico, and that a port be opened on the Texas coast to enable the inhabitants to import the goods they needed and export the products they raised. He elaborated on the danger from the United States, and pointed out various reasons for checking the aggressive pioneers of the West at the Sabine. The popular notion that there was nothing to fear from the Americans was a serious mistake to make, he declared, emphatically.

The governor discussed at some length the importance of maintaining friendly relations with the Indians. Control over the natives was of the utmost importance for the defence of the province. He warned that although all the border Indians were then at peace, the Government would have to offer them greater trade inducements in order to retain their friendship. The Spaniards would lose their influence over the Indians unless they could offer goods at lower prices than the American traders. He suggested, therefore, the establishment of several new trading houses among the northern Indians and the erection of several presidios in the lands of the more important tribes.

In connection with the Indians he discussed the mission system which he asserted was outmoded, incapable of coping with the present situation. There were only 343 Indians in the six missions of the province. The Indians, he contended, had been attracted to the missions by the assurance of food, clothing, and gifts rather than by a desire to be instructed in the teachings of Christianity. Their conversion and civilization could be more effectively attained by increasing the number of settlements and promoting more intercourse with the Spaniards. Closer relations would teach them Spanish and acquaint them with the customs and ways of civilized life.

Governor Salcedo concluded his report with the statement that the most important matter to be attended to was that of increasing the population of the province. He agreed that adequate precautions should be taken to prevent the entrance of disloyal or undesirable settlers from Louisiana, but he maintained that these restrictions should not prevent the immigration of honest and hard-working colonists who desired to move to Texas. He expressed the conviction that a larger number of troops, as well as the appointment of an independent commander for the Eastern Interior Provinces, was essential to the defence and prosperity of Texas.[1]

---

[1] Report of Governor M. de Salcedo, August 8, 1810. *A. G. M., Historia, Operaciones de Guerra, Años 1810-1812.*

Indians in Texas. As early as 1806, Cordero had made a detailed report on the Indian tribes in the province. At that time the Tonkawas occupied the area between the Trinity and the Brazos and roamed both north and south of the road to Nacogdoches. They had established *rancherías* on most of the river crossings, and were generally friendly towards the Spaniards, with whom they engaged in trade.

The Tawakonis had their *rancherías* along the Brazos, with their chief pueblo at Tortuga. They were suspicious of the Americans, whom they had come to know while trading with them on Red River. They were well acquainted with the various routes to East Texas and had furnished the Spaniards with guides and interpreters on various occasions. They had expressed their desire for instructions and their willingness to coöperate with the Spaniards to prevent the intrusion of Americans into their lands.

The Taovayas, originally on the upper Red River in the vicinity of present Wichita, had been forced farther to the south and were now in the territory between the Trinity and the Brazos, above the *Camino Real*. The new chief, Elías Coq, was anxious to coöperate with the Spaniards, but found the members divided in their allegiance. Seven families had remained at their old *ranchería* on Red River. Cordero pointed out that these Indians were treacherous and should be treated with caution.

The Comanches, who ranged south of the Red River and west as far as the San Antonio, were implacable enemies of the American pioneers, declared the provisional governor, and were ready to help the Spaniards.

The former nations of the Assinai Confederacy: the Tejas, Ais, Ainaes, Nacogdoches, and Nacogdochitos, had grown cold but were not inimical to the Spaniards. Their friendship could be revived by trade and gifts. Although they accepted presents from the Americans, they were not known to have coöperated with them. In this same category, and living in the same area between the Neches and Trinity were the Quichas (Quitseys).

The Alabamas, Choctaws, and Coshates had of late joined the Orco-quisacs along the coast between the Trinity and the Colorado. These tribes were all friendly to the Spaniards. The new arrivals had, in fact, been driven from their former homes by the American frontiersmen and could, therefore, be counted upon in any activity against them.

West of the Colorado, roving along the coast, southward as far as the San Antonio River, were the Karankawas. These fierce tribesmen had been cannibalistic, but they were now civilized and reported regularly to the commander at La Bahía and the missionary at Refugio everything that occurred on the coast. They had recently established a *ranchería* on the lower Colorado, not far from the crossing on the lower La Bahía Road.

West of San Antonio, principally along the Nueces River, were the Lipan-Apaches and the Canosos, a kindred tribe, who wandered south and west to the lower Río Grande and into Coahuila itself. These Indians had been driven into this area by their deadly enemies, the Comanches. They were less treacherous and committed fewer depredations than in past years.[2]

A more comprehensive report made in 1809, based on information furnished by Samuel Davenport, Indian agent of Nacogdoches, throws additional light on the movement and location of the different Indian tribes, particularly those driven into Texas by the Americans. According to Davenport, the Alabamas had emigrated from Louisiana and established their principal village on the west bank of the Neches River, about eight leagues above the confluence of the Neches and the Angelina. This would place the Alabamas in the vicinity of present Rockland. They had become somewhat sedentary, for the 200 warriors and their families raised corn, beans, and other crops.

On the east bank of the Neches, four leagues below the Alabama village, the ex-Louisiana Choctaws had established their *ranchería*. They numbered forty warriors, without counting the women and children. They cultivated some corn, but subsisted principally on fish and wild game.

The Coshates were at this time on the east bank of the Trinity. The principal settlement was about thirty leagues below Salcedo, in the vicinity of Kickapoo or Onalaska, where they cultivated corn and beans. They had 150 warriors. The Alabama and Coushatti Indian Reservation is today located in Polk County, midway between Kickapoo and Woodville.

The Orcoquisacs, once the dominant coastal tribe between the Trinity and the Brazos, had now moved to the Trinity to the land of the Bidais, with whom they lived. They had no fixed habitat and had been reduced in number to about fifty warriors. The Bidais had about sixty. The two tribes roamed south of the *Camino Real,* between the Trinity and the Brazos, as far as the coast, where they spent a good deal of the summer fishing. According to Davenport, they cultivated a little corn but, as a general rule, were not inclined to do much work.

[2]Cordero to N. Salcedo, June 16, 1806. *Béxar Archives.*

The nomadic Cocos, who could muster some sixty warriors, were living on the banks of the lake at the mouth of the Brazos, in the vicinity of present Freeport. Fishing was their chief occupation.

Along the coast, roaming between the Brazos and Matagorda Bay, lived about two hundred Karankawa braves and their families. This number did not include those who were living at Mission Refugio, where a good many had congregated and become civilized. The coastal Karankawas had intermarried with the Cocos. They too spent most of their time fishing in the numerous lakes and inlets of the coast, with which they were thoroughly familiar.

The Tonkawa, one of the strongest surviving nations, numbered about two hundred fifty warriors, who, with their families, made a considerable aggregate. They ranged from the Brazos to the San Marcos, along both sides of the *Camino Real,* from San Antonio to Nacogdoches. They depended on the chase for their food, principally deer and buffalo, as they did no planting. Each of their two tribes had its own chief.

About thirty leagues above the crossing of the *Camino Real* on the Brazos, probably near Chilton, lived about three hundred Tawakoni warriors and their families in three villages. This nation was industrious and their well-cultivated fields yielded an abundance of corn, beans, and other products.

About one hundred leagues northwest of Nacogdoches, on the Red River, there were three villages in which some four hundred warriors of the Taovayas, Wichitas, and Aquichis lived. Like the Tawakoni, these Indians were agricultural. In their irrigated fields they planted corn, beans, watermelons, and other products and obtained good returns.

The principal village of the Quitseys (called Quichas by the Spaniards) was located six leagues west of the Trinity, about ten leagues above the *Camino Real,* in the vicinity of Leona. They numbered fifty or sixty warriors, who, with their families, planted corn, beans, and other crops.

The old Tejas tribe was now divided into two pueblos. The first, called Nabdacos, was located three leagues west of the Neches River, and four leagues north of the *Camino Real,* near Slocum. Here lived about one hundred warriors and their families. The other village, called Aynais, was on the west bank of the Angelina, three leagues above the highway, in the vicinity of Rusk. Here lived sixty warriors with their families. Both pueblos planted corn and hunted.

The old tribe of the Nacogdoches had its *rancheria* about five leagues above the city of the same name. Only fifty warriors and their families remained. They lived on the products of the chase and did little or no planting.

On the Sabine, two leagues above the village of the Nacogdochitos was the pueblo of the Nadacos, now reduced to about one hundred persons in all. They planted corn and raised good crops.

The Cadodachos were also on the east bank of the Sabine, some nineteen or twenty leagues above the pueblo of the Nadacos. This tribe still numbered over two hundred braves. They planted some corn and lived from the products of the chase.[3]

The various tribes listed by Davenport, which lived and roamed from the Red River west to the San Antonio and south to the Gulf coast, could muster 2,250 warriors. This number does not include the Lipan-Apaches or the Comanches. The first of these were not numerous in Texas, but their kindred tribes ranging over the plains of West Texas into Coahuila and north into New Mexico constituted a potential danger to Spanish settlements. The Comanches were by far the most numerous, but they had no fixed habitat and they ranged in their constant wanderings and foraging expeditions from the Red to the San Antonio and even as far west as the upper Nueces.

Although these nations or tribes were all nominally at peace with the Spaniards, they constantly harassed the settlers by petty thievery on their visits and not infrequently by open raids. Villa de Salcedo was seriously threatened by the Indians of the north, who seem to have resented the establishment of this settlement in their hunting grounds. The Tonkawas were responsible for the repeated attacks on the struggling settlers of the Villa de San Marcos. So grave were the depredations committed that the abandonment of the villa was contemplated as early as 1810. In spite of remonstrances and threats, the Indians continued to prey upon the cattle of the new settlers and to raid the village until its final abandonment four years later.

Even San Antonio was frequently raided by roving bands. When the chiefs of the respective tribes were asked to explain these raids, they generally declared that the young men had gone on the warpath without

---

[3]Noticias de las Naciones Yndias de la Prova. de Texas que me dio Don Samuel Davinport en Nacogdoches desde cuyo punto se han de considerar sus situaciones y distancias. Dispatches with a letter of M. de Salcedo, April 24, 1809. *Nacogdoches Archives*, Vol. 11, pp. 254-257.

their permission. They expressed regret and promised to punish the offenders and return the loot, but their promises were seldom if ever fulfilled. Governor Salcedo informed Bonavía that the inhabitants of San Fernando de Béxar were determined to abandon the villa and return to Coahuila unless they were given adequate protection. Alarmed at the increasing hostility of the natives, which was naturally attributed to the activities of American agents and traders, the governor warned Bonavía that the whole plan for the development of the province would be seriously thwarted if the Indians were not controlled sufficiently to permit the settlers to cultivate their lands and tend their cattle.[4]

Bonavía protested to the various chiefs and made preparations for a campaign against the marauders. The serious tone of the commander and the angry attitude of the enraged settlers convinced them of the Spaniards' determination to stop these forays, and they sent a delegation to San Antonio to negotiate a new peace. Governor Salcedo was so anxious to come to an understanding that, instead of demanding reparations before making peace, he welcomed their overtures and gladly forgave them. The hatchet was buried and the peace pipe smoked. The settlers abandoned the plan to leave their homes and a period of false security followed.[5] The Indians were interested primarily in gifts. They lacked a sense of loyalty or attachment; they had no feeling of gratitude to either Spaniards or other Europeans. When in April, 1810, a French vessel surreptitiously entered the mouth of the Sabine with a cargo of goods to trade with the Indians, the news soon brought all the natives from far and wide. Miguel Crow, in reporting the incident, reclared that every man, woman, and child had gone to meet the foreigners in the expectation of gifts.[6]

The missions. It will be recalled that when the missions were secularized, there were a number of neophytes still under instruction and that the two missions at La Bahía were exempted from the secularization decree. In June, 1809, the governor made a detailed report on the San Antonio missions. In Concepción there were nine men and twelve women; in San José, twenty-nine men and twenty-six women; in San Francisco de la Espada, fourteen men and ten women; and in San Juan Capistrano, nine men and eleven women. Altogether there were one

---

[4]M. de Salcedo to Bonavía July 3, 1809. *Béxar Archives.*

[5]Bonavía to M. de Salcedo, July 4, 1809; M. de Salcedo to Bonavía, July 15, 1809. *Béxar Archives.*

[6]Ruiz to Guadiana, April 4, 1810. *Béxar Archives.*

hundred twenty men and women who were being taken care of by two missionaries. In addition to the Indians, some Spaniards had rented lands and were residing in the missions. These were distributed as follows: Concepción, eighteen men and fourteen women; San José, nine men and six women; San Juan, twenty-four men and twenty-two women; and San Francisco, fifty-one men and forty-two women, a total of one hundred eighty-six Spaniards. All the Indians had houses within the mission walls and each had been assigned a *suerte* for cultivation. According to the instructions of Pedro Nava, these Indians should have been given title to the lands assigned to them, but the officials had neglected to carry out this part of the instructions.

It is of interest to note the description of the boundaries of each one of the missions. Governor Salcedo reported that the lands of Mission Concepción extended from the mission one league to El Paso del Nogal, whence the line ran east for a league to Salado Creek, then one league north to the La Bahía Road, and hence eight leagues to the Cibolo and back to the mission. The area included some fifteen square leagues, of which only a small portion had been divided into *suertes* and was under cultivation.

The lands of San José were bounded by the Arroyo de la Piedra on the south and by the ranch of the curate, Valdés, on the north. The eastern boundary was formed by the San Antonio River and the western by the Medina. In addition to these lands, the mission owned eleven *sitios* in San Lucas, on the Medina River, which had been bought from the king by the *padres* in 1766. The deed, issued by the Royal *Audiencia* of Mexico, was recorded in the mission archives. The mission also owned and operated a good wheat mill.

San Juan Capistrano extended five leagues east from the mission to El Aguila, on the La Bahía Road. The line then followed the road to Pataguillos Lake for a distance of ten leagues, and from the headwaters of the Cibolo to San Bartolomé. Its extensive lands were being cultivated in part by Spaniards.

The boundaries of San Francisco de la Espada were more vague. The governor commented that he had determined them from the tradition common among the oldest settlers in Béxar. They appear to have run from the back of the mission north to a small dam on the river and west from this point to the ranch of Luis Pérez. Its lands were bounded on the east by the property of Delgado, and on the south by Atascoso Creek.

Indefinite as these boundaries are, they give an indication of the extent of the lands assigned to the various missions. The governor pointed out that these vast properties were being administered by an Indian governor in each mission and by the *padres,* but that neither had the ability to manage them properly. Valuable lands were thus being held without yielding a fair return. The missions had become a haven for idlers and gamblers. The churches, according to the report, were in a fair condition.[7]

At La Bahía there were two missions still in operation, Rosario and Refugio. The number of Indians in the first had greatly diminished, as most of the Cocos had run away. In Refugio there were still numerous Karankawas, who spent most of the year in the mission, but who in the summer frequently abandoned the mission to go to the seashore.

When Mission Valero was secularized, the lands were distributed among the remaining neophytes and Spanish settlers for cultivation. But it seems that after the lands were assigned, many failed to develop them as agreed. In August, 1809, the lieutenant governor of Valero and Doctor Vicente Amador reported on the state of cultivation of the former Valero Mission lands. They declared that Antonio Vaca had five fields which he had permitted to lie fallow during the last six years; Agustín Hernández was reported as having neglected his land for three years; Andrés Vallejo had not planted his field for the last twelve years; and Guadalupe Carmona for four. Among the negligent landholders was the former curate of San Antonio, Clemente Arocha, who had asked for and received two *suertes* from the lands of the secularized mission, but had failed to cultivate them for three years. José Antonio de la Garza had a farm which had not been plowed for seven years; Roberto Núñez neglected his, as did Juan de la Cerda, during the past twelve years; and Gertrudis Torres failed to keep her farm under cultivation for the preceding seven years. Six persons, to whom lands had been granted in the secularized mission, had since died and their lands had remained uncultivated for ten years.[8] It is of interest to note that the high expectations of Pedro Nava had not been fulfilled and that instead of making the lands of the former mission more productive, the actual yield had fallen far below that of the days when, under the careful supervision of the zealous missionaries, the few remaining neophytes had industriously applied themselves to their cultivation.

---

[7]Provincia de los Texas. Padrón General de las quatro misiones. *A. G. I., Audiencia de Guadalajara,* 104-2-25 (Dunn Transcripts, 1800-1819, pp. 222-225).

[8]Report on the lands of Mission Valero, August 18, 1809. *Nacogdoches Archives,* Vol. XV, pp. 43-44.

First hospital in Texas. Mission Valero, the first to be founded and the first to be secularized, was also the first to have a hospital in Texas. When Cordero brought the first large contingent of soldiers to protect the remote province from the threatened invasion of the land-hungry frontiersmen, he was obliged to establish a military hospital. A part of the abandoned mission was reconditioned at a cost of 352.50 *pesos,* and on January 1, 1806, the first patients were admitted.[9] It was the establishment of the hospital that brought the young Doctor Frederick Zerban from New Orleans to San Antonio. The staff consisted of Francisco Amangual, superintendent, and Doctor Frederick Zerban, physician and surgeon. An orderly was detailed to act as hospital steward, and a cook and one servant were hired. A weekly allowance of two *reales* (25 cents) was made for each patient.[10] Amangual found the position of superintendent incompatible with his military duties and resigned shortly after his appointment. Timothy Nemesio, a citizen of San Antonio, took his place.

Orders were immediately issued to the commandants on the eastern frontier to send all serious and chronic cases to the hospital for treatment.[11] It will be remembered that malaria had almost decimated the Nacogdoches troops. Unfortunately we do not have the complete records on the nature of the cases or the number of patients treated during the first seven months. But the requisition sent by Francisco Amangual for expenses incurred in hospitalizing the soldiers during the first nine months may give some idea of the number of patients treated. Their bill came to 516.37 *pesos.* We do know, however, that there were forty-two patients in the hospital in September, 1806, and that the physician had reported a shortage of essential drugs. Steward Lázaro Orrantí complained that he was unable to take care of the patients without assistance and demanded either the appointment of additional help or a salary increase. His pay was insignificant enough—only eight *pesos* a month, and room and board. He was given a two-*peso* raise, which was charged to the food account. Whether or not this action affected the quantity or quality of food served we do not know. The services of others had been secured in the meantime, another soldier to help the orderly, and two

---

[9]Report on expenditures for hospital, December 16, 1806. *Béxar Archives.* The bill was paid out of the Mesteña Fund.

[10]Cordero to N. Salcedo, January 11, 1806. *Béxar Archives.*

[11]Sebastián Rodríguez to Cordero, January 13, 1806. *Béxar Archives.*

women servants. The latter received room and board plus four *pesos* a month. The total cost of operation for the first year was 864 *pesos*.[12]

Doctor Zerban did not prove popular. The people of San Antonio complained to Governor Cordero that Zerban failed to show proper interest. They protested that the medicines he prescribed, besides being expensive, were ineffectual and that, as a matter of fact, their own home remedies brought much better results. He had not held the position four months before they signed a petition asking that he be not permitted to practice at all. Their antagonism was due in part to his nationality, for they declared frankly that the people of San Antonio preferred a Spanish doctor.[13] An investigation disclosed that the movement had been started after the arrival of a Spanish doctor. The newcomer seems to have desired to eliminate all medical competitors. Cordero retained Zerban, although he had no personal affection for him. In a letter to Salcedo some years later, he admitted that Zerban was a scoundrel, but that he was obliged to keep him because physicians were few and far between.

An effort was made to secure adequate medical supplies and the necessary surgical instruments. Cordero sent to Salcedo a long list of drugs and instruments needed for the treatment of the troops. Salcedo immediately replied that he had forwarded the order to Mexico City together with instructions to forward the supplies without delay to Saltillo and thence directly to San Antonio.[14]

Texas' first dentist. This same year San Antonio received its first dentist, Pedro Lartigue. In a petition to the governor for permission to practice, Lartigue declared that he was a master surgeon and dentist of twenty-three or twenty-four years' experience in Louisiana, and offered to furnish his patients free drugs and medicines. Cordero referred the petition to the *Cabildo* of the Villa de San Fernando de Béxar as coming under their immediate jurisdiction. The City Council voted to grant the request and Pedro Lartigue thus became the first licensed dentist in Texas. The members of the *Cabildo* who signed the resolution were José Antonio Saucedo, José Felix Menchaca, Vicente Travieso, Francisco Arocha, José Benito Duton, José Erasmo Seguín, and Toribio Durán.[15]

---

[12]Francisco Amangual to Cordero, October 10, 1806; Accounts rendered, December 16, 1806. *Béxar Archives.*

[13]Alcalde Toribio Durán to Cordero, April 24, 1806. *Béxar Archives.*

[14]Salcedo to Cordero, July 13, 1806. *Béxar Archives.*

[15]Petition of Pedro Lartigue and accompanying documents. August 7, 1806. *Béxar Archives.*

San Fernando de Béxar. When the site of present San Antonio was first occupied, the first mission established was called Nuestra Señora de Valero and the military post, San Antonio de Béxar. Twelve years later (1730), plans for a formal civil settlement with an independent administration were begun, and resulted in the establishment of the Villa de San Fernando with colonists brought from the Canary Islands. Ever since that time there had been a tendency to use the names San Antonio and San Fernando de Béxar indiscriminately to designate both the presidio and the civil settlement. In October, 1809, Governor Salcedo decided to eliminate the resulting confusion. In a formal proclamation he declared that in view of the fact that the civil settlement—now grown into a town—had superseded the presidio in importance, all legal documents were henceforth to be drawn up in the name of the Villa de San Fernando de Béxar. The town was to be divided into four wards: the north ward, the south ward, the Valero ward, and the Laredo ward, each of which was to have a commissioner (Alcalde) and its own citizens' committee to maintain order and street sanitation.[16]

The mobilization of troops to protect the province had brought new life to the indolent outpost neglected for so many years. Shortly after Cordero's arrival in 1805, plans were drawn up for new barracks in anticipation of the new contingents. The plans called for rock and mortar quarters to accommodate larger numbers of troops and eliminate the necessity of having to house them in the unsanitary villa. Commandant General Salcedo formally approved the project in December, 1806, and the work which had been started as early as October went forward at a more rapid pace.[17]

Chaplain José Vicente Arispe, of Monclova, who came with the troops from Coahuila, took sick shortly after his arrival and died in San Fernando. Fortunately for the soldiers, Father José Rumayor was on hand to take over the chaplaincy. José Rumayor had accompanied the Agua Verde detachment to Nacogdoches as chaplain and had been sent back to recuperate in the new military hospital. But before the end of the year, Chaplain Rumayor became dissatisfied with conditions at the presidio, and left without permission—much to the chagrin of the governor, who reported the matter to the commandant general.[18]

---

[16]M. de Salcedo to the citizens of San Fernando de Béxar, October 5, 1809. *Béxar Archives.*

[17]Salcedo to Cordero, December 6, 1806. *Béxar Archives.*

[18]Cordero to N. Salcedo, December 29, 1806. *Béxar Archives.*

Royal instructions on education. The concern of the king for his subjects' education reached even the natives of distant Texas. The governor received a copy of a royal decree issued in 1807, enjoining him to carry out the provisions of the royal instructions of May 10, 1770, November 28, 1772, and November 24, 1774, concerning the establishment and maintenance of schools in all Indian pueblos. The natives congregated in the various missions were to be taught in Spanish and made to learn to read, write, and speak the language. They were to be strictly forbidden to speak their own tongue in order that they might more easily master Spanish and communicate more freely with the Spaniards. The governor was ordered to establish schools, if they were not already in existence, to employ teachers who by experience and training were qualified for this work, and to draw on the royal treasury for their salary which had been stipulated in the former instructions.[19] The number of Indians in the missions, however, was too small to justify the expenditure involved in fulfilling these orders, and nothing was done about the matter, although the citizens of San Fernando tried to establish a school.

Among the various craftsmen, the carpenters' services seem to have been most in demand. Of the nine in San Antonio listed for 1809, only Manuel Cabrera, a journeyman, was native to San Antonio. Two were designated as masters: Luis Beltrán who had come originally from Zacatecas, and Antonio Canavés from New Orleans, who had resided in San Antonio for thirty-one years. Two others came from the United States, Robert Ringlain and William Rolan (Roland). Joseph Winet had come all the way from Canada. The other three journeymen carpenters were from Mexico. Monclova lost Tomás Sánchez; San Luis Potosí gave up Manuel Arenales, and Monterrey was forsaken by José Juan María González.[20]

The first large San Antonio bakery was established by Pedro Gerónimo Longueville. This Louisianian signed a contract with the *Cabildo* on January 23, 1806. By the terms of the agreement, he was granted an absolute monopoly on flour, its purchase and sale in the neighborhood. In return for his concession, Longueville was to set up a bakery which could supply whatever bread, Spanish white (water), and French, the

---

[19]Order of the king transmitted by N. Salcedo, May 1, 1807. *A. G. I., Audiencia de Guadalajara*, 103-4-1 (Dunn Transcripts, 1800-1819, pp. 177-178).

[20]Noticia de los carpinteros que existen en esta Villa hoi dia. May 17, 1809. *Béxar Archives*.

citizens needed. He was further allowed to bake other kinds of bread if he had time. To insure his monopoly, the city agreed to impose a fine of six *pesos* on anyone found guilty of making bread for sale without permission.

The city specified certain standards which he had to meet. A city inspector was to examine the bread for texture, weight, and amount of cooking. Loaves that were short of weight, burned, or not well done, were to be condemned and given to the prisoners in the jail. To prevent excess profits from the monopoly, it was stipulated that the maximum profit was not to exceed twenty-five per cent. The monopoly was binding on the city only until a better offer was made.[21]

Ordinances. Parking meters are comparatively modern, but Governor Salcedo initiated the idea and for the same purpose—to obtain revenues. In his proclamation of January 16, 1809, he pointed out that the city needed money to keep the plazas and streets clean and to furnish entertainment on holidays. To that end, riders and muleteers would be charged twenty-five cents, he said, for the right to hitch their mounts and beasts of burden. The hitching zone was restricted to the area in the rear of the church on the main plaza. Hitching elsewhere was liable to a fine of two *pesos*.[22]

The registration of vehicles and the issuance of license plates is not new to Texas either. In December, 1809, Governor de Salcedo ordered owners to register their vehicles with their ward commissioner. Each registrant was to receive a numbered license which was to be attached to the front of the vehicle. This regulation applied to all residents within the jurisdiction of Béxar, which extended for almost thirty miles in all directions. Failure to comply with this regulation made the owner liable to confiscation of his property.[23]

A regulation was adopted prohibiting a man and a woman riding the same horse, particularly on feast days. The custom was considered indecorous. Galloping and racing on the streets was likewise declared unlawful. The reason given was that it endangered the lives of pedes-

---

[21]Agreement entered into between the Villa de San Fernando de Béxar and Pedro Gerónimo Longueville, January 23, 1806. *Béxar Archives.*

[22]M. de Salcedo to the Citizens, January 16, 1809. *Nacogdoches Archives*, XII, pp. 1-2.

[23]M. de Salcedo to the Citizens, December 3, 1809. *Nacogdoches Archives*, XII, pp. 11-12.

trians and caused unnecessary disturbance, scaring women and children. This in a way may be called the first Texas speed law.[24]

Many other regulations were adopted during this year. The governor decreed that all women desirous of practicing midwifery must first register with the city council, and pass an examination to obtain a license. This obstetrical law was adopted to reduce infant mortality which was attributed in part to the lack of knowledge and experience of many women who posed as midwives. Those who secured the coveted license by presenting evidence of their skill and ability were to indicate their rating on a sign affixed to the door of their homes.[25]

An effort was made to secure funds to repair the church and improve the cemetery. In a notice to the citizens in October, 1809, the governor explained that liberal residents had contributed 586 *pesos* for church repairs that were long needed. Part of this money had already been spent on materials. And those who cared to, could examine the account books at any time in the governor's office. But 300 *pesos* more were needed for the cemetery. The citizens were asked to contribute in accordance with their means.[26]

It has erroneously been held that land-fencing was a late development in Texas. Early in 1810, Governor Salcedo issued an order for the fencing of all privately owned lands, whether planted or pasture. It seems that many persons were in the habit of pulling up fence posts to use them for firewood. The new ordinance imposed serious punishment on those found guilty of such a crime, and imposed heavy fines on those who failed to fence their property or to denounce fence-post thieves.[27]

As early as 1810 a public abattoir was operated under city supervision. The governor ordered all slaughtering to be done by the city abattoir. But individuals wishing to slaughter a beef or a hog for home use could secure permission.[28]

---

[24]M. de Salcedo to the Citizens, July 25, 1810. *Nacogdoches Archives*, XII, pp. 60-61.

[25]M. de Salcedo to the Citizens, September 27, 1809. *Béxar Archives*.

[26]M. de Salcedo to the Citizens, October 4, 1809. *Nacogdoches Archives*, XII, pp. 3-4.

[27]M. de Salcedo to the Citizens, January 12, 1810. *Nacogdoches Archives*, XII, pp. 24-25.

[28]M. de Salcedo to the Citizens, July 25, 1810. *Nacogdoches Archives*, XII, pp. 61-63.

In November, 1810, Governor Salcedo, alarmed by the revolution spreading in Mexico, published a long proclamation on good government. It contained numerous regulations to safeguard the public peace and welfare and to improve conditions in San Antonio. The curfew law of the previous July was to be strictly enforced. After the curfew, persons failing to halt when challenged were to be fired on as suspicious characters. Employers were charged with the responsibility of keeping their servants and members of their household at home after curfew. Husbands were to be held accountable for wives out after curfew, as were parents for children. All business places were to close when curfew rang and to remain closed until daylight. First offenders were liable to a fine of ten *pesos;* and second offenders to confiscation of their place of business.

Shouting and shooting in or near the city were strictly prohibited, in order to save wear and tear on nerves. A three-*peso* fine was to be imposed on persons burning trash, as the smoke was at least obnoxious and might even be used as a signal to Indians. As a fire prevention, all open-air fires were prohibited. Persons who built fires which spread to neighboring property were to be held responsible for the damages. Property owners were ordered to keep their yards clean and free of weeds.

Public amusements came in for regulation, too. Dances were henceforth not to be given by private individuals or public concerns without a permit. Upon application, permission would be granted by the city officials provided the dance was held in a "house of good repute." No liquor could be sold or dispensed in or near the place of the dance. Professional gambling was declared illegal and the carrying of firearms prohibited under heavy penalties. Crowds were forbidden to gather outside — at doors, windows, and other points of vantage — in order not to block traffic.

The proclamation ended with the warning that ignorance of the new regulations would not excuse from the penalty of the law.[29]

The rumblings of the revolution became more and more audible. The dissatisfaction of ambitious Creoles, the century-old oppression of the masses, and the pernicious activities of French and American agents were constantly reaching the ears of the Texas officials. Finally in December, 1810, Governor Salcedo ordered all foreigners in, or recent immigrants to, the province to register—whether they lived in towns, missions, or on ranches. Married women were exempt, as were those on active duty in the armed forces. But servants were to register. Foreigners living on

---

[29]M. de Salcedo to the Citizens, November 18, 1810. *Nacogdoches Archives,* XII, pp. 67-77.

ranches were allowed one week in which to report and those who failed to register in accord with the new regulations, were to be fined twenty-five *pesos* and classified as suspicious character.[30]

The amount of royal revenue collected in San Antonio was meager indeed. In June, 1809, Erasmo Seguín, collector for the *Estafeta* (Royal Revenue Office) reported the total amounts collected from 1804 to 1808, and indicated the annual increase over each previous year. The total revenue for 1804 from sealed paper, tobacco, and other royal imposts was $666.87. It reached $859.50 in 1805, and in the following year, $1,479. The 1807 revenue showed an increase of $475 over the previous year. But the 1808 total of $2,069.37 represented an increase of only $115.37.[31] These figures serve as an index of the growth of business in the struggling frontier outpost, but they at the same time reveal how little the community contributed towards the support of the administration and the defence of the province. The revenue from both La Bahía and Nacogdoches could not have been more than that of San Antonio.

Ranches and haciendas. As a result of the orders for the registration of foreigners and the taking of a census of the inhabitants and resources of the province, a list was prepared of all the ranches in the vicinity of San Fernando (San Antonio), their owners, the number of persons and the amount of stock on each, and the general conditions. This document gives an excellent idea of the rural establishments in 1810.

Francisco Montes, a 54-year-old native of San Fernando de Béxar, lived on his ranch, San Juan Bautista del Puente de Piedra, with his family. His 45-year-old wife from San Fernando, María Josefa Sambrano, had borne him three children: Juan, Antonio, and María Antonia, aged 12, 8, and 4, respectively. He had two menservants: Apolinar Pérez, aged 70, from Punta de Lampazos, whose family was at La Bahía; and bachelor José María Pérez, a 52-year-old native of Béxar. Montes owned 125 milch cows, 53 bulls, 30 yearlings, 132 heifers, 20 tame horses, 24 mares, 11 ponies, 2 mules, 1 stud, 1 jackass, 9 yoke of oxen, and 3 cars. Manuel Rodríguez also lived on this ranch. This married 40-year-old native of San Fernando had 11 horses, 50 cows, 32 bulls, 32 heifers, 10 bullocks, and 2 oxen.

The widow of Francisco Pérez, Josefa de la Garza, lived on her ranch, Nuestra Señora del Refugio, at Paso de José Miguel, with her children:

---

[30]M. de Salcedo to the Citizens, December 8, 1810. *Nacogdoches Archives*, XII, pp. 82-83.

[31]Report of Erasmo Seguín, June 25, 1809. *Nacogdoches Archives*, XV, pp. 10-11.

Francisco Casanova, 18 years of age, María Antonio, 15, José de los Dolores, 8, Anacleto, 7, and Juan Díaz, 5. Her property consisted of 25 tame horses, 28 colts, 100 milch cows, 62 heifers, 44 bullocks, 350 sheep, 40 hogs, 7 yoke of oxen, 4 mules, 1 stud, 1 jackass, and 3 carts.

In addition to her family there were a number of servants and tenants on the ranch. Among her helpers were bachelor Nicolás Cantú, a 30-year-old native of Cadereita, Nuevo León, who had his own horse, and a cowboy from La Bahía, Matías Peña, 21, who was married to 22-year-old Josefa Valdez of Santa Rosa. He possessed 3 horses. A Lipan, only 19 years old, Francisco Pérez, was employed to break horses. From Monterrey had come Marcelo Barcota to tend the sheep, and from Chihuahua, Miguel Herrera, the 22-year-old caretaker. He and his 30-year-old wife, Perfecta Díaz, of Béxar, had 6 cows and 9 bullocks.

The two tenants living on the ranch, José Leal, a soldier, and his wife, María Josefa Casanova, a native of Béxar, possessed 20 cows and 4 bullocks.[32]

Rancho del Sabinito was owned by Felix Estrada, a native of Boca de Leones, Nuevo León. This 35-year-old rancher was married to a girl of 19, Josefa Rodríguez, a native of Béxar. Their son, José Manuel, was 2 years old. They possessed 80 milch cows, 30 heifers, 30 bulls and bullocks, 40 calves, 15 tame horses, 24 mares, 1 stud, and 3 mules. Their servants were: Siriaco González, a 55-year-old cowboy from Chihuahua, and Rafael González, another cowboy from La Mota, Nuevo León, aged 27. Estrada's mother-in-law, Luisa Guerrero, lived with her 18-year-old son, José María, on the same ranch. This 80-year-old native of Béxar had been widowed by the death of her husband, Salvador Rodríguez. She had two servants, an Indian slave named Manuela Pérez, 90, and a cowboy from Mayapil named Luis Fernando, 40 years old. She had 60 milch cows, 20 heifers, 30 calves, 18 bulls, 9 horses, 5 yoke of oxen, and 2 carts.

Miguel Flores, a native of Monclova, was the owner of Rancho de San Juan Nepomuceno located at Los Arroyos. He lived on the ranch with his wife, María Antonia de Abrego, who was also a native of Coahuila. They had five children: María Gertrudis, María Antonia, María de Jesús, Miguel, and José Francisco, the eldest of whom was 11 years of age, and the youngest, 3. He had 40 milch cows, 70 bullocks, 30 bulls, 50 heifers, 27 yearlings, 26 horses, 26 mares, 100 sheep and goats, 6 yoke of oxen, 1 stud, 1 mule, and 2 carts. His helpers were

[32]*Nacogdoches Archives*, XV, pp. 118-122.

Pedro Ricardo, a 40-year-old cowboy from Béxar, who had married Antonia Sabalza, 19, from Coahuila; Facundo Ricardo, 27, Ignacio Ricardo, 19, and Luciano Gámez, 16, Indian cowhands from Béxar; and 60-year-old Concepción Abrego, from Coahuila.[33]

Rancho de San Cayetano y Paso de las Huitas was the property of José Antonio Carvajal, a native of Béxar, 40 years old, who lived with his 33-year-old wife, María Gertrudis Sánchez, also of Béxar, and his three children: Teodora, José Luis, and José María, ranging from four to one years of age. His was not a very prosperous ranch. He possessed 3 cows, 1 heifer, 1 horse, 1 mare, 3 yoke of oxen, and 1 cart; and he had only one helper, Francisco Sosa, a young boy, 18 years old, from Béxar.

Ignacio Rodríguez, of Béxar, lived with his wife, Antonia Bueno, on his property, Rancho de la Candelaria. He possessed 25 milch cows, 25 heifers, 12 mares, 4 tame horses, 1 stud, 1 colt, 1 mule, 4 yoke of oxen, and 1 cart. His helpers were Francisco Hernández, of Santa Rosa, Coahuila; Miguel Silvia and his wife, María de los Dolores Villanueva, both from Béxar. An old bachelor of 46, Melchor Martinez, also lived on this ranch. He was a native of old Castile, and possessed 4 horses and 1 mule.[34]

José Flores, a native of Béxar, lived on Rancho de San Nicolas with his 33-year-old wife from Béxar, María Antonia Rodríguez, and their six children: Manuel, 11, Josefa, 9, José María, 7, Salvador, 5, Gertrudis, 3, and José Ignacio, 1. They had 45 milch cows, 37 heifers, 30 bullocks, 7 tame horses, 5 mares, 1 colt, 6 yoke of oxen, and 2 carts. Their servants were José María Garcia, 37, a cowboy from Aguascalientes, and Paulín Benítez, 36, a farmer from Béxar.

Santa Rita de las Islitas was owned by Joaquín Leal, a citizen of Béxar, who lived with his 37-year-old wife, Ana María Arocha, also of Béxar, and his five grown children: Clemente, 21, Simón, 20, Antonio, 19, Juana, 18, and Consolación, 17. He owned 160 milch cows, 29 bulls, 30 bullocks, 40 heifers, 105 calves, 36 oxen, 12 hogs, 11 tame horses, 11 mares, 1 stud, 1 mule, and 2 carts. He had two helpers: Miguel Montalvo, a native of Camargo, 58, and Pedro Ramírez, 57, a free Negro from Guinea, who owned 2 horses.[35]

[33]*Nacogdoches Archives*, XV, pp. 122-125, 130-131.
[34]*Nacogdoches Archives*, XV, pp. 127, 129-130.
[35]*Nacogdoches Archives*, XV, pp. 125-128.

On Rancho de San Bartolomé lived a couple from Béxar. The 42-year-old owner, Manuel Salinas, and his wife, María Ignacia Flores, 37, had five children: Margarita, 21, Gertrudis, 16, Pablo, 20, Antonia, 13, and José María, 12. A sister-in-law named María Flores, 50, was staying with them also. The servants were a motley group. Sixteen-year-old Encarnación Jiménez was a former neophyte of Mission San Juan. José Rosalío, a 54-year-old widower, was a free Negro who had come from Mexico. Pedro Xavier Salinas was a cowboy from Béxar, aged 62, who owned 3 mares, 1 stud, and 5 milch cows. Then there were Ignacio Rios, 27, from La Bahía, and his wife, Paula Salcedo, 23, of Béxar, and José Montalvo, 33, of Río Grande, and his wife, Polonia de la Garza, 24, of Béxar.

On Cibolo Creek was Rancho de San José, owned by Juan Martín Veramendi, 32, a native of Béxar. Here he lived with his 18-year-old wife, Josefa, also from Béxar. They had 180 milch cows, 50 bulls, 105 bullocks, 48 heifers, 20 yearlings, 70 calves, 1,890 sheep, 33 horses, 58 mares, 6 yoke of oxen, 4 ponies, 2 studs, 1 jenny, 1 jack, and 1 cart. Their servants were Francisco Gamaba, 26, from Béxar; Domingo Bruno, 34, cowboy, and his wife Estéfana Sosa, 22; Rafael Sosa, 40, and his wife, Eufrasia Jiménez, 20, and their children: Juana, 13, María Guadalupe, 8, Francisco, 6, Juan, 4, and María Ignacia, 9 months, all from Camargo; Antonio Guerra, 34, and his wife, Guadalupe Rios, 26, from San Fernando, Coahuila; Francisco Holanderos, 25, Ignacio Sánchez, 29, and his wife, Juana Antonia Flores, 27, who came from Linares to take care of the sheep and goats; and Pablo Torres, 24, from Béxar, who was employed to break horses.[36]

Vicente Micheli, 51, a native of Brecia, Italy, owned Rancho de San Francisco, where he lived with his wife, María Susana Maró, 36, of Natchitoches, and their two children: José Vicente, 18, and María Nieves, 15. He possessed 70 milch cows, 20 bulls, 5 horses, 7 mares, and 1 yoke of oxen. He had three helpers: Juan José Gámez, 50, widower, a cowboy from La Bahía, Prudencio Quintero, 42, from Saltillo, and his wife, María Guadalupe Ruiz, 50, from La Bahía.

Rancho de las Mulas, one of the more prosperous establishments, was the property of 44-year-old Vicente Travieso, who declared he was a native of Saltillo. He was married to María Luisa León, of Béxar, 24 years old, by whom he had had three children, Juan, 9, Jacoba, 6, and Melchor, 4. His property consisted of 313 milch cows, 43 bulls, 110

---

[36]*Nacogdoches Archives*, XV, pp. 146-149.

bullocks, 186 branding calves, 1,128 sheep and goats, 20 oxen, 34 horses, 54 mares, 26 colts, 3 studs, 7 mules, 3 jackasses, 3 jennies, 3 hogs, and 2 carts. Among his servants were María Cabrera, 24; Fernando Martínez, 33, and his wife, Gertrudis Menchaca, 21; José Sánchez, 24, and his son, José Francisco, 8; Luis Núñez, a 44-year-old cowboy, his wife, Francisca Morales, 22, and his son, Marcos, 20, all from Béxar; Severiana Guardado, 57, who had left his family in Aguascalientes; José Antonio Jiménez, 37, from Río Grande, his wife, Regina Pérez, 27, from Monclova, and their daughter, María de los Dolores, 8; and Joaquín Rodríguez, 56, and his wife, Jacoba Segura, 36, both from Río Grande, and their daughter named María de los Dolores.[37]

Fernando Veramendi lived with his wife, from Béxar, 21-year-old Antonia Flores, on his property, Rancho de San Bartolo. Veramendi had 190 milch cows, 25 bulls, 122 branding calves, 5 bullocks, 5 yoke of oxen, 5 horses, and 2 mules. Among his helpers were Antonio Martínez, 23, from Río Verde, and José Bárcena, a 34-year-old cowboy from Béxar, who was married to Juana Flores, 21, by whom he had two children, José, 6, and José II, 2. This couple had some property of their own, 5 milch cows, 3 heifers, 1 ox, and 8 horses.

The ranch really formed a small rural community, for several other families lived on it. José Andrés Hernández, 65, a widower, from Béxar, owned 50 milch cows, 16 mares, 8 wild horses, 1 stud, 8 colts, and 9 oxen. With Hernández lived his son, José Vicente, 25, and his son's wife, María Antonia Calvillo, 16, besides a single son, José Felipe, 20, and a spinster daughter, Juana, 16. These Hernández families had two servants: Francisco Mireles, 35, and Manuela Jiménez, 26, his wife, both from Río Grande. A third Hernández family also lived on this ranch. Francisco, a 50-year-old native of Béxar, and his wife, Rafaela de León, 50, from Aguascalientes, who had three children, José, Juan Nepomuceno, and Cándida, ranging in age from 15 to 10. They had 50 mares, 16 horses, 40 milch cows, 8 heifers, 4 yoke of oxen, and 1 cart. They employed José Vicente García, 34, from Santa Rosa, to help with the stock. Bárbara Sánchez, 30, from Béxar, widow of José Hernández, also lived on the ranch with her son, José, 20, and José Antonio Llanos, 19, of Monterrey, caretaker of her stock. She had 28 milch cows, 10 horses, 3 mares, 1 jackass, 6 yoke of oxen, and 1 cart.

José Erasmo Seguín, 28, was the owner of Rancho de San Juan Nepomuceno de la Mora, where he lived with his wife, Josefa Becerra,

---

[37]*Nacogdoches Archives*, XV, pp. 153-158.

19, from La Bahía, and their three children: Juan Nepomuceno, 5, María, 3, and Leonidas, 2. His property consisted of 326 milch cows, 110 bulls, 20 calves, 30 hogs, 20 mules, 18 mares, 10 horses, 1 stud, 1 jackass, 6 oxen, and 1 cart. His hired help were Máximo Vasquez, 27, a cowboy, and his 18-year-old wife, Gertrudis Vazquez; Antonio Bueno, 25, from Béxar, his wife, Antonia Hernández, 18, and their son, Francisco, 2; Alejandro González, 26, native of Pilón; José Ramos, 16, from Saltillo; Anselmo Pres, 45, and his 25-year-old wife, Feliciana Hernández, both of whom were from Béxar.[38]

These 14 ranches were all located within the jurisdiction of San Fernando de Béxar and formed a part of the district of Béxar. Taken as a whole, the 172 persons listed as owners of or residents on the 14 ranches, looked after 1,921 milch cows, 452 bulls, 488 heifers, 650 calves, and 417 bullocks—some 3,928 head of cattle; 312 mares, 268 horses, 14 studs, 64 colts, 15 ponies; 42 mules, 12 jacks and jennies; 168 oxen; 3,730 sheep and goats; 85 hogs; and 21 carts.

Renewal of the Río Frio project. It will be remembered that in 1806 José Antonio Ramírez had asked permission to be established on the Río Frio a settlement which was to be called Nueva Jaén. The commandant general refused to grant the request at that time, because, as he said, it would be better to concentrate on the settlements already authorized rather than to attempt new projects before the others were finished. The petitioner was promised that his proposal would be filed for later consideration. Early in 1809, Ramírez again asked to be permitted to carry out his proposed settlement on the Frio River. Cordero, who was still in Texas, immediately transmitted the request to Don Nemesio Salcedo with a plea for its approval. But the commandant general could not bring himself to grant the desired authorization for a new settlement. As a matter of fact, conditions had become more disturbed than ever, and the old guardian of the frontier had grown more wary of all new enterprises. Following his usual procrastinating policy, Salcedo informed Ramírez that the project would have to be postponed again until a more opportune time.[39]

Cordero's efforts in behalf of the colony on the Frio was one of his last official acts in Texas. Early in May the veteran commander and experienced administrator of affairs in Texas was recalled to Coahuila,

---

[38]*Nacogdoches Archives*, XV, pp. 150-153, 156-157.
[39]N. Salcedo to Cordero, April 17, 1809. *Béxar Archives.*

where his services as governor were greatly needed and had long been missed.[40] The liberal party in Texas lost one of its most able and courageous leaders. Cordero's associates thereafter did not dare openly oppose the commandant general. They resorted to less direct methods, which were as effective in obtaining their end. Bonavía and Manuel de Salcedo seemed to be possessed of a blind faith in the goodness of human nature and believed that immigration would solve the problem of defending the province and of developing its resources. The commandant general, more experienced in dealing with men, had long since learned to distrust all Louisiana immigrants, whether American, French, or Spanish. Numerous cases of treachery and deceit had increased this distrust of his, and subsequent events in Texas amply vindicated him in his opinion about the majority of the immigrants who gained admission in spite of his determined opposition.

Conditions in East Texas. Early in 1809 Governor Salcedo had informed the commandant general that he was about to undertake an inspection of the province. Summer came and went, but there was no inspection. Commandant General Salcedo, uneasy over the disquieting news concerning French agents and American filibusters, wrote the governor in August to urge him to proceed without further delay to execute the long-postponed tour of inspection. He instructed the governor to make a list of all persons, particularly of all foreigners and recent immigrants, in order that those who had violated any regulation might be expelled immediately as provided by the *Laws of the Indies*.[41] In spite of this peremptory order, the tour was not undertaken until some six months later. Instead, Governor Salcedo contented himself with ordering all local officials to take a census, which he sent to the commandant general. A careful study of the reports convinced the commandant general that many foreigners had succeeded in evading the immigration laws, and were now living in the five Texas settlements. Many of these, especially in Villa de Salcedo, should never have been admitted under any circumstances. In despair, Commandant General Salcedo now appealed to Bonavía, pointing out that many of the settlers were undesirable on account of their religion, their nationality, and their questionable character. He severely criticized the Texas officials for their negligence in enforcing the laws designed to keep this type of immigrant out of the country, and instructed Bonavía to request Governor Salcedo to start

---

[40]N. Salcedo to Bonavía, June 6, 1809. *Béxar Archives.*

[41]N. Salcedo to M. de Salcedo, August 7, 1809. *Béxar Archives.*

at once on his tour of inspection with an adequate number of troops to expel immediately all who had gained admission illegally. The governor was to be told not to return to Béxar until he had satisfactorily carried out this important mission.[42]

Upon being informed of the commandant general's serious charge of negligence preferred against him, Governor Salcedo made a spirited reply. He disclaimed responsibility for the admission of objectionable characters, defended the integrity of the immigrants in general, and protested against their arbitrary expulsion. He declared that the majority of the settlers, impelled by a desire to continue to live under the benevolent laws of the king of Spain, had moved either prior to or immediately after the retrocession of Louisiana. Their long residence in Texas and the circumstances under which they had felt compelled to immigrate were eloquent proof of their loyalty to Spain, he naively contended. Arbitrary expulsion at this late hour, he warned, would but increase the number of dissatisfied squatters forced into the Neutral Ground, where numerous disreputable characters had already found refuge and were constantly harassing the province and carrying on a profitable contraband trade. More pressing duties had prevented him from undertaking the long-contemplated tour of inspection, the governor explained, and although a year had elapsed, he assured the commandant general the delay had been unavoidable. He concluded by presenting an earnest plea against the arbitrary expulsion of foreigners, and asked to be authorized to use his own discretion in disposing of individual cases. He ventured to suggest that undesirable settlers found in East Texas be removed to the interior of the province instead of being expelled, pointing out that their removal from the frontier would put an end to their illegal activities.[43]

When Bonavía transmitted the reply, he took occasion to endorse Governor Salcedo's suggestion for removing undesirable settlers farther into the interior. He maintained that the expulsion of all foreigners at this time would result in unnecessary excitement and confusion on the eastern frontier. The governor was right, Bonavía asserted, in that those who would be expelled would probably join the already too numerous desperados in the Neutral Ground and add to the worries of frontier officials. In an effort to allay the fears of the commandant general, Bonavía declared that the danger of French attack was remote, since

[42]N. Salcedo to Bonavía, January 9, 1810. *Béxar Archives.*
[43]M. de Salcedo to N. Salcedo, January 21, 1810. *Béxar Archives.*

England was now the ally of Spain. This factor would also deter the Americans from an open break.[44]

The commandant general was shocked by and indignant at Bonavía's support of the governor, but he was furious with the governor for boldly disregarding his formal and explicit instructions. He immediately wrote a sharp rebuke to Governor Salcedo for having presumed to interpret definite orders, for having dared to suggest modifications of the order for the expulsion of foreigners, and for having suspended execution of his formal command. He reminded the governor that orders were to be carried out literally and commanded him to undertake the tour of inspection without further delay. He instructed the governor to make a thorough investigation of the defences of the province, to suggest a means of improving them, to list all Indian tribes, and to report on their general attitude towards the Spaniards and their desire for missionaries. Bonavía was similarly reprimanded and ordered to coöperate with the governor in immediately executing his instructions without exception.[45]

In spite of these explicit orders to start at once, Governor Salcedo still delayed his departure from Béxar for more than a month. In the meantime, the commandant general regained his composure and reconsidered the whole matter. The previous warnings of Onís and other Spanish agents in regard to the presence of a large number of French and American revolutionists in New Orleans made him conclude that the arbitrary expulsion of foreigners from Texas would but furnish additional information and recruits to this band of filibusters. Perhaps the governor was right. Consequently the orders of February 6 were modified by supplementary instructions on March 1 and 13, 1810. Commandant General Salcedo again ordered Governor Salcedo to leave at once on his tour of inspection. He was instructed to investigate carefully the character of all foreigners and the circumstances under which they had been admitted. He was, likewise, to warn those who had entered the province illegally that their cases would be taken under advisement and that they would be expelled if there were no attenuating circumstances. Those who desired to leave at once were to be allowed to go, and those who desired to await the decision in their cases were to be permitted to stay. One thing they were not to be permitted to do: move into the interior.[46]

---

[44]Bonavía to N. Salcedo, January 23, 1810. *Béxar Archives.*

[45]N. Salcedo to M. de Salcedo, February 6, 1810; N. Salcedo to Bonavía, February 6, 1810. *Béxar Archives.*

[46]Bonvía to M. de Salcedo, March 1, 1810; N. Salcedo to M. de Salcedo, March 13, 1810. *Béxar Archives.*

Villa de Salcedo. Unable to find a good excuse for postponing his inspection any longer, the governor set out from Béxar on March 11. He made his way directly to Villa de Salcedo, where he arrived on March 24. Half-heartedly he gathered the required information on the foreigners. He found that there were ninety-one persons living in the settlement, not including several families who resided on nearby ranches. The governor frankly admitted that he did not have the heart to tell them that they either had to burn their property and move within the two leagues of the municipality of Salcedo or leave the country. He was equally lax in carrying out his instructions concerning irregular marriages. Instead of summoning the immigrants and ordering them to abide by the laws on matrimony, he contented himself with having a confidential talk with the parish priest and inquiring about their character and behaviour. Fortunately for the immigrants, Father José Francisco Maynes was a tolerant and kindly shepherd, who hoped to convert the immigrants from their erring ways by kindness and understanding.

The list of foreigners residing in Villa de Salcedo proper showed only twenty-seven names, although it should have included a good many more. For example, the governor admitted that he did not take the trouble to investigate Jacob Dorst, who was absent, and in whom the commandant general was particularly interested. Rather, he pleaded in Dorst's behalf, declaring that he was a German who had lived in Arcos, Louisiana, for many years prior to his coming to Texas. He had three sons, all Catholics, one of whom lived with him in Salcedo; the other two were in Nacogdoches. Neither Vicente Micheli, another suspicious character, nor Juan Lorenzo Boden, a native of Natchitoches who had married an Indian woman, was included in the list.

In making out his report, the governor made bold to defend practically all the foreigners in Texas. He stoutly declared that there was nothing to fear from the American pioneers who had moved into the province. They were almost all good farmers, who loved the soil and were thoroughly happy if allowed to settle on rich, well-wooded lands. Those who had lived under the Spanish flag in Louisiana had become loyal supporters of Spain. It is interesting to note that Governor Salcedo insisted that Protestantism did not constitute a serious objection to their settlement in Texas, because "they are so poorly instructed in their beliefs that under the influence [guidance] of a priest, it would not be difficult to convert them to our faith." It was the educated Americans, such as doctors, lawyers, and merchants, who were to be feared. These were the ones who were constantly starting trouble. Governor Salcedo branded all Frenchmen as restless, and said that whether they were Catholic or Protestant, educated or uneducated, they all had a bitter hatred in their heart for Spaniards and everything Spanish. These were the two types of immigrants that should be barred from Texas. Turning from the general to the specific, he maintained that the records of almost all the foreigners now living in Salcedo showed conclusively that they were faithful and peace-loving settlers who deserved to be allowed to remain in the province. The governor informed the commandant general that in view of the circumstances, he had disregarded the explicit instructions of March 1 and 13, and permitted all foreigners to remain until their cases were individually decided.[47]

In support of the governor's testimony, Father Maynes, parish priest of Salcedo, made a formal statement that the foreigners in his jurisdiction were peaceful, law-abiding citizens and loyal subjects of the king. He testified that as a general rule, the Protestants attended his religious services equally as well as the Catholics and had offered no open offence to the Church. He admitted that the foreigners did not go to confession regularly, but he attributed their failure to receive the Sacrament of Penance to their inability to express themselves in Spanish with ease.[48]

The persistence of Governor Salcedo and the blandness of Bonavía wore down Commandant General Salcedo's resistance. He gave up, and sent to Bonavía two copy books with the names of the foreigners in Salcedo and the evidence gathered against them by the governor, and instructed Bonavía to decide the fate of these immigrants.[49] Bonavía lost no time in informing the governor that he had decided that all foreigners who had resided in Texas for any length of time were to be permitted to stay, and that those who were considered disloyal or suspicious characters were to be removed to the interior in order to prevent them from communicating with their friends and accomplices in Louisiana. The commander in Texas had taken upon himself to reverse the explicit order of March 13, which provided that no foreigner was to be permitted to move farther into the interior regardless of the circumstances. On May 30, he reported his action to the commandant general, who seems not to have bothered to give his formal approval.[50]

[47]M. de Salcedo to N. Salcedo, March 30, and April 6, 1810. *Béxar Archives.*
[48]Father José Francisco Maynes to M. de Salcedo, May 30, 1810. *Béxar Archives.*
[49]N. Salcedo to M. de Salcedo, May 14, 1810. *Béxar Archives.*
[50]Bonavía to N. Salcedo, May 30, 1810. *Béxar Archives.*

In forming his policy concerning foreigners, Bonavía decided to share with the governor the discretionary power granted to him and to permit the governor to pass on the admission of those residing in Salcedo. He was to submit a formal list with his recommendations to Bonavía for final approval. Bonavía reported to the governor on June 6 that he had studied the various cases submitted and found eight which needed to be decided individually. Of these, Juan Magui (John McGee), Miguel Quin, and Juan McFarland were involved in the scandalous contraband case against Enrique Kuerke, a Kentuckian resident of Nacogdoches. Bonavía instructed Governor Salcedo to suspend final action on these three until the trial of Kuerke was terminated. Bonavía, who was inclined to be lenient, declared that three of the other five might be permitted to stay, since, judging by the records, their conduct should give little uneasiness to the authorities. Of the two remaining, the commander pointed out that one of them needed instruction rather than expulsion and the other, a habitual drunkard and a Protestant, could adduce no grounds for clemency. Governor Salcedo, therefore, was ordered to expel Guillermo Burxer as a hopeless case. But it seems that not even he was ever forced to leave the province.[51]

Nacogdoches. Flushed with success, Governor Salcedo proceeded to Nacogdoches, where he directed his attention to the disposition of foreigners and undesirable immigrants. After holding a review of the garrison and inspecting the weak fortifications of this important outpost, he summoned all foreigners and had each family head fill out a rather detailed questionnaire. Each had to give his name, age, birthplace, religion, length of time and places of residence under Spanish jurisdiction prior to his coming to Texas, date of taking and the name of the person administering the oath of allegiance for the first time. More embarrassing—because it was incriminating in many instances—was the demand for a statement of the number of times the declarant had absented himself from the province and the reasons for the absences.[52] It is strange that Nacogdoches, with a population of more than six hundred, had registered and questioned at this time only twenty-nine foreigners, for there had been almost twice that many listed as foreigners in 1801. This disparity may be accounted for by the fact that the inhabitants of Bayou Pierre had not been notified, consequently did

---

[51]Bonavía to M. de Salcedo, June 6, 1810; Causa seguida a Kuerke, Magui, McFarlan . . . por contrabandistas . . . *Béxar Archives.*

[52]Expediente sobre Extranjeros de Nacogdoches, May 8, 1810. *Béxar Archives.*

not register. The governor had neglected, likewise, to investigate the ranchers in the vicinity just as it happened in the area of Villa de Salcedo.

Many were the nationalities represented on the list. There were one Irishman, one Italian, one German, several Englishmen from England and Canada, and several Americans from different states of the Union. Not all were Catholics and many had made frequent trips to Louisiana. It was difficult to find a reason for permitting some of them to stay. But the governor pursued his usual policy of trying to find justification for their permanent residence in the province. He called upon the two priests in Nacogdoches for certificates of good conduct and loyalty of the immigrants.

Less optimistic and tolerant than Father Maynes, perhaps because they were more experienced in the ways of the frontier, the two missionaries refused to give a general approval of all the foreigners. Father Mariano Sosa, who had been in Nacogdoches for only a short while, regretted his inability to be of better service because he was unfamiliar with conditions. He stated, however, that the Spaniards in the settlement were all good, practical Catholics. Although not well acquainted with all the people of the vicinity, he expressed serious doubts about the character of a certain Bernardo Dortolán, who had been too intimate with the scheming General D'Alvimar during the latter's stay in Nacogdoches. Dortolán was an old settler, who had come into the province in 1779, with the famous French trader and Indian agent, Athanase de Mézières. Two others were singled out by Father Sosa, Santiago Dill and Christian Hesser. Neither one observed his religious duties as Catholics. Hesser, moreover, lived well in spite of the fact that he had no visible means of support. He always displayed an inordinate admiration for everything French and American. Father Sosa wondered if he were not a paid agent.[53] Father José María Huerta de Jesús also began by deploring his unfamiliarity with conditions on this frontier, but he concurred in his superior's opinion of Dortolán and Hesser. He admitted he knew a little more about Santiago Dill, who, he declared, was not a Catholic. Dill, in fact, prided himself that he was not, and had often declared that he would never become a Catholic. His family, however, were good Catholics.[54]

---

[53]Father Mariano Sosa to M. de Salcedo, May 4, 1810. *Béxar Archives.*

[54]Father José María Huerta de Jesús to M. de Salcedo, May 31, 1810. *Béxar Archives.*

Governor Salcedo forwarded the list of Nacogdoches foreigners and the report on his investigations concerning them, in which he frankly admitted that there were a goodly number who should never have been allowed to enter the province. He maintained, however, that since they had been admitted to or had succeeded in establishing themselves in Texas, they should be allowed to remain, provided their conduct had been above reproach. Many of them were not Catholics and since they had never taken the oath of allegiance, he contended that they could not be properly called Spanish subjects. Consequently they could not claim the right to admission as former subjects of the king. He expressed no concern over the conduct of Dortolán and his relations with D'Alvimar, or over the illegal trading activities of Kuerke and his associates who were convicted. As a matter of fact, he recommended that all foreigners in Nacogdoches be granted permission to stay.[55]

Much light is thrown on conditions at Nacogdoches by a more detailed report of Father Mariano Sosa. He declared that the principal occupations of the settlers were farming, cattle raising, and contraband trade. The chief products were corn, beans, pumpkins, cotton, various vegetables, watermelons, melons, and wheat. He criticized the soldiers for their bad habits of gambling and petty thievery. The conduct of the civilians was not much better, but he attributed their laziness and dishonesty to their inability to dispose of their products advantageously. The lack of an incentive to raise larger or better crops under the existing regulations accounted for the prevalence of contraband trade among them. The character of these shiftless frontiersmen could be improved, he thought, by adopting a number of constructive policies. He made bold to suggest that the soldiers be paid more regularly and in specie. Under the system in force they had to purchase all their supplies from the commissary. If, however, they were paid in specie and allowed to buy from the local merchants, they would help in improving trade. Another way he suggested of stimulating business was to permit the settlers to sell their produce either in the interior of Mexico or in Louisiana. With such a market, the farmers would exert themselves to produce larger and better crops, there would be more money in circulation, and the merchants and townsmen would not be compelled to resort to contraband in order to make a living. He recommended the establishment of a school to teach the children reading and writing, good manners, and moral principles. The ignorance of the young people, he believed, was not conducive to

---

[55]Informe of M. de Salcedo, May 19, 1810. *Béxar Archives.*

either interest or ambition in life. Education would, in his opinion, change the indifferent attitude of the Nacogdoches people to give them a goal in life.

Father Sosa's last recommendation concerned the Indians in the vicinity and those who frequented the outpost, who, he declared, were friendly. He admitted that while some Indians were interested only in gifts, there were others who seemed anxious to be instructed in the faith. Among those tribes desirous of religious instruction, he thought missions might be established, but he was of the opinion that these should be organized differently. He believed that in the past the Indians congregated in the missions had been pampered too much and given too many things for nothing. The new missions should be for only those Indians who wanted to be instructed and were willing to adopt European customs and habits; those who wanted to be allowed simply to idle in the mission when they were not on a hunting expedition or on the warpath should be excluded.[56] It is a pity that these constructive suggestions of Father Sosa were not given a trial.

Bayou Pierre. Although a large number of foreigners were located at Bayou Pierre, Governor Salcedo did not bother to visit the settlement. He contented himself with referring to the July census taken at his request. According to this census report, there were seventeen men and their families at Bayou Pierre. They were Juan Bilberg and David Gaulteman (Waltman), natives of Germany; Juan Bolbado, from Nantes, and Juan Duponey and Carlos Bruillar, from France, and Vicente Nolan, who claimed to be from that country also; Miguel Benson, from Canada; Pierre Bonet Lafitte, Luis Beltrán, Sylvestre and Atanacio Poisset, Pedro Dolet, and Remi Christi, natives of Natchitoches; Miguel Roben, from Natchez; Bautista Colet, from Louisiana; Santiago Guales (Wallace), a native of the United States; and Guillermo Estretche, from Nueva Mercia.[57] Needless to say, no investigation was conducted to ascertain the manner in which they had come in or the length of time that they had been residing in Texas.

Atascosito. Because of the rains the governor did not visit Atascosito. The very name, which means "muddy," indicates the character of the terrain. Little wonder that Governor Salcedo, who was not interested in

---

[56]Father Mariano Sosa to M. de Salcedo, May 26, 1810. *Béxar Archives.*

[57]Affidavits and census of settlers at Bayou Pierre, July 26, 1809, and August 2, 16, and 17, 1809. *Béxar Archives.*

expelling anybody, did not consider a trip to Atascosito in the rainy season essential.

Depopulation. While the commandant general seemed to be of the opinion that undesirable settlers ought to be expelled, the authorities in Texas were becoming quite concerned over the fact that many settlers were leaving the province and going to New Orleans. So great was the fear that the entire eastern frontier might become depopulated that Governor Salcedo, who had succeeded in persuading the commandant general to abandon his policy calling for the expulsion of foreigners, took the liberty of issuing a proclamation to the inhabitants of Nacogdoches on July 29, 1810. He promised a pardon upon return to all who, because they had been accused of dealing in contraband trade, had fled the country, and to any others who may have left Texas.[58] He held out to them the inducement of a more liberal trade policy and various other measures to promote prosperity. All those who had fled either through fear of punishment or in despair of ever improving their condition under the existing regulations, he invited to return to help develop the country and to enjoy the fruits of the new regulations which the Government planned to adopt. He reminded them of the great danger to their Catholic faith resulting from contact with heretics and unbelievers and urged them for the sake of their religion and out of their loyalty to Spain to return to Texas. In the name of Ferdinand VII he offered a full pardon to all those who had fled to Louisiana, even if they had taken their stock with them, on condition that they returned before November 1 and presented themselves to the proper authorities to be placed in possession of their lands again. He assured the foreigners residing in the province, whose cases were still pending, a favorable decision which would permit them to remain permanently in secure possession of all their property. "Be relieved of your forebodings," the governor entreated, "and enjoy the paternal solicitude of the kindest and wisest government."[59]

Governor Salcedo became alarmed at the number of foreigners and Spanish subjects who, instead of seeking admission were now anxious to leave, impelled by the fear of impending revolution and political persecution. He appealed to Bonavía to do something to check the outflow

---

[58]Proclamation of Governor M. de Salcedo to the Inhabitants of Nacogdoches, July 29, 1810. *Béxar Archives.* The text of the proclamation is reproduced in a poor English translation as Appendix 19 in Hatcher, *The Opening of Texas to Foreign Settlement*, 332-333.

[59]Proclamation of Governor M. de Salcedo to the Inhabitants of Nacogdoches, July 29, 1810. *Béxar Archives.*

of settlers. He pleaded with the military commander to make these people see what they were losing by their rash action. The governor believed that Bonavía should give them assurance so as to allay their fears and that they should be detained by force if necessary. He should show them that they were throwing away the rights they had acquired at great personal sacrifice, that they were endangering their faith, and that they were branding themselves as traitors by leaving at this time.[60]

Bonavía tried to reassure the governor, who seems to have been unduly concerned about the panic that had seized the inhabitants of East Texas. He pointed out that there were no legal means to prevent foreigners from leaving the province if they chose to depart. It was also impossible to prohibit Spanish subjects from emigrating except those who were fleeing from justice. In that case, they could be apprehended and put in prison until their trial. As for those who had succeeded in leaving and were now in Louisiana, Bonavía believed that the only recourse was to request the Spanish consul at New Orleans to make an effort to induce them to return to their former homes in Texas.[61]

When Commandant General Salcedo learned of the proclamation issued by Governor Salcedo in Nacogdoches, he was again furious. Unacquainted with the conditions that had prompted the governor to take this step, he judged the action as an unpardonable disregard of authority. The governor had not only exceeded his authority by inviting foreigners into Texas, but had also taken to himself sovereign powers by granting a pardon in the name of the king without consulting royal officials. He reminded the governor that even he, the commandant general of the Interior Provinces, had no power to grant such a pardon or to offer complete amnesty to criminals. Those who had left the province with their stock had violated the trading regulations, he asserted, and should be tried for this crime upon their presentation to the authorities. He, therefore, ordered Governor Salcedo to issue strict instructions to all frontier officers to disregard the terms of the proclamation, and to arrest all those who in response to it presented themselves within their jurisdiction. They were to be held until they were tried for the crimes they had committed prior to their leaving the province.[62]

Governor Salcedo suddenly found himself in a dilemma, but was just as suddenly relieved from his embarrassing position by an unexpected

---

[60]M. de Salcedo to Bonavía, October 5, 1810. *Béxar Archives.*
[61]Bonavía to M. de Salcedo, October 6 (?), 1810. *Béxar Archives.*
[62]N. Salcedo to M. de Salcedo, October 2, 1810. *Béxar Archives.*

change of mind on the part of the commandant general. By the time he issued his irate order annulling the governor's proclamation, the standard of rebellion had been raised in the interior of Mexico and the Capital itself had been seriously threatened by the masses under the leadership of Miguel Hidalgo y Costilla. The cry for emancipation from the tyrannical Government of Spain had been taken up and had been reëchoed throughout Mexico. There was no time for quibbling. Measures that could not be effectively enforced would but lead to a whole train of evils. Hurriedly, the commandant general wrote the governor again on October 13, approving the general terms of the proclamation of July 29. All those returning to Texas in response to the call were to present themselves to the Spanish officials for readmission after giving the reason for their departure from the country, the number of animals they had taken with them, and the places where they had resided during their absence. This information was to be duly filed before the *emigrés* were permitted to return.[63]

Once again the commandant general had been forced to reverse his policy within a year. The power of Spain in America was rapidly crumbling and the imposing edifice of Spain's colonial empire was about to crash upon the heads of its devoted defenders. The ruling of the commandant general was in itself an admission of weakness. He well knew that he had no means of enforcing his orders. His outbursts of temper were but the rage of his impotency.

Villa de Palafox. Villa de Palafox, established by Governor Cordero, of Coahuila, was not within the province of Texas at the time of its founding. Since it was located east of the Río Grande and within the present limits of Texas, its establishment, nevertheless, deserves to be included in this history. On April 27, 1810, Governor Cordero instructed Captain Juan José Díaz, the commander of Presidio de Río Grande (located near present Eagle Pass), to distribute lands to such settlers as wished to establish their homes in the new villa, which was named Palafox, in honor of a Spanish patriot who had fought with distinction against the French invaders of the Peninsula. The villa was located on the east bank of the Río Grande, about half-way between Presidio de Río Grande and modern Laredo. The settlers were to be drawn from older establishments in Coahuila. A regular map was drawn for the lay-out of the town and Captain Juan José Díaz was put in charge of

---

[63]N. Salcedo to M. de Salcedo, October 13, 1810. *Béxar Archives.*

its development.[64] Not until September did the commandant general approve the project officially. He expressed regret at the inability of the king's treasury to bear the customary expense of erecting the public buildings for the new villa. The details of the history of this little known settlement are, indeed, meager.[65] Stephen F. Austin's map of 1829 indicates the location and notes tersely but significantly "Destroyed by Indians." The country was not suitable for a settlement, and to this day there is not a town of any great size along the Río Grande between Laredo and Eagle Pass. The story of the hardships and sufferings endured by the brave pioneers will remain unknown unless it will be found among the documents of some unexplored archives.[66]

New Spain in revolt. With lightning rapidity the wave of discontent was spreading from Villa de Dolores over all New Spain. Thousands of natives flocked daily to swell the advancing hordes that were threatening the Capital itself. The viceroy and his advisors attributed the revolt to the activity of French agents, who, they claimed, had vigorously fanned into flames the smouldering fire of dissension between Creoles and Spaniards. But the rebellion had gathered force from three hundred years of misgovernment and exploitation to drive the masses of the people to join Hidalgo. Aware of the dangerous consequences of help being given the rebels from Louisiana, the commandant general urged the governor of Texas early in October, 1810, to redouble his vigilance along the frontier and at the first sign of conspiracy or revolt, to employ vigorous means to stop it.[67] The governor replied immediately that he had taken all necessary precautions against surprise, but because of the inadequate means at his disposal, he would be unable to act effectively in the event of an emergency or insurrection. It was at this critical moment that Bonavía was ordered to return to Durango, where his presence was needed to check the advance of the revolution into the northern provinces of New Spain.[68] Thus, Governor Salcedo was left practically alone to continue the policy of appeasement with the Indians, to stop American and French filibusters from crossing the frontier, to

---

[64]The original map is reproduced in Hatcher, *The Opening of Texas to Foreign Settlement,* opposite page 202.

[65]The only available sources on Palafox are in Volume 58 of the *Records* in the Land Office (Austin, Texas), and the account in Hatcher, *Op. Cit.,* 202.

[66]All efforts to find additional details have proved futile.

[67]N. Salcedo to M. de Salcedo, October 2, 1810. *Béxar Archives.*

[68]M. de Salcedo to N. Salcedo, October 27, 1810. *Béxar Archives.*

stamp out sedition, and to put an end to contraband trade. To accomplish these arduous tasks, he had a greatly reduced military force, an empty treasury, a semi-hostile population, and a group of fickle Indian allies.

Undismayed, the governor issued detailed instructions to the commandant of Nacogdoches to watch closely the movement of foreigners and suspicious Spaniards within his jurisdiction. He authorized him to call upon the commander at Villa de Salcedo in the event of an emergency. He informed the officials on the frontier of the insurgents' plan to murder those who remained loyal to the king and warned them against even their intimate friends. Disloyalty, he declared, had permeated all classes and no one could be trusted. Suspects should be immediately arrested and tried.[69] To keep foreigners and filibusters out and to put a stop to contraband trade from Louisiana, he commissioned an officer from the garrison in San Antonio, Cristobal Domínguez, to supervise all frontier outposts from Nacogdoches to Orcoquisac and charged him with the full responsibility of closing the frontier.

Efforts to arouse loyalty. Commandant General Salcedo issued a proclamation to all the inhabitants of the Interior Provinces on October 24, 1810. He asserted that French emissaries were misleading the loyal subjects of the king; that the real purpose of Napoleon was to gain control of the colonies, destroy religion, and enslave America. Through deceit he had imprisoned Ferdinand VII and made Pope Pius VII a virtual captive. Salcedo urged all to remain loyal Spaniards and oppose the spread of the rebellion. He exhorted the governors, commanders, and all public officials to maintain order as the best means to promote the general welfare and insure peace. He warned the people that idleness in times like those they were facing was conducive only to evil. For this reason all unemployed persons were to be classed as vagabonds and regarded as suspicious characters. He concluded his proclamation with a restatement of the decree issued by the viceroy concerning the treatment to be accorded French sympathizers and other seditious leaders. Anyone giving aid or comfort to, or harboring French agents was to be arrested and tried immediately on the charge of high treason, and if found guilty, he was to be executed within twenty-four hours after pronouncement of sentence. Those found guilty of spreading propaganda to stir up rebellion were to be condemned and hanged as traitors. Persons

---

[69]M. de Salcedo to the Commandant at Nacogdoches, October 26, 1810. *Béxar Archives.*

found guilty of spreading false rumors concerning the strength of the rebels and the danger of attack were to be tried for cowardice or malicious intent and punished accordingly. Officials found guilty of failing in their duty to maintain strict vigilance were to be tried on the charge of and sentenced for criminal negligence. But those who loyally contributed to the maintenance of public tranquillity by aiding officials to stamp out rebellion were to be duly rewarded by the king.[70] Thus did the commandant general and the viceroy attempt to allay public fear, discourage rebellion, and excite loyalty.

In a similar proclamation, the governor extended his New Year's greetings to the "Faithful Inhabitants of Texas" on January 6, 1811. He restated the charges against the treacherous character of Napoleon and his agents; denied vehemently the charge that Spaniards either in Spain or America had ever intended to sell out to the French; warned the Creoles against the perfidy of the leaders of the rebellion, and appealed to subjects of Spain in the name of religion, patriotism, and gratitude to remain loyal to the king.[71]

As early as January, 1809, the *Suprema Junta Central* of Cádiz had declared that the overseas possessions of Spain formed an integral part of the Spanish nation and as such were entitled to representation in the *Cortés* that was soon to meet. New Spain, Peru, New Granada, Buenos Aires, Cuba, Puerto Rico, Guatemala, Chile, Venezuela, and the Philippines—each was to elect its own deputies to the *Cortés*.[72] This was a step of transcendental importance taken by the Supreme Council to win the whole-hearted support of the colonies in the struggle against the French. For the first time the Spanish possessions overseas were incorporated into the Spanish nation.

When the decree was transmitted to the Interior Provinces by Viceroy Pedro Garibay in April, with the comment that perhaps only the city of Durango was entitled to elect a representative, the *Auditor* in Chihuahua protested the interpretation. His reply furnishes eloquent proof of the penetration of liberal, democratic ideas into these remote provinces. He boldly declared that the intent of the *Supreme Junta* was to give the

---

[70]N. Salcedo to the People of the Interior Provinces, October 24, 1810. *Nacogdoches Archives*, XV, pp. 110-117.

[71]M. de Salcedo to the Faithful Inhabitants of Texas, January 6, 1811. *Béxar Archives*.

[72]Decree of the Junta Suprema Central issued in the name of Ferdinand VII, January 22, 1809. *Nacogdoches Archives*, XV, 4-5.

people of America a just and proportional representation in the *Cortés*. If such was the case, Sonora, Coahuila, Texas, and New Mexico were, likewise, entitled to select their own representatives. To deprive them of this right was to deprive the inhabitants of these four provinces of their just representation in the *Cortés*.[73] The protest was heeded and representatives were elected to represent Durango, Sonora, New Mexico, and Coahuila and Texas.

But this belated concession did not suffice to avert the spread of the revolution to the Interior Provinces. Hidalgo and his confederates soon turned their eyes to the distant outposts of Texas in the hope of securing aid from the successful Democracy to the north. Before long the leaders of the rebellion dispatched an emissary to the United States by way of Texas. Hidalgo and his companions, unaware of their fate and that of their sympathizers in the Interior Provinces, themselves soon afterwards sought refuge in the north. They were betrayed and returned to Monclova and Chihuahua for trial and execution.

January, 1811, saw Governor Salcedo faced with open rebellion. Although he was overthrown and put in chains, he was, however, restored to office before the end of the year. The Mexican Revolution had, meanwhile, spread to Texas, and Texas was not to stop short of complete independence from Spain. The struggle was soon to be renewed against Mexico. But the history of the struggle for independence first from Spain and later from Mexico will be developed in the subsequent volume.

---

[73] Transmittal of Decree of January 22, 1809, by the viceroy, April 12, 1809; Opinion of the *Auditor,* May 10, 1809. *Nacogdoches Archives,* Vol. XV, pp. 6-8.

BIBLIOGRAPHY

Printed Works

Alamán, Lucas
   *Historia de Méjico desde los primeros movimientos que prepararon su inde-
   pendencia en el año de 1808, hasta la época presente.* Méjico, 1849-1852.
   5 vols.

Altamira y Crevea, Rafael
   Historia de España y de la civilización española. Barcelona, 1900-1930. 5 vols.

American Historical Review
   New York, London. Vol. VI.

Bancroft, Hubert Howe
   *History of Mexico, being a popular history of the Mexican people from the
   earliest primitive civilization to the present time. . . .* San Francisco, 1882-
   1890. 39 vols. (The Works of Hubert Howe Bancroft.)
   ——*History of the north Mexican states and Texas.* San Francisco, 1884. 2 vols.

Bolton, Herbert Eugene
   *Athanase de Méziéres and the Louisiana-Texas frontier, 1768-1780; documents
   published for the first time, from the original French and Spanish manu-
   scripts, chiefly in the archives of Mexico and Spain; translated into English;
   edited and annotated by Bolton,* Cleveland, 1914. 2 vols.
   ——"The Beginnings of Mission Nuestra Señora del Refugio," in *The Quarterly,*
   Vol. XIX.
   ——*Texas in the Middle Eighteenth Century; studies in Spanish Colonial history
   and administration.* Berkeley, 1915.

Castañeda, Carlos Eduardo
   "Communications Between Santa Fe and San Antonio," in *Texas Geographic
   Magazine,* Vol. V, No. I, Spring 1941.
   ——*Morfi's History of Texas.* (See Morfi.)
   ——*The Passing of the Missions, 1763-1795,* Vol. IV of *Our Catholic Heritage in
   Texas.* Austin, 1939.

Cavo, Andrés
   *Los tres siglos de México durante el gobierno español hasta la entrada del
   ejército trigarante, obra escrita en Roma por el padre Andrés Cavo. Publícala
   con notas y suplemento.* México, 1836-1838. 4 vols.

Clark, Daniel
   *Proofs of the Corruption of General James Wilkinson, and of his connexion with
   Aaron Burr.* Philadelphia, 1809.

Cox, Isaac Joslin
   The West Florida Controversy, 1798-1813: a study in American Diplomacy.
   Baltimore, 1918.

[439]

Cox, I. J.
    "The Louisiana-Texas Frontier," Texas Historical Association, *The Quarterly*,
    Vol. X.

Davis, Matthew Livingston
    Memoirs of Aaron Burr: with miscellaneous selections from his correspondence.
    New York, 1836. 2 vols.

Dunn, William Edward
    "The Founding of Nuestra Señora del Refugio, the last Spanish Mission in
    Texas," in *The Quarterly*, Vol. XXV.

Ellicott, Andrew
    *The journal of Andrew Ellicott, late commissioner on behalf of the United
    States during part of the year 1796, the years 1797, 1798, 1799, and part
    of the year 1800: for determining the boundary between the United States
    and the possessions of His Catholic Majesty in America, containing occasional
    remarks on the situation, soil, rivers, natural productions, and diseases of the
    different countries on the Ohio, Mississippi, and Gulf of Mexico, with six
    maps comprehending the Ohio, the Mississippi from the mouth of the Ohio
    to the Gulf of Mexico, the whole of West Florida, and a part of East Florida.
    To which is added an appendix, containing all the astronomical observations
    made use of for determining the boundary . . . likewise a great number of
    thermometrical observations.* Philadelphia, 1814.

Filisola, Vicente
    *Memorias para la historia de la guerra de Tejas, por el señor general de división
    . . . Don Vicente Filisola.* México, 1848-1849. 2 vols.

Fisher, Lillian E.
    The Background of the Revolution for Mexican Independence. Boston, 1934.

Fortier, Alcée
    A History of Louisiana. New York, 1904. 4 vols.

Geer, Curtis Manning
    The Louisiana Purchase and the Westward Movement. . . Philadelphia, 1904.
    (History of North America, Vol. VIII.)

Hale, Edward Everett
    "The Real Philip Nolan," Mississippi Historical Society, *Publications*, Vol. IV.

Hatcher, Mattie Alice (Austin)
    The Opening of Texas to Foreign Settlement, 1801-1821. . . Austin, 1927.
    (University of Texas Bulletin No. 2714, April 8, 1927.)

King, Grace
    "The Real Philip Nolan," in *Louisiana Historical Society Publications*, Vol. X.

Louisiana Historical Quarterly. New Orleans, 1917. Vol. IX.

McCaleb, Walter Flavius
    *The Aaron Burr Conspiracy; a history largely from original and hitherto
    unused sources.* New York, 1903.

Morfi, Juan Agustín
  History of Texas, 1673-1779, by Fray Juan Agustín Morfi . . . translated with biographical introduction and annotations, by Carlos Eduardo Castañeda. Albuquerque, 1935. 2 vols.

Músquiz, Miguel
  "Diary", translated by J. A. Quintero in "Philip Nolan and his Companions." *The Texas Almanac, 1868,* pp. 61-64.

Napoleon I, Emperor of the French
  The Confidential Correspondence of Napoleon Bonaparte with His Brother Joseph, Sometime King of Spain. Selected and translated, with explanatory notes, from the "Memoires Du Roi Joseph." New York, 1856. 2 vols.

——*Correspondance de Napoléon Ier; publiée par ordre de l'empereur Napoleon III.* Paris, 1858-1870. 32 vols.

Oman, Charles William Chadwick
  A History of the Peninsular War. Oxford, 1902. 7 vols.

Orleans Gazette
  October 3, 1806.

Pichardo, José Antonio
  Vida y martirio del protomártir mexicano San Felipe de Jesús de las Casas, religioso del hábito y Orden de san Francisco de Manila. Guadalajara, 1934.

Pike, Zebulon Montgomery
  Exploratory travels through the western territories of North America; comprising a voyage from St. Louis, on the Mississippi, to the source of that river, and a journey through the interior of Louisiana, and the northeastern provinces of New Spain. Performed in the years 1805, 1806, 1807 by order of the government of the United States. London, 1811.

Priestley, Herbert Ingram
  José de Gálvez, visitor-general of New Spain (1765-1771). Berkeley, 1916.

Quintero, J. A.
  "Philip Nolan and his Companions," in *The Texas Almanac,* 1868, pp. 61-64.

Recopilacion de leyes de los reynos de las Indias. Mandadas imprimir, y publicar por la Magestad catolica del rey don Carlos II, nuestro señor. Va dividida en quatro tomos, con el indice general, y al principio de cada tomo el indice especial de los titulos, que contiene. . . Madrid, 1756. 4 vols.

Rose, John Holland
  The Life of Napoleon I. New York, 1907. 2 vols. in 1.

Rydjord, John
  Foreign Interest in the Independence of New Spain; an introduction to the war for independence. Durham, North Carolina, 1935.

Smith, Ashbel
  Reminiscences of the Texas Republic. Galveston, 1876.

State Papers and Publick Documents of the United States from the accession of Thomas Jefferson to the Presidency, exhibiting a complete view of our foreign relations since that time, 1801-1806. Boston, 1814-1815. 5 vols.

The Texas Almanac for 1868, Galveston, 1867. (W. Richardson and Company Publishers.)

United States Treaties, etc.
Treaties, Conventions, International Acts, Protocols, and Agreements between the United States of America and other powers, 1776-1909. Washington, 1910.

Ward, Sir Henry George
Mexico in 1827. London, 1828. 2 vols.

Wavell, Arthur
"Account of the Province of Texas," in Ward, H. G., *Mexico in 1827.* Vol. II, Appendix B.

Whitaker, Arthur Preston
The Spanish-American Frontier: 1783-1795; the westward movement and the Spanish retreat in the Mississippi Valley. Boston, New York, 1927.

Wilkinson, James
Memoirs of My Own Times. Philadelphia, 1816. 3 vols.

MANUSCRIPT SOURCES

An alphabetical order has been followed in listing all the manuscript sources cited in the text. These have been entered whenever possible under author and arranged in chronological order in each case. The archival depository of the originals has been indicated in every instance. The abbreviations used to designate them are A. G. I. for Archivo General de Indias, Spain; A. G. N. for Archivo General de la Nación, Mexico; B. A. for Béxar Archives; N. A. for Nacogdoches Archives; and S. A. for Saltillo Archives. With very few exceptions, all the sources cited and used are in the University of Texas Library.

Affidavits and census of settlers at Bayou Pierre, July 26, 1809, and August 2, 16, 17, 1809. *(B. A.)*

Aguilar, Juan José
to Manuel Muñoz, February 23, 1795. *(B. A.)*
——to Manuel Muñoz, July 30, 1795. *(B. A.)*
——to Manuel Muñoz, [August 8, 1795 ?] *(B. A.)*
——to Juan Bautista Elguezábal, May 11, 1797. *(B. A.)*

Alberola, José María
al Exmo Señor Ministro de Estado, Don Mariano Luis de Urquijo sobre el Plan sometido para una peregrinación conducente a la conversión de los Indios. Febrero 6 de 1800. *(A. G. I. Papeles de Estado, México, Leg. 10, Núm. 113.* Dunn Transcripts, 1795-1817.)
——to Felix Berenguer de Marquina, April 17, 1801. *(A. G. I. Papeles de Estado, México, Leg. 10, Núm. 113.* Dunn Transcripts, 1795-1817.)
——al Exmo Señor Virrey Don Felix Berenguer de Marquina, August 21, 1801. *(A. G. I. Papeles de Estado, México, Leg. 10, No. 113.* Dunn Transcripts, 1795-1817.)

———a Felix Berenguer de Marquina, sobre el plan sometido por Alberola para la conversión de los Indios, octubre 7 de 1801. (*A. G. I. Papeles de Estado, México, Leg. 10, Núm. 113.* Dunn Transcripts, 1795-1817.)

———Dictamen del Fiscal sobre las representaciones hechas por el Doctor Manuel Clavijo en lo escrito por Fray José Alberola, Enero 31 de 1802. (*A. G. I. Papeles de Estado, México, Leg. 10, Núm. 113.* Dunn Transcripts, 1795-1817.)

Alderete, José
    Report on the death of, October 5, 1806. (*B. A.*)

Amangual, Francisco
    to Cordero, October 10, 1806. Accounts rendered December 16, 1806. (*B. A.*)

Amparán, Miguel José de
    August 10, 1796. (*B. A.*)

Arocha, José Clemente
    Estan prestadas a la Capilla de la Compa. del Alamo las alajas siguientes que pertenesen a la Mision de San Antonio Valero . . . Bachiller José Clemente Arocha. (*N. A., Vol. VIII.*)

Arrambide, Juan Ignacio
    to Manuel Antonio Cordero, March 30, and April 2, 1806. (*A. G. I. Audiencia de Guadalajara. 104-2-9.* Dunn Transcripts, 1800-1819.)

———to Francisco Viana, December 9, 1806. (*B. A.*)

Bahía, Presidio de la
    Expediente relativo a ornamentos para la capilla del Presidio de la Bahía, 1791. (*S. A., Vol. V.*)

Bastrop, Baron de
    Petition of Baron de Bastrop, June 20, 1796. (*A. G. I. Santo Domingo, Louisiana, and Florida, 86-7-17.*)

Berenguer de Marquina, Felix
    Auto del Virrey Berenguer de Marquina, August 12, 1800. (*A. G. I Papeles de Estado, México, Leg. 10, Núm. 113.* Dunn Transcripts, 1795-1817.)

———Auto del Virrey, September 22, 1801. (*A. G. I. Papeles de Estado, México, Leg. 10, No. 113.* Dunn Transcripts, 1795-1817.)

———to Pedro Ceballos, May 27, 1802. (*A. G. I. Papeles de Estado, México, Leg. 10, Núm. 113.* Dunn Transcripts, 1795-1817.)

Bexar, Presidio de
    Estado que manifiesta los Extranjeros Desertores que existen en el Real Presidio de Béjar desde el año de 1808. (*B. A.*)

Blanc, Louis
    to Manuel Muñoz, April 26, 1793. (*B. A.*)

Blanco, José
    to the commanders of Refugio, Reynosa, Camargo, Mier, Revilla, and Laredo, November 20, 1800. (*A. G. M. Historia, Vol. 413, Part 1.*)

———to Felix Calleja, January 15, 1801. (*A. G. M. Historia, Vol. 413, Part 1.*)

Bonavía, Bernardo
to Nemesio Salcedo, April 26, 1809. *(B. A.)*

——to Francisco Saavedra, June 28, 1809. *(A. G. I. Audiencia de Guadalajara, 104-2-25.* Dunn Transcripts, 1800-1819.)

——to Nemesio Salcedo, June 28, 1809. *(A. G. I. Audiencia de Guadalajara, 104-2-25.* Dunn Transcripts, 1800-1819.)

——to Manuel de Salcedo, July 4, 1809. *(B. A.)*

——to Francisco Saavedra, July 26, 1809. *(A. G. I. Audiencia de Guadalajara, 104-2-25.* Dunn Transcripts, 1800-1819.)

——to Nemesio Salcedo, July 26, 1809. *(A. G. I. Audiencia de Guadalajara, 104-2-25.* Dunn Transcripts, 1800-1819.)

——to Antonio Cornel, August 9, 1809. *(N. A., Vol. XI.)*

——to Francisco Saavedra, September 20, 1809. *(A. G. I. Audiencia de Guadalajara, 104-2-25.* Dunn Transcripts, 1800-1819.)

——to Nemesio Salcedo, September 20, 1809. *(A. G. I. Audiencia de Guadalajara, 104-2-25.* Dunn Transcripts, 1800-1819.)

——to Nemesio Salcedo, September 20, 1809. *(A. G. I. Audiencia de Guadalajara, 104-2-9.* Dunn Transcripts, 1800-1819.)

——to Nemesio Salcedo, November 29, 1809. *(A. G. I. Audiencia de Guadalajara, 104-2-9.* Dunn Transcripts, 1800-1819.)

——to Francisco Saavedra, December 27, 1809. *(A. G. I. Audiencia de Guadalajara, 104-2-25.* Dunn Transcripts, 1800-1819.)

——to Nemesio Salcedo, January 23, 1810. *(B. A.)*

——to Manuel de Salcedo, March 1, 1810. *(B. A.)*

——to Nemesio Salcedo, March 12, 1810. *(N. A., Vol. XV.)*

——to Francisco Saavedra, May 16, 1810. *(N. A., Vol. XV.)*

——to Nemesio Salcedo, May 30, 1810. *(B. A.)*

——to Manuel de Salcedo, June 6, 1810. *(B. A.)*

——to Manuel de Salcedo, October 6, 1810. *(B. A.)*

——to Nemesio Salcedo, November 23, 1810. *(N. A., Vol. XV.)*

Boone, Daniel
Petition of, June 11, 1806. *(B. A.)*

Brady, Juan
to the Bishop of New Orleans, October 29, 1800. *(B. A.)*

——(and Bernardo Martín Despallier) to the Commandant General, April 10, 1804. *(B. A.)*

Branciforte, Marqués de
to Antonio Ventura Taranco, September 30, 1794. *(A. G. I. Audiencia de Guadalajara, 104-1-1.* Dunn Transcripts, 1794-1798.)

——to Eugenio Llaguero, January 15, 1795. *(A. G. I. Audiencia de México, 88-1-15.* Dunn Transcripts, 1792-1799.)

——to the Duque de Alcudia, July 3, 1795. *(A. G. I. Papeles de Estado, México, Legajo 4, Núm. 7.* Dunn Transcripts, 1795-1817.)

——to the Count of Sierra Gorda, July 10, 1795. *(B. A.)*

——to the Principe de la Paz, May 27, 1796. *(A. G. I. Papeles de Estado, México, Legajo 5, Núm. 64.* Dunn Transcripts, 1792-1799.)

Bucareli y Ursua, Juan Antonio
al Exmo Señor Frei Juan Julian de Arriaga, el Virrey de Nueva España. Repite la necesidad que pulsa de que al Baron de Riperda se le releve del Govierno de la Provincia de Texas que está exerciendo, Abril 26 de 1776. (*A. G. I. Audiencia de Guadalajara*, 1755-1776, Dunn Transcripts.)

Caballero, José
to Miguel Cayetano Soler, Minister of War, May 22, 1804. (*A. G. I. Audiencia de Guadalajara*, *103-6-17*. Dunn Transcripts, 1800-1819.)

Cabello, Domingo
to Gil Ibarbo, March 11, 1780. (*B. A.*)
——to Teodoro de Croix, May 20, 1784. (*S. A., Vol. V.*)
——a Señor Commandante General Don Felipe de Neve. Decreto del Gobernador Cabello relativo al pago de reses orejanas y caballerías mesteñas, Mayo 20 de 1784. (*B. A.*)
——al Exmo Señor Don Mathias de Galbes. Informe general sobre el estado de la provincia a su cargo, septiembre 30 de 1784. (*A. G. M. Provincias Internas, Vol. 64, Part 1.*)
——to Teodoro de Croix, December 17, 1799. (*B. A.*)

Cadena, José Antonio
to Manuel Muñoz, June 8, 1794. (*B. A.*)
——(and José Plácido de Monzón), Declarations of. (*A. G. I. Audiencia de Guadalajara, 104-2-9.* Dunn Transcripts, 1800-1819.)

Calahorra, José de
Diario del Viage que hizo Fray Joseph de Calahorra. (*A. G. I. Audiencia de México, 96-6-22, Part 2.*)
——to Angel Martos y Navarrete, May 27, 1760. (*A. G. I. Audiencia de México, 92-6-22, Part 2.*)
——to Angel Martos y Navarrete, October 18, 1766. (*A. G. I. Audiencia de México, 96-6-23?, Part 2.*)

Calleja, Felix
to José Ramón Díaz Bustamante, December 21, 1800. (*A. G. M. Historia, Vol. 413.*)
——to Simon de Herrera, December 21, 1800. (*A. G. M. Historia, Vol. 413.*)
——to Viceroy Berenguer de Marquina, December 22, 1800. (*A. G. M. Historia, Vol. 413.*)
——to the Viceroy, February 27, 1801. (*A. G. M. Historia, Vol. 413, Part 1.*)

Cárdenas, José Luis Mariano de
to Manuel Muñoz, October 31, 1793. (*B. A.*)
——to Pedro de Nava, July 6, 1794. (*S. A., Vol. VI.*)
——to Pedro de Nava, July 20, 1794. (*S. A., Vol. VI.*)
——to Manuel Muñoz, October 2, 1794. (*B. A.*)
——to Manuel Muñoz, January 1, 1796. (*B. A.*)
——to Manuel Muñoz, January 1, 1798. (*B. A.*)

Carondelet, Baron
    to Manuel Muñoz, September 9, 1794. *(B. A.)*
——Proclamation of, May 30, 1797. Spanish translation by José Piernas. *(B. A.)*
——to Francisco Rendón, January 13, 1798. *(A. G. M. Historia, Vol. 413, Part 1.)*

Carrasco, Pedro Nolasco
    Instructions to, September 17, 1805. *(B. A.)*
——to Manuel Antonio Cordero, January 4, 1806. *(B. A.)*
——to José Cayetano Valle, June 27, 1806. *(B. A.)*

Casa Calvo, Marqués de
    to Juan Bautista Elguezábal, March 1, 1800. *(B. A.)*
——to Marqués de Someruelos, June 15, 1801. *(A. G. I. Audiencia de Santo Domingo, 86-7-27.* Dunn Transcripts, 1763-1818.)
——to Manuel Antonio Cordero, December 8, 1805. *(B. A.)*

Casili, Juan Carlos
    Petition of, May 12, 1806, and accompanying documents. *(B. A.)*
——Petition of 1811. *(B. A.)*

Castro, Ramón de
    to Viceroy Revillagigedo, May 15, 1792. *(A. G. M. Historia, Vol. 93.)*

Ceballos, Pedro
    to Comandante General de las Provincias Internas, November 21, 1807. *(A. G. I. Audiencia de Guadalajara, 104-3-15.* Dunn Transcripts, 1800-1819.)

Census reports
    (N. A., Vol. VI.)

Charles III
    Real Orden aprobando la remesa de ganado de Texas a Luisiana para remediar la escasez en ésta última. [De José de Galvez a Teodoro de Croix.] Mayo 1, de 1780. *(A. G. M. Historia, Vol. 413, Part 1.)*
——Real Orden de Enero 31, 1784. *(A. G. I. Indiferente General, 154-7-14.)*
——Cédula of September 21, 1787. *(S. A., Vol. 5.)*

Charles IV
    al Virrey de Nueva España [Conde de Revilla Gigedo] sobre los limites entre la Luysiana y Nacogdoches, 1 de noviembre de 1789. *(A. G. I. Audiencia de México, 96-2-12.* Dunn Transcripts, 1787-1791.)
——Ynstruccion que devera observar el . . . principal Comisionado para el importante desempeño de reconocimientos que han de hacerse en la Provincia de Texas una de las internas de este Reyno consiguiente a Soberanas Resoluciones, Abril 27 de 1791. *(A. G. I. Audiencia de México, 89-6-14.* Dunn Transcripts, 1787-1791.)
——Al Virrey Revillagigedo de Nueva España. En que resuelve que se deje para más tarde la extensión del territorio de Natchitoches, Septiembre 21 de 1793. *(A. G. I. Audiencia de México.* Dunn Transcripts, 1787-1791.)
——Real Cédula de 28 de Mayo de 1800 pidiendo informes sobre las Minas de cobre, su situacion, propietarios, y cantidad de metal que producen, Mayo 28 de 1800. *(B. A.)*

——Real Cédula del Rey haciendo nombramiento del comandante General de las Provincias Yntas de Dn Pedro de Nava. 26 de agosto de 1800. *(B. A.)*

——Cédula of September 24, 1803. *(B. A.)*

——Royal orders of July 31, 1804. *(A. G. I. Audiencia de Guadalajara.* Dunn Transcripts, 1800-1819.)

——Real Cédula de 6 de agosto de 1804. *(A. G. I. Audiencia de Guadalajara.* Dunn Transcripts, 1800-1819.)

——Royal orders of August 13, 1804. *(A. G. I. Audiencia de Guadalajara.* Dunn Transcripts, 1800-1819.)

——Real Orden de Junio 24 de 1805. *(A. G. I. Audiencia de Guadalajara, 103-6-17.* Dunn Transcripts, 1800-1819.)

Clavijo, Manuel
[Investigation conducted by Manuel Clavijo], January 25, 1802. *(A. G. I. Papeles de Estado, México, Legajo 10, No. 13.* Dunn Transcripts, 1795-1817.)

Clouet, Brogné de
Passport issued by, and letter to Gerónimo Herrera, December 17, 1807. *(B. A.)*

——to Manuel Antonio Cordero, June 22, 1808. *(B. A.)*

Compromiso celebrado por el Cavildo, y Vezindario de este Preso de Sn Anto de Bexar de la Prova de Texas con las Missiones de ella sobre las Recogidas de sus Ganados assi Herrado como orejanos Alzados y Mostrencos. Mayo 20-Junio 20, 1787. *(N. A., Vol. VI.)*

Conception Mission
Ynventario de los bienes de Temporalidad de la Mision de la Purisima Concepción. Año de 1794. *(S. A., Vol. VI.)*

Consejo de Indias
Informe del Consejo, November 23-December 15, 1804. *(A. G. I. Audiencia de México, 88-1-4.* Dunn Transcripts, 1800-1819.)

——Informe del Consejo, January 4, 1812. *(A. G. I. Audiencia de Guadalajara, 104-2-9.* Dunn Transcripts, 1800-1819.)

Consulta del Fiscal y Asesor General, August 4 and 12, 1800. *(A. G. I. Papeles de Estado, México, Leg. 10, No. 113.* Dunn Transcripts, 1795-1817.)

——September 16 and 19, 1801. *(A. G. I. Papeles de Estado, México, Leg. 10, No. 113.* Dunn Transcripts, 1795-1817.)

——October 29, 1801. *(A. G. I. Papeles de Estado, México, Legajo 10, No. 113.* Dunn Transcripts, 1795-1817.)

Copia del Informe General instruydo en cumplimientos de el Orden de 31 de Eno. de 1784 Sobre las Misiones del Reyno de Nueva España. . . . *(A. G. I. Indiferente General, 154-7-14.* Cunningham Transcripts, 1780-1804.)

Cordero, Manuel Antonio
to Manuel Muñoz, March 28, 1797. *(B. A.)*

——to Simón de Herrera, January 17, 1801. *(A. G. M. Historia, Vol. 413.)*

——to Francisco Viana, September, 1805. *(B. A.)*

——to Nemesio Salcedo, September 24, 1805. *(N. A., Vol. X.)*

——to Nemesio Salcedo, September 25, 1805. *(B. A.)*

——to Nemesio Salcedo, October 5, 1805. *(N. A., Vol. X.)*

——to Nemesio Salcedo, October 14, 1805. *(N. A., Vol. X.)*

——Proclamation of Governor Cordero, October 18, 1805. *(B. A.)*

——to Nemesio Salcedo, October 18, 1805, transmitting a copy of the permission issued to Clouet on the same date. *(B. A.)*

——to Nemesio Salcedo, November 19, 1805. *(N. A., Vol. X.)*

——to Nemesio Salcedo, November 22, 1805. *(N. A., Vol. X.)*

——to the Commandant of La Bahía, November 25, 1805. *(B. A.)*

——to Nemesio Salcedo, January 11, 1806. *(B. A.)*

——to Nemesio Salcedo, February 15, 1806. *(B. A.)*

——to Francisco Viana, April 21, 1806. *(N. A., Vol. X.)*

——to Nemesio Salcedo, May 1, 1806. *(B. A.)*

——to Nemesio Salcedo, May 20, 1806, transmitting the text of the royal order of September 9, 1805, concerning the settlement on the Trinity. *(B. A.)*

——to Nemesio Salcedo, May 21, 1806. *(A. G. I. Audiencia de Guadalajara, 104-2-9. Dunn Transcripts, 1800-1819.)*

——to Nemesio Salcedo, May 28, 1806. *(B. A.)*

——to Nemesio Salcedo, June 12, 1806. *(N. A., Vol. X.)*

——to Nemesio Salcedo, June 16, 1806. *(B. A.)*

——to Nemesio Salcedo, June 29, 1806. *(N. A., Vol. X.)*

——to Nemesio Salcedo, July 24, 1806. *(B. A.)*

——to Nemesio Salcedo, July 30, 1806. *(B. A.)*

——to Nemesio Salcedo, August 23, 1806. *(N. A., Vol. X.)*

——to Simón de Herrera, October 18, 1806. *(N. A., Vol. XI.)*

——to Nemesio Salcedo, December 3, 1806. *(B. A.)*

——to Felipe Roque de la Portilla, December 16, 1806. *(B. A.)*

——to Nemesio Salcedo, December 29, 1806. *(B. A.)*

——to Francisco Viana, July 1, 1807. *(B. A.)*

——to Nemesio Salcedo, August 29, 1807. *(N. A., Vol. XI.)*

——to Nemesio Salcedo, January 6, 1808. *(B. A.)*

——to Manuel de Salcedo, January 19, 1808. *(B. A.)*

——to Nemesio Salcedo, March 14, 1808. *(B. A.)*

——to Francisco Viana, July 1, 1808. *(B. A.)*

——to Nemesio Salcedo, August 11, 1808. *(N. A., Vol. X.)*

——to Nemesio Salcedo, August 11, 1808. *(N. A., Vol. XI.)*

——to José María Guadiana, August 12, 1808. *(N. A., Vol. XI.)*

——Certified statement by, September 8, 1808. *(N. A., Vol. XI.)*

——to Manuel de Salcedo, November 28, 1808. *(N. A., Vol. XI.)*

——to Manuel de Salcedo, December 1, 1808. *(B. A.)*

——to Nemesio Salcedo, December 15, 1808. *(B. A.)*

——to Bernardo Bonavía, April 23, 1809. *(B. A.)*

——to Bernardo Bonavía, July 21, 1809. *(B. A.)*

Cortés, Juan

    to Manuel Muñoz, May 6, 1793. *(B. A.)*

——to Manuel Muñoz, July 13, 1793. *(B. A.)*

——to Manuel Muñoz, August 23, 1793. *(B. A.)*

——to Manuel Muñoz, January 16, 1795. *(B. A.)*

——to Manuel Muñoz, February 21, 1795. *(B. A.)*

——to Manuel Muñoz, April 22, 1795. *(B. A.)*

——to Manuel Muñoz, April 24, 1795. *(B. A.)*
——to Manuel Muñoz, May 8, 1795. *(B. A.)*
——to Manuel Muñoz, May 16, 1795. *(B. A.)*
——to Manuel Muñoz, June 20, 1795. *(B. A.?)*
——to Manuel Muñoz, July 7, 1795. *(B. A.?)*
——to Manuel Muñoz, August 8, 1795. *(B. A.)*
——to Manuel Muñoz, August 28, 1795. *(B. A.)*
——Informe del estado de la artillería del Presidio de la Bahía, September 23, 1795. *(B. A.)*
——to Manuel Muñoz, January 15, 1796. *(B. A.)*
——to Governor Manuel Muñoz, February 13, 1796. *(B. A.)*
——to Pedro Nava, March 11, 1797. *(B. A.)*
——to Manuel Muñoz, March 24, 1797. *(B. A.)*
——to Manuel Muñoz, April 7, 1797. *(B. A.)*
——to Manuel Muñoz, April 22, 1797. *(B. A.)*
——to Manuel Muñoz, July 21, 1798. *(B. A.)*

Council of War, September 5, 1808. *(N. A.)*

D'Alvimar, Octaviano
    to Manuel Antonio Cordero, August 9, 1808. *(N. A., Vol. XI.)*
——to José María Guadiana, August 29, 1808. *(N. A., Vol. XI.)*
——to Nemesio Salcedo, August 29, 1808. *(N. A., Vol. XI.)*
——Passport issued to, Bordeaux, November 27, 1808. Copy sent to Cordero, August 9, 1809. *(N. A., Vol. XI.)*

Dannequien, Louis
    (and José Nicolas Landrés) Petition of, July 16, 1806. *(B. A.)*

Davenport, Samuel
    Noticias de las naciones yndias de la Prova. de Texas que me dio Samuel Davenport en Nacogdoches desde cuyo punto se han de considerar sus situaciones y distancias, April 24, 1809. *(N. A., Vol. II.)*
——Affidavit of Samuel Davenport, June 16, 1809. *(B. A.)*

Desgraviers, Francisco Marceau
    (and Juan Francisco Warnet) Petitions of, October 22, 1806. *(B. A.)*

Despallier, Bernardo Martín
    (and Juan Brady) to the Commandant General, April 10, 1804. *(B. A.)*
——to Salcedo, December 5, 1804. *(A. G. I. Audiencia de México, Leg. 18, Núm. 28.)*
——Diario de, February 15-March 4, 1806. *(B. A.)*

Díaz Bustamante, José Ramón
    to Manuel Muñoz, March 1, 1797. *(B. A.)*
——to José Blanco, December 29, 1800. *(A. G. M. Historia, Vol. 413, Part 1.)*

Dictamen de la Contaduría, June 14, 1811. *(A. G. I. Audiencia de Guadalajara, 104-2-9. Dunn Transcripts, 1800-1819.)*

Dictamen del Fiscal Posada, June 26, 1792. *(A. G. M. Historia, Vol. 93.)*

Dictamen del Real Fiscal. *(A. G. I. Audiencia de Guadalajara, 104-1-1. Dunn Transcripts, 1794-1798.)*

Discretorio del Colegio de Zacatecas
  to Manuel Silva, November 7, 1796. *(B. A.)*

Dortolán, Bernardo
  to Manuel Muñoz, September 6, 1795. *(B. A.)*

Durán, José Luis
  Merced a, January 23, 1806. *(B. A.)*

Durán, Toribio
  to Manuel Antonio Cordero, April 24, 1806. *(B. A.)*

Ecclesiastical Cabildo
  to Juan Bautista Elguezábal, December 30, 1799. *(B. A.)*

Elguezábal, Juan Bautista
  to Pedro Nava, May 27, 1797. *(B. A.)*
——to Manuel Muñoz, May 28, 1797. *(B. A.)*
——to Manuel Muñoz, June 8, 1797. *(B. A.)*
——to Pedro Nava, June 25, 1797. *(B. A.)*
——to Manuel Muñoz, July 3, 1797. *(B. A.)*
——Capitán de la Bahía de Espíritu Santo, al Gobernador Manuel Muñoz. Julio 20 de 1797. *(B. A.)*
——to Manuel Muñoz, August 3, 1797. *(B. A.)*
——to Manuel Muñoz, August 7, 1797. *(B. A.)*
——to Manuel Muñoz, January 17, 1798. *(B. A.)*
——to Manuel Muñoz, February 4, 1798. *(B. A.)*
——to Manuel Muñoz, March 28, 1798. *(B. A.)*
——to Manuel Muñoz, April 22, 1798. *(B. A.)*
——Decree, May 20, 1799. *(B. A.)*
——Ymbentario de los Documentos y Papeles correspondientes álos gastos erogados en la manutencion de los Yndios y distribucion de los regalos que se les ha subministrado desde 3 de Diciembre de 1786 hasta 27 de Julio de 1799. Que entrega al Gobernador de esta Provincia Dn Juan Bautista de Elguesaval, Dn Gabriel Gutierrez, 1 de Mayo de 1800. *(B. A.)*
——to Pedro Nava, November 12, 1800. *(Quaderno Borrador de los oficios, Vol. II.)*
——to Pedro Nava, November 30, 1800. *(Quaderno Borrador, Vol. I.)*
——Carpeta general que abrasa los Documentos correspondientes al numero de Yndios de las Naciones amigas del Norte que se presentaron en esta Plaza en todo el proximo pasado año de 1800. y los importes de los gastos mensuales erogados en la manutencion y obsequio de ellos á consequencia de libramientos expedidos por el Governador interino de la Provincia de Texas. Teniente Coronel Dn Juan Bautista de Elguezabal. 31 de Dice de 1800. *(B. A.)*
——to Pedro Nava, January 8, 1801. *(Quaderno Borrador, Vol. I.)* *(Photostat.)*
——June 20, 1801. *(B. A.)*
——to José María Guadiana, August 12, 1801. *(B. A.)*
——to Francisco Xavier Uranga, October 5, 1801. *(B. A.)*
——to Nemesio Salcedo, June 20, 1803. *(B. A.)*
——to the Commandant General, January 18, 1804. *(Quaderno Borrador, January 4, 1804-December 19, 1804.)* *(B. A.)*
——to Nemesio Salcedo, February 29, 1804. *(B. A.)*
——to Manuel Salcedo, April 11, 1804. *(B. A.)*

——to Nemesio Salcedo, April 25, 1804. *(B. A.)*

—— to Nemesio Salcedo, June 20, 1804 *(B. A.)*

——to Nemesio Salcedo, August 15, 1804, draft No. 276. *(Quaderno Borrador, January 4-December 19, 1804.)* *(B. A.)*

——to Nemesio Salcedo, November 21, 1804. *(Quaderno Borrador, January 4-December 19, 1804.)* *(B. A.)*

——to Nemesio Salcedo, December 5, 1804. *(A. G. I. Audiencia de México, Leg. 18, Num. 28.)*

Espadas, Manuel de
Calculo prudencial que forma al Comdte. Into. de la Bahía de Esptu. Santo, Don Manuel Espadas. *(A. G. M. Historia, Vol. 93.)*

——to Manuel Muñoz, March 10, 1791. *(A. G. M. Historia, Vol. 93.)*

Espíritu Santo Mission
Relación de los Yndios de la Misión del Espíritu Santo. dependiente. . . *(S. A., Vol. VI.)*

——Report on Mission Espíritu Santo. *(S. A., Vol. VI.)*

Estado relativo al número de Vasallos y Habitantes en Texas, 1783. *(B. A.)*

Farías, Juan José
a José Manuel Castro. Noticia de lo que corresponde a dha. micion entregada por el cavo . . . Septiembre 13 de 1793. *(B. A.)*

——to Manuel Muñoz, October 22, 1793.

Ferdinand VII
Decree of January 22, 1809. Transmittal of, by the viceroy, April 12, 1809, and opinion of the auditor, May 10, 1809. *(N. A., Vol. XV.)*

Fernández, Bernardo
Memoria de los Efectos que de los Destinados a regalo de Yndios se le entregaron al Teniente Dn Bernardo Fernández para el mismo efecto, consiguiente a orn de 21 de Noviembre proximo pasado del Sor Comte Gral Mariscal de Campo Dn Pedro de Nava. 16 de enero de 1795. *(B. A.)*

——Relativo a la aparición de los franceses Dupont y Caekan entre los Indios y a su posible aprehensión, September 23, 1795. *(B. A.)*

——Relativa a una communicación del Gobernador de Nueva Orleans, Barón de Carondelet, acerca de D. Dionicio Dessesant y de los efectos que a éste se le embargaron. September 23, 1795. *(B. A.)*

Fernández, Santiago
——Derrotero, diario y calendario de leguas que hago Yo el abajo firmado (Santiago Fernández) en descubrimiento desde esta de Santa Fe a los Pueblos de Jumanos por orden Superior del Sr. Governador Dn. Fernando de la Concha, a condución y guia de Pedro Vial, y es como siguen. Santa Fe, December 17, 1788. *(A. G. M. Historia, Vol. 43, 62.)*

Fernández Tejeiro, Vicente
to Felix Trudeau, November 7, 1800. *(A. G. M. Historia, Vol. 413, Part 1.)*

——to Elguezábal, May 23, 1801. *(B. A.)*

Flores, Manuel Antonio
 to Juan Ugalde, September 30, 1788. *(A. G. M. Historia, Vol. 93.)*
——to Juan Ugalde, February 3, 1789. *(A. G. M. Historia, Vol. 93.)*
——Auto del Virrey [Florez?] con referencia al restablecimiento de la Misión abandonada de los Orcoquizas. 10 de febrero de 1789. *(A. G. M. Historia, Vol. 93.)*
——Auto del Virrey, February 19, 1789. *(A. G. M. Historia, Vol. 93.)*
——Decreto concerniente a la petición del Fiscal de Real Hacienda con respecto a las solicitudes de los Yndios Atacapa, Bidais y Orcoquizacs, Abril 21 de 1789. *(A. G. M. Historia, Vol. 93.)*

Foronda, Valentín de
 to Nemesio Salcedo, January 6, 1809. *(B. A.)*

Fort Claiborne
 Commander of, to Manuel de Salcedo, July 7, 1810. *(N. A., Vol. XV.)*

Fragoso, Francisco Xavier
 Derrotero, diario, y Calculación, July 16, July 20-23.
——Derrotero, Diario, y Calculación de leguas, que en descubrimiento por derecho desde esta provincia del Nuevo México hasta el Fuerte de Natchitoches y la de los Texas de orden superior voya practicar en compañia de Dn Pedro Vial, comisionado a este propósito, yo el abajo y a lo último firmado (Francisco Xavier Fragoso) Villa de Santa Fe, Veinte y quatro de junio de mil setecientos ochenta y ocho. *(A. G. M. Historia, Vols. 43, 52, 62.)*

Fuentes, Pedro
 to Domingo Cabello, May 13, 1784. *(S. A., Vol. V.)*

Garavito, José Antonio Mariano de Jesús
 to Francisco Gomarra, September 23, 1796. *(B. A.)*
——to Manuel Muñoz, June 4, 1797. *(B. A.)*
——to Juan Bautista Elguezábal, June 30, 1797. *(B. A.)*
——to Juan Bautista Elguezábal, March 25, 1798. *(B. A.)*
——to José Miguel del Moral, October 13, 1798. *(B. A.)*
——to José Miguel del Moral, October 27, 1798. *(B. A.)*
——to José Miguel del Moral, March 12, 1799. *(B. A.)*

Garnier, Juan
 Affidavit of, October 10, 1805. *(B. A.)*

Garza, José Mariano Francisco
 Memoria de lo que por ahora se juzga precisamente necesario para la nueva fundación del Refugio presentada por. . . *(A. G. I. Audiencia de Guadalajara, 104-1-1.* Dunn Transcripts, 1790-1793.)
——Memoria de lo que ahora se juzga precisamente necesario para la nueva fundación del Refugio. *(A. G. I. Audiencia de Guadalajara, 104-1-1.* Dunn Transcripts, 1794-1798.)
——to Manuel Muñoz, February 24, 1793. *(B. A.)*
——to Manuel Muñoz, April 1, 1793. *(B. A.)*
——to Manuel Muñoz, May 17, 1793. *(B. A.)*
——to Manuel Muñoz, June 17, 1793. *(B. A.)*
——to Manuel Muñoz, July 21, 1793. *(B. A.)*
——to Manuel Muñoz, September 11, 1793. *(B. A.)*

Gasiot, Juan
 to Felipe Neve, October 9, 1783. (*San Francisco El Grande Archivos, Vol. XXXIII.*)

Glass, Anthony
 Petition of, October 31, 1807. (*B. A.*)

Gomarra, Francisco
 to Pedro Nava, September 26, 1795. (*B. A.*)
——to José Mariano Cárdenas, October 31, 1796. (*B. A.*)
——to Pedro Nava, November 7, 1796. (*B. A.*)

Granados, José Manuel
 Diary of José Manuel Granados, September 15-25, 1795. (*B. A.*)

Grand Pré, Carlos de
 Passport to Herman Wallet, October 7, 1805. (*B. A.*)

Guadalupe, Colegio de
 Petición del Discretorio del Colegio de Guadalupe al Commte Gral. Theodoro de Croix relativo a que se exima a los Ministros de la Provincia de Texas de tener en lo postero introducción en las temporalidades de aquellos neófitos. Enero 13 de 1780. (*S. A., Vol. V.*)

Guadiana, José María
 to Manuel Muñoz, Nacogdoches, October 23, 1796. (*B. A.*)
——to Manuel Muñoz, October 25, 1796. (*B. A.*)
——to Bernardino Vallejo, February 26, 1797. (*B. A.*)
——to Manuel Muñoz, February 28, 1797. (*B. A.*)
——to Manuel Muñoz, May 9, 1797. (*B. A.*)
——to Manuel Muñoz, March 20, 1798. (*B. A.*)
——to Manuel Muñoz, January 3, 1799. (*B. A.*)
——to Manuel Muñoz, March 19, 1799. (*B. A.*)
——to Manuel Muñoz, April 2, 1799. (*B. A.*)
——to Manuel Muñoz, May 14, 1799. (*B. A.*)
——to Manuel Antonio Cordero, August 5, 1808. (*N. A., Vol. XI.*)
——to Manuel Antonio Cordero, August 29, 1808. (*N. A., Vol. XI.*)

Herrera, Gerónimo
 Diario de acontecimientos, November 21, 1806. (*B. A.*)

Herrera, Simón de
 to T. H. Cushing, August 6, 1806. (*N. A., Vol. X.*)
——to Colonel Manuel Antonio Cordero, September 20, 1806. (*B. A.*)
——to Manuel Antonio Cordero, December 1, 1806. (*B. A.*)
——to the Governor, August 14, 1808. (*N. A., Vol. X.*)
——to Bernardo Bonavía, 25, 1809. (*B. A.*)

Huerta, José María de Jesús
 to Manuel de Salcedo, May 31, 1810. (*B. A.*)

Huizar, Pedro de
 to Manuel Muñoz, March 4, 1791. (Transmitted by Manuel Muñoz to the Viceroy, March 26.) (*A. G. M. Historia, Vol. 93.*)

Ibarbo, Antonio Gil
Junta Superior de Real Hacienda. Relativo a que se exima la responsibilidad con referencia a los cargos que se le hacen a Dn Antonio Gil Ybarbo. Abril 15 de 1789. *(A. G. M. Historia, Vol. 93.)*

Instrucción y Orden a qe. se deve arreglar el Sargento Mariano Rodríguez en esta Nueba Mision de Ntra. Señora del Refugio, con los catorce hombres de Tropa de la Rl. Compañía de Sn. Antonio de Béxar. *(B. A.)*

Instructions for the Establishment of the New Villa of Pitic in the Province of Sonora, Approved by His Majesty and Ordered Adopted for Other Projected New Villas to be Established in this General Commandancy. (Spanish copy in B. A.)

Iturrigaray, José de
to Diego (James) Wilkinson, January 21, 1807. *(A. G. I. Audiencia de México, 90-1-8.* Dunn Transcripts, 1800-1819.)
——al Principe de la Paz, March 12, 1807. *(A. G. I. Audiencia de México, 90-1-8.* Dunn Transcripts, 1800-1819.)

Jaudenes, José Francisco
to Pedro Nava, November 17, 1793. *(B. A.)*
——to Manuel Muñoz, September 9, [1796]. *(B. A.)*
——to Manuel Muñoz, October 23, 1796. *(B. A.)*
——to Juan Cortés, April 5, 1797. *(B. A.)*

Jones, Daniel Colman
(and others), Petitions of, June 9-August 13, 1806. *(B. A.)*

Junta de Guerra
Monclova. December 9-11, 1777. *(A. G. M. Provincias Internas, Vol. 64, Part 1.)*
——Enero 5 de 1778. *(A. G. M. Provincias Internas, Vol. 64, Part 1.)*
——Minutes of the, June 19, 1809. *(A. G. I. Audiencia de Guadalajara, 104-2-25.* Dunn Transcripts, 1800-1819.)
——Minutes of the, July 20, 1809. *(A. G. I. Audiencia de Guadalajara, 104-2-25.* Dunn Transcripts, 1800-1819.)

Junta Superior de Real Hacienda
July 13, 1792. *(A. G. M. Historia, Vol. 93.)*

Junta Suprema Central
Decree of the, issued in the name of Ferdinand VII, January 22, 1809. *(N. A., Vol. XV.)*
——Copy of the decree of, transmitted with the letter of Nemesio Salcedo to Manuel Antonio Cordero, March 13, 1809. *(B. A.)*

King, Charles
(and Stephen Richards), Testimony of. *(Nolan Documents, Vol. I.)*

Kuerke, Enrique
(and John Magui, Juan McFarlan) Causa seguida a, . . . por contrabandistas. *(B. A.)*

Landrés, José Nicolás
(and Louis Dannequien) Petition of, July 16, 1806. *(B. A.)*

Lanee, Nicolás
to Juan Bautista Elguezábal, July 31, 1801. *(B. A.)*

Larrua, Miguel de
(and Party) Report on, October 11, 1808. *(B. A.)*

Lartigue, Pedro
Petition of, and accompanying documents, August 7, 1806. *(B. A.)*

Lastrope, Juan
to Juan Bautista Elguezábal, October 13, 1801. *(B. A.)*

Layssard, Valanteín
a Dn José Vidal, Consul de España en Natchez. 15 de Septiembre de 1800.
[Traducción del francés del documento de Layssard a Fransamashtabé, Gran
Jefe de las Naciones Chocta y otras. Septiembre 15 de 1800.] *(B. A.)*

León, Prudencio de
to Manuel Antonio Cordero, March 15, 1806. *(B. A.)*

Leonard, Gilbert
List of merchandise sent by Gilbert Leonard from New Orleans to Nacogdoches,
June 26, 1800. *(B. A.)*

López, José Francisco
Razon e Ynforme que el Padre Presidente de las Misiones de la Provincia de
Texas o Nuevas Filipinas, remite. . . *(University of Texas Archives.)*

McGee, John
to Manuel Antonio Cordero, August 30, 1806. *(B. A.)*

Magui, John
(and Enrique Kuerke, Juan McFarlan) Causa seguida a, . . . por contrabandistas. *(B. A.)*

Marchand, Juan Eugenio
to Francisco Viana, November 24, 1806. *(B. A.)*

Mares, José
Derrotero y diario que corresponde al número de Leguas que hay desde la
Capital de San Antonio de Béjar Provincia de los Texas hasta la de Santa Fe
del Nuevo México, que hago yo, José Mares, cabo ymbalido de la compañía
de ella por los terrenos que me conducen los Yndios Amigos Comanches, para
descubrir camino de derechura. *(A. G. M. Historia, Vol. 43, 52, 62.)*
——Por el nombre de Dios Todopoderoso, y de la Santísima Virgen María mi Señora
del Rosario Conquistadora del Reyno, y la Provincia del Nuevo México,
concevida en gracia Amen. yo el cavo José Mares Ymbalido del Rl. Presidio
de la Capital Villa de Santa Fe, hago este derrotero para inteligencia, y
conocimiento del transito que comienzo a hacer para el Presidio de San Antonio
de Béjar, hoy el día 31 último del mes de Julio del presente año de mil
setecientos ochenta y siete. *(A. G. M. Historia, Vol. 43, 62. B. A. . . . Original.)*

Martínez Pacheco, Rafael
——to Jacobo Ugarte y Loyola. October 14, 1787. *(S. A., Vol. V.)*
——to Juan de Ugalde, October 20, 1787. *(Spanish Archives of Texas,* University of Texas.)
——to Jacobo Ugarte y Loyola, December 1, 1787. *(S. A., Vol. V.)*
——to Reyes, September 13, 1788. *(A. G. M. Historia, Vol. 93.)*
——to Juan Ugalde, September 15, 1788. *(A. G. M. Historia, Vol. 93.)*
——to Juan Ugalde, March 9, 1789. *(A. G. M. Historia, Vol. 93.)*
——Diary of events, December 3-29, 1789. *(N. A., Vol. VI.)*
——to the Viceroy Revillagigedo, March 1, 1790. *(N. A., Vol. VI.)*

Maynes, José Francisco
to Manuel de Salcedo, May 30, 1810. *(B. A.)*

Minor, John
to Nemesio Salcedo, October 16, 1804. *(B. A.)*

Monzón, José Plácido de
(and José Antonio Cadena) Declarations of. *(A. G. I. Audiencia de Guadalajara, 104-2-9.* Dunn Transcripts, 1800-1819.)

Mora, José María
to Manuel Antonio Cordero, March 26, 1806. *(B. A.)*

Moral, José Miguel del
May 13, 1798. *(B. A.)*
——to Manuel Muñoz, May 28, 1798. *(B. A.)*
——to Manuel Muñoz, June 5, 1798. *(B. A.)*
——to Manuel Muñoz, September 14, 1798. *(B. A.)*
——to Manuel Muñoz, October 1, 1798. *(B. A.)*
——to Manuel Muñoz, October 27, 1798. *(B. A.)*
——to Manuel Muñoz, November 13, 1798. *(B. A.)*
——to Manuel Muñoz, November 21, 1798. *(B. A.)*
——to Manuel Muñoz, January 5, 1799. *(B. A.)*
——to Manuel Muñoz, January 13, 1799. *(B. A.)*
——to Manuel Muñoz, January 18, 1799. *(B. A.)*
——to Manuel Muñoz, January 23, 1799. *(B. A.)*
——to Manuel Muñoz, February 4, 1799. *(B. A.)*
——to Manuel Muñoz, March 13, 1799. *(B. A.)*
——to Manuel Muñoz, March 17, 1799. *(B. A.)*
——to Juan Bautista Elguezábal, October 28, 1799. *(B. A.)*
——to Juan Bautista Elguezábal, January 28, 1800. *(B. A.)*
——to Manuel Muñoz, January 28, 1800. *(B. A.)*
——to Juan Bautista Elguezábal, March 5, 1800. *(B. A.)*
——to Juan Bautista Elguezábal, April 26, 1800. *(B. A.)*
——to Juan Bautista Elguezábal, June 26, 1800. *(B. A.)*
——to Juan Bautista Elguezábal, July 11, 1800. *(B. A.)*
——to Juan Bautista Elguezábal, July 27, 1800. *(B. A.)*

Morales, Francisco
to José de Iturrigaray, May 12, 1806. *(B. A.)*

Moreno, José Francisco
to Juan Bautista Elguezábal, August 26, 1800. *(B. A.)*

Moya, Juan de
   to Antonio Ventura de Taranco, February 11, 1794. *(A. G. I. Audiencia de Guadalajara, 104-1-1.* Dunn Transcripts, 1794-1798.)

Muñoz, Manuel
   to Pedro Nava. *(S. A., Vol. VI.)*
——to Revillagigedo, concerniente a las obra para asegurar el vecindario de San Antonio de Bexar, March 26, 1790. *(N. A., Vol. VII.)*
——to Revillagigedo, January 14, 1791. *(N. A., Vol. VII.)*
——al Exmo Señor Virrey Conde de Revilla Gigedo [Da cuenta de los bienes recogidos de la Misión del Rosario] 30 de enero de 1791. *(N. A., Vol. VII.)*
——to Viceroy Revillagigedo, February 9, 1791. *(A. G. M. Historia, Vol. 93.)*
——to Viceroy Revillagigedo, February 9, 1791. *(B. A.)*
——to Viceroy Revillagigedo, March 10, 1791. *(A. G. M. Historia, Vol. 93.)*
——to Viceroy Revillagigedo, March 26, 1791. *(N. A., Vol. VII.)*
——to Viceroy Revillagigedo, May 9, 1791. *(N. A., Vol. VII.)*
——to Viceroy Revillagigedo, July 14, 1791. *(B. A.)*
——to Viceroy Revillagigedo, August 15, 1791. *(N. A., Vol. VII.)*
——to Viceroy Revillagigedo, August 29, 1791. *(B. A.)*
——to Viceroy Revillagigedo, August 29, 1791. *(N. A., Vol. VII.)*
——to Viceroy Revillagigedo, October 1, 1791. Sobre el informe que mandó el Padre Misionero de la Misión del Rosario sobre la condición y pide auxilio. *(N. A., Vol. VII.)*
——to Viceroy Revillagigedo, October 10, 1791. Sobre el estado de los ganados de la Misión del Rosario. *(N. A., Vol. VII.)*
——to Viceroy Revillagigedo, November 7, 1791. *(N. A., Vol. VII.)*
——to Gaspar González de Cardamo, November 21, 1791. *(N. A., Vol. VII.)*
——al Virrey Conde de Revillagigedo. Contestando a orn de de [sic] 4 de Enero ultimo informa sre el destino, conducta, y suficiencia del Pe Fr. Josse Mariano Garza . . . 13 de Febrero de 1792. *(N. A., Vol. VII.)*
——to Viceroy Revillagigedo, March 12, 1792. Hace referencia a los gastos que originó la compra de menesteres p'a proveer a los Indios de la Misión del Rosario. *(N. A., Vol. VII.)*
——to Viceroy Revillagigedo, October 21, 1792. *(N. A., Vol. VII.)*
——to Pedro Nava, January 26, 1793. *(A. G. I. Audiencia de Guadalajara, 104-1-1.* Dunn Transcripts, 1794-1798.)
——Auto del Gobernador Manuel Muñoz referente al informe del Conde de la Sierra Gorda con respecto a las Misiones (al Conde de Revillagigedo?) Febrero 23 de 1793. *(S. A., Vol. V.)*
——to the Viceroy, March 12, 1793. *(B. A.)*
——to Juan Cortés, March 23, 1793. *(B. A.)*
——Auto del Gobernador Manuel Muñoz, Relativo al reparto de bienes a los Indios de San Antonio Valero. 11 de abril de 1793. *(S. A., Vol. V.)*
——Auto del Gobernador Manuel Muñoz relativo al recibo de ganado y otros bienes del campo de los indios de San Antonio de Valero. Abril 15 de 1793. *(S. A., Vol. V.)*
——Expediente y autos del gobernador Muñoz relativos a los útiles de la misión de San Antonio, April 24, 1793. *(S. A., Vol. V.)*
——Ordenando que se traslade el Indio Lipan Mariano y los suyos a la mision de San José, April 24, 1793. *(S. A., Vol. V.)*

——al Comte Gral Brigr Dn Pedro de Nava. Da parte de la provda qe tomó pa qe los capitanes dela Nación Lipana pasasen a aquella Capital pa formalizar el tratado de paz, con todo lo demas qe haze preste qe suplica se lea, 20 de Mayo de 1793. *(S. A., Vol. V.)*

——to Juan Cortés, June 7, 1793. *(B. A.)*

——to José Francisco Mariano Garza, September 12, 1793. *(B. A.)*

——Orden a Juan José Farías de que haga entrega de la vigilancia de la misión del Refugio al Cavo José Manuel Castro. Septiembre 13 de 1793. *(B. A.)*

——to Luis Mariano de Cárdenas, May 15 [1794]. *(B. A.)*

——to Juan Cortés, May 16, 1794. *(B. A.)*

——to Pedro Nava, June 6, 1794. *(B. A.)*

——to Juan Cortés, June 10, 1794. *(B. A.)*

——to José Mariano Cárdenas, June 25, 1794. *(S. A., Vol. VI.)*

——to José Mariano Cárdenas, June 25, 1794. *(S. A., Vol. VI.)*

——to Pedro de Nava, June 25, 1794. *(S. A., Vol. VI.)*

——to Pedro de Nava, July 18, 1794. *(S. A., Vol. VI.)*

——to Pedro Nava, August 4, 1794. *(S. A., Vol. VI.)*

——to Pedro Nava, August 17, 1794. *(S. A., Vol. VI.)*

——to Pedro Nava, August 18, 1794. *(B. A.)*

——to Pedro de Nava, September 21, 1794. *(S. A., Vol. VI.)*

——to Pedro de Nava, October 13, 1794. *(S. A., Vol. VI.)*

——to Pedro de Nava, October 25, 1794. *(S. A., Vol. VI.)*

——to Pedro Nava, November 7, 1794. *(B. A.)*

——to Pedro Nava, November 30, 1794. *(B. A.)*

——to Juan Cortés, December 7, 1794. *(B. A.)*

——to Baron de Carondelet, January 18, 1795. *(B. A.)*

——to Commandant-General Pedro de Nava, January 26, 1795. *(A. G. I. Audiencia de Guadalajara, 104-1-1.* Dunn Transcripts, 1794-1798.)

——to Pedro Nava, January 26, 1795. *(B. A.)*

——to Pedro Nava, January 31, 1795. *(B. A.)*

——to Manuel de Silva, February 20, 1795. *(B. A.)*

——to Commandant at Nacogdoches, March 12, 1795. *(B. A.)*

——to Pedro de Nava, June 15, 1795. *(S. A., Vol. VI.)*

——Extracto de la Revista pasada por mi el Tente Corl de Cava Dn Manl Muñoz, Govor de dha Prova como Capn de ella, alos Ofizs, Capellan, Cavos, y Soldados que existen en el dia de la fecha 1 de agosto de 1795. *(B. A.)*

——to Juan Cortés, August 10, 1795. *(B. A.)*

——to Pedro Nava, October 26, 1795. *(B. A.)*

——to Pedro de Nava, November 8, 1795. *(B. A.)*

——Certification of Governor Muñoz, February 12, 1796. *(B. A.)*

——Contestación a la queja presentada por los vecinos de la villa de San Fernando sobre los daños q' hacen los Comanchez y las naciones del Norte. Septiembre 22 de 1796. *(B. A.)*

——to Bernardo Fernández, September 25, 1796. *(B. A.)*

——to Bernardo Fernández, September 27, 1796. *(B. A.)*

——to Juan Cortés, April 1, 1797. *(B. A.)*

——to José María Guadiana, April 25, 1797. *(B. A.)*

——to Juan Bautista Elguezábal, May 29, 1797. *(B. A.)*

——to Juan Bautista Elguezábal, October 17, 1797. *(B. A.)*

——to Juan Bautista Elguezábal, April 3, 1798. *(B. A.)*

——to José Miguel del Moral, September 23, 1798. *(B. A.)*
——to José Miguel del Moral, October 8, 1798. *(B. A.)*
——to José Miguel del Moral, November 6, 1798. *(B. A.)*
——to José Miguel del Moral, January 14, 1799. *(B. A.)*
——to Pedro Nava, June 12, 1799. *(Quaderno Borrador, 1799-1801.)* *(B. A.)*
——to Francisco Xavier Uranga, April 4, 1801. *(B. A.)*
——to Francisco Xavier Uranga, April 28, 1801. *(B. A.)*

Músquiz, Miguel
    to Juan Bautista Elguezábal, January 2, 1801. *(Miscellaneous Correspondence
    . . . 1800-1803.)*
——to Juan Bautista Elguezábal, April 20, 1801. *(B. A.)*
——to Juan Bautista Elguezábal, May 1, 1801. *(B. A.)*
——to the Governor of Texas, August 20, 1803. *(N. A., Vol. X.)*

Nacogdoches
    Relación de los Ranchos y Habitantes pertenecientes a esta Jurisdicción de
    Nacogdoches que se Hallan Situados en la Parte Oriental del R. De Sabinas,
    February 26, 1797. *(B. A.)*
——Expediente sobre Extranjeros, May 8, 1810. *(B. A.)*

Nava, Pedro
    to Colonel Manuel Antonio Cordero, May 26, 1788. *(B. A.)*
——to Marqués de Branciforte, March 20, 1789. *(A. G. M. Historia, Vol. 413,
    Part I.)*
——to Manuel Muñoz, March 20, 1789. *(A.G. M. Historia, Vol. 413, Part I.)*
——to Ayuntamiento, August 17, 1789. *(B. A.)*
——to Governor Manuel Muñoz, June 20, 1793. *(S. A., Vol. V.)*
——Decreto de secularización del comandante Don Pedro de Nava relativo a las
    temporalidades de las Misiones. Abril 10 de 1794. *(S. A., Vol. VI.)*
——to Manuel Muñoz, May 7, 1794. *(B. A.)*
——to Manuel Muñoz, May 24, 1794. *(S. A., Vol. VI.)*
——to Manuel Muñoz, July 5, 1794. *(B. A.)*
——a la Catolica Real Persona de V.M. El Comandante Gral. de Provincias Ynternas
    de N.E. Ynforma sobre el estado de la Mision del Refugio de la Provincia
    de Texas. Noviembre 6 de 1794. *(A. G. I. Audiencia de Guadalajara, 104-
    1-1. Dunn Transcripts, 1794-1798.*
——to Manuel Muñoz, November 29, 1794. *(A. G. I. Audiencia de Guadalajara,
    104-1-1. Dunn Transcripts, 1794-1798.)*
——to Manuel Muñoz, January 9, 1795. *(B. A.)*
——to Manuel Muñoz, January 15, 1795. *(B. A.)*
——to Manuel Muñoz, January 26, 1795. *(B. A.)*
——to Manuel Muñoz, January 27, 1795. *(B. A.)*
——to Manuel Muñoz, February 10, [1795]. *(B. A.)*
——to Manuel Muñoz, February 26, 1795. *(B. A.)*
——to Manuel Muñoz, March 13, 1795. *(B. A.)*
——to Manuel Muñoz, May 5, 1795. *(B. A.)*
——to Manuel Muñoz, May 10, 1795. *(B. A.)*
——to Manuel Muñoz, June 4, 1795. *(B. A.)*
——to Manuel Muñoz, July 2, 1795. *(B. A.)*
——to Manuel Muñoz, July 8, 1795. *(B. A.)*
——to Manuel Muñoz, July 15, 1795. *(B. A.)*

——to Manuel Muñoz, July 18, 1795. *(B. A.)*
——to Manuel Muñoz, July 29, 1795. *(B. A.)*
——to Manuel Muñoz, July 30, 1795. *(B. A.)*
——to the Duque de Alcudia, August 6, 1795. *(A. G. I. Papeles de Estado, Mexico, Legajo 13, No. 2.* Dunn Transcripts, 1792-1799.)
——to Manuel Muñoz, August 26, 1795. *(B. A.)*
——to Duque de Alcudia, November 3, 1795. *(A. G. I., Mexico, Legajo 18, Núm. 5.* Dunn Transcripts, 1792-1799.)
——to Manuel Muñoz, July 16, 1796. *(B. A.)*
——to Manuel Muñoz, September 3, 1796. *(B. A.)*
——to Manuel Muñoz, October 1, 1796. *(B. A.)*
——to Manuel Muñoz, October 16, 1796. *(B. A.)*
——to Francisco Gomarra, October 18, 1796. *(B. A.)*
——to Manuel Muñoz, October 18, 1796. *(B. A.)*
——to the King, November 11, 1796. *(A. G. I. Audiencia de Guadalajara,* 104-1-1. Dunn Transcripts, 1794-1798.)
——to Manuel Muñoz, January 1, 1797. *(B. A.)*
——to Manuel Muñoz, March 7, 1797. *(B. A.)*
——to Manuel Muñoz, March 10, 1797. *(B. A.)*
——to Juan Bautista Elguezábal, March 21, 1797. *(B. A.)*
——to Manuel Muñoz, April 4, 1797. *(B. A.)*
——to Juan Bautista Elguezábal, April 21, 1797. *(B. A.)*
——to Manuel Muñoz, May 2, [1797]. *(B. A.)*
——to Manuel Muñoz, May 16, 1797. *(B. A.)*
——to Andrés Llanos y Váldez, May 24, 1797.
——to Manuel Muñoz, May 24, 1797. *(B. A.)*
——to Manuel Muñoz, May 24, 1797. *(S. A., Vol. VI.)*
——to Manuel Muñoz, June 7, 1797. *(B. A.)*
——to Manuel Muñoz, June 13, 1797. *(B. A.)*
——to Manuel Muñoz, July 1, [1797]. *(B. A.)*
——to Manuel Muñoz, July 17, 1797. *(B. A.)*
——to the Principe de la Paz (Godoy), August 1, 1797. *(A. G. I. Papeles de Estado, Legajo 18, Núm. 21.* Dunn Transcripts, 1792-1799.)
——to Manuel Muñoz, August 4, 1797. *(B. A.)*
——to Principe de la Paz, September 5, 1797. *(A. G. I. Papeles de Estado, Legajo 12, Núm. 22.* Dunn Transcripts, 1792-1797.)
——to Manuel Muñoz, September 25, 1797. *(B. A.)*
——to Philip Nolan, October 31, 1797. *(B. A.)*
——to Juan Bautista Elguezábal, January 19, 1798. *(B. A.)*
——to Manuel Muñoz, January 19, 1798. *(B. A.)*
——to Manuel Muñoz, January 31, 1798. *(B. A.)*
——to Manuel Muñoz, March 8, 1798. *(B. A.)*
——to Manuel Muñoz, May 24, 1798. *(B. A.)*
——to Manuel Muñoz, July 10, 1798. *(B. A.)*
——to Manuel Muñoz, July 20, 1798. *(B. A.)*
——to Manuel Muñoz, July 24, 1798. *(B. A.)*
——to Manuel Muñoz, August 17, 1798. *(B. A.)*
——to Manuel Muñoz, August 28, 1798. *(B. A.)*
——to Manuel Muñoz, October 30, 1798. *(B. A.)*
——to Manuel Muñoz, January 9, 1799. *(B. A.)*
——to Manuel Muñoz, February 19, [1799]. *(B. A.)*

———to Manuel Muñoz, April 30, 1799. *(B. A.)*
———to Manuel Muñoz, June 15, 1799. *(B. A.)*
———to Manuel Muñoz, September 18, 1799. *(B. A.)*
———to Manuel Muñoz, October 1, 1799. *(B. A.)*
———to Juan Bautista Elguezábal, October 29, 1799. *(B. A.)*
———to the Governor of Texas, November 20, 1799. *(B. A.)*
———to Juan Bautista Elguezábal, December 24, 1799. *(B. A.)*
———to Juan Bautista Elguezábal, Governor *ad interim*, December 25, 1799. *(B. A.)*
———to Juan Bautista Elguezábal, April 14, 1800. *(B. A.)*
———to Juan Bautista Elguezábal, July 10, 1800. *(B. A.)*
———to Juan Bautista Elguezábal, August 4, 1800. *(B. A.)*
———to Juan Bautista Elguezábal, August 5, 1800. *(B. A.)*
———to Juan Bautista Elguezábal, August 8, 1800. *(N. A.)*
———to Juan Bautista Elguezábal, September, 1800. *(B. A.)*
———to Manuel Muñoz, December 28, 1800. *(B. A.)*
———to Manuel Muñoz, May 12, 1801. *(B. A.)*
———to the Governor of Texas, June 26, 1801. *(B. A.)*
———to Juan Bautista Elguezábal, August 4, 1801. *(B. A.)*
———to the governor, October 12, 1801. *(B. A.)*
———to Juan Bautista Elguezábal, October 13, 1801. *(B. A.)*
———to Juan Bautista Elguezábal, November 11, 1801. *(B. A.)*
———to Felix Berenguer de Marquina, November 27, 1801. *(Historia, Vol. 413, Part 1.)*

Navarro, Galindo
    Galindo Navarro al Comdte General relativo a la Real Cedula del 14 de Junio de 1780 en que se manda se formen nuevas ordenanzas para el régimen de las Misiones. Julio de 1781. *(S. A., Vol. V.)*
———to Pedro Nava, May 10, 1793. *(S. A., Vol. VI.)*
———al Señor Comandante General Pedro de Nava. Informa sobre la fundación de la Misión en el Caballo del Refugio para la reducción de los Carancaguaces, 26 de junio de 1794. *(A. G. I. Audiencia de Guadalajara, 104-1-1.* Dunn Transcripts, 1794-1798.)
———to Pedro Nava, May 10, 1797. *(S. A., Vol. VI.)*
———Dictamen del Auditor Galindo Navarro, August 1, 1797. *(B. A.)*

Navarro, José
    (and Antonio Samper) to Miguel Cayetano Soler. *(A. G. I. Audiencia de Guadalajara.* Dunn Transcripts, 1800-1819.)

Neve, Felipe
    El Comdt. Gral. Don Felipe Neve hace relación concisa y exacta del estado en que ha encontrado las Provincias Internas y la divide en los 4 ramos, Justicia, Policía, Hacienda, y Guerra. *(A. G. I. Audiencia de Guadalajara, 103-4-10.* 1783.)

New Orleans, Bishop of
    Testimony of the Bishop of New Orleans, October 1, 1801. *(B. A.)*

Nolan, Philip
    to Pedro Nava, November 25, 1797. *(A. G. M. Historia, Vol. 413, Part 1.)*
———to Francisco Rendón, November 25, 1797. *(A. G. M. Historia, Vol. 413, Part 1.)*

———to John Cook, November 20, 1799. *(N. A.)*

———to John Cook, October 23, 1800. *(Miscellaneous correspondence concerning Philip Nolan.)*

———to Vicente Fernández Tejeiro, November 6, 1800. *(Nolan Documents, I.)*

———to William Barr and Samuel Davenport. *(Nolan Documents, Vol. I.)*

Nolan Documents
Photostat copies in University of Texas Library.

Noticia de lo subministrado a los Pobladores de San Marcos, April 3, 1808. *(B. A.)*

Noticia de los carpinteros que existen en esta Villa hoi día, May 17, 1809. *(B. A.)*

Noticia de los efectos de regalo que se le entregaron a José Cal Morin pa. el capitan Quiscat de la Nacion taguacan, 13 de Marzo de 1795. *(B. A.)*

Onís, Luis de
to Francisco Xavier Lizaña, October 21, 1809. *(A. G. M. Operaciones de Guerra.* Barker Transcripts.)

———to Francisco Xavier Lizaña, November 24, 1809. *(A. G. M. Operaciones de Guerra.* Barker Transcripts.)

Ortiz Parilla, Diego
to the Viceroy, November 8, 1760. *(A. G. M. Historia, Vol. 84, Part 1.)*

Pedrajo, José Manuel
to Manuel Muñoz, June 12, 1795. *(S. A., Vol. VI.)*

———to Manuel Muñoz, June 28, 1795. *(B. A.)*

Piernas, José
Spanish translation of the Proclamation of Governor Carondelet, New Orleans, May 30, 1797. *(B. A.)*

Portilla, Felipe Roque de la
to Manuel Antonio Cordero, August 29, 1808. *(B. A.)*

Posada, Dictamen del Fiscal de Real Hacienda
Ordenando se lleve a cabo lo propuesto por el Comandante de las Provincias de Oriente, Dn Juan Ugalde, con respecto a la forma en que Fray José Mariano Reyes ha de servir a los Orcoquizas desde la misión de Nacogdoches. Febrero 10 de 1789. *(A. G. M. Historia, Vol. 93, Exp. 15.)*

———Ordenando proceda el Señor comandante de las Provincias de Oriente, Don Juan Ugalde, a la investigación de los cargos instruídos contra Don Antonio Gil Ybarbo. Mayo 28 de 1789. *(A. G. M. Historia, Vol. 93, Exp. 15.)*

———Sobre la petición de los Orcoquizacs, 21 de abril de 1789. *(A. G. M. Historia, Vol. 93.)*

———Ordenando que el Gobernador M. Muñoz adquiera con sigilo la verdad sobre las acusaciones contra Gil Ybarbo y que disponga lo conveniente con respecto a la fortificación de S. Anto de Bejar, a la Saca de Agua del Río, a la reedificación de la Bahía de Esp. Sto. y otras cosas. Noviembre 22 de 1790. *(A. G. M. Historia, Vol. 93, Exp. 15.)*

———Ordenando se remita al Comandante General, Dn Ramón de Castro, el expediente relativo a la restauración de la misión de los Orcoquizacs y a otras mejoras propuestas, Mayo 31 de 1791. *(A. G. M. Historia, Vol. 93.)*

Prieto, A.
    to Manuel de Salcedo, December 4, 1809.

Primo, Obispo de Nuevo León
    to José Caballero, Secretario de Estado, March 7, 1804. *(A. G. I. Audiencia de Guadalajara, 104-2-19.* Dunn Transcripts, 1800-1819.)
——to José de Iturrigaray, June 20, 1806. *(A. G. I. Audiencia de Guadalajara.* Dunn Transcripts, 1800-1819.)

Provincia de los Texas
    Padrón General de las quatro misiones. *(A. G. I. Audiencia de Guadalajara, 104-2-25.* Dunn Transcripts, 1800-1819.)

Puelles, José Mariano
    to Manuel Muñoz, November 6, 1797. *(B. A.)*
——to Manuel Antonio Cordero, September 4, 1805. *(B. A.)*
——to Manuel Antonio Cordero, December 5, 1805. *(B. A.)*

Padrón General, July 12, 1809. *(B. A.)*

Rábago y Terán, Felipe de
    to the Viceroy, March 2, 1761. *(A. G. I. Audiencia de México, 91-3-3.)*
——to the Viceroy, July 12, 1761. *(A. G. M. Historia, Vol. 94.)*

Refugio, Misión de
    Memoria de lo que por ahora se juzga precisamente necesario para la nueva fundación del Refugio. Undated. *(A. G. I Audiencia de Guadalajara, 104-1-1.* Dunn Transcripts, 1790-1793.)

Report on expenditures for hospital, December 16, 1806. (Bill paid out of Mesteña fund.) *(B. A.)*

Reports of Indian Nations and expenses of entertainment in San Antonio, 1796. *(B. A.)*

Reports on Mesteñas, 1786-1788. *(S. A., Vol V.)*

Representación de Salvador Rodríguez, Vicente Amador, Luis Menchaca, Joaquín Leal, José Antonio Saucedo, José Hernández, Felix Ruiz, y Manuel Serbán. September 22, 1796. *(B. A.)*

Revillagigedo, Conde de
    al Rey. Remite Copia de la Representacion de la Audiencia sobre honores. 10 de Enero de 1790. *(A. G. I. Audiencia de Mexico.* Dunn Transcripts, 1787-1791.)
——al Gobernador Manuel Muñoz, 10 de Dice de 1790. *(A. G. M. Historia, Vol. 93.)*
——to Manuel Muñoz, April 13, 1791. *(A. G. M. Historia, Vol. 93.)*
——to Antonio Porlier, April 27, 1791. *(A. G. I. Audiencia de México, 89-6-14.* Dunn Transcripts, 1787-1791.)
——Auto del Virrey relativo al restablecimiento de la Misión para los Yndios Orcoquizac, al reedificio del Presidio de la Bahía de Espíritu Sto, a la Saca de Agua del Río de Sn. Anto y a la fortificación del Preso de Sn Anto de Béxar. Noviembre 1 de 1792. *(A. G. M. Historia, Vol. 93.)*

——to Conde del Campo de Alanza, January 31, 1793. *(A. G. I. Audiencia de México, 89-6-21.* Dunn Transcripts, 1792-1799.)

——to Diego de Godorqui, April 30, 1793. *(A. G. I. Audiencia de México, 96-2-12.* Dunn Transcripts, 1787-1791.)

Reyes, José Mariano
   to Rafael Martínez Pacheco, September 13, 1788. *(A. G. M. Historia, Vol. 93.)*

——to Juan Ugalde, October 30, 1788. *(A. G. M. Historia, Vol. 93.)*

Richards, Mordicai
   Declaration of, December 13, 1800. *(A. G. M. Historia, Vol. 413, Part 1.)*

Richards, Stephen
   Testimony of Charles King and Stephen Richards. *(Nolan Documents, Vol. I.)*

Río, Ignacio del
   Guardian of Zacatecas to Viceroy Felix Berenguer de Marquina, December 23, 1801. *(A. G. I. Papeles de Estado, México, Legajo 10, No. 13.* Dunn Transcripts, 1795-1817.)

Robin, C. C.
   Memoire par, Auteur du Voyage a la Louisiane les Colonies et Conduite que doit tenir la France Relativement continent de L'Amerique Septentrionale par C. C. Robin. *(Paris Archives. Affaires Etrangeres, Etats Unis, Vol. 61.)*

Rodríguez, Mariano
   Diario. March 13-May 23, 1793. *(B. A.)*

Rodríguez, Sebastián
   to Manuel Antonio Cordero, January 13, 1806. *(B. A.)*

——to Manuel Antonio Cordero, February 19, 1806. *(N. A., Vol. X.)*

——to Manuel Antonio Cordero, March 4, 1806. *(B. A.)*

Rosario, Misión de Nuestra Señora de
   Estado que manifiesta el que tiene esta Mision de Nuestra Señora del Rosario segun existen sus individuos hoy 26 de Septiembre de 1794 y es . . . A saver. . . *(S. A., Vol. VI.)*

——Report on Mission Rosario, September 26, 1794. *(S. A., Vol. VI.)*

Rua, Luisa Gertrudis de la
   to Nemesio Salcedo, December 17, 1809. *(A. G. I. Audiencia de Guadalajara, 104-2-9.* Dunn Transcripts, 1800-1819.)

Rubí, Marqués de
   Inspection of Presidio de San Sabá by the Marqués de Rubí, July 27-August 4, 1767. *(A. G. I. Audiencia de Guadalajara, 104-6-13.)*

Saavedra, Francisco
   to Lizaña, December 12, 1809. *(A. G. M. Operaciones de Guerra.* Barker Transcripts.)

Salcedo, Bruno Díaz de
   al Gobernador Manuel Muñoz. Circular sobre la propagación de malestar llamado *Mosezuela.* Diciembre 17, de 1796. *(B. A.)*

Salcedo, Juan Manuel
    to Nemesio Salcedo, November 11, 1803. *(B. A.)*

Salcedo, Manuel María de
    Appointment of, April 24, 1807. Titulo de Governador de la Provincia de Texas, May 1, 1807. *(A. G. I. Audiencia de Guadalajara, 103-4-1.* Dunn Transcripts, 1800-1819.)
——to Manuel Antonio Cordero, November 27, 1808. *(N. A., Vol. XI.)*
——to Nemesio Salcedo, November 30, 1808. *(B. A.)*
——to the commander of Atascosito, Demember 5, 1808. *(B. A.)*
——to the Citizens, January 16, 1809. *(N. A., Vol. XII.)*
——to Manuel Antonio Cordero, June 14, July 12, 1808, and January 19, 1809. *(B. A.)*
——to the commander of Trinidad, February 4, 1809. *(B. A.)*
——to the commander of Trinidad, March 21, 1809. *(B. A.)*
——to Bernado Bonavía, April 24, 1809. *(B. A.) (N. A., Vol. XI.)*
——to Nemesio Salcedo, May 7, 1809. *(B. A.)*
——to Bernardo Bonavía, June 26, 1809. *(N. A., Vol. XI.)*
——to Bernardo Bonavía, July 3, 1809. *(B. A.)*
——to Bernardo Bonavía, July 15, 1809. *(B. A.)*
——to Bernardo Bonavía, July 24, 1809. *(B. A.)*
——to Bernardo Bonavía, July 30, 1809. *(B. A.)*
——to Bernardo Bonavía, September 15, 1809. *(B. A.)*
——to the Citizens, September 27, 1809. *(B. A.)*
——to the Citizens, October 4, 1809. *(N. A., Vol. XII.)*
——to the citizens of San Fernando de Béxar, October 5, 1809. *(B. A.)*
——to the Citizens, December 3, 1809. *(N. A., Vol. XII.)*
——to Bernardo Bonavía, December 17, 1809, Constancias. *(A. G. I. Audiencia de Guadalajara, 104-2-9.* Dunn Transcripts, 1800-1819.)
——to the Citizens, January 12, 1810. *(N. A., Vol. XII.)*
——to Nemesio Salcedo, January 21, 1810. *(B. A.)*
——to Nemesio Salcedo, March 30, 1810. *(B. A.)*
——to Nemesio Salcedo, April 6, 1810. *(B. A.)*
——Informe of, May 19, 1810. *(B. A.)*
——to the Citizens, July 25, 1810. *(N. A., Vol. XII.)*
——Proclamation of, to the Inhabitants of Nacogdoches, July 29, 1810. *(B. A.)*
——Report of Governor, August 8, 1810. *(A. G. M. Historia, Operaciones de Guerra, Años 1810-1812.)*
——to Bernardo Bonavía, October 5, 1810. *(B. A.)*
——to the Commandant at Nacogdoches, October 26, 1810. *(B. A.)*
——to Nemesio Salcedo, October 27, 1810. *(B. A.)*
——to the Commander of Fort Claiborne, November 17, 1810. *(N. A., Vol. XV.)*
——to the Citizens, November 18, 1810. *(N. A., Vol. XII.)*
——to the Citizens, December 8, 1810. *(N. A., Vol. XII.)*
——to the Faithful Inhabitants of Texas, January 6, 1811. *(B. A.)*

Salcedo, Nemesio
    to Juan Bautista Elguezábal, July 14, 1801. *(B. A.)*
——to the Governor of Texas, May 23, 1803. *(B. A.)*
——to Pedro Ceballos, June 7, 1803. *(A. G. I. Audiencia de México, Leg. 18, Núm. 27.)*

——to the Governor of Texas, March 13, and 25, 1804. *(B. A.)*
——to Juan Bautista Elguezábal, March 27, 1804. *(B. A.)*
——to the Governor of Texas, May 8, 1804. *(B. A.)*
——Copia de los once capitulos de Orn del Sor Comdte gral de 22 de Mayo de 1804.
    (N. A., Vol. XI.)
——to the Governor of Texas, May 22, 1804. *(B. A.)*
——to Juan Bautista Elguezábal, May 23, 1804. *(N. A., Vol. XI.)*
——to Juan Bautista Elguezábal, July 17, 1804. *(B. A.)*
——to William Barr, August 29, 1804. *(B. A.)*
——to Juan Bautista Elguezábal, September 11, 1804. *(B. A.)*
——to Juan Bautista Elguezábal, October 22, 1804. *(B. A.)*
——to Manuel Antonio Cordero, January 1, 1805. *(B. A.)*
——to Pedro Ceballos, January 8, 1805. *(A. G. I. Audiencia de México, Leg. 18,*
    ——*Núm. 27.* Dunn Transcripts, 1795-1817.)
——to the Governor of Texas, April 8, 1805. *(N. A., Vol. X.)*
——to Juan Bautista Elguezábal, May 20, 1805. *(N. A., Vol. X.)*
——to Manuel Antonio Cordero, June 17, and August 6, 1805. *(N. A., Vol. X.)*
——to Juan Bautista Elguezábal, July 1, 1805. *(B. A.)*
——to Manuel Antonio Cordero, July 7, 1805. *(B. A.)*
——to Juan Bautista Elguezábal, July 9, 1805. *(B. A.)*
——to Manuel Antonio Cordero, July 29, 1805, and November 4, 1805. *(N. A.,*
    Vol. X.)
——to Manuel Antonio Cordero, August 20, 1805. *(N. A., Vol. X.)*
——to Manuel Antonio Cordero, October 8, 1805. *(B. A.)*
——to Manuel Antonio Cordero, November 2, 1805. *(B. A.)*
——to Manuel Antonio Cordero, December 2, 1805. *(B. A.)*
——to Manuel Antonio Cordero, December 6, 1805. *(N. A., Vol. X.)*
——to Manuel Antonio Cordero, December 16, 1805. *(B. A.)*
——to Manuel Antonio Cordero, January 1, 1806. *(B. A.)*
——to Manuel Antonio Cordero, January 17, 1806. *(N. A., Vol. X.)*
——to Manuel Antonio Cordero, January 28, 1806. *(B. A.)*
——Proclamation of, February 11, 1806. *(B. A.)*
——to Manuel Antonio Cordero, February 23, 1806. *(N. A., Vol. X.)*
——to Manuel Antonio Cordero, February 24, and April 4, 1806. *(N. A., Vol.*
    X.)
——to Manuel Antonio Cordero, March 11, 1806. *(B. A.)*
——to Manuel Antonio Cordero, April 9, 1806. *(B. A.)*
——to Manuel Antonio Cordero, May 6, 1806, and July 13, 1807. *(B. A.)*
——to Manuel Antonio Cordero, June 16, 1806. *(N. A., Vol. X.)*
——to Manuel Antonio Cordero, July 13, 1806. *(B. A.)*
——to Manuel Antonio Cordero, July 14, 1806. *(B. A.)*
——to Manuel Antonio Cordero, July 15, 1806. *(B. A.)*
——to Manuel Antonio Cordero, August 4, 1806. *(B. A.)*
——to Manuel Antonio Cordero, August 16, 1806. *(B. A.)*
——to Manuel Antonio Cordero, August 24, 1806. *(B. A.)*
——to Manuel Antonio Cordero, August 25, and September 18, 1806. *(N. A.,*
    Vol. X.)
——to Governor Claiborne, September 18, 1806. *(N. A., Vol. X.)*
——to Manuel Antonio Cordero, October 24, 1806. *(B. A.)*
——to Manuel Antonio Cordero, December 4, 1806. *(N. A.)*

———to Manuel Antonio Cordero, December 5, 1806. *(B. A.)*
———to Manuel Antonio Cordero, December 6, 1806. *(B. A.)*
———to Manuel Antonio Cordero, December 9, 1806. *(B. A.)*
———to Manuel Antonio Cordero, December 10, 1806. *(B. A.)*
———to Manuel Antonio Cordero, December 15, 1806. *(B. A.)*
———to Manuel Antonio Cordero, February 24, and April 27, 1807. *(B. A.)*
———Ordero of the King transmitted by, May 1, 1807. *(A. G. I. Audiencia de Guadalajara, 103-4-1.* Dunn Transcripts, 1800-1819.)
———to Manuel Antonio Cordero, September 11, 1807. *(N. A., Vol. XI.)*
———to Manuel Antonio Cordero, January 12, 1808. *(B. A.)*
———to Manuel Antonio Cordero, February 13, 1808. *(B. A.)*
———to Manuel Antonio Cordero, March 8, May 31, and August 5, 1808. *(B. A.)*
———to Salvador de Soto, March 13, 1808. *(B. A.)*
———to Manuel Antonio Cordero, May 27, 1808. *(N. A., Vol. XI.)*
———to Manuel Antonio Cordero, May 31, 1808. *(B. A.)*
———to Manuel Antonio Cordero, July 12, 1808. *(N. A., Vol. XI.)*
———to Manuel Antonio Cordero, August 23, and December 3, 1808. *(B. A.)*
———to Manuel Antonio Cordero, August 23, 1808. *(N. A., Vol. XI.)*
———to Mariano Velasco, August 24, 1808. *(B. A.)*
———to the Governor, August 31, 1808. *(N. A., Vol. XI.)*
———to the viceroy, November 8, 1808. *(B. A.)*
———to Manuel Antonio Cordero, December 11, 1808. *(B. A.)*
———to Manuel Antonio Cordero, December 11, 1808. *(N. A., Vol. XI.)*
———to Manuel Antonio Cordero, March 13, 1809. *(B. A.)*
———to Bernardo Bonavía, March 24, 1809. *(B. A.)*
———to Manuel Antonio Cordero, March 24, 1809. *(B. A.)*
———to Manuel de Salcedo, March 24, 1809. *(B. A.)*
———to Manuel de Salcedo, April 2, 1809. *(N. A., Vol. XI.)*
———to Manuel de Salcedo, April 8, 1809.
———to Manuel Antonio Cordero, April 17, 1809. *(B. A.)*
———to Bernardo Bonavía, May 12, 1809. *(B. A.)*
———to Bernardo Bonavía, May 13, and June 22, 1809. *(A. G. I. Audiencia de Guadalajara, 104-2-25.* Dunn Transcripts, 1800-1819.)
———to Bernardo Bonavía, June 6, 1809. *(B. A.)*
———to Bernardo Bonavía, June 22, 1809. *(N. A.* and *A. G. I. Audiencia de Guadalajara, 104-2-25.* Dunn Transcripts, 1800-1819.)
———to Bernardo Bonavía, June 27, 1809. *(B. A.)*
———to Bernardo Bonavía, July 9, 1809. *(B. A.)*
———to Manuel de Salcedo, August 7, 1809. *(B. A.)*
———to Bernardo Bonavía, August 13, 1809. *(B. A.)*
———to Bernardo Bonavía, August 21, 1809. *(A. G. I. Audiencia de Guadalajara, 104-2-25.* Dunn Transcripts, 1800-1819.)
———to Bernardo Bonavía, September 7, 1809. *(A. G. I. Audiencia de Guadalajara, 104-2-25.* Dunn Transcripts, 1800-1819.)
———to Bernardo Bonavía, October 6, 1809. *(B. A.)*
———to Bernardo Bonavía, October 27, 1809. *(A. G. I. Audiencia de Guadalajara, 104-2-9.* Dunn Transcripts, 1800-1819.)
———to Francisco Xavier Lizaña, Viceroy of Mexico, October 31, 1809. *(A. G. I. Audiencia de Guadalajara, 104-2-9.* Dunn Transcripts, 1800-1819.)

———to Francisco Saavedra, November 7, 1809. *(A. G. I. Audiencia de Guadalajara, 104-2-9.* Dunn Transcripts, 1800-1819.)
———to Bernardo Bonavía, January 9, 1810. *(B. A.)*
———to Bernardo Bonavía, February 6, 1810. *(B. A.)*
———to Manuel de Salcedo, February 6, 1810. *(B. A.)*
———to Manuel de Salcedo, March 13, 1810. *(B. A.)*
———to Manuel de Salcedo, May 14, 1810. *(B. A.)*
———to Manuel de Salcedo, October 2, 1810. *(B. A.)*
———to Manuel de Salcedo, October 13, 1810. *(B. A.)*
———to the People of the Interior Provinces, October 24, 1810. *(N. A., Vol. XV.)*

Salcedo, Villa de la Trinidad de
Census report of the, October 6, 1809. *(B. A.)*
———Commander of Salcedo to Manuel de Salcedo, including the statement by Father Sosa. *(B. A.)*
———Samper Antonio
(and José Navarro to Miguel Cayetano Soler. *(A. G. I. Audiencia de Guadalajara.* Dunn Transcripts, 1800-1819.)

San Antonio
Estado que manifiesta el Numero de Basallos y Habitantes qe tiene el Rey en esta Jurisdiccion con distincion de Clazes, estados, y Castas de todas las Personas de ambos sexos, inclusos Parbulos. Real Preo. de Sn. Anto de Bexar y Dizieme 31 de 1786. *(N. A., Vol. VI.)*

San Antonio Missions
[Autos sobre secularización.] Diligencia del reparto de tierras á los Yndios de San Anto Valero. Abril 12 de 1793. *(S. A., Vol. V.)*
———[Autos sobre secularizacion.] Entrega á los Yndios del maiz y demas auxilios que tienen pedido como ofrece el pe López. Abril 12 de 1793. *(S. A., Vol. V.)*
———[Autos sobre secularización.] Auto relativo en que se manda la entrega de Bueyes, Bacas, y demas auxilios de Semillas, Erramientas, y tierras a los Yndios que se secularizan. *(S. A., Vol. V.)*
———[Autos sobre secularización.] Entrega hecha a los Yndios de la Mision de San Antonio. *(S. A., Vol. V.)*

San Francisco de la Espada, Misión de
Ynventario de los bienes de Temporalidad de la Misión de Sn Franco de la Espada. Año de 1794. *(S. A., Vol. VI.)*

San José, Misión de
Ynventario de los bienes de Temporalidad de la Mision de S. S. José. Año de 1794. *(S. A., Vol. VI.)*
———Relación de lo que adeudan á esta Misión de Sor. Sn. José. . . June 5, 1795. *(S. A., Vol. VI.)*

San Juan Capistrano, Misión de
Ynventario de los bienes de temporalidad de la Misión de Sn. Juan Capistráno. Año de 1794. *(S. A., Vol. VI.)*

Sant-Maxent, Celestino
to Juan Bautista Elguezábal, October 14, 1801. *(B. A.)*

Sedella, Antonio de
  to Juan Bautista Elguczábal, July 6, 1806. *(N. A., Vol. X.)*

Seguín, Erasmo
  Report of, June 25, 1809. *(N. A., Vol. XV.)*

Sierra Gorda, Conde de
  Informe sobre el plan de Fray José M. Reyes para la conversión de los Indios desde el Presidio de la Bahía del Espíritu Santo hasta el pueblo de Nacogdoches. Septiembre 7 de 1792. *(N. A., Vol. VI.)*
——to the Viceroy, September 7, 1792. *(S. A., Vol. V.)*
——to the Viceroy, September 27, 1792. *(S. A., Vol. V.)*
——to the King, December 30, 1792. *(A. G. I. Audiencia de México, 98-6-23. Dunn Transcripts, 1792-1799.)*
——to Manuel Muñoz, October 23, 1796. *(B. A.)*

Silva, Manuel de
  to the King, March 7, 1793. *(A. G. I. Audiencia de Guadalajara, 104-1-1. Dunn Transcripts, 1790-1793.)*
——to the Secretary of the Council of the Indies, March 18, 1793. *(A. G. I. Audiencia de Guadalajara, 104-1-1. Dunn Transcripts, 1790-1793.)*
——to Manuel Muñoz, August 8, 1793. *(B. A.)*
——to Manuel Muñoz, September 3, 1793. *(B. A.)*
——to Manuel Muñoz, September 21, 1793. *(B. A.)*
——Petition to the King, October 10, 1793. *(A. G. I. Audiencia de Guadalajara, 104-1-1. Dunn Transcripts, 1790-1793.)*
——to Manuel Muñoz, November 1, 1793. *(B. A.)*
——al Sr. Governador Dn Manuel Muñoz. Noviembre 20 de 1793. *(B. A.)*
——to Manuel Muñoz, December 12, 1793. *(B. A.)*
——to Manuel Muñoz, December 19, 1793. *(B. A.)*
——to Manuel Muñoz, January 3, 1794. *(B. A.)*
——to Manuel Muñoz, January 12, 1795. *(B. A.)*
——to Manuel Muñoz, January 28, 1795. *(B. A.)*
——to Manuel Muñoz, April 22, May 10, 1795. *(B. A.)*
——to Manuel Muñoz, May 18, 1795. *(B. A.)*
——to Manuel Muñoz, June 23, June 29, August 22, and September 27, 1795. *(B. A.)*
——to Manuel Muñoz, September 9, 1795. *(B. A.)*
——to Manuel Muñoz, September 30, 1795. *(B. A.)*
——to Manuel Muñoz, January 12, 1796. *(B. A.)*
——to Manuel Muñoz, March 27, 1796. *(B. A.)*
——to Manuel Muñoz, June 22, 1796. *(B. A.)*
——to the *Discretorio* of the College of Zacatecas, September 11, 1796. *(B. A.)*
——to Manuel Muñoz, September 13, 1796. *(B. A.)*

Solana, Domingo Joaquín de
  to Manuel Antonio Cordero, September 25, 1806. *(B. A.)*

Someruelos, Marqués de
  to Viceroy Pedro de Garibay, February 2, 6, and 12, 1809. *(N. A., Vol. XV.)*

Sosa, Mariano de Jesús
 to Manuel Antonio Cordero, December 4, 1805. *(B. A.)*
——to Manuel de Salcedo, May 4, 1810. *(B. A.)*
——to Manuel de Salcedo, May 26, 1810. *(B. A.)*

Soxas, Captain
 A bill of the gifts given to Captain Soxas of the Comanche Tribe, two other
 lesser chiefs, 55 Indians, 40 women and 11 babies of the same tribe, all of
 whom leave today, March 12, 1800. *(B. A.)* (Translations by Edward
 Hancock.)

Suprema Junta Central
 Order of the, March 1, 1809, transmitted with letter of Salcedo. *(A. G. I.*
 Audiencia de Guadalajara, 104-2-25. Dunn Transcripts, 1800-1819.)

Taranco, Antonico Ventura de
 to the Council, March 17, 1794. *(A. G. I. Audiencia de Guadalajara, 104-1-1.*
 Dunn Transcripts, 1794-1798.)

Testimony of the Bishop of New Orleans, October 1, 1801. *(B. A.)*

Ugalde, Juan de
 to Manuel Antonio Flores, October 30, 1788. *(A. G. M. Historia, Vol. 93.)*
——to Viceroy Flores, December 9, 1788. *(A. G. M. Historia, Vol. 93.)*
——to Manuel Antonio Flores, April 18, 1789. *(A. G. M. Historia, Vol. 93.)*
——to Viceroy Revillagigedo, September 21, 1790. *(A. G. M. Historia, Vol. 93.)*

Ugarte, José Joaquín
 to Juan Bautista Elguezábal, April 3, 1804. *(B. A.)*
——to Juan Bautista Elguezábal, October 1, 1804. *(B. A.)*
——to Manuel Antonio Cordero, February 20, 1806. *(B. A.)*

Ugarte y Loyola, Jacobo
 to Martínez Pacheco, December 1, 1787. *(S. A., Vol. V.)*

Valdez, Gabino
 to Juan Bautista Elguezábal, July 9, 1800. *(B. A.)*

Valero, Misión de
 Expediente sobre el recibo de los vasos sagrados, y demás utensilios de la
 misión de San Antonio de Valero. *(S. A., Vol. V.)*
——Report on the lands of, August 18, 1809. *(N. A., Vol. XV.)*

Valle, José Cayetano
 to Juan Bautista Elguezábal, June 12, 1804. *(B. A.)*

Valle, Dionisio
 to Juan Bautista Elguezábal, April 5, 1805. *(B. A.)*

Vallejo, Bernardino
 to José María Guadiana, February 20, 1797. *(B. A.)*

Vázquez, Francisco
 to Fray Jaudenes, August 11, 1794. *(B. A.)*
——Diario de Francisco Vázquez, June 3-5, 1798. *(B. A.)*

Verger, Rafael José
    Proclamation of, April 19, 1784. *(S. A., Vol. V.)*

Vial, Pedro
    Diario que por la gracia de Dios comienzo [yo Pedro Vial] a hacer desde este
        Presidio de Sn. Antonio de Béjar hasta arribar al de la Capital Villa de
        Santa Fe por comision de mi Governador Dn. Domingo Cavello, Governador
        de la Provincia de los Texas, con expresión de las jornadas desde el día 4
        de octubre de 1787. *(A. G. M. Historia, Vols. 43, 52, 62.)*
——Derrotero, diario y calculación de leguas, que en descubrimiento por derecho
        desde esta Provincia del Nuevo México hasta el Fuerte de Natchitoches a
        la de los Texas orden superior voy a practicar en compañía de Dn. Pedro
        Vial, último firmado [Francisco Xavier Fragoso.] Villa de Santa Fe veinte
        y quatro de Junio de mil setecientos ochenta y ocho. *(A. G. M. Historia,
        Vol. 43, 52, and 62.)*

Viana, Francisco
    to Commander of American Expedition, May 10, 1806. *(N. A., Vol. X.)*
——to Manuel Antonio Cordero, June 3, 1806. *(B. A.)*
——to Manuel Antonio Cordero, October 22, 1807. *(B. A.)*

Vidal, José
——to Miguel Músquiz, October 6, 1800. *(Miscellaneous correspondence concerning
        Philip Nolan, 1800-1803.)*
——to Marqués de Casa Calvo, October 11, 1800. *(Nolan Documents, Vol. I.)*
——to the Governor of Texas, October 4, 1803. *(B. A.)*
——to Pedro de Garibay, February 13, 1809. *(N. A.)*

Villa de San Fernando de Béxar
    Agreement entered into between them and Pedro Gerónimo Longueville, January
        23, 1806. *(B. A.)*

Warnet, Juan Francisco
    (and Francisco Marceau Desgraviers) Petitions of, October 22, 1806. *(B. A.)*

Wilkinson, James
    to José de Iturrigaray, November 17, 1806. *(A. G. I. Audiencia de México,
        90-1-8. Dunn Transcripts, 1800-1819.)*

Wilson, Maurine T.
    Philip Nolan and His Activities in Texas. M.A. Thesis, *University of Texas,*
        1932. (Unpublished.)

Zárate, Miguel Ignacio de
    to Juan Bautista Elguezábal, October 12, 1801. *(B. A.)*

Salcedo, Manuel María, analysis of conditions in Texas by, 368, 370-372, 375, 376; appointed governor of Texas, 349; in relation to American deserters, 392, 393, city ordinances, 412-415, colonization policy, 349-353, 374, 376, 421, 422, De la Rosa incident, 356, 358, 359, East Texas, 422-432, foreigners, 430-433, immigration, 415, 421, Nacogdoches, 427-430, mission report, 406-408, neutral ground difficulties, 393-396, Salcedo, 425-427; measures taken by against revolution, 434; overthrow of, 437; report of on economic conditions, 400, 401; warning against Indians sent to, 405.

Salcedo, Nemesio, commandant general, 203; in relation to aggression, French and American, 363-365, Claiborne, 268, 269, Clouet's colony, 307, 308, D'Alvimar incident, 340-348, De la Rosa incident, 354-359, defence plans for Texas, 361-369, Despallier's settlement, 298-302, foreigners on frontier, 323, French agents, 398, Glass expedition, 283, hospital supplies, 410, immigration, 287, 292-294, 308, 309, 322-329, 349-353, 393-395, 360-363, 375, Indian policy, 321, 322, instructions of to Cordero, 260-262, 283, to Elguezábal, 393-395, to Herrera, 266, Jaen settlement, 319, *Junta's* proposals, 379, Louisiana frontier crisis, 230, 253-260, 268, measures against revolution, 422-427, military policy of, 393-397, Minor's colony, 305-307, 390, Neutral G r o u n d Agreement, 260, Orcoquisac Mission, 303-305, Pike, 280-283, policy toward settlers in East Texas, 360, 362, 363, 375, reports of Bonavía, 383, 384, of Cordero, 262, 265, 266, 285, 286, of M. Salcedo, 412, requests for troops, 260-262, 272, 384-386, Río Frio project, 421, 422, Salcedo's colony, 310, 311, 314, San Marcos de Neve, 332, trade, 383, 384, Wilkinson, 272.

Salcedo Settlement, Villa de, 309-319, 322, 325, 326, 360-363; Atascosito settlers removed to, 376; base for troops, 366; commandant of, 435; Coshates near, 403, 405; De la Rosa at, 353, 355; efforts of Cordero to promote, 370; immigrants to, 368; plans to strengthen, 372; progress of, 332, 335; runaway slaves, 349; Salcedo in, 425-427; Tessier at, 352, 353.

Salinas, José, San Marcos settler, 334.
Salinas, José María, agent of De la Rosa, 353, 354.
Salinas, Manuel, ranch owner, 419.
Salinas, Pedro José, sent to Mission Refugio, 89.
Salinas, Pedro Xavier, cowboy, 419.
Saltillo (Coah., Mex.), fair at, 383; in relation to Cortés, 209, immigrants from, 419, Silva, 92, 93, 172, trade, 410, Váldez, 199.
Salt Fork, Vial at, 170.
San Agustín Presidio, 16.
San Agustín de Laredo Mission, finances of, 78.
San Ambrosio, danger of Apache attack to, 9.
San Andrés River, Comanche rendezvous, 117.
San Andrés de Nava (Coah., Mex.), established by Cordero, 309, 314.
San Angelo (Texas), visited by Terán, 147.
San Antonio (Texas), American prisoners taken to, 269; archives at, 202; bakery in, 412, 413; Burling at, 277; Calbert at, 207; Castro at, 200; communications with East Texas, 285, 286, 353, 354, 366, with Santa Fe, Chapter V; conditions in, 195-197; D'Alvimar at, 345-347; defence of, 255, 256; depredations on, 152; description of, 169; deserters at, 330, De Meziérès in, 5, 6, difficulties with curate of, 197-199; Elguezábal at, 293; first hospital at, 408-410; Granados at, 183; Herrera at, 262, 344; in relation to Grimarest expedition, 272; guardhouse, 201; horse thieves, 226, immigrants, 293, 294, 299, 330, 334,

THE CHICANO HERITAGE

An Arno Press Collection

Adams, Emma H. **To and Fro in Southern California.** 1887

Anderson, Henry P. **The Bracero Program in California.** 1961

Aviña, Rose Hollenbaugh. **Spanish and Mexican Land Grants in California.** 1976

Barker, Ruth Laughlin. **Caballeros.** 1932

Bell, Horace. **On the Old West Coast.** 1930

Biberman, Herbert. **Salt of the Earth.** 1965

Casteñeda, Carlos E., trans. **The Mexican Side of the Texas Revolution (1836).** 1928

Casteñeda, Carlos E. **Our Catholic Heritage in Texas, 1519-1936.** Seven volumes. 1936-1958

Colton, Walter. **Three Years in California.** 1850

Cooke, Philip St. George. **The Conquest of New Mexico and California.** 1878

Cue Canovas, Agustin. **Los Estados Unidos Y El Mexico Olvidado.** 1970

Curtin, L. S. M. **Healing Herbs of the Upper Rio Grande.** 1947

Fergusson, Harvey. **The Blood of the Conquerors.** 1921

Fernandez, Jose. **Cuarenta Años de Legislador:** Biografia del Senador Casimiro Barela. 1911

Francis, Jessie Davies. **An Economic and Social History of Mexican California** (1822-1846). Volume I: Chiefly Economic. Two vols. in one. 1976

Getty, Harry T. **Interethnic Relationships in the Community of Tucson.** 1976

Guzman, Ralph C. **The Political Socialization of the Mexican American People.** 1976

Harding, George L. **Don Agustin V. Zamorano.** 1934

Hayes, Benjamin. **Pioneer Notes from the Diaries of Judge Benjamin Hayes, 1849-1875.** 1929

Herrick, Robert. **Waste.** 1924

Jamieson, Stuart. **Labor Unionism in American Agriculture.** 1945

Landolt, Robert Garland. **The Mexican-American Workers of San Antonio, Texas.** 1976

Lane, Jr., John Hart. **Voluntary Associations Among Mexican Americans in San Antonio, Texas.** 1976

Livermore, Abiel Abbot. **The War with Mexico Reviewed.** 1850

Loyola, Mary. **The American Occupation of New Mexico, 1821-1852.** 1939

Macklin, Barbara June. **Structural Stability and Culture Change in a Mexican-American Community.** 1976

McWilliams, Carey. **Ill Fares the Land:** Migrants and Migratory Labor in the United States. 1942

Murray, Winifred. **A Socio-Cultural Study of 118 Mexican Families Living in a Low-Rent Public Housing Project in San Antonio, Texas.** 1954

Niggli, Josephina. **Mexican Folk Plays.** 1938

Parigi, Sam Frank. **A Case Study of Latin American Unionization in Austin, Texas.** 1976

Poldervaart, Arie W. **Black-Robed Justice.** 1948

Rayburn, John C. and Virginia Kemp Rayburn, eds. **Century of Conflict, 1821-1913.** Incidents in the Lives of William Neale and William A. Neale, Early Settlers in South Texas. 1966

Read, Benjamin. **Illustrated History of New Mexico.** 1912

Rodriguez, Jr., Eugene. **Henry B. Gonzalez.** 1976

Sanchez, Nellie Van de Grift. **Spanish and Indian Place Names of California.** 1930

Sanchez, Nellie Van de Grift. **Spanish Arcadia.** 1929

Shulman, Irving. **The Square Trap.** 1953

Tireman, L. S. **Teaching Spanish-Speaking Children.** 1948

Tireman, L. S. and Mary Watson. **A Community School in a Spanish-Speaking Village.** 1948

Twitchell, Ralph Emerson. **The History of the Military Occupation of the Territory of New Mexico.** 1909

Twitchell, Ralph Emerson. **The Spanish Archives of New Mexico.** Two vols. 1914

U. S. House of Representatives. **California and New Mexico:** Message from the President of the United States, January 21, 1850. 1850

Valdes y Tapia, Daniel. **Hispanos and American Politics.** 1976

West, Stanley A. **The Mexican Aztec Society.** 1976

Woods, Frances Jerome. **Mexican Ethnic Leadership in San Antonio, Texas.** 1949